Writing Scripts

for

TELEVISION, RADIO, AND FILM

Third Edition

EDGAR E. WILLIS

The University of Michigan

CAMILLE D'ARIENZO, R.S.M.

Brooklyn College, City University of New York

Harcourt Brace Jovanovich College Publishers

Fort Worth   Philadelphia   San Diego   New York   Orlando   Austin   San Antonio
Toronto   Montreal   London   Sydney   Tokyo

Editor-in-Chief	Ted Buchholz
Acquisitions Editor	Stephen T. Jordan
Developmental Editor	Cathlynn Richard
Senior Project Editor	Cliff Crouch
Production Manager	Debra A. Jenkin
Senior Book Designer	Don Fujimoto

Library of Congress Cataloging-in-Publication Data

Willis, Edgar E.
  Writing scripts for television, radio, and film / Edgar E. Willis, Camille D'Arienzo.—3rd ed.
    p. cm.
  Includes bibliographical references and index.
  ISBN 0-03-075011-3 (paper)
  1. Television authorship. 2. Radio authorship. 3. Motion picture authorship. I. D'Arienzo,
    Camille. II. Title.
  PN1992.7.W49 1992
  808.2'2—dc20   92-53792
                                                                             CIP

Address editorial correspondence to: 301 Commerce Street, Suite 3700
                                        Fort Worth, Texas 76102
                   Address orders to: 6277 Sea Harbor Drive
                                        Orlando, Florida 32887
                                        1-800-782-4479, or 1-800-433-0001 (in Florida)

Cover illustration by Lamberto Alvarez

Printed in the United States of America
2 3 4 5 6 7 8 9 0 1 2   016   9 8 7 6 5 4 3 2 1

CONTENTS

PICTUREBOARDS AND STORYBOARDS

SCRIPTS AND SCRIPT EXCERPTS

To Zella, who
helped in so many ways
EEW

To Barbara Valuckas, my
first partner in writing
television programs
CD

PREFACE

As was true of previous editions, this edition has two main objectives: (1) to provide practical instruction for those hoping to become writers in broadcasting and film, and (2) to guide students whose goal is a liberal, rather than professional, education toward fruitful creative experiences. In pursuit of these objectives, we describe the theories and techniques underlying the writing of the principal broadcast and film forms, and we illustrate professional practice with a wide variety of scripts and script excerpts. In the concluding chapter, we also discuss some of the routes aspiring writers may take to gain entry into the professional world.

In preparing this new edition, we have made a number of changes:

1. The organizational pattern is new. The plan of the last edition, which divided programs into persuasive, informative, and entertainment types, did not work as well as we had hoped because some programs fit into more than one category. We have replaced it with one that divides the principal forms into two main groups: nondramatic and dramatic material. The discussion of comedy writing is now in a separate section because it can be found in both of these groups. Because writing for children requires unique approaches, we have also put our consideration of this material into a separate section. The book begins with a prologue that discusses the talents writers must have and the techniques they can learn; it ends with an epilogue that describes what life for writers is like in the real world.

2. Most of the script examples are new and up-to-date. We have, however, retained some from the last edition that instructors told us had worked particularly well. These excerpts all fill at least one of two distinct purposes: to demonstrate how a professional writer puts a device or theory into practice, or to illustrate a script format.

3. We have added many new comments and statements from professionals now working in the field.

4. The consideration of comedy writing, an important field that many textbooks either ignore or touch on lightly, has been expanded to show how the principles of humor are actually applied to constructing comedy material.

We have tried to be specific in explaining principles and techniques. It is not good enough, for instance, to simply tell students to arouse audience interest at the beginning of a script. They need to know specific ways of accomplishing this goal, and we have tried to provide those details. In the same way we have outlined specific methods for plotting a drama, explained how to build a commercial around a key selling idea, and have identified the elements that make a situation funny. We have been similarly specific in describing the writing of other forms.

Because writers of short stories, novels, and stage plays share many interests with the writers of television and movie scripts, and contend with the same problems, we have not limited our references to broadcasting and film only. Writers of all types often say things relevant to script writers. We recognize this linkage by using the term *play* to signify television and film drama as well as stage drama, and we call those who write plays for the electronic media "dramatists" or "playwrights." It follows that this is not just a book about writing for television, radio, and film. It is a book about writing in general.

Those who have provided us with illustrative material are acknowledged fully at the end of this text. In identifying various scripts we have used italics to signify the titles of films, plays, books, radio and television series, and one-time specials. We have used quotation marks to indicate the titles of short stories and the programs or episodes making up a series. The editor of the *Chicago Manual of Style* has informed us that that publication will recommend this format in its next edition.

Besides illustrating the application of principles and techniques, our exhibits also show how various types of scripts are set up on the page. These formats exemplify generally accepted practices, although those used by any particular organization may differ in some details.

We expect that the main activity of students will be writing scripts and reading them in class. A list of questions and projects at the end of each chapter may suggest some useful variations. We have also included a bibliography (which lists relevant books, films, and videocassettes), and a glossary of terms television and screen writers should know.

A great many people have provided us with material and ideas for this book. We are especially pleased that a number of the exhibits came from former students who are now professionals. We were also delighted to discover that some providers of material whom we had not known previously had used our book during their student days.

Some people deserve special notice. One who made an invaluable contribution was Terri Sarris, a lecturer in broadcasting at the University of Michigan, who used our book as both a student and a teacher. We incorporated many of her ideas into this revision. Mary Lou Teel, a writer-producer for *CBS Sunday Morning,* through a generous gift of her time and wisdom, provided us with insights, information, and contacts. Among the most valuable of those contacts is her husband and co-worker, Peter Freundlich. David Black, a producer-writer of dramatic series, including *Law and Order,* and a Pulitzer Prize-winning author, responded to lengthy, probing interviews. He went beyond the craft of writing to describe his own internal philosophical conversations about storylines and human values. Media creator-consultant Tony Schwartz likewise generously shared his commitment to the common good; this commitment has led him, after a long, fruitful career in commercial and political advertising and the authorship of numerous books, to devote his energies to public service announcements. Peggy Charren, the founder of Action for Children's Television, provided us with valuable insights into the nature and needs of children.

We could fill a chapter with our conversations with secretaries and production assistants, as well as writers and broadcasters. So many busy people gave us valuable information along the way. We hope they realize our gratitude. One person we must name is Cathlynn Richard, developmental editor at Harcourt Brace Jovanovich College Publishers. Her perceptive comments guided us in improving the manuscript, and she was able to provide us with material not available elsewhere. Thanks also go to those who read the manuscript at various stages and made constructive comments and suggestions: Mario Acerra, Northampton Community College; Lewis Barlow, Boston University; Chris Campbell, Xavier University; Irving Fang, University of Minnesota; John Kelly, Boston University; Donna Munde, Mercer County Community College; and Diane Waldman, University of Denver.

E.E.W.

C.D.

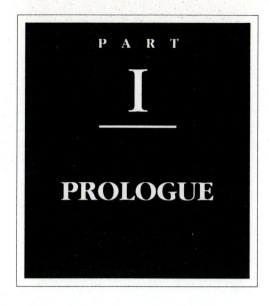

PART

I

PROLOGUE

People looking forward to careers as scriptwriters for the broadcasting and film media need to know the answers to a number of significant questions. Do these media confront writers with any unusual problems or demand of them any special talents? Which of these talents must writers possess as innate gifts and which can be acquired through training or experience? What are the conditions under which the television, radio, and film industries operate, and do these conditions impose any restrictions on the writer's creativity? How does the task of writing take place? These are the questions we address as we consider the general situation of the writer in the broadcasting and film industries. Those who are thinking about writing professionally for television, cable, radio, and film will also want to know employment opportunities and the best ways of finding them. We deal with this subject in the final chapter of the book.

C H A P T E R

1

THE WRITER'S CHALLENGES

Writing involves a craft that you have to learn and a talent that you must possess. Neither is common and both are essential.

JOHANN WOLFGANG VON GOETHE
(1749–1832)

THE MEDIA'S DEMANDS ON THE WRITER

The experience of a number of writers who have made successful transitions into the broadcasting and film fields from other types of writing suggests that the techniques demanded by television, radio, and film can be mastered by those whose general writing skills are fully developed. Walter Cronkite and Harry Reasoner first established their reputations as newspaper reporters before going on to distinguished careers in broadcast journalism. Archibald MacLeish's poetry brought him his first national notice; when he turned to radio, such poetic dramas as *The Fall of the City* were acclaimed as classics almost immediately. Evan Hunter drew attention originally as a novelist with *The Blackboard Jungle* and then went on to create television and film scripts as well as many more novels. In one instance, he wrote a police novel, *Fuzz*, under the pseudonym Ed McBain and later adapted it for the screen under his real name. Movement in the other direction has also taken place. Sidney Sheldon earned his living as a scriptwriter for television and film before *The Other Side of Midnight* and *Bloodline* made him one of our best-selling commercial novelists. Their careers indicate that people who have mastered the art of writing can apply it in a number of ways.

Although the broadcasting and film media do not constitute forms that have a unique identity or embody special demands all their own, they encompass a number of different fields which do have separate identities and impose unique requirements. Various skills are needed in broadcasting and film, among them the ability to move people emotionally through drama; the wit to contrive comedy situations; the ingenuity to think up game show ideas; the capacity to influence behavior and opinions with commercials, documentaries, and editorials; and the gift of writing clear exposition in newscasts and in scripts designed to inform. Individuals who are effective in writing one type of material may not necessarily be effective in writing another type. This situation is also true outside the broadcasting and film fields. Charles Dickens and Henry

James are among the English-speaking world's most acclaimed novelists; yet, though they both yearned for success as playwrights and sought it by writing for the stage, they were never able to achieve it. To reverse the coin, George Bernard Shaw's novels are now ignored; only when he turned to drama did he find the vehicle that has made his name live.

The career of Paddy Chayefsky provides a good illustration of the point that one does not master a medium such as television or film, but rather that one masters a type of writing that can be expressed effectively through them. Chayefsky achieved fame overnight when his drama *Marty* was broadcast in the early days of television. Later he wrote successful plays for the Broadway stage and then turned to writing for the movies, where his script for *Network* won an Academy Award. Chayefsky mastered the art of creating dramas in television and then applied that skill to writing dramas for the stage and screen. To cite MacLeish again, he was primarily a poet who found radio a natural outlet for his special gifts. What counted for MacLeish was his essential talent as a poet; he found that adapting his talent to the special demands of radio was relatively easy.

One of the things beginning writers must do is undertake a voyage of exploration to discover the nature of their own resources. The result of that search should lead to some conclusions about the kind of material they are best qualified to write. One step in that process is practice in writing various types of scripts. This book, by providing instruction for writing in the various script categories, can assist you as you test your own abilities. But before setting out to learn the special techniques and demands of various media and script forms, you need to think about the characteristics that distinguish all good writing no matter what its nature. In the next section we discuss the talents, both innate and acquired, which

you must possess if you are to be a successful writer in any field.

INNATE TALENTS OF THE WRITER

It is commonly held that writers are born, not made, and that writing cannot be taught. This statement rests on the assumption that writers must have within them certain innate talents. It does seem to be true that instruction cannot bring certain necessary talents into being, though it may be able to nurture them if they do exist. Let us begin, then, by considering what capacities aspiring writers must bring with them to their teachers. These capacities will differ, of course, according to the type of writing the student plans to do.

Something to Write About

An obvious necessity for writers is material on which to base their work. The immediate inspiration for beginners is usually their own experience, and an essential is the capacity to live fully. Writers cannot afford to let experience merely wash over them. It must mark them with indelible imprints. But to provide all of the substance required for writing, observation must reach beyond the bounds of immediate reality. Writers need a native curiosity that will lead them to gain a sense of what Hippolyte Taine, a French historian, called the "moral temperature of their times" and an understanding of the world that existed before their own day. Only in this way can they gain the sensitivity to the present and the sense of the past that are necessary to measure the relevance of their own experiences. To put it another way, they must have the capacity to escape the limits of their own backgrounds, for one who relies entirely on personal experience soon exhausts those resources and becomes shallow and monotonous. Moreover, even works that find their main inspiration in the lives of writers must reflect faithfully the personalities and experiences of others involved in the story, people whose passions and ways of life may be utterly alien to their own. For the dramatist, the ability to project into other lives is an absolute requirement.

Language Facility

The tools of writers are words and they must have a special way with them. Clarity and precision in word choice, for example, are essential for the newswriter who must describe events accurately. This skill can be sharpened with instruction, but some innate feel for language is necessary. Another basic requirement for all writers is the ability to see on their own what hangs together and what does not, as well as to recognize whether what they write at any given moment stems from what they have just written and whether it will lead directly into what they are about to write. Only if they have this capacity for self-criticism will their work have unity and coherence, qualities especially important to the documentary writer, who must analyze a problem and handle its treatment with clarity and logic.

David Black, a versatile writer, whose successful novel *Murder at the Met* was spun from a sensational murder case, also researched and authored a Pulitzer prize-winning book on AIDS, *The Plague Years*. As a writer-producer of several dramatic television series, he says, "In this business, coherence is genius." He also places strong emphasis on the importance of research, no matter what the writing form. Not even coherence can compensate for shallow information about subjects and characters. Coherence itself is enhanced by descriptive clarity, achieved by the use of the appropriate words.

Always choose your words carefully so that they will convey precisely the meaning you intend. If a word or expression seems awkward or inexact, a dictionary or thesaurus will suggest alternatives. The commentator Eric Sevareid, conceding that there are times when a picture may be better than a thousand words, also insisted that there are times when one well-chosen word may be better than a thousand pictures.

Writing for the Ear

The writer for broadcasting and film must be particularly sensitive to the sound of spoken language. "Word deafness" may be a handicap to a novelist, but in a television or film writer it is a fatal flaw. If people lack this sensitivity, no teacher can give it to them. Audience members must be able to absorb the material without having the opportunity to study it; they cannot ask a speaker to repeat a fact or request clarification of a complex point because they do not understand it. This factor has important implications for all those who write material for the ear—among them the writers of newscasts, feature talks, commentaries, continuities, and dramas.

The first fact the writer of radio and television material should understand is that the audience is composed of isolated people who cannot experience the social facilitation operating in a group assembled in one auditorium. Even though millions may be listening, you are writing, not for a mass audience, but for a single person sitting at ease in a home setting. This means that you should employ the direct, informal style characteristic of conversation. To attain a conversational style use contractions ("don't," not "do not"); give your language an informal tone by avoiding inversions and relative clauses; use shorter sentences than you generally would in writing material to be read, though not to the point of becoming monotonous; proceed directly from the subject to the predicate in most instances.

Because you are writing material to be read out loud, you should take special pains to avoid tongue twisters that might trip up the announcer. Numerical figures should be spelled out because words can be converted into language more easily than numbers. Beware of homonyms, words that sound alike but have different meanings. The following sentence, though clear when read, might perplex a radio listener. "The young man got his girl a ring and thus he got her, too!" The sentence "She gasped in surprise at the bear keeper" is subject to misinterpretation when only heard. Unless the reader is very skillful, the sentence, "While we were drinking, the river, previously quiet, began to eddy and swirl," might mislead listeners. We shall have more to say about achieving a conversational style in Chapters 7 and 14, on writing news and drama.

The Ability to Create

Experience and knowledge make a major contribution to a writer's work, but most forms require writers to create something that never existed before. If they are to bring new ideas into being, they must be gifted with native inventiveness. The commercial writer needs it to find a new way of presenting an old appeal. The documentary writer needs it to devise a framework for presenting factual material in an interesting way. Television or film dramatists need it to work their way out of plotting cul-de-sacs which might prevent a story from flowing credibly and inevitably to its end. The task of bringing new characters into being requires, in addition, the gift of creative imagination. These characters may reflect real persons but if that is all they do, the dramatist has failed to move beyond the achievement of mere verisimilitude. The most satisfying characters emerge when reality is enriched with imagination. The ability to recombine and modify familiar elements into something that never existed before cannot be created by instruction. It must be there when instruction begins.

The Capacity to Re-experience

Writers must have good memories, and there are some who have displayed a gift of almost total recall, but the mere recollection of events is not enough. If writers are to infuse their work with the vibrations of actual existence, they must be able to live through experiences again. Many people can recite accurately the facts of a past event, but only a few have the ability to bring back those facts clothed with the emotions and sensations they originally aroused. The writer of comedy must add to this talent the knack of seeing people and events from a unique point of view.

Storytelling

The ability to tell a good story is of crucial importance in creating drama and some types of documentaries. The great dramatists seem to know instinctively how to grip the attention of an audience from the first moment and hold it to the end. Instruction can provide writers with some knowledge of the techniques involved in the art of storytelling, but much of this understanding must come to them naturally.

Self-Evaluation

The practice of writing is a lonely art and loneliness seems particularly to be the fate of broadcast writers—one they share with poets and novelists—who rarely see the reactions of their audiences. For the professional, solitude can be both gift and asset. Peter Freundlich, a writer and associate producer for *CBS Sunday Morning,* broadcast weekly on the CBS television network, believes "the real work of a writer is done in solitary fashion. The best is done by soloists."

In most instances, radio and television writers have access only to the reactions of those who put on the program, and their judgments, like the writer's, may be warped by this participation. Broadcast writers need a generous gift of self-criticism to be able independently to measure the reach of their accomplishment. The ability to maintain a fresh and objective eye for something as personal as a piece of writing, into which one's whole being may have been poured, is not a common one. People fired with dedication and commitment may easily confuse the high purpose they set out to achieve with what they have actually written.

ACQUIRED SKILLS OF THE WRITER

The argument that writing cannot be taught seems to imply that it is impossible to acquire any writing skills at all. It is axiomatic, of course, that a teacher cannot give a person the innate gifts we have just considered, but it seems equally clear that certain skills can be acquired through instruction. Though students cannot learn to be inventive, they can learn how to apply what gifts they do possess. Almost all writing demands a mastery of the art of writing correct English. Instruction in the principles of grammar can help achieve it. Students can also learn the lore and disciplines of the media; they can be taught how to adapt to a particular medium's demands; they can discover the ways in which an idea may be framed for

presentation on radio or television. In this way the talent they have can be expanded and developed. Knowledge of the principles involved in such functions as designing dramatic scripts, selecting items for a newscast, persuading people to buy products, or motivating laughter also can provide students with criteria for evaluating their own work. As a result, they may flounder less in error and spend more time in rewarding trial. Most important of all, a teacher can be a first audience for writers, providing the feedback that lets them know that they are either on target or have completely missed the mark.

D. H. Lawrence's statement regarding the novel, that "all rules of construction hold good only for novels which are copies of other novels," seems to be true only in part. There is need, at the very least, for criteria that give the various forms of writing their shape and identity. And while the writer's skill is still untested and unproved, it may be dangerous to disregard practices that experience has shown are effective. Some rules are made to be broken, perhaps, but not by beginners.

Still, the study of writing may have its dangers. Young writers desperately seeking guidance may assume that there are certain techniques and formulas that can be used in script after script. Such an assumption may carry them into prescribed channels which repress their imaginative powers and limit their capacity to find new ways of expressing ideas. Principles should not become frozen into detailed procedures which become so inflexible that they enclose and stultify. Beginning writers can use the patterns of the past as reference points, but in the end they must try not to write like someone else but to write in their own individual way.

Thus far we have been discussing challenges related to what might be thought of as the artistic side of writing. There are also challenges of a practical nature. Foremost among them is the problem of finding employment as a writer. If successful in that venture, writers then find that the broadcasting and film industries make special demands on them and impose certain restraints. National and state laws add further restrictions as do the customs and mores of society as a whole. Copyright law, for example, places limits on the use writers may make of other people's works, and state laws prohibit defamation and the invasion of privacy. Writers must also recognize that people worry about the amount of violence in television and films and often react negatively to offensive language and to the stereotyping of various groups in our society. We take up these matters in Chapter 19. There we discuss the steps one should follow to become established as a writer and review the practical problems of working in the broadcasting and film fields.

GETTING DOWN TO WRITING

The task of writing involves more than putting down words on paper. The process varies with the type of writing being done, but we can discern a number of steps that apply to all. The first is to find something to write about. For news writers the subject matter is the events that are happening locally, nationally, and around the world; for documentary writers it is the list of social issues and informational subjects that deserve exploration and treatment; for writers of editorials and short talks it is the day-to-day happenings that call for criticism and comment; for writers of drama it is ideas produced by their own imaginations and powers of invention. The next step is a period of reflection and research. For news writers the main task is to choose the stories to be covered. Reports from news services and their own investigative staff provide the information. Writers of documentaries often

undertake long periods of research which involve visits to libraries and field interviews. Writers of commentaries must decide the approach they will take. Dramatists use this period to develop their plots and create their characters. Next comes the planning of the script. For news writers this amounts mainly to deciding the order in which the various events will be treated and giving some thought to the transitions that will connect them. Writers of informational programs must organize their material in a coherent way and develop a plan for presenting it. Dramatists must decide the order of their scenes and devise a means of introducing the characters. The writing of the script comes next, followed by a period of rewriting and polishing. For news writers the changes are likely to be minimal; for others a number of drafts may be written before the script reaches its final form.

Getting Under Way

One of the most difficult challenges writers face is reaching the point when they actually start to put words down on paper. For news writers delay is unacceptable—the next newscast may be only a few minutes away. Writers of other types of informational programs also face deadlines. They may have more leeway than writers of news, but they cannot delay indefinitely the time when actual script writing must begin. Staff writers, in general, must respond to demanding schedules. The problem of getting started is most likely to affect free-lance writers of drama and documentaries. It is said that Ernest Hemingway postponed the awful moment by sharpening as many as 20 pencils before finally taking one in hand to write. By constantly putting off the act of writing, it is possible to imagine for a whole lifetime that one is a writer without ever putting down a word. How can you get started? Most professional writers emphasize that one of the best ways of warming up the creative machinery is to apply yourself regularly to the task of writing. Do not wait for inspiration. As Guy de Maupassant said: "Get black on white—get down to work." Sitting down in front of a typewriter or word processor is the act that for some people starts their imagination working.

Once started it is important to keep writing for a certain period each day and to keep at a given writing project until it is completed. The warm-up period you need to get words flowing will be wasted if you do not continue writing for a considerable period. How long you spend writing at any one time is a matter to be decided, of course, by your individual bent. The important thing is to write regularly and for sustained periods.

Methods of Writing

Writers differ so greatly in the way they write that it is impossible to draw conclusions about the best practices. Some compose at great speed and turn out a prodigious amount of work in a short time. The novelist Georges Simenon completed a novel in as short a time as 11 days, and he revised very little.

Other writers, in contrast, find that rapid composition is impossible for them, and they must perfect each sentence and then each page before they proceed. The constant revisers are those who tend to hate what they write because it falls so short of their expectations; for them every word constitutes a drop of their life's blood. James Thurber sometimes spent as much as 2,000 hours perfecting a single short story and he once poured out a total of 240,000 words in various drafts for a story that in its final form totaled no more than 20,000 words. Some writers find that the best approach is to get something on paper as quickly as possible

and then polish the result through cutting and revision.

Writing is hard, hard work. The act of putting words on paper is arduous in itself, but writers do not stop working simply because they leave their desks. They may continue to wrestle for hours with a problem in plotting; they are constantly alert to soak up the impressions that can enrich their work; they are always watching for the idea or event that may be the root of a new script. The glazed look one sometimes sees in the eyes of writers at social occasions reveals that they have deserted the immediate world of cocktails, chatter, and laughter for a world of their own creation.

What is the reward for all this hard work? For a few it brings some fortune and a little fame, but the majority who aspire to a writing career are doomed to insecurity, frustration, and anonymity. Yet many make the try year after year. Rod Serling, one of television's best-known writers in its early years, explained how that can happen. "Writing is a demanding profession and a selfish one. And because it is selfish and demanding, because it is compulsive and exciting, I didn't embrace it. I succumbed to it."

QUESTIONS AND PROJECTS

1. Compare and contrast the innate talents needed by a news, commercial, or continuity writer with those needed by a drama writer. Evaluate your own natural abilities in these terms.
2. List the specific proficiencies you are interested in mastering in taking a course in television, radio, and film writing.
3. Can you think of other innate talents a writer needs besides those mentioned in the text?
4. Are there other acquired skills writers can gain as the result of instruction besides those mentioned?

5. The novelist John O'Hara once said that it would be better for a person who hoped to be a writer to go to sea for four years than to spend that amount of time in college. What is your reaction to that statement?

6. After you have attended a current movie or watched a television drama, consider whether the script revealed that the writer possessed special knowledge of a particular field or area.

7. Examine your practices for planning, getting started, maintaining progress, revising, and evaluating that will lead to your optimum achievement.

PART

II

WRITING
NONDRAMATIC
MATERIAL

Because commercials provide the main support of American broadcasting, the eventual survival of most programming depends on their effectiveness. They may be routine sometimes, a fault from which other types of writing are not immune, but often they are marked by a high degree of craftsmanship—even artistry in some instances. What ultimately counts when commercials are evaluated, however, is not the creativity they manifest but their power to sell. The most finely crafted commercial fails if it does not move the product it advertises off the merchants' shelves. To achieve this end, broadcasters spend much more time and money producing one minute of a commercial than they do in producing one minute of regular program material.

We should note that this concentration on selling has generated much criticism. Commercials have been subjected to more attack than any other aspect of broadcasting. Critics complain that advertisers tend to deal in threats, promises, and certainties. Many worry particularly about the influence of commercials on children. Congress has demonstrated its concern by passing a law limiting the amount of advertising that can be included on programs aimed at children to 12 minutes an hour on weekday programs and 10.5 minutes on weekends.

Those who write commercials should be alert to the ethical questions involved in advertising. It is not the purpose of this chapter, however, to examine these questions but rather to describe the approaches and techniques that make commercials effective. The existence of much of our pre-

C H A P T E R

2

COMMERCIALS AND PUBLIC SERVICE ANNOUNCEMENTS

Nothing except the Mint can make money without advertising.
THOMAS BABINGTON MACAULAY
(1800–1859)

sent broadcasting system depends on their power to sell goods. The material that follows should, however, provide valuable insight: Those who are the targets of advertising campaigns (and that in one way or another includes everyone) may learn some of the methods advertisers use to persuade people to buy their products.

Writers of commercials work in a variety of situations. Some are employees of local radio or television stations who, for relatively modest stipends, turn out a whole series of commercials every week for as many as 50 different clients. The writer may be the person who secures the client in the first place, gathers the information for the commercial, writes it, and may even be the announcer who delivers it on the air. Employees of a national advertising agency, in addition to being more highly paid than local station writers, usually concentrate their efforts on extolling the virtues of only a few products. They do not work alone, either; the preparation of commercials in a large advertising agency is a team operation in which the initial writer's work is reviewed and revised until every sentence and effect is finely honed.

TYPES OF COMMERCIALS

There are a number of ways in which radio and television commercials can be classified. We shall examine them in terms of three different elements: the general arrangement for presenting them; the nature of the techniques employed in producing them; and the kind of selling approach used.

The Advertising Arrangement

In the early days of broadcasting when advertising on radio first began, a single company usually sponsored an entire program on which only its products were advertised. Often the title of the program identified the sponsor; *The A&P Gypsies* and *The Palmolive Hour* are examples. The single sponsor arrangement continued to dominate through the radio period and into the beginning of the television era. With the costs of television production sharply higher than those of radio, it soon became impossible for most companies to pay for an entire program. Advertisers began to share sponsorship either on the same program or by alternating from week to week. As costs continued to rise, this process accelerated until a large number of different advertisers were buying time on programs for the insertion of commercials. This is called a *participating* arrangement. The occasional company still sponsors an entire program—the *Hallmark Hall of Fame* program is one example—but the concept of sponsorship in its original meaning has virtually disappeared, although use of the term persists. The same development has taken place in radio, but for a different reason. There it was brought about by the disappearance of specific programs and their replacement with continuous musical entertainment punctuated by regular newscasts and commercials.

In the radio era, when commercials and most programs were produced by advertising agencies, program content and advertising frequently were linked. With the development of the participating arrangement, this connection has disappeared; programs and commercials now are produced in completely separate situations. The advertising agency itself may produce commercials, or companies specializing in this function may film or tape them. For many years the standard length of both radio and television commercials was one minute. In the 1970s a transition toward the 30-second length began, and since then the trend toward increasing brevity has accelerated, particularly in television. Now many commercials last no more than 15 seconds, and commercials as short as 10 or seven seconds are appearing in greater numbers. Sometimes commercials are written to permit presentation in either a 30-second form or in a shorter version excerpted from the longer one.

Stations insert commercials for local companies or national advertisers into their own programs or during the station breaks that interrupt network programs. Commercials for national products broadcast by local stations are called *national spot announcements*. The same national commercial may appear as participating advertising on a network program or as a national spot announcement during a station break. Through a scheduling mischance, in fact, viewers may see a commercial during a network program followed by exactly the same commercial in the station-break period.

Production Techniques

Another way in which commercials differ is in the techniques used to produce them. Most of the commercials presented on large stations and on networks are transcribed, filmed, or video taped. The preponderance of the recorded commercial can be attributed to several advantages it brings the advertiser:

1. It ensures uniformity in presentation.
2. It eliminates the possibility of a mistake which may distort the commercial message or make it seem ridiculous.
3. It permits the use of a wide variety of production devices.

Not all of the advantages are on the side of recordings, however:

1. The live presentation is much cheaper to produce than a recording or film.
2. The live presentation can be revised to reflect changes in prices or to announce special sales.
3. The immediacy and spontaneity of the live presentation may help a popular personality to sell the product.

A great many different techniques are used in the production of commercials, among them:

1. two or more voices to present sales messages;
2. interviews;
3. dramatizations;
4. music—instrumental or sung;
5. sound effects;
6. live action with the announcer in view;
7. live action with voice-over announcing;
8. computer graphics;
9. candid recordings or films;
10. still-picture sequences with voice-over narration;
11. animation;
12. puppets;
13. a combination of devices.

The Selling Approach

The ultimate aim of commercials is to sell products, but there are marked differences in the way they approach this objective. Some seek immediate sales, others eventual ones; a few merely seek to develop a feeling of good will toward the advertiser. The approach may vary also from the light and subtle to the direct and obvious.

Making the Name Familiar   One of the ways in which commercials accomplish eventual sales is to imprint the name of the product on consumers' minds through constant repetition. Seeing the product in a store, we respond to it as something we know and thus are more likely to buy it than the unadvertised product next to it on the shelf, even though we actually know nothing about the relative qualities of the two brands.

Persuading the Audience to Buy   In addition to establishing the brand name, many commercials present a persuasive argument designed to get the audience to buy the product. The persuasive commercial can take many forms. It may be presented in dramatic form, as a testimonial from a satisfied user, through a demonstration of the product's advantages, as a means of solving a problem, through a comparison showing its advantages over its competitors. We shall have more to say later in this chapter about the specific techniques of writing persuasive commercials.

Message Intensity   Another way in which commercials differ is in the relative intensity with which the message is delivered. A commercial designed to enhance the reputation of the advertiser rather than to convert listeners into immediate buyers of its products is called *institutional.* Manufacturers whose products are not sold directly to consumers frequently make use of this kind of advertising. Its tone tends to be stately and dignified and the message is often educational in nature. This restrained approach to advertising, we should note, is much less common than the more intense appeals that we discuss next.

A commercial that exemplifies the characteristics of institutional advertising exceptionally well was produced for the BellSouth telecommunications company. Like many commercials of the institutional type, its objective was to enhance the image of the company rather than to sell a product or service directly to consumers. In this way it differed in its purpose from commercials presented by telephone companies that are designed to enlist customers for their long-distance services. The BellSouth commercial was aimed at creating a

BELLSOUTH
"CHURCHILL"

COMM'L NO.: YOBB 0609

LENGTH: 60 SECONDS

(MUSIC UNDER THROUGHOUT)

FIRST MAN: Churchill was one of the greatest leaders

the world's ever had.

SECOND MAN: He got the Nobel Prize for oratory and for writing.

He was a great statesman.

THIRD MAN: Oh, Churchill loved to paint.

He always said that he did his best thinking with a brush in one hand, and a cigar in the other.

FIRST MAN: He was an innately brave man, he was totally fearless. The moment he realized the importance of the airplane, he got a pilot's license. Typical of the man.

ANNCR: (VO) The sum of Winston Churchill was much greater than the parts.

Because real greatness is doing more than one thing well. That's the vision of BellSouth. To be a network of companies doing a lot of things well.

To help manufacturers, state governments and others do what they do even better.

BellSouth...

(MUSIC)

(MUSIC)

(MUSIC)

Everything you expect from a leader.

favorable impression not just among private telephone users but also among the company executives and public officials whose enterprises might become customers for their wide array of communications services. The key idea was that BellSouth did many things well, just as one of the world's great men, Winston Churchill, did. The themes the commercial struck were *versatility* and *leadership*. It was dignified in tone but not stiff or formal in its language. The comments of the men who spoke about Churchill and the speeches of the announcer had a conversational quality. The commercial is presented in the form of a *pictureboard,* which is made up of stills taken from the film or tape of the commercial after production is completed. Later in this chapter, we review the formats most widely used by those who create commercials.

A somewhat more intense approach attempts direct selling but keeps it low pressured. Listeners are appealed to as reasonable, thinking individuals by an announcer who does not exhort them to immediate action— "before it is too late!"—but speaks instead in a relaxed and well-modulated tone in language written to match. This *soft-sell* approach would be used by a bank to persuade listeners to open savings accounts or to use the bank as a source of loans, or by a telephone company that wishes to convince listeners of the desirability of an extension phone.

The most intense approach attempts persuasion through high-pressure methods. The tone of such commercials is strongly emotional. The announcer is likely to race through the copy at breakneck speed, emphasizing points with forceful gestures and in a loud and high-pitched voice. The copy is filled with admonitions to act now and is likely to resound with superlatives that emphasize the special nature of the offer and its short duration. Listeners may get the feeling that the advertiser is trying to bludgeon them into buying. Commercials of this type are described as *hard sell.*

The Humorous Versus the Serious

Another way to classify commercials is to put those that use humor in one group and those that depend entirely on a straight or serious approach in another. Though the use of humor in commercials is not a new development, the number of advertisers using it has been growing rapidly in recent years. There are a number of reasons for the increasing use of humor in commercials. The trend toward shorter lengths and the growth in the amount of program time devoted to advertising has increased sharply the number of commercials that regularly bombard radio and television audiences. It is estimated that the average American family sees from 70,000 to 100,000 TV commercials a year. Advertisers have turned to humor as a way of making their messages stand out among the myriad appeals to which the industry exposes the public. Many believe that humor catches and holds the attention of people better than a straight appeal and is more effective in making them remember the product name.

A second reason for using humor is that it makes watching commercials more endurable; by softening the innate hostility many people feel toward commercials, it creates a more positive attitude toward the product. Some commercials achieve this end by obviously striving to become part of the entertainment. The commercials presented to persuade the public that Miller Lite beer tastes great and is less filling almost became a comedy series on their own. This use of humor in this series of commercials paid off handsomely. It made Lite beer the leading product of its kind.

The Wellness Plan, a health maintenance organization (HMO) enterprise, has also used a situation-comedy framework to bring its message to the public. The following radio commercial exemplifies the approach used. The two characters it features also appear in animated form in a shorter TV version.

Wellness Commercial
60 seconds

ANNCR: And now, The Wellness Plan presents Mr. and Mrs. Isaac Newton.

MUSIC: CHAMBER MUSIC UNDER

ISAAC: (SPEAKING AS A SHAKESPEAREAN ACTOR) To be or not to be, that is the question. . .

WIFE: Isaac, you're supposed to be discovering gravity, not reciting Shakespeare.

ISAAC: (IN HIS REGULAR VOICE; DEJECTED) I'm thinking about getting into another line of work.

WIFE: Now, dear, don't get so discouraged. Go outside, sit under that apple tree, and see if anything comes to you.

ISAAC: Good idea.

WIFE: I'm going to stay here and read all about the great benefits of our new HMO— The Wellness Plan.

ISAAC: (VOICE FROM AFAR) Okay. I'm here. And thinking. Wait. I think something's coming. . .

SFX: BOINK OF APPLE HITTING HIM

WIFE: Isaac. . . are you all right? Oh, thank goodness we have The Wellness Plan. Aside from wellness programs to keep us well, they have great doctors, fine hospitals, and convenient health care centers.

ISAAC: (PROFOUNDLY) What goes up, must come down.

WIFE: Isaac. . . Isaac. . . you've got it!

ISAAC: (IN ACTING VOICE AS AT BEGINNING) Hark! What light through yonder window breaks?

WIFE: On the other hand, maybe you haven't.

ANNCR: The Wellness Plan. An HMO that's good for you. Call 875-WELL.

(MUSIC OUT)

Sometimes the vehicle for conveying a commercial message is a comedy routine. The following commercial for *Time* magazine, produced by Dick Orkin and Bert Burdis, who specialize in producing humorous commercials for a variety of clients, illustrates this type. It features rapid-fire comedy interchanges, but at the same time it clearly communicates the value of reading *Time*.

TIME COMMERCIAL
60 seconds

PROFESSOR: Mr. Funster, you've been a major disappointment at college.

FUNSTER: Why do you say that, sir?

PROFESSOR: According to university records you've attended six classes in four years.

FUNSTER: Four classes in six years.

PROFESSOR: All right, I'll correct the record.

FUNSTER: I don't feel I've really missed anything, sir.

PROFESSOR: You don't?

FUNSTER: I know everything I need to know.

PROFESSOR: You do?

FUNSTER: I read *Time* magazine.

PROFESSOR: Young man, reading a section or two of *Time* magazine. . .

FUNSTER: No, No. I read all of *Time* magazine, cover to cover each week.

PROFESSOR: Why don't you live on campus?

FUNSTER: Ohio State allows off-campus housing.

PROFESSOR: Not in Aspen, Colorado.

FUNSTER: But, sir. . .

PROFESSOR: *Time* alone does not a sheepskin make, young man.

FUNSTER: Ask me anything, art, music, medicine, religion. . .

PROFESSOR: Why is it. . .

FUNSTER: And *Time* is so entertaining.

PROFESSOR:	Why is it. . .
FUNSTER:	Much more so than your class, if I may say so, sir.
PROFESSOR:	Why is it you don't participate in extracurricular activities?
FUNSTER:	Oh, that's not true, I'm social chairman of Sigma Sigma Si.
PROFESSOR:	That's a sorority!
FUNSTER:	But I *am* participating.
PROFESSOR:	Mr. Funster, a college education is the key that unlocks the door of success. No man ever achieved anything. . .
SFX:	*TELEPHONE RINGS*
PROFESSOR:	Hello. . . yes. . . It's your broker.
FUNSTER:	Well, ask him if it's the oil merger or the land deal in downtown New York.
PROFESSOR:	Is it the oil mer. . . mer. . . good grief.
ANNOUNCER:	*Time* magazine, the most colorful coverage of the week. Pick up a copy.

· In a few commercials the comedy element takes over almost completely. This was true of a series presented on behalf of Residence Inns, a motel chain. The main feature was a stand-up comedy routine by Henny Youngman presenting a number of the rapid-fire gags for which he is noted. In one commercial viewers heard as much about Youngman's mother-in-law as they did about Residence Inns.

Humor is not nearly so prevalent in print advertising as it is in broadcast commercials, but one ad, whose writers may have been influenced by the fact that they were publicizing a situation comedy, did employ it. The ad announced a new CBS show, *Good Sports,* starring Farrah Fawcett and Ryan O'Neal. It closed with this wisecrack: "That body. That hair. That smile. Those teeth. That's right, Ryan O'Neal is back. And Farrah looks good, too."

Some commercials introduce a humorous point into an otherwise straight selling approach. Even when the commercial is seen again and again, viewers may still look forward to enjoying the humorous twist. And it is important that commercials retain their effectiveness through many showings, because the high cost of producing them requires that they be repeated many times. A good example of an advertisement that lightens a straight appeal with a humorous element is a commercial for Skippy Dog Food. It emphasizes the idea that dogs like this dog food, and the sign of their appreciation is a wagging tail. The expounder of the commercial message is a woman sitting in a rocking chair. As she rocks, her dog wags its tail in time with her movements. His tail slips under the rocker as it rises and slips out as it descends. Watching this canine coordination remains amusing through several viewings.

Though the use of humor is widespread, not all advertisers are convinced of its effectiveness. Some believe that humor may obscure the basic advertising message because the machinery of joke making takes so much time that there is little opportunity to stress important selling points. There are also some types of humor that do not wear well with repetition. The commercial that depends on a gag is an example. Once heard, it is never fresh again. It is also obvious that certain products are not suitable for humorous treatment.

People like humorous commercials, and research indicates that the commercials we like are the most effective. Somewhat surprisingly, however, studies have shown that commercials the audience dislikes rank next in selling power. One of the most disliked advertising campaigns of recent years was the series of commercials depicting Mr. Whipple admonishing his customers not to squeeze the Charmin. Despite the audience's aversion to this approach, it was employed for many years. Why did this advertiser continue using it? The answer is that though they irritated people, the "Mr. Whipple" commercials were highly successful in moving the product off the shelves. One reason for this paradox, perhaps, is that they effectively spotlighted a product advantage. Another reason may be that the irritation itself helped etch the product name in viewers' minds.

PLANNING THE COMMERCIAL

Your first step in planning a commercial is to gain as much knowledge of the product as possible. These are among the questions you need to ask at the beginning: What are the peculiar advantages of this product? Does it have a unique quality on which the commercial can focus? Is its major appeal its price, its quality, its convenience, or its beauty? Is it primarily an item of intrinsic value? Does it have major shortcomings which must be taken into consideration?

The place the commercial is to occupy in the overall campaign to sell the product is also a matter of importance. Sometimes advertisers integrate printed and broadcast advertising so completely that they use the same language in both media. Radio commercials frequently serve as reminders to reinforce the ideas presented in television advertising. A given commercial may feature a certain appeal that other advertising repeats over and over again, or it may make a selling point constituting one step in a campaign the advertiser develops in stages.

The writer must also be keenly aware of the commercial's target audience. Advertising presented during breaks in one of the popular prime-time shows requires no special audience adaptations, for the millions of viewers who watch these programs include all kinds of people. Some network shows do select a particular kind of audience. Daytime programs are still directed toward women even though increasing numbers of them leave their homes to work; men, on the other hand, are the main targets of the advertising included in sports programs; the commercials in Saturday morning cartoon shows obviously are aimed at children. At the other extreme from the mass audience of network television is the small audience of an FM radio station specializing in classical music. This type of service draws the intellectual, the well educated, the well-to-do. The products advertised on such a station and the appeals used to sell them are quite different from those employed on a big network show. There is an affinity between certain types of programs or program times and certain types of products. Daytime programs tend to advertise products used in the home. People who like to watch football and baseball games often enjoy drinking beer. For that reason, commercials for beer are among those most frequently presented on sports broadcasts. Golf on television attracts people who play the game. They are obvious targets for the advertising of golf equipment. The audiences for televised golf also include a higher percentage of business executives than is found in the audiences of most other programs. Commercials in golf broadcasts, by advertising products and services that can be purchased only by large companies, often appeal to executives in their business roles rather than as private individuals. Advertisers of steel, industrial components, or of space in a magazine may buy time on a morning radio program and direct their commercials to the few hundred business executives who may be driving to their offices while the commercial is on the air. The writer of commercials must understand who the audience is and take its characteristics into account in planning and writing the advertising appeal.

Determining the Key Selling Point

Most successful commercials are built around a particular attribute that sets the product apart from its competitors and gives potential consumers a specific reason for buying it. The commercial is then organized around this attribute by devising a key selling appeal that promotes it. With the trend toward shorter TV commercials, the emphasis that comes from concentrating on a single selling appeal is more crucial than ever.

David Ogilvy, founder of one of the world's largest advertising agencies, said that the writer should begin by asking two questions: What does the product do? What is the product for?[1] Thinking about these questions can lead to the development of a key selling point.

If possible, the writer should try to find an attribute that distinguishes the product in a unique way from its competitors. The makers of Crest toothpaste began advertising years ago that Crest protects its users from developing cavities better than any other toothpaste. This claim was bolstered with evidence obtained from controlled experiments. As a result of this campaign,

Crest became the leading seller of toothpaste, and for a while it was the product most often purchased in drugstores. Another example of a unique attribute is one claimed by American Express Company for its traveler's checks. In a series of commercials, it maintained that lost or stolen American Express checks are easier to replace than those of other companies. This boast helped give these checks a 60 percent share of the market.

One of the problems faced by the makers of instant coffee is the conviction of many consumers that it lacks the flavor and aroma of the brewed variety. The manufacturer of Folger's Coffee Crystals made the refutation of this belief the key selling point of a series of commercials. In a number of notable American restaurants, diners were unwittingly served Folger's instant coffee instead of brewed coffee. Their comments indicated that they hadn't noticed the switch and were, in fact, impressed by the excellence of the coffee. McDonald's took advantage of many people's concern with eating too much fat by introducing the McLean hamburger. The key selling point of the advertising campaign was the claim that this new type of hamburger was 91 percent fat-free.

The effectiveness with which some key selling points have become ingrained in the popular consciousness is illustrated by the slogan used in the Lite beer commercials, referred to earlier. If students at one end of a football stadium shout, "Tastes great," the students at the other end are likely to shout back, "Less filling."

If a writer is not able to find an attribute unique to the product, the next best thing is to find a feature shared with competitors that no one else is exploiting. The makers of Gleem toothpaste did this when they began advertising that their product was especially made for people "who can't brush after every meal." When one thinks about it, it is obvious that few people can always brush immediately after eating, yet by emphasizing that Gleem helped to meet this problem, its makers managed to invest it with what seemed to be a unique attribute. Sometimes competitors may settle on the same basic feature but advertise it in different ways. The American Express company, for example, once pointed out that its credit card gives owners the recognition they need to purchase products. MasterCard advanced the same basic point in claiming that its clients gain "clout."

Sometimes key selling points of competing products run into one another head on. Anacin argues that its combination of ingredients provides faster relief. Bayer counters with the claim that its product is composed only of "pure" aspirin. The maker of one television set may argue that its modular units make it possible to repair sets quickly and easily with little chance of human error. Another maker, emphasizing that its sets are the product of the finest hand craftsmanship, may argue that true quality comes only when workers apply their individual skills throughout the entire manufacturing and repair process. These claims, though completely contradictory, still result in sales for their respective makers.

Centering the commercial on one compelling reason for buying a product does not mean that the writer should ignore all other points in its favor. The effect of absolute concentration might be rather stark and somewhat repetitive, especially in commercials longer than 30 seconds. Details are needed to flesh out the appeal and give it dimension and depth. Too many details and too many different appeals, however, can obscure the basic message. The key to the process is *emphasis*. The writer must always know what the key selling point is and concentrate on establishing it.

Designing the Persuasive Appeal

Most commercials aim at activating the audience to make an immediate purchase of the product. In planning an advertising appeal, therefore, writers must be aware of the stimuli likely to impel a person into a buying action. The process through which the advertiser accomplishes this end is called persuasion. Its success is related both to the way the message is presented and to its content. Successful commercial appeals usually contain four distinct steps. They do not always occur in the same order, but they need to be there if the commercial is to have a strong and complete persuasive structure.

Gaining Attention To get listeners to respond to a commercial's persuasion, you must first gain their attention, a formidable task when you consider the multitude of appeals cascading constantly from radio and television receivers. Breaking through the clutter so that listeners will take special note of your commercial among the thousands that bombard them every year confronts you with one of your most challenging tasks. That is why techniques for compelling attention loom so importantly in the construction of a commercial. In some instances, TV commercials seem to concentrate almost entirely on the task of making people look at them.

The use of beautiful women and attractive men in commercials has long been a way of capturing attention. Sometimes they seem to have little relevance to the product being advertised but they catch the viewer's eye nevertheless. Cute children, dogs, cats, and other intriguing animals perform the same function. The use of a celebrity as a spokesperson for a product, usually a person from the world of entertainment, catches viewer attention and gives credibility to the message. Angela Lansbury's performances as the mystery writer in *Murder, She Wrote* have made her a household name. When viewers see her testifying that Bufferin has cured her headaches, they are likely to listen carefully. Other means of gaining attention are to use special sound effects, music, and visual devices; to tie the commercial in with a recent news event, a sports happening, a prominent personality, or a holiday; to emphasize the new, novel, or the latest; to ask a rhetorical question; to make a sincerely personal approach. With so many special devices being used to gain attention these days, a single, unadorned voice may have the quality of unusualness that makes us listen.

A commercial that combined unique attention-getting quality and a deft and economical transmission of a key selling idea advertised the lasting qualities of Energizer batteries. The audience was fooled into thinking that it was watching a regular commercial only to have it interrupted by a pink rabbit rolling across the screen and the sound of an announcer's voice intoning the words: "Still going. Nothing outlasts the Energizer. They keep going, and. . ." The product advertised in the interrupted commercial did not exist, of course; it was the invention of a creative copywriter. Below you can see how one of these Energizer commercials was visualized in a storyboard.

Some commercials, however, take up so much of their time arousing interest that the articulation of the selling argument is left to the audience, and the mention of the product name becomes almost incidental. An example of this approach was a series of

Figure 2–1 Energizer Storyboard

1

SFX: ALARM GOING OFF.
MUSIC: TYPICALLY BAD
SOAP JINGLE UP.
SINGERS: Alarm!

2

It'll start your day!

3

Alarm! You'll be on your way!

4

Ring in your day—with Alarm!
SFX: BOOM, BOOM, BOOM. . .

5

MUSIC: JINGLE DIES.
ANNCR VO: Still going.

6

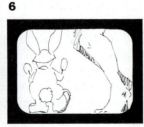

Nothing outlasts the Energizer

7

They keep going and going. . .
SUPER: Alarmingly fresh!

8

. . .and going and going. . .

commercials presented on behalf of Taster's Choice coffee. It portrayed the development of a romantic relationship between a woman who knocks on a neighbor's door to borrow some coffee and the man who answers. Another commercial of this type was presented by the makers of Dentyne chewing gum. It spent most of its time telling the story of a waitress who discovered that an attractive male customer had come into the restaurant to meet a blind date. She decided to change her appearance by switching from her uniform into a dress and rearranging her hair. She then went out the back door and re-entered the restaurant at the front, pretending to be the woman the man was expecting. The picture of a Dentyne package at the end of the commercial was the only reference to the product.

A number of commercials for Nike athletic shoes concentrated mainly on holding the attention of the audience. One was almost entirely taken up with Michael Jordan, the basketball star, making a series of fabulous dunk shots. Other commercials featured the football and baseball player Bo Jackson. A memorable entry showed a crowd of Bo Jacksons occupying the screen in a variety of costumes and personas. The reference to Nike shoes in these commercials was fleeting, but because they held attention, they were effective. During the period they were on the air, sales of the product doubled.

The fact that a commercial holds attention may not be enough, however. Some years ago a commercial for Schlitz beer was so attractive and interesting that it won a Clio award as one of the best commercials of the year. When viewers were asked about the commercial, however, they all remembered it advertised beer but few of them could name the brand.

Establishing Need   The most crucial step in the development of an action appeal is to make the listener feel an overwhelming need for the product. The normal individual experiences a number of basic needs which commercial products can help satisfy. These innate drives have been catalogued in a number of different ways. One authority simply listed them as self-preservation, security, sex, and status. In the classification that follows, needs are described in terms that are particularly meaningful to the writer of commercials.

1. *Self-preservation.*   The desire to preserve one's life and health is one of the most powerful of all drives. A great many products are relevant to this need—among them, medicines, anti-blowout tires, and safety belts.

2. *Security and Ease.*   Most people have the desire to live comfortably and well and want to feel secure against catastrophes which may threaten their particular way of life. When the American Express company shows people being robbed of their money and advises viewers to protect themselves by carrying traveler's checks, they are appealing to the desire to be safe, especially in a foreign country. The basic technique of this approach is an arousal of fear, as it is in many commercials that address the urge to be secure. This desire is also manifested in the concern people have for the well-being of their loved ones. Thus parents react favorably to appeals promising better things for their children. People not only want to be safe, they also seek ways of improving their lot and adding to the general joy of living. Many products contribute to satisfying these needs—among them tasty food, central heating, life insurance, and fine automobiles.

3. *Response to Others.*   Another of the powerful human urges is the desire to be accepted by others, particularly by members of the opposite sex. The advertising of numerous products is specifically directed toward satisfying this need—personal items in particular, such as deodorants and soaps.

4. *Status.* An innate desire of almost everyone is the urge to be important, to count in this world. This drive is related to the desire to be accepted by other people, but it goes beyond it to the point where we want to be looked on as superior to others. Some products, such as clothes that get attention or an automobile that bespeaks wealth, help to express the ingrained snobbery characterizing most of us.

The necessity for giving time and attention to developing a need for the product varies according to its nature. There is a clearly felt need for many of the articles advertised on radio and television even before the commercial begins. Most people, for example, want to have on hand a product that will help them if they develop headaches. The problem for advertisers in this instance is not to develop a sense of need, but to persuade audiences that their product provides the best remedy. There are some products, however, for which the average person may not be able to visualize any need at all. Because most people do not on their own recognize the value of home insulation, the advantages of a filter on the furnace, or the benefits of a water softener, the development of a feeling of need for these products is one of the most important parts of the commercial.

Somewhere between these two examples is the product for which most people feel a need but not a strong enough one to motivate buying. A writer confronted with this situation must recognize that some desires are more powerful than others. The urge to preserve one's life, for example, is stronger in most people than the longing for status or even for a response from the opposite sex. On the other hand, some people may be willing to sacrifice some of their security and ease and even their money to win the affection of another person. When the need most closely related to the product is a weak one, the writer reviews the basic human desires in an attempt to discover a need connected to the product that will have a more powerful persuasive effect than the more obvious one. The advertising of some toothpastes provides an example.

The basic function of toothpaste is to clean teeth and gums. Many manufacturers, however, obviously believe that appealing to the simple desire to be clean is not as persuasive as showing that their product can enhance dental health. As we noted earlier, Crest became a leader in the field by making the key selling point of its advertising the claim that Crest reduced the number of cavities. Other manufacturers quickly followed suit. In recent years some have turned to another aspect of the health problem by claiming that their product can prevent gum disease and the loss of teeth by removing plaque. A few concentrate on neither dental cleanliness nor health, but by emphasizing that their toothpaste freshens breath and whitens teeth they imply that its users become irresistible to the opposite sex, which is one variation of the response urge. The same appeal is used in advertising household soap. In promising users smooth, beautiful hands, some commercials suggest that washing dishes can be a beauty treatment instead of an onerous chore. Such appeals are not just limited to women. Advertisers of men's hair dressing have the response urge in mind when they emphasize its contribution toward developing an attractive appearance.

The commercials of the Hallmark company, the nation's leading manufacturer of greeting cards, make their appeal to the response urge. The message they communicate is that we can express affection, friendship, and admiration by sending greeting cards. With heart-tugging effectiveness these commercials create a feeling of warmth for others that enhances the desire of people to respond. The slogan "When you care enough to send the very best" makes the point that sending a Hallmark card expresses sentiments in the finest possible way.

The pictureboard that follows shows in detail how one Hallmark commercial developed. The central figure is a young boy who stays behind after his classmates have left to give his teacher a card expressing his appreciation for her special help in teaching him to read. The master touch in the commercial is the closing scene in which he shows that he

---

LEO BURNETT COMPANY, INC.   HALLMARK CARDS, INC.

AS FILMED AND RECORDED   (11/90) "Mrs. Lagow's Gift/Stereo" 2:00   HMHF1379
                                                                          Page 1 of 2

1. MRS. LAGOW: OK everyone, now I want you all to have a really good Christmas vacation.

2. Have lots of fun...

3. but...uh, don't forget everything we've learned so far this year...

4. 'cause when we get back... (SFX: BELL)

5. MRS. LAGOW: we're going to start on long division.

6. Everybody have a good Christmas. I'll see you in a couple of weeks.

7. (SFX: KIDS RUNNING AND TALKING)

8. MRS. LAGOW: Merry Christmas ...do your homework.

9. Merry Christmas...bye-bye.

10. Merry Christmas...bye-bye.

11. ...

12. ...

13. (MUSIC:UNDER THROUGHOUT) MRS. LAGOW: Peter, the bell rang...school's out...you can go.

14. PETER: I know. I just wanted to tell you something. I mean, my Mom...wanted me to tell you something.

15. My Mom wanted to thank you for helping me out with my reading, because she thinks...

16. it was really nice of you to take all that time after school...

17. and during lunch...and even that one day before school, just to help me learn how to read better.

18. Because if you hadn't spent all that extra time with me...

19. I probably wouldn't be able to read much of anything. And my Mom just wanted me to thank you...

20. MRS. LAGOW: Peter...

21. PETER: and this is from me.

22. Merry Christmas, Mrs. Lagow.

23. ...

24. ...

25. MRS. LAGOW: Thank you.
PETER: You're welcome.

26. Mrs. Lagow?

27. Want me to read it for you?

28. MRS. LAGOW: I'd like that.
I'd like that very much.

29. ...

30. PETER: (READING CARD)
"There are some special people,
we meet along life's way..."

is able to read the card to her, thus demonstrating how effective her help has been.

Commercial writers often take advantage of the affection parents have for their children. In the early 1950s the television industry, recognizing that nothing is more likely to make parents feel guilty than the charge that they are failing to provide their children with the advantages available to other boys and girls, conducted a campaign emphasizing that children living in a home without a television set were underprivileged. This campaign was harshly criticized for its cold-blooded assault on parental emotions, but it undoubtedly motivated a great many mothers and fathers to buy TV sets. Food makers frequently try to sell their products by arousing concern for the welfare of children. One bread manufacturer presents the product not merely as a wholesome, tasty food but as an absolute essential to the development of a sound, healthy body. Another type of product for which this type of appeal is ideally suited is the vitamin tablet designed for children.

The basic needs we have described are common to most people, but writers of commercials must recognize that their effectiveness in influencing behavior varies from person to person. People who smoke cigarettes, for example, obviously find the pleasure they get more important than the threat cigarettes pose to their health and life expectancy. Advertisers sometimes conduct research that analyzes in minute detail the way consumers differ in their sensitivity to various needs. As a result of a study conducted by the Young and Rubicam advertising agency, women were divided into various categories in terms of what they were looking for in a detergent. Some were more influenced by practical advantages, others were convenience oriented, and still others were economy minded. Procter & Gamble, manufacturers of Downy and Bounce fabric softeners, conducted a similar study to determine why consumers chose one of these products over the other. The study found that Downy appealed to a group characterized as "dedicated softness seekers." Bounce, on the other hand, was preferred by those who look for convenience above everything else. Other studies have investigated the lifestyles, aspirations, self-images, and product use of consumers in general. Some of the labels devised to describe the characteristics of various groups are "money and brains," "outgoing optimists," "conscientious vigilants," "frustrated factory workers," and "militant mothers." The challenge faced by the writers of commercials is to create key selling ideas appropriate to the varying needs suggested by these classifications.

Satisfying Need Once the need has been established, the next step is to convince the audience that the product not only satisfies that need, but satisfies it better than anything else on the market.

1. *Demonstrations.* One of the best ways to convince an audience that a product will meet a need is to show it being used. Demonstration is easy on television but it is not impossible on radio. The skillful use of words and sound effects leads the radio listener to visualize the product in action. In television, however, it is the picture that sells the product. What you show in action is more important than what you say. Sound and voice are used mainly to emphasize what the pictures demonstrate. This brings up the further point that the video and the audio should be firmly linked. Nothing can so quickly disperse a commercial's effect than a series of pictures that go in one direction while an announcer goes wandering off in another.

A commercial for Band-Aids illustrates the effectiveness of making the picture the primary persuasive element in a TV commercial.

The compelling reason for buying projected by this commercial was that a Band-Aid would stick to everything under any conditions. The picture that established this point was a Band-Aid firmly stuck to an egg suspended in boiling water. No supporting words were really necessary to establish the selling argument. The picture told the whole story.

Some advertisers are now presenting demonstrations in two phases. A commercial which Kellogg's has used to advertise its Crispix cereal illustrates this approach. The key selling idea was that Crispix stays crisp indefinitely even when covered by milk or cream. The first phase of the commercial showed a consumer pouring milk over a bowl of Crispix. At that point a commercial for another product came on. At its conclusion the Crispix advertisement returned to show that the cereal was still crisp despite the time taken up by the intervening commercial, as the following pictureboards (A and B) show.

2. *Science.* One of the best ways of convincing an audience that a product will satisfy a need is to associate it in some way with science. The use of scientific terminology is a common method of accomplishing this objective. The makers of Nuprin advertise that "metroprophin" is part of the formula used in manufacturing this medicine. Average viewers are not likely to know what this term means, but it has a reassuring scientific ring to it and thus their confidence in the product is enhanced. Saying that "precollagen molecules" are contained in Revlon's Ultima II performs a similar service. At times copywriters have even made up scientific-sounding names to give products an attractive aura. At one time the maker of Pepsodent toothpaste claimed that it contained an ingredient called "irium." A creative copywriter invented the name for a commonplace element.

A second major means of providing scientific support for a selling argument is to sub-

Kellogg's   "SCIENCE EXPERIMENT A" :15   CRISPIX

1. RANDY: We're gonna do an experiment to prove to you...

2. and my special assistant, Bobby, that Crispix stays crispy in milk.

3. Go ahead, Bobby.

4. (SFX: PITCHER SLIDING)

5. (SFX: MILK POURING)
RANDY: That's it. Fill it up.

6. We'll be right back.
(CUT AWAY)

mit or seem to submit the product to a scientific test. The outstanding surge in the sales of Crest toothpaste referred to earlier followed a series of commercials that reported the results of controlled experiments comparing the development of cavities in two groups of people: those who used Crest and those who didn't. The findings that Crest users developed far fewer cavities than nonusers persuaded millions of consumers to switch to Crest. Sometimes experiments of a simple nature are actually shown in the commercial. In one of them the late actress Nancy Walker, playing a waitress, spilled coffee on a counter. Using both Bounty paper towels and a competitive product, she convincingly demonstrated that Bounty is "the better picker-upper."

3. Foreign Words.   Recently some advertisers have turned to an unusual means for creating a tone that may help convince viewers that the products they advertise will satisfy their needs—the use of foreign words. Listeners to one commercial heard an Italian matron imploring them to *mangia* Uncle Ben's risotto. In commercials for its French-roast coffee, the Folger Coffee company translated part of the catchy "best part of waking up" song into French. Volkswagen has used the German word *Fahrvergnügen* in its commercials without explaining that it means "love of driving." Bill Young, president of Volkswagen of America, said they used the word "to get away from the customer coming and asking, 'What's the price?' Now people go into a

Kellogg's   "SCIENCE EXPERIMENT B"   :15   CRISPIX

1. (CUT BACK)
RANDY: We're back.

2. Give it a try, Bobby.

3. (SFX: CRUNCH)

4. RANDY: You heard it.
Scientific proof that Crispix
stays crispy and very tasty in
milk.

5. See, learning can be fun.

6. RANDY (VO): Crispix.
(SFX: LOCKING SOUND)
RANDY (VO): Crisp that just
won't quit.

dealership to ask, 'What does *Fahrvergnü-gen* mean?'"[2] One can assume that, after finding out, they may take a test drive.

4. *Testimonials.*   Another device that persuades listeners they will be satisfied with a product is the testimonial. The statement of a beautiful movie star that she uses a certain soap or shampoo carries the inescapable implication that all who do likewise will acquire her beauty and glamour. Children following the example of a famous athlete in eating a certain breakfast food see themselves attaining similar physical prowess. The virility and good looks of the baseball players who shave on television provide a subtle but powerful impetus toward purchase of the product. Arnold Palmer's ingra-

tiating smile and the image of trustworthiness he projects as he drinks a glass of orange juice after a round of golf helps to establish the idea that orange juice "isn't just for breakfast anymore."

Testimonials by celebrities are effective because people feel they can trust someone they know. However, not all members of the audience trust them; some people place little credence in a testimonial they know is paid for. Advertisers try to minimize suspicion of this type by showing celebrities actually using the product and reflecting obvious personal appreciation. It should be noted that the FTC requires that people who say in commercials that they use a product must actually be users of that product. Celebrities are not always asked to give personal testimony to the worth of the product, however. Sometimes they serve only as spokespersons who present the advertiser's message; as we noted earlier, their effectiveness comes from their ability as public figures to attract the audience's attention and from their skill as performers.

Testimony in advertising is not the sole province of celebrities. Advertisers often contrive situations in which unknown people become effective testifiers for a product. The best example is the "candid camera" setup, in which an advertiser's representative manipulates a passerby, who doesn't know the scene is being filmed for a commercial, into making favorable statements about the product. The taste tests conducted by the makers of soft drinks are an example of that practice. Agents for the Pepsi Cola or Coca-Cola companies, for instance, hide the labels on cans of Pepsi Cola and Coca-Cola and then ask people walking by to sample the two beverages and state which one they like better. Those who make the proper choice may appear in a commercial. The Shell company at one time arranged to have an actor posing as a gas station attendant suggest to customers that they might be using the wrong gasoline. Those who defended their choice of Shell with appropriate ardor had a chance of appearing in a commercial. To capture just the right responses, it was necessary to film hundreds of unsuspecting customers with a hidden camera. Testifiers in commercials need not even be human beings. In live commercials for Alpo dog food, the wagging tails of dogs as they eat Alpo provide convincing testimony of canine satisfaction with the product.

Another type of testimony advertisers make use of when it is available is a favorable statement or finding from an organization not connected with the company, which the public sees as being objective and authoritative. A government testing laboratory is an example. When government findings favoring a product or an ingredient are published, they often become a part of commercials. At one time the American Dental Association carried out research that showed a certain fluoride substance was effective in reducing cavities. The makers of Crest, which used this substance in their toothpaste, made the ADA statement a part of their advertising. Later, another company introduced a new toothpaste containing the same ingredient, and it also used the ADA statement.

Choosing the Presentational Appeal

Having decided what appeals to use, the writer must then determine how to present them to the audience. The dramatization is a commonly used framework which often uses a problem/solution approach. One commercial showed a small child crawling into a tablecloth covering a table loaded with food and drink. The pull on the tablecloth sent a glass of wine cascading to the floor despite the mother's desperate effort to catch it. The mishap created no great problem, however, for the remedy was already in place—a stainless carpet from which the spreading wine was mopped up easily without leaving a mark. The American Express company has long used dramatic vignettes to advertise its traveler's checks. A typical commercial shows a thief making off with cash a family is using for a vacation. Then the actor Karl Malden appears to tell viewers that this kind of disaster doesn't need to happen. The solution is American Express traveler's checks. "Don't leave home without them," Malden advises.

Writers of commercials use many other presentational frameworks besides the dramatization. Sometimes the focus is on an announcer who communicates the main message. In others, a singer or musical group carries out this function. Among the other frameworks used in commercials are interviews, a *cinéma vérité* style, an experimental setup, or a documentary approach.

The maker of Krylon paint used a visual effect in a striking way to drive home the key selling point that Krylon dries quickly. The commercial opened with Johnny Bench, the former all-star baseball catcher, painting one side of a picnic seat with Krylon, the other side with a competitive product. Twelve minutes later he confidently sat down on the part of the seat painted with Krylon. Then along came Bob Uecker wearing white shorts. Before Bench could stop him, Uecker had plopped himself down on the part of the seat painted with the competitive product. The shot of the two of them as they walked away effectively showed that the Krylon had dried, while the other paint hadn't. Bench's clothes were unmarked; Uecker's shorts were stained with red.

One of the most important objectives of commercial writers is to show the product being used in circumstances that will persuade audiences to use it also. Television is the obvious means for accomplishing this objective, but a skillfully contrived radio commercial can do it also by stimulating listeners to use their imaginations and thus "see" the product being used. In developing a plan for a commercial, particularly for television, visualization must be included. However, in carrying out this function, writers of commercials often have difficulty finding qualities that distinguish the product they are advertising from its competitors. What can you say about one brand of beer that will make people want to buy that particular brand instead of others? The problem is compounded by the fact that most people actually can't recognize the brand they say they prefer when they are asked to choose it from among its competitors during a blindfold taste test. What most

advertisers fall back on in these circumstances is a commercial that visualizes their product being used in connection with a happy or exciting event. Pabst commercials show people relishing a beer after triumphing in a stirring athletic contest. In Miller commercials, men turn to beer for relaxation after carrying out a challenging job assignment. In Lowenbrau and Michelob commercials, people make beer part of a pleasant evening with friends in a restaurant or at home. The makers of soft drinks face a similar problem and their solution is similar. The drinking of Coca-Cola, Pepsi Cola, and 7-Up is almost always visualized in situations in which people are having fun—at picnics, amusement parks, county fairs, dances.

Adapting to Special Problems

In working out a plan for a commercial, writers must often take into account special circumstances or conditions that complicate their task. Their problems arise from a number of sources, such as general restraints on advertising practices, the nature of the competition, selling objectives, and product disadvantages.

Responding to Restraints There are a number of governmental and industry policies that limit what advertisers can do. By congressional decree, for example, cigarettes cannot be advertised on radio or television, and broadcasters have agreed among themselves not to accept advertising for hard liquor. Advertising for such services as fortune telling, astrology, and phrenology, once barred by the now-defunct *TV Code*, is still not accepted by many broadcasters, although this barrier is breaking down. There are also restraints on the claims advertisers can make. If they cannot be substantiated, the Federal Trade Commission (FTC), which is responsible for policing the advertising industry, may order advertisers to stop using them. It forbade the use of the word *liver* in the name Carter's Little Liver Pills because the product had no effect on liver function, and it also ordered the maker of Listerine to stop claiming that it could prevent colds. The FTC is also empowered to prevent the use of techniques that will mislead or deceive the public. When a manufacturer of an auto safety glass claimed that its product did not distort the passengers' view of scenery, and tried to prove it by photographing scenery with the window rolled down, the FTC ordered the company to withdraw the commercial. In another celebrated case it stopped the Colgate-Palmolive company from using a commercial which purported to show that Rapid Shave could shave sandpaper. The demonstration did not involve sandpaper at all but sand placed on plexiglass.

There is a special sensitivity about commercials aimed at children. To keep them from being unduly influenced, for example, there is general agreement that hosts and characters in programs cannot deliver commercial messages. Broadcasters usually do not urge young viewers to pester their parents into buying the product or attempt to frighten them into a purchase. Because children often have difficulty distinguishing programs from commercials, a number of broadcasters use special signals and devices to let the children know that a commercial is coming on.

There are also some restraints on commercials meant for general audiences. Commercials for medical products, for instance, usually do not employ the terms *safe, without risk,* and *harmless.* For many years there was a prohibition against commercials in which spokespersons attired in the white coats commonly worn by physicians, nurses, dentists, and pharmacists urged viewers to buy medical products. The American Broadcasting Company (ABC) television network has now relaxed that restriction provided the person in the white coat is an actual medical or dental professional. Like almost all broadcasters, ABC will not permit people to drink beer on camera in commercials, but it now permits off-camera drinking. The National Broadcasting Company (NBC), in contrast, maintains its restriction against "white coat" commercials and will not permit beer to be consumed in commercials even off-camera. The trend, however, is to ease restrictions of this type.

Writers of commercials that advertise products relating to intimate bodily functions face special problems. Creating a feminine-hygiene product commercial that will not transgress the bounds of good taste, for example, requires great skill and sensitivity.

Besides being controlled by government and industry restrictions, writers of commercials are also affected by public and media reactions to their work. A case in point was a commercial for Reebok athletic shoes which showed two men, attached by long ropes to a bridge, jumping off into space. One was wearing Reebok shoes, the other Nikes. The one wearing Reeboks was jerked to safety, but the camera showed only an empty pair of Nikes at the end of the other line. Presumably their owner jumped to his death. Condemnations of the commercial by outraged editorial writers and protests from the public caused the Reebok company to withdraw it. Sometimes the broadcasting industry itself draws attention to questionable advertising practices. On November 6, 1990, ABC's *Good Morning America* reported a finding by the Texas attorney general that the maker of Volvo automobiles had employed deception in one of its commercials. It showed a huge tractor running over a row of cars, one of which was a Volvo. All were crushed except the Volvo. The ABC report revealed that the support bars in the other cars had been removed, whereas the support bars in the Volvo had been reinforced.

Naming Competitors The number of commercials in which the names of competing products are used has increased greatly in recent years. They now constitute about one-fourth of all commercials. The maker of Tums, for example, tells listeners that its competitor Rolaids "consumes one-third less acid than Tums." During a TV golf broadcast, the maker of Pro-Staff golf balls advised viewers that its product won more money and more tournaments than its chief competitor Titleist. The maker of Tylenol, a non-aspirin remedy for headaches, won first place in the market by comparing its product directly with aspirin remedies. AT&T uses counters to show how much speakers on competing AT&T and MCI lines are being charged for making identical long distance calls. When the calls come to an end, the counters indicate that both cost about the same despite MCI's claim that its rates are lower.

Sometimes comparative advertising can be quite elaborate. A commercial produced for the Pepsi Cola company, for example, showed a mix-up in the delivery of Pepsi Cola and Coca-Cola. The case of Pepsi Cola meant for a fraternity party was sent instead to a retirement home and the Coca-Cola ordered by the senior citizens arrived instead at the fraternity fest. The results of this mistake carried out the key selling idea that Pepsi Cola is supposedly for the "young at heart." After drinking the Pepsi Cola, the old folks began to boogie; the young people at the fraternity party, after downing their Cokes, decided to play bingo rather than dance.

In some instances the reference to a competitor is carried out in a subtle way. An example was a commercial produced for the maker of the sugar substitute Sweet 'n Low, whose main competitor is a product called Equal. The commercial for Sweet 'n Low concluded with the line, "For millions of people around the world, there's just no equal."

When broadcast advertising began, competing brands were never named. One reason was that the networks would not accept comparative advertising. NBC abolished this restriction in the late 1960s, and CBS and ABC took the same step in 1972. The FTC decided about the same time that comparative advertising helped consumers to make wise decisions, and actively encouraged it. The Federal Communications Commission (FCC) warned, however, that when advertisers claim their product is better than another they must take particular care to make sure their facts are right. It also counseled advertisers to avoid mere disparagement.

Advertisers took their first timid steps toward comparative advertising by referring to competitors in a general way. An example was the use of the term "Brand X." Writers of commercials for margarine even avoided the word *butter* in referring to their competition, using instead the phrase "higher priced spread"—a substitute that carried a built-in argument for the use of margarine. Sometimes the names of competitors, though ostensibly spoken, were covered by beeps. In other instances the main competition was referred to as the "leader" in the field, leaving the audience to identify it. The Gillette company became bolder when it produced a commercial showing a hand pushing away the clearly labeled packages of its competitors before picking up a Gillette package.

The advertising industry is not of a single mind about the use of comparative advertising that names names. Some say such advertising may backfire by arousing audience hostility. Others point out that naming a competitor's product may actually give the competitor free advertising. On the other side of the argument, the National Advertising Review Board says that "truthful and significant differences in competitive products should be made known to the public and comparative advertising is a proper technique for accomplishing this purpose." It adds, however, that "improper comparative advertising, which misleads or deceives, is not acceptable even though offered under the umbrella of 'free competition.'"

Obviously, writers using a comparative advertising technique to portray a competitor's product in an unfavorable light must construct their commercials with great care. For one thing, they must be absolutely certain they can back up their claims. They also need to be sure that they do not go beyond the bounds of good taste and fair play.

Enlarging the Market Most manufacturers constantly look for ways to increase their sales. One way to enlarge the market is to develop uses for the product not previously contemplated. In this type of campaign, commercials can play a significant part. A good example is the effort by the makers of Florida orange juice to persuade people to drink orange juice not just at breakfast but during all times of the day. The slogan "Orange juice isn't just for breakfast anymore" is repeated over and over again as celebrities and other people drink orange juice after sports and opera rehearsals, for lunch, and as an afternoon refresher. Johnson's Baby Shampoo, originally developed for the children's market, was advertised as a gentle product that wouldn't sting children's eyes. An obvious way of increasing sales was to encourage adults to use it, too. That is just what the company has been doing in recent years. The key selling point is that Johnson's Baby Shampoo is so gentle it can be used every day without damaging hair. In one commercial, the husky football player Fran Tarkenton testified that he used that particular baby shampoo because football practice required him to wash his hair every day.

Commercials produced for Kellogg's cereals illustrate how ads can further campaigns designed to enlarge markets. One

series of commercials aimed at persuading young adults to buy Bran Flakes, a cereal usually thought of as a favorite of older people. In one commercial a young man was afraid to admit to an attractive woman he met in the supermarket that the Bran Flakes he held in his hand were meant for him rather than for his father. Confirming her supposition, he said, "Yes, they're for Dad." Another commercial placed a young woman in a similar situation.

A second series of commercials was also directed at young adults, but in this case the objective was to enlarge the market for Kellogg's Frosted Flakes, usually considered a children's cereal. The commercials struck a theme similar to the one used in the Bran Flakes series: Some people were so embarrassed to admit that they still liked Frosted Flakes that they tried to hide their identity. A pictureboard (page 36) of the Frosted Flakes commercial illustrates this approach.

Dealing with Disadvantages Sometimes a product has certain inherent disadvantages with which a writer of commercials must contend. The Avis company boldly admitted in its advertising that it was number two in the car-rental business, then proceeded to take advantage of that problem by arguing that because it was second, it "tried harder." The Lipton tea company attempted to negate the feeling that tea drinking is for sissies by advertising its brew as "strong and hearty."

When Miller first brought out its beer, it called its product "The Champagne of Beers" and put that slogan on its containers. As the years went by, however, it became clear that the idea of champagne is not appealing to most of the people who enjoy drinking beer. Though it still appears on Miller containers, the company no longer uses the slogan in its advertising. They have gone even further to negate its effect with a series of commercials connecting Miller's use to husky working-

LEO BURNETT COMPANY, INC.　　　　　　　　　　　　　　　　　　　KELLOGG CO.

AS FILMED AND RECORDED　　(5/91)　　"SHADOWS/CONGRESSMAN-CC"　　:30　KLSF7723

1. GUY: Here I am, a pillar of the community. And I love Kellogg's Frosted Flakes.

2. (AVO): Brave adults challenge the notion that Kellogg's Frosted Flakes is just a kids' cereal.

3. WOMAN: In business meetings I look around and wonder...am I the only one?

4. (AVO): Those sweet, crunchy flakes...

5. and a splash of cold milk.

6. What could an adult like better for breakfast?

7. GUY: I'm crazy about the taste. Hey, I've got nothing to hide!

8. TONY: It's easy to see! Frosted Flakes have the taste...

9. adults have grown to love. They're grrrreat!

men who drink it after they have completed a challenging day's work in such places as a steel factory or a coal mine.

SCRIPTING THE COMMERCIAL

In planning a commercial, writers make a number of important choices. They decide the presentational framework for the appeal—whether it is to be presented by an announcer, in dramatic form, as a demon-stration, in a "candid camera" format, or in some other way. They also devise the key selling point and decide how to emphasize it. They consider any special problems that advertising of the product may present and develop ideas to meet them. After all this is done, the task of turning these ideas into a script that can be produced for radio and television still lies ahead. Using the right for-mat is simple, for it is necessary only to fol-low the formats that have become standard in the industry. Achieving *memorability* and *persuasiveness,* the two greatest challenges, is another matter. It involves an arduous process of finding the right words and pictures to communicate the message and planning devices to support it.

The Commercial Format

The examples of radio and television commercials included in this chapter illustrate the formats used by broadcasters. The main rule to remember is that everything spoken by someone is typed in regular upper- and lower-case letters. Everything else—such as character names, sound effects, music designations, and production instructions—is typed in capital letters. The precise style may vary from place to place, but this rule is generally followed.

TV commercials usually come into being first in storyboard form. Artists draw the pictures and put in the audio material accompanying them to show the relationships between the video and audio elements. The storyboard can be turned into a script that describes the video elements of the commercial on one side of the page and the audio

---

Energizer Commercial

VIDEO	*AUDIO*
	SFX: ALARM CLOCK.
OPEN ON SHOT OF ALARM SOAP.	*MUSIC:* TYPICALLY BAD SOAP JINGLE UP.
HAND OPENS SOAP WRAPPER.	SINGERS: Alarm! It'll start your day!
GUY IN SHOWER.	Alarm! You'll be on your way!
GUY LOOKS DOWN.	Ring in your day—with Alarm!
	SFX: BOOM, BOOM, BOOM. . .
BUNNY WEARING A RAIN SLICKER.	*MUSIC:* JINGLE DIES.
	ANNCR (VO): Still going. Nothing outlasts the Energizer.
SHOT OF FEET AS GUY SHUFFLES TO AVOID BUNNY.	
BUNNY PASSES THROUGH END PRODUCT.	They keep going and going. . .
SHOT OF SOAP.	and going. . . and going. . .
SUPER: ALARMINGLY FRESH!	

elements on the other. In typing this script, the rule that everything spoken is typed in regular upper- and lower-case letters and everything else is typed in capitals also applies. After the commercial has been produced, it may be recorded in a pictureboard or photoboard. It is similar to the storyboard, except that the visualization is accomplished by using stills from the commercial after it has been produced. Examples of storyboards, pictureboards, TV commercial scripts, and radio commercial scripts appear at various places in this book. Earlier in this chapter, for instance, there is a storyboard for one of the Energizer "pink rabbit" commercials. The script that follows shows how this storyboard was converted into script form.

Making the Audience Remember

The principal technique for making the audience remember the product name and absorb the key selling point is to repeat it constantly. Even though repetition may irritate, there is no doubt that it is the copywriter's most effective selling tool. As noted earlier, some commercials do little more than repeat the product name. Such commercials are often referred to as *name* copy. One TV commercial for a clothing store consisted of nothing more than the store's name bouncing around the screen, breaking up, reassembling in a multitude of variations, advancing and retreating as the letters changed, switched, and combined. A one-minute Gallo commercial included 30 mentions of the product name.

Commercials for Nike shoes do not usually employ repetition as a selling technique, but there was at least one exception. Even this commercial, however, was different from most in that the repetition did not focus on the product name, as most name copy does, but rather on the product itself. (The part of Mars Blackmon, incidentally, was played by the commercial's director, Spike Lee.)

Wieden & Kennedy
As-Produced Script
for Nike Shoes

Video	*Audio*
TITLE CARD AGAINST BLACK SCREEN: AIR. BY MICHAEL JORDAN AND MARS BLACKMON.	MUSIC: UP AND THROUGHOUT
OPEN ON MARS BLACKMON AS HE ENTERS CHICAGO STADIUM.	MARS: "Yo, Mars Blackmon here at NBA Finals to see what makes Michael . . ."
CUT TO FOOTAGE OF JORDAN IN ACTION.	MARS: ". . . Jordan the best!"
CUT TO CROWD CHEERING.	
CUT TO MARS STANDING ON STAIRS IN STADIUM HOLDING SHOE.	MARS: "Is it the shoes?"
CUT TO JORDAN FOOTAGE.	

CUT TO MARS IN FRONT OF CHICAGO BULL ON WALL.	MARS: "It's gotta be the shoes!"
CUT TO MARS SHOWING SHOE TO BULL MASCOT.	MARS: "It's gotta be the shoes!"
CUT TO MARS WALKING WITH SHOE IN EACH HAND THROUGH COLISEUM MEZZANINE.	MARS: "The shoes!"
CUT TO MARS WITH SHOE INTERRUPTING CONCESSION-STAND WORKER.	MARS: "It's gotta be the shoes!"
CUT TO MARS HOLDING SHOE UP AT REFEREE.	MARS: "The shoes!"
CUT TO MARS WITH SHOE AT SOUVENIR BOOTH.	MARS: "The shoes!"
CUT TO MICHAEL JORDAN FOOTAGE.	MARS (VO): "Gotta be the shoes!"
CUT TO MORE MICHAEL JORDAN IN ACTION.	MARS (VO): "The shoes . . . the shoes!"
CUT TO MARS STANDING UP IN CROWD HOLDING SHOE.	MARS: "It's gotta be . . ."
CROWD STANDS UP.	CROWD/MARS: ". . . the shoes!"
CUT TO FULL SCREEN OF SCOREBOARD READING: IT'S GOTTA BE THE SHOES!	ANNCR (VO): "It's gotta be the shoes!"
CUT TO REFEREE HOLDING SHOE TO CAMERA.	REFEREE: "The shoes!"
CUT TO CONCESSION STAND CLERK HOLDING SHOE.	CLERK: "The shoes!"
CUT TO CU OF MARS WITH SHOE.	MARS: "The shoes!"
CUT TO BULLS MASCOT HOLDING SHOE.	MASCOT: "The shoes!"
CUT TO SOUVENIR CLERK HOLDING SHOES.	CLERK: "The shoes!"
CUT TO CROWD HOLDING UP SHOES.	CROWD: "The shoes!"
CUT TO ANOTHER SECTION OF CROWD.	CROWD: "The shoes!"

CUT TO A LARGER SECTION OF CROWD.	CROWD: "The shoes!"
CUT TO SCOREBOARD READING: DA SHOES!	
OUT OF CENTER OF SCOREBOARD A NEWSPAPER SPIRALS OUT TO FULL SCREEN READING: BULLS WIN! WAS IT THE SHOES?	
CUT TO LAKER A.C. GREEN IN LOCKER ROOM AFTER GAME, HOLDING SHOE. TITLE: <u>45–A.C. Green</u>	A.C. (TO CAMERA): "It had to be the shoes."
CUT TO FULL-SCREEN TITLE: AIR JORDAN FROM NIKE.	
FADE TO BLACK	<u>MUSIC:</u> DOWN

A second major tool for attaining memorability is music, for melodies may linger tenaciously in our minds. How often have we found ourselves humming the tune from a commercial, even though we may hate ourselves for it? One of the first singing commercials began with the lines: "Pepsi Cola hits the spot; twelve full ounces, that's a lot." The jingle became so ingrained in public consciousness that a survey once showed it to be the second most recognized song in the United States, ranking below only "The Star-Spangled Banner."

Moreover, music helps to make the repetitiousness of a commercial palatable, for we are accustomed to repetitions in songs and the musical setting permits writers to repeat the name many more times than they would be able to in straight copy without becoming ridiculous. Music for commercials may be specially composed; some of it is so well done that it has become popular on its own. Some is adapted from melodies in the public domain that through the years have demonstrated their staying power. Some contemporary composers have also permitted melodies of theirs that are still under copyright to be used in commercials in return for a fee. An example of public-domain music that has been heard in a number of commercials is the majestic opening of Richard Strauss's "Also sprach Zarathustra," used so memorably in the film *2001: A Space Odyssey*. The wake-up song used in Folger's Coffee commercials is an example of specially commissioned music. Contemporary music licensed for use in commercials includes two Beatles songs, "Help" (which became part of a Mercury automobile commercial), and "Revolution" (used by the Nike company). McDonald's purchased the right to use the music to "Mack the Knife" from Kurt Weill's *Three-Penny Opera* in its hamburger commercials.

In using music there are two points to remember in particular. First, avoid music that is strongly connected in people's minds with certain lyrics because the message of these lyrics may compete with the message of the commercial. Remember that popular lyrics entrenched in memory because of their association with a party, a person, or a place are almost bound to win over an advertising message. Though only the melody is used, it often recalls the original lyrics to the listener's mind and thus defeats the purpose of the commercial. There are exceptions to this rule, of course. AT&T effectively utilized both the words and music of the song "Feelings" in a series of commercials it ran to promote telephone use. The second point to remember in using music is that the unauthorized use of copyrighted melodies and arrangements opens the door to lawsuits. Always seek express permission to use music under copyright and be prepared to pay fees for its use.

A third technique for making a product name and message memorable is to incorporate them in a catchy slogan. The history of advertising abounds with examples. Many years ago the slogan "Ask the man who owns one" was used by Packard Motor Car Company. The Clairol company helped to make the dyeing of women's hair an acceptable practice with the slogan, "Does she or doesn't she? Only her hairdresser knows for sure," and incidentally increased its sales by 40 percent. Modern-day slogans include McDonald's "You deserve a break today," Hallmark's "When you care enough to send the very best," American Express's "Don't leave home without it," and Pepsi's "You've got the right one, baby," delivered by Ray Charles. Sometimes slogans can help sell products even though (or perhaps *because*) their meaning is ambiguous. "Coke is it," a slogan of a few years ago, and the Nike slogan "Just do it," are examples.

A fourth device for imprinting product names and messages is to connect them with an easily remembered symbol. Insurance companies often use visual devices for identification in their television advertising. The stag of the Hartford company, the umbrella of Travelers, and the Rock of Gibraltar of Prudential come to mind. For many years the Hathaway shirt company used a model with a black eye-patch to advertise its shirts. Texaco was one of the earliest advertisers on television with its *Texaco Star Theatre,* the show that made Milton Berle into "Mr. Television," and it continues to use a star as a company symbol in its current advertising. Animals are often used to identify products or services. Many

TV-watching people who see an orange cat are inevitably reminded of Morris, the supercilious cat of the 9 Lives cat-food commercials. A tiger is used by both Esso and Kellogg's to help give memorability to their commercials. A bull identifies the investment firm Merrill Lynch, and a team of Clydesdale horses make many people think of Budweiser beer.

Making the Audience Buy

Copy designed to influence audiences to purchase the product immediately is often referred to as *action* copy. The first essential in such a commercial is *clarity.* Use words and phrases the audience is sure to understand and be certain that your ideas develop in logical progression. Writers sometimes use scientific or pseudoscientific terms, whose meaning is not made clear, simply to add dressing or persuasive appeal, but the main ideas should always be expressed in familiar terms. Avoid giving the impression that you are talking down to your audience. Your tone should be conversational and informal, and it should show some respect for the listener's intelligence.

In addition to being clear, it is important to choose words that are appropriate to the product. "Efficient" may be an accurate word with reference to some perfumes, but it is not an appropriate one. Your words should match the product. Often writers use double adjectives to catch the quality they are attempting to communicate. Bread is "oven-fresh," beer is "cool-brewed," grapes are "sun-ripened." Verbs are important in commercials because they are the words that suggest action.

Research into the effect of commercials shows that certain words have more selling power than others. You can enhance the impact of the commercial by sprinkling these persuasive words at intervals through your copy. David Ogilvy, in his book *Confessions of an Advertising Man,* listed a number of expressions that have unique selling force, among them the following: "introducing, it's here, just arrived, new, sensational, remarkable, startling, magic, quick, easy, hurry, last chance." Other words occurring frequently are "natural" and "new and improved."

A further characteristic of effective selling copy is that it is *concrete* and to the point. Generalizations and unsupported superlatives have little selling effect. Because buyers like to feel they are motivated by facts in choosing one product in preference to another, commercials should provide them with specific information.

Many commercials, particularly those of the high-pressure type, contain a concluding step designed to provide the final impetus toward a sale. This step may be a summary of the main points followed by an admonition to "Act now. . . Don't delay. . . Do it today. . . Try it now." If the offer is part of a special sale, the listener may be warned, "Act now before it's too late. . . This is your last chance. . . The offer may never be repeated." If the product is not one for which there is an immediate need—viewers watching an aspirin commercial may not have a headache at the moment—they are urged to buy immediately anyway, "for a headache may strike at any time!" Sometimes this last step involves the mention of a merchandising scheme calculated to impel listeners to action: "See your dealer tomorrow. You may already have won a new car!" In short, the action step aims to develop the highest degree of compulsion possible. When it is over the listener's lethargy should have been drained away. He or she should turn from the commercial with an irresistible urge to buy.

Reviewing the Copy

Once written it is important to review and revise the copy with great care. These are some of the questions you might ask yourself as you examine your work: *Will I catch the attention of the audience? Have I created enough desire for the product? Do I show it in action? Have I focused on a key selling point which emphasizes that the product is different or better than its competitors? Have I provided enough information about it?*

In addition to these basic points there may be minor matters needing attention. You may discover that you have unintentionally used alliteration in such a way as to make your product seem ridiculous, or your copy may contain a verbal pitfall that will trap an unwary announcer. It is also possible that an idea you have expressed may not have come out quite the way you intended. The writers of the following material probably wished they had reviewed their copy with more care: "All hats half off"; "When I see a lady who does her own housework and dishwashing and who has soft, pretty hands, I know she has been using her head"; "We stand behind every bed we sell"; "When clothes get dirty, just throw them in our washer and let 'er rip."

It may be well to recall a point made at the beginning of this chapter—namely, that the one goal of a commercial is to sell the product. In seeking this goal, the commercial may be humorous or dramatic, artistic or entertaining, but if it succeeds only in achieving these qualities without promoting product sales, it has failed. There is no question that the writers of commercials need to exercise great ingenuity. It is misdirected, however, if it aims only to win audience appreciation. The payoff for a commercial comes not in winning a Clio award, which is an accolade given by the industry for skill in the production of commercials, but at the merchant's cash register. It may happen, in fact, that a device is so attention-getting in itself that the audience will remember it rather than the sales message or the product name. Some years ago the Alka Seltzer company ran a series of commercials that concentrated on people's "tummies." They were funny and entertaining and audiences enjoyed watching them. They were not successful in promoting the sale of the product, however. This may be a case where the distinctiveness of the attention-getting device and the wit of the writer obstructed the attainment of the commercial goal. The writer may have been too clever for the product's good.

THE PROMOTIONAL ANNOUNCEMENT

Among the commercials broadcast by radio and television stations, the announcement that draws attention to coming programs plays an important role. Its purpose is to keep the audience tuned to the station.

Promotions to Inform

In many instances the promotional announcement does no more than inform audiences about programs on the broadcast schedule. A station that carries play-by-play broadcasts of a local team's games may remind listeners of the time of the next game when it is reporting the results of the most recent action. That is a natural time for such promotion since audiences to sports reports are most likely to be interested in play-by-play coverage.

Promotions to Persuade

In addition to drawing attention to coming programs, promotional announcements often include some material designed to persuade people to become listeners or viewers. It may be nothing more than the admonition, "Tune in for all the exciting action." Most promotional announcements, however, are directly persuasive in their approach. In this persuasive classification we can identify two general types.

The first includes those announcements that aim at persuading people to become regular members of the audience for an entire series of programs. Examples of this type are the announcements the networks present at the beginning of each new season to drum up interest in their new offerings. They emphasize the values of the series as a whole rather than focus on a particular episode. In carrying out this kind of advertising, the networks bring into play the devices that are familiar to all watchers of commercials, among them the use of slogans and identifying symbols. NBC, for example, has called itself "the place to be," while CBS argued that "the look is CBS." (The NBC peacock and the CBS eye also provide identification.) Such announcements feature exciting or hilarious action scenes, high-pressure appeals, and hard-sell approaches.

Local stations also engage in this kind of promotional advertising. The announcement below, for example, is designed to build the general audience for WXYZ-TV's 11 P.M. newscast. Note that it focuses on a quality that distinguishes all of those newscasts—namely, that each segment is a brand–new entity, not just a rerun of a previous newscast.

Channel 7 Promotion

VIDEO	AUDIO
OPEN ON NEWSMAN ABSENTLY GETTING READY TO DELIVER 11 O'CLOCK NEWS. HE LOOKS A LITTLE RUMPLED.	NEWSMAN: Good evening. Here's the very latest 11 o'clock news.

HE HOLDS UP SCRIPT. . . BLOWS OFF LOTS OF DUST.	In the news tonight. . .
	ANNCR VO: Do you get the feeling your 11 o'clock news is just a re-hash of your early news?
CUT TO: VARIOUS SHOTS OF CHANNEL 7 NEWS TEAM GETTING READY TO GO ON AIR WITH 11 O'CLOCK NEWS SHOW. SHOTS OF BONDS EDITING COPY. HODAK CONSULTING LATEST WEATHER. ACKERMAN GETTING READY WITH SPORTS. LEWIS TALKING TO SEVERAL STREET REPORTERS.	Then turn to Channel 7. Because our 11 o'clock news is an all-new newscast. With fresh film coverage. Up-to-the-minute weather. More street reporting than any other station in town. That's why on Channel 7 you're not just getting the late news, you're getting the latest news.
TEAM SHOT. SUPER: LOGO.	The kind that can make a difference in your tomorrow.
ZERO IN ON HODAK.	HODAK: Here's a last-minute weather forecast. . .

A second type of promotional announcement is one designed to build the audience for a particular program rather than to promote an entire series. In promoting a specific newscast, stations often use a "teaser" approach that contains just enough information about an event to arouse interest but does not reveal the whole story. The following announcement presented by WJBK-TV illustrates this technique.

Channel 2 Promotion

VIDEO	AUDIO
CU	SHERRY: The three-day-old coup collapses . . . and Mikhail Gorbachev is back in power.
SOVIET COUP PICTURES; RELATIVE OF GORBY WITH CATHERINE	JOE: (VO) Tonight TV-2's Catherine Leahan tracks down one of the Soviet leader's long-lost relatives. . . who lives, incredibly enough. . . in Roseville, Michigan.
WIDE TO SHOW STORE SHELVES LINED WITH BOXES OF HEARTBURN REMEDIES	SHERRY: (VO) Also tonight. . . heartburn. . . you know, that awful, bloated feeling. . . but tonight we'll set the record straight and show you how to use the right heartburn remedy for you.
TWO-SHOT JOE AND SHERRY	JOE: Get the facts on TV-2 "Eyewitness News" at eleven.

On the local station level, the strongest promotional advertising is used to build audiences for newscasts because that is the program field in which major stations in a large city compete head to head. Their success in winning number one status in news is of critical importance in determining which station will be considered the leader in its area. The use of persuasive slogans in promoting a station's news programming is widespread. The phrases "Action News" and "Eyewitness News" come immediately to mind.

The promotion of newscasts is not the only area in which the teaser technique is used, however. Stations and networks that carry such tabloid shows as *A Current Affair* and *Inside Edition* often announce the topic of the current day's episode and show one or two scenes. They use the same techniques in promoting a movie to be shown later in the day. Networks also present teaser promotional announcements for coming programs. They are marked by the use of brief scenes from the programs, transition music, and announcer copy. Many individual programs also conclude with scenes from the next week's offering. Like the previews seen in movie theaters, they picture the most exciting action in an effort to stimulate audience interest.

PUBLIC SERVICE ANNOUNCEMENTS

The announcement on radio or television promoting the cause of a nonprofit organization devoted to serving the interests of the public is known as a public service announcement, or PSA. In many instances, stations provide the broadcast periods for such announcements free of charge, inserting them where they have not sold the slot for regular commercials. However, public service organizations usually pay for the services of those who write and produce the announcements.

A PSA usually is persuasive in nature, since, in most instances, it seeks financial support for its enterprise. It may also try to persuade audience members to give up a dangerous habit such as cigarette smoking.

Because they are attempting to persuade, writers use the devices common to commercials in preparing PSAs. In a sense, the challenge these writers face is even greater than that confronting the writer of regular commercials. People listening to commercials probably are going to buy one brand or another of the product being advertised. The problem is merely one of persuading them to buy a particular brand. Furthermore, when people spend money for advertised products, they usually receive something of value in return. Writers trying to persuade people to contribute to a charity, on the other hand, must realize that most people who hear the message have no intention of giving away any of their money. Neither can they argue that audience members will receive something in return except for the prospect of feeling good about what they have done.

Some PSAs simply declare that a campaign is on. They probably accomplish little except to remind those who plan to give anyway that the time has come for another donation. Organizations carrying out medical research may eventually benefit listeners and their families with the discoveries they make. This possibility can become part of an approach designed to motivate giving to the organization. The announcement below, presented on behalf of the Juvenile Diabetes Foundation, is an example of the type designed to generate giving.

Juvenile Diabetes Foundation Announcement

VIDEO	*AUDIO*
CU MOTHER WASHING BABY'S HANDS. CAMERA PULLS BACK TO SHOW MOTHER WASHING CHEST OF CUTE NINE-MONTH-OLD BABY SITTING IN SMALL TUB.	BABY: (GURGLES) ANNOUNCER (VO): This child doesn't look sick. But she may be blind before she's thirty. She could have a heart attack. Or kidney failure.
WAIST SHOT OF MOTHER LIFTING BABY OUT OF TUB AND CUDDLING IT ON TOWEL DRAPED OVER HER SHOULDER.	ANNOUNCER (VO): You see she has diabetes. Insulin can keep her alive. And with luck it may prevent the complications that come from diabetes. But there's no guarantee because there's still no cure. Insulin is not a cure.
WAIST SHOT OF MOTHER RUBBING BABY'S BACK.	
CU OF MOTHER'S CONCERNED FACE. WAIST SHOT OF MOTHER PREPARING TO ADMINISTER INSULIN IN BABY'S BUTTOCKS.	
GRAPHIC: INSULIN IS NOT A CURE. JUVENILE DIABETES FOUNDATION BOX 9999 NEW YORK, N.Y.	ANNOUNCER (VO): Help us find one.

Another group that appeals to audiences for donations is made up of the operators of public broadcasting stations. These contributions provide a significant portion of their financial support. Often, however, they have difficulty in prompting such giving. The problem is that audience members know the station is likely to continue broadcasting even though they do not personally contribute. They can, therefore, continue to enjoy the station's programming without spending their money. The announcement that follows shows how one public TV station, WQED in Pittsburgh, attempted to persuade viewers to give to the station by taking a soft-sell approach.

Music to Write Checks By

Good evening.

I'm Lloyd Kaiser, president of Metropolitan Pittsburgh Public Broadcasting, Inc., and I'm here at Studio C at WQED tonight delighted that you have joined us for the debut of this marvelous series, *Edward the King*.

We're going to attempt an experiment tonight. It could well make television history. . . or could well turn out to be a bomb.

It might be the greatest idea since Xerox. . . or the worst idea since the Edsel.

And there's always the possibility that it could be something dreary in between.

In a few minutes you'll be watching *Edward the King*, a distinguished television series about the son of Queen Victoria. It's quite a story.

When it was shown last year on commercial television—elsewhere, but not in Pittsburgh—people called WQED wondering why we weren't carrying it. It isn't ours, we said. It's a sponsored, commercial television series. But it must be yours, they said. . . these kinds of programs are always on WQED.

Well, we took your comments to heart and when *Edward the King* wasn't brought to Pittsburgh under commercial auspices we bought it for you, using some of our precious program acquisition funds. And now because it is a special series, we are going to do something equally special with it.

For some years we here at QED have said to ourselves, wouldn't it be wonderful to find a better way of raising the money we need to operate Channel 13 without interminable on-air pitches for money? Often we

have dreamed about something we called "Music to Write Checks By."

We'd just play soft, pleasant music and ask people to write us a check. Sound ridiculous? We'll see, right after we watch this episode of *Edward the King*. We're going to take a couple of minutes at the end of the show and try this soft-sell attempt, "Music to Write Checks By," again responding to what you've indicated you'd like. We'll see if it works.

Now sit back and enjoy *Edward the King*.

(Televise remainder of program.)

Marvelous program. Now it is time to try the experiment we talked about before this program began tonight. You've asked for a softer approach to public television fundraising—so now we present "Music to Write Checks By." A lot of people wonder whether it will work. But there were people who said that public television wouldn't work and it has. So we'll see. Call us at 621-5808 and tell us how much your check is going to be so we can flash our total on the screen. You decide the amount of course: $100, $75, $50, $20, whatever you think is an appropriate amount for you and your family to participate in the magic of public television. You know that contributions of $20 or more bring a year's subscription of the monthly *Pittsburgh* magazine. What follows now is designed as the softest sell in the history of public television. Other than music, the only sound you'll hear is the scratching of your pen. Call us.

Some groups present public service announcements not to inspire donations but to provide helpful information or to persuade people either to carry out activities that may benefit them or to give up habits that could threaten their health. The campaign of the American Heart Association alerting people to the dangers of high blood pressure and urging checkups is an example. The anti-smoking announcements of the American Cancer Society provide further illustrations of public service broadcasting.

Tony Schwartz has spent 45 years in the advertising business and now specializes in the production of this type of public service announcement. He has a number of suggestions for improving their effectiveness. He believes that celebrities should be used only when they have a direct link to the cause or problem on which the announcement focuses. When the actor Yul Brynner, best known for his role as the King in *The King and I,* warned television audiences—just before he died from cancer induced by smoking—about the danger of cigarettes, his words had a profound effect because he was so widely known. Equally arresting was a similar message delivered by NBA basketball star Earvin "Magic" Johnson that he had tested HIV positive and would therefore retire from professional sports. His popularity, especially among young people, augmented the power of his admonition to avoid AIDS through either sexual abstinence or the practice of "safe sex" with condoms.

One PSA created by Schwartz illustrates another effective use of a celebrity. The person was Edward Koch, who at the time the announcement was produced was mayor of New York. Koch was not a willing participant. The statements he made were excerpted out of context from a speech he had delivered about another subject. Quite unwittingly, he became the instrument for saying words that became an insistent chorus highlighting the theme of the announcement.

Anti-Smoking Announcement

ANNOUNCER: Mayor Koch, the mayor of New York, made a statement about New York city's bathhouses being closed down due to AIDS. He said:

KOCH: "This is a matter that earns a lot of money for these people. They are selling death, places where death can be distributed. We don't want that to go on."

ANNOUNCER: But I wonder, Mayor Koch, did you ever stop to think that you can make the same statement about cigarette companies?

KOCH: "They are selling death."

ANNOUNCER: So why does the city allow cigarettes to be advertised on city bus shelters?

KOCH: "They are selling death."

ANNOUNCER: Why does the city allow cigarettes to be sold on public property?

KOCH: "They are selling death."

ANNOUNCER: Why does the city allow cigarettes to be advertised in the city's radio stations' guide?

KOCH:	"They are selling death."
ANNOUNCER:	Any why does the city allow cigarettes to be advertised on subways trains, buses, and city-licensed taxi cabs?
KOCH:	"They are selling death."
ANNOUNCER:	Mayor Koch, cigarette companies are selling death.
KOCH:	"We don't want that to go on."
ANNOUNCER:	And, like you, we don't want that to go on. Paid for by D.O.C., representing thousands of physicians who really care.

One of Schwartz's most striking anti-smoking messages was presented by someone who was not quite a celebrity but whose words nevertheless carried a great impact. He was Patrick Reynolds, the grandson of R.J. Reynolds, founder of the well-known tobacco company.

Anti-Smoking Announcement

My name is Patrick Reynolds. My grandfather, R.J. Reynolds, founded the tobacco company which now manufactures Camels, Winstons, and Salems. We've all heard the tobacco industry say that there are no ill effects caused by smoking. Well, we have plenty of cigarette-caused disease and death right in the R.J. Reynolds family itself. My grandfather, R.J. Reynolds, chewed tobacco and died of cancer. My father, R.J. Reynolds, Jr., smoked heavily and died of emphysema. My mother smoked and had emphysema and heart disease. Two of my aunts, also heavy smokers, died of emphysema and cancer. Three of my older brothers who smoke have emphysema. I smoked for 10 years and I have small-airways lung disease.

Now tell me, do you think the cigarette companies are truthful when they tell you that cigarette smoking isn't harmful? What do you think?

Sometimes one cannot find a luminary directly connected to a health cause. Schwartz believes that, in such a case, a person suffering from the disease can convey a great impact even though he or she is not a household name. It is better to feature such a person, he suggests, than to employ an actor to portray an illness victim or to spotlight a celebrity who merely speaks for the cause.

Another unique PSA created by Schwartz was designed for just one listener—Fred L. Hunter, chairman of McDonald's—and was broadcast by a station Hunter listened to each morning while driving to his office. The PSA presented an appeal to McDonald's to stop using beef tallow (a product high in saturated fat) for frying, and use vegetable oil instead. Apparently Hunter heard the message—shortly after, the company made the switch.

Schwartz recommends asking questions to get attention and to pique the audience's curiosity. He also suggests taking advantage of current events to generate interest and make the point being advanced more vivid. An example was his use of a highly publicized plane crash that killed more than 500 people. He pointed out that even if two such disasters took place every day of the year the number of victims would still not equal the total of those who die each year from smoking. Another principle Schwartz follows is putting at the end of the announcement the information or points he most wants the audience to remember.

QUESTIONS AND PROJECTS

1. Write two commercials for the same product, one of the name or reminder type, designed to establish the product name, the other of the action type, aimed at immediate sales. Write the action commercial in both a soft-sell and a hard-sell version.
2. Write a 60-second commercial that can be cut without rewriting to a 30-second version.
3. Define the key selling point of a widely advertised product. Devise a new and different key selling point for this product.
4. Define the key selling points in the commercials for three competing products and decide which is the most effective.
5. What in your opinion is the place and function of humor in broadcast advertising?

6. Analyze the persuasive steps (attention, need, satisfaction, and action) in three commercials and evaluate their effectiveness.
7. Find and evaluate a commercial in which a stronger need for a product was used than the more obvious and relevant need.
8. Write commercials for one product in three different presentational frameworks.
9. Make your own list of words that have a powerful persuasive appeal to potential buyers.
10. In a national advertising campaign, identify a number of different situations in which the key selling point remains constant. Plan your own campaign in which you create a variety of situations to exemplify the same key selling point.
11. Plan a public service campaign for a nonprofit group in which you make known the mission of the group and enlist public support for it. Write a series of radio and television commercials designed to achieve these objectives.

NOTES

1. Arturo and Maureen Gonzales, "David Ogilvy: The Day I Almost Created a TV Scandal," *TV Guide,* March 16, 1985, p. 18.
2. Marcus Mabry, "Sprechen Sie Advertising?" *Newsweek,* December 10, 1990, p. 58.

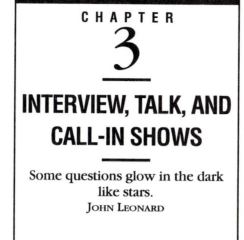

CHAPTER 3

INTERVIEW, TALK, AND CALL-IN SHOWS

Some questions glow in the dark like stars.

JOHN LEONARD

In the early days of broadcasting, the host and guest on interview programs often would meet before the broadcast to prepare a completely written interview which they then read word for word on the air. This technique served as a security blanket, assuring control over program content and timing; however, even the most skillful readers had difficulty in maintaining naturalness and spontaneity. As broadcasting matured and as hosts and guests grew more relaxed before microphone and camera, the technique of ad-libbing both the questions and the answers gradually replaced the scripted interview. The ad-libbed method is now the prevailing one.

With the transition from verbatim reading to ad-libbed conversation came a different set of demands on the interviewer. Careful and thorough preparation must still precede the broadcast, but the host and guest cast their questions, answers, and comments into final form while the interview is actually in progress. In wording questions on the air, interviewers actually carry out a writing function. They are also performers, and it is sometimes difficult to decide where writing ends and performing begins. In effect, they are oral writers. Although our focus in this book is on writing, it is inevitable that in discussing the preparation and presentation of interviews we shall deal with functions and qualities that some might call performance aspects. We shall also discuss the preparation that precedes the broadcast. This function, which belongs in the writing area, may be carried out by the interviewer, or it may be assigned to assistants who provide information about the subject and guest and who may also draw up a list of questions to guide the interviewer on the air. Contemporary interviews are potentially more exciting and involving than the formal exchanges they replaced. Some of that results from what Eric Sevareid, CBS news analyst and interviewer of powerful people for almost four decades, once called "a cast of mind," a general attitude toward people, events, and the task at hand. We shall now explore the major implications of the altered attitudes toward the interviewing function.

APPROACHES FOR THE ORAL WRITER

The major "recasting of mind" that accompanied the shift from scripted to unscripted interviews replaced interrogation with conversation. Though the art of conversation is worth recapturing, it should not be confused with idle chatter.

Good conversationalists are people interested in the views and feelings of others. They are listeners, reacting to bits of information with a good sense of the mood and meaning of what is said, or left unsaid, by their guests. Successful interviewers put their guests at ease in order to draw from them information they may not have shared elsewhere. Their attentiveness enables them to respond to the unexpected confidence, to encourage the disclosure, and to remain flexible enough to lay aside the prepared questions, should more interesting information begin to surface. Yet good interviewers must remain firm enough to redirect the evasive guest to the body of information both agreed they would discuss. Interviewers must be aware of their responsibility to ask the questions members of the audience would raise, were they in a position to do so. If they tend to be thorough researchers, they must take special care not to overlook the obvious, yet often necessary, questions important to their listeners.

Styles of Interviewing

Name a popular interviewer, and that name will evoke a *modus operandi* different from that of the competition. Ed Bradley, Morley Safer, and Mike Wallace are hard-hitting investigators. Oprah Winfrey and Jane Pauley are concerned friends. Arsenio Hall is a good-natured explorer, testing the waters. Joan Rivers is a caustic comedienne, Phil Donahue a passionate observer, John McLaughlin a no-nonsense overseer. Some interviewers succeed in presenting interesting people and stimulating ideas; others find a hundred ways to focus attention on themselves. Oblivious to their personal limitations, they run the risk of becoming tedious bores with an audience transformed into mindless blotters.

Types of Interviews

Each interviewee is selected with an intended audience in mind. The interviewer plans the public conversation by structuring a series of observations and questions which will capitalize on what each guest has to offer the listening audience. The choice of interviewee pretty much guarantees that the interview will fall into one of the following types: Personality/Celebrity, Authority/Information or Combination/Hybrid.

Personality/Celebrity　The focus in Personality/Celebrity interviews is the individual being interviewed. The more widely known such subjects are, the more neces-

sary it is to search out unpublished information about their personal histories and behind-the-scenes activities.

Authority/Information　People with exclusive or extraordinary information about a matter of interest or importance are sought after, not for their personal stories, but for data about their areas of expertise. The emphasis is on information and authority. If, for example, a doctor at a local hospital were to develop a cure for AIDS, every interviewer, reporter and talk show host would be on his or her doorstep, microphone in hand. The first rush of questions would focus on the nature and availability of the cure.

Combination/Hybrid　Fame, such as would ensue from the discovery of a cure for a deadly disease, might give to a formerly "ordinary" person the luster of celebrity. Once questions about the medical triumph were satisfied, the world would want to know more about the individual. This is one way in which a hybrid or combination interview develops. Other similar directions may be generated in conversations with a president or some other politician who was formerly an entertainer, an expert who is also eccentric, or any number of individuals whose outstanding gifts and life qualities fall into more than a single category.

Later in this chapter we examine the creative implications of each of these types, along with illustrations from some who have met the challenges.

Writing Introductions

Interviewers who set the stage for their guests by providing an honest depiction of their accomplishments and personalities and by announcing the intended direction of the upcoming conversation win the respect of their audiences. One caution for the overeager interviewer: Don't promise more than you can deliver. It's not wise to confound the expectations of your audiences. Inflated promises may motivate them to stay tuned, but are unlikely to bring them back.

One long-running, successful radio interview program is *Focus,* which airs daily on WJR in Detroit. Bob Talbert, a reporter for the Detroit *Free Press,* once called it "the best forty-five minutes in American radio." An aspect of the interview that is clearly a writing function is preparing the introductions. The popular host of *Focus,* J.P. (Joseph Priestly) McCarthy, entertains three guests during the course of each program. He begins by naming and identifying each briefly, then prior to each interview he provides a full introduction.

One of J.P.'s flamboyant programs featured a transsexual, a popular athlete and a singer. The introductions to these guests were written by Hal Youngblood, at that time the program's producer.

In Focus today. . . .
Mario Martino! A bearded, manly male transexual. . . who began life as a Marie Martino. . . and who has very candidly and explicitly chronicled the amazing medical and psychological transformation that turned him from female to male!
Then we'll introduce Mario to the Detroit Legend. . .
Number 9. . . Mr. Gordy Howe, who thought he would be part of the NHL this morning, but isn't! Then we'll introduce both to The Lady Who Sings the Blues like nobody else—and has packed houses and sold out albums to prove it—Miss Thelma Houston.

(Commercial Break)

Our first guest has lived two lives. . . as two different people. Born (ostensibly) a female,

Marie Martino discovered that there was a man living inside her!
Through the incredible miracle of transsexual surgery and personality therapy, Marie became Mario!
He has very frankly and sensitively told of that transformation (surgically) and transmorphus (emotionally and intellectually) in a new book called *Emergence.*
We welcome to Focus. . . Mario Martino.

In the ensuing interview J. P. McCarthy probed intimate details related to human sexuality, asked questions about Martino's struggle to identify and redetermine his own sexual preference, and discussed the consequences of his decisions on his family, his friends, and his professional life. The topic, which would have been forbidden during the broadcasting era of scripted interviews, carried with it the danger of resorting to a line of sensationally erotic questioning. Although that emphasis might have rendered the interview more entertaining for some listeners, it would have done a disservice to the transsexual's personal struggle and impugned the respectability of the psychosurgical alterations provided by modern science.

The interviewer maintained a delicate balance in his conversation, satisfying the curiosity of his listeners without compromising the integrity of his guest.

The second introduction reflects the familiarity of the listening audience with this particular athlete and also underscores J. P.'s interest in sports:

Gordy Howe obviously needs about as much of an introduction to anybody in this town or anywhere else as a hockey puck needs to the ice! We welcome 'Number 9' back to our arena. . . as a member of the Lincoln-Mercury Sports Panel. . .

In terms of content, J. P. was, for the second time in the same hour, faced with a sensitive topic. Gordy Howe, one of Detroit's most popular sports figures, had just been involved in a brouhaha in Canada that had earned him highly negative publicity in that country, a fact the host could not ignore. J. P. did not avoid the hard question, but posed it diplomatically. He began by reminding the hockey player of the high regard in which he was held by the Detroit audiences and, that established, in a tone carrying just a trace of incredulity, asked how it was that the Canadians hated this hero so much. Gordy Howe laughed outright and the dialogue began.

The final introduction provided by Youngblood asked:

Can a little girl from Leland, Mississippi, find happiness and contentment singing the blues?
She can and does. . . and according to most jazz critics and blues buffs. . . does it better than anybody else!
Currently "knocking 'em dead" out at "db's" in the Hyatt Regency. . . she will be off shortly to do a film about no one other than Bessie Smith.
We welcome to our little Piano Bar. . . the great Thelma Houston!

J. P. McCarthy, following his instincts and the leads of his guests, had spent most of his program time interviewing his first two. Miss Houston did, however, receive an opportunity to mention her current engagement and promote her film. That opportunity might be considered a professional courtesy, given in exchange for her presence on *Focus*. Although a fully scripted interview would have apportioned the time more equitably, it probably would have produced a less dynamic presentation.

To review the writing tasks in this particular program: Youngblood skillfully set the stage for the three guests, incorporating significant facts about each one in the written introduction and transitions. McCarthy kept the audience enthralled by verbally posing those questions best calculated to draw from his guests information of interest to his audience. An examination of Youngblood's introductory remarks prepared for the host reveals that each one establishes a mood of expectancy. Although the third interview was abbreviated, the content of the first two more than adequately satisfied the expectations raised by the introductions. Audience satisfaction, as well as professional integrity, depend on the interviewer's ability to deliver what the introduction promises. Exaggeration about the talents or accomplishments of guests can lead only to the embarrassment of host and guest and disappointment for the audience.

Modes of Preparing and Reacting

Successful interviewers follow different methods of preparing and conducting their programs. One interviewer may vary the approach or adapt it to individual guests and particular circumstances. McCarthy admits that this is so in his case. If the interviewee is a public figure, McCarthy makes sure he knows in advance everything the audience is likely to know. Youngblood considers him to be the best-informed man around, a fact attributable in part to his voracious reading habit. McCarthy's immediate preparation, however, like that of retired television host Johnny Carson, is intentionally thin. He conducts no extended preliminary conference, no rehearsal; indeed, more often than not, he doesn't meet the guest until air time. He doesn't want to distance himself from the audience, to sacrifice spontaneity to certainty. Perhaps Bob Talbert offered the most incisive commentary on McCarthy's singular success in achieving audience identification when he wrote, "The question on the tip of my tongue is sliding smoothly out of J. P. McCarthy's mouth even as I think of it. Most of the time, before I think of it."

The secret of that success cannot be seen by the radio audience any more than it can be missed by the live studio audience: the host's absolute attentiveness to every guest. Here, perhaps, more than in any other facet of the unscripted interview, performance plays a major role in eliciting responses from the interviewees. McCarthy is presence personified. His body language—eye contact, facial expression, and intimate conversational tone—obliterates the intimidating presence of microphone and studio. Host and guest talk person to person, while the audience settles into a most comfortable and comprehensive eavesdropping experience.

Attitude, approach, and performance skills are, undeniably, qualities apart from those needed for carefully constructed questions, but they are the raw material from which questions and responses arise. The ability to listen well and to "read" the face of a guest allows the host to register the emotional response, to catch the key word and use it as a transition linking ideas or bringing them forward. This ability leads to both good organization and flexibility.

Focus provides us with one successful style of hosting a program. Interviewers must determine the preparation and approach that work best for them. Individual decisions reflect the "general cast of mind" described earlier. In his discussions with political figures, for example, Mike Wallace employs confrontation, a kind of cross-examination of the architects of world events. Wallace has, on several occasions, succeeded in stirring up a cauldron of hostility, as was the case in a much publicized 1992 exchange with Henry Kissinger, many

years after his term as U.S. Secretary of State (1973–1977). Wallace alleged that Kissinger had used for personal gain knowledge he had obtained as a government agent—using especially his knowledge of U.S.–Chinese relations in the aftermath of the failed Tiananmen Square revolt. Wallace's allegations resulted in a series of charges and countercharges. During the program, it became apparent that the "interviewer" had in fact become the inquisitor.

Bill Moyers, by contrast, prefers to behave as the guest's "friend." Conscious of the distractions and the sometimes intimidating surrounding technology, he makes a real effort to put his guests at ease. Barbara Walters shifts between positions of confronter and friend to accommodate her different guests. She justifies the seeming vacillation in this observation: "Until the celebrity feels comfortable with you, it's not likely that he will feel like disclosing anything more intimate than his hat size." Phil Donahue shows similar adaptability. His show draws an audience predominantly composed of women. He probes with a wit that can be gentle or harsh, successfully elicits important responses from the shy, and sometimes disconcerts those who are noted for personal poise. Unlike Mike Wallace, Donahue spends much of his time interviewing not public personalities, but private citizens involved in societal problems or public issues. He has drawn sensitive and illuminating responses, for instance, from battered wives, homosexuals, and single parents. On the other hand, his questions to former First Lady Rosalynn Carter, concerning her husband and her diplomatic activities in his behalf, reduced this ordinarily poised woman to tears. Questions that evoke tears or laughter from guests or audiences are rarely intellectual in their concerns. Questions that move people in this fashion reflect emotions; they register the way people feel rather than how they think.

Preliminary Interviews

Writers and research assistants are often assigned the task of conducting preliminary interviews with celebrities scheduled to appear on talk shows. This enables them to gather information that will help the shows' hosts formulate their questions. (Award-winning documentary writer and producer Richard Kotuk considers the pre-interview valuable in determining the direction and extent of the on-camera exchange.)

One celebrity with whom host Jay Leno has talked on *The Tonight Show* is film actor Clint Eastwood. We have made here educated guesses about the kind of facts and suggestions a writer might have given to Leno before a typical program went on the air. The hypothetical notes that follow would supplement Leno's own knowledge of his guest and would help him guide the interview into fruitful channels.

1. Be aware that Eastwood, as an amateur jazz musician, knows several members of the band and may wish to comment on the fine music they play. Eastwood himself plays jazz piano, and did so in the movie *City Heat.* He also directed the film *Bird,* about saxophonist Charlie Parker, and may wish to talk about the careful work that went into restoring old musical recordings for the movie.

2. Mention that in switching around the TV dial a month or so ago, you came across an episode of a 1950s crime series, *Highway Patrol.* As you watched, you saw a kid go by on a motorcycle and suddenly realized he was the youthful Clint Eastwood. This should draw from Eastwood some recollections of his early days as a contract player at Universal Studios and a description of what it was like to work with Broderick Crawford, the star of *Highway Patrol.* At times two different episodes of the series would be in pro-

duction simultaneously and Crawford would have to move back and forth from one sound stage to the other. To help him remember which show he was doing, he would paste lines of dialogue on the furniture and even pin them to the clothes of other actors.

3. Remark that Eastwood has made a lot of cop movies. This should trigger his memory of the first one he made, *Coogan's Bluff,* and of his most famous picture in this category, *Dirty Harry.* Eastwood probably will comment on why audiences like police movies. You might mention that one of your favorite Clint Eastwood movies, *Bronco Billy,* happened to be one that didn't center on police action. Eastwood may tell you that among his movies, *Bronco Billy* is also one of his favorites. He is likely to explain why this story of a character who seems to belong to another era particularly appeals to him.

4. Refer next to one of Eastwood's more recent pictures, *White Hunter—Black Heart,* which dealt fictionally with the making of John Huston's movie *The African Queen.* Eastwood is likely to reply that he has great respect for Huston's work, and he may mention some of his films. Say that you don't want to invite a "Dirty Harry look," but you have heard some critics say that Eastwood deserved an Academy Award for his performance in *White Hunter—Black Heart.* Eastwood probably will respond modestly and may add that your reference to the Dirty Harry look reminds him of an encounter he had with Muhammad Ali, the former boxing champion, while the two of them were waiting to go on a *Tonight Show* some years ago. Ali took Eastwood to a secluded corner, where Ali asked Eastwood to give him one of those "Dirty Harry looks" and tell him that he has 10 minutes to get out of town.

5. Move to the two films Eastwood directed that featured Clyde the orangutan, and ask him what it was like to work with an ape. Eastwood may say that apes have short attention spans—and is likely to add that some actors do, too. Asked whether he prefers acting or directing, he probably will say that directing is more satisfying because it involves all aspects of a production.

6. Bring up the fact that he has received some criticism from feminists because of the way the characters he has played in his films have treated women. A case in point was his smashing actress Jessica Walters through a window in *Play Misty for Me*. Eastwood probably will reply with a smile that the psychotic character she played deserved to be smashed through a window.

7. Mention that you have recently seen *The Rookie*, which he also directed. Comment on the wonderful action scenes and ask particularly about the difficulties involved in filming an especially exciting episode showing a police car chasing a tractor-trailer loaded with automobiles. You might add that as a car lover, you cringed to see brand-new Porsches and Mercedeses crashing into the street. Eastwood probably will say that most were old cars fixed up to look new, but that some new cars had to be sacrificed to make the scene. Contrast the modern setting of *The Rookie* with the backdrop of his most recent film, *Unforgiven*, a western which he once again directed. Because Eastwood first became a star in movies like *A Fistful of Dollars* and *High Plains Drifter*, he may want to talk about what made him want to return to the western and make this particular picture. After showing a clip from the film, he may also have stories to tell about his co-stars, Morgan Freeman, Richard Harris, and Gene Hackman.

8. Say that you know he has to leave to catch his plane to Carmel (which he once served as mayor) but before he goes, you want to get his reaction to former president Reagan's use of the line "Make my day" from his film *Sudden Impact*. Eastwood, a steadfast conservative, may say he was flattered and probably will add that when he first saw the line in the script he knew it was a good one, but had no idea it would catch on the way it has. He probably will add that if he had a nickel for every time he has heard the line shouted at him by passersby, he could retire rich. He may mention that one girl even put the line "Clint Eastwood: Make My Day" on a banner carried by an airplane.

9. Conclude with another reference to *Unforgiven* and emphasize what a terrific picture it is.

PERSONALITY INTERVIEW

Many interviews with figures from the entertainment or sports worlds are designed to illuminate their personality and background. Interviewers need to know something about their guest's experiences and accomplishments, so they can direct their questions toward bringing out the information of greatest interest to the audience. It is important to consider what the celebrity would like to be asked. One question movie stars and recording artists wait for anxiously is a query about their latest release, since they probably are making the rounds of radio and television stations just to promote that picture or record. To fail to ask that key question is a serious error, one that J. P. McCarthy skillfully avoided in his brief exchange with Thelma Houston.

An equally grievous mistake is to ask a question about a subject the guest prefers not to discuss. Writers can direct interviewers to ask pertinent questions and to avoid embarrassing ones. A major difficulty arises when the embarrassing question is pertinent, a circumstance typified by the previously mentioned McCarthy interview with Gordy Howe. To spring the embarrassing question on the unsuspecting guest may be construed as hostile or deceptive.

On the other hand, the sensitive and enterprising interviewer may find a way to interject a delicate or controversial question without committing a breach of ethics. Mike Wallace, interviewing Johnny Carson on *60 Minutes,* apparently "won one, lost one" before the interview began. There were two sensitive areas in Carson's personal life at the time of the interview, both of which had surfaced in gossip columns. The line of questions made it clear that Carson had agreed to answer questions about his problems with alcohol. Apparently he was not willing to answer questions about his marriages and undoubtedly had informed Wallace of that decision in advance of the taping.

Interviewers, particularly inexperienced ones, sometimes allow themselves to be overawed by popular entertainers who are the recipients of enthusiastic hero worship. Extensive adulation does not produce good interviews. Questions that probe experiences common to most human beings reduce the distance between host and guest. Questions about family, background, education are obvious unifiers, but even more relevant are some that relate to those common factors of human experience. "What effect has your popularity (increased fortune, traveling, success) had upon those who were closest to you before you became a star?" is the kind of question that can result in an interesting insight into a performer. Another: "You're at the top of your profession, a position thousands of people would love to achieve. Can you describe the joys and sorrows that go with that popularity?" Or, "You're a star. What's next?"

Not all interviews of the personality type are with celebrities. Interviews with contestants on quiz shows, or with the individuals who phone in their opinions on a controversial subject also belong in the personality category. Where there is no opportunity for previous contact with the individual, questions about name, age, marital status, occupation, children, and hobbies are about the only ones that can be asked. Where contestants are available ahead of time, a writer through some discerning research may be able to develop questions that will carry the program away from the rut of clichés.

Barbara Walters has a special set of questions that she reserves for the "over-interviewed." Note the personal dimensions they include:

1. If you were recuperating in a hospital, who would you want in the bed next to you, excluding relatives?
2. What was your first job?
3. When was the last time you cried?
4. Who was the first person you ever loved?
5. What has given you the most pleasure in the last year?[1]

The personality interview runs the risk of sounding like an examination or a questionnaire for a census report. Avoid that pitfall by exploring the human interest angles. Prepare questions that will direct your guest toward revealing anecdotes, including names and dispositions of the people and relationships described. Don't stop with eliciting the fact; invite the example. Facts tend to center on abstractions; examples and anecdotes come dressed in human experience.

AUTHORITY INTERVIEW

The second major type of interview is designed to bring out the special information possessed by an expert or a prominent person involved in government, business, religion, or some other institution that affects society. The stature of the authority may create the additional aura of the celebrity, but revealing the person is only an incidental element in the interview. The focus is not on the celebrity, but on the information the expert can convey. Writers can be of material assistance to interviewers in preparing this type of program.

The first matter to be considered is the interviewer's introduction to the guest. Unless the guest is already well known to the audience, the interviewer needs to establish the interviewee's position as an expert. This introduction should not be long or involved, because such openings are interest-killers, but should center on the

points that will make the guest most intriguing to the audience The second part of the introduction should stimulate the interest of the audience in the subject to be discussed. A question that will arouse audience curiosity, followed by the promise that the question will be answered during the interview, helps to attract listeners.

Many of these elements are discernible in the introduction that Bill Moyers used in the first of a six-part series of conversations with Joseph Campbell. Moyers faced a three-pronged challenge. He had to establish his guest as one of the world's foremost authorities on mythology, lay the groundwork for the entire series, and announce the specific subject matter that would shape this initial discussion: the place of the hero in mythology.

Joseph Campbell and the Power of Myth—with Bill Moyers

1. The Hero's Adventure

BILL MOYERS: Joseph Campbell believed that everything begins with a story, so we begin this series with Joseph Campbell with one of his favorites. He was in Japan for a conference on religion, and he overheard another American delegate, a social philosopher from New York, say to a Shinto priest, "We've been now to a good many ceremonies and have seen quite a few of your shrines. But I don't get your ideology. I don't get your theology." The Japanese paused as though deep in thought, and then slowly shook his head. "I think we don't have ideology," he said, "we don't have theology. We dance."

Campbell could have said it of his own life. When he died in 1987 at the age of 83, he was considered one of the world's foremost authorities on mythology, the stories and legends told by human beings through the ages to explain the universe and their place in it.

The 20 books he wrote or edited have influenced artists and performers, as well as scholars and students. When he died, he was working on a monumental *Historical Atlas of World Mythology,* his effort to bring under one roof the spiritual and intellectual wisdom of a lifetime.

Some of his books are classics: *The Hero with a Thousand Faces,* which established his fame 40 years ago; and his four-volume study of mythology, *The Masks of God.*

Joseph Campbell was one of the most spiritual men I ever met, but he didn't have an ideology or a theology. Mythology was to him the song of the universe, music so deeply embedded in our collective unconscious that we dance to it, even when we can't name the tune.

Over the last two summers of his life, we taped these conversations in California, at Skywalker Ranch, the home of his friend, George Lucas, whose movie trilogy *Star Wars* had been influenced by Campbell's work. We talked about the message and meaning of myth, about the first storytellers, about love and marriage, gods and goddesses, religion, ritual, art and psychology. But we always came around to his favorite subject, the hero with a thousand faces.

(interviewing) Why the hero with a thousand faces?

Introductions to the remaining programs were shorter, containing less about the man, more about his ideas. This is apparent in the introduction to the fifth program, "Love and the Goddess."

Joseph Campbell and the Power of Myth—with Bill Moyers

5. Love and the Goddess

BILL MOYERS: One of Joseph Campbell's most eloquent essays was called simply, "The Mythology of Love." "What a wonderful theme," he wrote, "and what a wonderful world of myth one finds in celebration of this universal mystery." Stories of love fascinate the human race, and Campbell made their interpretation one of the great passions of his life as a scholar, teacher and philosopher. Like a weaver of fine cloth, he spun the tales and legends of love into an amazing tapestry of the human psyche.

He gathered his materials everywhere, from the erotic mysticism of India to the Old Testament Song of Songs; from the life of Christ and teachings of Ramakrishna, to Saint Paul and Bernard of Clairvaux, and William Blake, Thomas Mann, and many others, for whom love was the controlling principle of art.

Campbell thought the greatest love stories were told in the Middle Ages, when "noble and gentle hearts," as he called them, produced the romantic love that transcended lust. This love between individual men and women, Amor, was celebrated by wandering minstrels, who sang of "what the eyes have made welcome to the heart." It helped create a distinctive Western consciousness that exalted the individual experience of men and women over the authority and traditions of the church and state.

(interviewing) Let's talk about love.

The second step is to plan the way in which the material is to be covered. The procedures for doing this are basically the same as those used for planning any program of a factual nature. The outline for an extemporaneous interview, however, must be more flexible than an outline for a fully scripted show. The interviewer must be left free to follow leads that may develop while the show is actually on the air. This permits the whole exchange to have a natural, conversational flavor.

The final step in preparation is to design the question the host is to ask of the authority. Again, they must be considered not as absolutes, but as ideas which an adept interviewer can weave into a smoothly flowing conversational pattern.

In the construction of these questions, certain practices should be followed.

1. Arrange the questions to maintain an even balance of interest throughout the sequence. Interviews often start with stimulating questions, but slide steadily downhill in interest value thereafter.
2. Design questions requiring comment and interpretation from the authority rather than a mere "yes" or "no."

3. On the other hand, do not ask questions so broad that answering them requires long unbroken speeches from the authority. The most natural-sounding interviews feature frequent exchanges between guest and host.
4. Construct questions that permit natural transitions from one question to another. An interview composed of an unrelated and unconnected series of questions sounds mechanical and artificial.
5. Ask only one question at a time. When two or more questions are asked together, one of them is likely to be overlooked. Consider the following "double-barreled" question: "Are you happy to be relieved of your duties as emcee, or were you looking forward to meeting the new year's crop of celebrities?"

    Answer: "Yes."

    The audience trying to follow the discussion may well ask, "Yes, what? What's that supposed to mean?"

    An alert host will recognize the error and rephrase the question. There are other occasions, however, when a well-phrased question may, nevertheless, draw an ambiguous response, leaving questions in the minds of listeners. A simple "What do you mean?" or "I don't quite understand that" may encourage clarification. Questions beginning, "What exactly. . . ?" should be avoided. Interviews should not sound like an examination or a cross-examination.
6. Try to guide your guest toward a "human interest" framework for the discussion. "How did you become an investigative reporter. . . or a neurosurgeon. . . or a guidance counselor" can be directed toward more interesting responses by rewording: "Who and what inspired you to become a. . . ?"

COMBINATION/HYBRID

The first task in a combination interview is deciding which area of interest—personality or authority—to explore, or, perhaps, how to structure the conversation around a comfortable blend of the two. James Day, host of the highly successful public television series *Day at Night,* was uniquely adept at this. The following example displays his style and reveals his skill.

DAY AT NIGHT / WGBH-TV BOSTON

JAMES DAY WITH ANNE SEXTON

Anne Sexton is a Pulitzer Prize poet.

Her first book of poetry, *To Bedlam and Part Way Back,* was published in 1960. It was a way, she had said, of fighting off madness. The poems are as personal as a confessional, anguished, intimate, and deal with her innermost thoughts, fears, and anxieties, and her hospitalization for mental illness. In 1966, her third book of poems, *Live or Die,* was chosen for the Pulitzer Prize in poetry. She had been writing verse less than ten years at the time. Critics have treated her books well. The critic of *The New York Times* described her fifth book of poems, *Transformations,* as "a funny, mad, witty, frightening, charming, haunting book." Her seventh and most recent book, *The Death Notebook,* was published this year. Concurrently with her writing and poetry-reading, Anne Sexton teaches creative writing at Boston University.

Sometimes, despite the most conscientious determination to pursue one dimension over another, interviewers find themselves being led in an unexpected direction. The decision whether to redirect the conversation or follow the guest's lead cannot be preprogrammed. Intuition and experience may be the best mentors for that moment.

AUDIENCE INTERACTION PROGRAMS

Two broadcasting formats that have grown increasingly popular in recent years are those which include interaction with the studio audience, or which encourage telephone feedback from audiences at home. A television program hosted by Phil Donahue incorporates both. These two formats are loosely related to the traditional in-studio interview. They extend the concepts of conversation and discussion, but in a manner considerably less structured. Those who conduct them seldom choose in advance the individuals who will question them or respond to the topics they introduce. What the studio interaction and telephone call-in programs have in common for the scriptwriter is a range of opportunities to develop what we have come to regard as "oral writing" skills. Qualities important to the interviewer apply here. Beyond the scripting of introductions, transitions, and filler material, those who help prepare for or conduct such programs assert their influence in three ways: by choosing the goal of the program; by selecting the subject or theme, where specific ones exist; and by establishing the style of the exchange. In order to provide potential writers with some assistance in designing formats that generally defy attempts at categorization, we shall mention two specific television programs that suggest patterns for the future, and then we shall concentrate on the radio call-in, taking note of some of the diverse styles and shapes it takes.

Studio Interaction

One of the first television programs to incorporate interaction between host and studio audiences successfully is *Donahue.* Phil Donahue, whose topics often include subjects once forbidden on the airwaves, after an exchange with an invited guest, invites reactions from the studio audience. A limited number of telephone calls from the home audience are taken as well. A program addressing the problem of suicide demonstrated the control needed by a host who must integrate so many fragments of content. After several members of the studio audience had talked about the suicides of people who had been close to them, and others had admitted considering or attempting suicide themselves, a woman caller confessed that she was at the very moment contemplating taking her own life. In a suspense-filled few minutes, Donahue pleaded with the caller not to do anything, but to wait until some people associated with his program could get professional help to her, an effort, he assured her, that would proceed at once.

Responses from the studio and at-home listening audiences became commonplace throughout the 1980s into the '90s. Geraldo Rivera, Oprah Winfrey, Sally Jessy Raphael and others have abandoned the interviewer's seat on the set for a microphone with a long wire with which to weave through the studio audience or to take phone calls fed through the intercom.

Personality interviews, as well as audience interaction programs featuring celebrities, are increasingly intertwined with videotaped segments of the guest star. Barbara Walters uses this to introduce virtually all her guests from the entertainment world. Jane Pauley, hosting the interview show,

Real Life, did this as well. One particularly effective application of this technique was evident in an interview with Oprah Winfrey. Although *Real Life* originated from its own studio set, much of the content came from Oprah's set. *Real Life* incorporated video-taped segments from Oprah's own show, including portions of audience reaction.

This Personality/Celebrity interview, unlike the others included in this chapter, does not have a traditional introduction. Jane Pauley, instead, reveals the personality, history, and accomplishments of her multifaceted guest one layer at a time. The articulation of each insight is supported by excerpts from *Oprah.* The outstanding distinction from a writing perspective is the program's extraordinary reliance on editing. More of the "writing" was done in the editing room than at the word processor. The kaleidoscopic revelation of so many seemingly unrelated experiences and expressions, free-flowing as it may appear, is the result of tight organization and careful structure.

This is apparent in the following transcript of the first third of the Oprah Winfrey *Real Life* interview. We reproduce here only the audio portion of the program.

Real Life with Jane Pauley
September 6, 1991

JANE PAULEY: Chicago, the windy city, indeed. This is the capital of talk. When Oprah arrived nearly seven years ago, Phil Donahue had a lock on the market and Oprah's mission was to "make a little dent." Within a year, she owned Chicago. Today, Oprah has the number-one syndicated show in America, and on Monday, she celebrates the fifth anniversary of her national program.
Two hours before show time, the faithful gather at Harpo Studios. Upstairs, the star, and owner, is hard at work.

OPRAH WINFREY: Well, I think the first question is "Who's black enough?"
UNIDENTIFIED MAN #1: Black enough. (*Unintelligible.*)

WINFREY: I think that's why we did the show.

PAULEY: Her hair and make-up call is 7 AM, but Oprah's day started two hours earlier, reading research for today's show on Supreme Court nominee Clarence Thomas.

WINFREY: We had an outhouse [as Thomas's family once did]. You never forget it. No matter how many bathrooms you get, you never forget it.

PAULEY: While Oprah gets her briefing, the audience members get theirs on videotape.

WINFREY: (*Giving instructions on videotape*) Please stand up so everyone can see you. If you don't stand up, then the cameraman misses the shot.

PAULEY:	Guests may be unpredictable, but the show runs like clockwork.
WINFREY:	Okay, are we going to be ready—ready to roll on time?
UNIDENTIFIED MAN #2:	Yes, ma'am.
UNIDENTIFIED WOMAN #1:	All right, what are we going to do when Oprah comes to us? All together. . . .
AUDIENCE:	*(In unison)* Stand up!
WOMAN #1:	Very good, class.
PAULEY:	The audience is in place, waiting. Backstage, Oprah's still making mental notes.
WINFREY:	I don't have the *USA Today* article. . . *(unintelligible)*
PAULEY:	Then it's show-time.
WINFREY:	*(To the studio audience)* Hi, everybody.
PAULEY:	Two shows a day, three days a week, adoring fans pack this studio, anxious to see Oprah and hoping to be seen by the more than 14 million viewers who tune in daily to see what Oprah will say next.
WINFREY:	*(To the studio audience)* Y'all look nice and fresh and bathed.
WINFREY:	I love it. They get up, they get dressed and they come here with the intention to be on this show. I respect that.
PAULEY:	Before the taping starts, Oprah fills the time with banter, folksy and soothing. But as she takes her place and waits for her cue, she's all business.
WINFREY:	I am a viewer. I really consider myself a surrogate viewer. That's what I—that's what I am.

(During her program) There are nine people in this country ma—who make decisions that affect each and every one of our lives, and you may not know. . .

I ask the questions that they want to know, because I also want to know them.

(During her program) If and when women can have abortions, if women are paid the same as men, if blacks, Hispanics or Asians should benefit from affirmative action. And the list goes on.

PAULEY:	I was telling a group of people that I was excited to interview you because "Well, Oprah and I have—have so much in common," and a lady I was talking to, who happened to be black said, "May I ask

	what?" And I'm not sure I could articulate what it is, but I was being quite sincere.
WINFREY:	Right. I understand that.
PAULEY:	I didn't mean to imply, "Well, like Oprah, I am a high-powered woman in broadcasting." In. . .
WINFREY:	Or, "Like Oprah, I was born in Mississippi as a black woman," yes. Well, I—I think that is why I feel so comfortable with our audiences, because I feel like I have so much in common with them.

(During her program) Is your husband or your boyfriend happy with the way you dress? Well, a lot of them think that they can dress you better than you can dress yourself.

PAULEY:	Will you do 220 shows a year?
WINFREY:	There—and there are no new ideas. There are just different ways of—of doing them.

(From another program) So what would you do if your husband got another woman pregnant?

UNIDENTIFIED WOMAN #2:	I'd be very upset.
WINFREY:	Very upset?
WOMAN #2:	I'd kill him!

PAULEY:	The topics can be hot and deeply personal, but her audience isn't shy.

UNIDENTIFIED WOMAN #3:	Well, I'd be really hurt also, but I would hope that he'd take responsibility for a child—for making. . .

PAULEY:	You make people feel so safe that they say anything on their minds.
WINFREY:	There have been moments on this television show when people have said things that—that made me cringe. We had wives on with husbands, who—and the husbands were having an affair and we had the three of them on—and a husband said on the air that his girlfriend was having a baby. And his wife didn't know about it. It was a moment that I thought should not have happened. And I—and I—I said that to her, "I'm sorry that your husband said that to you on television. You should not have had to hear that on TV."
PAULEY:	Don't you get frustrated, though at—at what thick skulls so many of us have?
WINFREY:	Well, it's—what does—I'll tell you what frustrates me the most. What frustrates me the most is these women who still live their lives for men. I want to just shake them sometimes! But I've been one of those women, so understand. I understand that you have to come to it in your own time, and that it just takes some of us longer than others. And so you may have six children and three husbands before you can figure it out.

VANNA WHITE:	The Emmy goes to. . . Oprah Winfrey!
PAULEY:	In five years, the Oprah Winfrey show has won 11 Emmy Awards, and her ratings are 50 percent higher than her closest competitor, the man who created the talk-show format, Phil Donahue.
WINFREY:	I'm a mimic. I used to watch Phil all the time when I was in Baltimore. I watched him all of the time. When I first started doing my own talk show in 1978, I found myself saying "Is the caller there?"
PAULEY:	"Help me out."
WINFREY:	And "Can you help me out here?" And I stopped watching him, because. . .
PAULEY:	But Phil Donahue wasn't Oprah's first role model.
WINFREY:	And I really have missed an entire era of television, because I stopped watching television the night Mary Tyler Moore went off the air. It was my social life. The big M—I wanted a big "O" to go near my refrigerator because Mary had the "M."
PAULEY:	Okay, so that's what—we do have a great deal in common. We spent Saturday nights together, apart.
WINFREY:	Um-hm, right.
WINFREY:	Because she worked in the newsroom, and that's what I did.
PAULEY:	So it wasn't Mary Tyler Moore at all; it was Mary Richards. And all those little girls growing up, and they're doing that to you. You're Oprah Winfrey.
WINFREY:	I know. I can't imagine it. But I'm really proud of this television show. Every day, my intention is to empower people, and my intention is for other people to recognize by watching our show that you really are responsible for your life.
PAULEY:	Every show comes to the end and you've got 15 seconds. You've got to say something that kind of sums everything up and—and. . .
WINFREY:	Um-hm. Oh, but I know that it doesn't sum everything up. I know that this is really just a talk show. But that's all it is, and that's all I am is a talk show host. But I think I can be a catalyst for people beginning to think and—and to think more insightfully about themselves and their lives.
PAULEY:	One reason Oprah is so understanding about other people's troubles is that she's had her own to contend with.
WINFREY:	I ju—I started crying uncontrollably. I could not stop. It was all of my own stuff coming out on national television.

PAULEY: But right now her mind is on the business. When we come back, Oprah's spectacular success story.

(Commercial break)

Radio Call-in

Although some television programs, particularly those offering advice to viewers, have begun to include telephone calls from their audiences, telephone talk began back in radio and flourishes there. Lively call-in programs gain high ratings and, therefore, are not likely to go away.

Program Goals   There are three major goals of the call-in program: to examine or raise issues of interest, to provide listeners with a forum for feedback, and to present entertainment. Having indicated some differences in emphases, we are quick to add that the majority of programs are hybrids. All programs within the call-in category depend for their survival on audience response. Some, however, perceive interaction with the audience as a form of public service. They are conscious of the need individuals have for a forum which serves as an outlet for confrontation as well as for personal catharsis.

Raising Interesting Issues   A sampling of popular talk show hosts indicates the variety of approaches used and topics covered.

Some, like *The Mike Cuthbert Show,* which was broadcast from public radio station WAMU-FM, Washington, D.C., reflect controversy; others, such as the nationally syndicated show of the outspokenly conservative Rush Limbaugh, regularly generate it. Still others, such as Bernard Meltzer's program, provide a service by offering callers advice, especially in the areas of health and finance.

In May of 1989, while the United States was divided over providing military aid to the Nicaraguan *contras,* one priest found himself forced to choose between providing humanitarian aid to the Nicaraguan people and remaining in the Society of Jesus (or Jesuits), a Catholic order devoted to missionary and educational work. Mike Cuthbert of WAMU-FM, Washington, D.C., interviewed the Reverend William Callahan about the spiritual and political aspects of his dilemma before opening the phone lines for audience response.

Cuthbert's introduction to his guest reflected the position of a disinterested outsider. It allowed Callahan to present forcefully his own view of the events which led to his censure. Cuthbert, who identified himself as a non-Catholic puzzled by the internal struggles within the Church leadership, referred to examples from traditional U.S. politics to provide insights into his guest's struggle before inviting his callers' participation.

Mike Cuthbert
WAMU-FM, Washington, D.C.

This hour we're delighted to welcome to our studios Father William Callahan, S.J. He is embroiled in a separation, if you will, from his friends and colleagues in the Society of Jesus, the Jesuits.

Father Callahan, I have a lot of correspondence here that continues to rain back between the various Church officials and yourself. What's the current status of you with the Jesuits and, briefly, how did you get here?

(Extended conversation between the two)

My guest is Father William Callahan, now with the Jesuits—in the future, we're not sure yet. I have a feeling you have a pretty good presentiment of what that will be. We'll get into that as the hour proceeds. Our number is 885-8850, if you're calling. All lines are filled. Lee, good evening. You're on the air.

One of the longest running call-in hosts is Bob Grant, who has been called alternately "the man you hate to love" and "the man you love to hate." Deliberately abrasive, Grant rarely announces a specific topic. His technique is to discuss whatever subjects are raised by members of his listening audience.

An insight into this provocative host is provided by reflections he offered a reporter who interviewed him for a feature story in *New York* magazine:

"I've called for mandatory sterilization for welfare mothers with two or more illegitimate children."

"You're not kidding?" queried writer Cynthia Heimel.

"Well, it would be nice if they would volunteer," Grant acquiesced. "If they volunteer, they should be given a cash award, or a case of gin, or whatever it is they want. . . We pay for their prenatal, natal and postnatal care, and a few years down the road, what do these offspring do? They mug old ladies and disrupt classrooms. Why the heck should we spawn the seeds of our own destruction?"

It's hard for audiences to remain indifferent to such remarks. Callers jam the airwaves to register their reactions as Grant rains the verbal equivalent of fire and brimstone on his audiences. One criticism of Grant's name-calling ("sickolas," "mutants," and "savages" are among his oft-used nomenclature) is that he inflicts psychological damage on some callers who are quite obviously already disturbed. Others argue that his program provides a catharsis for the pent-up aggressions and anger of people who feel victimized by society and its criminals and have no other way of fighting back.

Philosophically miles apart is Bernard Meltzer, favorite uncle for a New York audience. Focused on *What's Your Problem?*, Meltzer conveys the image of a compassionate, intelligent, financial counselor, an economic doctor of the airwaves. He performs a public service for his listeners by untangling their financial problems. He accepts their compliments, listens carefully, requests clarification, demands honesty, and offers straightforward advice while promising follow-up if more help is required.

Presenting Entertainment When Art Dineen was talk-show host at WXYZ-Detroit, he said he got involved in radio because he didn't like to work. His approach to his program and its callers was designed, with an occasional exception, to provide fun. His listeners were as free as he was to introduce a topic during his nocturnal show. The years spent with night people taught Dineen a few good techniques to keep the program running smoothly. While accepting a caller with "Hello, you're on the air," he was bound to hear the conventional opening, "Hello, Art, how are you?" The worst thing, he says, is to reply, "I'm fine. How are you?" Nervous callers may echo,

"I'm fine, thank you. How are you?" Others may plunge into a recitation of their medical history. Art's standard reply was, "I'm fine. What's on your mind?"

The demographics for Art's program revealed an older audience comprising more women than men. He approached his listeners as one would guests across a kitchen table. He saw his major responsibility as being to his listeners rather than to his callers, who comprised only a small percentage of the audience. With this in mind, he was careful not to let the program get bogged down in narrow interests. He says, "It may be okay to discuss photography, but when you get to talking about f-stops, you've become a bore to the majority."

A Radio Call-In Exercise It is possible, even within the limitations of a classroom situation, to experience the demands and challenge of call-in radio. Realizing that a live program would use a sophisticated system of screening, holding, and delaying callers while enlisting one or several operators trained to assist the program host, it is possible to simulate the situation as part of an interesting learning experience.

Those with access to a radio studio should utilize two microphones connected to a tape deck. The host, speaking into a desk microphone, sits facing the timekeeper, who also signals the host when a caller approaches the stand-up (telephoner's) microphones. A screen or chalkboard between host and caller increases the sense of distance. The callers, of course, are members of the class.

Student hosts are responsible for a 10-minute program to prepare according to the following directive.

Mindset You are a radio personality with a two-hour nighttime program. Each evening you discuss a timely topic (promoted the previous evening) about which

there is vigorous controversy at best or, at least, room for opposing viewpoints.

You, presuming nothing—

1. give the time;
2. identify the station;
3. identify the program;
4. identify yourself;
5. summarize the subject and indicate the major opposing positions, linking them, when possible, to specific information recently reported in the news or public affairs programming;
6. encourage audience response;
7. give the phone number.

Items 1 through 7 should fit into a prepared script of no more than 90 seconds. (Everyone enrolled in the class is expected to be a caller during the exercises. Participation is essential.)

Response to Callers

1. *Be ready for anything.* Listen without unnecessary interruptions. If, however, someone makes a speech or takes you on a tangent, assume control with an appropriate comment and word of dismissal. Although many different types of people call the station, you alone remain the host. Still, you must retain an identification with the audience. You are the only one with the opportunity to request clarification, or to correct where there is an obvious misunderstanding.

2. *Be ready for silences.* It's your job to fill them, while again inviting callers and repeating the phone number. It's helpful to have spread out before you index cards with "filler material," short pieces of information—anecdotes, statistics, quotes from reliable sources—which you can give while waiting for the next caller. After each filler, repeat the phone number. In considering filler material, remember that human interest anecdotes often make a point faster and more convincingly than philosophical or informational exposition.

3. *Prepare for the crackpot.* People who are disturbed or cantankerous are just as likely to get your ear as are the serious and sensible. Keep control. Remember, you have to return to the air tomorrow night. Your professional reputation is at stake.

4. *Prepare for the expert.* Know what you're talking about. Don't pretend to know what you don't know. Be honest. If you doubt the correctness of a caller's observation, appeal to members of the audience to react to what the person said.

5. *In presentation, be relaxed, be alive, be grammatically correct.* Avoid vocalized pauses and needless repetition. On the other hand, be alert to "lift" a key word or phrase from a caller's comment and use it as a transition into a prepared filler or an unscripted reaction.

This exercise has been put to the test in at least two major universities for several years and, with some variations, has, according to students and professors, proved a valuable learning experience.

QUESTIONS AND PROJECTS

1. The major portion of an interview is presented extemporaneously. Which segments generally require advance scripting?

2. Review the introductions used by the *Focus* programs. What elements do they contain to arouse and sustain audience interest?

3. Devise a list of five subjects of contemporary interest that you think would stimulate enthusiastic participation by a radio audience.

4. What are some of the nonwriting skills that are of particular importance to interview and audience interaction programs?

5. Some interviews, like those with celebrities, are designed primarily to entertain. Others, like those with authorities, aim mainly to provide information. How would your preparation for these two kinds of interviews differ?

6. Assume that you are preparing questions for a host who is to interview the President of the United States. What questions would you list?

7. Write a 30-second introduction to the celebrity or authority of your choice.

NOTES

1. Listed in John Brady, *The Craft of Interviewing* (Cincinnati: Writer's Digest Books, 1976), pp. 85–86.

Many people think of radio, television, and films as media whose primary objective is to entertain the audience. Material designed to achieve this goal unquestionably takes up more time than any other, but the broadcasting media particularly also devote a considerable amount of effort to providing audiences with information. News programming is the most obvious and common example of this program form, but there are a number of other types that involve the delivery of facts or are based on actual events, among them, interviews, discussions, commentaries of various kinds, and instruction in many different fields. Even game shows and commercials may dispense some information. In other chapters of this book we discuss the writing of this sort of material. In this chapter we focus on the writing techniques employed in creating four particular types of factual programming: documentaries, feature programs, magazine programs, and reality programs.

CHAPTER

4

DOCUMENTARY, FEATURE, MAGAZINE, AND REALITY PROGRAMS

The original documentary maker—known as Homer—achieved a unique kind of magic that was not to be equalled until Shakespeare.

GORE VIDAL

as "the creative treatment of actuality." In the broadest sense, a documentary is any program or film based on "documents." Defined this way, it is a form directed toward presenting a factual record about real people, things, and events, one that sets out mainly to explore a subject rather than to entertain. Under this definition, any material that simply dispenses information about historical or biographical subjects without reference to current social problems would be placed in the documentary category. It would even include material aimed mainly at providing cultural information, such as programs on Michelangelo, Shakespeare, and the Louvre.

Some would narrow this definition to make the term refer only to programs or films that deal with facts in a social context or those which concentrate on probing a social, economic, or political issue. In such presentations, opinions play an important role, and because they frequently conflict, controversy often erupts. Documentaries of this type may pursue one of several purposes:

1. Their goal may be to arouse public concern by making audiences aware of the existence of a pressing social problem. One of the most notable documentaries ever presented, CBS's "Harvest of Shame," narrated by Edward R. Murrow, made many people conscious for the first time of the desperately deprived lives of migrant farm workers.

2. The documentary producer may aim at securing some type of remedial action. "Harvest of Shame," in addition to making audiences aware of a problem,

DEFINING THE TERMS

We must concede that defining the nature of material we explore in this chapter is not an easy task. Through the years different terms have been used in referring to the various forms, and the same term often means different things to different people. In this section our purpose is not to settle the argument, but to explain what these terms mean to us.

DOCUMENTARIES

John Grierson, the British filmmaker who invented the term *documentary,* defined it clearly indicated that something needed to be done to correct it.

3. The goal may be simply to inspire or uplift the audience. A good example of this type occurred at the beginning of World War II when Norman Corwin wrote and produced a radio documentary called "We Hold These Truths." It depicted the sacrifices people had made to erect the structure of freedom we call the Bill of Rights, which the nation was defending against dictators who would destroy it.

Documentaries that strive to influence people's thoughts and actions are often imbued with a strong emotional quality which gives them a tone different from that of other factual forms. Their purpose is not merely to present facts about an issue but to create deep feeling about it. Writers therefore look for the most moving events they can find. They must be reported, as A. William Bluem put it in his book *Documentary in American Television,* "in as compelling a fashion as possible." In this sense, the documentary can be said to be dramatic. It is dramatic also in that it adds an artistic purpose to journalistic and sociological aims. John Grierson has remarked, "The documentary idea, after all, demands no more than that the affairs of our time shall be brought to the screen in any fashion which strikes the imagination and makes observation a little richer than it was."

One reaction makers of documentaries have learned to expect is violent criticism from some people of the way they treat certain subjects. That is because a documentary does not limit itself, as a news broadcast does, to telling *what* is happening, but goes further to explain *why* it is happening and may even suggest steps for *correcting* whatever wrongs may exist in the situation. As British TV producer Philip Donnellan said, it is a function of a documentary "to rock the boat." When it does so, those whose interests it threatens are likely to respond with angry counterattacks. They may start by questioning the right of the documentary producers to make their statement and may end up by trying to destroy their reputations.

When Murrow, a pioneer producer of TV documentaries for CBS, became one of the first journalists publicly to question the motives and methods of Senator Joseph McCarthy's anti-communist crusade of the 1950s, the senator responded by questioning Murrow's loyalty to the United States and accusing him of harboring pro-communist sympathies. The makers of another CBS documentary, "The Selling of the Pentagon," which accused the Pentagon of spending a great deal of money to generate public support for increased arms expenditures, were accused by the defense lobby of selectively editing their material to mislead viewers. The House Committee on Special Investigations demanded that CBS president Frank Stanton submit all of the sequences produced for the program, including those that had been discarded. When Stanton refused to surrender the "out-takes," as they are called, on the grounds that they were protected by the First Amendment, the committee asked the House to cite him for contempt. For a time it seemed that a documentary a network had produced would send its president to jail. The House, however, failed to act on the committee's recommendation.

CBS ran into trouble of a different sort with its documentary "The Uncounted Enemy: A Vietnam Deception," which accused General William Westmoreland, a commander of U.S. troops in Vietnam, of sending false reports to his superiors in Washington about enemy troop strength. Westmoreland sued the network for $120 million, stating that his reputation had been damaged by a program that twisted and warped the facts. Though Westmoreland ultimately chose to withdraw his suit before the jury reached a verdict, CBS still had to pay $2 million to defend itself.

When documentary makers deal with social and political problems, they are bound to treat issues about which people feel deeply. They must, of course, do everything they possibly can to discover the facts and present them accurately. They must, furthermore, strive for complete fairness in their overall treatment of the subject. No matter how well they do on both these counts, however, they are not likely to avoid some hostile reactions. The essence of most documentaries is controversy. To avoid it is to neglect the documentary's natural subject matter. To deal with it is to invite criticism.

The type of program we have been discussing, one which deals with social and political issues, is what most people think of first when the term documentary is mentioned. We, however, expand the category to include any program that explores a subject in a creative and imaginative way, even though no social or political issue is involved. Thus we would call a program that analyzed the contributions of Shakespeare to our cultural heritage a documentary. We would also place other programs and films that present facts and interpretations of events in nondramatic form in the documentary category: programs about nature, science, and anthropology, for example. The mini-series *The Civil War,* presented by the Public Broadcasting System (PBS), enhanced viewers' understanding of a significant historical event and thus qualified as a documentary even though its purpose was to present facts and impressions rather than explore an issue.

Another characteristic that distinguishes documentaries from other types of programs dealing with facts is the means used to present the information. The documentary form is marked by the use of a wide variety of production techniques. The information delivered by the CBS documentary "Harvest of Shame" could conceivably have been given by a single speaker or in interview form. No one would call such presentations documentaries, however. "Harvest of Shame," in contrast, showed migrant workers moving from one place to another, working in the fields, and living in primitive quarters. It featured interviews with a variety of people: the workers themselves, the farmers who employed them, executives of farm associations, and the children whose lives were blighted by the way their parents earned a living. Tying all these segments together was the eloquent narration of Murrow.

In recent years the commercial networks have reduced sharply the number of hour-long documentaries they produce. In the 1960s viewers could expect to see some 40 a year on NBC, CBS, and ABC, but by the late 1980s the number had declined to about a dozen. The Ralph Nader group reported that from 1979 to 1989 the amount of issue-oriented programming in general had dropped by 51 percent. A major reason for this reduction was that although critics admired them, documentaries drew a small percentage of regular viewers. The documentary of the week almost always ended up last on the ratings charts.

The decline in documentary production by commercial broadcasters has been made up to some extent by public broadcasters. Such series as *Frontline, Nova,* and *The American Experience* regularly bring imaginatively produced documentaries to viewers, and the PBS network often offers mini-series of a documentary nature. One already cited, *The Civil War,* drew the largest audience in public broadcasting history. Special programs produced by such cable networks as the Cable News Network (CNN), Arts and Entertainment (A&E), and the premium movie channels have also helped make up for the decline in documentary production by the broadcast networks. Documentary *films* continue to be produced, but they are not usually available to general audiences. Each year the movie industry recognizes outstanding work in this field with Academy Awards.

One documentary film in particular has gained a special place in the pantheon of documentary productions. It is Robert Flaherty's 1922 production *Nanook of the North*. Its essential achievement was the development of understanding in its viewers of a way of life utterly different from their own through an in-depth portrayal marked by unique and creative insights. The film aroused admiration for the courage and ingenuity of a people who clawed a meager living from a harsh and threatening environment. Many have called it the first documentary. Two films of the 1930s also portrayed life in difficult circumstances and gained wide critical acclaim—*The Plow that Broke the Plains* and *The River,* both produced by Pare Lorentz.

The documentary form has attracted writers for two main reasons. It gives them a chance, first of all, to use the media to explore the significant issues of life rather than expending their resources on what may be frivolous and ephemeral. Second, it provides opportunities for experimentation and the exercise of one's ingenuity not often possible in such formula-obsessed fields as drama and comedy. Because the expected audience is small to begin with, the writer can afford to use venturesome new techniques which may disenchant some listeners, whereas the writer of entertainment scripts, committed to attracting millions, may fear to try the innovation that will lose even one of them. Thus entertainment writing often follows the well-worn trail of what has been tried and found safe; documentary writing can explore new paths of subject and technique. Bill Moyers is an example of a writer and a producer who found that more than anything else he wanted the challenge of creating documentaries. When CBS failed to provide him with the opportunities he sought, he shifted to PBS. There he has become a prolific producer of documentaries.

Feature Programs

Feature is another term that has been used by broadcasters in a number of ways. The short talks on a variety of topics presented by news personalities such as Dan Rather on the commercial radio networks have been called features. So have the talks dealing with such subjects as health, show-business events, business affairs, and political events that are distributed to stations by both networks and producers of syndicated programs. At times stations schedule a cooking demonstration as part of a news show, and the morning programs of ABC, CBS, and NBC regularly include segments that describe and demonstrate the way various dishes are prepared. These, too, are called features.

The type of feature we discuss in this chapter is a brief program segment that deals with a social, economic, or political issue in the same way a documentary does. We can think of it therefore as a short documentary. It is usually presented as part of a news broadcast and may last anywhere from two to six minutes. Sometimes a single topic is considered in a series of features that runs for an entire week. Features take up problems that have a continuing existence. In this way they contrast with the "hard news" section of the broadcast, which deals with events that have just occurred.

The subjects treated by the producers of features run a very wide gamut indeed. They may focus on such topics as parking problems, garbage collections, an individual's contribution to the community, a local unsolved mystery, or the tragedy of child abuse. They are not always serious in nature but may be introduced to provide a touch that softens the sometimes depressing impact of the news stories. (One local station, for example, presented a series of five features on stand-up comedy in the area.) Sometimes their purpose is to educate, as cooking demonstrations do. Four times each year TV stations are particularly interested in attracting as large an audience as possible. These are the so-called "sweeps" periods, when the ratings they receive determine how much they can charge for commercials during the ensuing months. When this time comes the topics treated in features frequently veer into the sensational. A *TV Guide* survey in 1990 found stations presenting such special reports as "Secret Obsessions," "Prison Moms," "Too Stressed for Sex," and "Wedding Horror Stories."[1]

In recent years the national broadcast networks have softened their hard-news format by regularly scheduling features. *NBC Nightly News* provides an example of this practice. Each day it includes a segment with the general title, "The Daily Difference." On Mondays it is subtitled "In the '90s" and deals with "How Changes in the World Affect You." The subjects for the other days are: Tuesdays, "What Works? People and Ideas That Make a Difference"; Wednesdays, "Vital Signs: The Latest News in Health and Medicine"; Thursdays, "Crime and Punishment: America's War on the Streets—How We Fight It"; Fridays, "The Friday Follow-Up: Yesterday's Newsmakers—Where Are They Now?"

CBS Sunday Morning regularly includes features of various types. The segment below is from one that falls in the "human interest" category. Charles Osgood, one of the regular participants on the program, is the narrator.

Good Friends
Denny Zeitlin M.D.

VIDEO	AUDIO
ON CAMERA	ZEITLIN (VO): Good friends are good medicine—better medicine, at times, than doctors can provide. And good friends are easier to take. Especially they are easier for children to take. Charles Osgood now and "Good Friends."
ARTHUR USING WALKER, LEAVES HOUSE	OSGOOD (VO): Every week, on Thursday, as a rule, Arthur Lusignan [Loo-SIG-nan] sets out to meet a friend. It takes him a while to negotiate the elevator, and the doors, and the parking lot. Arthur doesn't move as fast as he used to, but that doesn't deter him. His wife, Lillian, gives him a lift whenever she can. She
RIDES OFF IN CAR DRIVEN BY WIFE	
CAR STOPS	

ARTHUR GOES INTO HOUSE	knows how important Arthur's friend is to him.
	ARTHUR AND DAMON GREET EACH OTHER.
KISSES DAMON	OSGOOD (VO): Arthur Lusignan is 84. His friend Damon is six. They've been friends for a long time now. . . ever since Damon was two.
ARTHUR AND DAMON	THE TWO CHAT: ARTHUR MENTIONS THAT DAMON IS ALWAYS A GOOD BOY.
	OSGOOD (VO): Arthur and Damon share a lot of memories.
	THE TWO EXCHANGE REMINISCENCES.
DAMON SHOWS NINJA TURTLES	OSGOOD (VO): Damon is a lot like most six-year-olds. He likes dinosaurs and Teenage Mutant Ninja Turtles. . . Unlike most six years olds, Damon can't run around and play. . . He has muscular dystrophy.
THE TWO LOOK AT A BOOK	THE TWO COMMENT ON THE PICTURES.
DAMON AND ARTHUR TALK	OSGOOD (VO): So Arthur comes over. They read, or play board games. . . And sometimes they just talk, as friends will.
	MORE REMINISCENCES
ARTHUR COMES UP TO PLATFORM TO GET CERTIFICATE FROM BARBARA ABROMOVITCH	OSGOOD (VO): Arthur is one of a small army of senior citizens all around the country who have volunteered to become Family Friends. . . a program that operates under the auspices of the National Council on the Aging. Once or twice a week. . . sometimes every day, when

they're needed, these volunteer friends visit families with chronically ill and disabled children.

The feature continued with scenes showing other volunteers providing services to people who need their special kind of help.

A feature of quite a different sort was presented by a local station, WDIV-TV in Detroit, as part of its early evening newscast. The reporter was Asa Aarons, who regularly deals with topics of particular interest to consumers. The segment began with an interchange between Aarons and Mort Crim, one of the newscast's anchors, and continued with scenes showing the use of the gear and statements by coaches and players about it. It concluded with a return to the studio where the newscast's anchors reacted to the report. Its main point was that safety gear not only protects young people but also makes them better players. The script format used here divides the page between video and audio information. Although Aarons used an ad-lib, conversational style in presenting his report, it is clear that the feature was carefully planned.

Consumer Report
Station WDIV-TV Detroit
Reporter, Asa Aarons

VIDEO	*AUDIO*
MORT CRIM (ANCHOR)	CRIM: Baseball, our great American pastime, isn't without its dangers. Our consumer reporter, Asa Aarons is here now to continue his look at summer safety and especially as it affects the little ones.
PAN TO INCLUDE ASA AARONS	
AARONS TURNS TO TALK TO TV AUDIENCE	AARONS: When you think of sports injuries, don't you immediately think of football? That always comes to mind for me and yet the really funny thing about it is that our children are really in greater danger when they're out there on the baseball diamond. My source for that is the Consumer Product Safety Commission. I've got part of a study they did. I've brought it with me. They studied a ten-year period during the 1980s and the figures they came up with are absolutely shocking. There
ZOOM IN ON AARONS	
HOLDING REPORT	

	were 86,000 emergency visits for kids eight to fourteen years old, all baseball and softball related. And then it really gets serious here. When you look down a bit it shows fifty-one deaths related to the game and again all concerning young children. Two of those deaths hit very close to home for a pair of Detroiters.
REFERRING TO REPORT	
CONSUMER BEAT TITLES	
PLAYER ON FIELD	AARONS (VO): The relative non-violence of the game may be just tradition. For some reason we don't think of protecting ourselves against a speeding projectile that moves at seventy miles an hour even in the hands of a Little Leaguer. What can severely damage a bat can destroy a human heart. Barb Demarco found that out when her young cousin died of a blow to the chest during a baseball game.
BATTER IN HELMET GETTING HIT	
FALLING	
LITTLE LEAGUER	
DENTED BAT	
LITTLE LEAGUER PITCHING	
DEMARCO	DEMARCO: At the time we all stood there and talked about what a horrible, awful, freak kind of accident it was. Come to find out this is not such a freak accident.
SAM MARION	AARONS (VO): Not freakish at all. Former Little League coach Sam Marion watched a little boy die in his arms, again from a blow to the chest.
ZOOM IN ON NEWSPAPER HEADLINE REPORTING THE TRAGEDY	
BACK ON MARION	MARION: When he swung, he exposed his chest and the ball hit him in the sternum area and he went down. We grabbed him and put him in a car and took him to the St. Johns hospital. When we got there, they hit him with the paddles and I

	broke down crying. And that was the end of it.
PROTECTIVE VESTS	AARONS (VO): The episode launched Marion on a research project that led to these protective vests, designed and distributed by his own Detroit company. The mix of dimpled nylon and canvas provides something light enough to play in and yet is protective. They're designed to allow movement and yet they fit snugly.
AARONS HOLDS VESTS	
VESTS	AARONS (VO): The jackets interested concerned parents and this season some coaches decided to try them out. Many reported noticeable results.
LITTLE LEAGUERS WEARING VESTS	
COACH	FIRST COACH: The bumps and bruises weren't as bad. We've had some kids hit with thrown balls and it didn't even faze them.
SUPER: DAVID KENNEDY, MANAGER COMMERCE BLUES	
COACH	AARONS (VO): Some even felt the jackets helped the kids to play better.
SUPER: TOM RYAN, MANAGER, COMMERCE BLUE JAYS	SECOND COACH: Especially some of the younger kids that maybe weren't as good as the older ones. They became much more confident and they weren't afraid to stand close to the plate.
	AARONS (VO): But the real judges are the players.
FIRST LITTLE LEAGUER	FIRST PLAYER: They're comfortable and they help you a lot, because I got hit right here and it didn't even hurt.

SECOND LITTLE LEAGUER	SECOND PLAYER: I think it makes the pitchers feel safer, too. You don't have to worry about hitting them in the ribs or something and hurting them that bad.
AARONS	AARONS: It's too early to have any hard and fast stats about the jackets but some municipalities aren't waiting for them to come in. Union Lake, Walled Lake, and Mount Clemens have all passed ordinances requiring protective jackets just like this for their Little Leaguers and more folks are expected to follow. And, Mort, as you can see for yourself, it's very hard to pull apart. It's snug and it'll stay on because it's a Velcro fit.
HOLDING UP JACKET	
PULLING ON JACKET	
PAN TO INCLUDE ANCHORS, MORT CRIM AND CARMEN HARLAN	CRIM: It looks like sponge, but when you feel it, that's really pretty tough stuff there.
AARONS PUNCHES VEST	AARONS: And it's designed to deflect the energy from the ball and send it out.
	CRIM: It's lightweight and it looks like it would not be too restrictive. It's certainly worth the effort and the cost.
	AARONS: It's a wonderful idea and coming from a Detroiter, no less.
	CRIM: Thanks. A good report as always.

Magazine Programs

Magazine programs are shows that present a number of relatively short documentaries during an hour or half an hour. CBS's *60 Minutes* and ABC's *20/20* are examples of this form. More recent entries in this field include ABC's *Prime Time Live* and NBC's *Dateline*. These programs run for an hour and take up three or four different topics. They may also include special additional segments; *60 Minutes* for example, often concludes with a commentary, presented in documentary fashion by the satirist Andy Rooney. Such programs may also present brief excerpts from letters sent to the program by viewers incensed or gratified by previous programs. The nature of this content, which resembles in its variety the material available in magazines, led to the term applied to this particular program type.

Other programs that use the magazine approach are the so-called "tabloid television" programs which are distributed mainly to stations on a syndicated basis rather than by networks. They acquired this name because they tend to deal with topics even more sensational than those usually treated by the network magazine shows. *TV Guide* has described their content as "gut-grabbing emotion; sex, murder, mayhem, madness, corruption, greed. Better yet if celebrities are involved."[2] Among the programs that fall in this category are *A Current Affair, Inside Edition, Hard Copy,* and *Inside Report.*

The most successful network entry in the magazine field, and the program that established the formula, is *60 Minutes.* After a slow beginning in 1968, its popularity steadily increased until it regularly ranked among the 10 most-watched programs of the year and in a given week sometimes attained the number-one position. The program *20/20* has not quite matched the success of *60 Minutes,* but in the 1990–1991 season it rose from the previous year's 44th place to rank 35th among all prime-time programs. The other ABC show in this category, *Prime Time Live,* after initially emphasizing live interchanges with studio audiences (the element that gave the show

its title), has turned to a format that closely resembles that of *20/20* and *60 Minutes. Dateline,* NBC's 1992 entry in this field, and its eighteenth attempt to develop a successful magazine format, featured Jane Pauley as its anchor.

Richard Campbell has written a study of *60 Minutes* from a viewer's perspective and attributes most of the show's success to a narrative approach that gives dramatic impact to stories and makes the reporter a principal figure in the "telling." Under this treatment, news becomes a mystery, an adventure, a therapy session, or an arbitration procedure, and the reporters are correspondingly detectives, tourists, analysts, or referees.[3]

The following excerpt from a *60 Minutes* segment deals with the quality of health care available to inmates in federal prisons. It exemplifies the *60 Minutes* practice of asking officials to answer difficult questions about the deficiencies in their operations while a camera registers their expressions and reactions. Thus it provides a good example of the probing, hard-hitting investigative journalism that has made *60 Minutes* so popular. This concept also demonstrates how the focus shifts back and forth between the narrator's statements and the answers and statements of the people being interviewed. The narrator and interviewer was Stephen Kroft, a relative newcomer to the program.

That's The Law
Produced by Lowell Bergman and Isidore Rosmarin
March 17, 1991
© *MCMXCI CBS Inc. All Rights Reserved*

VIDEO	AUDIO
STEPHEN KROFT	KROFT: More than a million Americans are in prison tonight, which means, among other things, that we imprison more of our countrymen

than any other nation in the world. But that's not the only noteworthy thing about our prison population. All inmates, no matter what they're in prison for, are entitled to adequate food, housing and the same kind of medical care they would have gotten on the outside. That's the law. But complaints are growing, not just from inmates, but from prison doctors, that medical treatment in prison is woefully lacking and that even a minor jail term can turn out to be a death sentence.

SCENES IN FEDERAL PRISONS

KROFT (VO): There are 65,000 inmates in the overcrowded federal prison system, spread around the country at 66 institutions. Before you ask why you should care about a bunch of prisoners, it's important to remember one thing. Not everyone in federal prison is a criminal. On any given day there are 4,000 inmates in federal custody: people who are awaiting trial, people who haven't been convicted of anything. In November of 1987, one of them was a 41-year-old single mother named Isabelle Suarez. Isabelle Suarez was arrested on a federal assault charge after she got into a fight with her mail carrier about the delivery of her welfare check. The crime carried a maximum penalty of 90 days in jail and a $100 fine.

STEPHEN KROFT ON CAMERA

KROFT: Isabelle Suarez was brought from her home in northern Michigan to the Metropolitan Correctional Center, the federal jail, here in Chicago. She had a medical problem. Isabelle

	Suarez was an epileptic and without her antiseizure medication, she would go into convulsions. That medication was confiscated when she was brought here to Chicago.
GEORGINA LAWSON	KROFT (VO): Georgina Lawson was an inmate at the Metropolitan Correctional Center when Isabelle Suarez arrived.
	GEORGINA LAWSON: She started getting seizures, one after another, and she started biting her tongue and foaming through her mouth.
CELL	KROFT (VO): According to medical records, the prison staff thought Isabelle was faking—"attention-seeking behavior" they called it —so they locked down Isabelle Suarez, isolating her in her cell where she continued to have seizures. Desperate, Georgina
PHONE	Lawson got to a prison pay phone and called 911.
KROFT AND LAWSON	LAWSON: The ambulance had came, but they didn't leave them in the building.
	KROFT: Prison officials wouldn't let them in?
	LAWSON: No.
CELL	KROFT (VO): It was only after a week, when Isabelle Suarez went into a coma and was taken to a local hospital, that she was finally examined by a doctor. In the meantime, the prosecutor decided to drop all charges against her. Two weeks later, Isabelle Suarez died.

DR. MORITSUGU	KENNETH MORITSUGU: It is always tragic and unfortunate when something of that sort occurs.
	KROFT (VO): Dr. Kenneth Moritsugu, who's wearing the uniform of the Public Health Service, is the head of health services for the U.S. Bureau of Prisons. We asked Dr. Moritsugu about an investigation that he ordered into the death of Isabelle Suarez that resulted in this report.
KROFT READS FROM REPORT	And I quote, "In my opinion, the medical care provided to Mrs. Suarez during her incarceration in the MCC was abysmal."
KROFT AND MORITSUGU	MORITSUGU: I understand what you're saying. And what I'm—
	KROFT: It's not what I'm saying. It's what your own doctors say.
	MORITSUGU: Well, again. I don't feel that I can quote—or comment further on that report.
	KROFT: You think the care that she received was adequate?
	MORITSUGU: I think the care that she received balanced the care and custody issues that we are concerned with. I think that obviously, in retrospect, one may think in the other professional judgments, but at that point that was a professional judgment.
	KROFT: You have to forgive me. It didn't seem to balance very well for

Isabelle Suarez. She's dead. And the charges against her were later dropped.

MORITSUGU: I really don't feel that I can comment further on that.

MARION FEDERAL PRISON

KROFT (VO): As we said, every federal inmate is entitled to quality medical care, even at the Marion Federal Prison, the top-security penal institution in the United States housing 435 of the nation's most dangerous convicts.

Later in the segment, two inmates who claimed they had received inadequate medical treatment made appearances. One said that although he was suffering from cancer he had been treated by an unlicensed physician. The other claimed that an operation to remove a small growth in his groin area had sterilized him. Mixed in with their appearances were interviews with two other prison officials who were challenged to defend what had gone on. At the end of the segment, Kroft reported that the doctor who had performed the botched operation had been promoted. He closed the sequence with this comment:

VIDEO	*AUDIO*
KROFT ON CAMERA	KROFT: The United States Bureau of Prisons insists that it has thousands of inmates who are satisfied with the medical care that they've received in prison and the government points to a study of 8 of their 67 institutions, which concludes that prison health care is, quote, "adequate." About that doctor practicing in prison without a license, the Bureau says he's been told to go out and get one.

(Commercial break)

Reality Programs

A type of documentary that differs somewhat from the programs we have been discusing depicts a sequence of actual events connected with a particular kind of activity. The camera focuses on the people involved in these events as they experience what is happening. In essence, the TV audience sees a slice of life as it takes place. Once called *actualities,* this material is now usually referred to as *reality* programming. One of the first programs of this type was the 1973 PBS series *An American Family.* The Loud family (their real name) permitted cameras to photograph them in various situations, and it was clear from the naturalness and spontaneity of their responses that even when private matters were being discussed, the presence of the cameras did not inhibit them. They acted, in fact, as if they were unaware that the scene was being recorded for the TV audience.

The reality shows of today follow a similar pattern. *Rescue 911,* for example, let viewers eavesdrop while a rookie police dispatcher carried out tense negotiations over the telephone with a gunman who was holding an elderly woman hostage. The series *Cops* sometimes showed a crime that was still underway when the cameras arrived. Another type of material is represented by *Yearbook,* which showed the ups and downs of student life at a suburban Chicago high school during the final year before graduation. That most states now permit cameras in courtrooms made possible the production of a series called *Verdict,* which edited the tapes of particular trials into half-hour presentations. A reality program that explored a variety of situations from week to week was the CBS series *48 Hours.*

WRITING AND PRODUCTION

In discussing the writing and production of the forms just described, we simplify matters by using the term *documentary* for all of them. As we pointed out, the reality show is a form of documentary programming, and magazine and feature segments are simply short documentaries. Even though such programs differ in length, the techniques used to write and produce them are essentially the same. Whether they run for two minutes or for three hours (as one ABC documentary did), they use the same mix of narration, shots of real events, interviews, vintage movies, and stills.

We include some discussion of production in this section because in preparing documentary programs the writing process often merges so completely with the production process that one is indistinguishable from the other. Only rarely does a script represent everything appearing on the program; the rest is inherent in the tapes or films that make up a major share of the program. This does not mean that a writing function cannot be identified, however. The producer who shoots a piece of film in the field and the editor who cuts it are carrying out a writing function. In this section, therefore, we shall be thinking not only of the writer who creates a documentary at the typewriter but also of those who work in the field or at the editing table. In some instances all these functions are carried out by the same person.

When radio was the only broadcasting medium, the writing of documentaries was carried out quite separately from production. The disk-recording equipment of that period was too clumsy and ponderous to take into the field. Documentary subjects were dramatized in scripts, which were then produced in studios. If interviews were included, those questioned came to the studio instead of being interviewed in their homes or offices as they are now. In some instances, the questions and answers were written out and read from scripts during the broadcast.

Before the arrival of television, the makers of filmed documentaries had demonstrated how effective it was to show people reacting to events in their own environments. Television producers began using movie cameras to record materials in the field. At about the same time the development of audio tape made it possible for makers of radio documentaries to use the same technique. The introduction of videotape a few years later gave television producers still another means of capturing events as they occurred on the scene. These developments brought an end to the studio production of documentaries and brought about the blending of the writing and production functions. Now almost the only documentary segments produced in studios are narration, opening and closing frames, and the occasional interview.

The rise of television also brought an end to most radio documentaries. Some are still produced, however, particularly by public radio stations. In this chapter we concentrate on the television form, but what we say applies equally to the radio documentary.

Taping or filming material in the field requires the use of special techniques. One objective is to attain natural responses to a situation even though the artificial element of a camera has been introduced. To accomplish this purpose, producers developed the *cinéma vérité* technique, which makes the camera operator a part of a given situation for a relatively long period and requires that the camera be used as unobtrusively as possible.

Besides film or tape specifically shot for a program, a major ingredient of most documentaries is the interview, which is usually produced nowadays where an event is taking place or in the interviewee's office or home. In editing this material into the final program the interviewer's questions may be retained along with the responses, or the questions may be eliminated, leaving only the answers, which then appear to be spontaneous comments on a situation.

The skill with which interviewers carry out their function is of crucial importance to the success of a documentary. They must have a clear idea of what they are seeking in the interview and be prepared with questions that will draw it out. Getting ready for this step by carrying out preliminary research

is essential, a step we shall discuss in more detail shortly. Fred Freed, a noted maker of documentaries, distinguishes among three different purposes interviewers may have in asking questions. In some cases, interviewers merely want to get information from the people they question. In other instances, they may also want a statement of an opinion on an issue. In still other instances, they may hope to draw out statements or facts they know the person being interviewed does not really want to make or reveal. It is obvious this situation requires the greatest interviewing skill of all. We have more to say on the general function of interviewing in the chapter dealing with that subject.

The nature of the ingredients that eventually make up a documentary depends largely on the kind of subject being explored. Those that deal with today's issues or events can use film or tapes showing what has happened and interviews with the people involved. In some instances films or tapes made in previous years can provide background information. When Kenneth Burns began planning his documentary on the Civil War, he recognized that none of these possibilities was open to him. There was no movie footage showing the Northern and Southern armies in combat, of course, but some of the battlefields looked much as they had when the encounters took place. There were also thousands of still photographs depicting battle action. By combining these old pictures with new film of the deserted battlefields, backed by explanatory narration, Burns drew his audience into visualizing the contending armies. Other stills pictured incidents and people—pictures of political leader, soldiers, and generals; views of Lincoln visiting his troops; scenes of prison camps—in a way that amplified the viewer's understanding of the total event that was the Civil War. From the 16,000 pictures that Burns managed to collect, he chose 3,000 for his documentary.

Makers of documentaries dealing with contemporary events can interview those who have taken part in them. Burns was denied this opportunity, of course. His solution to this problem was as ingenious as the technique he used to bring battlefield scenes to life. He found some 900 first-person accounts of the war and used such actors as Morgan Freeman, Julie Harris, Sam Waterston, and Jeremy Irons to read passages from them. Hearing the words that actual participants had written, viewers could almost believe they were listening to the voices of those who took part in the struggle.

This point brings us to a question that has long been a matter of controversy. Should episodes in documentaries ever be staged? Burns, of course, had no choice if he wanted the words of people who figured in the Civil War to be heard as they might have said them. Many argue, however, that such staging is improper in documentaries dealing with modern subjects. This opinion is not unanimous; producers of tabloid television shows regularly stage events.

The technique has also been used on documentary programs produced by networks. NBC's now defunct *Yesterday, Today, and Tomorrow* regularly re-created events. So did the CBS show *Saturday Night with Connie Chung,* which also had a brief existence. Chung vigorously defended the practice, contending that it permitted the introduction of material that otherwise could not have been presented. An example she cited was a staged episode in a segment about American hostages in Lebanon. It showed how they were blindfolded and shut up in tiny rooms which permitted them no communication with the outside world. Chung argued that this harrowing story could be told in no other way. She also pointed out that staged episodes were always clearly identified as re-creations. When *Face to Face with Connie Chung* replaced her *Saturday Night* show, how-

ever, she no longer used re-creations, concentrating instead on interviews.

One complaint is that staged episodes breed confusion even when the staging is made known. An actor on *America's Most Wanted,* for example, was turned into the police by a viewer who mistook him for the criminal he had played in a re-enactment. The principal argument against re-creations in documentaries, however, is that they simply go against the grain of their chief purpose: to convey reality to audiences. Staging may sometimes be more dramatic than the real thing and create impressions that conventional means cannot provide, but no matter how well they are done, they are still a producer's idea of what reality is like, not reality itself.

The validity of staging in documentaries will probably continue to be a matter of dispute. Critics and broadcasters are almost unanimous, however, in saying that they should not be used in regular news programming. Dan Rather was accused of staging some of the combat scenes he showed in reporting on the war in Afghanistan for CBS. Although the accusation was never confirmed, the idea of doing such a thing was roundly condemned. Staging did take place on ABC's *World News Tonight.* The episode showed an alleged "spy" passing a briefcase to a "Soviet agent." The clip was not identified as a staged event, and viewers had no way of knowing that they had not seen the actual participants. Later Peter Jennings, the program's anchor, apologized for the deception.

RESEARCH FOR THE DOCUMENTARY

Since writers and producers of documentary programs deal with facts, they must develop a technique for discovering what the facts are. The resources available for carrying out a program of research vary in terms of the size of the organization and its standing in the marketplace. Those preparing programs for a public broadcasting station or a commercial station operating in a small market may find they must gather information entirely on their own. Larger organizations may provide some assistance in carrying out this function and in a network operation, where the budgets for producing documentaries are the largest of all, a corps of skilled researchers may be available to take over the primary task of digging out information. Even in these circumstances, however, writers cannot entirely escape research responsibility. They must immerse themselves sufficiently in the subject to develop a point of view. They must also know enough about the subject to realize what else they need to know to complete the documentary.

One way in which the research procedure for the documentary differs from the research carried out for some other factually based programs is that the process continues even while the documentary is being produced. Writers of historical dramas, in contrast, complete their research and then write their scripts. When producers of documentaries film or tape interviews, they often unearth new facts, which can become part of the finished program. A camera held in the hand of a person who unobtrusively shoots a "slice of life" in the *cinéma vérité* fashion becomes a research tool that produces information. Before shooting or taping, producers must carry out some research, of course. They must explore the subject sufficiently beforehand to know at the very least where to send their cameras and who to interview.

How preliminary research can guide the filming process is illustrated by an episode included in the CBS documentary "Harvest of Shame," which dealt with the lives of migrant farm workers. Research for the program indicated that migrant workers, as

they travel from one job to another around the country, are not treated even as well as farm animals. To support this point, film was first shot of workers as they journeyed a full day without being given any rest. Then film was shot of farm animals in transport being given respites for water and exercise every four hours. These two episodes, shown one after the other on the program, constituted graphic evidence of the condition the producers aimed to expose. Capturing this film material became possible because preliminary research revealed the existence of the condition it illustrated. The producers then established a shooting plan that directed the camera crew to film these specific scenes.

Later in this chapter we reproduce excerpts from the script of a documentary called "Guns," broadcast by the ABC television network. An examination of this script indicates that considerable research was carried out before the program went into production. The impetus for the documentary came from the killing of five children and the wounding of 30 others in a Stockton, California, schoolyard by a man wielding an AK-47 assault rifle. The producers discovered that in response to this tragic event, the Stockton city council was considering the passage of an ordinance banning the use of such weapons within the city limits. Knowing of this development ahead of time made it possible to incorporate the testimony of citizens attending the council meeting and the comments of the mayor and council members into the broadcast. (The ordinance, incidentally, passed unanimously.)

The producers decided that to give unity to the program, they would concentrate on the Stockton area, covering not only the massacre of the children, but the unrelated deaths by gunfire of other Stockton people following the incident in the schoolyard. This meant that they had to keep track of these events and round up witnesses, law-enforcement officials, and relatives and friends of the victims. As a result of this research, the statements of these people became part of the program.

Preliminary research is just as important in planning interviews. Before talking with informed people, you should know enough about the subject to plan the general nature and direction of the program and thus know what kind of information you need. It is clear that the producers of "Guns" had a number of questions ready when they interviewed people, among them:

1. What can be done to solve the gun problem?
2. Why do people carry guns?
3. How does a gun differ in its use and effect from other weapons?
4. Are too many people carrying guns?
5. Why are so many people in this country killed by guns?
6. Will gun-control laws help solve the problem?

These questions and others like them were put to a number of different individuals: police officers, an assistant district attorney, city officials, a judge, a police pathologist, the president of a Stockton citizens group, sports shooters, Stockton residents, witnesses to killings committed with guns, and friends and relatives of victims. Their answers to the questions, of course, differed widely.

Undoubtedly, these interviews revealed information not previously known to the producer. Thus the camera and the interviewer continued the research process. It may be that filming or interviewing in the field develops new ideas which indicate the need for filming and interviewing not previously contemplated. A production plan developed as the result of preliminary research must, therefore, always be a flexible one that can be revised when the revelation of new information calls for it. Most producers hope for a lucky accident or unlooked-for development that will add excitement or an unexpected angle to their program. Capturing them is no accident, however. They are the product of a careful program of preliminary research and the alertness to take advantage of events as they develop in the field. For that program and for all good documentaries, research is a process that begins as the project first gets under way and continues until the last editing decision is made.

There are three stages in the research process for a documentary program or film. One is a general phase in which you explore the subject to establish the dimensions of the finished program and to define the areas needing further investigation. The second is a phase in which you devise a production plan and seek answers to specific questions that arise during the period of general research. This is also the time when you look for visual materials that can contribute to the program, such as existing films or still pictures. In a large production organization, a film specialist would be assigned this task. The third stage is the research you carry out during the production phase while you are filming scenes or recording interviews.

ORGANIZING THE DOCUMENTARY

The documentary must be based on a coherent and logical organization of the material if it is to be clear and effective. Documentary producers should go through the same process that speakers do when they plan speeches aimed at influencing or informing audiences.

Defining the Organizing Function

When you organize material for a documentary, you arrange the information you have discovered into a logical pattern that indicates the relationship among the various facts and ideas of the program. We call this pattern a structural or logical outline. It lists the ideas of the documentary and shows which are the main ideas and which are the subordinate ones. This logical outline does not necessarily indicate the order in which these ideas appear on the program, however. That is the function of the program plan which adds the ingredient of showmanship to the program. The outline provides the structural foundation on which you base the program plan.

Many people find the making of an outline tedious and difficult work and are tempted to skip this part of the process. To do so may be a grievous mistake. Neglect at this point can lead to a program that at best may be fuzzy and at worst may be completely formless. The main ideas may remain unclear and unestablished or they may not come to light at all, for writers often perceive the points they wish to make while they are going through the process of organization. An outline, furthermore, helps to avoid overstressing or understressing supporting points and it is a guide toward including those ideas essential to the achievement of the program's objectives. At the same time it leads to the exclusion of irrelevancies and thus helps to ensure that the program will move directly to its objectives.

The organizational plan of a documentary should have several qualities—simplicity, unity, logical connection, and clarity. A major step toward creating a plan with these qualities is to make sure that the script is dominated by one overriding thought to which all the other ideas in the program are related. These supporting ideas in turn should be arranged to show their relationship to the main thought and to one another.

There is no ideal time in the process of producing a documentary for constructing a structural outline. Some writers feel that drawing up an outline too early in the process thrusts them into a rigid, inflexible groove. Others feel insecure even in the early stages until they test the relationships among ideas by casting them into outline form. Others postpone making an outline until the script plan is completed, at which time the outline becomes the final test of the program's organizational strength. Some who produce fine documentaries never draw up an explicit outline at all but trust their experience to lead them to an organized handling of the material.

Your outline, whenever it is constructed, is not likely to remain intact throughout the research and production process. You should look on its listing of ideas and its pattern of logical relationships as tentative until all the facts are in. Just as your attitude toward your production plan should be one that welcomes revisions leading to improvements, so should your attitude be toward your structural outline. You should be fluid enough to revise and tighten it when such action will improve the overall arrangement of your program's material.

Developing the Ideas

The first step in outlining your material is to determine the basic purpose of your script. It may seek one of several purposes:

1. To arouse concern about a social problem or political issue.
2. To convince people to accept an idea or develop a certain attitude.
3. To reinforce an existing attitude or opinion.
4. To motivate your audience to carry out a specific course of action.
5. To inform your audience about a subject area, a problem, or a person.

The next step is to develop a preliminary statement of the central idea of the program. The nature of the central idea is implicit in its name: It is a one-sentence expression of the main point you want your program to communicate. This statement may also include the basic purpose of the program. Thus a purpose and central argument might be expressed as follows: *to convince the audience that capital punishment is wrong.*

The reason you should consider your statement of the central idea to be tentative is that as you develop the supporting points, you may discover that you need to modify the central idea. One of your supporting points may take you in an unanticipated direction. Your most likely step then is to revise the supporting point so that it directly reinforces the central idea. But it may happen that the supporting point suggests a more promising general approach than the one you originally envisioned and you therefore revise your central idea.

The final step in organization is to set the central idea, the main supporting points, and the sub-supporting points down in outline form to make their relationships perfectly clear. A satisfactory outline is not something that springs immediately into being. A long, arduous process of expressing points, examining them critically, and then reworking them may be necessary before your outline is completely clear and consistent.

A good first step in creating an outline is to write down the ideas of the program in a list without giving any particular thought to order or arrangement. Then examine this list with these questions in mind: What seem to be the main ideas of the program? What are the subordinate points? What is clearly the supporting material? The responses to these questions will guide you in setting down the outline. There are certain patterns of organization that naturally suit certain subjects. You may find that your material fits into one of the following patterns: a chronological order; a space order; an order that adopts an existing classification (for example, the effect of a certain problem on various age groups—the young, the middle-aged, the old); a cause-and-effect order; a problem-solution order. If none of these patterns is suitable, you must find your points in the topic itself. To establish an organizational plan in which the relationships among the ideas are clearly defined, you should observe the following rules:

1. Write the outline in complete sentences. Incomplete sentences or single words mask muddy thinking and fail to reveal that some ideas which seem to be related are not really related at all.
2. Make certain that the ideas of the program are set down in such a way as to reveal their true relationships. Use a consistent set of symbols to reveal which ideas are the main points, which are subordinate, and which are equal to one another or coordinate.
3. Restrict the number of main points to a reasonable number. Most programs should have no fewer than two main points and no more than five.
4. Be sure that your outline does not omit an essential step in the development of your main idea. You should also make certain that you have enough supporting material to establish your main points adequately.
5. Avoid the use of compound or multiple-idea sentences. There should usually be only one simple sentence after each symbol in the outline.
6. Express points as positive statements, not as questions. When a point is introduced in the actual program it may be worded as a question, but questions in outlines may hide fuzzy thinking or faulty structure.
7. Make sure that there are at least two subordinate points following a main point.

If there is only one, make it part of the main point. An exception to this rule is that an example or illustration supporting a point may be listed singly or it may be made part of the point it supports.

Testing the Relationship of Ideas

When you have completed your outline, you should examine it carefully to make sure it expresses logical relationships. If the program is designed to persuade an audience to accept an idea or to carry out some action, a simple test can be used to check the relationship between the main and subordinate ideas. See whether one of the following words, "for," "because," or "in that," can be used as a natural link between the main idea and its supporting point. The following outline provides an example:

I. Capital punishment should be abolished.
    A. It is morally wrong.
    B. It does not deter crime.
    C. It makes judicial mistakes irretrievable.

Let us suppose that in constructing this outline, you have put these arguments in a different order, as follows:

I. Capital punishment does not deter crime.
    A. It should be abolished.
    B. It is morally wrong.
    C. It makes judicial mistakes irretrievable.

This outline has the same ideas as the first outline, but it does not reveal the relationships among them properly. Point I is connected to point A, but the word that links them is "therefore" rather than "for," "because," or "in that." This indicates that you have reversed the order; point A is the main idea, point I is a subordinate idea that

supports it. Points B and C are obviously divisions of the subject equal in standing to point I rather than being subordinate to it as this version of the outline indicates.

When you actually present your documentary, of course, you may choose to present the supporting ideas first and then conclude with the main idea: Capital punishment is morally wrong; it does not deter crime; and it makes judicial mistakes irretrievable. Therefore capital punishment should be abolished. In constructing a structural outline, however, you make your conclusion a main point and your supporting arguments the subordinate points. The reason for doing this is that you must recognize the difference between the conclusions you are advancing and the arguments you use to support them if your documentary is to be clear and convincing.

Thus far we have been discussing the preparation of structural outlines for documentaries aimed at influencing the audience's opinions or actions. The test words *for, because,* and *in that* do not work as well, however, in evaluating the logical relationships among the items in the structural outlines of documentaries whose main purpose is to provide information. Assume that the purpose of your documentary is the simple one of explaining the process of driving a car. You might construct a structural outline as follows:

I. The process of driving involves three steps.
    A. The car must be started.
    B. The car must be driven in traffic.
    C. The car must be parked.

The question you must ask yourself is whether points A, B, and C comprise complete and logical divisions of the subject matter indicated in point I. If the outline passes this common-sense test, it constitutes a clear and coherent organization of the material. It appears that this outline does pass that test.

A Documentary Outline

In 1990, ABC presented a documentary titled "Guns," which dealt with one of the most controversial issues now facing the American people: Should the government control the sale and use of guns? People interviewed for the program expressed sharply contrasting opinions but the producers took no stand on the issue. Their objective was not to persuade viewers to accept a particular point of view, but rather to describe the conditions that gave rise to the gun-control issue and to indicate how greatly people differ in their responses to it. Their basic purpose, therefore, was to convey information.

We analyzed the script of this program to determine the ideas it presents and the way in which they are related. The result of this analysis is shown in the following outline. It indicates the main ideas the program dealt with and the major subpoints. It does not, however, include all of the information that supported them. A little later in this chapter we include some excerpts from the script which show how some of these ideas came out in the actual program.

"Peter Jennings Reporting: Guns"
Broadcast by ABC News

Central idea and purpose: To inform viewers about the nature of the illegal gun use problem and the arguments for and against gun control as a means of dealing with it.

I. The use of guns confronts society with a serious problem.
    A. Guns are widely available.
        1. There are 200 million guns in the United States.

2. Twenty million of those are assault rifles.
3. A gun is manufactured every nine seconds.
4. San Joaquin County in California has 500,000 residents and 200,000 guns.
    B. Many people are killed each year by gunfire.
        1. In the U.S. 30,000 people die in this way.
        2. In the past 20 years the number of young people killed by guns has increased by 50 percent.
        3. Stockton, California, is a microcosm of this problem.
    C. The judicial system is overwhelmed by crimes in which guns are used.
    D. The ownership of guns in California is difficult to trace.
II. People own guns for several reasons.
    A. Most use them for sport.
    B. Some acquire them for protection.
    C. Others find that the ownership of guns gives them a feeling of power.
    D. Some use them to carry out planned crimes.
III. The illegal use of guns is marked by certain salient characteristics.
    A. Most of the victims are poor.
    B. Victims tend to be killed by their own kind.
    C. Guns are used illegally to express anger, settle disagreements, acquire money, or in response to a dare.
    D. People who use illegal guns impulsively often deeply regret their act.
IV. Gun laws fail to solve the problem.
    A. They often lack the proper rationale.
        1. The banning of assault rifles by a unanimous vote of the Stockton city council was an emotional reaction to the schoolyard massacre; despite this, the city's supply was quickly sold out, and fewer than 20 assault rifles were turned in.

    2. The ordinance left untouched such powerful weapons as deer rifles.

    3. The ordinance left untouched other weapons that kill.

B. Gun laws in general have had no effect.

    1. In 50 years the level of violence has not gone down.

    2. If a law restricts the use of one type of gun, people turn to other types.

C. Gun laws attack the wrong problem.

    1. People kill people, not guns.

    2. The solution is to get criminals behind bars.

    3. The problem is a sick society; 75 percent of those shot are gang members and drug dealers.

D. Taking guns away from people would deprive them of the means of maintaining the freedom some governments might want to destroy; students in China found out how important this principle is during the Tiananmen Square massacre.

V. The arguments against gun control do not eliminate the necessity of doing something about the problem.

A. The arming of citizens does not deter crime.

B. A deadly mixture of three elements results in killings:

    1. A precipitating event occurs.

    2. Drugs or alcohol are often involved.

    3. The gun is there waiting to be used.

C. The passage of the Stockton ordinance constituted a step in the right direction.

    1. It was logical to ban assault weapons because they can kill so many people so fast.

    2. It made the point that violence by guns is unacceptable.

    3. Somewhere a line has to be drawn.

You will note that points IV and V in this outline state opinions about gun control. As pointed out earlier, these were not the opinions of the producers but of people who were interviewed. Including them showed the wide variations in people's views about this issue.

Whether the producers actually drew up an outline similar to the one we constructed we do not know. People who have experience in this field may find it unnecessary to go through this step. That does not mean that they neglect the organizing function. They simply carry it out intuitively. Those who are starting out, however, probably would be wise to make out a structural outline at some stage in the preparation of a program, for nothing is more important to the achievement of clarity in a documentary than a firm grasp by the writer of the ideas to be presented and an understanding of their relationships. The best way of making sure of this is to give the ideas concrete expressions in an outline. This may be done before the program plan is devised or it may be done after it is completed as a final test of the plan's organizational effectiveness.

THE PROGRAM PLAN

After the ideas for this program have been assembled and the relationships among them worked out, the writer's next task is to plan the program. One important step in the process is to choose the way the ideas are to be presented—in narration, interviews, statement, or scenes. Another is to decide the order in which the ideas will be presented. As pointed out before, they will not necessarily come in the order they appear in the outline. Simply following the outline probably would result in a program so rigid in style and unvaried in approach that it would fail to attract an audience.

Let us cite an example. To make sure of representing the logical relationships of ideas clearly, you always list a main point first in an outline and follow it with a statement of the subpoints supporting it. In presenting the program, however, you may very well reverse this order. Some years ago NBC presented a documentary called "Trip to Nowhere" that dealt with drug use by teen-agers. One of the main points made by this program was that "drug use has serious consequences." One of the subpoints supporting this statement was that "drug use sometimes results in death." In the program itself the producer presented the subpoint first and did so in a most effective and dramatic way. The audience saw a funeral procession winding its way through the streets of Phoenix, Arizona. It was revealed then that it carried the body of a young woman who had died from a drug overdose. Viewers would realize with jolting force that drug use has serious consequences without anyone having to tell them that in so many words. The point appeared in the outline because it was part of the structural foundation of the documentary. It did not have to be stated explicitly in the program itself, however. Permitting audiences to arrive at conclusions on their own by presenting them with the evidence first often has a more profound persuasive impact than stating the point and following it with evidence.

In a sense we can say that when the writer moves from constructing an outline to planning the program itself, the logical organizer steps aside to make way for the creative artist. In making this transition, the writer must keep several objectives in mind, among them: to seize and hold the attention of the audience, to give the main points the proper emphasis, to invest all the ideas with an emotional charge powerful enough to sustain interest.

Developing a Program Framework

The first step in drawing up a program plan is to look for a framework that can provide an overall design for structuring the documentary. It is a pattern you find inherent in the material that gives form to the presentation. Some examples will illustrate this.

One of the most ingenious frameworks ever conceived was that used for the CBS series *You Are There*. The idea was to present historical happenings as if they were taking place at the moment of the program, employing the technique of the special events broadcast. CBS commentators, whose voices and faces were familiar to the audience as newsmen, described such occurrences as the fall of Pompeii and the execution of Mary, Queen of Scots as if they were actually present as witnesses, and they further developed an atmosphere of immediacy by interviewing the leading participants in these events.

The documentary "Harvest of Shame" found a framework in the annual migration of farm workers that began at a camp in Florida where the workers spent their winters, turned north as the migrants followed the various crops as they matured, and then, when the northern winter began, went back south to conclude at the same workers' camp. At various stops along this route the program revealed the poverty-stricken lives of the migrants.

Lou Hazam, for many years a documentary writer for NBC, was an ingenious contriver of frameworks. Assigned to do a program on budgeting, he decided that the problem of budgeting has three aspects: the burden of debts accumulated in the past; the problem of paying current expenses; the necessity of planning for future expenses. As a frame for his program, he established a budgeting clinic with specialists who counseled clients with money problems in these three areas—the past, the present, and the future. Another program by Hazam, which dealt with the problems of adolescents, used songs played by a juke box as a means of focusing on each problem. One episode dealt with a music-loving boy whose mother could not bear to hear him practice. The jukebox song initiating this episode was "Mama Don't Allow No Music Played Around Here!"

In the days when documentaries were produced in studios, dramatic frameworks often were used. The development of the field-recording technique brought an end to this approach, but it did not eliminate dramatic elements from documentaries.

An example was a *CBS Reports* program made up of existing and specially shot film about Dr. Tom Dooley, who gained fame for his efforts to bring modern medical practice to the natives of Laos. In this case the program centered on Dr. Dooley's personal battle with disease. Entitled "Biography of a Cancer," the story provided an ideal structure for a drama with a line of action rising toward a climax, which was resolved with the young doctor's tragic and untimely death.

Interviews in "Guns" with the grieving relatives of victims and other shocking eyewitness accounts of violence gave the documentary a strong dramatic flavor. Reality programs, which record everyday lives in telling and revealing detail, can become dramas that deliver a powerful emotional impact. Often needing no narrators, they use the faces of real people reacting to events in actual places to communicate the ideas of the documentary.

At times you may find that nothing in the material provides you with a program framework of the kind we have been describing. When that happens, don't try to force a pattern on the material that does not arise naturally from it. To do so is likely to make your program sound artificial and contrived. The best step in such circumstances is to present your ideas in as interesting a way as possible, using a narrator to link the interviews and scenes and provide whatever comment you think is necessary. This is the framework more documentaries

employ than any other and, in most instances, it is fully satisfactory. At times you can enhance its effect by reinforcing an idea through repetition. A good example of this technique occurred in "Trip to Nowhere." The producers repeated the scene showing the funeral procession of the young victim of a drug overdose at intervals through the program. Each time it appeared, its power to touch the audience grew. It became an arresting motif that emphasized in most affecting terms the tragic consequences that can arise from drug use.

The documentary "Guns" achieved the same kind of effect by returning at regular intervals through the program to the accounts of violence resulting from the use of guns.

Selecting Material and Writing the Script

After you have completed your field work, you will find that you have more material than you can use for the program. The makers of network documentaries, in fact, often shoot 20 times as much material as they can use. Producers working in less affluent situations do not enjoy the luxury of a 20-to-1 ratio, but they are still likely to have more material than they can use and must select from it those elements that best suit their purpose. In carrying out this editing process, there are certain criteria to keep in mind.

Gaining Attention Like all programs, documentaries face the challenge of capturing an audience. In their case, the attention step is a particularly crucial one, for the mere promise of information held out by a documentary is not a powerful attraction in itself for most people. You must therefore depict the subject of the program in the most powerful terms you can devise. You must make it vital and meaningful to the average person. You must surround it with an aura of excitement. You must create suspense by leading your audience to wonder about possible solutions.

"Trip to Nowhere" shocked viewers into watching by beginning with scenes showing pushers actually selling drugs to addicts on the streets of New York. An NBC *White Paper* on the miscarriage of justice opened with a man telling the audience in a quiet yet poignant way that he had spent 16 years in prison for a crime he did not commit.

The ABC documentary "Guns" caught attention immediately by referring to violence committed in the city of Stockton by means of guns. The narrator, Jennings, presented some of that information. Other facts came from a picture, an assistant district attorney, and police officials.

1. JENNINGS ON CAMERA

JENNINGS: Last January, in Stockton, California, there was a shooting—a massacre— five children killed and thirty others wounded in a schoolyard. All over the nation people were affected. All over the nation in the last year, other people have died as the result of gunfire. In this hour we're going back to Stockton, because other people have died in Stockton since.

2. HIGHWAY AND SIGN: "STOCKTON CITY LIMITS, EMERGENCY 911."

JENNINGS: In the whole of San Joaquin county, 60 miles east of San Francisco, there are almost 500-thousand people—and about 200-thousand guns.

3. BLANSETT (ASSISTANT DISTRICT ATTORNEY) ON CAMERA.

BLANSETT: Her ex-husband stepped from the shadows with a shotgun in his hands.

4. SPANISH WOMAN ON CAMERA.

WOMAN: And we were just watching TV and I heard this boom, boom.

5. BLANSETT ON CAMERA.

BLANSETT: His assailants were armed with a handgun, shotgun and rifle.

6. BLACK WOMAN ON CAMERA.

BLACK WOMAN: Yeah, there was a lot of blood. You get shot about, by a, so many, so many. He got shot so many times. Well, they couldn't even count the times. Yeah.

7. CHINESE MAN ON CAMERA.

CHINESE MAN: They found the body right over there in the corner, right there, you know.

8. LAWRENCE (POLICE PATHOLOGIST) ON CAMERA.

LAWRENCE: He jammed the weapon against the door to block her egress, pushed her back in the room and fired.

9. LAWRENCE SLIDE PROJECTED ON SCREEN, DEAD MAN AND WOMAN ON FLOOR OF HOUSE.

10. WINGO (POLICE OFFICER) ON CAMERA.

JENNINGS: Have you ever kept a count of how many people you've seen shot?

WINGO: Oh, no. Hundreds and hundreds and hundreds. And the thing is when I tell you how many murders, I mean I couldn't even guess and tell you how many shootings. There's a lot of them.

A technique commonly used to gain attention is a "teaser." It is a shocking statement, an exciting scene, or a portion of a challenging interview taken from the body of the program and placed at the beginning specifically to seize attention and stimulate interest. The *60 Minutes* magazine series regularly opens with scenes from the three documentaries making up each program.

Introducing Conflict   The attribute most likely to capture audiences is conflict. The main reason dramatic programs are so popular is that they focus on situations filled with conflict. Producers of documentaries treating social and political issues have the advantage of presenting material with con- flict built into it. They should not neglect the opportunity this element provides for building audience interest. One method of enhancing the effect of conflict is to alternate interviews of people who hold clashing views on the subject. This technique also may help to clarify the issues at the same time that it is building audience interest. The "Guns" documentary alternated interviews with people who had conflicting views about gun control to achieve these purposes. Among those interviewed was Gene Kurilow, a member of the Stockton Rifle Club, a group that opposes any kind of gun control. At one point Kurilow responded to a question from Jennings in this way:

---

17. KURILOW ON CAMERA.

JENNINGS: Is there any firearm presently available in the United States which in your view should be banned?

KURILOW: I would suggest atomic bombs but not much less than that.

Another spokesperson for those who opposed gun control laws was Dale Thurston, who formed a group in Stockton to overturn the city ordinance banning assault rifles. Late in the program Jennings asked him for his views on gun control.

95. THURSTON ON CAMERA.

JENNINGS: Do you think there are too many guns out there?

THURSTON: Well I think the current estimate is about 200 million guns in the United States. We manufacture millions more each year.

JENNINGS: One every nine seconds, I'm told.

THURSTON: Is that what it is? And I think that's probably up to the American public to decide.

JENNINGS: What's your own view?

THURSTON: Once they decide not to buy any more, that'll be enough.

JENNINGS: What's your own view, though? Are there too many guns out there to, to make it as safe as you'd like it to be?

THURSTON: I don't really think the guns contribute to the safety one way or another. As a matter of fact, I believe the fact that a law abiding citizen is armed is a deterrence to crime. Surveys have shown that criminals deliberately look for unoccupied homes just out of fear of the fact that, that they may be shot if they were to break in. And for good reason. Armed citizens shoot twice as many criminals as the police do because the armed citizen has the first opportunity. He's first aware.

Standing in opposition to these statements from representatives of anti-gun control groups were people who believe that some kind of restraint is needed. One of them was Barbara Fass, the mayor of Stockton. She vigorously supported the ordinance that banned assault rifles.

131. FASS ON CAMERA.
FASS: I think you have to do it a step at a time and I think that is what the NRA is most concerned about, is that it will happen one very small step at a time so that by the time people have woken up, quote, to what's happened it's gone farther than what they feel the consensus of American citizens would be. But it does have to go one step at a time, and the beginning of the banning of semi-assault military weapons that are military weapons, not household weapons, is the first step.

Other people who believe some type of gun control is necessary included Dr. Robert Lawrence, the police pathologist who conducted autopsies on those killed by guns; and Jack Calkins, the Stockton police chief.

137. LAWRENCE ON CAMERA.

LAWRENCE: I think their stance is somewhat hysterical, and it's based on their fear that someone's going to take away their guns. These are people who like guns. I would not want to take away guns from people like that. I would not propose to take away guns from anybody. But I want people who are thinking to realize that we shouldn't have them in our pocket, and we shouldn't have them in our cars. It's stupid. It's just stupid.

138. CALKINS ON CAMERA.

CALKINS: I think in terms of not only what my people have to put up with every day here in the police department with guns, but I start thinking about all of our children, our grandchildren, our great grandchildren. Where are we headed? Where are we headed in this whole attitude we have about guns and violence?

Jennings remained neutral as he presented narration and carried on interviews. His purpose was to present information and draw out statements that would represent the various views on the gun-control controversy. At one point, however, he did correct a statement made by one of the participants. This was Thurston's comment: "Armed citizens shoot twice as many criminals as the police do." In narration immediately following the statement, Jennings pointed out that records of the Federal Bureau of Investigation (FBI) show that citizens and police are just about even as far as the shooting of criminals is concerned.

Another way in which conflict can be introduced is to feature direct confrontations between the program's interviewers and those to whom they direct questions. In its early years *60 Minutes* sometimes caught people unawares with sharp accusations of misconduct. In one instance Mike Wallace questioned a sham doctor about the people he was cheating in his health clinic; in another, Dan Rather confronted a crooked store buyer with evidence that he was accepting payoffs. Still another episode on *60 Minutes* showed a reporter questioning a gas station attendant whom he caught red-handed creating tire trouble for an unsuspecting motorist. Audiences watched enthralled as these people and others like them squirmed under the relentless eye of the camera. Concluding that ambushing people in this way is not quite fair, the producers abandoned this technique, but interviews with people who are often hostile remain an integral element in the series.

Emphasizing Emotional Values To arouse concern about a social problem and motivate people into taking the steps needed to correct it, a documentary maker must appeal to the emotions of the audience. The best way to do this is to present the issues as they affect individuals. A writer content with discussing problems in general terms will leave the audience uninvolved. The memorable documentaries are those that focus on people.

"Harvest of Shame" was filled with unforgettable portraits. One showed a migrant family composed of a weary father, a dull-eyed wife, and two unkempt-looking children standing at the foot of a tree that had been their only shelter the night before as the father told the audience that all he had in the world was $1.65. In another scene a group of children, still bright-eyed despite the privations of their life, talked about their ambitions. One wanted to be a teacher, another a nurse, still another a doctor.

These statements, coming just after the audience had learned that most migrant children never even completed elementary school, had a special poignancy.

In "Trip to Nowhere," the tragedy of drug use was translated most effectively into human terms. In one sequence, a number of high school students who seemed to be fine, healthy, normal examples of American youth stated that they used drugs. The contrast between their appearance and the habit they confessed had a jolting, emotional effect. In another scene, a man and woman, their tear-streaked faces showing their anguish, struggled to realize that the son they loved had been a drug user for a number of years.

The testimony of grieving relatives and the accounts of violence given by unbelieving witnesses imbues "Guns" with an intense emotional atmosphere. Seeing and hearing people touched by these violent incidents provided far greater impact than merely telling about them. In one scene, the father of one victim speaks at his son's funeral.

---

85. WILLIE PRUITT SR. PREACHES TO FUNERAL CONGREGATION.

PRUITT: I want you to know something. All the peoples can't do Willie no good. All the singing can't do Willie no good. All the preaching can't do Willie no good. No regards on how much we miss him, can't do him no good. He thought he had everything. You can see it ain't all in the selling drugs, and it ain't all in being rich, and it ain't all living in a fine car. I must warn you today, too late, too late.

86. MOURNERS FILE PAST WILLIE'S OPEN CASKET.

JENNINGS: The death of Willie Pruitt went unnoticed in most of Stockton. There was certainly no public outcry to ban the gun used by his killer. There was confusion in Stockton last year over which gun deaths are beyond gun control.

87. YOUNG WOMAN CRIES AT CASKET.

Maintaining Fairness One of the greatest challenges facing the producers of documentaries is to be absolutely fair in the treatment of issues. It may be tempting sometimes to warp the truth a little to strengthen a persuasive appeal or to ignore evidence conflicting with the producer's point of view. Such action is never warranted. Resorting to such measures, in fact, can get documentary makers into trouble. One of the problems faced by CBS in defending itself against the libel action brought by General Westmoreland was that its own internal investigating committee concluded that the producers of "The Uncounted Enemy: A Vietnam Deception" had failed to follow the network guidelines for making documentaries. Had Westmoreland not withdrawn his suit, it is quite possible that the court would have found that the producers were guilty of using selective editing to support a conclusion not warranted by the facts.

Documentary makers should be resolute and hard-hitting in their programs, but knowing that inaccuracies can unfairly damage peoples' reputations, they must make sure that the facts they present are unimpeachable. Even when documentaries are completely fair and accurate, the people and groups who appear in an unfavorable light are likely to react with great hostility.

When the ABC network broadcast a program on psychiatry called "Madness and Medicine," for example, the American Psychological Association called it a vicious, one-sided attack on psychiatry. It accused the network of news-slanting and clamored for time to make a reply.

Writing Narration   Chief among the tools a writer of documentaries needs is a mastery of the art of writing narration, for it is the rare documentary, indeed, that does not employ narration in some form or other. Its chief function in most instances is to reinforce what is presented by filmed or taped segments. Narration in this instance is written after the editing process is completed, for only then can the writer know what material needs narrative support. Sometimes writers create narration that relates directly to what is being shown on the screen. This is known as writing *to* the scene. At other times, they compose narration that has only an indirect relationship to the picture element. This is known as writing *away* from the scene.

Narration can reinforce the effect of a program in a number of ways. It can clarify the meaning of the tapes and pictures. The identification of people in a scene is an example of such clarification. In providing explanation the writer must walk the narrow line that divides saying too little from saying too much. Unnecessary narration may clutter a documentary, but too little may leave a viewer unsure of what is going on.

Narration also may provide an interpretation which enriches the contribution of a taped or filmed excerpt. It can serve also to make a transition from one idea in the documentary to another. Viewers need to be told regularly where they have been, where they are now, and where they are going to be taken. Narration is also an effective tool for presenting the basic ideas of a script, for defining its attitudes, and for summarizing its conclusions. Finally, narration may enhance the emotional effect of a scene or taped insert with a vivid sentence or an appropriate quotation.

An excerpt from a documentary entitled "Who Are the DeBolts and Where Did They Get Nineteen Kids?" illustrates how narration can provide basic facts while scenes and interviews flesh them out with incidents and ideas that give warmth and dimension to the program. Winner of an Academy Award for best documentary and a *Humanitas Prize*, an award given to programs that communicate "those values which most fully enrich the human person," the documentary told how Dorothy DeBolt, the mother of four children, began with her first husband to adopt needy children, mainly Koreans and Vietnamese, some severely handicapped. She continued to adopt children after she was widowed and, with her second husband, added still more children to her household until the total had reached 19 by the time this program was written. They have since adopted another child.

Who are the DeBolts. . . ?

VIDEO	AUDIO
CHILDREN SCREAMING, LAUGHING	RAG TIME MUSIC
SHOTS OF FAMILY	NARRATOR (VO): This is a story of a family, a big family, a special kind of family, but a fam-

ily more like your own
than you might think.

SINGING: "Has Anybody Seen My Gal?"

NARRATOR: You're not going to be able to
remember all the names or
keep straight all the personal
visitors, but you're not going
to forget the DeBolts.
In 1957 Dorothy and Ted
Atwood had four children of
their own when they saw a
picture of a Korean child that
needed a family.

(Interview: Marty, the first child adopted, talks about his experiences.)

MARTY

MARTY AND KIM

FAMILY

NARRATOR: Marty was soon joined by Kim,
and in a couple of years they
became big brothers to a new
baby named Melanie. Their family circle seemed full and complete . . . then . . . Ted Atwood
died of cancer at 49. Suddenly
Dorothy was a widow with 7
children. She recovered, not by
withdrawing, but by extending
her family again. Tich arrived
from Vietnam in need of medical help and specialized equipment. They opened the eyes of
the family to the world beyond
Piedmont, California. Then, Bob
DeBolt appeared, an only child
himself. He had always wanted
a big family. In June of 1970 he
found one . . . Almost 20 years
have passed since that first
adoption. All the oldest children
are out on their own . . . The
Vietnamese are young men
and their garden's thriving.

CU

MRS. DE BOLT: Being the mother of 19 can
be pretty hilarious. I'm

always tearing around and one day I picked up the phone. It was Jennifer saying, "Mom, this is Jennifer. Can I stay at the playground?" and I said, "Sure, but be home by 5 o'clock." I hung up the phone and realized we don't have a kid named Jennifer.

| CHILDREN LAUGHING | MUSIC |
| | CHILD SINGING |

Note that the content of the interview is not recorded in full but is merely summarized. This technique is used also in the following excerpt from a script titled

"Reading, Writing and Reefer," an NBC production narrated by Edwin Newman and written, produced, and directed by Robert Rogers.

READING, WRITING AND REEFER

VIDEO	*AUDIO*
ADULTS SMOKING MARIJUANA	EDWIN NEWMAN: For years we have debated the legal and medical ramifications of marijuana smoking, but for the most part we've talked about adults. This report is not about adults and it is not about the occasional use of marijuana. It is about chronic marijuana smoking by American youngsters.
NBC NEWS PRESENTS READING WRITING AND REEFER REPORTED BY EDWIN NEWMAN	
ACT I 12-YEAR-OLD BRIAN WALKING ON THE BEACH	EDWIN NEWMAN: Brian lives in Florida. But there are children like Brian in almost every American city.

Children who even before they enter high school have become veteran marijuana users.

Interview: Brian says he began smoking pot when he was eight or nine, gets stoned every day, says most of his friends smoke pot.

BRIAN RIDING BUS TO SCHOOL

EDWIN NEWMAN: Often, by the time Brian boards the morning school bus, he and some friends have shared their first joint. Sometimes they decide not to go to school. There was a time when Brian was an excellent student, interested in school. That has changed.

Interviews: Brian says he often falls asleep in class. His mother says that smoking pot has made his grades go down, adding that she found out only recently how much he was using it.

EDWIN NEWMAN: Experts like Dr. Robert Dupont believe that many adults are not aware of the extent of their children's smoking.

Statement: Dr. Robert Dupont, Former Director of the National Institute for Drug Abuse, says adults, most of them nonusers of marijuana, don't realize how much young people are smoking it. If they do, they try to ignore the problem.

Statement: 15-year-old Lisa says parents don't know their kids are getting high.

Interview: Dr. Lloyd Johnston, Institute for Social Research, University of Michigan, says a 1978 survey of high school seniors shows 11 percent reporting daily or near-daily use of marijuana, up from 6 percent in 1975

GRAPH SHOWING INCREASE IN DAILY USE
BY HIGH SCHOOL SENIORS

EDWIN NEWMAN: An official government report says that in 1977 more than four million young Americans ages 12 to 17 were what the report called "current users of marijuana."

This excerpt illustrates a format that can be used by students to practice the writing of documentaries without trying to find experts who can be interviewed or going to the expense of recording material in the field. Your experts can be authorities who write books or articles on various subjects. What they say can be summarized as an interview or statement just as the above excerpt has done. From these same books and articles you can gain information to guide you in creating the video portion of your documentary and provide you with material—a sentence or an appropriate quotation. As we point out in Chapter 14, where we discuss the function of narration in dramatic scripts, narration need not always be spoken. A title card that shows a person's name or official position or indicates the time or place of an event is also a form of narration.

DOCUMENTARY SCRIPT FORMAT

A script does not play quite the same role in documentary production that it does in many other types of programs. Scripts for newscasts and dramas, for example, are completed before production begins, and those for dramas, in particular, may be revised a number of times before the director throws the first cue. Much of the script for a documentary, on the other hand, takes form as the process of production goes on. Interviewers may prepare notes before they begin asking questions and producers may draw up a plan for shooting a scene in advance, but the actual content of these segments comes into being only after the cameras or tape machines start to roll. Documentary scripts, rather than being guides for production, are records of what was said and done while the production was taking place. The main exception to this rule is the narrative portion, which is generally scripted before it is delivered.

Documentary scripts are typed in a variety of formats. A common technique is to put the video elements on the left side of the page and the audio elements on the right. The words actually heard by the audience are typed in regular upper- and lower-case letters, the rest in capital letters. Most of the script examples reproduced in this book use this format. The "Guns" script represents a variation; the writer does not divide the page between video and audio information but lists video information across the page in a numbered sequence. Below each video item is the audio material that accompanies it. The writer, however, does follow the practice of typing the spoken words in upper- and lower-case letters and everything else in capital letters.

QUESTIONS AND PROJECTS

1. Construct a number of main statements (in full sentence form) expressing a point of view about a current social problem. Support each of these main statements with a number of subordinate ideas. Check the relationship between the main ideas and the subordinate ideas by using the testing words: "for," "in that," or "because."

2. Prepare structural outlines for the magazine segment "That's the Law" from *60 Minutes* and for the Detroit station's consumer report on protective gear for children playing baseball. Use these outlines to evaluate the strengths and weaknesses of the two programs' organizational structures.

3. Watch a current documentary or feature with paper and pencil in hand and note the principal ideas it presents and the main supporting points.

4. Compare the structural outline of the documentary "Guns" with the script of the program. Make note of the way in which several of the principal ideas in

the outline were communicated to the audience by the program.

5. Compare the way ideas were presented in the outline of "Guns" with the way they were presented in the program.

6. Observe a number of documentaries with special attention to: (a) attention-getting devices. (b) methods of defining and clarifying the subject of the program (c) the use of human-interest material to arouse interest and achieve emotional response.

7. Choose five subjects that might be given documentary treatment in radio, television, or film. Develop a schedule of interviews for one of these subjects.

8. Collect information by reading books and magazine articles and by interviewing people. Present it in a sequence of narration, interviews, and statements with various scenes indicated, using the "Reading, Writing and Reefer" script excerpt as a model. In this type of outlining, you will remember, statements and interview responses are not presented in their entirety as they occurred in the program but are summarized only. The narration, however, is written out in full. This exercise will provide a worthwhile experience in documentary creation without requiring any filming or taping.

NOTES

1. Joanna Elm, "What Shows Featured These Topics? Geraldo? Oprah?" *TV Guide*, February 3, 1990, pp. 24–25.
2. Monica Collins, "Extra! Extra! Tabloid Clones Invade TV," *TV Guide*, November 18, 1989, p. 14.
3. Richard Campbell, *60 Minutes and the News: A Mythology for Middle America*, Champaign, Ill.: University of Illinois Press, 1991, pp. xxiv and 25–136.

Programs described as "educational" have a bad name in the broadcasting industry because education is usually equated with dullness. Long ago, broadcasters began avoiding use of the term. Early in its existence NBC changed the name of its "education" division to its "public service" division. More recently, noncommercial radio and television stations have stopped referring to their broadcasting as "educational" and are using the term "public" instead.

It cannot be denied that many educational programs are dull, as are many classroom presentations. Dullness is not inevitable, however. Educational programs can be as exciting and stimulating as anything television and film can offer. The critical element is the treatment writers develop. If they resort to routine, shopworn approaches, they are certain to end up boring their audiences. On the other hand, if they use the audio and visual media imaginatively and resourcefully, they can capture the interest and attention of their audiences at the same time they are educating them. Before we discuss the means for achieving these goals, we need to decide just what distinguishes an educational program from other types of broadcasts and films. There is some disagreement about what the term means.

CHARACTERISTICS OF EDUCATIONAL PROGRAMMING

That people define the word *educational* in different ways became clear some years ago when a network and an educational organization each classified the network's offer-

CHAPTER 5

EDUCATIONAL AND CORPORATE PROGRAMMING

Let early education be a sort of amusement.
PLATO

ings in a number of categories. It turned out that the network placed a far higher percentage of its programs in the educational group than the educational organization did. The reason was that the network classified all of its new broadcasts as educational, whereas the educational organization placed them in an informational category.

Defining Educational Programming

Is a news program educational? Since a quiz program provides bits and pieces of information about a variety of subjects, should it be called educational also? Some would say "yes." A few would even go so far as to argue that all experiences have educational value and that all programs and films are, therefore, educational to some degree. To apply the term this broadly, however, deprives it of any special meaning whatsoever. We suggest that if a program or film is to be called educational, it should meet two general criteria: It should explore a subject or develop a treatment in a systematic, organized fashion, and it should aim to improve its recipients in some kind of permanent way.

Newscasts do not treat information in an organized manner but skip from item to item depending on what is happening. Quiz programs present information, but in an aimless, haphazard way. In a sense the information provided by newscasts is of strictly temporary use, being valuable only until the next news program comes along. The information provided by quiz programs has little value or none at all. The newscast and quiz program, therefore, fail to meet the two criteria we described. We would classify newscasts as informational and quiz programs as entertainment.

Types of Educational Programs

The most structured type of educational program is one that takes over the task of directly teaching a lesson in the regular curriculum. TV instruction that explains the concept of fractions in an elementary school arithmetic class or teaches subjects not included in the regular curriculum, such as a language, is an example of direct teaching. This type of broadcasting is also referred to as instructional television or ITV. The armed services and many corporations use training films in the same way to teach certain functions to their personnel.

A second type of educational program provides a *supplement* to the teaching done by the regular teacher. A class of elementary school children studying the history of the United States might watch a film or television program dealing with some aspect of George Washington's life, for example. A university class concerned with the way in which films and television present stereotypes of certain minorities might watch a film called *Geronimo Jones*, which depicts the emotional damage caused by ethnic stereotyping.

A third type is the program that integrates education and entertainment. The programs *Captain Kangaroo* and *Sesame Street* have clear educational objectives, and *Sesame Street*, particularly, engages at times in what might be called direct instruction in seeking to teach preschool children to recognize numbers and letters, but both programs also include segments obviously designed to entertain. The series *Victory at Sea* provided viewers with knowledge of the naval history of World War II at the same time that it gave them entertainment of the first order.

In this chapter we talk mainly about television and filmed educational programs. At one time school systems used radio to bring educational experiences to students, and numbers of radio stations broadcast educational programs for adults. Television has now taken over virtually all of this activity.

Advantages and Disadvantages of Educational Programs

Writers should realize that using the various media for educational purposes entails both advantages and disadvantages. Among the advantages are the following:

1. Broadcasting can be more up to date than printed material and films.
2. Broadcasting and films can present notable people, other places, and a realistic portrayal of events in a way that is beyond the reach of the classroom teacher.
3. Broadcasting and films can integrate learning by breaking down the rigid compartments into which much instruction is organized, thus approaching the situation prevailing in real life where people carry out such functions as spelling and reading together instead of practicing them separately as children do in school.
4. Broadcasting and films provide the writer with a host of special devices and means for accomplishing educational purposes which, used imaginatively, can often make a concept or a function clear in a way that no other teaching method can match.
5. Broadcasting and films, by providing a variation in the traditional approach to teaching and by promising the pleasant experiences most people associate with television and the movies, can make learning more exciting.

If these advantages are to be realized, it is important to recognize that though television programs and films under ordinary circumstances are isolated experiences, educational material succeeds only to the extent that viewers integrate it into the broader context of their lives. Instructional programs, in particular, require preparation, appreciation, and follow-up—all forms of integration. Teachers who fail to utilize educational programs as part of the whole learning experience diminish their effectiveness. Writers often play a part in preparing utilization materials.

These advantages of the media are countered by some of the following disadvantages:

1. There is a lack of intercommunication between the presenter and the audience. Presenters are, in fact, blind as well as deaf, for they cannot see, as a teacher can, when their audiences are becoming inattentive, and because they cannot hear the sound of television dials whirling or the click of switches turning sets off, they do not even know when they have lost audience members completely. Some attempts have been made to meet this problem by providing a two-way communication system that permits viewers to ask questions and, in some cases, even take part in discussions. This is possible in broadcasting, however, only when use is made of the Instructional Television Fixed Service (ITFS), provided by the FCC for educational institutions. In 1970 the University of Michigan, in Ann Arbor, became the first public university to use an interactive, multi-channel system to broadcast engineering courses to people in the field. Most of them were in the Detroit area, 40 miles away, where they received the instruction in their workplace. Of some 14,000 students enrolled a large number earned Master of Science degrees entirely by means of these televised courses.

2. A program or film is fixed in content and approach whereas its audience is heterogeneous in its background and interests. It may strike one member of the audience where the need is greatest, shoot over the head of a second person, or disappoint a third with its obviousness. This lack of adaptation to individual needs is a principal problem. It may mean that a program provides an educational experience for some people in the audience, but not for others. Thus a music-appreciation program may educate those whose tastes are subject to sharpening but may be no more than entertainment for those with an already developed appetite for fine music.

3. It is difficult or impossible to schedule programs for schools at the optimum time for all classes. Schedules vary greatly, and even in the same school system classes in the various subjects meet at different times. Even when classes meet simultaneously, the speed with which they cover a specific course of study varies greatly. That is why broadcasters tend to concentrate on programs that simply enrich or supplement the curriculum instead of trying to provide direct instruction that must fit it precisely. Films do not share the scheduling inflexibility of broadcasts, for they can be shown where they best fit the course of study. This can also be done with television programs that are recorded, of course. The development of the *video cassette recorder* (VCR) has gone a long way toward solving the inflexibility problem. That programs are broadcast at fixed times can also create problems for programs directed at general audiences. People are not likely to see all of the programs in a certain series, a fact writers must take into account in planning and writing them.

4. A disadvantage applying only to radio is its limitation to a single physical sense. Music, of course, suffers least from this

restriction and may actually benefit from it by centering attention on the sound; it is not surprising, therefore, that a substantial proportion of educational radio programs deals with music. But because the teaching of most subjects requires visualization or demonstration, television lessons for schools have largely supplanted radio lessons.

PREPARING EDUCATIONAL PROGRAMS

The preparation of an educational program usually includes the writing of a script, but before that task begins, a number of preliminary steps are necessary.

Selecting Goals

To organize and prepare a successful educational series, writers must be keenly aware of the goals they seek. Defining goals in the educational field is a more complex challenge than it is in other fields. Writers of dramas know what they want to do—namely, hold the attention of an audience by entertaining it. The comedy writer's goal is equally clear—amuse people. Attaining these goals is not easy, of course, but defining them is. Educators, on the other hand, must choose from a wide number of goals. They must ask themselves whether they seek simply to add to a viewer's store of knowledge, or whether they also want to promote understanding of an issue. Perhaps they hope to develop a certain attitude or build a set of values. Their goal may be the utilitarian one of teaching viewers a certain skill or showing them how to carry out a particular process. They may be interested in building tastes and appreciation for literature, drama, or music. Because the attainment of these various objectives requires a diversity of approaches, writers must know what their objectives are before they begin planning the program.

Sesame Street, one of the most successful educational children's series ever produced, provides an excellent example of care in defining objectives. Before the first program went on the air, the Children's Television Workshop, producer of the series, carried out a carefully planned research effort designed to explore children's needs and to determine which ones should be focused on by a television program. From this effort came a set of goals that outlined in specific terms exactly what the programs should try to accomplish. Chief among these goals was teaching preschool children to recognize letters and numbers. The Workshop went on to describe in precise detail the conditions under which this recognition should take place. There were other goals also. The programs taught children to recognize and name parts of their body, to discriminate among various visual forms, to distinguish one sound from another, to understand size relationships, to classify and order objects, to solve problems, and to recognize causality. The programs also presented facts about the physical and social environment and encouraged meaningful and satisfactory interaction with others. Children tuning in the television set to watch *Sesame Street* may have been seeking entertainment. They were entertained without a doubt, but at the same time they benefited in a most constructive way from programs carefully designed to achieve certain educational objectives.

In the same way, Fred Rogers, creator and producer of *Mister Rogers' Neighborhood*, carefully defined his goals before he wrote the scripts. One of his objectives was to build attitudes that would help children feel good about themselves and the world around them and cope with some of the problems that concern them. Research carried out at a number of institutions showed that the young viewers of the program improved in such characteristics as rule obedience, tolerance of delay, and task persistence. (We make further reference to these programs in the section on writing for children.)

Defining goals of an educational program aimed at adults is just as important as defining them for children's programs. This task may be somewhat easier on the adult level where it is assumed that basic attitudes and values already have been formed. The emphasis is, therefore, usually on transmitting information that will deepen understanding and widen knowledge of a particular field or on providing instruction aimed at developing or heightening a skill.

Planning a Series

The way you plan a series depends in large measure on the conditions under which you expect the programs to be received. If teachers plan to use them in the classrooms to teach a part of the regular curriculum, you have reasonable assurance that your audience will see all or most of the programs. Adults tuning in to earn credit in a course, as some do, are likely to be regular listeners also. Being able to count on regular listening means that you can begin with a preview program to introduce the telecourse, you can link one program to another, and you can conclude with a review that looks back at the programs in the series to summarize and integrate them.

A series broadcast as a supplement to regular classroom lessons or as a general educational experience is quite another matter. In these situations, you cannot expect your audience to receive all or even most of the programs in the series. This circumstance affects planning in a number of ways. First, you should probably skip the introductory and review programs because they are not likely to be meaningful to most of your viewers. Second, you should plan each program to provide a satisfactory educational experience on its own. Some references to

previous and succeeding programs may be in order, but you must be careful that viewers' knowledge of what has been presented before is not critical to what you are presenting now.

An early step in planning is to decide how many programs the series will include. There is no automatic "right" number. In commercial broadcasting, programs often are produced in groups of 13 because that is a quarter of the calender year. Educators have tended to follow this pattern in planning programs, but there is no reason they should, and in doing so they have often made a series too long or cut it off abruptly.

A series should have as many programs as the material itself dictates. This means that some series may have only three programs, others 30 or more. Some subject areas, of course, are flexible ones that may be given extended or brief coverage. A series produced by the University of Michigan, called *Genius*, provides an example: It can be short or long, depending on how many geniuses you choose to include. A series on *Marriage*, another University of Michigan program, in contrast, demands coverage of certain aspects of the subject if the series is to treat it in a complete and satisfactory way. The producer settled finally on the following 15 programs:

University of Michigan TV Series

Marriage

1. Dating
2. Choosing Your Partner
3. Mixed Marriages
4. Love
5. What It Means to Be Married
6. Tremendous Trifles
7. Marital Counseling
8. Divorce
9. Companionship and Recreation

10. Money and Marriage
11. In-Laws
12. Physical Adjustment
13. Children and Marriage
14. Remarriage
15. Marriage in the Older Years

Planning and Writing a Program

Having decided on the general structure of a series, the writer's next task is to plan the specific content that will go into each program. Among the matters to be determined are the divisions of the subject matter; their order and organization; the means for communicating the main and subtopics: audio, video, or a combination of both; and the use of complementary material to lighten and add interest to the basic content.

Research, Analysis, and Organization

Let us assume that you have been assigned to write a TV program explaining how TV and radio programs are sent and received. If you are not familiar with this subject, you must gather information about it by reading and consulting with experts. You must then decide how to divide the information you obtain into major and minor topics. You might begin by describing such basic concepts as atoms, electromagnetic energy, and the electromagnetic spectrum, particularly that part connected with the transmission of radio and television programs.

With this foundation in place you can then move to an analysis of the broadcasting process. This would involve a description of radio waves, the way they are generated and propagated, and the means used to make them carry the information we see and hear on radio and television programs. This last topic probably would call for a treatment of the difference between AM and FM transmission. Your next step might be to explain how radio and television differ in the way programs are sent and received.

Because this subject matter is highly technical, you must take special pains to make your presentation clear. Most crucial in attaining this objective is the use of visual information and devices to support the audio exposition. You must also think up ways of making this subject exciting and interesting, for it is one that could well make the average viewer's eyes glaze over.

Organizing the material in a logical and understandable way is also of the utmost importance. We discussed organizational principles in the previous chapter, on documentaries. If you have not yet read that material, you should do so now, for the principles that apply to organizing documentaries apply equally to educational programs. The divisions of subject matter that we have suggested for a program on the broadcasting process would constitute your major topics. You need to determine, further, what the minor topics are and how they relate to and support the major topics. You must make sure that your topics represent logical divisions of the subject and that they are relevant and supportive of the main topic.

The way in which weakness in an organizational pattern can obstruct the attainment of clarity and understanding was illustrated by an educational program on the subject of heredity. In one part of the program the writer made the point that the influence of heredity causes parents and children to resemble one another. In the course of this discussion, the writer showed a man and boy, identified as father and son, who looked strikingly similar. The audience had the right to assume that they illustrated the point that parents and children tend to look alike. At the end of the segment, however, the writer surprised the audience by revealing that the boy was the adopted, not the natural, son of the father. The only result of this revelation was confusion. The appearance of this father and son did not support in any way the point the program was making—that resemblances run in a family. In fact, it illustrated quite another point—that people who are not related may look alike. Casting this material into an organizational outline would have immediately revealed the existence of this irrelevancy, which should then have been promptly eliminated. Perhaps the writer put it in simply as a "gimmick" to divert the audience. You should avoid such tricks in writing educational programs. Never use a "gimmick" that gets in the way of achieving clarity.

In discussing the writing of documentaries, we made a distinction between the outline of the content and the program plan. That distinction applies equally to educational programming. The outline identifies the ideas to be presented and shows their relationships. The program plan indicates the order in which those ideas will be presented on the actual program. That order is not likely to be the same as that of the outline, for to follow it rigidly probably would result in a program that sounded stiff and didactic. In an outline, for example, the major topic is always stated first, followed by the points that prove or support it. In designing your program plan, however, you might choose to present the supporting points first and thus lead viewers into arriving at the conclusion—or main topic—on their own.

In designing your plan, one of your principal challenges is to catch the attention of the audience. Arousing and holding interest is far more critical for television and film educators than it is for classroom educators. One reason is that viewers whose interest flags can easily leave the audience by throwing a switch. Students do not usually walk out on a dull classroom lecture, though they might be tempted to do so. A second reason why arousing interest is urgent is that most people turn on a television set in the expectation of being entertained. Recognizing

this, the Children's Television Workshop took over a number of the devices used in commercial television programs and applied them with great success in such programs as *Sesame Street* and *The Electric Company*.

Choosing the Presentational Framework The most obvious procedure in presenting educational material on film and television is to follow the usual classroom practice of using a lecture. Those who do so are often denounced for relying on a "talking head" to present their material. The trouble with this approach is that it ignores the opportunities the visual media offer. A person who simply stands in front of a camera and lectures for the duration of a program is almost bound to be dull. Writers of educational scripts have found it difficult to eliminate talking heads entirely, however. Programs that present information usually need a host or narrator to introduce the material and to provide linkage as the program moves from one segment to another. This technique is entirely acceptable if these segments utilize the media's various resources in an interesting and stimulating fashion. Even talking heads in and of themselves may work well at times. A good example of effective use occurs in every episode of *Mister Rogers' Neighborhood*, when Fred Rogers talks directly to his young viewers, often in a camera shot that does not change for a considerable period. The reason this approach succeeds is that Mister Rogers has established himself as a trusting, caring individual who talks about subjects directly relevant to children's lives, such as the fears associated with what he calls "the universal growth tasks of human development." Children, therefore, watch with fascinated interest. It is like a personal visit through an electronic medium.

In addition to the host-narrator framework, there are other possibilities for structuring educational programs. The program may be built around interviews with experts in the field or may feature discussions by informed individuals, as PBS's *Washington Week-in Review* does. Some stations have dealt with public issues by presenting the debates printed in the *Congressional Record*. A quiz format has even been used as a means of leading into the discussion of a serious question. Excellent programs have used still pictures as the primary visual element. Biographies of Abraham Lincoln and Mark Twain have been presented in this way. A memorable film was Pierre Berton's *City of Gold*, which, with a combination of still pictures and poetic narration, brought the Klondike Gold Rush back with such vivid reality that its participants seemed to breathe. Kenneth Burns used still pictures in the same creative way in his striking PBS mini-series *The Civil War*.

Writing the Script   Your primary concern in writing an educational program is to achieve clarity. Your secondary goals are to sustain interest and create memorability. All are essential to the writing of a successful program. In reaching these goals, you must use the resources of the audio and visual media in an inventive and imaginative way. To accomplish this you must become familiar with what the resources are. One of the best ways of doing this is to learn something about production. Only by seeing such elements as cameras, slides, switching techniques, and film inserts actually being used can you acquire the understanding needed to employ them in a practical and creative way.

The Budget Situation   One factor you cannot overlook is the budget under which you operate. It will determine what resources you may consider using. An excellent way to demonstrate a process, for example, is to produce an animated film. This is an expensive undertaking, however, which only the best-financed production organizations can afford. If animation is beyond your financial reach, you must think of cheaper ways to attain your goals. A number of production organizations have approached the effectiveness of animation in a much less expensive way by creating graphics with movable parts that can be pulled to illustrate the steps in a process. You must demonstrate similar ingenuity in developing a wide variety of means for conveying information in a clear yet striking way. In doing so, do not forget the people who take part in your program. They are probably your most important resource and you must do everything you can to use them well.

Opening the Script   The way you begin the program is crucial, for it is at that point that many people will decide whether to listen or turn to something else. Somehow you must create curiosity and expectation. Educational broadcasters often employ the "teaser," a technique many dramatic programs use as a way of stimulating interest at the opening. A teaser may take the form of a curiosity-arousing question to which the program promises an answer. A program dealing with medical matters, for example, might open with the question: "Are we gaining on cancer?" and then provide a "yes" by describing recent advances in the treatment of leukemia.

Another way to tease an audience into watching is to open the program with an exciting segment taken from the body of the script.

This technique has two disadvantages, however: Its artifice is too obvious for some, and it may disorient the audience because it presents material out of context. For this reason, some prefer a straight introduction that seeks to stimulate interest by using such traditional devices as a striking statement, a quotation, a reference to the familiar, a promise of the unusual, or a recounting of a recent event. In addition to seizing attention, the introduction should also indicate the program's subject matter. It is well to remember that not everyone tuned in when your program comes on is going to be interested in watching it. You need to let potential viewers know what the program is about, recognizing that while some will say "this is not for me," others will be attracted by the content you promise.

The Body of the Script   We emphasize again that your most important responsibility in writing an educational script is to be clear. Only if you are clear can your viewers understand what you are presenting, and only if they understand are they likely to continue listening. Clarity, then, is essential if you are to hold attention and sustain interest.

There are also other attributes that help to make educational programs interesting. Many are those we associate with dramatic writing. Writers of educational programs, in fact, have often used a dramatic format in presenting information, especially when the material is biographical or historical. The techniques of writing this type of drama are covered in the chapters on dramatic writing.

It is not necessary, however, to employ a dramatic format to attain many of the qualities we associate with drama. Just as dramatic writers do, you should try to develop expectation and even, to some degree, suspense when you are writing an educational script. You should parcel out information in a gradual way through the program so that complete satisfaction does not come all at once but is provided step by step. In some instances you can even include a conflict situation.

The final revelation can, in a sense, provide a climax to the program. Thus you should build an educational program as you would a drama, on a plane that rises in interest to the conclusion.

Special Problems   Creating educational programs for children confronts writers with a number of unusual problems. This is a matter of such importance that we have devoted a separate chapter to the nature of children and the problems of writing for them. That chapter, which appears later in the book, covers educational programs as well as other types of programs for children.

Earlier we mentioned that writers must be keenly aware of the budget restraints under which they operate. Limited financial resources create many problems to which there are no pat answers. Writers must be ingenious in responding to them. They must also be aware of the conditions under which the production of programs takes place. For example, in producing *Mister Rogers' Neighborhood*, Fred Rogers, in addition to talking directly to children in his own person, also provides the voices for many of the puppets who appear in a fantasy segment called "the Neighborhood of Make-Believe." Mister Rogers, who creates most of the programs, is well aware of this circumstance, of course, and so are the others in the small group who write scripts. To help acquaint possible new writers with the circumstances under which *Mister Rogers' Neighborhood* is produced, some guidelines were prepared. These instructions, which follow, provide a good example of the way writers must adapt to a production situation.

Neighborhood of Make-Believe (NOM) Limitations

Fred Rogers does all the puppets except the Platypus family. Hence, except in unusual circumstances (either when Platypus family is involved or when an extra puppeteer is hired), no more than two of the puppets can be in conversation with one another—although the two puppets will usually be augmented by at least one live person.

Because of the similarity in voices, the following groups of puppets cannot talk in direct dialogue with other puppets in the same group—but they can talk with those in the other group, or with those in their own group if a live person speaks intervening lines.

King Friday / Queen Sara
Grandpere / Lady Elaine Fairchilde
Corney / Henrietta
X the Owl / Collette
Edgar Cooke / Daniel

Donkey Hodie falls somewhere in-between. The NOM should be written, insofar as possible, as a "live" program. This means that you must allow time for Fred Rogers to move from one set piece and puppet to another. Edits are expensive and our budget is small; use both sparingly! Since the NOM is, psychodynamically, a dream, it is preferable to introduce key elements in the NOM (prop, talent) in the segment(s) which precede it.

Script Formats A script for an educational program may be written out in full, or it may be only semiscripted for presentation by a host or narrator who speaks extemporaneously. The format for the fully scripted program often follows the pattern used for the documentary.

The ad-libbed or extemporaneous method is more common in educational broadcasting than it is in other kinds of programs. The script format below illustrates a common pattern for semiscripted shows. Note that the lines provide cues or reminders of content, which the narrator then converts into full exposition. The writer has written out the roll cues for the films in full, however, to guide the director in inserting the films into the program at precisely the right moment. The writer also has described the ending of the film in detail so that the director may know exactly when to cue the narrator for the next segment.

Format for Semiscripted Show

VIDEO	*AUDIO*
CHART: DIAGRAM OF CYCLE SLIDE #1	Concept of green leaves as food factories: 1) Oxygen = CO_2 Cycle 2) Water and nourishment up from roots 3) Manufacture of chlorophyll Role of chlorophyll in growth of vegetation
FILM: 1' 20"	FILM ROLL CUE: Now suppose we take a look at the inside of a green leaf and see for ourselves how the little dots of chlorophyll flow through the cells of the leaf substance. FILM ENDS WITH SHOT OF PULSING DOTS SLOWING DOWN TO A DEAD STOP

A Program Analysis

One of the most basic educational objectives is teaching people how to read. A series of programs designed to achieve this goal was broadcast by a Detroit TV station, WXYZ. Titled *Assignment Education: Learning to Read*, the venture was supported by the Chrysler and Michigan Bell corporations. An analysis of the content and presentation of Program 10 in the series illustrates the application of the principles we have been discussing.

The episode began with a review of the letters of the alphabet, which had all been covered in the previous nine programs. The discussion of each letter was marked by a number of carefully planned steps:

1. The presenter articulated the sound of each letter.
2. The presenter showed the letter in a number of words, pronouncing them and showing them on the screen.
3. The presenter distinguished between the upper- and lower-case forms of the letter.
4. The presenter directed viewers to practice writing down these forms.

These steps constitute the division of the subject matter for this particular segment and the sequence demonstrates an excellent organizational plan. The audio instruction was consistently backed up with video supporting material.

The presenters, and there were several of them, dealt with a number of other divisions of the subject matter in the segments that followed. One of them concentrated on the five vowels, considering them in the steps we have just outlined. A second showed how letters combine with other sounds to make words, followed by sample sentences showing the words in use. A third segment concentrated on "sight words," described as elements for binding sentences together. Other segments demonstrated how adding the syllable "er" to a word like *fat* extends its meaning, and how single words like *sink* and *hole* can be combined to make the new word *sinkhole*.

Variety and interest were added to the program by using more than one presenter, by using common signs such as "No Park-

ing," "Exit," and "Stop" in the opening format, and by introducing a lighthearted character named Les the Letterman, who talked about disappearing letters. He pointed out that one does not hear the *w* in *who,* for example. He then disappeared from the screen.

The presenters encouraged viewers to work on exercises after the program, writing sight words on pieces of paper, for example, and reviewing them until they could recognize them instantly. They added that constant practice would make them skilled readers eventually, just as practicing cooking and sewing promotes skill in those arts. A successful student then provided personal testimony about the value of acquiring reading skills. Before he mastered the process, he could only pretend to read bedtime stories to his children. He had to look at the pictures for guidance and then make up the rest. By the time his grandchildren came along, however, he had learned to read. Now he can use the author's words instead of his own-and he can still talk about the pictures.

All of this material was covered in just half an hour. It was possible to make it meaningful in so short a period because the producers made excellent divisions of the subject matter and presented them in an understandable and orderly way. Contributing immensely to the clarity of the program was the efficient working together of the audio and video elements. The use of several speakers, the alternation of different types of segments, the touches of humor and human interest, and the occasional words of encouragement helped to hold attention and promote learning.

CORPORATE EDUCATIONAL PROGRAMMING

Many corporations now use television and film programming to achieve a variety of educational objectives. One of the principal applications is its use in the training of employees. The installation of a new computer system, for example, may require workers to become familiar with new and more sophisticated techniques. A training film or television program can contribute to attaining this objective. On a more elementary level, newly employed secretaries can learn about the company's filing methods by watching a film or tape. In the same way, workers in a factory can be taught a new manufacturing process. Television can be used to introduce a new product to the corps of salespeople both at the company's headquarters and, through special television hook-ups, around the country. These examples constitute just a few of the ways in which corporations use film and television for the internal instruction of their employees. The United States government, particularly the armed services, also makes extensive use of instructional films and tapes.

Sometimes corporations produce instructional material designed for people other than their own staffs. A good example is the film or tape some airlines show to instruct passengers in the use of seat belts and breathing devices. Such presentations relieve flight attendants of the boring task of repeating the instructions every time a plane takes off, and they have the further advantage of being more visible and interesting than demonstrations in the plane. Grocery and department stores can use video or audio presentations to inform people in the store about special offers.

Hospitals also employ instructional films or tapes to provide information to patients and potential patients. Such tapes can show in a clear and dramatic way what precautions, for example, a patient should observe. One good example of this use can be seen in the following excerpt, taken from a script for a videotape produced by the communications division of St. Joseph Mercy Hospital in Ypsilanti, Michigan. The tape, aimed at people about to undergo surgery to replace defective hip joints with artificial ones, shows viewers the reasons for their affliction, the nature of the surgery, and the steps patients should take to get ready.

PATIENT EDUCATION VIDEO SCRIPT
Writer/Producer: Joyce B. Williams, RN, MA
THE NEXT FEW STEPS: PREPARING FOR TOTAL HIP REPLACEMENT

VIDEO	*AUDIO*
INTERVIEWS, ONE OF WHICH IS WITH BURNETTE, THE "PATIENT" IN THE VIDEO, OVER THE FOOTAGE	"When the pain got so great that I just couldn't stand it anymore, I had my operation and it feels great so I know I did the right thing."
DOMENIC IN DR. HENKE'S OFFICE	
BURNETTE PLAYING WITH CHILD	"Now I can get down on the floor and play with my grandkids!"
FORMER PATIENT WORKING	"Now I can work all day without feeling that pain and stiffness."

MIDDLE-AGED WOMAN CYCLING

NARRATOR (VO): Many people have discovered the positive changes that can occur after having hip joint arthroplasty, also

BURNETTE PACKING TO LEAVE HOSPITAL

known as total hip replacement surgery. It is one of the most consistently successful surgeries performed in the U.S. today. Although

OLDER PEOPLE GOLFING

hip replacement is not without risk, 95% of patients who have the procedure experience

FADE OUT
FADE IN

smooth, uncomplicated recoveries. For them, the reward is a less painful, more active life.

COMPUTER GRAPHIC OF HIP ANATOMY

NARRATOR (VO): The hip joint is the largest weight bearing joint in your body. It is formed where the thigh bone and the pelvis meet. The round head of the upper leg bone fits into the hollowed out socket of the pelvis. It's known as a ball and socket joint.

COMPUTER GRAPHIC OF HEALTHY HIP JOINT

NARRATOR (VO): Your hip joint once had smooth surfaces that created pain-free movement. Now, due to disease, injury, or

COMPUTER GRAPHIC OF DISEASED HIP JOINT

the effects of aging, the joint has become rough and pitted. During Total Hip Replacement, we will replace your worn out hip

COMPUTER GRAPHIC OF PLACEMENT OF HIP PROSTHESIS

joint with a smooth artificial joint, or prosthesis, made of plastic and metal.
Your physician will discuss the type of artificial joint that will be best for you.

QUESTIONS AND PROJECTS

1. *Sesame Street* and *Mister Rogers' Neighborhood* employ markedly different approaches to educating children. The first presents specific information in short bursts, as commercials do, the second integrates information with philosophical discussion over a longer time span. Is one approach better than the other or does each have a place?

2. One effective way of presenting information clearly is to employ comparison and contrast. What other techniques would you recommend for making an idea clear?

3. Choose a general subject, such as "safety on the highway" or "energy conservation," and after identifying your target audience, devise a series of program titles that will encompass this general subject in a complete and reasonable way.

4. Discuss the experience that students may have had in elementary and high school with educational programming. Evaluate its effectiveness.

5. Take note of some of the educational programming that students may encounter outside the classroom and analyze its goals.

6. How would you define educational programming?

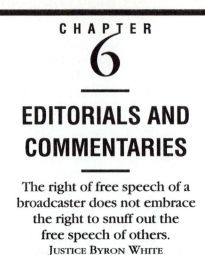

EDITORIALS AND COMMENTARIES

The right of free speech of a
broadcaster does not embrace
the right to snuff out the
free speech of others.
JUSTICE BYRON WHITE

Among the types of programming that many radio and television stations broadcast are editorials and commentaries. They range in their approaches from those that consciously try to influence the actions and beliefs of audience members to those that aim merely to reinforce the beliefs most people already hold. Some may seek no more than to provoke an emotional response. Others present the opinion of a broadcaster or a station on an issue or an event without trying to persuade the audience to accept that opinion.

EDITORIALS

The editorial page on which publishers, through their editorial writers, express opinions about issues of the day, is a traditional part of most newspapers. Editorials were commonplace in radio and television for more than 40 years; however, as a consequence of broadcasting policy, they survive today at the whim of prevailing political and managerial winds. The controlling factor is the attitude of the Federal Communications Commission (FCC) toward the propriety of a broadcasting station presenting an opinion about an issue. Because the president appoints members to replace those whose terms expire, the commissioners' policies generally reflect those of the administration currently in power. In 1941 the FCC encountered the question of advocacy in connection with a license application and decided, in what came to be known as the Mayflower Decision, that a station should not be an advocate. Because a station uses a public frequency to broadcast programs, the FCC first said it was improper for the station to use this frequency as a vehicle for broadcasting its own opinions about issues.

In 1949 the FCC reversed itself on this question by granting stations the right to broadcast editorials. It added an important requirement, however, namely, that the station provide a reasonable opportunity for the airing of all sides of a controversial issue. This was the beginning of what has come to be known as the Fairness Doctrine. Newspapers were not subject to this requirement because they do not use public broadcasting frequencies to express their points of view. The influence of the Fairness Doctrine is the reason that many broadcast editorials have traditionally ended with an invitation to those with differing views to call or write the station. Those who respond may then get what is deemed a "reasonable" opportunity to air their views through what has been designated "editorial feedback" or "editorial reply."

During the presidency of Ronald Reagan, and with his encouragement, the FCC advanced the principle of deregulation. It removed from broadcasters the stipulation that they expose conflicting opinions on important issues. While some stations reduced the number and vigor of the editorials, or eliminated them entirely, other stations did not. They believed that maintaining the spirit of the Fairness Doctrine is one way to "serve the public interest," a responsibility articulated in broadcast law since 1927.

Where editorials continue to be aired, the challenge to the writer is unchanged: to express the official opinion of the management on an issue of importance to the audience.

Deciding Editorial Subjects

Because an editorial expresses a station's point of view rather than that of an individual, there needs to be a procedure for deciding the issues editorials will cover and the positions the station will take. Editorial boards, traditionally the vehicle for formulating position statements, might include the general manager, station manager, program director, executive producer, community affairs director, editorial director, and news director. The precise procedure for deciding editorial subjects varies from station to station, but most have a process that permits input from several staff members. The editorial voice may be the station's general manager, or someone assigned the duty, generally on a regular basis.

Many of the editorials contain filmed or taped inserts, and some feature the editorial director speaking "on location," as did Richard Hughes of independent WPIX-TV.

Editorial: "Productivity and the Sanitation Workers"
WPIX-TV, New York

(On location: Lower Manhattan)

The attitude which makes dealing with New York City's budget gap such a horrendous problem can be seen in an argument now raging between the sanitation workers' union and the city government.

Because of the mandatory recycling program in the city, sanitation trucks are picking up 20% less trash in many neighborhoods than they were before recycling began. The obvious response to that should be "three cheers for recycling." At last we've found a way to improve productivity

—by 20%. That is a very big deal. Garbage collection in New York City costs $130 million a year. Save 20% of that [and] you've picked up 26 million bucks to help close the budget gap.

So, since the garbage crews have less work to do because of the recycling, the city wants to extend the routes. That would reduce the number of trucks, and sanitation workers, needed to do the job.

Now, understand, all the city wants is for the sanitation workers to pick up the same tonnage of garbage that they did before recycling began. Is that an unreasonable policy?

The Sanitation Workers Union thinks it is, and will not even discuss the proposal, unless it is part of a larger package that includes wages, work-force size, health benefits, the works.

That attitude, or a variation of it, is being played out in many departments of city government, and it is reprehensible. It could be the death of the city.

Maybe it's time for the "P word." Privatization.

What's your opinion? We'd like to know.

WPIX-TV regularly broadcasts editorials. The one above, which was delivered by the station's editorialist, won an "outstanding editorial" award from the New York State Broadcasters Association.

Why do you think the judges selected this editorial for commendation? You might read and analyze it with these questions in mind:

1. Is there something particularly effective in the organizational structure? What is it?
2. Does it contain compelling evidence or arguments?
3. Is its primary appeal to the head or heart of the viewer?"
4. How is that appeal supported?
5. Does the piece contain persuasive anecdotes?
6. Is the station's position clearly stated?

7. Do you agree with the point of view expressed by the station?

Writing the Editorial

Because an editorial is designed to persuade, writers must be concerned about constructing a strong structural framework. This framework is expressed through an outline. What we said in Chapter 4 about drawing up outlines for documentaries also applies to the editorial.

Preparing the Structural Framework
You may prepare the outline before you write the editorial or, if you wish to avoid being controlled by too rigid a pattern which some people feel an outline forces on them, you may defer drawing up the outline until after you have written your first draft. The outline then becomes a test of the structural soundness of your presentation. If you are especially experienced and secure, you may rely on your intuition to provide the proper organizational form without putting it into written form.

As is the case with the documentary outline, the order of ideas in the outline for an editorial does not necessarily indicate the order in which you will present the ideas in the editorial itself. In writing your copy, you need to think about catching attention, about leading the audience to reach conclusions on its own, about using devices that will influence thought and action. You may therefore present the evidence before you present the conclusions. In the outline, however, which lists your arguments and shows how they relate to one another, you always list the conclusions first, followed by the arguments and evidence that support them.

The outline that follows shows the organizational structure of an editorial presented by station KGO Radio in San Francisco. It was the first in a series of four editorials that demanded new legislation to combat rape in California. They followed a 10-part series of news reports, featuring the voices of victims and rapists telling their stories, which detailed the causes and consequences of rape. The San Francisco Bar Association gave this campaign a first-place award for community service.

The first editorial in the series, shown first in outline form and then as presented, emphasizes the severity of the problem. It is brief and therefore the outline is brief, containing just two major points. The first is supported by reminding listeners of the information given in the news reports and also by listing figures showing how rape has increased. The second point is merely mentioned, but there is a promise that succeeding editorials will deal with it. Note that the order of ideas in the outline is somewhat different from their sequence in the editorial; point A precedes B in the outline, but follows it in the editorial.

Editorial: "The Ravages of Rape—I"
KGO Radio, San Francisco

Outline

General Purpose: To arouse public concern about the rape problem.

I. California needs more effective laws to control rape.
   A. Rape has tragic consequences.
   B. The state is failing to cope with this crime.
      1. Last year rape increased statewide more than 12 percent.
      2. In San Jose it increased 47 percent.
      3. In San Francisco it increased 26 percent.
II. Public participation will determine success or failure in this fight against rape.

The Editorial

California urgently needs far more effective prosecution and punishment for the crime of rape. There are glaring failures at every stage of the state's efforts to cope with this socially devastating and fast-rising crime.

Rape increased statewide by more than twelve percent last year. Today the worst two problem cities of highest incidence are in the Bay Area—San Jose, up an amazing forty-seven percent and San Francisco, up twenty-six percent.

KGO Radio listeners recently learned, in an exclusive ten-part series of news reports, the primary causes and tragic consequences of rape. The voices of victims and of rapists told their own stories. Now KGO proposes practical methods to help stop the spreading rape epidemic, and then to reduce its scope.

Public participation in this statewide effort can without a doubt produce either its success or failure. We will disclose in our next editorial the major moves now underway to strengthen the forces of law against rape, and then detail how citizens can directly help make that happen.

Choosing Appropriate Language   To persuade audiences to accept a certain point of view, editorial writers must provide their audiences with enough information to understand the issue. They must express their viewpoints with strength and conviction and be fair at the same time. Because the time allotted to them is brief, they must strive to accomplish their objectives with language that is succinct and to the point. They must also keep one other factor of overwhelming importance firmly in mind;

namely, that what they write is to be heard, not to be read. In Chapter 1 we summarized some of the considerations to keep in mind when you are writing for the ear. It would be helpful to review them before beginning each assignment.

COMMENTARIES

A type of writing on radio and television stations and networks heard more often than editorials is the commentary. Although similar to editorials, which often convey a particular perspective, opinion, insight or analysis, commentaries differ in a number of ways. First, the commentary does not necessarily express the official position of a broadcasting organization on an issue but presents the opinion of a private individual who is permitted by the station or network to offer a point of view. Second, the commentary sometimes deals with topics that are not as serious as those usually discussed by editorial writers. Third, because commentators do not represent the station officially, they generally experience greater freedom in expressing passionately held perspectives.

General-Purpose Commentaries

Andy Rooney, who provides a conclusion to the CBS program *60 Minutes*, presents wry and perceptive commentaries on various aspects of American life. He often provides comic relief after the program's audacious exposures of a cast of scoundrels. Rooney, in contrast to his colleagues, will more often toy with a perplexing question ("Where do lost socks go?") or ponder the irrelevance of slogans on license plates than tackle a thorny political problem.

60 Minutes
"Advertising"
by Andy Rooney

ROONEY: There ought to be some places where we're safe from being advertised at. There ought to be some open spaces left in the world, some pieces of paper, some painted surfaces that aren't covered with advertisements. Advertising doesn't belong on license plates, either. Of the 50 states, 27 of them have slogans trying to sell themselves to the rest of us.

ROONEY **(VO as license plates are shown):** The license plate has an important function and I think it's a cheap trick to tack something else on to it. Most of the legends the states put on them aren't really true anyway. Rhode Island, for instance, calls itself the "Ocean State." There are 15 states with more ocean than Rhode Island has. If they want to say something on their plate, why don't they explain why they call it an island when it isn't one.

Florida says it's the "Sunshine State." I like Florida but why don't they say that Miami also has more rain than any other city in the country except for Mobile, Alabama. North Carolina says it's "First in Freedom." Doesn't say anywhere on here who they think is Second in Freedom. Connecticut says it's the "Constitution State." We called the License Bureau in Connecticut yesterday and no one there could tell us why they call themselves the "Constitution State." They're not the "Constitution State," of course, Pennsylvania is the "Constitution State." And Pennsylvania, of course, on their license plate, they call themselves the "Keystone State." Maine says it's "Vacationland." How would you like to drive a garbage truck for 8 hours in Augusta with a sign hanging on the back that says "Vacationland"?

Montana. . . ."Big Sky." Same sky as the rest of the 49 states as far as I know. Here's New Hampshire. New Hampshire has this pretentious legend on it, "Live Free or Die." And some religious organization complained and they taped it over. And it went all the way to the Supreme Court, and the religious group won the right to tape it over. "Land of Enchantment" . . . New Mexico. I ran out of gas in a helicopter in New Mexico once. That was some enchanted afternoon.

Hawaii. I have a hard enough time as it is taking Hawaii seriously without reading on every one of its license plates that it's the "Aloha State." Here's Wisconsin . . . "America's Dairyland." Never mind that, Wisconsin. What ever happened to heavy cream? That's what I want to know. Here's the topper though . . . Idaho. How would you like to work hard for ten or fifteen years, save maybe $18,000, buy yourself a new Cadillac, and then drive around all day with a sign on the back that says "Famous Potatoes."

ROONEY: "If a state is any good," I imagine my grandfather would have said, "it shouldn't have to advertise."

Charles Osgood, a seasoned broadcaster for the CBS radio and television networks, is famous for his rhyming commentaries, virtually unique among successful broadcasters.

The Osgood File
CBS News

There is so much we have to avoid nowadays,
The list seems to get longer each day. . . .
Of the things that one should just say No to,
And from which we should all stay away.
This causes cancer and that puts on weight
And cholesterol TOO, I suspect.
And THAT isn't aware or it poisons the air
And produces a greenhouse effect.
And be careful indeed lest some sex, race
    or creed
Take exception to that or to this.
We don't want, goodness knows, to be step-
    ping on toes
Or someone inadvertently DIS.
What we eat, do and wear,
We must take special care
for the handicapped, homeless and poor.
That we must shun,
It no longer is done,
It's offensive to someone I'm sure.
A neighbor of mine
With an antenna fine,
Taking note of the no's and the yesses. . .
Makes a case rather strong
That you cannot go wrong in avoiding things
starting with s's.
Stand by.

Among the things you must avoid and eschew
Lest you err or offend or transgress
Are many activities, tastes and proclivities
That happen to start with an s.
Doctor Ron Brenner, my neighbor next door,
Pointed this out yesterday.
Perhaps it is just a coincidence. . .but things
Do seem to work out that way.
Here we are now in the middle of June with

The heat of the summer in store.
But watch out everyone. . . don't go out in
    the
Sun. . . you cannot sunbathe any more.
To lie on the beach on a hot summer day
May please you make you feel nice.
But sunburn is dangerous business and skin
Cancer is too high a price.
There also are S's we have to avoid
When it comes to the food that we eat.
Snacks . . . and salami and sausage and
Scotch . . . and SUGAR . . . or anything
    sweet.
Too much sweets are BAD for your health
    if we
Take in much more than we need.
As out on the highway observe the speed
Limit . . . a terrible killer is speed.
Salt is another S word to cut down on. . .
The world's getting much too complex.
It's not just sexism we have to look out for,
We now have to watch out for sex.
It's OK to go swimming or snorkling. . .
But you'd better watch out for the sharks.
Smoke is a no-no wherever you go go,
Don't smoke in the woods or the parks.
Cigarettes are verboten and pipes and cigars,
However the smoke is dispensed.
Sin of all kinds is discouraged today . . .
Sin is what everyone is against.
Avoid sensitive subjects whatever you
    speak. . .
Because as by now you suspect
It's like walking on eggshells for someone
    will tell you
Politically you're incorrect.
So avoid all those S's Dr. Brenner advises. . .
It's a dangerous letter, you see.
He's a psychiatrist. . . but that's OK
Since psychiatry starts with a P.
                    The Osgood File. CBS News.

Some commentators scrutinize their subjects, turning and twisting them under a mental microscope. They examine them with analytical precision, separately, as well as in some larger historical, artistic, ecological, religious, or philosophical context. Some aim to convince their audiences by the weight of carefully researched information. Others simply invite audiences to take a closer look at an issue, event or concept, holding it to the light of relevant information. Comparison and contrast prove valuable tools for writers of every genre, but especially in editorials and commentaries because of their brevity. The selection of a strong image likewise contributes to verbal economy.

For some broadcasters the most effective way to share an insight is to tell the story. Charles Osgood excels in this procedure. Indeed, he specializes in highlighting the human element in news events. He finds the right flesh and bones, names and personalities to go with the abstract qualities of valor and suffering, good and evil. He often introduces individuals by name and arouses our sympathy for their tribulations. Such was the case of a man trapped in a medical mix-up that changed his life.

Commentary: "HIV-Nightmare"
Charles Osgood, CBS Radio Network

It was just a clerical error, but the life of a United States Marines vet has not been the same ever since he was told something that wasn't true. He was told that he had AIDS. Stand by.

(Buick commercial)

. . . Dispatch reports on the living nightmare of Michael Peebles, a Marine vet who served in the Vietnam era. Earlier this year Mike entered a VA hospital in Chillicothe to be treated for alcoholism. Early in February he was given an AIDS test. On February 23rd he was told the test was positive. On that day a nurse noted on his medical chart, "Patient was upset and started crying." Well, who wouldn't?

Peebles was moved to an isolation ward. Looking back he says, "Everybody in the ward knew I had AIDS. I didn't know who to tell because of the stigma that comes with the disease."

Peebles then had to face the thought of telling his family. But before he could tell them anything, he claims the VA went ahead and broke the news to them first.

At the time Mike Peebles was engaged. And when his fiancee found out that she might have been exposed to AIDS, she broke off the engagement. And then she went to his boss and told him what happened and Peebles was then told he had lost his job.

But that's not all. Since before entering the hospital Peebles had been living with his fiancée. Now that the engagement was broken, he had no place to live either. At that point Peebles began to think about killing himself. He says, "I wrote a suicide note. I decided I was going to carry it out on the day before my birthday." His birthday was March 8th. The days went by until March 7th, the morning of the day that Michael Peebles was going to kill himself. It was then that the VA doctors gave him some more news. It seems there had been a mistake, a mix-up in the lab tests, and maybe he didn't have AIDS after all. There is another note on Peebles' medical chart for March 7th. It says, "The patient was somewhat upset and perturbed upon hearing the explanation but agreed to have the HIV test repeated."

The new tests showed that Peebles was not exposed to the AIDS virus. He's out of the hospital now. He does not have AIDS, but he lost his fiancée and lost his job. He still doesn't have a place to live. He's in a shelter for the homeless in Columbus.

How could such a mistake be made? Well, it seems that Mike and another patient had been assigned the same code number for their lab tests. What Mike needs now is the correct telephone number of a good lawyer.

The Osgood File. CBS News.

Osgood may go down in history as the world's most prolific radio commentator, broadcasting four fresh commentaries, an hour apart, each weekday during morning drive time. His work pattern is heavily influenced by the clock. Rising between 2 and 2:30 A.M., he is at his desk at CBS by 4 A.M. He first checks the notes and story suggestions left on his computer by his producer the previous evening. There may be as many as a dozen ideas from which to choose. There may be a rough draft to consider. Osgood's selections depend upon his reaction to what he finds.

He explains: "I look for something I can get my teeth into, not necessarily the most important event as much as grist for my own mill. The test is whether it makes me sad or amuses me."

He avoids dull subjects. Reports of most committee meetings are out. He says the subject "must have human interest, character and color." It must stimulate "some visceral reaction," he says, adding, "I don't try to posture myself as an investigative reporter with claws out all the time. I don't aim to leave someone in a pool of blood." His goal, he says, is "to interest and engage the audience, to inform them," to relate an event or issue in terms they can understand.

Gentle, amiable and witty as he is, Osgood admits that not everyone who listens to him loves him. "I have no political ax to grind," he says, "no particular point of view; nevertheless, if you express yourself as often as I do, you're bound to offend someone." With a twinkle in his voice, he repeats the wisdom of a colleague who cautioned: "When you say 'Good morning,' somebody's bound to say, 'What do you mean, good morning, you sonafabitch?'" It's just not a good morning for that person and now you've got him mad at you, he notes.

The content itself usually dictates whether his commentary takes the form of a spoken essay, a presentation with actuality, or a poem. Although commentaries express opinions, he avoids using the first person.

Although Osgood doesn't do all his own writing, he assumes responsibility for the final editing. In the wee hours of the morning, he divides the topics for research, verification of sources, and writing with his partner, Harry Poloshjian, who works on one commentary while Osgood concentrates on another. In addition to the 20 aired on radio, they develop three for television. Osgood considers his broadcast "thoughts. . . . a thought for the day."

Judy Muller, who for several years substituted for Osgood on his days off, uses a distinctly vibrant, conversational style. She incorporates images calculated to leave an almost palpable impression upon her listeners. This technique is apparent in a commentary in which she implicitly espoused the cause of animal rights' activists in their advertising war with fur merchants.

Commentary: "The Fur War"
Judy Muller, CBS Radio Network

The anti-fur folk have been getting a lot of publicity in recent weeks and that's no accident. It's part of a well-planned campaign to convince people that buying fur coats is contributing to cruelty to animals.

Slogans like "Buy a fur and slip into something dead" can take their toll on the fur trade. That's why the industry is fighting back. The fur is flying—after this.

(Commercial)

In the public relations war over the issue of fur, the anti-fur folk have been on the offensive for some time telling the public that animals caught in traps suffer greatly and that animals bred on farms are mistreated and killed inhumanely. One full page ad in *Spy* Magazine, for example, shows a photo of a trapper approaching a fox whose leg is caught in a trap, then standing on the animal and suffocating him. Not too subtle, but then it's not supposed to be.

At bus stops in New York City where many a fur can be seen so can ads depicting a leg-hold trap with a raccoon's foot caught in it. And a group of people called "People for the Ethical Treatment of Animals" is running an ad campaign which spoofs the famous black llama fur ads with the headline, "What disgraces a legend most."

The ad agency that produces the black llama is not amused, calling the spoof "libelous." The fur industry is not content with just complaining; it's fighting back with its own national ad campaign aimed at turning the issue into one of freedom of choice. In the words of one fur industry spokesman, "We want to tell consumers what these groups are really after," adding, "No one has the right to take away your freedom to buy and wear furs." Actually,

one furrier says, "these groups are threatening freedom of expression and freedom of choice, you know, First Amendment rights." Playing on that fear, the headline on one pro-fur ad reads: "Today fur, tomorrow leather, then wool, then meat."

The ad campaign is costing the fur industry about 2 million dollars. But that's squirrel feed compared to what's at stake. The Fur Vault, the country's second largest fur chain reports losses of over 7 million dollars in the last two years. Meanwhile, the other side is firing new ammunition as well. Posters throughout New York City show an animal's paw caught in a trap with the headline, "Get the feel of fur. Slam your hand in a car door."

The Osgood File. CBS News.

One Moment Please is a syndicated, daily radio program in which commentator Mort Crim presents his personal observations on a variety of topics. He ordinarily uses an objective, third-person approach; however, when the story of actor Michael Landon's losing battle with cancer was in the news, Crim addressed the dying man in a uniquely personal manner.

Commentary: One Moment Please
Mort Crim, "Tough Role"

ANNOUNCER: Now with today's "Personal Observation," here is Mort Crim.

CRIM: Shakespeare said, "All the world's a stage." But sometimes we don't get to choose the role we'll play. An open letter to Michael Landon, after this.

(Commercial, :30)

CRIM: Dear Michael Landon: The doctors say they can't cure you.
I heard the same gut-wrenching "sentence" delivered to my father.
To my uncle. And to my wife.
Many of us who know you also know about walking in the valley.
Oh, I realize, Michael, you haven't met most of us.
But we have been guests in your *Little House on the Prairie.* We've traveled with you on the *Highway To Heaven.* So you're like family.

That's why we're glad you've decided to fight.

They say where there's life, there's hope. But it's also true that where there's hope, there's life. A friend told me there is no form of cancer from which someone hasn't recovered. He told me *that* five years after doctors predicted he'd be dead. Michael, they say your odds aren't good. But people *do* win horse races against worse odds.

As an actor, you'll understand what I'm about to say:

Most roles you've played until now, you've sought. This one, you didn't audition for—didn't even want. But it may turn out to be the most important role of your life: Because people you've never met, Michael, look to you now to help them. In their own illness, their own sadness, their own fear. They're taking strength from your courage—inspiration from your determination.

We pray that the final curtain is a long way off.

But remember, Michael, the quality of a performance is never determined by its length.

And sometimes. . . sometimes, Michael, you just have to trust the outcome to the one who wrote the script.

With a "Personal Observation," I'm Mort Crim.

Might it be that Crim's approach reflects each person's desire to delay the inevitable, to control the uncontrollable? As you consider the above commentary, you may find yourself appreciating its public affirmation of a long-time television friend.

News-Related Commentaries

Commentaries are presented sometimes by newscasters who temporarily put aside the role of the objective reporter to express an opinion about a subject in the news. The role change is clarified by the superimposition of "Commentary" over the television image, or the verbal introduction that signals the transition: "And now a commentary by. . ."

Walter Cronkite was most famous as the anchor of the *CBS Evening News*, yet most of the time he was gaining his reputation there, as "the most trusted man in America," he was also presenting frequent commentaries on the CBS radio network. They were widely admired for their thoughtfulness and for the thoroughness with which they probed a wide variety of news-related issues. Other anchors who

have presented radio commentaries on a regular basis are Cronkite's successor, Dan Rather, and ABC's Peter Jennings. The reputation of broadcast journalists enhances the credibility of their presentations. This also applies to those whose careers in broadcast journalism as anchor or field reporter have preceded their role as commentator. Eric Sevareid, who was considered by many to be broadcasting's most eloquent commentator, began his writing career as a newspaper reporter. He was invited to work for CBS Radio by Edward R. Murrow, and started out as a European correspondent during World War II. After more than 40 years with CBS he retired, only to be recalled by American Public Radio for occasional reflections on matters of consequence up until his death in 1992.

Once asked by a reporter to identify the goal of his excursions into current events, Sevareid replied: "To get at the truth of things."

Most often Sevareid's talks were designed to clarify issues in the news; sometimes they concentrated on the less important happenings that illuminate the foibles of the human race; occasionally they reflected the deep emotions aroused by certain events. Clarity of thought, incisive wit, and grace of expression marked Sevareid's writing. An excellent example of his art was the eulogy he presented in 1967 on the day of the funerals for three astronauts killed while practicing for the first Apollo space mission. With quiet eloquence he reflected the feelings of a nation saddened, as it had not been since the 1963 death of President John F. Kennedy, by the tragedy of young men struck down at the height of their powers.

Commentary by Eric Sevareid
Talk broadcast on CBS News

Grissom and White and Chaffee—mortals who aspired to the moon and eternal space—were returned to the earth today from which they came and to which we all belong. They had lived life more intensely in a very few years than most of us do in our lifetimes, and they shall be remembered far longer. They were among the men who wield a cutting edge of history and by this sword they died.

Grissom and Chaffee were buried near the grave of Lt. Thomas Selfridge, the first American military pilot to be killed in an airplane crash nearly 60 years ago. Then, the air above the ground was as unfamiliar as the space above the air. The men who go first are accounted heroes and rightly so, whatever the age, whatever the new element and horizon. Space, said the late President Kennedy, is our new ocean and we must sail upon it. It was truly the hazards of the unknown oceans and territories that took the lives of earlier heroes, like Magellan or Captain Cook, men who went first and were killed by inhabitants of the Pacific.

It was not precisely the unknown hazards of space that killed our astronauts; it was the hazards of fallible man's calculations. It was not a technical failure; all technical failures are human failures. It was the

familiar, never totally escapable failure of the human brain to cope with the complexities it has arranged. A slight miscalculation, a single slip, then a spark, a flame, and the end of three remarkable products of those infinitely more complex mysteries, genetic inheritance and environment, the processes that occasionally produce personalities like Grissom and White and Chaffee—men who are brave but not brash, proud but not self-conscious, thoughtful but not brooding, men of a health, a wholeness we all aspire to but so few attain. We are told they will be replaced. This only means that other such men will take their places. The three cannot be replaced. There never was a replaceable human being.

There is no event so powerful as death to arouse thoughts about the value of life. Eulogies such as Sevareid's tribute to the three astronauts are usually commentaries reflecting deeply personal convictions. In addition, his effective use of a structure accented by punctuation, parallel phrases, and pauses illustrates how seasoned writers occasionally bend the rules to excel in their communication.

Another respected commentator, John Chancellor, who regularly appears on the *NBC Nightly News*, departed from his role as host of a prestigious awards ceremony to deliver a commentary critical of the tight military control over media coverage of the 1991 Persian Gulf War. The Alfred I. DuPont Columbian Journalism Awards ceremony was broadcast on the Public Broadcasting Service on January 29, 1991. At the time few broadcasters had challenged what they considered to be excessive secrecy.

Commentary by John Chancellor
Public Broadcasting Service

We meet this evening on the fourteenth day of the war. War time is not a good time for the liberties we go to war to defend. It is especially difficult for the craft of journalism and it is getting worse.

We all know there have to be restrictions on journalism in war time. The trouble is those restrictions have grown in the sixteen years since the end of the Vietnam War. During that time the technical ability of journalism to cover a military operation has increased. But during that time our access to the story has been decreased by our own government and that's odd. There's an epidemic of shooting and killing and death in American cities shown every night on our television screens, along with prime-time shows and movies about shooting and killing and death. But when young Americans go into combat, their government tries to control images of shooting and killing and death. That happened in Grenada. That happened in Panama.

This control of the images of war by the authorities, this sanitizing of the horrors of war takes away something important from those of us at home. It reduces our emotional understanding of what our country is doing in war, our knowledge of the true costs of war, and it robs us of a chance to grieve for the dead we never knew. Grief should be part of the national experience. Yet cameras have been banned at the country's largest military mortuary, at the Dover Air Force Base in Delaware. There will be no pictures from Dover of flag-decked coffins, or of ceremonies honoring our dead in this war. Death in battle is now hidden from view in a thicket of censorship and regulation, the way other painful matters are considered off budget and hidden in the smoke and mirrors of Washington.

And I ask myself, What is the American government afraid of when it shields us from the tragedy and ugliness of war? That images of dead and dying Americans will affect our will to fight? Our patriotism?

They should trust us. We are stronger than they think.

Charles Kuralt, the genial host of *Sunday Morning*, broadcast on the CBS television network, reads news headlines, provides transitions and introductions, and delivers a 60-second commentary. Called "Milepost," the commentary focuses on a single event by which one might remember the past week.

Although Kuralt has the final word on the selection, scripting and editing of each "Milepost," most of the writing is done by Peter Freundlich, writer and associate producer for *Sunday Morning*. He praises Kuralt for being an excellent editor whose "deft touches have an alarming ability to improve" a script.

Freundlich's description of the writing process departs significantly from other writers' models of careful organization and tight outlines. "There are no guidelines, no meetings or discussion," he says. Freundlich proposes topics from issues and events in the news, and Kuralt makes the selection.

Freundlich also advises writers to wonder from time to time what a writer is. "If they see writers as machine operators who put other people's ideas into words, they're probably in the wrong game." He advocates a more fluid understanding of the craft. Effective writers, he says, "are more like conduits . . . adjunct discoverers of things."

Freundlich's own talent as one of the "adjunct discoverers of things" is apparent in his contemplation of a penny on the occasion of Lincoln's birthday, noting Lincoln's accomplishments and leading Freundlich to the following conclusions.

Commentary: CBS Sunday Morning
Charles Kuralt, CBS-TV

VIDEO	AUDIO
KURALT	Did someone say, "A penny for your thoughts?" I have been thinking about—the penny. And the man whose sad, strong face is on that little copper coin. Today is his birthday. And our "Milepost."
HOLDS UP PENNY, AROUND WHICH IS MILEPOST LOGO	Abraham Lincoln was born 180 years ago today, in Hardin County, Kentucky. This is mostly how we see him now—as a profile stamped on a very small bit of money: bright, sometimes, or dull, or metal-red or green with age.
LOSE LOGO	At first thought, that does not seem right. To put THIS figure, of all figures, on the smallest and least valuable of all our coins. Why did we do that? This gaunt, wise, severely tested man, who gave us the Emancipation Proclamation, and the Gettysburg Address. We might not have a country today, but for him. Why did we put this giant on the one penny piece? Well, but: How else could we carry a giant around? How else could we be sure that some sliver of that spirit might be in every pocket, at all times, out of reach to no one, ready and common and familiar? What better token of Lincoln than a pretty penny? Lincoln's memory is far too great to carry around with us any other way. To stand for such spirits as his, human beings have always made little talismans to carry around with them: keepsakes to touch. The penny may be as good a keepsake as we have.

Special-Purpose Commentaries

A number of commentaries deal with designated subject matter or are broadcast with a special purpose in mind. The sports commentary is an example. We discuss it in the chapter covering various types of sports broadcasts.

This section will examine two other special-purpose commentaries: entertainment reviews and religious commentaries.

The world of entertainment has an ample share of critics. No longer confined to the pages of newspapers and magazines, reviews of films, books, cultural events, and television fare are regular offerings of broadcast stations and cable outlets.

Joel Siegel's review of the suspenseful film *The Silence of the Lambs*, which went on to sweep all the major 1992 Academy Awards, arouses in the viewer some of the tension that characterizes the film.

Film Review: The Silence of the Lambs
Joel Siegel, ABC-TV

Good morning.

Wednesday we talked about this year's Oscar nominees. Today we talk about next year's. This film is that good. And be warned, it's not for the faint of heart. Maybe it's the matter of fact way people speak ABOUT the unspeakable. Or the fact that the villain is so evil and so intelligent we can't write him off the way we do with other movie villains. But this is the kind of movie two hours AFTER it's over you are still shaking. The FBI uses a serial killer to help catch a serial killer. Jodie Foster is the pawn in the play.

You are scared to death and you still haven't seen anything. And just when you think your imagination is more terrifying than anything they could show, they show you things more terrifying than you could imagine. There are some very gruesome scenes. . . and some of the most frightening scenes I've seen on film.

Jonathan Demme, whose work I've liked a lot—*Married to the Mob, Something Wild*—joins the ranks of world-class directors. Last time out they gave Jodie Foster the Oscar. This time maybe they should just change the sign from Hollywood to Jodieville. . . She really is that good. And Anthony Hopkins? Such an incredible performance he's going to have to eat dinner alone for the rest of his life. *Silence of the Lambs* is one of the best thrillers ever made.

She's an FBI Trainee. Scott Glenn, who heads a serial-killer unit, uses her to question Hannibal Lecter. A psychiatrist, a serial killer himself, he may help solve these crimes. She risks her psyche and maybe her life.

(VIDEO CLIP: Instructions.)

Yes, there are instructions: pass him only papers, no pencils, no sharp objects. Use the sliding food tray. Don't touch him. He's walled in behind plexiglass four inches thick. . . Don't even touch the glass.

(VIDEO CLIP: Track up to show one of her eyes.)

We don't see it. . . Director Jonathan Demme never shows us the picture. But not seeing makes the picture more vivid. Makes the terror even worse. Demme drains terror out of every scene. This is the Smithsonian. The FBI found the pupa of a large insect in a victim's mouth. Two entomologists. . . playing checkers with beetles. . . will identify it. I couldn't watch this scene. I hate bugs. It's a Death's Head moth. They live in Asia. Nothing is shown and. . . the terror grows.

(VIDEO CLIP: Death's head moth.)

Jodie Foster, not only a perfect West Virginia accent. . . her make-up, thin lips, high cheekbones. . . a perfect Appalachian look. And Anthony Hopkins as Hannibal Lecter. A monster almost beyond description. Riveting. Mesmerizing. Not scary. . . Much deeper than that. Terrifying.

Another commentary with a specific focus is regularly written by one of the co-authors of this book, Sister Camille D'Arienzo. New York's all-news radio station WINS-AM provides a regular forum for four religion commentators. Every weekend one of the four delivers a one-minute reflection on some subject connected with religious values. The commentaries often provide a spin on political actions or public issues. Each commentary is followed by the disclaimer: "The preceding does not necessarily reflect the views of WINS." You may be surprised to discover that many religious commentaries make little overt reference to God or specific doctrines. Such remarks often spring from reflections upon moral precepts rather than upon any one denomination's practices. Much inspiration comes from Jesus's "second greatest commandment," recounted in the Gospel of Mark (12:31), "Thou shalt love thy neighbor as thyself." To the extent that governments and groups may victimize rather than help people, some religious commentaries may be political. The following is a commentary by Sister Camille D'Arienzo on the release of hostage Terry Anderson, who had spent years in captivity in the Middle East in the grip of a terrorist faction.

Commentary: Terry Anderson
Sister Camille D'Arienzo
December 22, 1991

Today, as I review the range of sermons I've read and heard during the weeks

before Christmas, none has touched me more than that expressed by Terry Anderson, who didn't mean his words to be a sermon. And so today I'd like to address an open letter to this inadvertent preacher.

Dear Terry Anderson, you were the longest held of the hostages. When the world rejoiced in your liberation from tortures most of us can't imagine, you missed your chance to express anger and demand revenge. The reporters were all around you.

Instead, you said, you weren't even angry—just determined to forgive those who had tormented you. That, you explained, was what Jesus expects of his followers, and you are Christian and Catholic. Your faith, you said, was rekindled in captivity. You may have been in solitary confinement, Terry, but you weren't alone. God was speaking to your heart. Thank you for listening and reporting that good news to us.

This is Sister Camille D'Arienzo.

The following reflection was presented by one of Sister Camille's fellow commentators.

The Poor and the Panhandlers
Rabbi Marc H. Tanenbaum
(Copyright 1988,
Jewish Telegraphic Agency, Inc.)

How should we regard the needs of genuinely poor people in our streets? With generosity, compassion, and cheerfulness.

That is a central teaching of Biblical and rabbinic ethics, and that obligation to relieve poverty, both personally and communally, should be the moral framework for dealing with the real problem of phony panhandlers.

No one in his right mind would advocate encouraging scam artists and professional hustlers. But most people, I believe, are reasonably intelligent, and are capable of judging who is really poor and who is a flimflam beggar.

Withholding charity from the phony beggar should not become a license for withholding aid from the truly needy.

That is not simply a do-gooder's sentimentalism. If you study Biblical and rabbinic ethics, you will know that nothing is more basic than the moral obligation of *tzedakah,* which means both "charity" and "doing justice."

The Talmud declares in fact that almsgiving—aiding the poor and feeding the hungry—is equal to all the commandments of the Torah.

The rabbis dramatize the point by saying, "He who has no pity upon his fellow creatures is assuredly not of the seed of Abraham, our father."

In Jewish communities from Biblical times to the present, there was free and generous giving of alms to all who were in need.

There was also much systematic and careful relief through established charitable institutions, such as the *tamchui,* or the public kitchen, and the *pushka,* or alms box.

But the highest degree of charity, Maimonides reminds us, is to help a person get work and thereby achieve dignity through self-support and independence.

QUESTIONS AND PROJECTS

1. Compare the editorials of a radio station and a television station in your community. Does the television station take advantage of its opportunity to visualize the issue?

2. Do the stations in your community make clear to their audience the point at which newscasters shift their role from being objective purveyors of facts to being people expressing their own opinions? What techniques are used to make the shift clear?

3. Rewrite a newspaper editorial for radio or television, using to best advantage the special characteristics of the medium you choose. In doing this, take notes on the facts in the printed piece, then put it aside, write your editorial and check for accuracy. Do not paraphrase the editorial.

4. Select a serious topic of your own. It must be timely or of enduring interest to your audience: drugs, leadership, racism, sexism, family values, unemployment, homelessness, equal opportunity. Write a two-minute commentary. Cut it to 90 seconds, then to 60.

5. Choose a lighter topic—a pet peeve, personal observation, a film or television review. Limit: 90 seconds.

6. One effective way of presenting information clearly is to employ comparison and contrast. What other techniques would you recommend for making an idea clear?

7. In recalling a commentary or editorial that caught your interest, what ideas do you remember and what techniques were used to make them especially memorable?

8. Choose a subject and write two commentaries, one designed simply to present information; the other to persuade your audience to accept a certain point of view.

Entire books have been devoted to the craft of writing news, an occupation that employs hundreds of thousands of people, most of whom never write or speak a single news word. The news-gathering process involves policy makers and executive and assignment editors who determine which issues and events should be pursued, and camera crews and technicians whose handling of equipment influences the angles and emphases given to the stories they cover. There are, of course, others too numerous to list. Having hinted at the vastness of the enterprise, this chapter will clarify the main characteristics of the newscast itself, particularly as they differ from those of newspaper accounts of the same events.

CHAPTER

7

NEWS

The newscaster writes the first draft of history.

ERIC SEVAREID

(1912–1992)

GATHERING INFORMATION

The purpose of a newscast is to report what is happening now in the community, in the nation, and in the world. It does not seek to interpret the significance of events; that is the function of news analyses, editorials, and documentaries. The newsroom is the center of a station's activities. In addition to the resource of its personnel, its grasp of issues depends on phone calls alerting the staff to stories in progress, mail deliveries providing press releases, and announcements of scheduled events. Increasingly, electronically transmitted messages and other forms of direct mail add to the volume of incoming information.

Integrating the Sources

The minimum requirement for obtaining the information needed for a newscast is service from at least one of the major press associations—Associated Press (AP) or the financially troubled United Press International (UPI)—which transmit their dispatches by teletype or, increasingly, by computerized information systems which feed directly into the newsroom. Most radio stations, in addition, avail themselves of the wire services' actualities or "voicers," taped reports of events occurring around the world, written and reported by professional field reporters. A large station or network generally utilizes additional press association services and has a local, national, and international reporting staff of its own. A TV operation would, in addition, employ a national video tape and news film company, or, in the case of network affiliates, the reports of the network. The greatest change in newscasting, however, is the result of electronic news-gathering devices (ENG), the industry's new lightweight camera and tape equipment. The portability and economy of the minicam units have contributed toward an increase of on-location reports and a trend toward longer newscasts. ENG, according to a viewer survey conducted by *TV Guide,* is meeting the primary interest of people who tune into TV news to see "eyewitness, on-the-scene reports." The desire to improve and expand that service while scooping the competition has led to a growing number of TV stations buying or renting helicopters as a way of overriding the traffic snarls and shortening the travel time between station and location.

Amateur photographers, equipped with camcorders, sometimes "scoop" the professional news-gathering teams. A furtive taping of an incident involving police brutality in Los Angeles gained a national audience, while first-on-the-scene reports of fires and accidents have become commonplace. Some stations, especially those with small staffs and low budgets, actively solicit such community involvement.

Traditional news divisions, while being augmented by the contributions of local amateurs are, additionally, being blanketed by global satellite transmissions. The challenge to traditional newscasts posed by the Cable News Network has motivated self-examination and restructuring at the local and network level.

Radio, which reports the news more often than TV and updates it more frequently, relies even more heavily than TV on actualities and "beepers." A beeper is a telephone report or interview recorded or aired live by the station. It calls for reporters who can, literally, think on their feet. All stations receive press releases and phone tips, check the newspapers, and monitor the broadcast competition; larger stations assign desk assistants to peruse the significant papers serving their broadcast areas. Reporters everywhere develop their own sources of information and frequently provide the station's most dependable news leads. Local reporters often cover stories suggested by the Daybook, a listing published by the wire services, outlining local occurrences of which they have been notified but which they do not plan to cover themselves. If the event is newsworthy, the assignment editor will dispatch a reporter or contact a stringer. (Stringers are part-time, usually free-lance, reporters who can be called upon to cover events, often in their own neighborhoods or areas of expertise.) The reporter will make the decision whether to file a beeper story or to collect whatever releases are provided and return to the station with them. The reporter may find the story sufficiently attractive to interview its key players, gather eyewitness accounts,

and find opposing viewpoints. Whatever the decision, it must take into account the interest of the community in the issue, as well as its significance for the local and broader neighborhood.

The ability to make the on-the-spot decision, subject, of course, to final judgments by the news director, is one of the qualities which distinguish the good reporter from the mediocre one.

When Bill Scott was executive editor for WINS-Radio, New York, he valued news staffers as sources of information. Says Scott: "The reporter on the scene is the best source—not the wire service story. If there is a discrepancy, we ought to advise our reporter on the scene that the wire story differs from the WINS report, but once the reporter is advised of that and determines that the WINS version is correct, we will always go with our WINS reporter over the wire service. We must have confidence in our people . . . and let them know that."

Establishing Criteria

The first task in preparing a newscast is to select the stories to be included, for even a 15-minute radio newscast cannot present all the dispatches that flow through a teletype machine or computer system. A television newscast, which must incorporate video, can cover even less. Two criteria should control the selection of news items: (1) those stories that are of the greatest *significance* to your audience, and (2) those stories that are of the greatest *interest* to your audience. Any story involving the security of the United States concerns every citizen. Such a story would have a prominent place on a newscast because of its significance. The story of a local crime may not be particularly significant, but because it involves people in the community, it is of interest to the local audience.

Deciding Which Stories to Use Sometimes factors other than those of significance and interest do influence the selection process. These may result from external sources, the size of the news-gathering staff, the quantity and quality of field equipment, the time of day or night for which the newscast is prepared, and the air time allotted for the report.

Sources of Information The wire services prepare summaries which can be read in their entirety with little editing or alteration, expressly to fill 15, 10, or five-minute periods. This "rip and read" service, however, places two major limitations on a station's news service. It precludes the use of news originating in the local community unless that news is significant enough to justify its inclusion on a national or state wire, and it prevents the station from developing a news service with an individual style and flavor. For these reasons, many stations do not present press dispatches as they come off the wire but use them merely as a source of information. The station's own newscasters, staff writers, or editors write the actual news stories. Consideration of two very different, successful radio stations will help illustrate possible uses of prepared copy.

WJR-Detroit, a full-service radio station, devotes a substantial block of its air time to news. During morning drive time the station broadcasts 15 minutes of news at the top of the hour and two minutes at the bottom. At noon, late evening, and overnight it airs 10 minutes at the top. It has, in addition, an afternoon news block, from 4:00 to 6:30, dedicated to news and sports.

According to WJR news director Dick Haefner, the station, which is now computerized, subscribes to the *Wall Street Journal* and AP wire services. Its nonlocal source of "sound" comes from the ABC radio network. WJR airs more than 150 taped voice reports and actualities daily.

The "sound" is provided by the network, and by its own 14 newscasters.

Unlike WINS, WJR does not have news writers, apart from the 14 newscasters who are themselves responsible for the stories. Three reporters have news beats outside the station. One is based in Lansing (the capital of Michigan), a second at City Hall in Detroit, and the third in Oakland County (a major suburban area).

At WJR, the "rip and read" approach to broadcasting is consigned to history. Today's reporters are expected to put the news into a style suited to the listening audience. Haefner says the writers are expected to present information accurately, clearly, simply, crisply, and, he adds, "It's not enough to a have a simple compilation of facts, one on top of another. Newscasts should have pizazz and sparkle."

Unlike the fast-paced WINS, WJR puts little emphasis on "a story count," according to Haefner. "The number of stories in a newscast isn't as important as our taking the time to tell a story well."

Actualities have become increasingly important to the presentation of news. Field reporters, he says, "let the players in the events tell the stories in their own words. It's better journalism and more appealing to the ear." So, Haefner concludes, actualities meet both journalistic and esthetic criteria. "The change of voice makes the newscast sound more active," he adds. "It's a radio version of television's visual variety."

WINS, broadcasting news only, covers more national and world events than does WJR; however, the emphasis is on the local. That, according to executive editor Steven Swenson, accounts for 60 to 70 percent of each hour's news, which on an ordinary day in the WINS listening area (New York and parts of New Jersey and Connecticut) may exceed the amount of news reported in some foreign countries. Four wire services provide the raw material for nonlocal news: Reuters,

ABC, CNN Radio, and AP Radio. The last vestige of the "rip and read" style of preparing news went out with the old teletype machines. Newscasters are expected to rewrite copy provided by the wire services. Each anchor has the assistance of a staff writer for the first or second of the five newscasts the anchors must prepare. Swenson describes "the mastery of basic broadcast writing—ear-catching, as opposed to what one might write for a newspaper"—as an ongoing concern.

The Relationship of Local to Network Newscasts A network can cover the major national and international events better than a local station. For this reason, the writers of a local newscast airing in the early evening just before or after a network news show give their major attention to the local scene. When writing for a late evening local newscast with a network news program nowhere near, they can cover stories strictly in terms of their news merit, whether they be national, international, or local.

The Availability of Film or Video Tape In an attempt to keep the TV newscast as visual as possible, the newscaster may be tempted to use a story simply because there is visual support for it rather than because it meets the criteria of interest or significance. If this film or tape deals with such predictable and unexciting occasions as the opening of a bridge or the inauguration of a public official and neglects the important events of the day, the program may lose its quality of immediacy and degenerate into a meaningless newsreel. Films of interviews with people who have been involved in the real news events of the day are more vital and interesting. They also reflect the problems of the community, which all responsible radio and television stations should cover in their news broadcasts.

The Influence of Air Time Most major news stories take place during the day and are reported soon after they happen on newscasts scheduled from 10 in the morning until 6 in the evening. Writers of late night or early morning newscasts must realize that most of the stories on the teletype happened hours before and already have appeared on previous news programs. In this situation, how can writers keep the program from sounding like a tired rerun? One approach is to search diligently for a new development in a major story and to update it. Another is to ignore the existence of the previous newscasts, or assume that the listeners did not hear them, and report the news as if it just happened. Finally, there are times when no news *is* news. This particularly applies to a story in progress which, at last report, was inconclusive. People whose last newscast of the day informed them of an escaped convict at large in the area, or a child missing from the neighborhood, probably will start the next day wondering about that person's fate. If the individual has not been found, then that failure is the main news story and should be reported in the morning news. The "no new development" report both satisfies the listener's need to know and sustains interest in an ongoing story, keeping the "cliff-hanger" effect in operation.

Fitting Time Requirements Newscasts vary in length and reflect the programming emphasis and "personality" of the station. The Radio Information Office of the National Association of Broadcasters describes the differences:

While a local rock station may carry three-minute newscasts and an easy listening station may carry five- or ten-minute newscasts, an all-news station may program news constantly. The local rocker may restrict news stories to twenty seconds in length; the easy listening station may prefer stories from twenty seconds to one minute in length, and the all-news station may carry some stories that range from twenty seconds to two minutes long.

A TV network news story may run a minute and a half. Related, or sidebar, stories may bring coverage of a major event up to three and a half minutes. The trend among the more than 8,000 licensed radio stations is toward many short stories, as opposed to a few long ones, and as many actuality reports as possible. This leaves the audience with more of a headline service than in-depth information. This concept is suggested by the promise WINS makes to its New York metropolitan area audience. "You give us twenty-two minutes and we'll give you the world." Capitalizing on the enormity of that claim, perhaps, *The New York Times* advertised on radio and television, "If you heard something on the news tonight that you would like to know more about, pick up *The New York Times* tomorrow."

The idea of "twenty-two minutes" can be applied to television news to identify one of the major differences between electronic and print journalism. Subtract the permitted eight minutes of commercials from network half-hour newscasts and you've got—22 minutes of news. Someone once said that a transcript of the network news would not fill half the front page of *The New York Times*. The comparison is an example of "good news and bad news." Although the volume of broadcast news may suffer from quantitative anemia against the printed page, the typed report rarely has the unique impact of, say, 30 seconds of film showing a boatload of Cuban refugees adrift on the open sea, or the reuniting of a kidnapped child with his mother. And yet, as George Will once wrote in *Newsweek*, "Taking twenty-two minutes to cover the world is a bit like taking a teacup to empty the ocean."

BEING PART OF THE NEWS TEAM

A writer for a small radio station may have the responsibility of an entire news department, from gathering information to reporting it on the air. The writer in a large, metropolitan station, especially if it is one under union contract, may be assigned to a single, carefully circumscribed function in the production of news. Those responsible for hiring people to work in news departments look for special qualities and interview prospective employees with an eye toward the station's needs and style. Those who directly cover the news have their perceptions, too. We shall review some of those ideas in the views expressed by several broadcasters, some in radio, others in television.

News Editors, Writers, Reporters

The roughly 70 news people employed by WINS are scheduled for different shifts and consist of reporters, writers, editors, and anchors. They include medical reporters, theater and entertainment reviewers, and several religion commentators. The station has street reporters whose on-the-spot accounts are carried live and on tape throughout the week.

Charlie Kaye, a former news director for WINS, responding to a question about the qualities he looks for in a potential newswriter, says he is most concerned about the mastery of basic newswriting and a good news judgment. Dave White, who filled the same position at WJR, on the other hand, emphasizes the ability to get along, to work well with those already employed at his station.

Doug Edelson, one of the WINS field reporters whose newscasting career has included the events surrounding seven presidents, numerous political campaigns, and the race riots of the 1960s, identifies other desirable qualities, including a "natural inborn curiosity, a real dedication to the profession and to the people in our stories."

WJR's news reflects its "easy listening" programming. WINS projects a sense of urgency. Its pace is fast, reflecting the tempo of a great metropolis. The background sound of tickertape increases the feeling of movement. News is cyclical, three newscasts per hour, 24 hours a day. The sum of people and words is enormous.

Anchors for the Newscast

Some radio stations opt to have all in-studio stories read by a single newscaster to give the station a smooth sound. The lone anchor's broadcast often integrates a variety of other voices on the taped actualities. WJR and WINS both prefer the single anchor. WCBS radio in New York, in contrast, regularly uses a pair of newscasters in a relaxed, interactive fashion. CBS-TV, on the other hand, featured Walter Cronkite as a single anchor for many years, followed by Dan Rather. Other network stations and a majority of local stations use a news team approach.

The single or multiple anchor presentation may reflect a decision made by management, or an established style. Audiences may respond to the presentation in terms of their perception of the entertainment quality or projected authority of the newscaster or news team, but there is another viewpoint worth considering here—that of the "anchorperson," whose main job is to integrate numerous bits and pieces of information prepared by other reporters and writers. Some anchors are little more than news readers, who are hired precisely because they sound as though they are telling stories rather than reading them. Others, like Jack Cafferty, reporter for WNYW-TV, New York, say they are much more comfortable reading their own words.

A citation on the wall of Cafferty's office reads, "Your performance on Saturday night's oil special was excellent. You operated in the true role of anchor, pulling all the diverse elements together, creating the feeling of a real focal point, completely in charge of the broadcast."

Cafferty sees himself as "the wallpaper paste that keeps the wallpaper from falling off the wall." He adds, "We lend a certain meaning (to the events of the day). We set up stories so they communicate some urgency. We provide an overview."

How much Cafferty writes depends on the day's assignments. Within a relatively short span of time, he might provide spot coverage for the funeral of a murdered mob leader, an announcement by President Bush of a new jobs initiative, the defection of a Chinese trade official at Kennedy Airport, and the visit of Pope John Paul II to New York. If a large portion of his day is spent doing on-the-spot reports, other people (often in large numbers) will write the news he reads.

MEETING THE DEMANDS OF TWO MEDIA

The differences between radio stations like the two used as references in this chapter are considerable; however, the media of TV and radio are marked by even greater differences. Radio newscasters lean heavily on actualities and voicers to provide the presence and immediacy that audiences appreciate. When TV writers begin to put their stories together, they realize two things: (1) many of their most significant "words" will be pictures, and (2) they, as writers, constitute only one small part of a large news-gathering team. They are, therefore, dependent upon many others who rely in turn on the news writer's good sense to arrange and incorporate the various elements of the newscast. The visuals selected to tell any particular story require introduction, context, and minimal explanation by the news writer.

The time of the occurrence of an event and its physical distance from the station are two factors which sometimes determine who actually writes the story for broadcast, according to Edith Cahill, who was for many years an assignment editor for NBC-TV, New

York. Cahill says, for example, that a story happening on the east end of Long Island, some 80 or more miles away from the station at Rockefeller Center, might call for the hiring of a helicopter to transport the reporter, along with technical crew and equipment. If the event can be covered, at least in part, from the air, the camera operator can film it while the reporter records personal observations on tape or paper. If the event warrants additional coverage, the crew will continue gathering information; the reporter will integrate the details, take notes, conduct interviews and, as far as time and circumstances permit, provide an eyewitness account. If there is a tight deadline, or if the reporter must rush to a second assignment, the editor will direct the reporter to take the tape or film and return by chopper. The crew and equipment, because of the additional time required to assemble and move both, will return to the city by car.

Ideally, the on-the-scene reporter would write the entire copy. However, the lack of time and station policy may require the sending of only a fact sheet along with the taped or filmed actuality, or, in some cases, the silent film. In that case, a staff writer or anchor will go to the editing room, write the lead and tag, and, when needed, the voice-over. Although the editor may recognize the individual reporter's desire to finish what he or she has begun, the interdependent nature of the broadcast operation may lead the editor to other decisions. If the story is ongoing, the editor makes every effort to keep the same field reporter on it, both for the efficiency resulting from having the same person on top of the information and for the sense of continuity provided the audience by the presence of the same reporter.

ORGANIZING THE NEWSCAST

A newscast made up of many diverse items cannot be organized like a program that revolves around a single theme, but it should have some order and arrangement. The first decision is to choose your opening story. Usually this will be the biggest story of the day, big, either because of its significance or because of its interest to the audience. Another criterion for making this choice is to consider what the audience is most anxious to hear. An important news story may be developing—an international crisis, for example, or a local kidnapping. People turning to the news expect, first of all, to hear the latest development in a big story that is already in the news.

After choosing the first story, you must next decide how to arrange the other items in the news. The importance of stories affects the order of items not only at the beginning but down through the newscast. Generally, newscasters deal with the most important news first. There is danger, however, that by putting all of the exciting items at the beginning, they will lose their audience for the rest of the show and cause unhappiness for a sponsor who is just as anxious that listeners hear the last commercial as the first. Because most people are eager to know what the weather is going to be like, newscasters hold their audiences by delaying the weather forecast until the end. As a further incentive to listening all the way through, human-interest stories and sports news frequently wind up a broadcast.

The nature of the news on a given day may decide what plan of organization is most appropriate. A common pattern is to divide the news into local, national, and international events. If the opening news item deals with a local event, other local events might be considered before the national and international news is covered. Some newscasters use a geographical plan, moving in order from one world capital to another. One of the best procedures is to present the news in terms of certain major topics, which may change from day to day according to what is happening in the world. The advantage of this plan is that it is flexible and is best adapted to showing relationships among the various news items. A topical arrangement might present news under such headings as political developments, labor happenings, world trouble spots, weather on the rampage. Another important criterion in the ordering of items on a program is the need for balance and variety in the visual aspects of a TV newscast.

Achieving a sequence that permits transitions from one item to another may dictate the placement of some stories. Two items concerning the same person should be put together because there is a natural linkage between them and one identification of the person will suffice for both items. Stories with other types of common elements should be presented in sequence to make transitions possible. A newscaster who has been considering international strife might move to a labor dispute with the line, "There was conflict of another type on the labor scene." But the best way to help the listener make transitions is to arrange the news dispatches into groups of related items.

Some newscasters make transitions through the use of the dateline technique, which calls for preceding each item with the place of its origin. This technique may work for the short newscasts, but in longer ones the repetition of place names becomes monotonous and mechanical. Moreover, this device makes for a disjointed program in which the single news items appear to bear no relationship to one another. Incidentally, you should be careful not to put a story of a tragedy right next to one with comic overtones or the transition problem will become difficult. What may be more important is that such juxtaposition may indicate an insensitivity to human suffering.

RECOGNIZING THE STORYTELLING FUNCTION

The need for sensitivity toward the characters involved in the human dramas that fill newscasts underscores what most of news

reporting is: storytelling. Much of the news printed and broadcast is bad news: accounts of sensational occurrences, accidents and earthquakes, murders and other crimes, wars and misfortunes of a thousand kinds. The stories have heroes and heroines, victims and villains. The news writer and reporter are at their best, however, when they recognize their responsibility to tell these stories *fairly, concisely, and accurately*, and in a way audiences can understand and relate to from their own sense of humanity.

Research shows that dramatic storytelling is what radio and television do best. The broadcast media are relatively poor conveyers of institutional and abstract information. Too often the effort to project authoritative knowledge produces lifeless expressions, laden with impersonal data and layered with jargon. It's no wonder that the average viewer retains only about 10 percent of a newscast. Successful broadcasters know they inform audiences better when they tell stories about other people. News programs share broadcasting's entertainment function. Disclaimers that reporters are committed solely to journalistic objectivity misrepresent the reality.

WORDING THE NEWSCAST

Effective writers in any medium are generally good conversationalists. They listen well, absorb and relate fragments of information, react intelligently and retell them accurately and interestingly, interpret when it is called for, and try not to be redundant. Clear and attractive writing is enhanced by human qualities of curiosity and compassion. It also is limited sometimes by those same qualities. Newsman Doug Edelson, speaking from his long experience, expresses what smart writers and audiences have always known: "I try to put myself in the role of the people I'm talking to, to afford them the same sensitivity

I would want to receive." Then he adds a preference denied many reporters: "Some of our best stories are of emotionally charged situations. Unless it can be done without inflicting additional harm, I don't want to intrude on tragedy. If it comes down to getting or not getting a story, I'd rather not get it." Commendable as is this ethical approach to news coverage, many reporters are not allowed the luxury of opting in or out of stories with great human-interest qualities, particularly if competing stations are likely to cover them. The questions for most, therefore, must be, "How deeply and in what manner do I probe? How much do I show?"

General Qualities

Should there be a difference between material written to be heard and material written to be read? Absolutely. The operators of the major wire services affirm this by writing the news in one version for newspaper use and in another for their radio and television clients. UPI, in a stylebook published for its reporters, cautions: "The broadcast writer has no readers, only listeners."

There are some obvious differences between the nature of print and electronic media which automatically justify differences in the way they adapt material to accommodate their audiences. Readers can pick and choose stories at random or in response to an attractive headline, an apt photo. If something is not clear at first glance, or if a distraction interrupts readers, they can go back over the material at leisure. Not so in broadcasting. Listeners can't recall the spoken word or linger over a piece of complicated information. Television commands more attention from its viewers than does radio. More often than not, radio listeners tend to engage in some other primary activity, like driving a car or preparing a meal. The audience applies attention selectively, tuning in and out without ever touch-

ing the dial. Some have described radio as "auditory wallpaper." It is often much more, but because that possibility exists, news writers must be more diligent in achieving simplicity, clarity, and accuracy than their print counterparts.

Newspaper stories are generally top-heavy. The "inverted pyramid" directs that answers to "who, what, when, and where" be provided, if not in the first paragraph, very early in the account. The reason is practical. The amount of space allowed is dependent on the quantity of advertising and the number of competing and related stories. Newspaper stories are designed to be "cut from the bottom." Essential facts comes first; details, often including quotes and anecdotes, are added to fit. Broadcast stories are written for time, not space. Air time, unlike newspaper space, is not expandable. All the advertising revenue in the world cannot add a single minute to a day.

Simple Precautions

The need to capture listeners does not give writers license to overdramatize or distort. It merely challenges them to unearth and present the compelling angle and fashion it into a lead that suggests the "feel" of the story, or sets the stage for the drama to unfold. Imagery helps. UPI introduced a complicated account of increasing antagonisms between Arabs and Israelis with the lead, "Peace in the Middle East hangs by the slender thread of land known as the Gaza Strip."

The UPI Broadcast Stylebook suggests an attitude helpful to the beginning news writer. "The broadcast writer is telling a friend about something that happened—not writing a story." For that reason—and others—radio and television writers learn to talk to their typewriters. This stops them from using long, complex, cleverly convoluted sentences. People with normal measures of breath control simply can't read them.

News director White has mixed reactions to the "telling a story to a friend" approach. "Telling a story to a friend is a good idea," he says, "but only as long as I remember that, listening along with my friend, are college professors, politicians, my wife, and people from every walk of life." Broadcast language, he insists, must be a cut above common conversation. Stories must be carefully crafted to present news in language that moves, involves, and impresses.

Reporter Cafferty, with another opinion, says he doesn't care who's listening. His responsibility is to the news. If he presents it properly, the classes within the audience will dissolve. The order of first importance is that the writer understand the story, the whole story, not just the lead. Cafferty, in guiding cub writers, shares with them what he calls "the greatest piece of training I know." He lets them write the story, present it to him for minor editing, then has them rewrite it. He sits back and tells them to read it aloud to him, then put the copy down, look at him and, without benefit of notes, tell him what happened. "Their job is not to write," he says. "Writing is a tool that enables them to speak."

Cafferty traces his own best training to his upbringing: "I was the product of a home where language was not to be abused. I developed good habits as a child. My father and mother were strict about the way we used language. What I do for WYNW is more or less automatic." Those who did not have this kind of experience at home may have to work harder to catch up with the competition.

Hearing the Story

Most news writers warn against the inclination to rewrite the news wire or newspaper copy while looking at it. This kind of paraphrasing, they insist, turns into a mediocre parroting. Better to read the copy, retell it in your own words without looking at the source of information, then check it for accuracy and completeness. When you are satisfied with the content, take a harder look at the form. For copy that sounds crisp rather than cumbersome, ideas should flow through a series of short, declarative sentences. Complex sentences tend to crowd in more information than the ear can comprehend; interrogative sentences sound artificial, more often than not. Read the following quote: "Are you wondering how to protect yourself against the increase in neighborhood crime? If so, the police chief has come up with a few practical suggestions." Now try this: "If you're wondering how to protect yourself against the increase in neighborhood crime, you might want to heed some suggestions from the police chief." Which *sounds* better? A superior performer may do equally well with either; however, most announcers will find the second wording more natural.

In general, broadcast style leans toward giving each idea its own sentence. Beware of adjectives. They are often carriers of preference and prejudice, twin enemies of objective news reporting. Verbs are your work horses, unless you turn them into nags by saddling them with the passive, rather than the active voice. A verb in the active voice, you will remember, follows this pattern.

Subject acts.
Subject verb object
Ellen wrote the story.

The subject, Ellen, performed an action conveyed in the verb "wrote." The story is the object or result of her writing. Substitute the passive voice and you create this pattern:

Subject receives.
The story was written by Ellen.

Your new subject, "story," does nothing. It is the receiver of Ellen's action. The sentence has picked up two extra words along the way, moving more slowly with this extra baggage.

Naming the Source

Telling the audience the exact source of information is vital to the newscast's credibility. The listeners have a right to know whether newscasters speak for themselves or from a source. The way in which people hear the news dictates the position of attribution. Oral attribution is best at the beginning of a sentence rather than at the middle or at the end of a sentence, positions which are better suited to printed stories. The following examples suggest the differences.

Poor—sandwiching the source inside the sentence:

Creatures from outer space, according to six-year-old Wayne Thompson, are hiding in an abandoned building on downtown Main Street.

Poor—leading with a startling statement followed by the attribution of source:

Creatures from outer space are hiding in an abandoned building on downtown Main Street, or so says six-year-old Wayne Thompson.

Poor—hitching the source to the end of the sentence:

Creatures from outer space are hiding in an abandoned building on downtown Main Street, six-year-old Wayne Thompson said today.

Better—identifying the source at the head of the story:

Six-year-old Wayne Thompson says there are some creatures from outer space hiding in an abandoned building on downtown Main Street.

Early, clear source attribution discourages a questionable technique used by some reporters—creating a needless sense of danger through the presentation of a startling statement. You can see this in the second of the examples just provided. Although it is true that the newscaster's tone of voice might negate the fear factor, the writer should not rely on it, particularly if writer and reader are not the same individual.

The way in which the newscaster identifies direct quotations often presents a problem. Audiences cannot see the punctuation available to the news reader. The awkward "quote . . . unquote" technique is rarely used today. The more direct "Senator Bob Dole said" is better form. If the quotation is a long one, it is wise to introduce, "Senator Dole went on . . . " in the middle and to remind the audience at the end that Senator Dole made the statement. The important point is to make sure that the audience differentiates the quoted material from the rest of the newscast, particularly if the quotation is controversial or opinionated. To be sure that there are no misunderstandings, identify the source before you give the quotation.

Finding the Lead

Stories must be timed and planned in a way to catch and hold audience attention, similar to the way a headline and photo arrest the reader. Broadcast writers, therefore, rarely use the inverted pyramid approach. To put it graphically, they get to the heart of the story, excise it, and dangle it before their audience at the beginning, in order to tease their attention. A newspaper account of a school bus which overturned on a major highway during the morning rush hour without inflicting serious bodily harm on any of its passengers might present the facts in the order just stated. The broadcast version, by contrast, is more likely to begin like this: "Forty schoolchildren are lucky to be alive tonight." Audience curiosity whetted, the newscaster will then flesh out the details. It ought to be noted here that an increasing number of print journalists are incorporating broadcast techniques into their writing styles. Consequently, some of the sharper differences are disappearing.

Sample Rewrite

A story in a metropolitan newspaper opened with this paragraph:

Four people were killed and six others were wounded early yesterday morning when an argument in a Queens cabaret exploded into a blazing gun battle that turned a joyous birthday party into a scene of carnage and terror, the police and witnesses said.

The article was a long one. Read aloud, it ran four minutes and 50 seconds, more than four times the length of a radio version.

Facts included were as follows:

Two innocent women were killed. Both had four-year-old children.
Witnesses fled the building, many of them bleeding.
They left behind toppled tables and chairs, blotches of blood, scattered shoes and a white teddy bear.
Police suspect drugs might have been a catalyst for the violence, but not that they were directly related to the celebration.
The neighborhood is known for drug-related criminal activities.
Relatives and friends express grief and outrage at the indiscriminate slaughter.

There are many ways to tell that story; many different angles to pursue. What follows represents one approach. Its running time is 50 seconds.

What started out as a birthday party in a Queens cabaret ended up as a gun battle waged by uninvited criminals. The celebration of life gave way to panic, danger and death.
Police and witnesses say the guests were enjoying a mariachi show when the shooting started. Lethal firepower from automatic hand-guns left at least six people wounded and four dead. Two of the victims were young mothers, one was the photographer for the party. The others were men involved in the battle.
Witnesses and neighbors complain that the neighborhood has become drug ridden. Shootings are common among rival Latino factions.
As police continue their investigation, unwanted memories haunt those who went to celebrate a birthday: gun shots, screams, overturned tables and chairs, blotches of blood and scattered shoes, a white teddy bear and two four-year-olds who wonder where their mothers are.

Using the Present Tense

Broadcast news, which does not have to wait for the next run of the printing presses, capitalizes on its ability to report what is happening now. It offers its audience an air of immediacy, a quality that increases its popularity with people who regularly ask one another—and their news sources—"What's new?" Broadcast writers, therefore, to keep their copy sounding current, use the present tense wherever possible. If, for example, the mayor, during a morning press conference, had issued a call for wholehearted cooperation in conserving energy, the evening newscast might report it this way: "The mayor is asking everyone to reduce home energy consumption. He says . . . " The press conference, though completed in the past, recommends a continuing effort. The sense of the information is an easy guide to the use of the tense. The person who wins a marathon race at the same moment the mayor is holding his press conference must have the achievement reported differently. It would be foolish to announce that the athlete "is winning the marathon" eight hours after the race was over. The rule of thumb on tense might be that unless the deed reported, in its essence, projects finality, news writers employ the present, continuing present, or present perfect tense.

Using Titles

When reports include newsmakers' titles, along with their names, the title always precedes the name. This, in general, reverses the style used for identification in printed versions of the same story. It must be noted, however, that written reports are becoming more flexible in their methods of identifying people. Consider the following sentence which appeared in a daily newspaper.

Robert C. Ode, a hostage from Falls Church, Virginia, sent "almost identical" letters to Carter and the Washington Post, *White House Press Secretary Jody Powell said Thursday.*

The man's name will have no meaning for most people, but the term "hostage," used at a time when world interest focused on the 50 Americans detained against their will in Iran, immediately placed Ode in a context that aroused sympathy. Individuals, for whom reading the newspaper is a primary activity, will be sure to go back and check the name as soon as it is linked with "hostage." The radio listener, on the other hand, may be distracted and inattentive until hearing the term "hostage." Radio listeners cannot go back and check what they heard. They are dependent on the broadcaster, and a short account or a passing reference may not be repeated in the newscast. The broadcaster, therefore, might rephrase that lead sentence in this way:

One of the hostages, Robert C. Ode from Falls Church, Virginia, has sent two letters to the nation's capital, one addressed to President Carter, the other to the Washington Post. *White House Press Secretary Jody Powell, in a statement delivered Thursday, described the letters as "almost identical."*

One clue writers and readers should be able to count on comes from punctuation. Quotation marks, periods, and—above all—the dash, aid the news reader in interpreting the material according to sense phrasing. Don't use exclamation points in news copy, but use the dash to help the news reader. It is the arrow pointing toward an important word or idea. It doubles for parentheses, preparing the announcer for an aside or for additional, often incidental, information. It suggests a pause longer than that indicated by a comma and a thought more related to the sentence's main idea than the words following a period. Newscasters will add their own commas, slashes, and dashes, but the news writers must chart the course with appropriate punctuation.

Some Words From the Wise

Many experienced broadcasters are eager to help aspiring writers. Allan Jackson, for many years a CBS newscaster, frequently lectured to college students on the craft of newswriting. His advice then holds good today: "Keep it tight, terse, simple—and make it flow." The need for directness and simplicity becomes apparent when one considers that the newscaster has only a few sentences to tell a story to which a newspaper writer may devote several paragraphs. The listeners, furthermore, must understand the story the first time through; they have no chance to go back over the material the way newspaper readers can. For this reason avoid inversions, long, modifying phrases, and involved constructions. Short sentences should predominate. Generally, take the normal route from subject to verb and keep them close together.

Sentences do not necessarily have to be complete. Lowell Thomas often used a headline approach—"New Floods in India"—to make a transition from one item to the next. Use easy-to-understand words instead of fancy and complex ones. Remember that verbs are more important in a newscast than adjectives, but when adjectives are used, there should be no doubt about the subject they modify. Be alert to the articulation problems that certain phrases may involve. Jackson cited "the Joint Chiefs' Chairman" and "the earth's first space" as phrases that might trip even the most fluent newscaster.

Imbue the newscast with an atmosphere of excitement, for it deals, after all, with events that often have a critical influence on everyone. This does not mean that the treatment should be sensational or shocking, but it should be forceful and active. The passive voice has little place in a newscast. Make each story sound as if it has just happened, and particularly avoid dating stories unnecessarily. When dealing with a story already in the news, start with a fresh angle or new lead before reviewing what is known by most listeners.

You may discover at this point that your copy is accurate and lively but that it lacks the conversational quality you hope to achieve. There are two additional suggestions which may help you unlock the secret of success.

First, having talked your copy to your typewriter in phrases and fragments, now read it aloud to someone else or onto an audio tape. Listen for contractions. Have you used them wherever possible? Few people use "do not" and "would not" in conversation in place of "don't" and "wouldn't" unless, of course, they are intent on emphasizing the negative aspect of a statement as in, "The commissioner said he would *not* tolerate insubordination."

Second, examine your copy for extra words, especially needless "that's." Excise them. Eric Sevareid once said he thought one could eliminate the vast majority of "that's" in any presentation without harming either the meaning or the grammatical structure. Try it. Is there an essential difference between, "The president said that he's withdrawing from the race," and "The president said he's withdrawing from the race"?

Before addressing some specific problems in newscasting, it might be well to address what could appear to be an inconsistency between principle and practice. You probably have noticed that the copy in this textbook includes what seem to be violations of the broadcast style it recommends. Contractions are used interchangeably with the longer forms; the overall style includes complex sentences and verbs in the passive voice. The reason is quite simple. This textbook is designed primarily for the eye, not the ear.

Special Problems

A number of special problems face the writer of news copy.

1. Since news often involves controversial matters, it is easy to let one's particular bias color the presentation. The hallmark of the straight newscast is objectivity. You must be certain that you report the facts accurately without letting that report be warped by your personal opinions.

2. You must guard against making judgments not warranted by the facts. To refer to an accused man as a killer or thief before the courts have decided his guilt or innocence is to be guilty of prejudgment and possible libel which can lead to damage suits. To report that an individual has jumped from a 10-story building is to say that he has committed suicide. This judgment may not be justified by what is known at the time of the newscast. To say that he fell is to imply an accidental death, which again the facts may not establish. The word "plunged" tells what happened without making a judgment.

3. Because a newscast is heard rather than read, you must be especially careful that the order of words does not create

misunderstandings. Make sure that the antecedents of pronouns are completely clear. Guard against misleading the audience with qualifying phrases. The best procedure is to place the qualifying phrase or clause ahead of the item it modifies. The danger of doing the reverse can be illustrated by the following example: "Iraq's Chief of State, the Iraqian counterpart of George Bush, died today." A person half-listening to the broadcast might gather that the President of the United States had died.

4. Television newscasters have the special problem of relating their copy to taped or filmed material. If there is a direct relationship between what they are saying and what is on the screen, they are said to have written *to* the film. This is what they are doing when they identify the people in the film or discuss the action directly. In other cases, however, writers let the film speak for itself while they cover another phase of the story. This is called writing *away* from the film. In writing this copy, the writers also must decide whether the film tells the basic news story or merely reinforces it.

5. A commonly used technique to arouse interest is to begin the newscast with a series of headlines. The purpose is to arouse interest in the story without revealing the story itself. If headlines tell too much, the audience will have its curiosity satisfied before the program is well under way. Thus the headline, "Chief of Staff resigns with blast at the Congress" contains too many details. "Turnover at the Pentagon" will hold the listener's attention better.

6. Dates, numbers, measurements can be overwhelming. "Three months ago" conveys a better sense of time to most listeners than does the mentioning of a specific date. "The pipe is 300 feet long"

might be well served by the addition, "Laid from ground upward, it would be about as long as a six-story building."

The following excerpt from an obituary published in *The New York Times* (August 24, 1991) illustrates the two forms of writing, the first designed for the eye, the other for the ear. if you read these two paragraphs aloud, you'll appreciate the differences more. Both paragraphs are rich in information about this outstanding individual. The tribute recognized the accomplishments and character of actress Colleen Dewhurst:

An imposing presence both in person and on stage, Ms. Dewhurst was known as a woman never hesitant about using her distinctive big throaty voice to express an opinion on almost any subject. In the theater, she conveyed a mature sexuality, a folkish earthiness; her feline smile, crinkly eyes and high cheekbones combined to soften her large stature and enable the audience to feel closer to her and to identify with her characters, who were often tragic.

Her friends considered her passionate and caring. "She's like an earth mother," the actress Maureen Stapleton once said, "but in real life she's not to be let out without a keeper. She's a pushover, a pussycat. She's the Madonna of the birds with broken wings."

Stapleton's spoken words formed short sentences and employed contractions. Their impact was intensified by the use of metaphors: "pushover . . . pussycat . . . Madonna of the birds with broken wings."

RADIO NEWS FORMAT

There is no single format, either for radio scripts or for television scripts. Stations develop their own styles. Some use capital letters for all audio and video directions, reserving standard upper and lower case for words spoken by the newscasters and others involved in the stories. Other stations employ all capital letters for the anchor and newscasters and use parentheses to enclose directions. It's important for each new station employee to learn the preferred format and use it consistently. One common demand, however, is that all copy be double- or triple-spaced; a second is that each story, regardless of length, have its own page.

Mike Lopiparo, news writer for WINS, provided the following four samples used to introduce, contain, or present news stories. The heading (slug) on each page identifies the story content, the writer, and breakdown of tape time and copy lines. Lopiparo has added a brief instructional guideline after each example.

Slug Example 1

Slug	Writer	Tape	Copy	Lines
Thomas/Nickolaides	Lopiparo	:40	0:23	11

ABORTION REMAINS THE CONTROVERSIAL ISSUE AT THE SENATE CONFIRMATION HEARINGS FOR SUPREME COURT NOMINEE CLARENCE THOMAS . . .

(Nickolaides . . . 40 . . . Cart)

Guideline: When a reporter files a story that'll be broadcast, the anchor reads a lead-in that allows listeners to know beforehand what they'll be hearing, as in the example above. Be careful not to write a lead that's similar to the one the reporter uses to begin the actual story. That's known as an echo lead, and it sounds amateurish.

Slug Example 2

Slug	Writer	Tape	Copy	Lines
Condoms/Russell	Lopiparo	(NA)	0:25	12

THE NEW YORK CITY SCHOOL BOARD IS DECIDING WHETHER PARENTS CAN KEEP THEIR CHILDREN FROM GETTING CONDOMS AT HIGH SCHOOLS . . . LET'S GET A LIVE UPDATE AT BOARD OF EDUCATION HEADQUARTERS IN BROOKLYN FROM W-I-N-S REPORTER JOHN RUSSELL . . .

(Russell)

Guideline: When reporters are at the scene of the story, they should be introduced by the anchor, who provides a short lead to let listeners know what the story will be about, as above. It identifies the reporter and the locations of the report.

Slug Example 3

Slug	Writer	Tape	Copy	Lines
Tyson/VC	Lopiparo	:08	0:40	19

MIKE TYSON HAS PLEADED NOT GUILTY TO CHARGES HE RAPED AN 18-YEAR-OLD BEAUTY PAGEANT CONTESTANT IN INDIANAPOLIS. TYSON'S TRIAL IS SET FOR JANUARY 27TH. THE FORMER HEAVYWEIGHT BOXING CHAMP SAYS HIS MAIN CONCERN IS GETTING HIS TITLE BACK ON NOVEMBER 8TH WHEN HE CHALLENGES CURRENT CHAMP EVANDER HOLYFIELD . . .

(Tyson . . . 08 . . . Fight)

PROMOTERS INSIST THE BOUT WILL TAKE PLACE DESPITE TYSON'S LEGAL PROBLEMS. TYSON FACES 63 YEARS IN PRISON IF CONVICTED ON ALL COUNTS.

Guideline: An actuality, or voice cut, is the sound of a newsmaker in the story. The actuality helps tell the story. The anchor must say who is about to speak and then "tease" into what that person will say. Never leave an actuality hanging. Always have at least one sentence after the actuality ends, as in the example above.

Slug Example 4

Slug	Writer	Tape	Copy	Lines
Welfare	Lopiparo	(NA)	0:47	18

NEW YORK STATE SENATE REPUBLICANS ARE PROPOSING A PLAN TO HELP CUT DOWN MEDICAID FRAUD. THEY'RE CALLING FOR PHOTO I-D CARDS FOR ALL MEDICAID RECIPIENTS IN THE STATE. THEIR PROPOSAL GETS THE ENDORSEMENT OF NEW YORK'S SPECIAL PROSECUTOR FOR MEDICAD FRAUD CONTROL. EDWARD KURIANSKY SAYS MEDICAID FRAUD IS COSTING STATE TAXPAYERS AS MUCH AS 150 MILLION DOLLARS PER YEAR. THE PHOTO I-D IS DESIGNED TO HELP CURB SCHEMES WHERE SO-CALLED "MEDICAID MILL" DOCTORS ILLEGALLY PRESCRIBE DRUGS TO PEOPLE WHO SELL THEM.

Guideline: The above is an example of a "straight" story. It's a story without any audio or video tape. In both radio and television news a straight story is 30 seconds or less. Try to have a good lead sentence in any type of broadcast story. The sentence should tell the listeners what they're about to hear. Don't put too many facts in the lead sentence.

TELEVISION NEWS STORY INGREDIENTS

The inherent components of each news story, the subject matter and availability of sound, pose specific challenges to the news writer. Two stories written and delivered by Ellen Fleysher of WNBC-TV, New York, illustrate the demands. The first dealt with the issue of cameras in the courtroom on the day that New York state decided to end its two-and-a-half-year experiment of allowing electronic coverage of courtroom proceedings.

Fleysher summarized the specific demands of this story. The issue of cameras in the courtroom is not as easily grasped by viewers as are some issues—for example, a highway proposed for their town. The concept of cameras providing public access to this part of the judicial process isn't easily visualized; neither is the determination to terminate the experiment. Its translation has to be in words, concepts, ideas. Fleysher, a longtime supporter of cameras in the courtroom, had to explain the significance of the action taken to forbid their presence. She had to do so, moreover, without providing editorial comment.

What resulted was Fleysher's delivery of a straightforward "standupper"—an on-camera presentation videotaped outside and inside the courthouse. She drew on file tape depicting the criminal proceedings mentioned in her script and ended her report outside the courthouse.

The report, including the announcer's Intro and Outro, ran three minutes, 10 seconds.

WNBC-TV
NEWS AT SIX
FLEYSHER REPORT

VIDEO	*AUDIO*
STUDIO: FRATANGELO GRAPHIC: CAMERAS IN COURTROOM	ANNCR: High drama in the courtroom. You see it live or on videotape in your living room. Cameras were in the courtroom for some of the most notorious cases in New York over the past few years, but now it's all over. It was an experiment that will not continue. News 4's Ellen Fleysher has this special report.
FILETAPE: COURTROOM SUPER: MANHATTAN SUPREME COURT FILE TAPE: DEFENDANTS	FLEYSHER (VO): For the last two years, television cameras and radio microphones have been allowed inside New York State courtrooms, like this one, making audiovisual coverage of trials a regular part of the news you see every day.

	(COURTROOM SOUNDS ON TAPE) In the beginning there were plenty of reservations about a camera possibly contaminating the sanctity of the courtroom.
JUDGE ROTHWAX SUPER: JUDGE'S NAME SUPER: MANHATTAN SUPREME COURT	ROTHWAX: I thought cameras in the court room would be distracting and that they would be disruptive and I felt that somehow having that kind of presence in the courtroom would impede the serving of the truth.
FILE TAPE: JOEL STEINBERG, LISA STEINBERG FILE TAPE: DEFENDANTS SUPER: QUEENS SUPREME COURT	FLEYSHER: But Judge Rothwax did a turn-around after presiding at the trial of Joel Steinberg, a trial that received national attention because it focused our attention on the problem of child abuse in the heart of the middle class. Cameras in the courtroom made us confront racism close to home in Howard Beach. The legislation enabling this coverage brought New York in line with the majority of states across the nation.
BARRY RYTTENBERG SUPER: NAME	RYTTENBERG: 40 some-odd states have audiovisual coverage. New York is the first one that in their infinite wisdom the legislators have decided to discontinue a successful experiment.
SHOTS OF FLEYSHER AND JUDGE	FLEYSHER (VO): All coverage in New York ended a month ago when the Assembly and the Senate couldn't agree on the same bill.
	JUDGE: It really hasn't been a problem and I don't know why the Legislature suddenly perceived it as such.

FLEYSHER OUTSIDE COURTHOUSE

FLEYSHER: In Albany the Assembly passed a bill continuing audiovisual coverage on an experimental basis, but in the Senate a bill drafted by Christopher Meaga, Chairman of the powerful Senate Judiciary Committee, gave witnesses the power to ban cameras from the courtroom, power previously held by judges alone. This, in effect, killed the bill.

MEAGA

MEAGA: If my daughter or my wife had to be a witness in a criminal matter, and should they be on camera without their consent and I'd say No.

FLEYSHER

FLEYSHER: Do you know of anyone who was ever forced to testify?

MEAGA

MEAGA: No. I don't know of anyone who was ever forced to testify.

RYTTENBERG

RYTTENBERG: You can't have witnesses run the courtroom. That's the judge's job. That's why the judge wears a robe, that's why he's elevated to the bench.

JUDGE

JUDGE: The experience over the last two and a half years has been that the judges have been able to control the process adequately.

FLEYSHER

FLEYSHER: Senator Meaga concedes that he thinks judges are sensitive to witnesses, which is why the death of the legislation is especially perplexing.

RYTTENBERG

RYTTENBERG: I want Senator Meaga to know, that, speaking on behalf of the 700 members of the New York Press Club,

	we hold him personally responsible for the defeat of that bill.
FLEYSHER OUTSIDE COURTHOUSE	FLEYSHER: There is some irony in the fact that while legislation permitting television cameras inside State courthouses has ended for the time being, for the first time television cameras are being permitted inside Federal courthouses, across the street. Ellen Fleysher, News 4, New York.
ANNCR IN STUDIO	ANNCR: It's interesting; New York state's program was the model for the experiment in the Federal court.

Her second story, "A Special Wish," provides a sharp contrast to the first. This was about a camp for dying children and their well siblings. Insofar as it was possible, no differentiation was made between the well and the dying. Filmed at the camp, the story, according to Fleysher, "was extremely visual and moving." Her judgment: "It required lean language." The characters had to speak for themselves, the writer providing context and only the sparsest commentary.

The story that was aired begins with a young man calling out: "Bingo!" His relationship with his younger sister provides the focus. As they express their concerns and aspirations, the audience is surprised to discover that he is the one who is dying and that she has become her big brother's protector.

Fleysher says she was so moved by the story that she spent sixteen hours of free weekend time composing it. Struck by the bond between well and ailing siblings, she highlighted the strength inherent in little Danielle's determination that her older brother David would get well. Their responses to Fleysher's questions reveals two elements in the dynamic between the children: David, despite his big-brother logic, cannot protect Danielle from the pain bound to follow his approaching death, and the little girl, in her unflinching love and confidence, becomes for at least this little while the older boy's protector.

This is a story that seems to tell itself, and it does so by having been introduced and bridged by the reporter's voice-over presence. Entirely visual, it comes together in the editing process.

A SPECIAL WISH

VIDEO	*AUDIO*
ELLEN V/O	BINGO NIGHT AT CAMP STAR TRAILS: HOT, HUMID AND STICKY. THE OVERHEAD FANS AT THE PAVILION ARE DOING THEIR

BUBBLE MONTAGE **FALSE TEETH**	DARNDEST—WHICH ISN'T MUCH—BUT NOBODY SEEMS TO MIND. WHEN YOU'RE PLAYING FOR GIANT WADS OF BUBBLE GUM OR A PRIZED SET OF THOSE WIND-UP FALSE TEETH, THE HUMAN SPIRIT CAN ENDURE JUST ABOUT ANYTHING.
NAT SOT (CAMPER) **SOT (DAVID)**	(BINGO!) (YES, WE HAVE A WINNER . . .)
ELLEN V/O CONTINUE VIDEO	WHILE THE GAME IS COMMON ENOUGH, THE PLACE AND PLAYERS ARE NOT . . . EXTRAORDINARY CHILDREN TRYING TO BE ORDINARY.
SOT (DAVID BENSON) **START WITH C.U. AT BINGO, DISSOLVE TO SOT, DISSOLVE BACK TO BINGO.**	(THEY'RE JUST AS NORMAL AS YOU OR ME OR ANYBODY EXCEPT FOR THE FACT THAT THEY HAVE LEUKEMIA OR WHAT-EVER CANCER OF SOME TYPE.)
ELLEN V/O	NOT EVERYBODY HAS CANCER HERE. HEALTHY BROTHERS AND SISTERS OF YOUNG CANCER PATIENTS COME TO CAMP TOO.
SOT (DANIELLE BENSON)	(EVERYBODY ASKS ME "DO YOU HAVE CAN-CER OR DOES YOUR LITTLE BROTHER?" I SAY "NO, MY BIG BROTHER DOES" AND THEY JUST LOOK AT ME LIKE "WHAAAAT?"
ELLEN V/O	IT'S PRETTY HARD TO TELL WHO DOES AND WHO DOESN'T, ALTHOUGH IT DOESN'T REALLY MATTER. A VERY SPECIAL BOND UNITES ALL 150 KIDS WHO CAMP HERE TWO WEEKS EACH YEAR . . . A BOND THAT YOU ONLY BEGIN TO UNDERSTAND WHEN YOU LISTEN TO THEIR SONGS.
NAT SOT "FRIENDS OF THE FAMILY" **(MONTAGE OVER SONG)**	("I MET SOME FRIENDS OF THE FAMILY/ LOVE CAN BUILD A HOME AWAY FROM HOME/YES I MET SOME FRIENDS OF THE FAMILY/FRIENDS AMONG THE BEST I'VE EVER KNOWN/YOU ARE MY FRIENDS AMONG THE BEST I'VE EVER KNOWN.")

ELLEN V/O	FOR HALF OF HIS 16 YEARS, DAVID BENSON HAS BEEN FIGHTING HIS OWN ENEMY WITHIN: ACUTE LUMPHOBLASTIC LEUKEMIA. HIS SIX-YEAR-OLD BROTHER, LINDLEY, IS STILL TOO YOUNG TO KNOW WHAT THIS IS ABOUT, BUT THEN THERE'S DANIELLE. SHE IS 10 YEARS OLD.
SOT (DANIELLE BENSON)	(LEUKEMIA IS A CANCER OF THE RED AND WHITE BLOOD CELLS.)
SOT (JANET JOHNSON)	(THE SIBLINGS TEND TO GROW UP A LITTLE BIT SOONER. . . .)
ELLEN V/O DROP AUDIO, CONTINUE PIX, THEN B-ROLL WITH WALK ALONG THE LAKE	JANET JOHNSON IS THE FOUNDER AND DIRECTOR OF CAMP STAR TRAILS. SHE IS ALSO CHIEF PEDIATRIC NURSE AT M.D. ANDERSON CANCER CENTER IN HOUSTON. THE CENTER SUPPORTS THE CAMP.
	OF THE 90 CAMPS IN THE NATION FOR PEDIATRIC CANCER PATIENTS, FEWER THAN ONE QUARTER OF THEM INCLUDE HEALTHY BROTHERS AND SISTERS.
SOT (JANET JOHNSON & EF)	(WHETHER IT'S THE SAME BOAT OF HAVING CANCER OR BEING A BROTHER OR SISTER OF SOMEONE WITH CANCER, IT'S THE GREATEST THING FOR THEM TO KNOW THERE ARE OTHER PEOPLE DOING THIS. *EF:* BECAUSE BOTH ARE DIFFICULT, AREN'T THEY? *ANS:* VERY. WE FIND WE SPEND AT LEAST AS MUCH TIME WITH THE SIBLINGS AS WE DO WITH THE PATIENTS AND SOMETIMES MORE.)
SOT (EF O-C BRIDGE)	(CAMPS LIKE STAR TRAILS WERE BORN NOT ONLY OUT OF LOVE BUT ALSO OUT OF NECESSITY. NOT THAT MANY YEARS AGO SUMMER CAMPS WOULD NOT ACCEPT CHILDREN WITH A HISTORY OF CANCER. AND SO THESE VICTIMS OF DISEASE WERE VICTIMIZED A SECOND TIME. THEY WERE OSTRACIZED. A LOT OF THAT'S CHANGED NOW. ADVANCES IN TREATMENT HAVE A WAY OF TEMPERING PUBLIC OPINION.)

SOT (DONALD PINKEL, M.D.)

(ONLY WHEN WE BEGAN TO BE ABLE TO CURE SOME CHILDREN OF LEUKEMIA DID SOME OF THAT PALL OF SILENCE AND FEAR BEGIN TO LIFT.)

ELLEN V/O DROP AUDIO, CONTINUE PIX

DONALD PINKEL IS DIRECTOR OF PEDIATRIC LEUKEMIA RESEARCH AT M.D. ANDERSON.

THE TREATMENT OF CHILDHOOD CANCERS IS BOTH INTENSE AND LONG-TERM. THE PROCESS CAN MAKE OR BREAK THE FAMILY, BECAUSE THE FOCUS CAN GET DISTORTED.

SOT (DAVID BENSON)

(IF I HAD A MESSAGE FOR EVERY BROTHER AND SISTER THAT HAS A BROTHER OR SISTER WITH CANCER I'D SAY "TELL YOUR PARENTS YOU NEED MORE ATTENTION." DON'T GO OUT AND TRY TO GET IT IN THE WRONG WAY LIKE THROWING FITS OR WANTING TO GET YOUR WAY ALL THE TIME AND DOING BAD STUFF JUST TO GET ATTENTION. FOR A WHILE, THAT'S WHAT MY SISTER WAS DOING.)

SOT (DANIELLE BENSON)

(I SOMETIMES FELT JEALOUS BECAUSE I DIDN'T KNOW WHY THEY WERE GOING TO THE HOSPITAL.)

BUTTED TO:

SOT (DANIELLE)

(I SCREAMED AND YELLED AND THEY NEVER LET ME GO BECAUSE DAVID DIDN'T WANT ME TO SEE THAT KIND OF THING HAPPEN.)

ELLEN V/O

DAVID LEARNED HE COULD NOT PROTECT DANIELLE.

SOT (DAVID)

(I JUST WENT THROUGH THE WHOLE BIT WITH HER AND SHE GAINED SORT OF A KNOWLEDGE AS TO WHAT CANCER IS.)

BUTTED TO:

SOT (DAVID)

(SHE ASKED ME OVER AND OVER AGAIN WHY THEY DO CERTAIN TESTS SUCH AS

	BONE MARROWS, ASPIRATIONS AND SPINAL TAPS. AND EVEN WHY THEY GIVE ME IV'S AND THINGS LIKE THAT. SHE ASKED ME, "DOES IT HURT?" AND OF COURSE IT HURTS.)
SOT (DANIELLE)	(IT HURTS YOU IN YOUR HEART AND YOU FEEL SORRY FOR THE PERSON WHO HAS IT AND IT'S LIKE YOU HAVE CANCER AND WHEN I LOOK AT DAVID, IT'S LIKE I HAVE CANCER.)
ELLEN V/O	AND SO THE PROTECTED HAS BECOME THE PROTECTOR.
SOT (DANIELLE)	(WE HELP HIM FIGHT, YOU KNOW. *EF:* HOW DO YOU HELP HIM FIGHT? *ANS:* WE CHEER HIM ON AND EVERYTHING AND I TALK TO HIM EVERYDAY.)
ELLEN V/O	THE T-SHIRT DAVID DESIGNS IN THE CRAFTS SHOP BEARS HIS MOTTO: LOOK TO THE FUTURE. HE DOESN'T THINK ABOUT THE RADIATION AND DAYS OF MORE CHEMO-THERAPY AHEAD. BUT DANIELLE DOES.
SOT (DANIELLE)	(IT'S LIKE BREAKING YOUR HEART Y'KNOW. AND I DON'T LIKE IT. 'CAUSE HE'S MY BROTHER. AND IF HE WOULD LIKE DIE OR SOMETHING, I WOULD LIKE DIE. A PART OF ME WOULD DIE. 'CAUSE I LOVE HIM A WHOLE BUNCH.)
SOT (DR. PINKEL)	(WE ALL KNOW FROM STUDIES IN WARTIME CONDITIONS THAT WHEN YOU HAVE TROOPS IN A VERY CRITICAL SITUA-TION, IF THEY HAVE EACH OTHER TO TALK WITH AND SHARE THE MISERY, THEY CAN SURVIVE A LOT BETTER THAN IF EACH ONE IS ALONE IN SOME ISOLATED FOXHOLE.)
NAT SOT "WITH YOUR FACE TO THE WIND" DANIELLE SINGS	("WITH YOUR FACE TO THE WIND/ I SEE YOU SMILIN' AGAIN/ SPIRITS MOVIN' WITHIN/ I KNOW THAT YOU'RE GONNA WIN.")

SOT (DAVID)	(THAT'S THE GLORY OF IT ALL. AND THAT'S WHY I'M A TRUE BELIEVER IN GOD'S WAY.)
SOT (DANIELLE)	(SOMETIMES HE HAS RELAPSES YOU KNOW. AND WHEN I PRAY FOR HIM, IT'S KIND OF LIKE I'M ASKING GOD, "WHY?" YOU'RE NOT SUPPOSED TO QUESTION GOD, BUT I DO. I DON'T KNOW WHY BUT I DO.)
ELLEN V/O **MUSIC UNDER: "SPIRIT OVERFLOWING . . ."**	FOR ALL CAMPERS EVERYWHERE, THE LAST DAY IS FILLED WITH BOTH EXCITEMENT AND SADNESS: THE MAGIC OF CLOSING CEREMONIES COUPLED WITH THE MELANCHOLY INHERENT IN KNOWING THAT THESE GLORIOUS DAYS ARE ABOUT TO BE RELEGATED TO MERE MEMORY. AT CAMP STAR TRAILS, TRADITION CALLS FOR EACH CABIN TO DELIVER A COLLECTIVE WISH.
SOT (CAMPER)	(OUR SPECIAL WISH FOR Y'ALL IS THAT EVERYONE MAKES IT BACK NEXT YEAR.)
ELLEN V/O	THE WISHES COME FORTH STATED SIMPLY AND PURE: THAT ALL THE SICK CHILDREN WILL BE WELL. THAT THE DOCTORS WILL FIND A CURE FOR CANCER. THAT EVERYONE WILL DISCOVER THE BEAUTY WITHIN. THE CANDLES SURROUNDING THE STAR REPRESENT EVERYONE'S DREAMS FOR THE FUTURE. SENT OUT INTO THE NIGHT, THEY CREATE A GLOWING PATH IN THE DARKENED LAKE. REKINDLING HOPE. (*Q:* DO YOU BELIEVE IN WISHES:? *ANS:* YES, I DO SOMETIMES. *Q:* CAN YOU TELL ME THE BIGGEST WISH? *ANS:* I WISH DAVID WOULDN'T HAVE CANCER ANYMORE. *Q:* IS THAT WHAT YOU'RE GOING TO WISH TONIGHT? *ANS:* I WISH IT KIND OF EVERY NIGHT.) FOR SUNDAY TODAY, ELLEN FLEYSHER, CAMP STAR TRAILS, NAVASOTA, TEXAS.

Note that capital letters are used throughout, a bolder type providing video instructions. All narration besides Fleysher's is enclosed in parentheses. What is important about a script, however, is that its format reflect a consistent style to achieve clarity, and that it follow a pattern approved by the broadcasting station for which it is prepared.

The two previous stories fulfill the criteria of "significance" and "interest." Each is self-contained; the first reports a significant legal action; the second, features an interesting insight into the courage of the human spirit.

The next report, written and delivered by Mary Murphy of WCBS-TV, New York, reflects the need for fresh angles to a story that continues over several days, weeks, or longer. During the 1991 Persian Gulf War, she visited a V.A. hospital in Brooklyn to poll hospitalized veterans on the subject. The story broadcast on the evening news was primarily a voice-over report which included responses from the veterans. Much of the story was "written" in the editing room, the audio track being laid first in preparation for the visual images, and with Murphy's memory of what she saw and felt during the visit.

The reporter's selection of a V.A. hospital as a site from which to present the sidebar stemmed from her sense that a hospital dedicated to the care of men and women with battle scars from earlier wars would have its own field of psychological warfare. Murphy, realizing that this latest conflict would be "a TV war," was especially curious about how the Vietnam veterans would perceive it. After some initial resistance to her and her video crew, she said she "talked her way" in. Listening to the veterans was the most important part of her information gathering, but all the while she did so, she kept her eyes open for unspoken clues: Some vets wore combat uniforms or military hats; a map on the wall showed Vietnam and Cambodia. She was alert to body language, the twitching of an eye or knee, a scowl, or some sign of enthusiasm.

While the veterans remembered their fighting days and reacted to the latest war, a doctor described their post-traumatic stress.

Three and a half hours at the hospital and several hours more spent editing tape and writing the script produced a concise report which ran 2 minutes and 5 seconds, complete with introduction.

VIDEO	AUDIO
IN STUDIO: ERNIE ANASTOS	ANNOUNCER: For veterans in our area the war in the Gulf is striking an emotional chord. Channel 2's Mary Murphy reports on those who have served our country and how they're reacting to this crisis.
CU VET'S FACE	MURPHY (VO): They wear the scars of battle in their weary eyes and the nervous tension in their legs. We met them in a place they call "The Hootch," a nickname for their sleeping quarters during the Vietnam War.
SUPER: BROOKLYN	
CU KNEES	
DOOR OPENS TO REVEAL VETS	

PAN WALLS, VETS, CU ON TV SET
SHOWING WAR REPORT

But this is part of the Brooklyn V.A. Hospital, where veterans get help for post-traumatic stress even as they watch a new war on TV.

CU VET #1
SUPER: BRUCE THIBOU VIET VET

BRUCE THIBOU: The sounds of rockets, bombs. That's what's terrifying me, the sounds. It's bringing back memories.

CU VET #2
SUPER: "ARKANSAS" SWISHER
FOUGHT IN CAMBODIA
HOLDS UP SON'S PHOTO

SWISHER: With the talk of terrorism coming here, makes me flash back and have nightmares, where in the last 19 years I haven't had too many nightmares. My son Jerry is in the service. He was in the last battle group that went to Saudi Arabia.

CU VET #3
SUPER: VICTOR MONTANEZ
EX-AVIATION FIGHTER

MONTANEZ: I picked up some wounded soldiers when I was in Nam and uh, I still get flashbacks about this.

MURPHY: Do you think we should be there?

ECU MONTANEZ

MONTANEZ: I think so. Yes, I think so. Why? I guess because we're Americans.

LS MURPHY AND MONTANEZ
PAN ROOM

MURPHY (VO): Victor Montanez is a father of five who used to manage a Red Apple Supermarket. He was sitting next to Sandy Cohen, who arrived wearing army fatigues.

CU VET #4
SUPER: SANDY COHEN
FOUGHT IN CAMBODIA

COHEN (VO): And I can picture myself in the place of these kids that are over there now. I went through the same thing.

MURPHY AND DOCTOR

MURPHY (VO): Dr. Thomas Horvath is an expert on post-traumatic stress. He estimates 50 to 60 per cent of all soldiers involved in heavy combat duty later exhibit some symptoms.

DOCTOR INTO GROUP SHOT STOP AT ZAMBOR	HORVATH: In many ways it's very similar to a number of chronic anxiety disorders that we now recognize in the general population.
	MURPHY (VO): Yet Horvath knows a good number of vets are relatively symptom free, even as he recognizes the non-stop war coverage could be upsetting. Kenneth Zambor is angry with anti-war protestors.
CU VET #5 SUPER: KENNETH ZAMBOR VETERAN	ZAMBOR: If it wasn't for veterans, not just these veterans, but all veterans who served their country, they wouldn't have the right to be doing what the hell they're doing.
EXT HOSPITAL, CU YELLOW RIBBON ON FENCE	MURPHY (VO): And so the war watch continues with yellow ribbons on the hospital gate, while veterans from World War II prepare care kits inside.
CU MONTANEZ	The pain of yesterday's still fresh in the minds of all who sit here. I'm Mary Murphy, Channel 2 News.

Reporter Lis Daily's story, which aired on WISH-TV, Indianapolis, was one of a series of crime reports delivered from the scene of the disturbance. In this instance she was in the studio, delivering a voice-over report connecting a series of tapes. Her transitions provide the background for the three elements important to the audience's understanding of the story: a physical confrontation between a black robbery suspect and the white officer giving chase, a confrontation that left the suspect dead; an allegation that the officer's use of deadly force might not have been warranted; and a further report alleging that the officer had been involved with the American Nazi Party. The report, which ends on the newsroom set, suggests that the story, and the investigation, are far from over.

This is a brief, fact-hugging report of a complicated issue. Its presentation required restraint, accuracy, and candor.

WISH-TV INDIANAPOLIS
P–SHARP–SHOOTING, 11 PM 6-18-91
LIS DAILY REPORTING

VIDEO	*AUDIO*
DAILY	LIS: IT BEGAN AT THIS K-MART STORE, WHERE AN EMPLOYEE ALLEGEDLY
K-MART	SAW THE SUSPECT SHOPLIFTING SOME CLOTHING. THAT WORKER CONTACTED POLICE AND PATROLMAN WAYNE SHARP CHASED HIM THROUGH THIS
PARKING LOT	APARTMENT COMPLEX PARKING LOT . . . WHERE HE APPARENTLY DITCHED THE CLOTHING IN THIS DUMPSTER. THE CHASE ENDED HERE. . . IN BACK
DAV SHOP	OF THE DISABLED AMERICAN VETERANS THRIFT SHOP. . .
HORTY SUPER: LT. TIM HORTY IPD SPOKESMAN	HORTY: The officer chased the individual to a dead end alley behind the thrift store here and as he turned the corner he was struck in the right arm with a large board.
DAILY	LIS: THIS IS THE BOARD IN QUESTION. . . A TWO BY FOUR. OFFICER SHARP
BOARD	RESPONDED BY SHOOTING THE SUSPECT ONCE IN THE HEAD . . . KILLING HIM. NO OTHER WEAPON WAS FOUND.
DAILY	LIS: ACCORDING TO POLICE CHIEF PAUL ANNEE. . . DEPARTMENT POLICY ON THE USE OF DEADLY FORCE APPLIES TO AN OFFICER WHO BELIEVES HE OR SOMEONE ELSE IS IN SERIOUS DANGER. . .
ANNEE SUPER: IPD CHIEF PAUL ANNEE	ANNEE: Or he may use deadly force to stop a fleeing felon who has been suspected of probable cause to believe that serious harm or death has occurred.

DAILY

LIS: OFFICER SHARP HAS BEEN INVOLVED IN AT LEAST ONE OTHER POLICE ACTION SHOOTING IN HIS 18 YEARS WITH THE DEPARTMENT. THE CHIEF IS URGING THE COMMUNITY TO BE PATIENT WHILE THEY INVESTIGATE THE INCIDENT.

ANNEE

ANNEE: I'm not here to pass judgment on the shooting. I'm not here to say whether it was appropriate or inappropriate. Those are all fair questions asked. I don't have the answers to them.

DAILY

LIS: THE CHIEF ALSO DID NOT RESPOND TO QUESTIONS ABOUT A 1981 INVESTIGATION INTO OFFICER SHARP'S ALLEGED INVOLVEMENT WITH THE AMERICAN NAZI PARTY. . . A WHITE SUPREMACY GROUP. THAT INVESTIGATION FOUND SHARP HAD NO TIES WITH THAT ORGANIZATION. . . EXCEPT THAT HE WAS PHOTOGRAPHED GIVING SPEECHES AT AT LEAST TWO NAZI MEETINGS . . .

ANNEE

ANNEE: We'll provide any information that we have relative to any background information on this officer when we have it. . . when I can talk about it.

DAILY

LIS: THE SUSPECT HAS STILL NOT BEEN IDENTIFIED. THERE WAS NO IDENTIFICATION FOUND. HE'S DESCRIBED AS A BLACK MALE. . . IN HIS LATE TEENS OR EARLY 20'S. OFFICER SHARP IS RECOVERING AT HOME FROM CUTS AND BRUISES TO HIS RIGHT ARM.

ANCHOR (NEWSROOM)

DEBBY: WILL OFFICER SHARP'S BACKGROUND HAVE ANY BEARING ON THIS INVESTIGATION?

DAILY

LIS: NOT ACCORDING TO CHIEF ANNEE, WHO SAYS "THIS INCIDENT HAS TO STAND ON ITS OWN." THERE'S NO QUESTION. . . THOUGH CLEARED IN THE FATAL SHOOTING OF A BLACK ROBBERY SUSPECT 10 YEARS AGO AND HIS ALLEGED TIES TO THE AMERICAN NAZI PARTY. . . THESE ARE ISSUES THAT WILL NOT BE IGNORED.

TELEVISION NEWS FORMAT

One of the main objectives in preparing copy for a television newscast is to show the relationship between what is seen and what is heard. To accomplish this purpose, most stations and networks set up the copy in two columns, with video information on the left and the newscaster's copy on the right. A common element in most television newscasts is the ever-increasing incorporation of electronically gathered news items.

The following is an abridged rendition of the 11 P.M. news broadcast from New York by WNBC-TV News Center Four. Chuck Scarborough, as anchor, worked with three other in-studio reporters and another 10 from field positions. Note that Scarborough bids for the audience's attention by headlining events to come at the show's opening and before commercial breaks. In this example the final story describes a "human-interest" dimension of the day's news. This newscast, which weaves nineteen news items and four commercial breaks into a 30-minute presentation, indicates both the increased reliance on ENG and the importance of the anchor who provides continuity for a newscast containing so many separate stories. The sequence for the newscast is detailed in a "topsheet," or rundown, which lists the stories in preparation for writing the script.

Although the approach to this format may vary from station to station, a rundown for the following newscast probably would include a short description of the segment, the name of the anchor, video sources and graphic directions, and the running time.

NBC NEWS CENTER 4
11:00 P.M. EST

VIDEO	*AUDIO*
CHUCK ON CAMERA	Hurricane David blasts Puerto Rico and continues north. A live report from the national weather service coming up. And a court does to the Lone Ranger what no bad guy ever could... News Center 4 is next.
EJ HURRICANE SUPER HEADLINE	An awesome hurricane named David continues on its murderous journey toward the U.S.
CHUCK AND	Good evening.
SATELLITE MAP	I'm Chuck Scarborough.

	This is News Center 4.
	One of the biggest, most ferocious hurricanes of the century has dealt a glancing blow to Puerto Rico . . . and is roaring northward . . . aiming its incredible 150-mile-an-hour winds at Haiti and the Dominican Republic.
	(EJ VO)
EJ HURRICANE VO RUNS :45	Hurricane David has already left a trail of death and destruction in the Caribbean.
	At least seven people were killed on the Island of Dominica . . . a modest number, really, when you consider that nearly every building on that island has been reported flattened. . . .
	Three-fourths of its population of 80-thousand are now homeless and without food.
	In Puerto Rico. . . . three were killed.
	I have Roberto Tschudin Lucheme on the phone in San Juan.
	(QUESTIONS AND ANSWERS)
WHEN EJ ENDS, TAKE SATELLITE PHOTO AT END OF PHONE CHAT TAKE CHUCK & CLIFF IN KEY	
CHUCK	Cliff Morrison is in the offices of the National Weather service with a live minicam.
	Cliff . . . what's the latest on Hurricane David?
REMOTE PHONE	(TO CLIFF)
CHUCK	Outgoing Ambassador Andrew Young today followed up yesterday's official U-S criticism of Israel and the P-L-O for the fighting in Lebanon.
	After today's security council debate ended, Young was even more explicit in his criticism of Israel.
	He said: "I can't see much difference between a bomb in a trash can and a bomb dropped from ten-thousand feet."
	Turning to news here in New York. . . .
	The police today started a crackdown on private boarding houses for former mental patients.
	It began in Queens and Bob Teague has the story.
EJ/SOT EJ SOT RUNS 1:14 SUPER: LOCATION AT TOP REPORTING:	(EJ)
BOB TEAGUE AT	:13
RESIDENT AT	:26
ELLEN GARY AT	:43
	OUT: "AT THE D.A.'S OFFICE IN QUEENS."

CHUCK	And once again the police had their hands full with bank robberies. . . . a dozen more since last night led to a one-month record of 137 bank heists. . . . a dozen more than the previous record set last month. One suspect was caught near the scene. . . . and another was caught for an earlier robbery. School days are getting close . . . and when we come back . . .
VO EJ TEASE DESEG	(VO) teachers face layoffs and a Queens district gets pressure to integrate.
1ST COMMERCIAL BREAK	(COMMERCIAL 2:00)
CHUCK	244 teachers have gotten layoff notices . . . just two weeks before the new term in New York City. The teachers are losing their jobs because of an 85 million dollar budget cut. The Board of Ed says it's already reassigned 29 of them . . . and plans to do the same for the rest. The union . . . however, is not totally happy with that . . . .
FILM INTLK RUNS: 28 SUPER SUSAN GLASS	(TO FILM SOF)
	OUT: "HAVE A GOOD EDUCATION"
CHUCK	Members of a local school board in Queens are meeting tonight . . . to draft an integration plan for I-S 231. Dave Gilbert has a report . . .
EJ RUNS 1:17 SUPER AT TOP: I.S. 231 AT:20..DAVE GILBERT AT :41 DOLORES GRANT	(TO EJ SOT)
CHUCK	OUT: "GILBERT, NEWS CENTER 4 IN QUEENS" In Yonkers, the N-double-A-C-P today issued a "black paper," charging the city with deliberately maintaining segregated housing and schools. The organization warned that . . . unless the city revises its policies . . . Yonkers stands to lose millions in Federal dollars. An N-double-A-C-P spokesman says the city also discriminates against Blacks in the government.
EJ SOT RUNS :48 SOT UP FROM 00:13 SUPER: KEITH	(TO EJSOT)
	OUT: "MINORITY COMMUNITY"
TO EJ VO EJ VO FROM :14–26	(VO EJ CONTINUES) Another spokesman cited a Federal report . . . which said that Yonkers had violated equal employment rules in the hiring and firing of workers for the local community development agency . . .
EJ UP SOT SUPER: BATTS	(TO EJ SOT UP)
	OUT: "AT THIS LEVEL."
CHUCK	And still ahead. . . . mysterious pigeon deaths . . .

VO <u>FILM</u> SOLAR	(VO)
	. . . and solar energy is tested in a low income neighborhood.
2ND COMMERCIAL BREAK	COMMERCIAL 1:40
CHUCK	Somebody is killing the pigeons of Queens.
	Just who—is a mystery.
VO NATSOF RUNS :47	(TO V/O-NATSOF)
VO - :00 - :12	Normally, this Long Island railroad trestle in Forest Hills is full of perching pigeons.
	But lately, they've been dropping dead like flies.
SOUND UP :13–:47	No suspects yet . . . but neighbors are having their say.
SUPER: JANINE VINCENT	SOT
SUPER: PEARL KORNBLUM	SOT
	ENDS . . . "ALL THE PIGEONS."
CHUCK	The Triple A says that gas will be plentiful this Labor Day weekend. But even so . . . the odd-even gas rationing plan will be in effect in the metropolitan area.
	Odd-even will be suspended tomorrow . . . however . . . as it is in every month with 31-days.
	But . . . Governor Carey . . . here on News Center 4 this week . . . said that most probably . . . he'll move to end the rationing plan sometime after Labor day.
3RD COMMERCIAL BREAK	COMMERCIALS
MARV ALBERT	(SPORTS REPORT INCORPORATING FILM AND TAPE)
CLIFF MORRISON	(WEATHER REPORT)
CHUCK	A masked man loses in court . . . when we come back
4TH COMMERCIAL BREAK	COMMERCIAL 1:00
CHUCK	When I was growing up and television came to my town . . . it wasn't long before I had a video hero.
	The Lone Ranger.
VO EJ	(EJ VO)
RUNS :14	So it pains me to tell you that a court has done to my childhood hero what no bad guy was ever able to do.
	Ordered him to take off his mask.
	If you've been following this story, you know a movie company that owns the rights to the character of the Lone Ranger doesn't want my Lone Ranger, Clayton Moore, to be the Lone Ranger any more.
CHUCK	That movie company won in court today.
	Moore . . . true to the ranger's creed . . . vowed to fight on.
SILLS SC	The New York City Opera opened its season at Lincoln Center tonite . . . and it was a debut for Beverly Sills.
	This is the first season for the well-known soprano as General Director of the Opera Company:

VO EJ RUNS: MAX THEN TRACK UP FROM :10- 29 SUPER: TONITE LINCOLN CTR AT TOP SILLS AT :11 TAPE KEEPS ROLLING AFTER SOUND BITE!	(TO VO EJ) The opening presentation is Naughty Marietta and among the first nighters tonite was Shirly Silverman, Ms. Sills' mother . . . who confessed to some nervousness. But not so Ms. Sills herself: (TRACK UP) OUT:
EJ ROLLING VO TAG MUSIC ON TRACT 2 UNDER THEN UP OUT ON TIME AT :47	(VO tag) Ms. Sills was backstage until minutes before curtain. Her innovations tonite include microphones to amplify on-stage dialogue. The singing will not be amplified. People . . . and nature . . . often have a way of bringing hope back to a scene of devastation. Mary Alice Williams is back from a largely burned out section of the Bronx. Mary Alice . . .
BRONX GARDEN TOP MARY ALICE	The people on Baretto Street planted the seeds of an idea to reclaim their decaying neighborhood. It took a lot of ambition, but they weeded through enough bureaucracy to get a government grant for the project. Tonight was the harvest:
EJ/SOT RUNS 1:01 SUPER: BARETTO STREET :02 SPER: HARRY DODSON :34 OUTCUE: "DID YOU PLANT OR DID YOU HARVEST?" (SHRUGS) "YES."	(TO EJ/SOT)
MARY ALICE	Baretto Street is not an isolated case. The same tenacious group has launched 14 other victory gardens in vacant lots. And when they're done with that, they say they'll try to reclaim vacant buildings, too.
CHUCK	That's the news. Join Pia Lindstrom and Melba Tolliver for the early edition of News Center 4 tomorrow afternoon at five. Jack Cafferty and I will be at the newsdesk an hour later at six. And I'll be back at eleven. I'm Chuck Scarborough. Thanks for joining us . . . Have a good night.
5TH COMMERCIAL BREAK	COMMERCIAL 2:00

QUESTIONS AND PROJECTS

1. Prepare a five-minute newscast using the stories from your daily newspaper. Describe your pattern of organization (topical; geographical; local, national, international) and briefly outline one other pattern you might have used.
2. Evaluate the headlines of a number of newscasts with the following questions in mind:
   (a) Do they tell too much?
   (b) Do they arouse interest?
   (c) Are they repeated without variation in the body of the newscast?
3. Evaluate the transitions in a newscast to determine whether they are clear, forced, or natural.
4. Select a number of stories from the newspapers and rewrite them for the ear, keeping within a 20-second limit for each story.
5. Arrange for the taping of a radio and a TV newscast presented at the same period. Compare these programs in terms of the number of news items covered and the way they are treated. How does television's need to be showing something instead of just telling about it account for some of these differences?
6. Listen to a number of newscasts to determine the various ways in which they deal with the problem of attributing sources. Are the sources clear or vague?

The coverage of sports through the broadcasting of news, features, and play-by-play descriptions is an important part of radio and television programming. The sports area in major stations and networks usually is assigned to a separate unit in the broadcast organization where it is handled by specialists in the field. In smaller operations, people in the news department cover all the news events including those in the sports world. For many years sports broadcasting was almost entirely a male activity; females were considered unfit because of their presumed lack of sports interest and knowledge. Enterprising women have now broken down that barrier and a number of them are enjoying careers as on-the-air sports personalities and writers.

C H A P T E R
8
SPORTS AND SPECIAL EVENTS

Perhaps it is the fate of every modern sports hero to be judged by his Nielsen points.
PETE AXTHELM

SPORT NEWS

Much of what we have already said about writing newscasts applies also to writing sportscasts. The sources are similar—among them teletype information, beeper reports, and ENG transmissions—and sportswriters need many of the same qualities required of newswriters. They must be accurate in their reports and in most situations must present them without bias or favoritism, though it is natural for them to concentrate on the fortunes or misfortunes of the home team.

They must be ingenious in making use of material that will sharpen interest—interviews with sports figures, audio or video coverage of sports events, and special features such as predictions of sports results. They should employ a brief, direct approach that carries the characteristics of oral communication over into the script.

Dave Cohen, who writes material for such sportscasters as Bob Costas and Jim McKay, and has had on-the-air experience as a television sports anchor, stresses the importance of writing sports copy in a conversational style. He starts by telling the story out loud. If it sounds conversational—the way he would tell it to a friend—then, and only then, does he transcribe it to paper. He never works the other way around—writing the story and then reading it aloud. He feels that if he wrote it first and then read it, he would be speaking the written form of the language.

The following introductions to excerpts from a taped interview conducted by Bob Costas illustrates Cohen's crisp, conversational style. The interview was one in a radio series featuring well-known sports personalities. The line following the "IN" contains the words that open a particular excerpt from the interview; the line following the "OUT" contains the words that close it. The numbers provide timing information.

APRIL 25 RICK MONDAY STOPS FLAG BURNERS

I'm Bob Costas with the Inside Sports Magazine.

1976 was America's bicentennial and there's never been a year when Old Glory's been displayed more often and more proudly. When two men ran onto the field at Dodger Stadium attempting to burn the American flag, Rick Monday came to the rescue and he became a national hero. We'll talk with him about that incident right after this.

[Commercial]

1976 would become the most productive year of Rick Monday's 19 year career. Playing for the Cubs, he had career highs in homers 32; RBI's 77; runs 107; while batting 272. But his greatest moment that season came on April 25. Standing in center field at Dodger Stadium, Monday watched two men run on the field, place an American flag on the grass and begin dousing it with lighter fluid.

IN: [389] I started running toward them
OUT: angered by it [45]

Monday became a national hero and every group, it seemed, wanted to honor him.

IN: [398] And every ballpark we went to
OUT: in front of him [35]

Rick Monday, now a baseball broadcaster. I'm Bob Costas. Join me again tomorrow for another edition of the Inside Sports Magazine.

Another requirement for sportscasters is that they write well under the pressure of time. Often games are still being played even while the broadcast is on the air. Sportscasters must be able to incorporate the latest developments into their presentations with split-second speed, for audiences want to know what the situation is at the moment.

Besides possessing the skills required for effective news writing, sportswriters need some special attributes. Though people may weep when their favorite teams lose or shout in exultation when they win, sports events are, nevertheless, not quite so significant in their impact as most news events. This fact is reflected in the tone of sports coverage. As part of the entertainment world, sports is usually treated in a lighter, more colloquial way than most news events. One can note this difference in style by comparing a news magazine like *Time* with its sibling *Sports Illustrated*. In addition to a grasp of this special style, the ability to leaven the report with humor is another valuable attribute which one finds in the writing of many leading sportscasters.

An item from a sports report written and presented by Paul Greenberg on WINS Radio, New York, illustrates the particular flavor characterizing many newscasts. Its style is less formal than that of the usual straight news item and it reflects the feeling and opinion of the presenter more than most newscasts would. It also has the attributes of crispness and directness.

Paul Greenberg
WINS-RADIO

THE BOYS OF SUMMER HAVE BEEN PLAYING LIKE A BUNCH OF OLD MEN . . . AND NOW THEY'RE PAYING THE PRICE. THE METS WAKE UP THIS MORNING TO FIND THEMSELVES

10 & 1/2 GAMES OUT BEHIND PITTSBURGH IN THE NATIONAL LEAGUE EAST, AND
THEY'RE NOW JUST ONE GAME ABOVE .500. TONIGHT THEY'RE HOPING FOR A CHANGE
OF PACE AGAINST A GREEN PITCHER . . . THE CARDS GIVE REAL CORMIER HIS MAJOR
LEAGUE DEBUT. WALLY WHITEHURST TRIES TO SNAP THE METS SIX-GAME LOSING
STREAK WHEN HE TAKES THE MOUND FOR NEW YORK, BUT IT MAY BE DIFFICULT. HE'S
ALLOWED 13 HITS OVER THE PAST 20-PLUS INNINGS.

Another essential for sportswriters is a thorough knowledge of various sports—particularly the major ones like baseball, football, basketball, and hockey—and a command of the jargon or special terms connected with them. Sportwriters must know what the following terms mean and the sports events to which they refer: blindside, RBI's, blue line, three-on-one, fair catch, trapped, top of the key, hang time, crease, three-second violation, audible, offside. This is just a sampling of a vast array of terms that every sportscaster should know. The use of sports jargon can be carried too far, of course. When George Allen described a play by the Los Angeles Rams football team for a national TV audience in the following manner: "The corners were in tight, Haden read the dog, audibilized, stepped out of the cup, and dumped off to the short man," he was probably intelligible only to former football players, and perhaps not to all of them.

Sports events are covered regularly by stations and networks either in segments in news periods, in separate programs, or as part of the overall news coverage. The major element in a sports news program is a report of the results of the day's sports events. Besides the scores, this coverage may include a description or video coverage of the key plays, information about the effects of the win or loss on the team's standing in the conference, and notes on significant injuries. Sports programs also cover other late developments, such as the firing and hiring of coaches, player trades, franchise moves, and sports awards. In addition to giving straight news, sports programs often include commentaries and features prepared ahead of time which may present interviews with sports personalities, anecdotes, and special coverage.

In organizing a sports news program, you should follow the principles applying to the news broadcast. If you ask yourself what the audience wants to know first, as you should, you will almost always conclude that it is the scores of the most recent games by the home teams. Only when a sensational development, such as the unexpected firing of a coach or a far-reaching player trade, has taken place would the latest scores receive anything but first place in the broadcast. You then move to the less important events, remembering to group items in a logical way so that you do not jump back and forth haphazardly from sport to sport. Though you put the most interesting news at the beginning, you should not permit your broadcast to run downhill. You can prevent that by saving coverage of intriguing sidelights and special features for later in the program.

SPORTS FEATURES

Sports programs, in addition to reporting the latest developments in the sports world, often include special features. Sometimes they stand on their own or are inserted into play-by-play broadcasts. Sports features take a variety of forms and deal with many different types of subject matter. Among the topics that may be covered are a notable event in past sports history, a profile of a current sports figure, predictions of football scores, reflections on recently concluded games, the greatest plays of the week or month, or unusual sports ventures.

A familiar figure on ABC's coverage of sport events is Jack Whitaker, a veteran sportscaster. One of the contributions he has made is to appear during breaks in the action to present a brief commentary that brings into focus some intriguing aspects of the event. In many instances these short features are delivered without supporting visualization; Whitaker simply stands before the camera and presents his thoughts in a direct, unvarnished way. The following example, presented during the 1991 coverage of the Kentucky Derby, illustrates his style and the nature of his subjects.

Sports Feature: Jack Whitaker
Kentucky Derby, 1991

The Kentucky Derby came into this world dripping in Americana. This sport of kings, inherited from the British, was going to have an American accent if it took another war, and with the arrival of Colonel Matt Wynn at Churchill Downs, the marvelous strains of county fair, Chautauqua, and circus all came together in this river town that is neither north nor south, east nor west. It's merely America.

Because it is so essentially American, it has attracted all types of Americans. The slick and the sleazy, the minks and the tanktops, the diamonds and the tattoos. Over the years it has become a measurement of who America's heroes are. Whoever the nation's celebrities were at the time, some of them showed up in Louisville in Derby week. Politicians and Hollywood stars, rock-and-roll entertainers and presidents have all made the trip down the Ohio River on the first Saturday in May.

This year, the winning celebrity by far is General Norman Schwarzkopf, fresh from a winter spent in the desert. He has been the number one topic aside from the race itself and was the marshal of Thursday night's Pegasus parade. And isn't that another piece of Americana. Where a grateful nation of England bestowed a spacious home in the middle of London on the Duke of Wellington for cornering the mad dog of Europe, we invite the man who curbed Saddam Hussein to be the marshal of a parade. It could only happen in America.

We mentioned earlier that sports broadcasting is often marked by a humorous approach not characteristic of regular news broadcasting. This quality is most often found in sports features. Al Ackerman, formerly a TV sportscaster for WDIV in Detroit, was even willing to make fun of himself when the situation called for it. That happened most often when he forecast the results of key college and professional football games. Because he made a practice of predicting upsets in a number of contests, he led a precarious life as a forecaster. When he was doing well, he called his predictions "Ackerman's Accurate Assessments." When his average dropped, he referred to them as "Ackerman's Abysmal Assessments." One of his successors at WDIV, Bernie Smilovitz, also presents broadcasts tinged with humor. This is particularly true of a feature he presents once a week, "Bernie's Bloopers," which presents excerpts showing hilarious mishaps and misplays from the taped coverage of whatever sports happen to be in season.

A sportswriter and broadcaster whose work is marked by gentle humor and unusual insights is Bill Geist, who regularly presents sports features on *CBS Sunday Morning*. Illustrative of his sometimes quirky approach is the sport he chose to discuss during one of the programs. Although played by millions of Americans, it is rarely covered by the nation's sportscast-ers. The sport is shuffleboard. The segment began with a brief ad-libbed chat between Geist and the program's host, Charles Kuralt, about the "cut-throat, breakneck, famously physical" game of shuffleboard. The feature followed.

SHUFFLEBOARD

VIDEO	AUDIO
CLUB EXTERIOR AND CLUB SIGN	GEIST (VO SOUND-ON-TAPE [SOT]): Welcome to St. Petersburg, Florida, the Mecca of shuffleboard, and home to the nation's oldest and largest shuffle-board club—a shrine of the game.
GEIST (ON CAMERA [OC]) COURTSIDE	GEIST (SOT): More than 200 players from trailer parks, retirement communi-ties, and shuffleboard clubs through-out the state gathered here last week for the Florida State Shuffle-board tournament, which determines the best shufflers in Florida—and therefore the world.
SHUFFLERS CONGREGATING, CHATTING, SHOTS OF CLUB LOGO, E.G., "LINIMENT LEAGUE"	
CLEANING COURTS, DUSTING WITH GLASS	GEIST (VO): Courts for such an important tournament are carefully groomed and lightly dusted with ground glass to make the discs slide true. Elabo-rate opening ceremonies feature a salute to the colors.
OPENING CEREMONIES	
	MUSIC: NATIONAL ANTHEM

| | PRAYER: [OPENS] . . . Thanks for this group to play our game of shuffleboard [CUT TO] . . . Help us refrain from using Your name in vain when we make a bad shot. |

HORDES PLAYING
SHUFFLEBOARD

GEIST (VO): It has to be three grueling days of 9 A.M. to 6 P.M. shuffleboard action on 60 courts to determine Florida's best.

LEW, GORDON, AND
GLEN
HALL OF FAME

The field of professionals . . . Oh, yes! there are professional shuffleboard players. Included are such greats of the game as Lew Tansky and Len Worden, both in the national Shuffleboard Hall of Fame . . . Oh, yes! there is a Shuffleboard Hall of Fame . . . Not to mention such young sensations as Glen Peltier, just 54 years old, if you can believe it—last year's champion.

VARIOUS SHOTS

All with their own unique styles. Players range in age from a 47-year-old rookie to a 97-year-old veteran. You need not be old to play serious shuffleboard, but you must be retired, as all the tournaments are held during the week.

PEOPLE PLAYING SHUFFLEBOARD
SCORES
KITCHEN
REFEREE ON HANDS
AND KNEES

For those who play once a year or once in a lifetime at a motel it seems a simple game. Scoring a ten . . . an eight . . . a seven . . . or ten off! . . . if you land here in the kitchen. On the line, of course, doesn't count.

KNOCK OFF DISC

Oh, it's simple enough to score in shuffleboard, but the next moment you're out looking for your disc in the parking lot.

The feature continued with demonstrations of various shots, interviews with players, and scenes from a shuffleboard match.

Andrea Joyce is often assigned to cover sports events by CBS. She was on the scene, for example, during the 1991 U.S. Open Tennis Tournament to present live interviews from the courts and to prepare and present features on key players.

She put together the feature that follows while the 1991 U.S. Tennis Open was going on. Her script began with continuity scribbled on a yellow pad. She then wove into the pattern other ingredients such as taped sound bites from Jimmy Connors, segments by Bud Collins (who provided commentary and analysis during the coverage), shots of tennis fans, and scenes of the action.

Andrea Joyce: Feature on Jimmy Connors
U.S. Tennis Open, 1991

VIDEO	*AUDIO*
ON CAMERA	JOYCE: Jimmy Connors is the U.S. Open's longest running act—21 years of gutsy dramatic moments.
COLLINS	(SOT—SOUND-ON-TAPE) REACTIONS TO CONNORS
FANS	
TIM GULLICKSON	
SCENES FROM FRENCH OPEN '91	(SOT) CROWD REACTIONS
ON CAMERA	JOYCE: Back in June . . . age betrayed Connors in a third-round match at the French Open against Michael Chang . . . when he was forced to retire in the fifth set. But last night . . . Connors turned back the clock.
DANA (UMPIRE)	(SOT) "Hardest crowd to control . . . "
CONNORS	(SOT) "When I play . . . then that's great."
COLLINS	(SOT) " . . . Wouldn't be surprised if he played 'til 45.
CONNORS WAVING RACKET	(SOT) CROWD REACTION
ON CAMERA	JOYCE: On just Day Three . . . Connors is the star of the show . . . and everybody knows it . . . including his next round opponent.
MICHAEL SHAPERS NEXT OPPONENT	(SOT) "This is his stage . . . He's an actor.
ON CAMERA	JOYCE: Stick around, folks. Last night was just Act One.

CONNORS AFTER	(SOT) CROWD REACTION
VICTORY UNDERNEATH	
STADIUM COURT	
WALKING OFF ADRENALIN HIGH	CONNOR'S COMMENTS
TALKING TO CAMERA	

SPORTS-EVENT COVERAGE

Most of the coverage of a sports event is ad-libbed by announcers who describe what they see happening before them. This description obviously can't be written out ahead of time, but in putting words together on the air, announcers are engaging in a writing function. That is why we cover play-by-play description in this book on writing.

In many instances on-the-spot description is complemented by background material which must be prepared ahead of time. Most announcers do this themselves, but they may be helped by writers in compiling this background information. Its nature depends on the event being covered. If it is a college football game, the announcer needs information about such items as the competing schools, the history of the competition between them, the significance of the contest in the conference race, and the players. This information is available in publicity material which the competing schools make available to all broadcasting organizations covering the game. It contains many more facts than can possibly be used. The task of the writer is to abstract the most pertinent and interesting items and set them up so that the announcer can easily refer to them during the broadcast.

Bill Flemming for many years broadcast play-by-play descriptions of football games for the ABC television network, as well as serving in many other sports programming areas. In preparing for football games, he constructs a chart composed of squares containing statistical and background information about the players on the offensive

and defensive teams of each school. He tacks the charts for each school on small boards, putting the offensive chart for a given school on one side, the defensive chart on the other. When the ball changes hands, Flemming has only to flip the two boards over to have information about the incoming players immediately available to him. Each square on the chart contains the following information: the player's number, his name, his position, his height, his weight, his year in school, other points of interest. Information about players who participated in a game broadcast by Flemming between teams of the University of Michigan and Northwestern University, illustrates the type of material appearing on the charts.

83 . . . Rocky Rosema . . . End . . . 6'2" . . . 214 . . . Junior. Grand Rapids, Mich. Early Mono . . . just getting back.

18 . . . Rick Sygar . . . Back . . . 5'11" . . . 185 . . . Senior Niles, Ohio . . . Second baseman, baseball team . . . P.A.T.'s—18 of 19, 1965, 26 of 26, 1966. Broke leg twice as a soph.

19 . . . Carl Ward . . . Back . . . 5'9" . . . 178 . . . Senior Cincinnati, Ohio . . . Started every game since soph. year. 48 yd. run in Rose Bowl high-point of football career.

33 . . . Dave Fisher . . . F.B. . . . 5'10" . . . 210 . . . Senior Ketterling, Ohio . . . B + student in Arch. and Design. Won "golden helmet" for combined abilities. High School All-American. Total loss—12 yards in two years.

Howard Kellman, who does play-by-play for the Indianapolis Indians, an American Association baseball team, spends two-and-a-half hours before each game listing statistics and other information for use during the broadcast. One item he always draws up is a statistical chart for each player. It contains his current batting average, of course, but it also contains many other facts—how he has hit against the opposing team, for example, or his record against the particular pitcher he will face. In addition to preparing this material, Kellman also spends an hour-and-a-half before the game talking with the players and managers of both teams. These interviews often provide insights that enhance his ability to explain what happens later on the field. During this period he also records an interview with a player, manager, or person associated with the game. This segment then becomes part of the broadcast.

Kellman believes that statistics and background facts should not be forced in gratuitously or obviously, but used only when the need naturally arises. When a player comes to bat the first time, listeners want to know what his batting average is, for example; when he returns to the plate as the game goes on, they need to be reminded of what he has done in his previous times at bat. Information like this must always be ready for use. To keep track of what happens during the game, Kellman maintains a chart for both teams. A diagram of the field showing the players assigned to each defensive position occupies one section. Another section lists the pitcher or pitchers and has spaces for numbers showing the innings pitched, hits, runs, bases on balls, and strikeouts. Below it there is a place for recording the game totals: the number of runs, hits, errors, and men left on base for each team, the name of the winning and losing pitchers, the name of the pitcher who registered a save (if any), the time of the game, and the attendance. The bottom part of the chart shows the batting lineup. Symbols are used to record the action as the game progresses. The line for one player at the end of the game might look like this:

RBI	Line up	Pos	1	2	3	4	5	6	7	8	9
28	Rey Sanchez	SS	BB		4-3			2 b 1 rbi 1 run			K

Figure 8-1

To simplify scoring, the defensive positions are assigned numbers: pitcher—1; catcher—2; first base—3; second base—4; third base—5; shortstop—6; left field—7; center field—8; right field—9. The symbol for a base on balls is BB; for strikeout—K; and hits are designated 1b, 2b, 3b, HR. This chart shows that Sanchez began the game with 28 runs batted in; received a base on balls in the first inning, was out second base to first in the third, hit for two bases in the sixth, batted in a run and scored a run, and struck out in the ninth.

An opportunity to use a number of the facts the announcer has on hand may not arise, but when the occasion does develop, they often provide pertinent information or add a human-interest element.

Ernie Harwell, whose excellence as a play-by-play announcer for the Detroit Tigers has earned him a place in baseball's Hall of Fame, is a master at inserting background information in so natural a way that it seems to arise spontaneously from the situation. When Cecil Fielder hit two home runs during a game, Harwell added in an almost casual way that this was the eighth time in his career that Fielder had hit more than one home run in a single game. The need for such information was not likely to arise, but when it did, Harwell was ready.

Tom Hemingway, who has broadcast radio coverage of football and basketball games for both commercial and public stations, prepares a chart similar to that of Flemming. In addition, he puts other information on three-by-five cards which he takes into the broadcast booth. He finds, however, that going through the process of abstracting the information from the material available to him and writing it down imprints it on his mind to the extent that he usually does not have to refer to the cards while the game is in progress. This means that he can insert background facts into his description in a more natural way than would be possible if he had to read them.

For many years Frank Gifford was the member of the ABC broadcasting trio who provided play-by-play description for the *Monday Night Football* broadcasts. He spoke with authority, for he was once a star running back for the New York Giants. He augmented his personal knowledge of the game by gathering extensive information about all the participants in the week before the game. He watched films, made telephone calls to ask about lineups, injuries, and the players who were performing particularly well. He gathered further information when he arrived at the game site. By the time the kickoff came, he was ready.

Gifford's successor as the play-by-play announcer on Monday nights is Al Michaels, who also served in the same capacity when ABC was broadcasting baseball. In covering Monday night football, he leaves most of the commentary to his associates in the booth, Frank Gifford and Dan Dierdorf, and concentrates on describing the action. Among the facts he gives are the nature of the play, the names of the ball carrier, tacklers, passer, receiver, safety men as they apply, the yards gained or lost, and a description of any penalties. Before the next play begins,

he mentions the number of the down, the yards needed for a first down, and, when it becomes a factor, the time left in the game.

Michaels had a unique experience while he was broadcasting a 1989 World Series baseball game between the San Francisco Giants and the Oakland Athletics from Candlestick Park just south of San Francisco. As the broadcast was getting under way, the stadium began shaking. When the tremors stopped, Michaels realized that he would not be broadcasting a baseball game that evening but rather the results of a devastating earthquake, an event he had not planned to cover. The skill he had developed in the ad-lib coverage of sports contests served him well as he reacted quickly to this totally unexpected situation. He described what he himself observed with great vividness and efficiently summarized other reports as they came flowing in to him. His performance earned him plaudits from around the nation.

Coming back to the somewhat more mundane task of reporting athletic events, we should note that various sports confront broadcasters with somewhat different types of challenges. Basketball, Tom Hemingway says, is easier to follow than football because it involves fewer players and no changes from offensive to defensive personnel. He characterizes the broadcasting of baseball as both easier and more difficult than broadcasting football; easier because the action is simpler to follow, more difficult because there are long pauses in the action which must be filled with chatter. Hemingway calls hockey the most challenging of all games to describe because of the constant and unobtrusive switching of players and the problem of following a tiny, swiftly moving puck. Someone has said that hockey is a game in which critical action always seems imminent but seldom actually develops, a condition that makes a balanced presentation harder to maintain than it is for other sports.

Are there differences in the way you describe a game on radio and on television? It would seem that because TV viewers can see what is happening and radio listeners can't, your techniques would change radically when you move from one medium to the other. That is true to a certain extent, but the contrast between the two approaches is not as great as you might expect. The major difference is that sports coverage on television is somewhat more interpretive and less descriptive than it is on radio. You do not give TV viewers extended delineations of what they can see for themselves. Still, you must remember that the TV audience's view of the action is more restricted than yours. A TV viewer also loses track of downs and the count of balls and strikes. To sum up then, your report on TV should be somewhat different from the one you would make on radio, but it should not be greatly different.

For most on-the-scene coverage, writers prepare rundowns that guide the presentation. These include stock openings and closings and indicate the number of commercials and the breaks in the action when they should be inserted. This rundown constitutes a framework within which the announcers who describe the action and provide color and interpretation develop their own on-the-air, ad-libbed continuity.

SPECIAL EVENTS

Covering special events presents problems similar to those involved in covering sports events, and much of what we have said about preparing for sports coverage applies also to special-events coverage. It is worth noting, however, that getting ready to cover sports is often easier than preparing for a special event because sports contests usually follow predictable lines, unless, of course, an earthquake intervenes, whereas the precise development of a special event is often difficult to foretell. The launching of space missions, for example, has often been marked by long and unexpected delays during which the announcers must continue the broadcast. It is obvious that extensive material must be ready for such eventualities. The information a writer prepares may be supplemented with special demonstrations and exhibits made ready for use in case there is a halt in the proceedings.

An event presents special problems when it includes a group of happenings so similar to one another that describing each one would become ridiculous. For example, a parade, particularly when it features not much more than marching soldiers, puts even the most eloquent of announcers to the severest of tests. Needed are background facts to leaven the running account of the event. A procession, such as the Mummers Parade in Philadelphia and the Tournament of Roses Parade in Pasadena, California, is more varied than the usual military parade, but information must still be compiled for those describing it.

Let us consider some of the items a writer might assemble for announcers assigned to these events. First in order is to prepare information about the units making up the parade; in the case of bands the identity of the leader, the number of marchers, and special distinctions would be listed. Ed McMahon told television viewers watching the Thanksgiving Day Parade in New York that in the city of Bristol, Virginia, no battery was safe. The reason was that the Bristol High School Band, just coming into view as he spoke, had collected and sold old batteries to finance the trip to New York. He concluded this segment by saying that there wasn't "a dead battery in the entire group." This material and much more like it was prepared for McMahon by writers. Information compiled by writers also can be used to guide the art department in making title cards to be superimposed over the various units for identification purposes.

Other notes of a miscellaneous nature add to the enjoyment of the audience. To cite some examples: TV viewers of the Mummers Parade were told that a local bridal shop in Philadelphia had been bought out by men participating in a marching exhibit satirizing the marriage of a president's daughter; the audience to a Tournament of Roses Parade found out that it was viewing the 46th appearance of the Salvation Army Band but the first appearance in that parade of a Navy Band; the racing car in one float, it was made known, had actually been used in the previous Indianapolis 500-mile race; data on the number and nature of the flowers making up the various floats in the Tournament of Roses Parade was included in the information provided the announcers—one float contained 500,000 individual blossoms, another 15,000 orchids, a third 28 varieties of roses. We might note that the work of writers in preparing background information for these parades is so important to the success of the broadcasts that the writers are identified in the credits at the end of the program.

Political events require the writer to assemble facts about the people involved, the background of the event, and its possible future consequences. In other instances, the writer must try to assemble the information that will be most interesting and relevant. In preparing for any special event or sports broadcast, forethought is of the utmost importance. Writers must be certain to gather enough material to permit the announcer to make a continuous running commentary. At the same time, they must recognize that much of what they go to great pains to provide probably will not be used. In this respect they keep company with the writer who prepares extensive notes for a symphony concert that ordinarily starts late, only to have the conductor raise the baton on time.

QUESTIONS AND PROJECTS

1. Watch a TV news program which includes a sports segment. Do the styles of the newscaster and the sportscaster differ and, if so, in what way?
2. Do you believe that sports news should be classified as information or as entertainment?
3. Assume that you have been assigned to prepare material on your football team for a broadcaster from a visiting school. Prepare information on six of the players who are most likely to be involved in the action.
4. Turn down the audio of a football telecast and record your own play-by-play description. Evaluate your performance in terms of the essential information you provide the listener.
5. Prepare continuity to open and close the broadcast of a special event soon to take place in your community.

The main concern of this book is the writing of scripts–the material that either forms the essential substance of a program or stands as a unit in a program that includes other segments. In addition to scripts, writers in broadcasting are often called on to prepare continuities that serve to introduce the selections played on a music program or to provide linkage on a program featuring a variety of entertainment forms. In such programs the continuity plays a subsidiary role: it reinforces or enhances the effect of the other elements, existing to make them clearer and more appealing rather than being important in its own right.

MUSIC, VARIETY, AND GAME SHOWS

Americans, with their millions of television and radio sets, apparently stand most in fear of a moment of silence.
GIRAUD CHESTER

MUSIC PROGRAMS

The most common type of program for which writers prepare continuity is the music program. As radio developed through its first three decades, music became a staple element on the broadcasting menu. In television the program consisting mainly of music is much rarer than it is on radio. There are, however, some outstanding examples of television shows devoted almost entirely to music. One was *The Lawrence Welk Show*, a program scorned by most young people but watched regularly by many adults. After its network run, it continued as a syndicated program and enjoyed further exposure as an offering of public television stations.

Few programs of this type are now presented by the regular networks, but cable movie channels, such as HBO (Home Box Office) and Showtime, occasionally present popular music concerts. The Boston Pops Orchestra has been a feature on the PBS network for 22 years. On the classical side, PBS and cable networks such as Bravo and Arts and Entertainment (A & E) regularly present operas, symphony concerts, and classical soloists.

The television industry has not neglected the musical interests of young people. A program that entertained an entire generation of teenagers with the latest popular music was *American Bandstand*, presided over for many years by Dick Clark. Since 1980 the cable network MTV (Music Television) has attracted the millions of people who enjoy rock music with its video interpretations of the latest hits. We shall have more to say about its offerings later in this chapter.

Music in the Radio Era

As radio began, the presentation of music quickly became one of the most common types of entertainment. The offerings ranged through a wide variety of musical types from the popular to the classical. An example of a popular music program was *Your Hit Parade*, a series, beginning in the middle 1930s, that played the songs shown by weekly surveys to be the ones most people wanted to hear. This series made a transition into television and lasted until a change in contemporary music tastes brought it to an end. Another type of program often heard in the radio era was a daily 15-minute presentation by a leading singer; among the personalities who were heard on this kind of program for many years were Bing Crosby and Perry Como. Daily programs by the big bands of the era were also common; the orchestras of Glenn Miller and

Benny Goodman were among those featured in such series.

Offerings were by no means limited to popular music, however. Religious music, familiar old-time favorites, light-classical selections, and symphonies and operas were among the types of music presented. From the beginning of the 1930s, for instance, people around the nation could hear the Saturday matinees of the Metropolitan Opera Company and Sunday concerts by the New York Philharmonic Orchestra. Operatic stars of the period often appeared in regular series and special programs to present music ranging from operatic arias to current hits. The Metropolitan Opera baritone Lawrence Tibbet sang popular music for a time on *Your Hit Parade*, and John Charles Thomas, another operatic luminary of the period, presented a weekly program largely made up of traditional and old-time songs.

The music for most of these programs was introduced by announcers who read from continuities prepared by a corps of writers employed by the networks and some of the large stations. Their work varied from the straightforward commentary that introduced numbers in a direct, simple way to those that provided the framework for an elaborate "idea" show. One idea show fondly remembered by some is *The Chamber Music Society of Lower Basin Street*, a program of popular music whose continuity adopted the dignified, stately style used in introducing classical music and even employed Milton Cross, famous for his announcing of symphony and opera programs, to read it. Virtually the only music programs not introduced from a written script were occasional late-night presentations from major hotels where the resident orchestras provided the music and announcers ad-libbed the introductions.

Radio in the TV Era

With the development of television after World War II, radio programming under-

went a drastic change. Programs with a definite, recognizable identity have given way to long stretches of music, often selected according to a specific station format, and introduced by an announcer, familiarly known as a disc jockey or "deejay," who ad-libs comments. Newscasts at regular intervals provide an occasional break from the music and commercials. There is a wide range in the nature of these offerings. Some stations, particularly those with a beautiful music format, play selections on a virtually continuous basis without giving them specific introductions. In others, the music plays a subsidiary role and the spotlight may rest on a number of other elements, among them the chatter of the disc jockey, call-ins, interviews, weather, sports, and Wall Street reports.

There were a number of reasons for this change. The principal one was the development of television, which took over the function of presenting specific, recognizable program units. The radio networks stopped presenting music programs, limiting themselves to news, feature talks, and the occasional coverage of special events. The number of radio stations sharply increased, a development that, with the competition of television, gave them a share of the market so small they could not support writing staffs. The disappearance of written music continuity also resulted, to a degree, from a change in the nature of popular music, especially that directed at young people. Prior to World War II the ideas communicated by popular songs tended to be simple and obvious. Some would describe them as clichés. Beginning in the late 1950s the themes of popular music became much more provocative than they had ever been before. Songwriters and singers such as the Beatles and Bob Dylan spoke through their music directly to the young people who were their principal audiences. The ideas that in previous years may have been presented in continuity now came through in the music and lyrics of the songs. Audiences wanted to concentrate on listening to the music, not the continuity introducing it.

Radio Station Formats   In radio, music is now most often selected in accordance with an entire station approach rather than in response to a specific program idea. Names for many of these formats have become standard in the industry, though the situation is a fluid one in which new patterns constantly emerge with new names to describe them. The term "contemporary," for example, is usually applied to music appealing primarily to teen-agers. Recently a modification of that format, called "adult contemporary," has appeared. The fierce competition among radio stations for listeners prompts most of these changes. To increase their share of the audience, stations constantly experiment with various approaches, and in a fairly brief period may adopt and then discard a number of different formats, or develop an entirely new format of their own.

In thinking about format names, one must also realize that a number of them are not easy to define in readily understandable terms. All but popular music specialists may have a difficult time distinguishing between "progressive rock" and "rock," for instance. The music designated by the various format titles also undergoes subtle changes as the years go by. The Middle-Of-the-Road (MOR) music of years past is not the same as it is today, for example.

The following is a listing of some standard terms used to describe the formats of stations which specialize in the presentation of musical entertainment. Some stations, of course, have other specialties like news, talk, or religion, and others employ an ethnic designation, such as Hispanic. A number of stations combine formats, such as those listed here, into a mixed pattern:

Jazz	Gospel
Rock	Golden Oldies
–*Mellow*	Classical
–*AOR (Album-Oriented Rock)*	
–*Progressive*	
Beautiful Music	Easy Listening

Disc jockeys, in making ad-libbed introductions to music, are carrying out what we have described in earlier chapters as an "oral writing" function. Their freedom to operate varies greatly from station to station. In some instances, they must follow a rigid formula that prescribes the selections to be played, the order in which one type of music follows another, and even dictates what they can say and how long they can spend saying it. In other instances, they may have to choose music of a particular type but are free to make personal selections and to determine the order in which they will be heard. In rare instances, they may even choose whatever records they wish to play.

If you are employed as a disc jockey, obviously you must conform to the station's program formula. You must use language that fits the particular type of music you play. Each type tends to develop its own particular jargon. In many situations it is likely that your work will be evaluated, not only by the station's program department, but also by an outside consulting agency which may have helped the station set up its program format. Your preparation for your air appearances can vary from the intense to the casual. Some deejays spend far more time preparing for a broadcast than they spend on the air, contriving ways of introducing music that will avoid repetitive language and clichés and assembling material to provide the substance for comments and quips. Others sit down before the microphone with only a list of the selections they plan to play in front of them, depending for their comments on the inspiration of the moment. Some may even wait until air time to choose their records, pulling them from the stacks while other music is playing. Some of these "inspiration-of-the-moment" disc jockeys do very well. Until you have had a good deal of experience, however, and can be sure that your wit will not let you down at a critical moment, you will be wise to follow the first pattern. Prepare for every appearance and prepare as well as you can.

Developing Programs Though specific radio programs have been largely replaced by overall station formats, they have not entirely disappeared. Some major commercial stations and a number of public radio stations still present music programs built around carefully constructed ideas. The continuities may be ad-libbed from notes or be scripted and read word for word by announcers.

Just as the freedom of disc jockeys to create their own formats varies greatly from station to station, so does the freedom of writers assigned to write continuity for a particular program. The concerts of leading symphony orchestras, which in radio's heyday were presented live by national networks, are now recorded as they are presented and are broadcast later by classical music commercial stations and by public radio stations. Writers preparing program notes for these concerts play no role in planning the program whatsoever but are merely given a list of the selections in the order they are to be played, and are required simply to write the material that will introduce those selections. At the other extreme, writers in some situations may be given the entire responsibility of developing a music show to be presented from recordings. In such instances, they have full authority to create the theme of the show and to select the music to illustrate it.

Approaches and Ideas Writers who have the responsibility for planning a music program may choose between two approaches.

They may create a straight program that is developed around no particular theme or idea but aims only for some uniformity of mood or a reasonable transition from mood to mood. The other approach is to build around an idea that gives both music and continuity a definite focus. Most unifying ideas apply to programs of popular and semiclassical programs of classical music. There are any number of such ideas. The unifying element may be:

1. A mood.
2. A personality associated with certain songs.
3. A season.
4. A composer.
5. A setting, such as Broadway.
6. Holidays.
7. A period in time.
8. Anniversaries.
9. Music of various nations.
10. Music associated with historical events.
11. A topic.

An interesting example of an "idea" series broadcast on a national network shortly after World War II was a 15-minute weekly series entitled *Something Old, Something New, Something Borrowed. Something Blue.* Each program featured four numbers representative of these ideas; the "something borrowed" was a theme from a classic that had become a popular number.

For many years Ted Strasser of station WJR–Detroit broadcast a program called *Patterns in Music* that ran for approximately four hours every Sunday morning. He was adept at matching his music to the season and to the various special occasions that occur throughout the year. His ingenuity in developing ideas and finding the music to implement them is exemplified by one of his Sunday morning programs. It was called "Music by the Numbers" and featured selections in which a number played a part.

He elaborated the idea still further by restricting each hour to music employing the same number. In the hour devoted to the number two, for example, among the selections he played were "Tea for Two" and "Two Sleepy People." Carrying out such an idea calls for an exceptional knowledge of various kinds of music, a challenge Strasser always met admirably.

The following music continuity shows how Meridith Gottlieb, a student at Brooklyn College, responded to an assignment requiring the development of a music program with a unifying idea at its center. She set herself the task of finding popular music that makes statements about political issues.

Music Continuity
Meridith Gottlieb

THEME: UP, HOLD FOR 5 SECONDS, THEN UNDER

ANNCR: A number of bands express their opinions about world problems through their music. Such bands as U2 and Midnight Oil have based their entire careers on presenting music dealing with issues of world concern.

Some of their songs, performed in benefits for organizations like Amnesty International, are designed to raise public consciousness about these issues. In some areas of the world, for example, people are imprisoned for voicing their beliefs. These artists have used their music to try to stop such violations of human rights. Other songs focus on problems on the home front in the countries in which the artists were born.

Tonight we hear examples of this type of political music.

MUSIC: "SECONDS," U2, UP, THEN UNDER

ANNCR: We begin with the Irish band U2. One of the most political albums in their career was "War" which pretty much says it all. This song from the album called "Seconds" centers on immediate death in war.

MUSIC: "SECONDS" UP TO COMPLETION

ANNCR: The war theme continued in U2's music with "Bullet the Blue Sky" from the "Joshua Tree" LP, which deals with American foreign policy.

MUSIC: "BULLET THE BLUE SKY"

ANNCR: We move now to another band, Midnight Oil, which hails from Australia. Its lead singer Peter Garrett once ran for the Australian Senate but lost by two votes. The song "Hercules" from the EP "Species Deceases" focuses on the destruction of Hiroshima. All profits from the EP sales went to the relief fund.

MUSIC: "HERCULES"

ANNCR: English-born Elvis Costello, who is best known for his romantic songs, took up a political issue when he wrote about the failures of America in his song "Brilliant Mistake" from the "King of America" album.

MUSIC: "BRILLIANT MISTAKE"

ANNCR: The unique sound of Depeche Mode takes a political turn in a song called "New Dress." Princess Di's new dress figures in comments about different problems of the world. The song encourages voting action to help solve these problems.

MUSIC: "NEW DRESS"

ANNCR: Our final selection comes from the human-rights activist Peter Gabriel. His song entitled "Biko" deals with inhumanity and political injustice. It tells the sad tale of the imprisonment of Stephen Biko in South Africa and his eventual death. Gabriel urges people to stand up and fight for their beliefs before it's too late.

MUSIC: "BIKO," SEGUE INTO THEME, THEN UNDER

ANNCR: You have been listening to a program featuring bands and performers who use their music to make statements about political issues. This is Meridith Gottlieb speaking for WTVR Radio and saying goodnight.

THEME: UP TO CONCLUSION

Writing the Continuity   A writer handed a list of selections to be played on a classical music program must usually do some research to discover the facts needed to write the introductions. There are a number of standard works, such as Grove's *Dictionary of Music and Musicians*, that can provide most of the information required. In writing continuity for classical programs you should recognize that, to a certain extent, you are conducting a class in music appreciation, since your audience is likely to include a number of people who may be receiving their first experiences with this kind of music. On the other hand, there may be others who have heard the particular selections many times before and for whom anything you write may be an old, old story. What you need to do is to strike a mean between the needs of these two types of people, writing material that will enrich the experience of the beginner without being too naïve for the sophisticated listener.

Classical music continuity may contain information of various types:

1. Facts about the composer's life.
2. An anecdote that throws light on the composition of the particular number.
3. The place of the music in the world of music in general.

4. The way in which the composition was first received and how it has been accepted since.
5. The place of the number in the repertory of the orchestra performing it.
6. Material about the artists performing the music.

When a concert is presented live, the continuity writer usually must write more material than will be used because the length of waits between numbers is somewhat uncertain and the precise time the conductor will begin the concert is not known. The writer, therefore, needs to prepare what almost amounts to padding, material that will be interesting if there is time for it, but which is not essential to an understanding of the program as a whole.

There is little that can be said to guide the writing of continuity for programs of semiclassical or popular music. Each program presents its own unique problems, but there are a few general principles that can serve as reference points for guiding the writing and evaluation of music continuities of all types.

1. With the music program as with any other, you should seize the attention of the audience immediately and tell the listeners what is in store. The opening music can assist in attaining these objectives but the continuity carries the main burden.
2. Write continuity that is in harmony with the mood and nature of the music, with the performers, and with the intended audience, and maintain a consistent style throughout the program. You might write material for popular selections in a snappy, colloquial—perhaps even a slangy style—whereas the language

you would employ in introductions to symphonic music would be stately and dignified.
3. Avoid the use of such trite expressions as "the orchestra will now render" or other such worn-out rhetorical devices.
4. Resist the temptation to be overly cute. In most instances, choose the straightforward word or approach rather that the elaborate one. It may be acceptable at times to say that a performer "tickles the ivories" or "jounces the old eighty-eights" but it is usually better to say simply that he "plays the piano."
5. Provide the information about the number that you think the audience would like to hear. If the selection is a long one, as is frequently the case on a classical music program, repeat the name of the selection at the end for the benefit of those who tuned in late.
6. Make your comments about selections pertinent and specific rather than permitting them to remain vague and generalized.
7. In most instances the music is the important element in the show, not the continuity. Your purpose should merely be to identify the music and to add to the listeners' enjoyment and understanding of it. An exception to this rule is the program that presents an idea which the music illustrates. In such cases the continuity is as important as the music.

The segment that follows is from a continuity written by Patricia Matusky for a program similar to many broadcast by FM (Frequency Modulation) stations around the country—*Music of the Masters*, a regular offering of the University of Michigan station WUOM. In its dignity of tone and in the nature of the information it provides, this continuity is typical of those used to introduce such programs.

ANNCR: We continue MUSIC OF THE MASTERS now with Liszt's "Faust" Symphony. The Faust legend is probably one of the oldest, if not most popular, in Western religious folklore. The story of the wise, just man, tempted by evil and either succumbing to or refusing the temptation has been the subject of countless legends, poems, and ballads for centuries.

The basic Faust legend as known to us today had its beginning in the puppet plays of medieval Europe. These little dramas were the connecting bridge between the earlier religious morality plays and the secular theatre which finally developed. The early versions were a mixture of religion, comedy, philosophical meanderings, and a good deal of pagan mythology. Faust has since then appeared in a number of versions for the stage, and a vast number of early Faust operas were brought out.

As one critic has said, the "Faust" Symphony is a musical dramatization—not a musical illustration. The first movement, entitled "Faust," is intended to represent the longings and sufferings of man, as reflected in the soul of Faust. The second movement, "Margaret," represents innocence and simplicity. The final movement. "Mephistopheles," is sneering, cynical, and diabolical.

And now—we hear a complete performance of "A Faust Symphony" by Franz Liszt. In this recording the Choral Art Society and the New York Philharmonic are directed by Leonard Bernstein. The tenor soloist is Charles Bressler.

MUSIC: "FAUST SYMPHONY" (70:55)

The operators of major AM (Amplitude Modulation) stations usually avoid broadcasting programs of classical music. Such music, therefore, is generally found only in the schedules of public stations, or of a few FM commercial stations which deliberately seek the limited audience this type of music usually attracts. A program that defied this tradition, called *Adventures in Good Music*, ran for more than two decades on one of the nation's leading AM stations, WJR in Detroit. It was also heard throughout the nation on many other stations which carried it on a syndicated basis.

The success of this program can be attributed in large measure to the approach of its host Karl Haas, who held out the promise that listening to classical music can actually be fun. Instead of writing a word-for-word script, he spoke extemporaneously from carefully prepared notes, and thus gained the flavor and spontaneity of everyday speech. His programs were also marked by his exceptional skill in organizing musical presentations around a theme identified by a catchy and clever title. An example was a program called "Tune Transplants," which traced the melodies of well-known songs to their original sources.

The following continuity for one of his programs, transcribed from the air, illustrates how clearly Haas defined his theme and then made it explicit in a well-chosen program title. In this program he also aroused interest by inviting his audience to guess the name of the composer whose work he was featuring, revealing it only after the first number had been played.

Adventures in Good Music
"A Case of Unmistaken Identity"

THEME: PIANO EST, THEN UNDER

ANNOUNCER: WJR takes pleasure in presenting *Adventures in Good Music.* Monday through Friday at this time we bring you a program of the world's great music discussed informally and played for you by WJR's Director of Fine Arts, Karl Haas.

THEME: UP, UNDER AND OUT

HAAS: Hello, everyone. I have the music for you that I know most of you like. There are some composers whose musical speech is so unmistakable that it's impossible to hide it. And then there are those that are on the fence and especially some compositions tend one way while others do another. Well, today we have the other kind. We have the unmistaken identity. And I would like to bring you a program today called "A Case of Unmistaken Identity."

(COMMERCIALS)

HAAS: Let us begin with a work which is typical of the identity of which I speak. For the first piece, I'm not going to identify the composer. I'll do so right after we hear this.

MUSIC: TRIO FOR PIANO, VIOLIN, AND CELLO—DVORAK

HAAS: Surely mercurial in nature from the very active to the meditative. But it also has the undertone of the Slavic melancholy. This is Slavic music, all right. This is unmistakenly Slavic music. In fact, it has to do with the original Russian term of *dumky,* which means a passing thought. It's a sort of a ballad of Slavic lands and this composer had used the term on various occasions and in various situations and this is, in effect, a series of dumkas or dumki. Each movement of this trio for piano, violin, and cello has that little bit of Weltshmerz that we associate with Slavic music. This is Dvorak, unmistakably Dvorak. What makes it so unmistaken? Well, first of all, it is nationally Bohemian of the nineteenth century and perhaps to put it in focus, we ought to remember that the tide of nationalism that swept over Bohemia in the—oh—the latter half of the nineteenth century carried Dvorak really to fame and greatness. He became the first Bohemian composer to achieve recognition outside the boundaries of his own country. In the beginning, he was a sort of imitator of German romanticism, but when he used his music as a sort of clarion call to proclaim his national feelings, he finally arrived at individuality, and so he retained his own Bohemian identity all through his life. This dumky trail, this trail which was, in effect, a series of Slavic ballads, if you will, is unmistakenly Dvorak. It was performed here by the Yuval piano trio. A typical Bohemian Dvorakian work. But Dvorak could sing many songs, and he did so in many different situations. I thought perhaps we ought to listen to two of his Slavonic Dances, those marvelous manifestations of his love of homeland. This is music of the soil, music which has its roots in the folk tunes of folk dances of Bohemia. Here is a vivacious one first.

MUSIC: SLAVONIC DANCE IN C MAJOR—DVORAK

Another broadcaster who ad-libs his comments is Hazen Schumacher, whose program *Jazz Revisited* has been a feature on the NPR public radio network for many years. It focuses on the popular music of the 1930s and 1940s. Because the continuity is not set before the program goes on the air and therefore cannot be timed, the ad-lib broadcaster must develop a technique for keeping it on schedule. Schumacher's method is to determine before he goes on the air when each selection should begin if the program is to end on time. He then records this information next to the basic information about the number to be played. The notes below were for a program titled: "A Jazz Sampler for 1941."

3:30	1.	Harry James and His Orchestra SHARP AS A TACK May, 1941
7:00	2.	Benny Goodman and His Orchestra JACK HITS THE ROAD Vocal Jack Teagarden March, 1941, "What's New" broadcast
11:00	3.	Count Basie and His Orchestra BEAU BRUMMEL Jan, 1941
15:40	4.	Will Bradley and His Orchestra BOARDWALK BOOGIE 1941
19:40	5.	Joe Bushkin Sextet SWEET GEORGIA BROWN March, 1941
24:25	6.	John Kirby and His Orchestra IT'S ONLY A PAPER MOON July, 1941

As the broadcast proceeds, Schumacher can tell as each selection begins exactly what his timing situation is. If the program is running longer or shorter than it should, he can vary the length of his comments accordingly. In addition to the timing data and the basic information about the selection, Schumacher also notes other facts that he may use in his introductions. These notes may include references to the original recording and to contemporary sources of the music or they may record interesting facts that will enhance the audience's appreciation for selections or the musicians. In preparing to broadcast "A Jazz Sampler for 1941," for example, Schumacher noted that the John Kirby Orchestra was the first Black group to own its own radio show. In the material he prepared for another program, "Sweet and Hot," he recorded the fact that the Hal Kemp Orchestra had been voted the "best sweet band" by the readers of *Metronome*.

Because the persons who prepared the comments for *Adventures in Good Music* and *Jazz Revisited* were the ones who presented them, they could be delivered extemporaneously. In many instances, of course, the person who announces the continuity is not the one who prepares it, which means that it must be written out and read word for word. That was true of a series called *Money, Machines, and Music*, produced in the studios of WUOM in Ann

Arbor and broadcast nationwide by public radio stations. It traced the development of the automatic music machines called nickelodeons and featured selections played by several of these instruments. The series was different form most music programs in that it was designed as much to provide information about an intriguing aspect of our cultural past as it was to provide a pleasant musical experience.

MONEY, MACHINES, AND MUSIC!
Program One

STANDARD OPEN

ANNCR: Money, machines and music! . . . Mechanical pianos, band organs, violin players . . . nickelodeons by the thousands were made just forty years ago.

(SOUND EFFECTS AND MUSIC UP THEN UNDER) They made music and they made money; and now they are museum pieces. (MUSIC UP AND OUT UNDER ANNCR)

As early as 1863 a player piano was patented by a Frenchman named Forneaux. But, the heyday of the nickelodeon was in the late teens and early twenties of this century. In 1923, the peak year of their manufacture, over 200,000 player pianos of all types were produced in the United States.

Forneaux's machine was called the Pianista. Later there were dozens of makers and literally hundreds of models with wonderful names such as: Pistonola, Auto-Grand, Air-O-Player, Dulcitone, Playotone, Vacuola and Wondertone to name just a few. One popular model was the Midget, or Baby, made by the Seeberg Company of Chicago. This was a 44-note coin-operated player piano with a mandolin attachment. It cost about $750 and was used in many pool rooms and cigar stores. Here from an autographed roll by James P. Johnson is "Teddy Bear Blues" as mechanically reproduced by a Seeberg Midget.

MUSIC 1:35   TEDDY BEAR BLUES

This relatively simple player piano without the mandolin attachment was used in many homes, especially farm homes. Large dance halls and amusement parks often had more involved machines. One, sometimes called the Workhorse, was the Seeberg model G . . . Here's this ingenious gadget with . . . "Paddlin' Madeline Home."

MUSIC 2:10   PADDLIN' MADELINE HOME

A third style of orchestration made by the Seeberg Co. was the model KT Special. This device consisted of a 65 note piano with the mandolin attachment, 39 whistles, castanets, triangle, and tambourine. It sounds like this playing "Toodle-Ooh" by Fats Waller.

MUSIC 1:57   TOODLE-OOH

In 1912, Henry K. Sandell patented one of the most intricate of all mechanical music makers, an electric self-playing violin. It was manufactured by the Mills Novelty Company as the Violano-Virtuoso, a violin and piano in the same case, controlled by one specially coded roll of music. One tune produced for this amazing machine was "I Wonder What's Become of Sally?"

MUSIC 2:25   I WONDER WHAT'S BECOME OF SALLY?

Carnivals and merry-go-rounds were the main customers for Band Organs. These machines produced a tremendous volume of sound for outdoor use. The Band Organ we will hear playing "The Drum Major" was made in North Tonawanda, New York.

MUSIC 2:05   THE DRUM MAJOR (START BACK-TIMED)

The nickelodeons we've heard today are part of the collection of Mr. Jack Wirth of Ann Arbor, and this is the first in a series of thirteen programs called Money, Machines, and Music. Next week, a conversation with Jack Wirth; and more from that roll of James P. Johnson played on the Seeberg Midget.

MUSIC UP

Your announcer has been Merril McClatchy. Scripts and production by Ralph Johnson. This is the University of Michigan Broadcasting Service.

MUSIC UP TO CLOSE

This is the National Educational Radio Network.

Television Music Programs

Most of what we have said about writing continuity for music programs broadcast on radio applies equally to music programs broadcast on television. In both instances they focus on the music; the continuity performs a subsidiary function. It lets audiences know what selections are to be played and provides additional information designed to enhance the audience's appreciation of the performance. Radio and television continuity for a symphony concert, for example, can be virtually identical. In radio the opening words are likely to be read as the sound of the orchestra members tuning their instruments is heard in the background. In television these same words can be spoken over shots of the orchestra. In both media, similar continuity can cover the entrance of the conductor.

There is one area, however, in which writers create television music programs radically different from those written by their radio counterparts. We are referring, of course, to the video interpretations of popular music broadcast by the cable network MTV. In a sense it has a forerunner in *Your Hit Parade*, a program transferred from radio to television in the early 1950s. The TV version featured dramatization or visualization of the popular songs of the period. The factor that made this approach possible was the projection by most of the songs of some sort of story idea. The advent of rock music brought *The Hit Parade* to an end, for its producers could no longer find in rock music's repetitive lyrics the story ideas they needed to create meaningful visualizations.

The producers of videos featured on MTV took a different approach and in so doing created the first TV format not based on a radio, theater, or movie form. The centerpiece of each video is a recording of a number by a solo artist or a group. In many instances the video focuses on the musical artists either lip-synching the lyrics or mimicking the playing of their instruments. The shots and images are wildly imaginative and are supplemented by other visual impressions that reinforce the mood of the music. The most characteristic feature of the videos shown on MTV is a furious pace, marked by quick cutting from one image to another. Many images stay on the screen for much less than a second.

MTV videos have had a profound effect on our culture. John Leland, in a *Newsweek* article published at the time of MTV's tenth anniversary, said that it "changed the way we talk, dress, dance, make and consume music, and how we process information."[1] Howard Polskin, writing in *TV Guide*, struck the same note, saying that MTV "created a new visual language, shaped fashion, and defined a youth culture." He added that "countless Hollywood movies and TV shows have adapted the quick-cut editing and slick, flashy imagery associated with the music videos on MTV."[2] They have also had a noticeable impact on the way TV commercials are made. Their status as major cultural artifacts is exemplified by the fact that the Museum of Modern Art has placed 40 music videos in its permanent collection.

Tom Freston, chairman of MTV, called it "one of the most successful ventures in TV history."[3] Observers who might be somewhat more objective than Freston agree with this verdict. One thing MTV did was to breathe new life into the rock-music industry, which was in the doldrums when MTV began operating in 1981. In recent years it has been a major factor in promoting rap music. Before MTV's arrival, the playing of new releases by radio stations was the most important factor in advancing the sales of records. Exposure on MTV is now more sought after by record promoters than any other means. Exposure on MTV helped make Michael Jackson's *Thriller* the best-selling album of all time. Appearances on MTV have propelled a new breed of visual pop stars from anonymity into world-wide recognition, among them Cyndi Lauper, Boy George, Janet Jackson, and Madonna, who, incidentally, has had more videos presented on MTV than any other artist.

MTV's influence reaches far beyond the United States. In 1984 it began operating in Japan and since then has extended its service to some 73 other countries in Latin America, Europe, Asia, and Africa. It is estimated that 34 million people a week watch MTV programs in the United States, and its services abroad add many millions more to this number.

MTV's success has prompted other cable networks and regular broadcast stations to schedule programs featuring video versions of popular songs. The MTV cable channel has diversified its offerings through the years. In 1985 it established a sister service, VH-1, designed to appeal to the tastes of the so-called yuppie generation. MTV has plans to set up three different channels that will cater to various tastes in music, including Top 40 selections, rap, rock, metal, dance, and oldies. It has also put such nonmusical programs as movie reviews and comedy presentations into its schedule.

The fact that producing music videos provides an almost unlimited opportunity to use one's imagination gives innovative people the chance to test their creative powers. Such well-known film directors as Brian DePalma and John Landis, attracted by this challenge, have made music videos. The task facing writers is obviously utterly different from the one they must deal with in preparing conventional music continuities. For one thing, the production and writing functions blend. For another, there is almost a complete absence of rules. You are free to go almost anywhere your imagination takes you. In one video, for example, Paula Abdul dances with a cartoon cat; in another, a clay hammer spurts from Peter Gabriel's clay head. You see David Byrne as a child and in the next instant glimpse his face projected on the side of a house. As social scientist Todd Gitlin has noted, images take the place of logic.[4] In creating these effects you must use all of the conventional instruments and devices of television, but in addition you must take advantage of the special-effects techniques developed in recent years, particularly those created by computers.

In noting that the creation of music videos demands that you let your imagination take off, we do not suggest that there are no limits at all. The restrictions against the presentation of indecent, obscene, or defamatory programming, or material that violates most people's ideas of what is right and proper, obviously apply as much to music videos as they do to any other kind of programming. MTV, in fact, has been criticized for the sexual suggestiveness of some of its presentations. In response, it has drawn lines which the videos it is willing to accept cannot cross. It refused to play Madonna's "Justify My Love," for example, because of its blatant sexuality.

VARIETY PROGRAMS

Local radio and television stations often produce programs which, like magazines, include a variety of material—interviews with visiting celebrities, local officials, and experts in various fields, household hints, answers to listeners' letters, contests, and other features. Writers who work with the personality who appears on the air in producing and preparing the material for the show have a number of functions. They include such duties as developing ideas for the show, finding material, creating outlines, keeping track of visitors

to the city, arranging interviews, preparing questions for these interviews, deciding the order of events on the show, reading letters, doing the research necessary to answer questions, and inventing contest ideas.

Prime-time network variety shows offering various types of entertainment were common when radio was the dominant medium. They featured music, comedy, and dramatic sketches. A variety show, in fact, was in the initial program broadcast by the first permanent network, NBC, in 1926. Its star was the comedian Will Rogers, and also included were performances by popular and classical orchestras, opera stars, and singers of popular songs. With the arrival of television, variety shows broadcast by the commercial networks moved from radio to the new medium. In the public radio area, however, a variety program, developed long after the television age had begun, was broadcast for 13 years on the American Public Radio network. Called *A Prairie Home Companion*, and produced by Minnesota Public Radio, it made Garrison Keillor a national celebrity. The series came to a conclusion in 1987 when Keillor left for Denmark, but on his return to this country he began a similar (if less popular) program, *The Amercian Radio Company*.

The concluding program in 1987 provides a good illustration of the diverse ingredients that made up variety shows on both radio and television. Keillor carried out a number of functions, as the Master of Ceremonies, or MC, as a singer, and most particularly as a monologuist, whose reports of the "News from Lake Wobegon" were a highlight of the series. Other features of the last program were a humorous dramatic sketch about "Buster the Show Dog," the reading of a poem by the writer Roy Blount, Jr., songs by regular members of the company, and by a visiting Hawaiian glee club, and several appearances by the well-known guitarist Chet Atkins.

The material written to introduce the segments on a variety show may simply announce them as a musical continuity does, but it is far more likely to have comedy overtones, thus amplifying the humorous effect produced by the sketches and monologues. Its function, therefore, is not merely to inform the audience of what is coming, but it also becomes part of the entertainment. This was true of the introductions given by Keillor on *A Prairie Home Companion*. In his last 1987 show he made frequent humorous references to his imminent departure for Denmark. At one point, he told a joke in Danish and when no one laughed he commented, "That's probably what will happen to me in Denmark."

Just as radio variety shows ranged through a wide spectrum of entertainment, so did those on television. The addition of the visual element, of course, made it possible for television to present acts that radio, with its reliance on sound alone, could not handle. Such performers as jugglers, magicians, and dancers joined the singers, comedians, and actors who had performed in radio and continued to do so on television. An outstanding example of the TV variety format was *The Ed Sullivan Show*, which had a network run of 23 years. In recent times the number of prime-time variety network shows has declined almost to the vanishing point. One of the notable survivors in this field is Bob Hope. He first performed on NBC Radio in 1938 and as we write this, he is still making regular appearances in variety specials. His shows open with a monologue by Hope and continue with comedy sketches featuring Hope and his guest stars, who may also contribute other entertainment such as songs or comedy routines. Specialty acts may also be included.

Though comedy was an important element in many variety shows, some had a different focus. For many years the popular singer Perry Como appeared in Christmas programs that offered seasonal music in a variety of regional settings. In addition to music, the programs presented information about unique Christmas customs and provided glimpses of picturesque holiday scenes. In 1991 the singer John Denver performed in a CBS variety special with a similar focus. Entitled *John Denver's Montana Christmas Skies*, it celebrated the art, culture, and traditions of the Assiniboin and Gros Ventre Indian tribes and featured music of the Montana region in which the program was filmed, some of it performed by American Indians. The various elements were filmed on location and were then edited into a program that moved smoothly from one element to another as Denver provided songs and guidance. The practice of creating music and variety shows by editing together elements or video taped separately is a common one.

The Christmas programs of Como and Denver differed from many variety shows because they concentrated on a particular theme or subject. For a number of years variety shows presented by AT&T followed this kind of pattern. The programs revolved around a major unifying idea. One of them focused on the music of the song-and-dance performers of America's vaudeville stage. The segment below illustrates the format in which the script was typed. Written by Will Glickman, it featured Donald O'Connor as host and Anthony Newley as his special guest. The show opened with a song and dance performed by the two stars and then continued with the following:

(*MUSIC:* CONTINUES AS DONALD AND TONY SPEAK)

DONALD O'CONNOR   Good evening, ladies and gentlemen. Tonight's hour is a sentimental look at the show-business personality called the Song and Dance Man. Perhaps you already guessed that by the little pasquinade that Tony and I just did.

TONY   Pasquinade means a brief musicalized scene of a slightly satirical nature. . . .
            Which is pretty fancy talk for a song and dance man!

DONALD   Sorry.

TONY   Remember, Donald, how Fred Allen described a song and dance man.

DONALD   "Half gypsy and half suitcase." And that's the kind of fellow our show's about
            this evening . . . !

(BILLBOARD)

(MUSIC: SEGUE TO BELL THEME)

(SLIDES: THE BELL TELEPHONE HOUR & THE SONG AND DANCE MAN)

BRANDT (VO)   The Bell Telephone Hour. . . Presents "The Song and Dance Man" . . .

(CUT TO CAST AS NAMED)

                        With Donald Voorhees and the Bell Telephone Orchestra . . .
                        Starring—
                        Janet Blair . . .
                        Shani Wallis . . .
                        Nancy Dussault . . .
                        The Nicholas Brothers . . .
                        Special Guest—
                        Anthony Newley! . . .
                        And your host, ladies and gentlemen,
                        Donald O'Connor!

(DONALD O'CONNOR: INTRO TO DOUBLE ACT)

(MUSIC: UNDERSCORE)

We have noted that variety programs on prime-time television appear to be a vanishing breed, but programs marked by a great deal of variety are broadcast at other times during the day. The morning shows presented by the full-service, regular networks are not usually thought of as variety programs, but they do range through a diverse group of material. Often they contain some type of musical presentation as well as news reports, weather forecasts, interviews with political, literary, educational, and entertainment figures, and presentations on special subjects. Such shows may in fact be produced by a network's entertainment division rather than its news division and feature music and comedy routines as well as news reports and weather forecasts. A better example of variety programs broadcast during non-prime-time hours are the late night shows such as *The Tonight Show*. In addition to the comedy monologues presented by host Jay Leno, it often features guest comedians, appearances by singers and musical groups, and interludes by the *Tonight Show* musicians. These supplement the basic entertainment provided by interviews with celebrity guests.

GAME SHOWS

One of the most durable types of programs is the show that puts its participants into some kind of contest, run according to a carefully established set of rules. These programs are now generally referred to as *game* shows; in the past they were also called *quiz*, *panel*, or *audience participation* programs depending on their specific nature. Game shows are an important element in the daytime schedules of TV networks, and syndicated versions are also scheduled by local stations during the "access" period following network news broadcasts.

Game-Show Formats

The first step in developing a game show is to devise the formula that will provide the basic framework. A common ingredient is testing the participants knowledge by asking questions. *Jeopardy* puts a twist on this approach by requiring contestants to supply the questions for the answers they are given. An element of risk is often part of the formula. On *Jeopardy* there are times when contestants can double their winnings by responding correctly, or lose as much as they have dared to risk by giving an incorrect response. Chance also plays a role in some instances. On *Wheel of Fortune* the spin of the wheel determines what the contestants can earn when they make the right choice. Some game shows feature participants doing stunts rather than answering

questions and the aim of others, such as *The Love Connection* and *Studs*, is to attract audiences with titillating revelations about relationships between the sexes. Many game shows mix celebrity contestants with those chosen from the audience. A number put the spotlight on the gags and chatter of show-business personalities as much as they do on a contest.

The development of a game-show formula begins with the invention of a root idea from which the rest of the formula springs. This root idea may be inspired by a parlor game like "Twenty Questions" or "Tick-Tack-Toe"; it may be a spin-off from a previous show a production company has developed; or it may be entirely original. Once the root idea has been established, the creator must define every step in the on-the-air presentation by delineating in a master script such elements as the opening and closing continuity, a statement of the rules, the method of introducing contestants, the way winners are announced, and the transitions from one segment to another. Once the formula has been devised, it must be evaluated to make sure that it meets the criteria characterizing successful game shows. Among them are a formula that is simple enough to be readily understood and executed; a catchy title that sums up the show's essence; a framework that involves the viewing audience; and elements of suspense and conflict. The formula must then be tried out in a studio to make sure that it works in actual practice. *Family Feud*, for example, went through a three-year period of trial and development before it went on the air.

Writing Individual Scripts

In the game-show business the most demanding and the most lucrative activity is the invention of the formula or framework. The task of preparing material for each individual show is usually carried out by staff writers. If they do their work routinely or indifferently, however, they may seriously damage the execution of an ingenious formula. The questions asked of participants, for example, must be difficult enough to challenge them yet not be so difficult that almost no one will know the answer. Obvious sources for these questions are encyclopedias, almanacs, popular magazines, history books, and newspapers.

Writing material for games focusing on unique competitive elements may require greater resourcefulness and ingenuity than writing simple informational questions. This is also true of game shows in which the emphasis is on humor. The writers of *Family Feud* provide examples of how ingenuity exercised in the day-to-day production of a program can keep it bright and interesting. Since the contestants in this program are entire families, what would be more appropriate than to bring in families bearing the names of the most famous family feuders of all time, the Hatfields and the McCoys, to challenge one another? That is exactly what they did. In another instance, they selected as contestants not real families, but the fictional families whose stories are told in a number of evening television programs. This idea held so much promise of arousing audience interest that it became the basis for a prime-time special.

QUESTIONS AND PROJECTS

1. Choose selections and write a continuity that indicates how the musical style and subject matter of a singing group such as the Beatles or U2 evolved through a number of years.
2. Write continuity for the following with the emphases as indicated.
   (a) Brandenburg Concerto No. 3 in G Major—J. S. Bach (facts about the composer's life).
   (b) Ninth Symphony . . . Beethoven (place of this music in the total work of the composer).
   (c) Concerto for Violin . . . Bartók (place of this in the music world).
   (d) "Toreador Song" from *Carmen* . . . Bizet (the way this opera was first received by the public).
   (e) Fourth Symphony . . . Tchaikovsky, played by the Houston Symphony directed by Christoph Eschenbach (facts on the orchestra and its director).
3. Decide on a theme for a half-hour music program. Then select music and write continuity that will bring out this theme.
4. Assume that you have your choice of a leading show-business personality and variety acts. Design a variety show, indicate the sequence of its segments, and write the connective continuity.
5. In your listening, have you heard a theme for a musical or variety program that you thought was particularly imaginative and well executed? What made it so?
6. Design a program that constitutes a tribute to a composer in connection with a significant anniversary or event in the life of the composer.
7. Do you have any explanation for the decline of variety shows which were once so popular?
8. Select a current popular song and discuss two different ways that it might be converted into a video for showing on MTV.
9. Watch three game shows. Describe the framework of each show as succinctly as you can and present your descriptions to the class. Do these shows meet the tests of simplicity, catchy and descriptive titles, suspense, and involvement by the audience?

10. Can you think of ways to apply game show techniques to the creation of educational or informational programs?

NOTES

1. John Leland, "Do you Still Want Your MTV?", *Newsweek*, August 5, 1991, p. 53.
2. Howard Polskin, "MTV at 10," *TV Guide*, August 3, 1991, pp. 4–5.
3. Ibid, p. 4.
4. See Note 1 above.

PART

III

Writing
Dramatic
Material

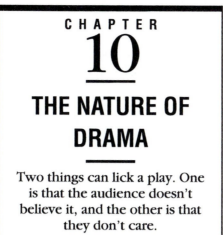

CHAPTER

10

THE NATURE OF DRAMA

Two things can lick a play. One is that the audience doesn't believe it, and the other is that they don't care.

HOWARD LINDSAY (1889–1968)

Drama is similar in some ways to other literary forms that tell a story, but in certain other aspects it is quite different. There are also variations in the nature of drama depending on the medium in which it is presented. These characteristics and distinctions are the main concern of this chapter. Some suggestions for the would-be dramatist who needs guidance in finding, developing, and evaluating ideas for plays are also included.

DRAMA AS A STORYTELLING FORM

When writers set out to tell a story, there are certain requirements they must fulfill if they are to be successful. These requirements apply whether the medium is the short story, the novel, the drama, or some other form. Let us consider these requirements now with special reference to the drama.

Audience Interest

Kenneth Tynan, a drama critic and essayist, once said that a play "is basically a means of spending two hours in the dark without being bored." That is to say, one of the inescapable requirements of drama is that it should interest some kind of an audience. It is not always necessary to attract the multitudes, for there is the *succès d'estime* that wins the plaudits of a small but perceptive group of people, but a play must reach to some degree beyond the dramatist's own peculiar concerns. Audience interest has played a major role in establishing the enduring place of works that we now accept as classics. The great plays of writers like Sophocles, Molière, and Shakespeare have attained their particular distinction because, having won audiences in their own day, they have continued to win them down through the centuries. They became classics simply because people keep wanting to see them.

The measure of the theatrical film writer's success or failure in arousing and maintaining interest is the number of people the film draws to the theater. The audience's response as it watches the film also provides some indication of its impact. Because the audience for a broadcast drama is broken up into small units that are widely separated, we must depend on the relatively crude measure of an audience rating to estimate interest. The reaction of the audience as it watches, so evident in a theater, is usually unknown. Occasionally, the impact of a TV program is so powerful that a significant number of viewers express their feelings by writing letters. The series *Cagney and Lacy* and *Designing Women* were saved from early extinction because a large number of people sent letters and telegrams demanding that they stay on the air. Praise from critics can also signal a program's success. This was true of the PBS series *The Civil War*, which received highly favorable reviews in newspapers and magazines. One result of these plaudits was that it became one of the most widely watched programs in public television's history.

Such striking evidence of viewer interest occurs infrequently, however. The success of a television play is usually evaluated by the small group of people who work on the production, but their involvement is likely to deprive them of the essential grace of objectivity. The reactions of those who really count, the people sitting in their homes, who may have been absorbed throughout the play or have disgustedly switched it off, generally go undocumented.

Appeal to the Emotions

Some people have a tendency to equate dialogue with drama. It is clear, however, that not everything written in dialogue is drama, as a study of Plato's *Dialogues* will reveal. There are a number of differences between his works and those we identify as drama, but the principal one is that Plato appealed primarily to the intellect whereas dramatists appeal primarily to the emotions. Though they may present ideas, of course, their basic emphasis must be on the arousal of feeling. A number of writers have stressed this point. The playwright and screenwriter John Osborne said in reference to his own work, "I want to make people feel. They can think afterwards."

Interest and Emotions   Not only is the arousal of emotion the heart of drama, but it can also contribute to gaining and holding the interest of the audience. The power of emotion to generate interest can be seen when we look into areas of life other than drama. People flock in large numbers to see a circus. Why? There is spectacle, of course—colorful parades, music, a constant change and flow of events—and there are feats of endurance and accomplishments that seem to defy natural laws. All of these have the power to hold attention. Various aspects of circus performance, however, differ in their holding power. Though most of the events arouse and sustain interest, there are some that fairly captivate the viewers, leaving them silent and expectant. The following illustration suggests how the emotions undergo gradual intensification.

Those who take their places under the Big Top first feel their interest aroused by a general response to the spectacle. They then apply selective attention to any number of acts and activities taking place around the ring, letting their eyes feast at random on animal trainers, clowns, beautiful girls on horseback, acrobats, and whatever else moves or calls from the sawdust. Then, at a signal from the ringmaster, the spectators raise their eyes to a tightrope where a lovely, fragile young maiden begins her death-defying act of walking above the animal cages. Now the viewers are not merely attentive, they are enthralled. To their interest in the circus as a spectacle has been added something else: *concern*. To increase the tension, the net beneath the tightrope is removed. There is nothing now to protect her from the snarling beasts in the cage below. Spectators see a human being in great jeopardy. Their emotions have moved from interest, to concern, to anxiety. They are worried about the outcome. Their interest has reached its apex. In the same way, the dramatist's best means of breaking down the viewers' detachment is to stir their emotions as soon as possible and keep them stirred throughout the play.

Types of Emotional Response   The emotions aroused by drama can be of various kinds. Sometimes a viewer may share the feelings that overwhelm a character in a play. A mother loses her child. We experience in some measure the shock of her bereavement. We may shake with the anger that convulses a character, tremble as danger approaches, or share the exultation of victory. This direct, personal identification, this feeling *with* the emotion of a character is called *empathy*. A dramatist who can arouse this response in viewers has found the most powerful means of exciting and sustaining interest.

Sometimes dramatists cannot cause people to feel what their characters feel, but they can create concern for them, make the audience feel *for* them. This response is called *sympathy*. To make the members of an audience anxious about a character's welfare is a guarantee of interest.

Creating a character for the audience to detest can also arouse interest. In this case the emotion the dramatist arouses is not sympathy at all but hostility. The pioneer screen villain, Eric von Stroheim, described as "the man you love to hate," entranced audiences with the prospect and hope of his eventual downfall. Scorn for a character can also induce interest as, for example, the distaste we experience for the weakling who, under the stress of fear, turns and runs from duty. Sometimes our emotional response is simply one of laughter. Characters in comedies frequently endure the most agonizing experiences, but their problems are presented in such a way that what results is merely ludicrous. We cannot empathize with their feelings or even sympathize with them; our laughter does indicate our interest, however.

The Place of Conflict The best way for a dramatist to arouse an emotional response is to present people torn by conflict. We might wish for a real world in which all problems are solved, but such a world can never be the province of the dramatist. Untroubled people have no power to arouse the emotion of an audience.

It is conflict that provokes the crises that are the high points of the play. Without conflict these crises would not develop and the play would lack the essential element we describe with the word "dramatic." Though conflict need not occur in every scene, it must have a significant place in the structure of the play as a whole. It is even possible to conceive of a play that begins after all of the actual conflict is over; existing only in retrospect, it still remains a vital element in arousing the emotions of the audience. The conflict in a drama may vary greatly in intensity and it may appear in many different forms, but it must always be there.

Types of Conflict What are the various types of conflict? It is conventional to categorize them as conflicts of a person against a person, a person against a group, a group against a group, and a person or a group against a natural force or obstacle. This list neglects the type of conflict that is most likely to move an audience—the spectacle of a person confronted by two or more courses of action who is trying to make a decision under the stress of conflicting drives. This is internal conflict, the most dramatic conflict of all. Even in cases where external obstacles create the conflict situation, the struggle within a person as he or she seeks ways of overcoming the obstacle is often more important than the clash with the obstacle itself.

It should be noted, however, that not all types of conflict are dramatic. An example is the conflict that arises when characters in a play do nothing more than argue over an issue. The advancement of the various points of view may have some attraction as an intellectual exercise, but it lacks the element so essential to drama—the capacity to move an audience to feel deeply. Yet some student writers, in their eagerness to be profound, mistakenly concentrate on this intellectual type of confrontation. Drama should not be permitted to degenerate into mere debate or it soon ceases to be dramatic. As the celebrated Swedish filmmaker Ingmar Bergman has said, "A film must strike you in the heart before it hits you in the head."

The Issues of Conflict The objective of a dramatist is to elicit from the audience the maximum possible emotional response. The extent of the response will depend on the significance of the issues at stake. Conflict over minor matters has little power to stir feelings. The conflict must focus on issues that are crucial, on such subjects as life or death, success or defeat, loyalty or betrayal, health or illness, freedom or captivity, honor or degradation. John Steinbeck said that "people are more interested in violence than in guilt, in murder and accidents than in uneventfulness, in divorce than in marriage." This does not mean that drama must always focus on unusual people and extraordinary actions. Characters like the boy across the street or the woman in the next block may be proper subjects of drama, provided that the situations into which we plunge them provoke conflicts involving issues of fundamental importance. It would be difficult, for example, to interest an audience in an individual whose basic problem is trying to decide whether to go to a movie or to stay home and read a book. A little girl with a coin clutched in her hand trying to decide which piece of candy to buy may be a completely satisfactory subject for drama, however. The decision she faces at that moment of her life is one of transcendent importance. Fortunately for the playwright, there are moments of extreme crisis in the experiences of almost all of us. Because they produce consequences that color life in a vital way, they are the stuff of which drama can be made.

Changes and Development

To create drama it is not enough merely to entangle a character in a predicament. The people involved in that problem must strive to free themselves, or the emotional response of the audience will soon subside. Drama comes from struggle, not from capitulation. Moreover, that struggle must bring changes and developments or, again, the attention of the audience will wander. The experience can be compared to watching a truck stuck in the mud. The sight of spinning wheels arouses our interest at first, but if the wheels continue to spin without visible results, we soon turn to more diverting activities. In the same way, the struggle of characters must advance them toward their goal or shove them further back, or they must make decisions that envelop them in new complications.

Interpretation of Life

Is it enough that a drama should merely hold the attention of an audience until the last scene is over? In the narrowest sense perhaps, we can say that a dramatist who succeeds in doing this has accomplished all that we should expect. It is certainly true that though much of TV and film drama diverts while it is on the screen, with the final fadeout, it immediately passes into oblivion. To write a truly significant drama, however, one that accomplishes more than temporary diversion, we must meet the challenge that George Bernard Shaw laid down. "The function of a playwright is to select incidents from the chaos of everyday living and arrange them in a pattern so that the spectator might leave the theater an enlightened man."

The reference of significant drama, then, is life. Its proper subjects are real people doing things for reasons that can be discovered by an audience. It gives a vision of the real by adhering to the surface of life as people live it. Achieving fidelity to human truth does not mean, of course, that life in all of its detail and ramifications must be presented. As we have noted previously, a normal life is dramatic only in its moments of crisis. Film director Alfred Hitchcock said, "A story needs to be true to life but never banal. . . . Drama is life from which we have wiped out the stains of boredom." The dramatist selects a vital moment of life and then intensifies it. By placing a magnifying glass over one human event, dramatists provide enlightenment about human existence in general.

THE SPECIAL CHARACTERISTICS OF DRAMA

To this point we have been considering some general requirements for effective storytelling that apply with particular emphasis to the dramatic form. But drama has some characteristics of its own, which set it apart from other types of stories such as the novel and the short story.

The Conventions of Drama

Though dramatic presentation seems to conform to reality, at least in some respects, it is never actually real. It becomes real only in the imagination of the viewer, who, in Coleridge's famous phrase, undertakes "the willing suspension of disbelief." The presentation may vary from one that provides only the barest clues to reality, from which viewers erect their own vision of the situation, to one that offers a virtually complete representation of reality. The radio drama, limited as it is to sound stimuli, presents the greatest challenge to the imagination of the audience. The stage drama employing a complete and realistic set presents a lesser imaginative challenge, but even in this case viewers must accept certain nonrealistic conventions. The room they see, for example, has only three walls, and they observe characters who are perfectly willing to carry on the most intimate conversations before a crowd of people.

There are conventions also in language. The play that employs naturalistic dialogue makes little demand on the credulity of the viewer, but the audience to the poetic dramas of a William Shakespeare, a Maxwell Anderson, or a Christopher Fry must be willing to believe in human beings who habitually and extemporaneously express themselves in soaring iambic verse. To cite another convention that applies particularly to television, the hands of the people who inhabit the world of the TV cartoon have only three fingers.

The Group Effort of Drama

The work of a novelist flows directly from the writer to the consumer by means of the printed word. But as Larry McMurtry, novelist and screenwriter (*Lonesome Dove*), has pointed out, "The screenplay is only secondarily a *written* thing; it is an elaborate notation . . . a kind of codified visualization."[1] It does not come into existence for an audience until the director, performers, designers, and production crew have made their contributions. If they are skilled, they can transmit with complete integrity what the dramatist has put into the script, and, in some instances, they may even reveal meanings richer than anyone in reading it thought were there. If they are clumsy or lacking in perceptiveness, on the other hand, they may distort or even destroy what the dramatist sought to accomplish.

The Present Tense of Drama

The playwright presents a story through the actions of characters living through situations that are actually experienced by the audience as they happen. The novelist merely tells the audience what has happened. The immediacy of the play contrasted with the retrospective quality of the novel constitutes one of the basic differences between the two forms. Because drama presents what is happening, it follows that all of its action occurs in the present. In a play it is perpetually now. Time within a play can change, of course; it can return to a past event or thrust forward into future time, but whatever takes place in a specific time period is produced as if it were happening in the present tense. This means that in any given scene the dramatist is bound to a large extent by what can actually happen in the real time devoted to the playing of that scene. Another aspect of this situation is that drama proceeds at an inflexible pace. The viewer cannot pause and seek clarification by going back and re-examining the previous action as the reader of a novel can; the audience of a play is irresistibly drawn forward at whatever rate the dramatist sets.

Restrictions on Comment

In addition to using dialogue—the main resource of dramatists—novelists have an unlimited opportunity to narrate, describe, analyze, and qualify. In so doing they can present their own views as observers of the scene. Dramatists, unless they resort to the unusual device of using narration as a vehicle for presenting their own views, are denied the privilege of expressing their own comments directly to the audience.

The Place of Implication

Because dramatists lack a direct route to the viewer, they must communicate with their audience largely through a skillful use of the technique of implication. This technique is employed, of course, in other forms of fiction, but in the drama its use is crucial. Unless viewers are permitted to gain most of their knowledge through their interpretation of implications, they cannot react to drama as something experienced. Without that experience, the form loses most of its special force and unique quality. Thornton Wilder, who was both a novelist and a dramatist, emphasized this point when he said, "A dramatist is one who believes that the pure event, an action involving human beings, is more arresting than any comment on it."

Drama's Emphasis on the High Points

One of the most perceptive distinctions between novel and play writing was made by William Archer when he said that drama is "the art of crisis, as fiction is the art of gradual developments."[2] The dramatist presents only the culminating events in the lives of the characters, the action that involves them at or near their moments of crisis. In addition to retaining only those details that have the maximum vividness and significance, drama presents changes in swift and startling succession. The audience has little time to wonder or reflect. The long slow buildup in which novelists may indulge is denied dramatists, for they simply have no time for such development and could not hold an audience with it anyway. Dramatists must begin when the situation is coming to a boil, not when the fire is first lighted. It follows that the choice of events to be dramatized is a matter of transcendent importance in the construction of a play. They must select only those events that contribute directly to the achievement of their purpose, rigidly excluding everything else. What actually occurs in the play, of course, can only be part of the complete story; the rest takes place outside of the action, between the scenes, or before the play begins, but these events are merely suggested by what is actually presented. Drama telescopes, focuses, and intensifies.

THE SPECIAL NATURE OF TV AND MOVIE DRAMA

Considering the difference in the size of TV and movie screens and the difference in the conditions under which viewing takes place, it seems reasonable to assume that there are basic differences in the nature of the drama presented by TV and the movies. This, in fact, was the conclusion of a number of critics who first wrote about television drama. Since those early days, however, television has become the chief vehicle for showing films originally made for theatrical release. More people by far see such films on television than see them in theaters. The practice of viewing films in the home on TV sets increased greatly with the development of the video cassette recorder, or VCR. Film companies now derive more income from selling and renting the video versions of their product than they do from theatrical exhibition.

Sometimes dramas created originally for television are later shown in theaters. This is particularly true of mini-series which are often edited into feature films and released theatrically in other parts of the world. In view of this constant interchange of product between the two media, can it still be argued that they are different in their essential nature? We shall examine that question and consider also the differences that distinguish film and TV drama from stage drama.

The Relative Intimacy of Television

The smallness of the TV screen in comparison to that of the movie theater gives rise to a basic principle: Television is a close-up medium. If viewers are to see what is happening, they need to be brought close to the action. The intimacy of the medium receives further enhancement from the fact that television is seen by one or two viewers per set who are separated completely from the millions of other people watching the program.

It follows that television is more often concerned with people in small groups engaged in sharply restricted activity. The large movie screen can present grand movements more effectively—the tumult at sea, the mob assaulting the castle, the ebb and flow of a battle scene. The activity presented on television is usually of a different order, intense and rigidly contained. When battle erupts it usually involves two people rather than thousands. And the movie screen can transmit the grandeur and presence of scenery far better than the smaller TV screen.

Does the intimacy of television mean that its peculiar province is the domain of the "average" person? There are some who think so, and many of the dramas broadcast when television was just getting under way supported that idea. They were referred to as "kitchen-sink" dramas, stories that immersed their audiences in the day-to-day crises that face ordinary human beings. That early period, however, was followed almost immediately by one in which wide-open western dramas, celebrating the exploits of heroic and legendary figures, dominated the TV screen. For a while the kitchen sink was nowhere to be seen. In the years that followed, almost every type of drama imaginable found a place in television. Even when programs were broadcast "live," there seemed no absolute limit on what could be done. A dramatization of Walter Lord's book *A Night to Remember* even accomplished the remarkable feat of sinking the *Titanic* in a TV studio. In the face of these developments, can we still say that television is ideally suited to dealing with the problems of the common person?

It cannot be denied that television has broadcast many different types of dramas with great success. It is still valid to say, however, that one of the types it does particularly well is the story of ordinary people meeting the crises that arise in circumstances that we all recognize. The success of such series as *thirtysomething* and *The Wonder Years* testifies to this fact. It can be added further that some types of dramas are not especially well suited to the TV medium. The critic Tom Prideaux has said, for example, that "epic Greek dramas, which need the illusion of outdoors and Godlike grandeur, look preposterously dinky on TV." It can be noted also that some movies are successful on TV, not because they are particularly suited to the medium, but because of such factors as the acclaim they received during their theatrical release, the presence of well-known stars in their casts, or the gloss that comes from high budgets.

Just as TV can handle almost every kind of drama, so too can the theatrical movie. There have been a number that have focused effectively on the problems of everyday people. One of the first great television successes, Paddy Chayefsky's *Marty*, which dealt movingly with the familiar problem of a man who believes that he is unattractive to women, was equally successful in its movie version, and its star, Ernest Borgnine, won an Academy Award for his performance. In communicating this type of personal drama, it should be remembered that the movie shares with television the advantages of using close-ups. It has the further advantage of portraying events of great sweep and scale with a special effect.

The Time Factor

Another way in which television differs from the movies, and also from the stage, is in the influence of the time factor. Television dramatists are more restricted by time than their counterparts in the other media in three different ways. The first is that in American television, they are required to fill a specific time period whether or not the dramatic idea fits comfortably into it. They cannot, like the stage or screen playwright, turn out a script that will be as short or as long as the idea itself dictates. Selecting concepts that fit the time period assigned to a drama involves one of the dramatist's most critical decisions. There are 15-minute ideas, half-hour ideas, hour ideas. The dramatist who decides to deal with a half-hour idea in an hour's time, or the reverse, is taking the first step toward trouble.

A second aspect of television's time restrictions is that whatever time may be available, it is often shorter than the time at the disposal of the stage or screen dramatist. TV programs in a regular weekly series are usually of the hour or half-hour variety. The panoramic approach, in which a drama wanders leisurely through many years and involves a multitude of characters, is out of place in this kind of time period. Instead, the drama must be sharply focused in its approach. Though the short time periods of television may seem restrictive, they do provide an opportunity for the treatment of ideas that lack sufficient substance for the longer periods of the stage and screen. The critic Marya Mannes pointed out that television can "open the door on one life in one room for one moment and . . . record one small shift in human relations . . . one half turn in a situation."[3]

Though most of television's time periods are relatively short, there are some opportunities for writing longer forms. One example is the movie written and produced especially for television to fit a two-hour period. Another opportunity is the TV mini-series, in which a story is told through a period of several days, with an hour or two-hour segment being broadcast every day. Some of the longer mini-series actually give their writers more time to develop plotting ideas and characters than conventional movies or stage plays. Other TV forms that give dramatists this kind of time are daytime and prime-time serials like *Another World* and *Knot's Landing* and series like *L.A. Law* that keep certain plot lines running through several episodes.

A third way in which time makes stern demands on TV writers is that the broadcast dates for specific programs tend to be inflexible. The date cannot be changed simply because the writer has not finished the script. There is somewhat more latitude in movie making, although budget considerations do dictate that production schedules be followed as closely as possible. Stage playwrights enjoy even greater freedom than movie writers. The production process is usually not scheduled until the script is completed.

Because TV writers must be ready for a specific broadcast date and because the time allotted to write and produce a script is relatively shorter than it is in the movies and theater, they frequently find that they are operating under extreme pressure. Sometimes a program idea is approved only a few months before the broadcast is scheduled. This condition is prevalent at the beginning of each new television season. Writers must be able to respond to this kind of pressure without becoming panic stricken.

Television, Movies, and the Stage

Television and movie dramas share an emphasis on the visual that sharply distinguishes them from stage productions. What is seen is relatively more important in TV and the movies than it is on the stage. By transmitting a delicate change of expression or a tiny gesture, the close-up camera sometimes can provide a deeper texture and richer insights than are possible in a stage presentation. Nuances of vocal expression can also be picked up by microphones in a way that is not possible on the stage.

Another advantage of television and the movies is that the audience's view of what is taking place can be constantly varied. The TV and movie drama, unlike the stage play, does not present a whole picture that is on display for long periods of time. Instead, it presents bits and pieces of a picture, selecting the specific image from the entire panorama of the action that will best advance the purpose of the drama at the given moment. The power to change the picture means that TV and movie dramatists do not, like stage dramatists, have to spend time arranging exits for people whose function is completed and who are merely cluttering up the scene. In most cases they eliminate the unwanted people simply by cutting away from them and taking the audience elsewhere. They have the further privilege of entering a scene to eavesdrop for a moment before moving to another scene. They can also develop parallel actions in widely separated locations, cutting back and forth between them, a method that is almost impossible on the stage. All of these visual means permit the TV and movie dramatist to open up a production in a way that is not available to the stage dramatist. One result of all this is that TV and film dramas have many more individual scenes than stage dramas.

Another factor that distinguishes TV and movie dramas from stage dramas is the relative emphasis on dialogue. Though the quality of the dialogue has a crucial effect on the success of a dramatist's work no matter what the medium, in TV and the movies, dialogue is not the whole play, as it so often is in the theater. With the probing eye of the camera available, the TV and movie writer does not need to depend on words to convey most of the meaning. A single close-up, imaginatively selected and skillfully produced, may create a stronger dramatic climax than a whole sequence of dialogue. This means that the TV and movie dramatists will usually contrive relatively more action and less dialogue than their stage counterparts, and the dialogue they write will be linked more directly with the action. The reliance of stage dramatists on dialogue has another effect. Because their plays tend to talk about events rather than show them, they depend more on the imagination of the audience to fill out the story than do TV and film dramatists.

THE NATURE OF RADIO DRAMA

Radio drama in the United States has reached a condition of near extinction. The National Public Radio network broadcast its *Earplay* series for a number of years and later added a *Masterpiece Radio Theater*, and the CBS network in the mid 1970s began broadcasting a series of suspense dramas followed by another series that dealt with general themes. No other commercial network followed its example, however, and radio drama activity remains sparse and sporadic with no indication that a general revival is about to take place. This in the eyes of some is unfortunate, for radio drama has certain qualities that establish it as a unique art form. More than any other dramatic medium it demands the active collaboration of the audience, for the listener's imagination is the stage of radio. Sound, moreover, has unusual power to arouse an emotional response, and radio, because it concentrates the listener's attention on sound, makes maximum use of this power. Of all the dramatic media, radio is most untrammeled in the form it can take. Radio dramatists can switch backward and forward in time without limit; through the use of the listener's imagination, they can place the drama in one setting for an instant and then snatch it suddenly away to another. Finally, radio drama can be produced quickly and inexpensively. If young dramatists have production facilities and performers available to them, such as they might find in a college workshop, the radio script provides them with the best opportunity they are likely to have to test their dramatic ideas in actual production.

THE SOURCES OF DRAMA

One problem facing aspiring dramatists is that, bursting with the urge to write, they sometimes experience difficulty in finding subjects to write about. Whether the desire to express oneself can exist separately from ideas one wishes to express is questionable, but it does seem that unchanneled creative energies occasionally need firm direction.

The Origin of Dramatic Ideas

Ideas for novels, short stories, and plays spring from every avenue of life, sometimes so insidiously that authors may be unable to explain how specific ideas came into their minds. The root of a story may be something seen, heard, told, or read, held in the brain like the image on a photographic film, ready for development at the proper moment. A story can be inspired by one of the dramas we sometimes see in everyday life: a woman in a railroad station holding a uniformed man tightly to her as though she can never let him go; a dazed motorist staring stupidly down at a body crushed beneath the wheels of his car; the adoring expression in a girl's face as she looks down at the ring on her finger; the teen-ager trying to tell his father that he has just smashed a fender; a lonely mother on a beach watching her deformed child play in the sand; the look of relief in a woman's eyes as she comes from the confessional. Or it may be as slight a happening as a chance remark heard in a subway, a cry of pain in the night, or the sound of a laugh with no mirth in it.

Katherine Anne Porter tells us that the process of creation that resulted in her masterful short story "Flowering Judas" began in Mexico when she saw a grossly fat man serenading a beautiful girl. Her story became an explanation for this situation. The movie production team of Don Simpson and Jerry Bruckheimer, who include among their films such hits as *Flashdance* and *Beverly Hills Cop*, regularly read out-of-the-way magazines to find ideas for stories. An item they found in one of them ignited the creative process that led to the movie *Top Gun*. Even another person's drama may give you a starting point for a story of your own. Johnathon Lawton, the screenwriter of *Pretty Woman*, said his idea for the film, originally a dark story entitled *3000*, came to him when he saw the movie *The Last*

Detail, which follows a convicted Navy criminal's final weekend of freedom.

The Writer's Direct Knowledge

The work of a great many writers suggests that the best writing often finds its inspiration in what the writer knows from direct, personal experience. One example is the work of the screenwriter and director Oliver Stone, whose film *Platoon* won an Academy Award as the best motion picture of 1986. It stemmed directly from his experience as a solider in Vietnam. Stone said of the film that it "was a summation of my feelings, my reaction to what I had seen over there." His film *Born on the Fourth of July*, which dramatized the real-life war and post-war experiences of Ron Kovic, also had its source in autobiography. Some critics have argued that the weaknesses of Stone's later films, such as *The Doors* and *JFK*, spring from the increasingly polemical (and less personal) nature of their screenplays.

Another writer whose work reflects personal experiences is Horton Foote, who first won recognition in the 1950s as a writer of TV dramas and went on to win Academy Awards for his scripts of *To Kill a Mockingbird* and *Tender Mercies*. In 1985 he earned his third Academy Award nomination for his script of *The Trip to Bountiful*. This adaptation of an original TV play was, like many of those he wrote during his TV period, set in a small town in Texas similar to the one in which Foote had grown up. At one point in his career, he published a number of his TV plays in a volume entitled *Harrison, Texas*, the name he gave to the tiny town that served as their principal locale.

The Literal Transcription of Life

Life, then, can be the inspiration for dramatic writing, but dramatists who try to pre-sent life exactly as they experience it usually will fail to write effective drama. One reason for this, oddly enough, is that actual happenings, even though unquestionably authentic, are sometimes so bizarre as to be utterly unbelievable when presented in a play. Novelist and dramatist Somerset Maugham (*The Razor's Edge*) said that "life is full of improbabilities that fiction does not admit of."[4] There is the added difficulty that people in real life are often so capricious and unpredictable that they do completely unexpected things. Dramatic characters must act in terms of the drives and values that have been established for them. They must be consistent. Above all, they must be believable.

A second problem with real life as dramatic material is that it is often routine and monotonous. The conflicts that exist, although they may be of sufficient urgency to arouse interest, generally fail to sustain interest because they remain constant and unresolved. Drama must have crises that gradually rise in pitch until they reach a climax, and these are infrequent in real life. The form and arrangement that drama demands are also missing in most real-life happenings.

We can conclude, then, that although events in one's own experience must usually be the inspiration for a dramatic idea, writers who attempt a literal transcription of these events are in danger of being either absurd or dull. On the foundation that life has provided, they must erect their own edifice of dramatic truth. The absurd and improbable must be rearranged and justified; the tediousness that is everyday life must be telescoped and heightened into a form that has order and development. In the words of George Bernard Shaw, "The dramatist picks out the significant incidents from the chaos of daily happenings and arranges them so that their relationship to one another becomes significant." It must be remembered also that life is dramatic only in its moments of greatest intensity, and only these moments should be selected for dramatic treatment. Whether the completed script reflects accurately the true event is quite immaterial. Katherine Anne Porter, commenting on the inspiration of her story "Flowering Judas," said that as soon as she saw the beautiful girl being serenaded by the fat man she "knew a story; perhaps not her true story, not even the real story of the whole situation, but all the same a story that seemed symbolic truth to me." The important question about a drama is not—is it true?—but rather—does it seem to be true? Will an audience accept and believe it?

Going Beyond Direct Experience

Though writers can find inspiration for dramatic material in what they know directly and use it to ensure authenticity and relevance to life, most of them cannot rely on it exclusively. Doing so would deny the power of the imagination to project writers into unknown realms and ignore their capacity to gain new understandings through vicarious means. It would restrict them to their own times, their own place, and their own acquaintances. William Faulkner, whose novels won him a Nobel Prize, found the inspiration for virtually all of them in his "own little postage stamp of native soil"[5] in Mississippi. But when he became a screenwriter, he had to reach far beyond that locale. In writing the script for *Land of the Pharaohs*, for example, a film that starred a youthful Joan Collins, Faulkner had to undertake research and use his imagination before he could convey an authentic vision of the Egypt of antiquity.

The screenwriters of *Grand Canyon*, Lawrence and Meg Kasdan, relied to a large extent on their own background as residents of Los Angeles to create the changing form and pattern of modern urban life that the film depicts. But the experience they brought to their task was not enough. They had little contact, for instance, with life in the minority-populated areas of the city, which was one aspect of urban experience they wanted to reflect. To fill this gap they undertook special research. Writers who are truly venturesome sometimes may escape the bounds of what they know almost entirely, using personal experience merely as a reference point from which imagination may soar.

QUESTIONS AND PROJECTS

1. Many authorities have described what they consider a "play" to be and have attempted to define the qualities inherent in the word, "dramatic." How would you define these terms?
2. Watch three TV dramas during a week, with the following objectives.
   (a) Note the conflicts they involve, and classify them as struggles involving person against person, person against a group, a group against a group, a person or a group against a natural force or obstacle, or internal conflict. Do any of the dramas seem to lack a readily identifiable conflict situation?
   (b) Be alert to the elements of violence the dramas contain; determine whether these elements are explicit, implicit, lacking in force, or too obvious.
   (c) Decide whether the dramas concentrate on the high points by summarizing the story as a whole and then differentiating between the action actually shown in the play and that which is merely described or implied or which takes place between the scenes.

3. List three incidents from your own experience that might be starting points for dramas.
4. Are there any subjects that you would rather see dramatized for a film to be shown in a theater rather than on television?

NOTES

1. Larry McMurtry, *Film Flam* (New York: Simon and Schuster, 1987), p. 34.

2. William Archer, *Playmaking* (Boston: Small, Maynard and Co., 1912). The discussion on this point occurs on pp. 31–36.
3. Marya Mannes, "Time for a Story," *The Reporter*, Vol. 21 (July 9, 1959), p. 34.
4. Somerset Maugham, "The Vagrant Mood," *The Decline and Fall of the Detective Story* (New York: Doubleday and Co., 1953), p. 109.
5. Quoted in Malcolm Cowley, "How Writers Write," *Saturday Review*, Vol. 40 (November 17, 1957), p. 36.

Inventing an intriguing plot and creating unique, full-bodied characters are two of the most important tasks involved in writing a play. Although these functions can be identified as separate processes in play construction, writers do not necessarily carry them out separately. What they do with one so directly affects the other that they often invent the plot and develop the characters in one simultaneous act of creation. Plotting and characterization make different contributions to the success of a play. A good plot is the most important factor in keeping an audience absorbed as the play is actually going on. Good characterization, on the other hand, is the element most likely to make people remember the play long after it is over. In this chapter we analyze plotting, and in the next take up the problem of creating and revealing memorable characters.

THE PLOTTING STRUCTURE

The plot is the basic pattern of events that constitutes the essential action of the play. It is the fundamental development through which the rise, progress, and resolution of the conflict are revealed to the audience. The plot reveals how one event influences another and why people act as they do. The plot is closely related to the story of the play and, in fact, many people use these terms interchangeably. Some think of the story as the sequence of events told in chronological order, whereas the plot is the arrangement of these events into a pattern that shows their relationships and causation. British novelist E.M. Forster (*A Passage to India*) made a distinction between

CHAPTER
11

INVENTING THE PLOT

Certain dank gardens cry aloud for murder; certain old houses demand to be haunted; certain coasts are set apart for shipwreck.
ROBERT LOUIS STEVENSON
(1850–1894)

story and plot that has become famous. In his book *Aspects of the Novel*, he wrote: "This is a story: The King died and then the Queen died."

And, "This," he wrote, "is a plot: The King died and then the Queen died of grief."

The Elements of a Plot

A number of people have tried to develop a formula for plotting that would simplify the writer's task of inventing stories. Unfortunately, there is no such easy route to the production of good plots. The problems of devising plots vary so much that finding principles having universal application is difficult. Still, there are some guidelines that can direct writers as they start down the road of invention. The first step is to consider the elements that make up a plot.

Decisions by a Character One element of great importance in the plotting structure of many plays is the sequence of decisions that characters make as they confront a problem. Let us suppose that a poverty-striken accountant whose wife desperately needs expensive medical attention considers the possibility of embezzling money to pay for her treatment. The decisions he makes, as he is pushed first in one direction by his need and then in the other by his desire to remain honest, constitute basic steps in the development of the plot. This movement, plus the intense internal conflict it generates, seizes the attention of the audience. The impact is heightened because the issues at stake, as they should be in all plots, are of vital importance to the character.

A Character's Struggle to Reach a Goal
Another element of major importance in plot construction is the struggle that follows a character's decision to reach a certain goal. If the accountant came to the conclusion that he could solve his problem only by embezzling money, the plot then would focus on his attempt to accomplish this goal without being detected.

In some instances the decision-making element may be of no importance because the goal is self-evident. An example is a situation in which a woman in danger struggles to save her life. The average person in such circumstances would not ponder the goal itself, for the urge to survive is instinctive, but would be entirely engrossed with accomplishing it. Decision making might be an element in the plot, however, as the woman considers various means of making her escape, but such decisions are usually of secondary importance to the struggle itself.

Dramatic Action

A criticism frequently made of a play that fails to sustain interest is that it lacks action. There is scarcely any fault more grievous than writing a play in which not enough happens. In fact, a play that is deficient in the quantity or intensity of the action may be worse than unsatisfactory; it may not be a play at all. The first step in avoiding this fault is to understand what action is.

The Nature of Action   Perhaps the most common mistake is to equate action entirely with activity. This is not completely an error, for activity is one of the principal ways of revealing action. It also has the important function of providing movement which keeps the picture on the screen from becoming static and dull. The director may introduce incidental activity or business—smoking, drinking, rises and movements around the set—to keep the picture animated. If action is to be equated with anything, however, it can be equated with change. There is action in a play when changes are constantly taking place. It is through change that a play develops and moves steadily forward to the final crisis. One type of change is connected with the decisions characters make as they try to determine their goals. The climax comes when the most important character makes the choice that sends the person irrevocably down one path instead of another. Activity usually indicates what this choice is. An example of this function occurred in the 1955 movie *Violent Saturday*. Its principal character, an Amish father, has abhorred violence all his life. One day an intruder enters his barn and attacks his family. The gentle father experiences an agonizing conflict at first but then in a wild burst, he seizes a pitchfork and kills the intruder. It was not the mere act of violence that gave this scene its overwhelming power. Its dramatic impact came from the viewer's realization that to save his family the Amish father had violated a principle in which he had always believed. This decision constituted the vital action of the scene, not the activity that expressed it.

A second type of change is the transition from success to failure, or from failure to success, that characters experience as they make various moves in their struggle to reach a goal. During this process, the variations in the equilibrium of the conflicting forces, the shifting from favorable to unfavorable and back to favorable again as the struggle goes on, constitute the action of the play. The final shift, for or against the character, occurs as the play reaches its climax.

Speech and Action   The most important method of revealing action to the audience is through the kind of activity we call speech. Does a scene showing two people sitting across a table from each other quietly talking contain enough action to hold the interest of an audience? We cannot answer that question until we know what the two are saying and its relationship to the vital issues of the play. Does the dialogue grow from a decision made by one of these characters or from a change in equilibrium between them that is leading inevitably to another change? If the answer is "yes," then the scene contains dramatic action and the dialogue helps to reveal it.

On the other hand, if the characters are talking about general matters not directly relevant to the basic issues of the play, the scene lacks action. The plot has stopped its forward movement; no change is taking place or is being prepared for; the play has become sluggish, static, and talky. A scene may also come to a standstill if characters merely argue a matter without settling it one way or another, for action occurs only when there are developments in the story.

Two Types of Plays

We have noted that a plot usually revolves around a conflict in which the significant elements are decisions and a struggle to reach a goal. In some instances a given play concentrates on one type of conflict or the other, particularly the shorter ones which are common in television, and this concentration often helps to provide a desirable unifying quality. A play plotted around the choices made by the leading character is decision centered. A play focusing mainly on a struggle by the leading character to achieve a goal is goal centered. Not all plays fit into these two categories, of course, since some deal equally with decisions and goals.

Basic Plotting Design

A general plotting pattern that fits most plays, whatever their forms may be, does exist, although the nature of the complications dif-

fers from one type of play to the other. In this pattern four main steps can be discerned.

Opening Situation Plays should begin with a character enmeshed, or about to be enmeshed, in a problem situation that involves the conflict at the center of the play's action. A beginning scene must meet two requirements. First, it must be clear. Above all, viewers must understand what is happening. If they become confused about who is who or what is going on, if facts and reasons get mixed up in their minds and the complications start before they get matters unraveled, the play is lost. This does not mean that the significance of every happening must be immediately obvious, for events often take place in the beginning that are not fully explained until later in the play.

The second requisite for the opening scene is that it seize attention immediately. This requirement sometimes presents writers with a dilemma. They must begin with a conflict and yet, to achieve clarity, they may need some time to explain the nature of the conflict. To start a play with a long exposition, however, as some playwrights for the stage used to do, is deadly. The conflict already developed is the best hook for the viewer's attention. The explanation of the conflict must be inserted skillfully into the scene so that it seems to be part of the dramatic action.

Complications The next step is to sharpen and deepen the conflicts until the final crisis is reached. The developments that intensify the conflict and make it more critical are called the complications. In the decision-centered play, they arise as the character is catapulted into a succession of circumstances, all of which force her or him to make a choice involving the same values. The accountant with the sick wife, referred to earlier, must be confronted with a series of events that force him to keep choosing between his wife's health and his desire to lead an honest life. As one decision follows another, he discovers that instead of solving his problem, he becomes even more deeply involved. The conflict within the character becomes more intense, his decisions more difficult, and the potential consequences more ominous.

The goal-centered play is structured in the same general way, but the nature of the complications is somewhat different. Instead of designing a series of developments requiring decisions, the writer must invent a series of situations in which there is a change in the balance of power involving the character and the threatening force. The best design presents situations in which the character first loses ground against the adversary and then gains it, and the maximum tension is likely to develop if, in balance, the hostile force constantly becomes more powerful and threatening.

The Final Crisis   The point in the story where the conflict reaches its greatest height is the final crisis, or the climax, as it is often called. In the decision-centered play, it is the instant when the character makes the choice that gives supremacy to one value instead of another. In the goal-centered play, it is the time of the final decisive struggle in which the character achieves a victory or goes down to defeat.

The Resolution   The part of the play in which the writer describes what happens as a result of the character's final climactic decision or struggle is the resolution. In some cases no explanation is necessary; the nature of the climax itself may be sufficient to indicate the consequences; at other times a brief explanation may be required. An extended resolution is undesirable, however, because the tension of the story has been dissipated with the climax.

Some of the most satisfying plays are those that do not really come to an end with the

final scene. Major problems of life are not solved completely in most cases, and even when they are, new problems rise to take their place. A sharper impact may be gained if the viewer can visualize life and its problems going on even after the play is over.

Analysis of a Decision-Centered Script

To make the general principles of plot construction more meaningful, we shall examine two scripts in considerable detail to illustrate how these principles apply to the design of actual plots. First, we analyze the 1991 film *Guilty by Suspicion*, written and directed by Irwin Winkler. Among the many films Winkler has produced are such notable successes as *Rocky* (which won the Academy Award for best picture in 1976), *Raging Bull* (cited by a number of critics as the best picture made in the 1980s), and *Goodfellas*. *Guilty by Suspicion* was, however, Winkler's first venture in either directing or screenwriting. Its story was set in the early 1950s, when the House Committee on Un-American Activities (sometimes called HUAC) investigated Communist infiltration in the United States. Accusations by anonymous informers sometimes led studios to blacklist film industry figures—an action that destroyed the careers, and, in some instances, the lives of a number of people in the entertainment industry.

The motion picture starred Robert De Niro, a leading Hollywood actor, in the fictional role of David Merrill, a film director who became one of the blacklist's victims. The part of his former wife, Ruth, was played by Annette Bening, who had received critical acclaim and an Academy Award nomination for her performance in *The Grifters*, released a short time before *Guilty by Suspicion*. George Wendt, best known for his role as the beer-drinking bar habitué in the TV situation comedy *Cheers*, played the deadly serious part of a Hollywood writer denounced by an informer. A cameo appearance by director Martin Scorsese added special interest, as did the casting of a number of actors who were actually blacklisted during the period. The picture gained a chilling verisimilitude by making a real person, Darryl Zanuck, production chief of Twentieth Century Fox when blacklisting was at its height, a character in the fictional story.

The Opening Situation   The picture begins with a brief scene depicting HUAC members in executive session, interrogating a film industry employee named Larry Nolan. The dilemma he faces is shared by all those called to testify. He can plead the Fifth Amendment and refuse to answer any questions, but doing so will almost certainly lead studio chiefs to put his name on a blacklist, guaranteeing immediate unemployment. He can also expect to be denounced in the press as a "Fifth-Amendment Communist." If he answers any questions at all, the committee will demand that he purge himself by naming associates who are Communists or Communist sympathizers. Nolan begs abjectly that he not be required to name his friends, but as the scene ends, the committee insists that he cooperate.

The film next focuses on a surprise party held at Nolan's home to welcome David Merrill back to America from a directing stint in Europe. The atmosphere is thick with anxiety as the party-goers talk about the investigation. A cut to a parking area shows a shadowy figure, later identified as an FBI agent, checking license plates. Because of his stay in Europe, Merrill arrives unaware of the HUAC investigation. A strange development makes clear to him, however, that something unusual is going on. He sees Nolan desperately throwing books into a fire. Then Nolan's wife, Dorothy, a film actor, denounces him for naming his friends as Communist sympa-

thizers. We soon discover that she is one of those named. We know then that Nolan yielded to the committee's pressure. The books he is burning are ones he fears would further implicate him as a Communist.

The Complications   The next day Merrill learns that he is caught in the same net now entangling some of his friends. The House committee, told by an anonymous informer that he once attended some left-wing meetings, considers Merrill to be a Communist sympathizer. This information comes to him from Zanuck, for whom Merrill is scheduled to direct a picture. Zanuck tells him the project cannot go forward until Merrill clears his name. He advises him to consult a lawyer named Felix Graff.

In a restaurant that evening, Merrill has a strange encounter with a producer of "B" movies who has apparently found out about the new addition to the blacklist. Knowing that Merrill's career as a director for movies for the top studios is now in jeopardy, the producer tries to inveigle him into directing for him. Upset by this proposal from a second-rate producer, Merrill is disturbed even more when he discovers that the lawyer Graff, fearful of being seen with him, demands that they meet surreptitiously. Merrill's agent also attends the meeting. Still unable to grasp the dimensions of the disaster enveloping him, Merrill is enraged at being told that to clear himself he must name others who attended left-wing meetings. One of them is his best friend, Bunny Baxter, a film writer. At this point, Merrill makes his first decision. Despite the protests of the lawyer and agent, he impetuously rejects their advice and stalks angrily out of the room.

A number of events occurring in quick order give Merrill a frightening grasp of the precarious situation in which he finds himself. Zanuck tells him coldly that if he expects to direct again he must purge himself with the committee. Next, Merrill's agent demands that he pay back $50,000 he has advanced. He then hears from Ruth, with whom he maintains friendly relations despite their separation, that Dorothy Nolan has sent out a desperate cry for help. Her husband Larry has gained custody of their son by denouncing her as a Communist and an unfit mother. Shortly afterwards Merrill runs into Joe Lesser, another director HUAC is investigating. Lesser tells Merrill that he is abandoning a picture before it is edited and is fleeing to England to avoid being pressured into naming his friends as Communists.

When Merrill comes to drive his son Paulie to school, his ex-wife Ruth, apparently concerned that his child support payments will stop, tells him she is going back to teaching. He tries to assure her that something will turn up soon, but his confidence is shaken once more by an encounter with a distraught Bunny Baxter, who has now come under the committee's fire. Merrill's anxiety intensifies when he finds himself denied entrance to the Twentieth Century-Fox studios. In desperation he begins calling friends for whom he has done favors in the hope that they can lead him to a job, but they refuse to come to the phone or return his calls. A demoralizing episode with his son follows. Paulie, hearing on television that Julius and Ethel Rosenberg are to be executed for giving atomic secrets to the Soviets, expresses fear that his father will suffer the same fate. Merrill tries to reassure him, then tells Ruth he is leaving Los Angeles for New York, where he thinks he can find theater work.

In New York, Merrill's situation darkens even further. Most of his friends are afraid to be seen with him, and those who do ask why he doesn't solve his problem by giving the committee what it wants. FBI agents constantly follow him and when he takes a lowly job in a repair shop, they threaten his employer for hiring a Communist. To pro-

tect him, Merrill quits and returns to Los Angeles on a bus.

Ruth, now returned to teaching, meets him at the depot and invites him to move in with her. That evening they join Dorothy Nolan for dinner. Certain that a person of his stature must have found a directing job in New York, she upbraids him for not casting her in his play. He has to tell her that no one would hire him. She shifts the conversation to the son she hasn't seen for a month and begins to drink. In the parking lot, Merrill offers to drive the intoxicated Dorothy home, but she obstinately climbs into her own car and then deliberately puts her car into reverse and crashes through a barrier into the rocky canyon below.

At Dorothy's funeral, an FBI agent quite openly takes pictures of those attending. Bunny Baxter hurriedly sneaks away to avoid being identified. Merrill is accosted once more by the "B" picture producer, who tells him he has had to fire a director in the middle of a picture and wants Merrill to finish the job. He will have to do so without getting screen credit, of course, the producer tells him. Now desperate for money, Merrill accepts the offer, but even this project collapses when the studio discovers that a Communist is directing one of its pictures and forces the producer to fire him.

Realizing he is at the end of his resources, Merrill seeks out the lawyer Graff and explores his options. He wonders whether it would help if he appeared before the committee and took the Fifth Amendment. Graff tells him that he can extricate himself from his dilemma only by giving the committee the names of Communist sympathizers. Shortly after, Baxter comes to see him and makes a peculiar request: To help his cause, he asks permission to name Merrill as a Communist when the committee calls him to testify, arguing that Merrill can't be hurt because he is already ruined. Merrill turns on his old friend in a fury, but when he think over what has happened, he realizes how desperate his situation has become. At that point Zanuck, in a final attempt to get him to act sensibly, calls him in and almost begs him to cooperate with the committee. To tempt him, he lets Merrill read a script that he knows will appeal to his directing instincts. It will go into production with him at the helm as soon as he stops being obstinate, Zanuck tells him. Now near the breaking point, Merrill talks with Ruth about his passion for filmmaking. She senses that he is ready to appear before the committee.

The Final Crisis Merrill's appearance before the House committee in public session brings the story to its climax. As he walks down the hall to the hearing room accompanied by Graff, he hears a committee member praising a previous witness for his helpful testimony. Grim-lipped, Merrill begins answering the committee's questions. He admits that he attended a number of meetings devoted to discussing leftist causes, but denies that he ever belonged to the Communist Party. The committee next asks him to name other people who attended those meetings. The moment of final decision has arrived as David stares silently at the committee. Graff implores him to answer the question. When his silence continues, Graff announces that he has been dismissed as Merrill's attorney and stalks from the hearing room.

The committee member presses him more heatedly, demanding to know whether the deceased Dorothy Nolan was one of those who attended the meetings. They ask him about the surprise party that welcomed him home from Europe. Quietly, Merrill tells the committee that he will talk about himself but about no one else. Its members threaten him with a contempt citation. He rises to his feet and denounces them. They angrily respond by demanding that he leave the stand to make way for the next witness.

That next witness turns out to be Bunny Baxter. As Merrill watches from the door with Ruth, he realizes that Baxter, whom he had last seen trembling with fear, has undergone an astonishing transformation. Now cool and self-possessed, he scorns taking the Fifth Amendment to protect himself from a contempt citation, but simply states that he will answer none of the committee's questions. He, like Merrill, has made a final, critical decision.

The Resolution As the movie closes, Merrill and his ex-wife walk down the corridor from the hearing room into what threatens to be a grim future. The film does not reveal what happened to them or to the other characters, but a title that concludes the motion picture tells the audience that those who refused to cooperate with the House committee remained under a cloud for the next 20 years.

A Summary of the Plotting The story of *Guilty by Suspicion* provides an excellent example of a plot whose complications are generated almost entirely by the characters' decisions. The ones we are most interested in, of course, are made by the leading character, Merrill, but the decisions of others also advance the action in crucial ways. The characters react differently to the problem they face. Larry Nolan capitulates under the pressure and names his friends. His wife, Dorothy, solves her problem by taking her own life. Joe Lesser, David's director friend, flees to England. Darryl Zanuck, though not personally accused, responds practically by advising David to cooperate with the committee. Bunny Baxter, after seeming to disintegrate under the pressure, eventually finds the strength to defy his accusers.

Because his stay in Europe kept Merrill from understanding the nature of the situation, he cannot believe at first that he is facing a threat to his career. In the beginning he decides in an almost casual way not to cooperate with the committee. Then the situation gradually becomes more ominous. Zanuck refuses to assign him to a picture and denies him entrance to the studio. His agent abandons him and other associates refuse to answer his calls. As his income dries up, his ex-wife is forced to return to teaching. His son is terrified at the menace enveloping his father. Merrill goes to New York only to find that he is as much a pariah there as he is in Hollywood. When he does find a menial position, the FBI tracks him down and threatens his employer. He returns to Hollywood where he is forced to sleep on his ex-wife's couch. He watches in horror as his friend Dorothy Nolan, reacting to the same situation he is in, commits suicide. Almost equally shocking are the panic-stricken actions of his best friend, Bunny Baxter.

These events, developing on a constantly accelerating plane, bring Merrill to the breaking point. He decides finally that he can continue the career he loves only by capitulating. In the committee room, however, the stark choice he is contemplating strikes him with overwhelming force. He can save himself only by betraying his friends. Confronted by that realization, he draw back and refuses to name them. He has now made his final decision and is willing to accept the consequences.

Analysis of Goal-Centered Script

The TV mini-series *Separate But Equal*, broadcast by ABC about the time that *Guilty by Suspicion* was playing in movie theaters, provides an excellent example of a plot that revolves around the struggle by a character to achieve a previously determined goal. *Separate But Equal* was awarded an Emmy in 1991 as the best drama special of the year. The script was

written and directed by George Stevens, Jr., who earlier won an Emmy for his production of *The Murder of Mary Phagan*. The stars were Sidney Poitier, in his first TV role since 1955, and Burt Lancaster, in one of his last performances. *Guilty by Suspicion* and *Separate But Equal* are similar in that each deals with real events. Most of the characters in the film, however, were fictional; the characters in the TV program, in contrast, were almost all real people who actually took part in the events depicted. Though some scenes and dialogue were created, as the introduction to the mini-series stated, its purpose was to tell a true story. It therefore falls into the category of dramatic writing called *docudrama*.

Poitier portrayed Thurgood Marshall, who, as the chief counsel for the Legal Defense Fund of the National Association for the Advancement of Colored People (NAACP), led the fight in the early 1950s to outlaw the practice of school segregation. Marshall was later appointed to the U.S. Supreme Court where he served from 1967 to 1991. Lancaster played the part of John W. Davis, Marshall's main antagonist in the desegregation fight. Davis in 1924 had run unsuccessfully against Calvin Coolidge as the Democratic presidential nominee, and had appeared before the Supreme Court on many occasions. In the 1950s he represented South Carolina in resisting the NAACP's attempt to abolish segregation. When the case came before the Supreme Court, it was known as *Brown v. Board of Education* and combined actions that took place in four different states. *Separate But Equal* focused on the events that occurred in Clarendon County, South Carolina. Other leading characters in the story were Marshall's wife Buster, who, though seriously ill of cancer, strongly supported her husband's effort; and Earl Warren, Chief Justice of the United States in 1954 when the case was decided. He played a vital role in determining the case's outcome.

Though the story is goal centered, decisions by the characters also are involved. From several options, for example, Marshall must choose his goal. He also must decide the best means of accomplishing it. But the focus is primarily on the events, some favorable, some unfavorable, that took place as he struggled to reach his objective.

The Opening Situation   In Clarendon County, one of many buses transporting White students passes a group of African-American children who must trudge five miles to reach their school. The father of one of them, Harry Briggs, complains to the teacher, the Reverend T.A. DeLaine, that his son, Harry, Jr., is so worn out by the daily 10-mile round trip that he can't study. DeLaine asks the superintendent of schools to provide at least one bus for the Negro children. The superintendent says that the county cannot afford another bus. DeLaine and others then seek the help of the NAACP, and it sends the chief counsel of its Legal Defense Fund, Marshall, to South Carolina to investigate the situation. Marshall immediately concludes that in providing buses for Whites but not for Negroes, the county is violating the Fourteenth Amendment, which guarantees all citizens equal protection under the law. He further believes that the practice of segregating children into all-White and all-Negro schools is at the root of the problem. He hesitates to make segregation the central issue, however, because the Supreme Court has ruled on seven different occasions that segregation is legal, provided that the facilities are equal. He decides that the lawsuit should focus on the fact that White children ride to school while Negroes walk. He suggests that the people who have called him to South Carolina draw up a petition complaining about that inequality, warning them, however, that their action is likely to provoke reprisals. His prediction is soon realized. Briggs loses his job, the Rev.

DeLaine is run off the road while driving his car, and later his house is burned down. Nevertheless, the group persists in gathering the required number of signatures, and the case comes before a South Carolina court.

The Complications   Marshall's decision to concentrate on school inequalities is immediately frustrated when the court rules that the petition challenges the provision in the state constitution that established segregation. He must therefore strike directly at segregation. Despite this unfavorable turn, Marshall perseveres. He presents striking evidence that segregation lowers the self-esteem of Negro children. His argument is so convincing that one of the three judges on the panel decides in his favor, but the other two vote against him. As Marshall leaves the courtroom, someone warns him that he had better not set foot in the state again.

It is clear now that continuing his battle may bring attempts on his life. Moreover, he must wonder what he can hope to gain by bringing the issue of segregation before the Supreme Court, considering it has supported segregation seven times in the past. If he is to overcome this precedent, he must accomplish the almost impossible task of convincing the justices that the framers of the Fourteenth Amendment had segregation in mind when they initiated the requirement that all people must receive equal protection under the law. Marshall is also confronted by opposition within his own group. Believing that he cannot win on the issue of segregation, some of his associates try to persuade him to go back to focusing on the issue of inequality. His wife's illness is also on his mind. He fears that his absorption with the case will cause him to neglect her.

Despite these obstacles, Marshall decides to make segregation the principal issue. He knows he can count on the votes of the court's two leading liberals. But he knows equally well that the majority is unlikely to overturn the precedent established by the court's previous rulings on segregation. Most of all, he worries that Fred Vinson, the Chief Justice, will not provide the strong leadership that so controversial a case demands. Marshall also learns that the redoubtable John W. Davis, who has argued 138 cases before the Supreme Court, will represent the South Carolina position.

After months of delay, the time for the argument before the Supreme Court finally arrives. Marshall presents the evidence he used in South Carolina, showing that segregation harms Negro children. Davis argues that the Fourteenth Amendment outlaws inequality, not segregation. To support this argument, he cites the fact that at the very time Congress passed the Fourteenth Amendment, it set up segregated schools in Washington, D.C. He also emphasizes the importance of maintaining the precedent established by the previous segregation decisions.

Marshall feels that many of the questions the justices ask are hostile to his case, particularly one suggesting that segregation helps to reduce racial tensions. He is deeply dissatisfied with his own performance, believing his responses to the questions weak and ineffective. The one bright spot he sees is a remark by Justice Douglas suggesting that the Fourteenth Amendment may need updating.

Grimly, Marshall and his colleagues wait for a decision they are almost certain will go against them. Then quite unexpectedly the court acts in their favor. It does not give them the victory they had hoped for, but it does offer them another chance. The court decides to ask for further argument and instructs Marshall to look for evidence indicating that, in passing the Fourteenth Amendment, Congress had segregation in mind. Immediately Marshall undertakes an intense research effort, but for many months he fails to find the evidence he needs. Other

circumstances work against him. The NAACP undergoes a financial crisis. Its electricity is cut off; the funds with which to pay employees run out. The situation threatens to become even more desperate when a South Carolina official suggests to Davis that he attack the tax-deductible status of the NAACP. Davis rebuffs him, however, with the comment, "That's not our style."

Then a development occurs whose impact cannot be foreseen. Chief Justice Vinson dies, and President Dwight D. Eisenhower appoints Earl Warren in his place. Marshall and his associates are dismayed. As governor of California, Warren had presided over the displacement of Japanese citizens during World War II into internment camps. A further count against him is that he has never before served as a judge. Their anxiety over this development is somewhat allayed when the research effort Marshall had instituted uncovers evidence that Thaddeus Stevens, one of the leaders of the Congress that passed the Fourteenth Amendment, had opposed segregation.

The case is reargued on December 7, 1953. Davis emphasizes steps that have been taken in South Carolina to make Negro schools equal to White schools, thus satisfying the requirements of the Fourteenth Amendment. Marshall counters with the evidence he has discovered about the intent of Congress. He also points out that White and Negro children play together in the streets and attend the same universities. Why then should they be separated from one another in public schools? Most of all he emphasizes the psychological damage caused by segregation.

Marshall does not yet know that the development most favorable to his cause was the appointment of Warren, who is convinced that moral and humanitarian considerations demand that segregation be outlawed.

The Final Crisis   As the story mounts to its climax, the burden of winning the battle against segregation passes from Marshall to Warren, who concludes that because of the controversial nature of the issue, the decision of the Supreme Court must be unanimous. Trying to achieve that goal complicates his task. He manages to win a majority of the court to his side, but the concern expressed by three of the justices seems to make the achievement of unanimity impossible. Nevertheless Warren perseveres as he delicately maneuvers to bring the recalcitrant justices over to his point of view. One of his principal challenges is to overcome their fear that the abolition of segregation will provoke unrest and violence. Day after day he goes from one to the other, pressing his view that segregation must be eliminated.

The Resolution In 1954 the Supreme Court takes one of its most significant steps when it nullifies precedent by announcing that segregation in the public schools is unconstitutional. In so doing, it adopts the argument, advanced by Marshall, that segregated schools are inherently unequal. Marshall calls his wife, greeting her with the triumphant statement, "We did it!" In another scene we see the joy on the faces of the Rev. DeLaine and Harry Briggs as they savor victory in the battle they had begun. Davis graciously acknowledges defeat. As the program closes, the audience is given a glimpse into the future. It is clear that the conflict feared by the reluctant justices does in fact lie ahead, and that years will go by before the nation as a whole accepts the Supreme Court's decision. The audience also learns that Marshall's wife died of cancer a year after the decision. In 1967, President Lyndon Johnson appointed him an associate justice of the Supreme Court, the first African-American to serve in that role.

A Summary of the Plotting The plot of *Separate But Equal* provides an excellent

example of the way the tides of fortune shift for and against a character striving to reach a previously determined objective. Thus it exemplifies the basic technique used in plotting goal-centered plays. Because writer George Stevens, Jr., was dramatizing an actual event, he could not invent incidents that would solve a plotting problem or intensify the conflict. Fortunately the real events which took place as Marshall and his associates struggled to eliminate school segregation made up the pattern of advances and retreats that characterizes a goal-centered play.

Among the unfavorable developments were the following: the refusal of Clarendon County to provides buses for Negro children; Marshall's defeat in the South Carolina Court; the opposition of some NAACP members to making the elimination of segregation the goal; the violence and threats suffered by those who were pursuing it; the precedent supporting segregation represented by seven Supreme Court decisions; the illness of Marshall's wife; the financial plight of the NAACP; the conservatism of many of the justices; the appointment of the formidable John W. Davis to argue for maintaining segregation; and the difficulty of finding an intent to eliminate segregation in the Fourteenth Amendment.

Balancing these unfavorable factors were a number of favorable developments: the psychological experiment showing that segregation destroys Negro children's self-esteem; the winning of one judge's vote in the South Carolina case; the presence on the Supreme Court of the liberal justices Hugo Black and William Douglas; the reopening of the Supreme Court case for further argument; the discovery that at least one member of the Congress that established the Fourteenth Amendment was opposed to segregation; the appointment of Warren to succeed Vinson as Chief Justice; the decision of Warren to support the anti-segregation cause and his commitment to persuading all his fellow justices to join him.

The writer took these opposing forces and fashioned them into a swiftly moving plot whose ups and downs consistently held the interest of the audience as events flowed alternately in the chief character's favor and then against him. In this case he won his battle. In some goal-oriented stories, of course, the character does not gain the sought-after objective.

Other Plotting Patterns

The technique we have described represents one approach to plotting dramas. Other writers have devised different ways of carrying out this step. William Miller, in his book *Screenwriting for Narrative Film and Television*,[1] divides the process into four phases as we do, but uses different words to describe them. His terms are *conflict, development, climax,* and *denouement.* Syd Field, in his book *Screenplay,*[2] structures a film script into three acts. The first act provides the setup for the story; the second dramatizes the confrontation; the third presents the resolution. Field also emphasizes the importance of what he calls "plotting points—an incident or event that hooks into the story and spins it around in another direction." They are similar to the instances in a decision-centered play where the focal character chooses one course of action over another, or places in a goal-centered play where events turn for or against the focal character. Like Field's plotting points, these developments change the direction of the story. Studying the ideas of these and other writers should provide you with further insights into the challenging task of inventing effective plots.

IMPROVING THE PLOT

An experience common to many writers is the discovery that a plot that seemed to be developing smoothly has suddenly hit a snag and come to a dead stop. What does the writer do in such a situation? To answer this question without reference to a specific story is somewhat difficult, but some general suggestions may be helpful. First of all, do not give up in despair. Very few stories suddenly spring full-blown into a writer's brain. The construction of almost every plot demands its moments of agony, and unfortunately there are no sure-fire formulas whose use is guaranteed to produce a satisfactory plot. There are certain basic procedures, however, which experience has shown to be effective. As an addition to the principles already discussed, let us consider a few more that may help the writer who is having plotting difficulties.

Trouble and Plotting

An old French proverb has this counsel for the playwright: "Get your character into a tree. Throw stones at him. Get him out." Exactly the same advice was offered by the American playwright and actor Frank Craven when he said, "Get your character into a pot. Light a fire. Get him out." These admonitions sum up succinctly the fundamental responsibility of the dramatist in plotting a play. Start with a person in trouble. Intensify that trouble. Resolve it. The resolution, by the way, despite the admonitions just quoted, does not always free the characters from trouble. As the play ends they may still be in the tree, perhaps with a storm coming up. Or if the pot is their fate, the fade-out may come with the water just coming to a boil. But whatever its precise nature, the playwright must be making some kind of trouble for somebody, at least until the resolution of the play is reached.

Yes, the aspiring playwright must be a trouble maker! Make as much trouble for your characters as you possibly can. Perhaps a guide to the most effective procedure is to combine the two pieces of advice with which this section began. Get your characters into a tree. Throw stones at them. Get them out of the tree. But do not let them escape safely to the ground just yet. Instead, let them drop from the tree right into Craven's pot of boiling water!

Intensifying Trouble

Assume that you have designed a plot that makes trouble for a character and yet still seems to lack sufficient impact to win sustained attention. What can you do to infuse such a pallid plot with a greater charge of excitement and power? One of the first questions you should ask yourself is: *Have I made the trouble for my characters serious enough?*

Remember that your primary challenge in writing a play is to make an audience react emotionally. One of the ways already noted for doing this is to portray characters twisted with indecision as they try to make a choice between two clashing values. To gain the maximum emotional response, those values must be as important to the characters as you can possibly make them. Moreover, they must involve a problem that has meaning and reality for the average listener.

Suppose that you are writing a play about a man who has lost his faith in God. This theme will probably strike a responsive chord with the audience, for most people believe in the existence of a God and, at the same time, most people occasionally experience doubt. You can therefore expect sympathy and understanding from your audience. Is this enough? Perhaps, but there is at least one way in which this particular problem can be made more serious. Suppose that the individual suffering the loss of faith is not an ordinary layman, but the representative of an organized religion. It is his responsibility not just to believe in God—that would be taken for granted—but to

enhance and sow that faith in other people. A loss of faith for such a person cannot be kept a secret. This complication of the problem will make his emotional response that much more intense, and it will have a similar effect on the emotional response of the audience.

Up to now we have been looking at this man's trouble only in terms of his personal involvement. What if the problem reaches out to affect other people? Suppose, for example, that he has a niece, a mature person who has already passed the age when most women are married. Now, however, there is a prospect in the offing, not a man she is in love with yet, but certainly one with whom a happy married life is a possibility. Suppose, furthermore, that this prospect is a devout believer who is attracted to the niece, at least at first, because of the position her uncle holds as a propagator of the faith. We have succeeded in making the main character's trouble even worse, for more than his own happiness is now at stake. If his loss of faith becomes known, it is likely to smash what may be his niece's last chance for a normal life as a married woman. (You may have suspected that this example is not a hypothetical one. It is the plot of a television play, so successful that it was repeated a number of times—Paddy Chayefsky's *Holiday Song,* the story of a Jewish cantor who temporarily lost his faith.)

The principle that intensification of trouble amplifies the emotional response applies just as much to the goal-centered play as it does to the decision-centered play. One effective technique is to show characters surmounting what seem to be the most difficult obstacles to attaining their goal only to find an even greater barrier in the way. This device was used effectively in Michael Crichton's movie adaptation of his novel *The Great Train Robbery.* Set in the mid-19th century, the story tells how a criminal named Edward Pierce attempts to steal a shipment of gold consigned to pay British troops in the Crimea. The gold, locked in two safes, is being carried on a train traveling from London to Paris. To open the safes, Pierce needs four different keys, all hidden in what appear to be inaccessible locations. He complicates his problem by deciding that he must possess the keys only long enough to make copies. To keep them permanently would notify the authorities that a robbery was being planned and they would then take steps to thwart it.

Pierce triumphs over what seem to be impossible odds to obtain copies of all four keys. The route to the gold now seems open. Pierce bribes a railroad guard to look away when an accomplice of Pierce enters the baggage car to replace the gold in the safes with lead shot and then throw the gold through the door to another accomplice waiting at a predetermined location. Chance interposes another enormous obstacle to the achievement of this objective. Because of a theft on another train, the railroad authorities impose new rules. They will permit no one to ride in the baggage car with the guard, and they place an outside lock on the door so that it cannot be opened from the inside. Pierce must now find a way to get his accomplice inside the baggage car; if he succeeds in doing that, he must then figure out how to get the gold from a moving train through a door that is locked from the outside. These successes and reversals are only a sampling of the pattern of events in this goal-centered script that shows Pierce surmounting one obstacle, only to be faced by another even more difficult one.

Surprise and Plotting

Another effective technique for making a story more interesting and intriguing is to surprise the audience at regular intervals. Some elements of surprise should be built into every plot. Some types of stories, of course, depend almost entirely for their impact on an unexpected plot twist. The type of detective fiction that makes the culprit the least likely suspect is an example. To make surprise the only objective of a story, of course, may be a mistake, for it can lead to an overall result that is thin and unsatisfying. T.S. Eliot struck the proper note of moderation when he said, "The audience should be kept in constant expectation that something is going to happen; and that, when it does happen, it should be different, but not too different, from what the audience had been led to expect."

How can you introduce the unexpected into your scripts? One means is to take an audience down a road and then suddenly push it further down that road than it expected to go. Viewers of the film *Chinatown*, knowing the corrupt nature of Noah Cross (played by John Huston), are ready to believe he engaged in fraud and conspiracy to commit murder. They are likely to be stunned, however, when they discover he is also the father of his own daughter's child.

Another effective technique is to make the audience think that the hero has surmounted the last obstacle in a goal-oriented play only to find that he is in even deeper trouble. This technique was used in the drama *Into the Night*, written by Mel Dinelli. It told of a young couple who become hostage to a criminal fleeing the law. When they stop at a farmhouse, the young man manages to tell the farmer about his plight and asks him to call the police, but his hope comes crashing down when the farmer indicates he is deaf. Even more disturbing, he realizes that the criminal has overheard the conversation and is about to kill the hostages, who have become a threat to him. Before the criminal can act, however, the farmer sneaks up behind him with a loaded shotgun. It turns out that the farmer had only feigned deafness to fool the criminal.

The technique of making an audience believe one thing and then reversing the situation by introducing new information is one of the most common devices for achieving surprise. It was used with great effectiveness in a script titled "Life Choice," an episode in the *Law and Order* television series. The central event in the story was the bombing of an abortion clinic. As was the practice in all episodes of this series, the story was divided into two parts: The first dealt with the police investigation of the crime, the second with the prosecution of those indicted by the district attorney's office.

Before the bomb exploded, an anonymous caller warned the abortion clinic personnel to evacuate the premises. Everyone escaped except a young woman named Mary Donovan, who had come into the clinic without being seen and was in the bathroom when the bomb went off. The police discovered she was carrying a fake identity card and was an active member of a right-to-life group. They therefore concluded that she had carried the bomb into the building and, because of a faulty timing mechanism, had failed to escape before it exploded. Further investigation revealed that another young woman, Celeste McClure, had purchased the materials for the bomb. The police conjectured that after constructing it, she passed it on to Rose Schwimmer, the head of the right-to-life group, who then instructed Mary Donovan to take it into the abortion clinic.

The surprise came after two assistant district attorneys began investigating the case. They discovered the shocking fact that Donovan, rather than being a member of the conspiracy, actually had come to the clinic to seek an abortion. To hide the fact that a member of a right-to-life group was actually taking an action the group publicly condemned, she had arranged with the man responsible for her pregnancy to obtain a fake identity card so that she could undergo the procedure under an assumed name. Hidden in the bathroom (where presumably she was trying to get up the nerve to carry through her plan), she failed to hear the warning to leave the building and thus became an innocent victim of the bomb. Further investigation pointed to Rose Schwimmer, the leader of the right-to-life group, as the person who had planted the bomb and called in the warning. Her crime, however, was no longer merely destruction of property. It had now become murder. This revelation set the stage for a dramatic scene after Schwimmer was indicted and brought to trial. Much to the surprise of the prosecution, she volunteered to testify in her own behalf and in the excerpt below, her attorney, Greg Molloy, has just begun his questioning. Representing the prosecution is Assistant District Attorney Ben Stone.

---

61   INT. COURTROOM—LATER

Schwimmer is sitting. Molloy is standing. Stone is seated.

JUDGE
Is the defense ready for its summation?

MOLLOY
Your Honor, at this time, against advice of counsel,
the defendant wishes to testify in her own behalf.

Stone and Robinette exchange an amazed look.

> JUDGE
> Miss Schwimmer, you realize that you
> will be subject to cross examination.

> SCHWIMMER
> I do, Your Honor.

> JUDGE
> While I urge you to reconsider and listen to advice
> of counsel, I won't prevent you from testifying.

Schwimmer, without even a glance at Molloy, stands and strides to the stand.

> BAILIFF
> Do you swear to tell the truth, so help you God?

> SCHWIMMER
> *(clear; steady)*
> I certainly do.

> MOLLOY
> Miss Schwimmer, did you conspire with Celeste McClure to bomb the
> Chelsea Women's Choice Center as well as seven other abortion clinics?

> SCHWIMMER
> Yes I did.

A rustle runs through the courtroom.

> MOLLOY
> Then you're guilty of the charges leveled against you?

> SCHWIMMER
> Not before God.

> MOLLOY
> Can you explain why you're innocent before God?

> STONE
> Objection. This case is being judged on the temporal plane, Your Honor.

> JUDGE
> Sustained.

SCHWIMMER
(quiet; commanding)
How dare you object, Mr. Stone. . . .
You've been baptized, you take communion . . .

JUDGE
That's enough, Miss Schwimmer.

SCHWIMMER
(ignoring him)
And you prosecute me! *All* the abortions in that clinic are murder . . .

STONE
Your Honor . . .

SCHWIMMER
Mary Donovan's death was tragic, but if it stops one abortion, the
scales are balanced! Are we a nation who will tolerate the abortionist
sticking his hand into a mother's womb and strangling the fetus . . .

JUDGE
(angry)
The Court Officer will remove Miss Schwimmer . . .

STONE
(holding up his hand)
Your Honor, please . . . I have only one question for the defendant . . .

SCHWIMMER
Which is?

STONE
If abortion is murder, no matter how you feel about Mary
Donovan, aren't *you* guilty of the murder of her unborn child?

The color drains from Rose Schwimmer. There's a rustle through the court.

STONE
(near sotto)
I'm finished with the defendant.

The main surprise of this story, of course, is the revelation that Mary Donovan was seeking an abortion. This twist gains added impact when Stone brings out the fact that the anti-abortionist Schwimmer is responsible for the death of a fetus.

Believability and Plotting

No matter what kind of plotting problem faces writers, they must always be concerned about attaining believability. The various segments of the plot must fit together in a reasonable, natural way. The resolution must be one that can be justified in terms of what has gone before. This test must also be applied to each development as it occurs. Does it grow naturally from the situation that just preceded it? Do the plot complications arise from factors that are inherent in the story? Solutions should not be thrust in suddenly from the outside.

One of the most important rules is that coincidence or fortuitous acts of fate should not be used to extricate a writer from a plotting dilemma. A coincidence may be employed to create a problem, but it should never be used to solve it. The use of coincidence or an act of fate to solve a problem, unless it develops inevitably from what has gone before, is a sign of plotting weakness.

ORIGINALITY IN PLOTTING

To the young writer who aspires to create a plot that is completely original, the best admonition is: *Quit trying*. At least as far as the basic elements are concerned, no new plots have been developed for thousands of years. Even when people first began to write dramas, there were not many plots to go around. Some authorities say that no more than seven completely different plots have ever existed.

Actually, concern with creating original stories is a relatively modern development. In Greek times, playwrights felt themselves limited to the dramatization of one of a few well-known legends. Their contribution was to promote new understandings of the characters and problems involved. Shakespeare's habit of borrowing plots or combining several of them to make a new story, as he did in

Macbeth, is well known. Only two of his plots have not been traced to other sources. What made his plays creative triumphs was not the plot but the sharp probing into human motives and the glorious dialogue through which plot and characters were revealed.

The impossibility of creating a new plot, at least as far as its fundamental structure is concerned, should not be taken, however, as minimizing the importance of designing a satisfactory plot. This means that it must meet the tests of credibility, of structural soundness, and of interest value. Great ingenuity and inventiveness are necessary to design a plot that will have these qualities.

And even though the basic elements of a plot cannot be new, the manner in which that plot is embodied in a script can be original with the writer. The use of new subject matter, for instance, can invest a familiar pattern of entanglements with qualities of freshness and distinction. Writers use a standard design when they constantly shift the balance of power in a goal-centered play, but the devices they use to cause that shifting can be their own creation. They cannot invent new values for use in a play of decision, but they can originate new circumstances in which old values can be tested. So far as these factors are concerned, almost every story confronts writers at times with a new frontier through which they must break the first path. In this strange territory they are pretty much on their own. For the unique problems they are likely to meet, they must find solutions equally unique. Their only resource in meeting this challenge is their capacity for imaginative and creative thinking.

Perhaps the best chance to achieve originality is in the characters that writers create. The pattern of entanglements can affect people who are uniquely their own creations. It is with the problem of creating characters that we are next concerned.

QUESTIONS AND PROJECTS

1. Recall some of the plays, movies, or television dramas you have seen. Do your most vivid recollections seem to stem from effectively created characters or from ingeniously contrived plots?
2. Watch a TV drama or film with particular attention to the activity of the characters (speech, physical activity, and so on) and decide whether it is effective in revealing the action of the play.
3. Diagram the plotting line of a TV play or film to determine whether it can be categorized as decision centered or goal centered. If it is the first, list the crucial decisions of the leading character; if it is the second, describe the turns in the situation and indicate whether they are favorable or unfavorable to the attainment of the character's goal.
4. Isolate the surprise elements in a number of TV plays or films and decide whether they add to the dramatic experience.
5. In several TV dramas, describe the nature of the trouble facing the leading characters. Could this trouble have been intensified to enhance the emotional impact in any instances?

NOTES

1. William Miller, *Screenwriting for Narrative Film and Television* (Boston: Hastings House, 1980).
2. Syd Field, *Screenplay* (New York: Dell Publishing Co., 1982).

In addition to inventing a plot, dramatists must create characters who will bring the plot into being in a memorable way, and they must also think about the theme or main idea the plot and characters will communicate to an audience. We consider the problems of developing effective characters in this chapter and then discuss the place of a theme in play construction in the next.

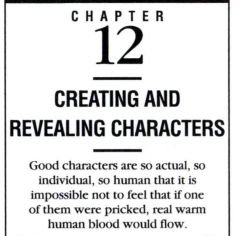

strated by the fact that three of the characters he created for *The Mary Tyler Moore Show* became the central characters of three new series: *Rhoda*, *Phyllis*, and *Lou Grant*.

The process of characterization involves two steps. First, the dramatist must bring into being the characters of the play, determining precisely what kind of people they are. Second, through such means as dialogue, setting, action, and reaction, these creations must be revealed to the audience. We concern ourselves now with the first of these steps.

CREATING CHARACTERS

Of the many challenges facing a dramatist, the most important of all is the challenge of bringing to life characters who have flesh-and-blood reality; who, because of their vitality and individuality, seize the attention of an audience and achieve existence as absorbing, believable human beings. The works that have won an enduring place in literature have done so primarily because of their characters. The brooding, hesitant Hamlet sticks more vividly in our memory than the precise series of events that entrapped him. The picture of a proud Oedipus propelling himself to doom in a relentless search for truth comes first to our mind rather than the specific complications that brought about his destruction. As David Black, a TV writer and producer, has said, series like *Hill Street Blues* remain memorable because of their characters. We remember them rather than the plots that involved them. James L. Brooks, the writer of such TV series as *The Mary Tyler Moore Show* and *Taxi* and writer-director of such films as *Terms of Endearment* and *Broadcast News*, has said that one of his principal goals is "to deliver characters that linger in your memory."[1] His success in doing so is demon-

A Definition of Character

The task of defining a person's character may be approached in a number of different ways. We may describe a certain woman as a selfish person, who in a crisis is likely to seek a solution that will be of benefit primarily to herself. We may characterize a person of the opposite stripe as kind or generous. We may say of a father that he always puts his work first, even at the expense of denying his family a much-needed vacation. Looking at character from still another viewpoint, we may attach the tag of "cold fish" to the individual who is difficult to know. When we think of a particular person, a tie that is always askew may come first to mind. These details are all reflections of the general qualities that add up to the complex concept we know as character. Let us examine the nature of these qualities.

Character Values   The ultimate test of character is the way people behave, particularly in critical situations. More important than anything else in determining that behavior are the values or drives that dominate them. These values determine the choices they make as they face critical decisions, and these choices, in turn, reveal what kind of people they are. Thus, a character is determined directly by a system of values. It follows that the most crucial step in the creation of a character is to decide the values that will control the behavior of the person.

What are some of the values that motivate our lives? A few people have an insatiable lust for power and are willing to sacrifice all else to gain it. Others give up everything for the love of a woman. Javert in Victor's Hugo's *Les Miserables* finally destroyed himself because of his insensate dediction to what he considered duty. Van Gogh's overwhelming desire to paint crowded all other values out of his life. Some men crave fame and attention; others deliberately avoid it. Bob Hope, for example, enjoys the adulation of the public; Woody Allen shuns it.

Some values may never interfere with one another, but if there is to be true drama in the decision-centered play, there must be a clash of values. We see this point vividly illustrated in the script of *Guilty by Suspicion*. The fictional David Merrill can resume his career as a film director and insure financial independence and peace for himself and his family if he purges himself before the House Committee on Un-American Activities. In doing so, however, he will be forced to denounce some of his friends as Communists and subject them to the same grim ordeal he is going through. In the end he refuses to cooperate and thus puts his future and that of his family at risk. Another character in the story, Larry Nolan, faced with the same clash of values, takes the opposite course.

The shocking ending of the 1991 film *Thelma and Louise* depicted the ultimate choice a human being can make. The title characters, played by Geena Davis and Susan Sarandon, have fled from stultifying existences—the first from a suffocating marriage with an overbearing, insensitive husband; the second from desperate loneliness. They find their escape in an exhilarating adventure on the open road. Unfortunately, their adventure also involves acts of violence, including robbery and the killing of a would-be rapist. As their crime spree widens, a small army of police close in and finally corners them on the rim of the Grand Canyon. What they value most is revealed when they reject a return to lives almost certain to include a long period of imprisonment, and choose instead the kind of freedom they believe they can win only by gunning their car into the abyss below.

People are not always aware of the desires that motivate their behavior. Extremely powerful drives, those controlling the individual's most vital decisions, may exist on a subconscious level, and, in fact, some people might actually be horrified if they understood the real nature of their motives. A citizen, for example, may gain a reputation for outstanding community contributions because of a willingness to head various campaigns. Is this an indication of a desire to help other people? It may be. On the other hand, his or her eagerness to assume these responsibilities may merely reflect a hunger for fame and praise or a lust for power—the desire to control people and things. Another example of the influence of hidden values is provided by the letter a young swain once wrote to his sweetheart: "I would go through fire and water or climb the highest mountain to be with you." Then he concluded with a P.S. "If it rains tonight, I won't be over."

That individuals are unaware of the values motivating their conduct does not in any way lessen their impact. Some hidden desires have tremendous influence and they are legitimate material for the dramatist's use.

Character Traits Another aspect of character is the trait or temperament that distinguishes one individual from another. These qualities are related to the values motivating behavior but in identifying them we can add further dimension to a character. One individual is cool and reserved, for example, difficult to know; another is friendly and gregarious. The characteristic way an individual reacts to a situation often provides a further revelation of basic temperament. In the face of a crisis one person may remain completely self-possessed, dealing with the problem in a rational way. Another may scarcely react at all; we would describe such an individual as phlegmatic. A third person may respond chaotically to a crisis in a hot-headed or impulsive way.

In the film *Thelma and Louise*, the title characters are strikingly different in temperament. Thelma is impetuous and uninhibited. During their highway adventure, she unthinkingly invites the attentions of a lout at a nightclub and shortly finds that she is about to become the victim of a rape. Later she finds sexual release with a hitchhiker even though he has confessed to her that he makes his living as a thief. Louise, in contrast, is reserved and self-contained. The action reveals, however, that this is merely a surface trait. Boiling beneath her cool exterior is the capacity for violence. She rescues Thelma from her attacker by holding him at bay with a gun; when he taunts her with obscene remarks, she shoots and kills him even though he no longer physically threatens them. It turns out later that she did so because apparently she was once a rape victim herself. The experience was so traumatic that she refuses to drive through the state of Texas, where the attack occurred.

Character Idiosyncrasies An idiosyncrasy that helps fill out a character can be a characteristic mode or peculiarity of speaking, dress, or behavior. Because so few men wear bow ties these days, those who do tend to be noticed. Television personalities who exhibit this idiosyncrasy include the political satirist Mark Russell, the NBC news commentator Irving R. Levine, and the conservative writer George Will. The title character in the *Columbo* series has a whole host of idiosyncrasies: the wrinkled raincoat, the ever-present cigar, the beat-up Peugot, the habit of walking out and then coming back with "just one more question."

Sometimes idiosyncrasies, at least on the surface, may appear to be in direct conflict with the character of the individual. Hannibal Lecter, the cannibalistic murderer in the film *The Silence of the Lambs*, concealed his horrible proclivity behind a cultured facade. A psychiatrist himself, he spoke with elegant precision about the impulses that drive people to commit unimaginable crimes.

This kind of contrast may have a shock value that serves to heighten the impact of the basic character traits. The idiosyncrasy, however, should not be confused with the trait, which is the reflection of the elemental character of each individual. An individual's peculiar way of doing things may be characteristic but, in the true sense of the word, it may not actually characterize. Idiosyncrasies are important, however, because they can make a character more interesting, richer, and in some instances more understandable. A villain shown doing what average people do—reading comic strips, quarreling with his mother-in-law or making model planes—takes on some of the characteristics of ordinary human beings.

Building the Character

The first step in characterization is to develop in your mind as complete a picture of the character as you can. This picture should include a full rendering of the values that will dominate behavior, the traits or temperament that will control the way the person reacts to people and situations, and the idiosyncrasies that will add interest and depth. Eugene O'Neill, it is said, wrote out the life stories of his characters before he began writing a single line of dialogue. Henrik Ibsen once remarked of his character, Nora, in *A Doll's House:* "The things I know about that young woman that aren't in the play would surprise you."

Selecting Character Elements

With a complete character in mind, the next step is to decide what facets of that character are to be emphasized in the play. You cannot hope, of course, to establish the whole character. Even in the longest movie or in the most elaborate TV mini-series, it would be impossible to communicate all aspects of a character. Were this possible, there is still some question whether you would want to do it, for as Tennessee Williams said, in discussing his play *Cat on a Hot Tin Roof*, "Some mystery should be left in the revelation of character in a play, just as a great deal of mystery is always left in the revelation of character in life."

Achieving Richness of Characterization If only a portion of a complete character can be presented in a play, how can dramatists give the impression they have created a real person, an individual, who, as the expression goes, is three dimensional? The answer is to select a few characteristics and treat them in depth rather than try to achieve breadth of characterization. If writers probe deeply enough into a character, even though what they reveal remains relatively narrow, they achieve a characterization that seems to be full and rich. Thinking about even the great characters of drama, we realize we know relatively little about them; what we do know, however, is so deep and satisfying we feel we have become acquainted with a real and complete person. The principal means of achieving in-depth characterization is to cre-

ate scene after scene in which you reveal the same characteristic in a number of ways. In the film *Frankie and Johnny*, for example, the deep love the short-order cook Johnny feels for the waitress Frankie becomes strikingly evident when he persists in his courtship even though she keeps rejecting him. The process of reiterating a character element is called *tagging*. We discuss it in more detail later in this chapter when we describe the methods for accomplishing character revelation.

Avoiding Stereotypes The stereotype is a character copied directly from the creation of some other writer, who may, in turn, have copied it from some writer before him. Even as early as the 19th century, the playwright Anton Chekhov identified alcoholic newspaper reporters, starving authors, and good-natured nurses as types to be avoided because they had been done over and over again. Despite Chekhov's stricture, these types persisted into this century, and stereotypes like them abound in today's dramas.

One reason for the prevalence of stereotypes is that creating new and original characters is a time-consuming process. Moreover, there are limits to creative resources; writers cannot keep inventing new characters indefinitely and yet they must keep writing to turn out their required quota of scripts. Another reason for the longevity of many stereotypes is that when first created they were original and arresting characters. In this sense, they resemble clichés which, because of their very color and vividness, tend to be perpetuated until ceaseless repetition dulls our reaction to them.

The constant employment of stereotypes will soon make writing sterile and routine; it will deprive the play of that quality which is most likely to make it memorable—the arresting character who seizes our interest because of his individuality. Stereotypes inhabit the program fillers; they may develop some temporary interest for audiences if the characters they are based on were sufficiently intriguing to begin with, but they do not linger in people's minds. It is the original creation that audiences remember, not the pale imitations. It is only through individual characterization that plays gain lasting memorability.

Another objection to the stereotype is that it often perpetuates false ideas about people, particularly the idea that certain characteristics, occupations, or human failings are associated with certain races or nationalities. Thus we are led to believe that policemen are always Irish, that the Oriental is undeviatingly wise and inscrutable, that Scotsmen are always inordinately concerned about money. Writers must recognize that most general statements about classes of people are untrue, at least in part, and they must realize that any given member of a national, racial, occupational, sexual, or educational group is a unique human being. The highest achievement in characterization is to establish the individuality and complexity of people—to show, in other words, how they differ from other people rather than to show how much they resemble them.

In only one instance may the use of stereotypes be justified, and even then the stereotype should not be one that perpetuates inaccurate or objectionable information about classes of people. Since time for characterization is always limited, writers may sometimes employ stereotypes as the minor or incidental characters in a script because their qualities will be recognized quickly by the audience. Doing this permits writers to spend their time portraying the major characters of the play, who become the original and unique creations of the script.

The Relationship of Character and Plot

It is obvious that there is a direct relationship between the characters of a play and the development of its plot, since the plot usually arises, either from the decisions characters make as a series of choices confronts them, or from changes in the balance for or against them as they strive to reach a goal. The decisions made or the willingness to continue or quit the struggle reflect, in turn, the character's basic values. If the values were different, the decisions would be different, and the design of the plot would change. Or, to look at it from the opposite point of view, if the plot takes a certain turn calling for a decision that is out of keeping with the character's previously held values, then either the character must be changed or that particular plot development must be abandoned.

Think for a moment what would have happened if Shakespeare had interchanged the characters or Romeo and Hamlet. The impetuous Romeo, confronted by the secret of his father's death, would have acted instantly instead of brooding and hesitating as Hamlet did. Hamlet in Romeo's role would not have undertaken the rash acts that made it possible for him to court Juliet. Before he had done anything at all, she would probably have been safely married to another man. The characters of Hamlet and Romeo dictated the action of the plays in which they appeared. To put it another way, their plots demanded the kind of characters that Hamlet and Romeo were.

That thought confronts us with a question: Which comes first, plot or character? If this is taken to mean which arises first in the writer's mind, there is no absolute answer. Either character or plot may be the starting point for a play. If the concept of a character sparks the creative drive, the writer must devise a series of situations, gradually developing in intensity, in which the character acts. The nature of these acts will reveal to the audience what kind of person the character is, for, in the words of Walter Kerr, "Character is best revealed by the response it makes to circumstance."[2] In constructing plots this way, the writer follows the characters, permitting them to create the complications.

It may happen, on the other hand, that the initial idea for a play is a plot twist or an exciting climactic scene. Now the problem of the writer is to create characters who will make the development of that scene believable. They must be imbued with the kind of drives that lead directly to the situation the writer originally conceived. In this instance, plot has given rise to character.

If a play depends for its interest primarily on plot action and gives little attention to character development, it is included in the class of plays called melodrama. The goal-centered play is more likely to fall into this category than is the decision-centered play, because the struggle to achieve a goal takes place primarily outside the chief character, and the focus of attention is on the activity that arises from the effort to overcome obstacles. The decision-centered play, on the other hand, spotlights an inner conflict; the emphasis is on the character values that will survive when the conflict is resolved.

Classes of Characters

There are a number of ways in which characters in a drama might be classified, and various terms have been used to denote the different characters in terms of their importance in the story.

The Focal Character   The character in the play who arouses the greatest audience interest is the focal character. It is the person on whom the attention of the audience chiefly focuses. In the decision-centered play, the focal character is the person who makes the decisions most vitally affecting the development of the plot; in the goal-centered play the focal character is the person who carries out the struggle constituting the most important action. The focal character may or may not be a person with whom the audience sympathizes. The question of goodness or badness is not at issue in deciding the identity of the focal character. The only legitimate question is: Which character draws the greatest audience interest?

The character of J.R. Ewing in the *Dallas* series, as played by Larry Hagman, became the modern version of "the man you love to hate," a phrase first applied to the early film actor Eric von Stroheim. Audiences may have despised J.R. for his sinister shenanigans, but they still watched in fascination as he planned the seduction of a friend's wife or plotted to destroy a rival in business. The episode that answered the cliffhanger question "Who shot J.R.?" drew one of the largest audiences in television history. The villainous J.R. was unquestionably the focal character of the *Dallas* series.

Though audience interest usually focuses on the decisions or struggle of one character, there are stories in which interest is equally divided between two or more characters, as it was in *Thelma and Louise*. The focal characters in the two scripts we analyzed in the previous chapter are easy to identify. In *Guilty by Suspicion*, it is the decision of David Merrill that the audience awaits with the greatest interest. In *Separate But Equal*, Thurgood Marshall is the clear leader of the struggle to outlaw school segregation.

Principal Characters   Those who take the leading parts in carrying out the action of a television or film play are known as principal characters. The focal character is obviously a principal character. The others are those whose actions have an effect on the development of the story next in importance to that of the focal character. In *Guilty by Suspicion*, Merrill's ex-wife Ruth and Darryl Zanuck are principal characters. In *Separate But Equal*, the characters of

John W. Davis and Earl Warren fall into this category.

Secondary Characters Less important than the principal characters, yet still playing significant functions, are the characters we label as secondary. They may be people who create the situation that provokes the conflict for the principal characters. Among the secondary characters in *Guilty by Suspicion* are Larry Nolan and his wife Dorothy, Bunny Baxter, and the members of the House committee. In *Separate But Equal* they include Marshall's wife Buster, Harry Briggs, the Reverend DeLaine, and the justices of the Supreme Court.

Sometimes a secondary character may play a supportive role or even be a *confidant* to the focal character. The use of a confidant permits the writer to transmit the thoughts of a focal character to an audience in a natural way by making them the subject of dialogue between the two characters.

Incidental Characters The characters needed to fill out a play or scene are called incidental characters. Usually they appear in a service function and, in many cases, are not even identified by name. Among the characters who fall into this category are taxi drivers, maids, gas station attendants, and hotel clerks.

Changes in Characters

If one is to write a satisfactory play, must the characters be portrayed as undergoing a change? Must they be significantly different from the kind of people they were at the beginning of the play? The answer to the question depends to a large degree on what we mean by change. If we think of it as transformation of a character's basic nature so fundamental that the values motivating his or her behavior are replaced by other and different values, we may well wonder about the possibility of achieving such a change. It has been accomplished, of course. In *A Christmas Carol* Charles Dickens enveloped Scrooge in events and experiences so cataclysmic we can believe he changed from a hard, self-centered old man into a kind, gentle one. Such personality transformations are usually difficult to believe, however. The character of Bunny Baxter in *Guilty by Suspicion* may be an example of this problem. For most of the film he is portrayed as a cringing, craven victim who appears willing to do almost anything to extricate himself from his dilemma. Yet when he actually appears before the committee, he defies it. He is not present in the hearing room while David Merrill is testifying, but the doors swing open momentarily to give him a brief glimpse of a heated exchange between Merrill and the committee members. It is obvious that he is refusing to answer their questions. Perhaps this example gives Baxter the courage he needs to make his own stand. Still, it is difficult to believe he could change so radically.

More believable than the 180-degree turn in Baxter's response to the committee's demands are some alterations in the way other characters react to their difficult situations. Merrill is not the same person he was at the beginning of the story. On his return from Europe he seems oblivious to the social and political currents that menace the freedom of artists. By the end of the story, he is fully aware of the threat they pose to his creative life. The stand he takes, moreover, strengthens the inner resources he needs to hold firm to his principles and to deal with the dire consequences likely to follow. In the same way, the struggle carried on by Thurgood Marshall makes him a more resilient and understanding individual. It helps him to prepare for the even greater influence he will wield as a Supreme Court justice.

The character of Nora in Ibsen's *A Doll's House* is often cited as a character who undergoes a basic transformation. At the beginning of the play she appears to be a flighty, improvident child who contrasts sharply with the mature, assured woman who slams the door at the end as she leaves her husband. Yet earlier events, particularly the forging of the note that saved her husband's career, reveal that she has always been a person of courage and resourcefulness. It seems clear that she assumed the doll-wife pose to please her vain and foolish husband and her willingness to play this role is a further reflection of her ability to adapt. Ibsen's achievement was not in bringing about a transformation of her character but in concocting a series of events that revealed her true nature. The process is similar to that occurring as we watch the development of a Polaroid film. At first the figures are unclear but they gradually emerge to become the images of real people. In the same way a dramatist's characters emerge into full reality as a series of scenes and incidents reveals their values, traits, and idiosyncrasies.

Sources of Characters

Where are writers to get their ideas for characters? They may come from almost anywhere, particularly from the people they know best.

The Writer's Character   Many characters reflect the writer's own thoughts, life, values, and feelings. An outstanding example of this practice was Thomas Wolfe who, despite vehemently denying he was doing so, wrote a series of novels that were mainly autobiographical in nature. The script of *Platoon* reflects Oliver Stone's own experiences in Vietnam and his reactions to them. In the same way *JFK* became a means for expressing his doubts about the

official report on the assassination of John Kennedy and his speculation regarding the reality. The plays of George Bernard Shaw frequently present characters whose personality, wit, and general attitude toward life are indistinguishable from that of Shaw himself. There is nothing wrong with this practice, incidentally, if the resulting character is unique and impelling.

Acquaintances   Most characters, of course, must come from outside the writer, for as Chekhov said, "A play will be worthless if all the characters resemble you." The most likely source of ideas is the experience you have with people in real life. Stories your friends or relatives tell you about people can also inspire character ideas. Probably nine-tenths of the characters you create will have their inspiration in a person who actually lived. This does not mean that this real person will be translated into a dramatic character without any change. For one thing, too-accurate a representation may entangle you in a libel suit. Some modifications may also be necessary to fit the demands of your plot or to point your theme more tellingly. Furthermore, it is impossible for you to depict a character in totality. As we have noted previously, you are limited to a consideration of those values and traits directly related to the play's basic issue. Finally, no matter how well you may think you know a person, your knowledge, like the part of the iceberg you see above the water, is an inadequate representation of the depths that are unseen.

Fictional and Historical People   Vicarious experience can furnish information about people you have never met who may provide the foundation for excellent characters. Your reading is an example. You cannot copy other writers' characters directly, but a character in fiction or in a play may start your mind working until you end up, not with the character you read about, but with one who is your own original, unique creation. The people of history may be another source of ideas. Sometimes they can be used in plays that are biographical or semibiographical in nature, in which case you attempt to portray a historical personage with as much fidelity to the known character as you can. In other cases, the actual person will merely serve to trigger your creative impulses; the final creation may bear no resemblance to its inspiration.

Steps in Creating Characters

Let us review briefly the steps you should follow in developing a character for your plays.

1. Seek a beginning idea for the character first. If the idea for your play has its origin in a plot twist, the basic nature of your character may be dictated to you. But the filling out of the character will depend to a large degree on your personal experience and recollections of real or fictional people.
2. Establish the basic motivations of the character. This means that you must decide the values that are to affect their choice of goals or determine their decisions. As you do this, you must keep in mind the plot line and the theme of the play. The values of your characters must be related to and reinforce these elements of the play.
3. Devise the other aspects of personality that will give depth and individuality to the characters. This involves the development of traits and idiosyncrasies that complement the basic values. Remember, too, that to present an effective characterization, you must see the person you are representing in far more detail than you can possibly reveal to the audience. This richness in your conception will help you to provide the touches and implications that

will aid the audience to amplify and round out the character.

REVEALING CHARACTERS

Thus far we have considered the first step in the process of characterization—the stage in which the writer creates the characters, deciding the fundamental values that will dominate their lives, and devising a combination of traits and idiosyncrasies to distinguish them from others. The second step in characterization is to reveal to the audience the characters the writer has created. If characters do not take form for the audience, dramatists actually accomplish nothing so far as characterization is concerned, no matter how vividly they may exist in their imagination. Character creation must be followed by character revelation.

Describing a Character Directly

It would seem that one means of revealing characters is to tell the audience directly what kind of people they are. If the father in a family is a vain, selfish person, whose concern with his own welfare is the dominating value of his life, why not tell an audience just that in so many words? There are at least two reasons why the technique of direct description should not be used.

First, the dramatist has no way of communicating directly with an audience unless a narrator is used. Second, describing characters violates the principle that the viewer of a play should be permitted to make inferences rather than be told things directly. What you should do as a dramatist is to provide your viewers with opportunities to observe the father's behavior in a situation and then let them decide what kind of person he is.

This process was illustrated in the film *Frankie and Johnny*. When Johnny (played by Al Pacino) comes out of prison, he fully expects that as an ex-convict he will have great difficulty in finding work. Yet when he applies for a job at a restaurant, the owner (played by Hector Elizondo) hires him immediately despite his prison record. This action reveals better than any explanation could that the owner is a kind, caring person who is willing to give people a second chance.

In giving audiences an opportunity to draw inferences from such actions, you are permitting them to arrive at judgments about a character's true nature in exactly the way we make up our minds about people in everyday life. Letting the audience draw its own conclusions is more important in characterization than it is in any other phase of dramatic writing. The same principle applies to other creative writers. John Ciardi said, for example, "A good novelist does not tell us that a given character is good or bad. . . . He shows us the character in action and then, watching him we know."

What a Character Does

Of all the acts performed by characters the most revealing are the decisions they make. In the goal-centered play, the things they decide to do to reach their goal tell the audience how important its attainment is to them. In the decision-centered play, the choices they make among the conflicting values in their lives reveal what kinds of people they really are.

Decisions as a Clue to Character   As we noted earlier, the decision by David Merrill to defy the House committee let the audience know that betraying his friends was unthinkable. He could not bring himself to do it even though he knew his choice would probably end his career. Thurgood Marshall's decision to make his goal the outlawing of segregation rather than the lesser objective of proving that

school facilities were unequal told us how resolute he was. He did not shrink from the major battle he might easily lose to achieve a smaller victory he could probably win. In the same way, a decision by John W. Davis, Marshall's main opponent in the struggle, revealed something vitally important about him. Though he deeply believed in the rightness of his cause, he was unwilling to use questionable means to win a victory. This became evident when he firmly rejected the recommendation of an associate that he weaken his chief adversary, the NAACP, by attacking its status as a tax-deductible organization.

The movie *The Deer Hunter* provides an example of how an unexpected decision can reveal that a character has substituted one value for another. In an early part of the film, Mike (played by Robert De Niro) goes on a deer hunt with some of his buddies. It is part of his creed that a stag should be brought down with a single shot, and he succeeds in doing so. He and his friends join the Army to fight in Vietnam, where they endure horrifying experiences of killing and destruction. Near the end of the film, Mike goes on another deer hunt. He gets a deer in his rifle sights and is ready to bring it down with the one shot his hunter's creed dictates. As he fires, however, he thrusts the muzzle of the rifle sharply upwards and the shot goes wild. The audience can infer from this action that his values have changed; war has made him so sick of killing that he now cannot bring himself even to shoot what before was fair game.

Incidental Action as a Clue to Character Sometimes small and seemingly unimportant actions provide a telling revelation of character. There is a good example of this technique in Arthur Hailey's television play *No Deadly Medicine*, which later became a movie. An old doctor, in company with a younger one, is conducting an autopsy. As he carries out the procedure, he carelessly permits the ashes from his cigar to fall on the body he is examining. He continues without even bothering to brush the ashes away. This incident gives a revealing indication of the old doctor's callousness. The obvious revulsion of the young doctor at this unthinking desecration of a dead human body shows, in turn, how different his attitude is from that of the older man.

A telling incident in *Guilty by Suspicion* reveals vividly what David Merrill's ordeal is doing to him. When his former wife Ruth meets him at the bus station on his return from New York, she suggests that he drive the car. Ordinarily he would have jumped at the chance. He has a passion for driving and prides himself on his skill. Uncharacteristically he declines and asks Ruth to drive. There could be no better evidence that his failure to find work in New York has broken his spirit.

What a Character Says

A second important means of revealing characters is to gives them words that will indicate what kind of people they are. In a sense this is also part of what they do, but speech is such an important aspect of behavior that it deserves special attention. Speech is the primary means through which the audience finds out about past actions and learns about those contemplated. It provides the main clues to the values dominating a character's life and thus reveals his or her true nature. Again, it is almost always speech that makes the decision a character has reached clear to the audience.

In the previous chapter we included an episode from the *Law and Order* series revolving around the bombing of an abortion clinic by the leader of a right-to-life group. The leader called in a warning but it failed to reach a woman who was in a restroom and she was killed in the explo-

sion. One thing the writers could not ignore was the fact that people have sharply different views about abortion. As one of the characters in the play said: "It's the most emotional issue the law has dealt with since suffrage." The program itself could not take a stand on abortion, of course, without arousing the antagonism of the large group who would disagree with it, whatever that stand might be.

What the writers felt they must do was to recognize that people do differ sharply in their views on abortion. They did this by revealing that some members of the enforcement team investigating the bombing were right-to-lifers whereas others believed in abortion rights. None of them, however, condoned the bombing of the abortion clinic. Though Assistant District Attorney Ben Stone was a strong opponent of abortion, he nevertheless carried out a vigorous prosecution of the person accused of planting the bomb. He also recognized the right of people to make their own decisions on the issue. In a discussion of the subject with District Attorney Adam Schiff, who viewed abortion as an acceptable procedure in some instances, Stone said: "And I've also never said women shouldn't have the right to choose. *Personally*, I'm also against smoking, but if people want to kill themselves, that's their decision."

People's differing views on abortion, and they have infinite gradations, reflect differences in fundamental values. In the *Law and Order* abortion episode these differences in values were made clear to the audience by what the characters *said*. The statements by Stone, for example, indicated that although he would never approve of abortion himself as a solution to a problem, he did not oppose making the procedure legal. Another character in the story, detective Max Greevey, took a much stronger position against abortion. His values were revealed during emotional exchanges with his detective partner Mike Logan, who had a different view. Logan felt the bombing of the clinic was a much more important issue than abortion, which he thought should be available to all women who chose to use it. Their contrasting values were vividly revealed by what they *said* in the following excerpt:

LOGAN
Quite a record Miss Schwimmer's got herself.
Trespass, disturbing the peace, harassment . . .
(looks up)
For a non-violent person, she sure does get around a lot.

GREEVEY
McClure's got nothing but a dismissed trespass.

LOGAN
And Donovan's completely clean—Not even a traffic ticket . . .

GREEVEY
(hard)
The methods are wrong, but they're trying to *prevent* murder.

LOGAN
(disgusted)
Spare me the rhetoric, all right, Max?
I don't consider abortion murder. . . .

Greevy stands up. The other cops stop working and watch. Logan stands, too.

LOGAN
And I don't care *what* you believe, trying to prevent
abortions by throwing bombs is *too far.*

GREEVEY
You and I both know they didn't mean to hurt *anybody.*

LOGAN
(vehement)
. . . Only an idiot thinks bombs don't hurt people.

The revelation accomplished through what characters say is most effective when their speeches permit the audience to make inferences about the kinds of persons they are. When Torvald in Ibsen's *A Doll's House*, on finding out that Krogstad no longer planned to press the charge of forgery against his wife, shouted, "Nora, I am saved" instead of "We are saved," he revealed his innate egocentricity far better than any direct statement could have done.

Sometimes a dramatist may characterize by actually having people make statements about themselves. The characters played by Woody Allen in a number of his movies constantly disparage themselves, particularly their attractiveness to women. What people say about themselves, of course, cannot always be accepted at face value, for it is virtually impossible to view oneself objectively. These statements, in fact, may suggest the exact reverse of the person's true nature. The fawning Uriah Heep's description of himself as "'umble" in Dickens' *David Copperfield* masked a consummate scoundrel who attempted to defraud his employer.

How a Character Speaks

Just as the choice of subject matter provides clues to an individual's basic nature, so does the manner in which that subject matter is expressed. Among the significant characteristics of language are vocabulary, the length and structure of sentences, and their basic rhythm. Grammatical usage, pronunciation, and the employment of particular epithets and idioms are other important speech factors that help to reveal character.

In his dramatization of a jury's deliberation in *Twelve Angry Men*, produced first as a TV play and then as a movie now regarded as a classic, Reginald Rose distinguished brilliantly among his characters by providing the most important jurors with distinctive word choices, language styles, and sentence structures.

The basic character of Juror 7, a loud, wisecracking, salesman type, is effectively suggested by such lines as, "How do you like him? It's like talking into a dead phone," "Stories this guy made up! He oughta write for *Amazing Detective Monthly*," "Why don't we have them run the trial over . . . "

Juror 4 is described as a man of wealth and position, a practiced speaker who expresses himself well at all times. Note the vocabulary that Rose provides him: "Potential menaces to society," "I can recount it accurately," "unshakable testimony," "exhibits in evidence," "insignificant details," "incredible coincidence." His use of language makes his breeding evident.

Juror 10's lack of breeding, on the other hand, is just as evident in the words and sentences he uses: "It don't mean anything," and "He's a common, ignorant, slob. He don't even speak good English," are examples.[3]

The portrayal of unique individuals demands dialogue reflecting that individuality. When characters in a play all express themselves in the same way, the dramatist has obviously failed to project people who are distinctive individuals. One of the dramatist's most critical challenges is to write dialogue that is appropriate only to the particular character who utters it.

What Others Say

Another means of revealing characters is to have people in the play describe them. This technique is an effective means for achieving characterization when it is employed skillfully. The most common fault is being too obvious. The discussion of a character by other characters in the play must occur in a natural way; it must be motivated by what is taking place in the play, rather than being forced in merely because something about a character needs to be told. What one individual says about another is not necessarily a correct description of that person's character, of course; sometimes it is a means of revealing the characteristics of the person who makes the statement. How characters describe other people may furnish one of the best clues to their own peculiarities and personality twists.

A good example of this occurs in Horton Foote's *The Trip to Bountiful*, which won an Academy Award for Geraldine Page, the portrayer of the leading character, Mrs. Watts. An old lady, she has a passionate desire to visit her childhood home in Bountiful but is constantly harassed by her selfish daughter-in-law Jessie Mae, who fears she will lose access to her mother-in-law's pension check. At one point Jessie Mae says of Mrs. Watts, "She's just spoiled rotten." These words utterly fail to describe the resolute, resourceful old lady who, despite the obstacles placed in her way by her daughter-in-law, manages to reach her goal. They are, however, an accurate description of the person who uttered them, Jessie Mae.

Other People's Reactions

Another means of revealing character is to show how people act in the presence of others. Thelma's husband in *Thelma and Louise* treats her as if she were a piece of furniture. His obliviousness to her needs and feelings demonstrates just how insensitive and uncaring he is. The character of Columbo as portrayed by Peter Falk is exactly the opposite. Even in the presence of people he knows are murderers, he is unfailingly deferential and courteous even when they taunt and insult him. When he finally closes in with conclusive evidence of their guilt, he does not exult in the battle of wits he has won. Sometimes he seems almost sad at what he must do. He makes his arrests firmly, but never gloats.

Setting, Costume, and Physical Appearance

When we see a man sprawled on a sidewalk in a skid-row section, we immediately gain some insight into the sort of person he is. We can make inferences about the general nature of the values ruling him, and we can make guesses about the actions that have brought him to this situation. The alcoholic white man in a South Seas island background tells us by his mere presence in that setting a good deal of what we need to know about him. Consider Laura in Tennessee Williams' play *The Glass Menagerie*. Her constant preoccupation with her collection of little glass animals becomes a symbol of her basic characteristic—her withdrawal from the world of reality. The setting in which we place people and the objects with which we surround them can supply significant information about their character.

Physical appearance and dress can perform the same function. Grooming, for example, or the lack of grooming can be a definitive clue to character. Setting and appearance may reveal a person's basic traits and values. The fact that individuals are dominated by selfishness or, in contrast, are inspired by concern for their fellow human beings can be communicated in part by their appearance, by the way they dress, and by the kind of environment in which they live. These elements can also illustrate an interesting mannerism. A personality quirk can be expressed in the clothes a man wears or the way he trims his moustache.

The character of Hercule Poirot as portrayed by David Suchet in the PBS *Mystery* series is immensely strengthened by his appearance. His impeccably knotted tie, fashionable clothes, and carefully waxed moustache suggest the fastidiousness and precision that mark his mental processes. Thus he is able to see solutions in circumstances that only confound others. Disclosure of personality characteristics through setting, dress, and appearance can be extremely telling, for by permitting the audience to make inferences, it reveals character in a natural way.

Repeating Character Qualities

Earlier it was pointed out that characters in a drama, although they may appear to be full, well-rounded individuals, are actually people about whom we know very little. The impression of completeness is achieved in a number of ways, but certainly one of the most important devices is to concentrate on one or two basic characteristics which are emphasized in scene after scene, a process called *tagging*. If your intention is to portray a person whose dominant quality is selfishness, you should show that person being selfish over and over again, until the characteristic is impressed on the audience with an indelible imprint. Obviously, the traits selected for this kind of repetitive treatment should be the traits that are at the core of the play. Only the traits should be repeated; the situations that reveal them must be different from one another or the play would sink to a deadly, monotonous level. Repetition of a trait in a number of situations and in different ways builds a powerful characterization, and the play gains color, depth, and variety.

Horton Foote's play *The Trip to Bountiful* illustrates the use of the tagging technique in revealing character. In that play Foote created the character of Jessie Mae, a woman whose principal traits are selfishness and insensitivity to the needs of others. She provides a home for her mother-in-law Mrs. Watts not because she cares for her but because she wants to get control of her money. When her mother-in-law goes for a walk on a hot summer's day and collapses on the sidewalk, Jessie Mae's first action after reaching her is to make sure Mrs. Watts hasn't lost her pension check. She berates her mother-in-law for being so foolish as to go out in the hot sun and, bemoaning the money an ambulance would cost, tries to persuade her to try to walk back to the house on her own, though the old woman is clearly unable to do so.

The daughter-in-law's selfishness is reflected in other ways. Her mother-in-law gets the meals while Jessie Mae sits idly and watches television. Even though Mrs. Watts

is washing the dishes, Jessie Mae asks her to bring her a soft drink from the refrigerator. She forbids the mother-in-law to hold a church meeting at the house and describes churchgoing as superstition, despite knowing that religion means more to her mother-in-law than anything else in life. When her mother-in-law becomes ill and has to be driven to the doctor, Jessie Mae sits in the car, loudly and impatiently honking the horn, while Mrs. Watts makes her slow and painful way down the steps to the car. Through all these situations the same trait of selfishness and insensitivity are reflected, thus building up a character concept that becomes fuller and richer as the script proceeds.

A principal trait of the character played by Rue McClanahan in the situation comedy *Golden Girls* was her interest in sexual dalliance. This trait was constantly reflected in story developments, incidental events, and particularly in gag lines.

It is not enough, of course, for dramatists to emphasize just one aspect of personality. Archie Bunker in *All in the Family* is a person whose dominant trait is intolerance. It would not have been enough for the writers to emphasize that alone. The characterization needed enrichment by supplementing the revelation of his bigotry with the revelation of traits often associated with it. Thus the harshness of his approach to other people was revealed also in the way he belittled his wife Edith and in his constant bickering with his son-in-law, whose values clashed diametrically with his. Archie's insistence that he always sit in one particular chair provided further reinforcement of a characterization that reflected a selfish, ego-centered life. To have revealed these traits alone, however, would have left the character too one-dimensional. Archie's personality was softened by showing his concern for his daughter, his obvious love for his grandchild, and even by portraying him in occasional tender moments with his wife.

QUESTIONS AND PROJECTS

1. Speculate on what might have happened to the plots of some familiar plays if qualities of certain characters were reversed. What would have happened to the story of *Gone With the Wind*, for example, if the traits of Scarlett and Melanie had been reversed?
2. In a number of TV plays or films, place the characters in the following categories: focal, principal, secondary, and incidental.
3. In viewing television dramas or films, be on the watch for devices that reveal character. Note the use of each one of the following devices described in this chapter:
   (a) what a character does
      (1) decisions
      (2) incidental action
   (b) what a character says
   (c) how a character speaks
   (d) what others say about a character
   (e) other people's reactions to a character
   (f) setting, costume, and physical appearance
4. Create a trait for a character, then tag that trait through the use of each of the devices listed above.
5. Use as many as possible of the devices listed above to reveal the following traits or characteristics:
   (a) a mother's inordinate fear for her child's health
   (b) deep religious belief
   (c) excessive pride in one's work

NOTES

1. Quoted in Syd Field, *Selling a Screenplay* (New York: Delacorte Press, 1989), p. 219.
2. Walter Kerr, *How Not to Write a Play* (New York: Simon and Schuster, 1955), p. 128.
3. Reginald Rose, *Twelve Angry Men*, in *Six Television Plays* (New York: Simon and Schuster, 1956), pp. 113–115.

CHAPTER
13
ESTABLISHING A THEME

The unbreakable rule of playwriting is that there is no unbreakable rule.

GEORGE BERNARD SHAW
(1856–1950)

Most people agree that to create drama you need at least one character, some kind of setting, and, if not a plot, at least a situation on which the action can turn. Does a play also need a theme? Some consider it an essential element, whereas others decry its importance and may even argue that too strong a theme may damage the dramatic impact. In this chapter we consider the importance of a theme in play construction, examine its nature, and consider its contributions and possible dangers to effective drama.

THEME AS SUBJECT MATTER

Answering the question of whether a theme is necessary depends to some extent on how the term is defined. It means different things to different people. To some, *theme* refers to the basic subject matter of the play; it is what the story is *about*. Sometimes this basic content can be summed up in a word or two. We can say, for example, that the theme of *Macbeth* is ambition; of *Othello*, jealousy; of *Hamlet*, revenge; of *Julius Caesar*, political power; and of *Romeo and Juliet*, young love. In other instances we need a longer phrase or a sentence to describe the subject matter of a play. We can say that *Separate But Equal* deals with the fight to eliminate one aspect of racism, school segregation, and that *Guilty by Suspicion* details the destruction of lives and careers brought about by the 1950s' Hollywood blacklist. Aric Press, writing in *Newsweek*, expressed the theme of the series *thirtysomething* in the form of a question: "What are you doing with your life?"

Individual episodes took up various aspects of this question, among them: workplace tensions, a sibling rivalry that never died, the lure of infidelity, and the struggle to make marriages work.[1]

Different Views of Subject Matter

People sometimes disagree on what a work of fiction is about. The 1991 film *Thelma and Louise* is a good example. One critic described it as simply the story of two women on the lam; another said it depicted the leading characters finding liberation in violent acts; still another argued that it portrayed women taking responsibility for their own destinies by calling the shots; a fourth took a still different tack by describing its theme as self-discovery. Some found the arid relationships of the two women with their men an important thematic element. *New Yorker* movie critic Terence Rafferty said it was about two women who go off in search of a little personal space and find that they have to keep going to find a space that's big enough.

Subject Matter and Unity

The answer to the question with which we began this chapter—Is a theme necessary?—is obviously "yes" if we think of theme as subject matter. Plays must be about something. It is possible, however, for a play to be about too many different things. Perhaps that is why critics varied so much in describing the subject matter of *Thelma and Louise*. In reviewing *Barton Fink*, a film about a Broadway dramatist experiencing writer's block after he goes to Hollywood to write a screenplay about wrestling, the playwright Arthur Miller complained that the screenwriters couldn't decide what they really wanted to write about, adding that there was no discernible theme to *Barton Fink*. The result, Miller argued, is that it constantly veers between farce and serious drama.[2]

A film that demonstrates how concentration on one type of subject matter can give unity to a script is Paddy Chayefsky's *Marty*, which he adapted from his television play. The subject matter is the title character's need for acceptance as he seeks a meaningful relationship with a woman. The theme is mainly reflected in Marty's actions as he makes tentative approaches toward the opposite sex, but one of the strengths of the script is the reinforcement of this theme in the actions of other characters. Marty's need is mirrored by the need of a woman he meets at a dance who also has endured the bitterness of constant rejection. The plight of Marty's Aunt Catherine, who is about to be evicted from her home by her son and daughter-in-law, provides another variation on this theme. Still another variation is projected by the action of Marty's mother who, discovering that her son may be developing a serious relationship, reacts sharply to protect herself from the loneliness that will inevitably follow his marriage. Echoing the theme of Marty's search for acceptance in other lives gives unity to the story and adds to its emotional impact. The use of the same technique amplifies the power of the film *Guilty by Suspicion*. The theme is made explicit mainly in the ordeal suffered by the focal character David Merrill, but its impact is unified and enhanced because others also suffer during the Hollywood blacklist. Dorothy Nolan's suicide, the flight of the director Joe Lesser to England, and the virtual disintegration of Bunny Baxter all reflect in varied tones the torment experienced by David Merrill.

Plays with Similar Subject Matter

A certain type of subject matter is not the exclusive province of one particular play. Many different dramas deal with the same kind of material. The fact that they take up the same topic does not mean necessarily that they are alike in other respects, however. Henrik Ibsen's *A Doll's House* and Garson Kanin's *Born Yesterday* both told the story of women who revolted against the domination of men. Yet the first was a serious drama, the second a comedy. Is it possible for a dramatist to find subject matter that is unique? This may happen on occasion. The 1991 TV movie *My Son Johnny* focused on a problem that involves millions of children and yet rarely had been the subject of any kind of drama. The subject was sibling abuse. The movie told the true story of a boy who killed his brother because he had constantly beaten him. He was one of an estimated 19 million children who regularly mistreat their brothers and sisters.

THEME AS THESIS

Theme, then, is often equated with subject matter. But there is a second major way in which the term is often defined. Many people think of theme as a statement about life and its meaning, an underlying truth that is communicated by the action of the play. The terms *thesis, proposition,* and *premise* are also used in referring to such statements. Another word commonly used in this way, particularly with reference to children's stories, is *moral*. In dealing with theme, we need to keep in mind whether we are thinking of it as subject matter or as a message or idea the drama transmits.

Dramas obviously must be about something—so they all have the kind of theme we think of as subject matter. Most of them also involve the second type of theme, the transmission of a basic proposition or thesis. The

TV play based on Walter Lord's book *A Night to Remember* illustrates these two kinds of themes. Its subject-matter theme was the sinking of the *Titanic*. The thesis the play projected was that fate had played a major role in bringing about a tragedy that cost more than 1,500 lives. This thesis was summed up in the concluding narration of the script.

NARRATOR

If the *Titanic* had heeded any of the six iceberg messages . . . if the night had been rough or moonlit . . . if she had hit the iceberg fifteen seconds later . . . if her watertight bulkheads had been one deck higher . . . if she had carried enough boats . . . if the *Californian* had only heeded and come. Had any of these "ifs" turned out right, every life might have been saved. But they all went against her. And never again has man been quite so confident. An age had come to an end.

The 1991 film *Prince of Tides* provides another illustration of these two kinds of themes. The subject it dealt with was the effect of a man's troubled childhood and youth on his adult life. Its thesis, according to Barbra Streisand, who starred in and directed the film, was the idea that we "need to love our fathers and mothers in all their flawed and outrageous humanity." Robert Towne, who wrote the screenplays for *Chinatown* and its sequel *The Two Jakes* (whose subject matter was political corruption) said that the two movies shared the same thesis—"the futility of good intentions."[3] The last line of the focal character, Jake Gittes, in *Chinatown* sums up this idea. He comments disconsolately that when he tried to help someone all he ended up doing was hurting them. The subject matter of the TV series *Law and Order* is the investigation of crime and the prosecution of its perpetrators. Its thesis, according

to David Black (one of the series' writers and producers), is expressed in the question: *How can just people survive in an unjust world*?

The Nature of Themes as Theses

The meanings that plays project are so diverse that it would seem impossible to establish a catalogue of criteria that can apply. Yet an examination of a number of themes—when the word is interpreted to mean the theses that express the essential meanings of the plays—reveals that there are some general observations one can make about them. If such a theme is to help invest a script with significance three attributes are necessary. First, the statement the theme makes about life should be an important one. Second, this statement should be one that is meaningful to as many people as possible; it should have the quality of universality. Third, the theme should concern one of the eternal questions of life and death that everlastingly face humankind. The best themes are those with potentialities for appealing to the deepest feelings of an audience. A theme whose point is dry and intellectual is a barrier to the achievement of a play's maximum emotional power.

One quality a theme need not have is originality. If you are to deal with the enduring questions of the ages, you cannot expect to say anything strikingly new. What marks writers as original and creative is not what their plays say but how they say it. Often writers will deal with the same themes over and over again as George Bernard Shaw did in his plays.

Must a theme make a true statement about life? Many times it does, and often the truth of the theme is so obvious that a play is scarcely necessary to establish it. The average individual going to see *Macbeth* does not need to be convinced that excessive ambition can be an evil thing. What this play does, however, is to overwhelm the audience with the truth of this observation. It projects its thought so forcibly that acceptance passes beyond mere understanding. A passive truth has been made vivid and alive.

A theme need not necessarily be true, however, at least for all of the audience. A good example is Arthur Miller's play *The Crucible*, first produced at the time Senator Joseph McCarthy's campaign to root Communists out of government was at its height. Miller's equating of that campaign with the witch hunt that took place in Salem, Massachusetts, in 1692 would be rejected by those in the audience who believed that McCarthy was conducting a righteous crusade against an evil and threatening force in our nation. To cite another example, some people would not agree that good intentions are futile—the theme cited by Robert Towne as the one communicated by his screenplays of *Chinatown* and *The Two Jakes*. Thus, themes need not be inevitably true nor universally applicable. What is crucial, however, is that the thesis of a particular play be true in terms of its characters and the action.

Is a Theme as Thesis Necessary?

In answering this question with respect to theme as subject matter our response was "yes." Is it also true that a play must communicate some kind of message or proposition that can be identified by the audience? The answer to this question is less obvious. In some cases such themes are clearly reflected by a play, although the precise language in which they are stated may vary somewhat from person to person. In other cases it is difficult to find a thesis or proposition, or, if it is identified at all, it will be stated by various people in widely different ways.

The presence or absence of a theme of the message type seems to have little bearing on the success of a play or on the judgments people make about its overall quality. As we have noted, Shakespeare's *Macbeth* advances a proposition about ambition that is easily identified. His *Hamlet* and *Julius Caesar*, on the other hand, defy the attempts of most people to condense their messages into single, declarative sentences. They are not for that reason any lesser dramatic achievements, however. Two plays generally considered among the best Arthur Miller wrote are *The Crucible* and *Death of a Salesman*. *The Crucible* is clearly a message play. In telling the story of the Salem witch trials, Miller's purpose was to put forward the idea that Joseph McCarthy's attacks on presumed Communists were unjust and irrational, the same message transmitted by the film *Guilty by Suspicion*. *Death of a Salesman*, on the other hand, seems to mean something different to everyone who sees it.

It is apparent, then, that a single, clearly identifiable theme is not an absolute requirement in play construction. This is not to argue that plays lacking one clearly defined message fail to project important ideas. Just the opposite is true. In fact, the problem in some great works is that the observations about life and people they reflect are so many-faceted that to encompass all of the meanings in a single statement is impossible.

The Contributions of a Thesis

Though the expression of a clearly defined proposition is not an essential element in a play, sometimes its presence can make certain contributions. They may be of various types.

Thesis and Substance One contribution a thesis may make is to cause the audience to ponder some aspect of life. This adds substance to a play. An example was an episode in the *Alfred Hitchcock* series, which had a long run on television and can now be seen in syndication. It is difficult to find a thesis or philosophical point in most of the scripts in this series, but at times the surprise twist at the end of the stories project a clearly identifiable thesis. An example was a television adaptation of John Collier's short story "Back at Christmas." It tells of an Englishman who murders his wife and buries her in the basement just before they are to set off for America on a trip that was to end at Christmas. It is the husband's plan to pretend that once in America they decide to stay there. His scheme appears to have worked perfectly until one day, safely in America, he receives a bill addressed to his wife. It seems that to surprise him when they returned to England at Christmas, she had arranged to have a wine cellar dug in the very place he had buried her body. The twist is ingenious and its effect is amplified by the thesis it expresses: "Murder will out."

Another story that illustrates how a strong thesis can add substance is Frank Stockton's "The Lady or the Tiger." It has had a number of television adaptations. Like the Collier story, it also is a work that depends for much of its effect on a surprise. The twist in this case is that Stockton left his story unfinished, leaving his readers to decide the ending for themselves.

The story tells how a princess living in a kingdom that often treated humans with primitive savagery falls in love with a common soldier. When their relationship is discovered by the king, he decrees that chance will decide whether the soldier will live or die. He puts him in an arena into which two doors open. Behind one door stands a vicious tiger, behind the other a beautiful maiden. The soldier is ordered to open one or the other of those doors, not knowing what is behind them. The princess, however, having discovered which door hides the tiger and which the maiden, catches her lover's eye and nods toward one of the doors. Without a moment's hesitation, the soldier strides toward the door and pulls it open. Stockton's story ends at that point. The television viewer, in deciding whether the open door will reveal the lady or the tiger, will decide the thesis of the play. Which would a savage princess choose: to see her lover torn to pieces before her eyes by a tiger, or to see him walk out of the arena in radiant happiness with another woman? In contemplating the answer to that question, the viewer has much to think about.

Martin Scorsese's 1991 remake of the 1962 film *Cape Fear* illustrates how the addition of a substantial thesis can enrich the audience's experience. The original version portrayed a struggle between a hero who was all good and a villain who was all bad. In the Scorsese remake the hero was ethically flawed. Years earlier, in defending the ex-convict now pursuing him and his family, the attorney had suppressed evidence that might have kept his sociopathic client out of jail. Scorsese's remake converted black-and-white conflict into shades of gray. In so doing, he invited the audience to contemplate the true nature of good and evil.

Thesis and Plot   Another contribution a well-defined thesis can make is to help a writer reach decisions about plotting. A certain thesis may take a story in one direction, another will guide it down a different road. Not dominating but serving, a thesis may lead a writer to those decisions that will best focus and crystallize the plot.

The impact of a thesis on a story and its role in determining story decisions is illustrated in a script written by a student at the Stanford-NBC Radio and Television Institute. The play *Chester Swivel Gets His*, by Alfred Wilkinson, is essentially one of the "gimmick" variety. At the beginning, a being identified as Fate tells the audience how an insignificant little man named Chester Swivel is that afternoon going to meet his end under the wheels of a truck—destined to come roaring down a certain street at the precise instant that Chester Swivel steps into the street from a drugstore. So that the audience will not grieve too deeply, it is demonstrated that Chester's existence under the thumb of a shrewish wife and a tyrannical boss is incredibly miserable; his imminent translation into the other world can be interpreted as nothing but a boon.

Events then occur exactly as Fate has planned them. The truck proceeds on schedule through the streets of the city toward its rendezvous with the insignificant Chester Swivel. Chester enters the drugstore just as planned; he purchases a newspaper; he starts for the door as the truck turns into the street a block away. And then the phone rings. The call is for Chester Swivel. He turns back to answer as the truck goes roaring by outside the door—leaving him unscathed. Overwhelmed at this incredible disruption of his plans, Fate storms at the audience, unable to believe that anything could have interfered. Then suddenly he knows what has happened. *A member of the audience had placed that telephone call to Chester Swivel to save him from his doom*!

That was the climax of the play and the "gimmick." How should the play end? Important decisions regarding both thesis and story are involved. Should Fate merely summon another truck and send Chester to his reward as previously ordained? That ending suggests the thesis: "You cannot avoid fate." Or should the audience member's intervention be permitted to succeed, with the result that Chester is doomed to spend 30 more miserable years oppressed by both wife and boss? The thesis suggested by that ending is: "Beware of interfering with fate." Which is the better thesis and which is the more satisfactory ending to the story? How would you finish this script?

The Dangers of a Dominating Thesis

Plays are written for various reasons. One dramatist may be motivated primarily by the desire to project a vivid character. Another may be inspired by a novel plot idea. Some set out merely to tell a good story in which character and plot ideas are of equal importance. Some dramatists, however, write scripts for the express purpose of communicating a social message or enunciating a proposition about life. Should a thesis of this nature ever be the main inspiration for a play?

Though a strong thesis may be an asset to a play, it can be damaging if it becomes too dominant. This is most likely to happen if you write a play primarily to make a social pronouncement. The critic Walter Kerr warned "that a good way to destroy a play is to force it to prove something."[4] One reason is that a thesis usually makes its appeal to the mind, whereas the success of a play depends primarily on its power to arouse the emotions. Writers who make their characters and plot serve the thesis rather than making the thesis serve them, will probably fail to move viewers, for they are concentrating on making people think rather than on making them feel.

Another damaging result of concentration on a thesis is that it subordinates characterization to the making of a social argument or the proclaiming of a text. When this happens, the people of the play never become living, breathing, humans at all but remain mere puppets being manipulated to express an intellectual or political idea. If the play is to succeed, its characters must become more than mere fleshless symbols whose sole function is to perform a role in developing a pattern of thought leading to a logical conclusion. They must become, instead, creatures of flesh and blood capable in themselves of arousing the passions of the audience. "It is better to make a man than to make a point," advised Walter Kerr.[5] The playwright Howard Lindsay struck the same note when he said, "A play doesn't have to have a moral. Human nature is good enough. . . . It is enough to see human beings acting in the circumstances of life."[6]

Finding a Thesis

As a matter of fact, if you succeed in depicting characters "acting in the circumstances of life," the enunciation of the thesis will take care of itself. Paddy Chayefsky's *Marty* obviously was written with the development of a character in mind. In creating a moving portrait of a human being, he was successful also in projecting compelling ideas about rejection.

In most of your dramatic writing the problem of deciding on a thesis will be of minor importance in the beginning. You will be absorbed in creating characters and filling them out; you will be concerned with developing the basic narrative line. Next perhaps you will ask yourself about the thesis. Must you then proceed to find or invent one? Probably not. As we have noted before, your play does not need to project a clearly identifiable statement about life to be a success. Even if it ends with such a statement, it probably will not be because you sought it out and put it there. In most cases you will see your thesis implicit in the characters and action you already have created. The thesis will be a by-product which comes into existence as your audience sees the play. You do not need to find a thesis. The thesis will have found you.

QUESTIONS AND PROJECTS

1. What is your opinion about whether themes are necessary in dramatic writing?
2. Can you define in one or two words the subject matter of three film or TV dramas you have seen recently?
3. Can you find a thesis or proposition in these same three dramas that you can express in a single sentence?
4. When asked to define the message he was trying to communicate in his play *The Hostage*, Brendan Behan responded: "Message? What do you think I am, a postman?" Consider this reply in a general discussion of the playwright's responsibility for enunciating a thesis.
5. Join with your classmates in defining the thesis of a common dramatic experience —a play, movie, TV production, or a dramatic script. Discuss the significance of your agreement or lack of agreement.

NOTES

1. Aric Press, "Michael, We Hardly Knew Ye," *Newsweek*, June 3, 1991, p. 8.
2. Arthur Miller, "Barton Fink," *Premiere*, October, 1991, p. 108.
3. Quoted in Fred Schruers, "The Two Jacks," *Premiere*, September, 1990.
4. Walter Kerr, *How Not to Write a Play* (New York: Simon and Schuster, 1955), p. 51.
5. Ibid, p. 58.
6. Quoted in A. S. Burack, *The Writer's Handbook* (Boston: The Writer, 1949), p. 370.

Most of the creative decisions we have been considering thus far are those dramatists make before they begin the actual writing of the script. They may have jotted down a few items that will become part of the final draft—a few lines of dialogue, perhaps—but the main task of deciding the order of scenes and casting them into dramatic form through the writing of dialogue and narration lies ahead.

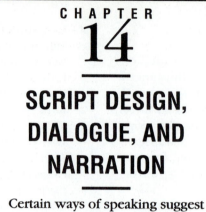

CHAPTER 14

SCRIPT DESIGN, DIALOGUE, AND NARRATION

Certain ways of speaking suggest certain shapes of flesh.
HENRY GREEN (1905–1973)

films. Don Simpson, co-producer of such films as *Beverly Hills Cop* and *Top Gun*, says, "In the first ten minutes of the movie the audience wants to know what they're sitting there for, and what it's going to be about."[1]

A Problem Already in Motion The single best way to arouse interest is to confront the audience at the beginning of your script with a character already enmeshed in a critical problem. If possible, your *point of attack*, as the entering moment is called, should show someone who has reached a turning point in life—who faces an agonizing decision or has begun a struggle to reach a highly desired goal. This approach presupposes a story that is under way before the opening scene flashes on the screen to illuminate this moment of crisis. The events that precipitated the crisis are then revealed as the play proceeds. To begin your play when the story itself actually begins probably would require you to precede the exciting events with a long, slow exposition not calculated to engage audience attention. This, in fact, is the way many stage plays once began. Two servants would sketch out the background of the situation and characters before there was any real action. As Eric Barnouw, a pioneer teacher of broadcast writing, wrote, "In radio drama the intriguing or arresting start, the quick plunge into essential conflict, have forever supplanted the two maids with the dusters."[2] His statement applies as much to television as it did to radio. At one time the opening credits usually were presented before television or movie dramas actually began. Now it is

SCRIPT DESIGN

Before you begin writing your script, you will be wise to work out its development in detail. In drawing up this plan, there are certain requirements you should keep in mind and certain overall qualities you should try to capture.

Gaining Attention

TV viewers are often chance wanderers through the channels, tuning in tentatively to find out what is in store for them. If you fail to engage their interest at once, they may turn restlessly to another channel or switch off the set entirely. In the case of movies, the darkened theater and the absence of household distractions help to focus attention on the screen. Moreover, viewers, having once paid their way into the theater, are not likely to leave even though their interest is not immediately awakened. Writers of movie scripts cannot wait too long to seize the attention of their audiences, however, or they will find that unfavorable word-of-mouth criticism will keep people from coming to see their common to delay them until the first scene is completed, or to superimpose them as the action begins.

The Promise of a Problem Sometimes the nature of a particular story makes it impossible for a writer to introduce engrossing action immediately. Before the audience can be plunged into the middle of the conflict, some preliminary exposition may be required. In such cases the writer can seize attention by promising a problem to come. One way to let an audience know that a crisis looms is to make some reference to it in the early lines of the play. A character may express dread of a meeting or event about to take place. The opening narration also can awaken audience expectancy in this way.

Another means of catching attention is to present scenes of exciting action appearing later in the script at the beginning of the play before the regular development of the story begins. This is called the *teaser* technique. The *Matlock* series used it consistently. Teasers do have the power to pique curiosity, but they have the fault of artificiality. They are so obviously devices for arousing interest that their power may be muted by that very obviousness. Another objection is that audiences may be disoriented by a scene presented completely out of context and without proper foundation.

The promise of a problem to come also can be made in opening narration. The MGM movie *House of Numbers* aroused interest by showing views of San Quentin Prison while a narrator spoke these words, "Authorities used to believe there were only two ways out. The main gate after you'd served your time . . . or the side gate, when you died. Two men and a girl found a third way out.*

The Appeal of the Unfamiliar An excellent way to arouse the interest of viewers is to provide them with novel or unusual experiences. Plays of the science-fiction or horror types often catch attention by generating a powerful atmosphere through the accenting of the bizarre and the macabre. An unfamiliar setting can excite interest, for most people are intrigued by places or activities they have never seen. The producer of *The China Syndrome*, a film about a TV reporter's investigation into trouble in a nuclear power plant, took advantage of two unfamiliar settings about which many people are curious. The film caught viewer attention at the beginning by focusing on the behind-the-scenes action involved in putting a TV news program on the air. Later it brought the audience into the control room of the nuclear plant to show the complicated process required to regulate and distribute the electrical energy produced by nuclear generation.

Another good way to catch attention is to depict an unusual or mysterious event at the beginning for which the play promises an explanation. The opening of *Hamlet*, with its references to the appearance of an unearthly being, is an example of this technique.

The Appeal of the Familiar Sometimes projecting a feeling of the familiar is as effective in arousing interest as novelty is. People are caught by stories that provide echoes of their own experiences.

An episode in the *MacGyver* series used this technique to capture attention. It opened with a scene, before the credits came on, that would evoke recognition from many in the audience—two people on a lake shore fishing, one a young boy, the other a grandfatherly type.

*With the permission of MGM from its motion picture *House of Numbers,* copyright © MCMLVII in U.S.A. by Loew's Incorporated.

MACGYVER: "COMA"
ACT ONE

FADE IN:

1 EXT. LAKESHORE—ESTABLISHING—DAY
Golden sun reflects upon the calm surface.

2 ANGLE—HARRY JACKSON
He expertly folds a piece of silver gum wrapper in origami fashion while a YOUNG BOY watches, wide-eyed. Both are dressed in favorite "fishin' duds." The Boy glances down and SEES:

3 BOY'S POV—A PLASTIC BUCKET
Depressingly empty. The CAMERA PANS to another bucket, this one made of metal and stuffed with freshly caught trout.

4 RESUME SCENE
The Boy returns his attention to Harry, impressed. Harry continues to work the foil wrapper.

> BOY
> (dubious)
> *That's* a fishing lure?

5 INSERT—SILVER FOIL
Harry intricately shapes it into a fishing lure.

6 RESUME SCENE
The Boy stares, fascinated.

> HARRY
> I call it the Harry Jackson Dazzler.
> (hands it to him)
> Might improve your luck.

> BOY
> Wow! Thanks!

Harry grins as the Boy admires the lure.

> HARRY
> You say your grandfather taught you to fish?

> BOY
> Yeah, long time ago, when I was a kid. But,
> he moved to California so I don't see him much.

                         HARRY
Know how that is. My grandson lives in Califor-
nia. Seems like an awful long way sometimes.
                         (beat)
Want to see a picture of him?

                          BOY
     Sure.

Harry digs out his wallet, opens it to REVEAL:

7 INSERT—PHOTOGRAPH OF MACGYVER
A head and shoulders shot of MacGyver.

8 RESUME SCENE
The boy's eyes widen.

                          BOY
     He's your grandson? Boy, he's old!
                    (beat, quickly)
     Uh, I mean, you don't look that old.

                         HARRY
                    (grins, winks)
     Let you in on a secret. I don't feel that old,
     either.

The Boy grins with him, then turns away, engrossed in his new lure.

9 ANGLE—HARRY
He gazes at MacGyver's photo, then slips it into his breast shirt pocket, picking up his rod.

                         HARRY
     Try keepin' your wrist stiff when you
     cast. You'll get more distance.

Harry suddenly stops in mid-cast, sharp pain shooting up his arm. He knows what it is.

                         HARRY
                  (under his breath)
          Damn . . . !

The Boy turns, frightened to SEE Harry collapse, pain hammering his chest.

                          BOY
     Hey, mister . . . you okay?

                              HARRY
                          (gasps, tightly)
                    Do me a favor, bud? Run to the cottage
                    back on the trail . . . tell 'em to call an
                    ambulance . . . fast as you can . . .

The frightened Boy obeys, bolting like a rabbit.

10 CLOSE—HARRY
clutching his chest, his fingers claw something from his shirt pocket. He SEES it's MAC-
GYVER'S PHOTO. He stares at it, growing faint as we DISSOLVE TO:

11 EXT. DOWNTOWN MUSEUM—ESTABLISHING—DAY

Note that the writers do not dally too long with the fishing scene, for its lack of critical action soon would lose the audience. Before too much time has gone by, a crisis develops as the old man collapses with an apparent heart attack. Moreover, the picture he carries has established his relationship with the title character. The audience knows that this event will soon involve MacGyver.

One problem with using an evocation of the familiar to capture attention is that what is familiar to one viewer may be totally unfamiliar to another. On the other hand, what appeals to one person because of its familiarity may appeal to another because of its novelty.

A Striking Characterization   A powerful means of gaining attention is to present a striking character. In the movie *The Silence of the Lambs* the appearance of the monstrous Hannibal Lecter, played with surpassing skill by Oscar winner Anthony Hopkins, immediately riveted audience attention. This character's sophistication and authoritative knowledge of psychiatric disorders, combined with his penchant for eating body parts of people he had killed, kept the eyes of the audience glued to the screen.

Sustaining Interest

It is not enough merely to excite the interest of an audience at the beginning of a play. To be successful you must sustain that interest as long as the play is on the screen. Your principal means for meeting this challenge is to develop a strong, accelerating plot involving striking characters caught in vital conflicts, but there are also other techniques that can be used.

Suspense   The best way for a dramatist to hold the attention of an audience is to develop an atmosphere of constantly increasing suspense. The writer creates suspense, in the first place, by arousing the audience's curiosity about the way things are going to turn out. This may involve a suspense question about the eventual result of the action, or if the nature of the outcome is fairly obvious—that the young lovers will live happily ever after, for example—the suspense question asks how this happy conclusion is to be reached in view of all the apparent obstacles. The writer develops suspense, in the second place, by creating characters who engage the interest and sympathy of the viewers. As these viewers begin to worry about whether these characters will find a way out of the troubles enveloping them, the feeling of suspense initiated by curiosity begins to mount. The playwright accentuates this process by multiplying both uncertainty and anxiety until the tension reaches a fever pitch at the climax of the play. Suspense, then, is composed of two ingredients: curiosity and concern.

Minor Suspense   Two types of suspense can be distinguished. Minor suspense is that created to catch the interest of viewers and persuade them to go on looking from minute to minute until the playwright has time to develop the problem that will produce the major suspense of the story. A car chase at the beginning of a police drama, for example, may create some minor suspense as the audience wonders how it will come out. This will hold interest until the writer can develop the main suspense question of the story.

Major Suspense   The most important suspense developed by a play is that related to the goal or decision on which the action focuses. In the goal-centered play, the dramatist develops suspense by making the audience both wonder and worry about whether the focal character will achieve his or her objective. In the decision-centered play, the dramatist creates curiosity and anxiety about the way the focal character will decide between difficult choices. As the action progresses, suspense about the major question of the play intensifies and gradually displaces the suspense generated by the minor questions.

Expectancy   Reinforcing the effect of suspense in holding the interest of an audience is the development of expectancy. The two are closely related in that both involve the arousal of audience anxiety, but they are different in that suspense is created when an audience wonders what will happen, whereas expectancy develops when an audience is led to believe that a certain something will happen. At times a situation develops suspense and expectancy in equal measure, a combination that has great power to hold the attention of the audience. Viewers seeing a boy swimming desperately to avoid being drawn over a falls may expect to see him fall over the brink to his death and at the same time may wonder whether some unexpected development will intervene to save his life. Prodded by expectation, curiosity, and anxiety, they are certain to keep their eyes fixed upon the event.

Sometimes writers develop so much expectancy for a particular incident or scene that they become obligated to present it. A good example of this occurs in the film *Thelma and Louise*. As the two women drive west, the obnoxious driver of an oil tanker pulls alongside their car and harasses them with crude gestures and facial expressions. Despite their effort to get away, he continues to hound them. Previous incidents in the film have shown that when these two women get caught in difficult situations, they can be counted on to extricate themselves with decisive action. In one instance, Louise shot a would-be rapist; in another, the two together locked a police officer (who was trying to arrest them) inside the trunk of his own car. With audience expectancy aroused by what has gone on before, the writer is virtually compelled to satisfy viewer anticipation with a scene showing them terminating this nuisance with a similar response. The audience is not disappointed. Thelma and Louise entice the driver out of his cab by pretending they are ready to cooperate, then blow the tanker sky high with a few well-placed bullets. Anyone who sharpens an audience's expectancy for certain exciting action and then neglects to include it is failing to deliver the goods the play's development promised.

Experiencing the Drama One of the major differences between drama and fiction is that drama reveals what is happening whereas fiction tells what has happened. Dramatists may fail to hold audience attention unless they take full advantage of the power of drama to give viewers the feeling they are experiencing an event as it is actually taking place. The mastery of a number of techniques is required if this impression is to be transmitted with the fullest possible effect.

Gradual Revelation The technique of gradual revelation has a role in all forms of storytelling, but it is particularly important to the dramatist. It consists of the ability to unfold the story by degrees, a method that provides viewers with the excitement of telling disclosures at regular intervals, but denies them full knowledge of the events until the play is almost over. This technique encourages the participation of viewers by inviting them to stretch forward from one revelation to the next. Gradual revelation also contributes to the effective pacing of a drama, for the movement of the play tends to accelerate when significant information is being revealed and to relax and slow down between disclosures.

In planning your play, no task is more crucial than that of deciding how you are going to make the disclosures that are fundamental to your plot and characterization. You should plan carefully what you are going to reveal at various points in your play and how you are going to reveal it. A certain sign of amateur writing is the disclosure that comes too early and too completely. To keep anticipation at fever pitch, you must dole out information in driblets, enough to keep the story moving, but not so much that the curiosity of the audience is muted because it is satisfied.

Implication Another primary tool in leading an audience to experience a play rather than merely to observe it is the technique of implication. Through the use of this technique the viewer gains information, not through direct statements, but by making inferences on the basis of indirect evidence and suggestion. Thus the audience becomes a partner in creating the action and the characterization. This process compares with the one that goes on in real life. On the basis of facts and observation we draw conclusions about people and events.

The television movie *When Every Day Was the Fourth of July* provided an excellent example of the technique of implication at work. Just before a trial is to begin, the judge is asked to prohibit the taking of pictures in his courtroom. He brusquely refuses and then is shown carefully combing his hair. His vanity and his thirst for publicity are effectively communicated without his saying a word.

The motion picture *Giant* told how a young lady, born and raised in a lush, green section of Maryland, is brought by her new husband to live on a bare and treeless Texas plain. Then one day she sees a tree and impulsively throws her arms around it and caresses it. Because the audience is permitted to see for itself how deeply she yearns for the trees of her native Maryland, rather than being informed of it directly in narration or dialogue, the power of the revelation is magnified.

A TV drama presented on the *Hallmark Hall of Fame* series provides an excellent example of the use of implication. In the course of its 40 years on the air this distinguished series has won 65 Emmys and has featured some of the world's leading actors. *Sarah, Plain and Tall*, written by Patricia MacLachlan and Carol Solieski, was adapted from a novel of the same title by MacLachlan. Broadcast in February 1991 with Glenn Close and Christopher Walken in the lead roles, it attracted the largest audience ever drawn by a Hallmark drama, earning the highest audience rating of the week as well.

Sarah, Plain and Tall tells the story of a widowed farmer, Jacob Witting, who for the six years following the death of his wife has been trying to work his Kansas farm, handle the household chores, and bring up two young children. Deciding at last that he needs the help of a woman, he places a discreet advertisement for a wife in a Maine newspaper. The understanding is that marriage would take place only after the woman has visited for a month and both agree that they can live happily as man and wife. As far as the Kansas community is concerned, she will be described as a family friend visiting from the East. The advertisement is answered by Sarah Wheaton, who is about to lose the home she has been sharing with her brother William because he is going to be married. She decides to make the journey west even though she wonders how she can be happy so far away from the ocean she loves. When Sarah arrives on the train in the little prairie town, she is filled with doubt about the arrangement. The writers do not communicate her uncertainty directly, however. Instead they let the audience learn about it through a telling action: Before Sarah leaves the railroad station, she buys a one-way ticket back to Maine. Through the rest of the play this ticket becomes a symbol of her indecision. It underscores the main suspense question of the drama: Will Sarah stay and marry Jacob?

There are major obstacles to a happy ending. Six-year-old Caleb, who has no memory of his mother (who died just after he was born), takes to Sarah immediately, but nine-year-old Anna, who does remember her mother, views her as an intruder whom she treats at first with cold hostility. As the story progresses, Sarah gradually wins Anna over, but one seemingly insurmountable stumbling-block remains. It appears that Jacob, still racked by the memory of his dead wife, will never be able to accept her. Early in the drama the audience sees Sarah looking at her return ticket and realizes that she is still wondering whether all of this will work out. One day Anna catches sight of the ticket in the open drawer of Sarah's bedside table and thus finds out that Sarah has not yet decided to stay. The ticket enters the picture again after a tense interchange between Jacob and Sarah. When she returns to her room, she sees it in the open drawer. Although Sarah shuts the drawer quickly, the audience knows that the idea of returning to Maine is still in her mind.

As the play reaches its climax, the railroad ticket plays a crucial role. Having survived a violent storm together, Sarah and Jacob appear to be growing closer. But once more the tension between them erupts in anger. Later, Sarah informs Jacob that she has learned to drive the horse cart and wants to go into town alone. Jacob, filled with misgivings, watches her go, as do the children—even Anna, who has finally been won over by Sarah's love and kindness. Then Anna remembers the train ticket and rushes to Sarah's room to see whether it is still there. To her dismay, she finds it gone. She immediately concludes that Sarah has left her luggage and even her cat, Seal, so that she can get away quietly. Fearing that the train is already taking Sarah away, Anna rushes out to tell her father. The following excerpt dramatizes this final crisis and its resolution.

SARAH, PLAIN AND TALL
CONCLUSION

EXT. WITTING FARM—DAY
Anna runs to the barn.

                              ANNA
                    Papa! It's gone!

Jacob is still sharpening his tool. Caleb helping him.

                              JACOB
                    What's gone?

                              ANNA
                    Sarah had a train ticket home. In her bed
                    stand. It's gone!

Jacob says nothing.

                              ANNA
                    You'll say it's not my place to know it. But
                    it's true, Papa. And it's gone!

Jacob stares at the children and then in the direction Sarah went.

                              CALEB
                    Go after her, Papa!

Jacob thinks a moment, then he gets up and runs to the barn for [his horse] Jack.

                                                                    CUT TO:

EXT. PRAIRIE TOWN—DAY

WIDE CAMERA VIEW SHOWS prairie town with a train having just come into the station.
Jacob far in the distance, is racing to get there before the train leaves. The train stops
momentarily, then after a moment begins to leave, Jacob just reaching the far side.

Frantically, almost irrationally, Jacob urges his horse after the train, but the train picks up
speed and slowly, in great despair, Jacob stops and watches the train go farther and farther
away. He sighs, then turns the horse around. There, from Jacob's POV, is Sarah, standing
on the station platform. He smiles, then gallops over to the platform. Jacob dismounts,
climbs the platform, staring at Sarah.

                              SARAH
                    (opening her hand)
                    Jacob, I—I turned in my ticket. I have this
                    money . . .

Jacob moves closer and takes her hands first, as he puts his arms around her, gently kiss-
ing her eyes and face as if just coming to know her. Then Sarah responds, throwing her
arms around him and they passionately kiss and then hug.

                                                                    CUT TO:

EXT. WITTING PORCH—DAY

Anna and Caleb sit on the porch steps, much as they did when Sarah first came. Anna stares down the road. Caleb plays his sad song on his harmonica over and over. Suddenly the dog, Nick, comes out from under the porch, his head lifting. Anna stands up quickly and Caleb climbs up on the porch railing excitedly. The children are all smiles.

CAMERA MOVES TO WIDE VIEW of the wagon coming down the road, Sarah and Jacob sitting in the wagon. Jacob's horse tied to the back of the wagon. Slowly the wagon comes around the windmill and into the yard, Nick jumping and BARKING with excitement. The wagon stops.

SARAH

Hush, Nick!

Caleb climbs down from the railing and stands staring at Sarah. She climbs down. And as if unable to hold it in any longer, Caleb throws himself at her, hugging her.

CALEB

Seal was worried!

Sarah bends down, looking him in the eyes.

CALEB

And the house is too small, we thought.
And I *am* loud and pesky!

ANNA

We thought you might be leaving us.
(beat)
Because you miss the sea.

SARAH

Well, I'll always miss my old home. But the
truth of it is . . . I'd miss you more.

She hugs the children as Jacob looks on.

Sarah gives a wrapped package to Anna.

SARAH

For you, Anna, and for Caleb. For all of us.

Slowly, Anna unwraps the small package with Caleb peering closely at it. Caleb reaches over and takes out three colored pencils.

CALEB

Blue . . . and gray.
(beat)
And green.

Caleb grins with understanding.

CALEB

Papa, look! Sarah's brought the seal

Jacob and Sarah look at each other over the heads of the children, then move toward each other.

Jacob puts his arms around her, suddenly swinging her up and around in his arms.

DISSOLVE TO:

SLOW MOTION—EXT. CHURCH YARD—SAME PICTURE—DAY

Sarah being swung in Jacob's arms, but they are dressed in wedding clothes, Sarah in a white dress, elegant and plain, carrying roses. Anna and Caleb, laughing; Maggie, Matthew and wedding guests in a wedding with the prairie stretches out around them.

FADE OUT

THE END

In using the technique of implication, dramatists must be careful, of course, to provide enough direct information to permit impressions to arise and conclusions to be drawn. Audiences must be told who people are and where they are. They must discover what actions or events in the past caused the present situation.

If viewers become confused about these points, they will lose interest. They do not need to know all the facts, only those necessary to follow the action. Writers walk a narrow line between excess explanation, which spoils the effect, and insufficient explanation, which permits no effect at all. The great artists include only what is necessary to establish the point; the rest they leave to the audience.

Showing the Action   Another technique, akin in its effect to the use of implication, is showing the critical action to the audience rather than merely talking about it. One of the unique strengths of drama is its power to portray events as they actually take place, yet writers often dissipate this strength by permitting characters to talk about vital occurrences instead of showing them happening. Viewers do not want to hear what has happened, they want to see it develop before their eyes. There is not enough time to dramatize all of the events, of course, so some of the incidental action must be communicated through exposition. But the viewers must witness the basic conflicts; they must agonize through the making of the vital decisions; they must see what produces the emotions and reactions of the characters.

Maintaining Plausibility

In addition to keeping the audience interested in the play throughout its presentation, the dramatist has the further duty of maintaining its believability. Once viewers begin to disbelieve, to question the plausibility of an action or motivation, to think, "I don't believe the character would act that way," the writer is beginning to lose them. Even if they continue to watch, they are no longer completely absorbed by the action of the play, for they have moved outside to look on instead of remaining inside and involved. Becoming objective and intellectual rather than remaining subjective and emotional, they can no longer experience the optimum dramatic impact.

The Problem of Preparation   One way to invite the audience's rejection of a situation is to fail to prepare for it. Preparation means to provide those details in advance that are necessary to get an audience ready for some later step in the action. If one character is going to snatch a knife from a table and attack another character, it is not enough that the knife merely be lying there ready to be used. Before the critical moment, the audience must be made specifically aware of the knife's availability. If a character is to die suddenly, the audience must have been given facts that make the death believable. The role of preparation has been aptly described by playwright John Van Druten (*I Am a Camera*): "Playwriting, apart from being like a lot of other things, is also very like chess, where a whole series of moves must be made to lead up to the one you want."

Other Problems of Plausibility   The playwright may be faced with a number of knotty problems that affect the plausibility of the action. The necessity of getting people out of a scene is a frequent cause of trouble. Using the hoary old device of having water boil over to lure a wife into the kitchen so that the other characters in the living room can talk about her reeks of contrivance. Arranging for a grandfather to forget his glasses so that another character can be asked to read a letter aloud for the audience's benefit is another example of conspicuous manipulation.

Sometimes the problem of maintaining plausibility involves what might be called simple reasonableness. A leading character in the *Mary Tyler Moore Show* was newscaster Ted Baxter, whose conceit, contrasted with his rank incompetence, provided much of the fun. There was a nagging question that bothered some viewers, however: How could a newscaster as incompetent as Baxter hold a job on a major television station? Most viewers were willing to accept this improbability, first, because they give writers of comedy more latitude with respect to plausibility than they grant to writers of serious drama, and second, because the situation, even though implausible, provided them with enjoyment. We see this saving principle at work in some of Shakespeare's plays. Shakespeare asks us to believe that a woman can hide her identity from her family and closest friends simply by putting on a man's hat. As the film *Guilty by Suspicion* begins, the focal character, David Merrill, seems unaware of the threat that the investigations of the House Committee on Un-American Activities pose for makers of films. His ignorance of what has been happening is difficult to believe even though Merrill has been away in Europe, yet the audience is willing to accept it to let the story go on. One of the most improbable events in all of drama is the marriage of Oedipus to his mother. What helps the audience to accept this action is that it took place before the play begins. We are more likely to believe implausible events in the past than we are those occurring before our eyes.

Sometimes writers justify their inclusion of events that defy belief by pointing out that they merely dramatized something that actually happened in real life. This is no defense. The old saying that "truth is stranger than fiction" explains why. Mark Twain commented that unlike truth, "fiction has to make sense." Or as critic Eric Bentley put it, "The truth doesn't have to be plausible, but fiction does."

There are no general rules for meeting the problem of avoiding implausibility. You must decide what an audience is likely to accept. If you feel that you are going too far, you must exercise your ingenuity to find a solution that will fit a specific situation without making your play shriek of contrivance.

Achieving Clarity

In addition to being interesting and plausible, a play also must be clear if it is to hold the attention of an audience. Viewers do not have to understand the significance of every event as it happens, but by the time the play is over, they should see how the parts have fallen into place and they should have answers to their most important questions. At no time should they become so confused that they lose touch with the development of events.

Opening the Script   One of the critical points as far as clarity is concerned is the beginning of a play. As the play opens, astutely designed visualization can function in a major way to provide needed information about the characters and situation. Narration and dialogue can, of course, aid in establishing this background. There are two main approaches to providing information through visualization at this point. By far the more common is to use an establishing approach, moving from the larger view down to smaller details. A much less used but sometimes effective approach is to begin with a close-up on a detail before pulling back to reveal the larger picture.

Transitions   It would be an unusual play, indeed, which, during its action, did not involve some transitions in time or place. A significant element in maintaining clarity is the skill with which the writer indicates the nature of these transitions.

Types of Transitions   Transitions can be classified into a number of categories depending on the nature of the change; it can be a change in place or time or in both.

In one type of transition a scene is followed by another in which both the time and place have changed. Time in most dramas moves forward, but on occasion a flashback takes place. A transition that goes back in time must be carried out with special care to keep the audience from becoming confused. A technique sometimes used to distinguish past from current action is to shoot the flashback scenes in black-and-white instead of color. Barbra Streisand used a variation of this technique in her film *The Prince of Tides*. Scenes depicting the lead character as a child are intercut with scenes of him as an adult in the present; the past scenes are suffused with an orange hue, while those in the present are shot in normal tones. A series of transitions that shows several incidents in the same general development is called a *montage* effect. In a television version of "Cinderella," this technique was employed to show the prince trying unsuccessfully to fit the glass slipper on the feet of several maidens in the kingdom before he finally found Cinderella.

A second type of transition shows the relationship between actions going on simultaneously in time but in different locations. A play of a man and woman about to be married might alternate between the bride and groom, showing their preparations for the wedding ceremony. A "chase" drama may show scenes of a detective pursuing a criminal intercut with scenes of the person being pursued.

A third type of transition shows the time relationships between actions occurring in the same location. In most instances the time of the following scene is later than of the preceding one, but this type of transition also may involve a flashback journey to a previous day or hour. Techniques that have been used to indicate this type of transition are such old reliables as the clock that shows the advance of time, the pages dropping from a calendar, the matched dissolve from an empty ashtray to a full one, and the trees in full leaf replaced by barren trees.

Clarity in Transitions   One good way to distinguish professional from amateur writing is to examine the nature of transitions. If they jump wildly in time and place without revealing clearly what changes are occurring, the audience can be quite sure that it is listening to the work of an amateur.

In radio drama, of course, transition devices must be entirely auditory in nature. Narration and dialogue are the most obvious means of informing an audience what kind of change is taking place, though sound effects and even music also may be used to give information about place and time. In television and the movies there are a number of visual effects that may be added to auditory techniques to indicate the nature of transitions, among them the cut, the dissolve, and the fade. Some degree of consistency in the transition devices used in a particular script helps the audience to follow the changes in time and place.

The Script Plan

A few writers plunge directly into writing without making specific story plans and without knowing for sure just where their writing will take them. That method may work with novelists, whose medium is much looser than the play, but dramatists who write a script without first drawing up a plan may discover that they have been indulging in a futile exercise. They may find that they have ended up with no play at all. TV producer Alan Armer stressed the importance of planning when he said, "Most scripts succeed or fail in the outline stage. If you build a strong foundation from a carefully detailed blueprint, your house cannot topple over. If the dialogue is corny, it can be fixed. If characters emerge colorlessly, they can be dressed up. But if the story is essentially wrong, it is headed for disaster."

There is no generally accepted term for the plan you prepare before you begin writing your script. Variously it is called a treatment, a breakdown, an outline, a scenario, or a script plan. There is no agreement either on the precise form it should take. It may be written as an outline, as a complete narrative, in an expository manner, or in any combination of these approaches. The analyses of *Guilty by Suspicion* and *Separate But Equal* in Chapter 11 illustrate the narrative approach to constructing a script plan. You will note that they are written in the present tense, as these narrative forms always are.

The particular form you use can be one that best fits your individual needs and preferences. There are certain indispensable functions it should accomplish, however. Obviously, it should make clear your plotting development, the nature of the characters, and the thematic message. It should indicate how the script is to be arranged into acts and scenes and the main devices you plan to use. These points should be clear not only to you as the writer but also to others, for scripts are frequently commissioned on the basis of plans or outlines.

One thing you should do during the planning stage is to determine the events that are crucial in changing the direction of the story so that you can place them at strategic intervals in its development. Syd Field, in his book *Screenplay*,[3] calls these events "plotting points," and he recommends that a major plotting point come at the end of the first segment of the script—which he calls Act One—and a second at the end of the second segment of the script—Act Two. The film *Thelma and Louise* provides illustrations of major events that substantially influence the course of the story. The first is the shooting of the would-be rapist by Louise. This event turns a happy-go-lucky outing into a grim race to escape capture. Even if they had been caught, however, they might have been able to convince the police that the shooting was justified. That possibility disappears when Thelma holds up a grocery store to replace the money stolen by a petty thief. That second major event makes the women outlaws without any question. It is thus a crucial development that materially alters the direction of the story.

By preparing a plan ahead of time, you will have a guide that can provide your script with the direction it needs to reach your goals. You will have tested the strength of your play ideas. It is likely that the act of committing those ideas to paper has revealed weaknesses which you can correct before beginning to write the script. Moreover, the writing of a plan is a creative process in itself which can stimulate you to think of ideas for your play that never occurred to you before. It is worth emphasizing at this point that throughout the entire process of preparing a script you should be alert to make improvements whenever they suggest themselves. At no time do you need to take the irrevocable step that will congeal your play idea into a final, inflexible mold. Plays are rewritten right up to the time of production.

Visualization   Once writers for the stage have described the setting and action of a play, which the audience sees from one unchanging point of view, they can concentrate on creating the lines for their characters. The responsibility of television or film dramatists for indicating the visual elements is much greater. They must be alert at all times to indicate the constantly shifting view of the action that is being presented to the audience.

Viewpoint   One of the decisions you may have to make in preparing your script plan is to choose a viewpoint. Viewpoint is to the writer about what it is to the artist. It determines what is to be seen and the angle from which the observation takes place. In the end it decides what is to be revealed to the audience. In this sense of the word, incidentally, viewpoint does not refer to the author's view or opinions, expressed through the script. That is another use of the word entirely.

The choice of a viewpoint from which the events are to be related is often not a significant matter unless you are using narration as an element in the script design. In that case we can distinguish three different viewpoints: (1) that of a narrator who sees all and knows all—the omniscient viewpoint; (2) that of the narrator who is the focal character in the story; and (3) that of a narrator, not the focal character, who may be a major or minor character in the story.

Of these viewpoints the easiest to use is the omniscient, for a writer whose narrator knows everything can reveal whatever item of information is needed to advance the plot. The writer who tells the story from the point of view of a character is always restricted by that character's view of the events. Sometimes, however, this restriction may work to the writer's advantage. A good example is the detective story, in which relating the events from the viewpoint of a minor character provides a natural way of keeping the audience in the dark about what is going on in the great detective's mind, and paves the way for the surprising revelation of the means through which the case is solved.

Generally, you should not switch the viewpoint from one character to another or you may damage the unity of the play. In some cases, however, a switch of viewpoint is justified if it adds an extra dimension to the story. There are some instances in which a switch of this nature is the major tool for achieving the effect the writer seeks. A case in point was the Japanese drama *Rashomon,* which related a single event as it was seen from the viewpoint of four different characters.

Dividing the Script into Acts Stage plays often require intermissions to provide opportunities for making set changes and other adjustments. It therefore became the practice of playwrights to divide their scripts into acts. Because most films run without interruption, a division into acts is not necessary, and usually they are not indicated in the script. In planning a script, however, it may be helpful to think of the development of the story in terms of acts. This approach is recommended by Syd Field in *Screenplay*. He sees the first act as providing the setup for the story; the second, the confrontation; and the third, the resolution.

TV plays are interrupted, of course, for commercials, and it is therefore necessary to indicate in the script the division of the story into acts. Half-hour shows usually have two acts, while hour shows have four. These divisions require careful planning. The way the acts end is of particular importance because audience interest must be carried forward through the commercial breaks.

Dividing the Script into Scenes The next step is to determine the content of individual scenes. A scene is defined as any sequence of action that continues in one place without a break in time. There may be only one scene between the television curtains that divide the play into acts, or there may be several, separated from one another by transitions in time, in place, or in both. In describing these scenes in your plan, you should include the following items of information:

1. The way in which each scene begins and ends.
2. The transition devices that will link one scene with another.
3. The nature of the sets.
4. The characters involved in each scene, how they appear, and how they are removed.
5. The way the action develops and what you intend to accomplish with each scene.
6. Key lines of dialogue, if they occur to you.
7. Major technical devices.

Some writers use a rather elaborate form that sets up the plan in three columns. One lists the characters in each scene; the second summarizes what they do or say; the third indicates what is to be accomplished in each scene in terms of character revelation, attention-getting devices, development of suspense and expectancy, exposition, preparation, complication, climax, and resolution.

The First Draft and After

With the script plan completed, you now are ready to put your play into the script from which it will be performed. One of the clichés of dramatic composition is that plays are not written, but rewritten. Writers, in fact, usually are obligated under their contracts with producers to revise their scripts a certain number of times. They generally go through several versions before a final draft is completed.

As you review your script, you should have certain questions in mind: Do your characters have depth and dimension and do they act with consistency? Are their motives clear? Do you capture interest at the beginning and sustain it with the development of suspense and expectancy? Does the plot rise to a satisfactory climax? Does your script have an essential unity, particularly of mood? Will the audience understand clearly what is going on?

It is possible to revise too much, of course. Developing a state of continuing dissatisfaction with what one has written may cause the discarding of existing values without substituting anything better for them. It is the rare writer, however, who can overdo rewriting or produce a first draft that needs no revision at all.

DIALOGUE

In the creation of a play nothing contributes more to the dramatist's success than the ability to write effective dialogue. It is the main channel through which the mind of the writer comes into contact with the mind of the audience. The playwright may have created vivid, individual characters whose conflicts are woven into an emotional, meaningful story, but if the dialogue fails to transmit these qualities, the previous creative effort is completely nullified.

The Functions of Dialogue

Since most plays are made up primarily of dialogue, it follows that dialogue must accomplish almost everything that the play itself sets out to accomplish. It provides the most important of all clues to character values and traits and is the primary means of advancing the story and revealing the theme. In addition to accomplishing these major functions, dialogue may also be used to solve a technical problem or to create a special effect. Making the audience laugh or gasp with horror is an example of a special effect. A technical problem that frequently arises is the necessity of getting certain characters out of a scene to permit the presentation of action that cannot involve them.

In writing dialogue to accomplish these purposes, a word of warning is in order. When technical problems arise they must be solved, and an audience reaction like a laugh is often desirable. But dialogue can be justified only if it is in harmony with character, plot, and theme. Even though a given dialogue section may have been motivated originally by the need to make a character exit, it must seem to come naturally from the characters who speak it, and it must flow out of the situation in which they are involved. The line designed to provoke laughter must pass this same test.

The Characteristics of Good Dialogue

At first thought it might seem that the best way to evaluate the effectiveness of dialogue is to determine how faithfully it reproduces the attributes of everyday conversation. Though much conversation is undeniably interesting for its participants, it is often not suitable for a drama. It is replete with awkward phrases, poor word choices, and boring repetitions; only occasionally is there an authentic *bon mot*. The conversation of everyday life, moreover, rarely goes anywhere, even in those situations that are filled with emotion. Drama, in contrast, demands changes and development, and dialogue must be purposeful language that accomplishes and reflects those changes.

In fact, conversation often stimulates not because of its brilliance but because it is part of a stimulating social situation. Most of what is said is too dull and static to be suitable for complete reproduction in a dramatic script. Does this mean that everyday conversation as a guide to writing dialogue must be totally rejected?

The Sound of Normal Speech Even though dramatists do not reproduce normal speech in most instances, they want their characters to sound like real people talking. This means they must write dialogue with *content* that rises above what people usually say but in the *form* of everyday speech. There are variations, of course, in the way this criterion is met. A naturalistic writer such as Harold Pinter may approximate the context of ordinary conversation as well as the form, and some writers may go in the opposite direction, investing speech with unnaturalistic opulence, as Shakespeare did. The usual objective, however, is to capture the illusion of everyday speech while surpassing it in direction, purpose, and diction. What are the characteristics that give conversation its particular sound?

Informal Words Everyday speech, first of all, abounds in *short, informal, colloquial* words. Elegant words may be chosen sometimes to reflect an ornate personality, and formal words help to flavor the speech of foreign-born people who, being unsure of themselves and having learned the language from books rather than from life, are likely to be more studied in their utterances than native-born people. These are the exceptions. Even the most educated people tend to use short, simple words when they are engaged in conversation. If you could listen to a group of college professors around a luncheon table, you would note the prevalence of simple words and colloquialisms— even slang expressions. They usually restrict the use of long, complicated, specialized terms to their textbooks and scholarly monographs.

Contractions The use of contractions is a second requirement for the dialogue writer. In ordinary conversation we do not say, "I am going," "I will be there," or "I could not do that," but rather, "I'm going," "I'll be there," and "I couldn't do that." There may be some occasions when the use of the non-contracted form is deliberate. When emphasis is sought, for example. "I do not!" is much more forceful than "I don't!" The noncontracted form, in addition, may be used to characterize the affected or pedantic person or to introduce a special quality into the dialogue.

Simple Sentences A third requirement is to use *short, simply constructed* sentences. Consider the following line, which appeared in a student-written script: "While helping me in the barn, Toby, who is too little to be much help anyway, backed into the pail of milk and kicked it over." The inverted order, the use of the relative clause, the length and complication of the sentence all help to disqualify it as effective

dialogue. In real life these thoughts probably would be expressed somewhat as follows: "What do you think Toby did? Kicked over my pail of milk. Backed right into it, he did. And the little guy was trying to help me. He's too little to be much help anyway." When talking, most people take the direct route from subject to verb. They rarely use inversions. They qualify ideas in separate sentences rather than in relative clauses.

Incomplete Sentences A fourth way to suggest the sound of normal speech is to use *incomplete* sentences regularly. People often start a sentence, forget what they were going to say, or feel their meaning is obvious, and break off in the middle. Or what is more likely, they are interrupted by someone else. The device of the broken sentence or the interrupted line can help immensely to give conversational quality to dialogue. Often a single word, or even a grunt, is sufficient to express an idea.

Short Speeches A fifth requirement in writing natural-sounding dialogue is to provide *short* speeches. Good dialogue is generally made up of a swift alternation among the various characters of words, parts of sentences, sentences, or, at most, short paragraphs.

Sounds Right When Spoken The final test is to read dialogue aloud to see how it strikes the ear. You should make sure you have avoided tongue twisters, too many alliterations, or accidental rhymes that can make lines meant to be serious sound absurd. You should also listen for anything that suggests the premeditated tone of written English and eliminate it. In its place strive to approximate the simplicity, informality and colloquial quality of spoken English.

Dialogue Appropriate to the Character and Mood Dialogue is the writer's most important tool for leading the audience into an awareness of a character's nature. This is primarily a positive process of finding the right words and phrases. But there is also a negative phase to the process—namely, to avoid putting anything into the lines that will be inconsistent with the character who says them. When a particularly neat phrase or witty line occurs to you during the process of composition, the temptation to use it is difficult to resist. Before you put it into the mouth of a character, however, you must ask yourself whether the character is the type of person who would be likely to say such a line. A line spoken by a character in a TV play about a crime investigation in a poverty-stricken area of New York illustrates this problem. A detective asked a 12-year-old who was obviously hostile to the police whether he had seen any suspicious people in his apartment building. The boy responded, "So what am I, the doorman?" It was difficult to believe that a child of his age who, later developments showed, had not yet learned to read would be capable of such a sophisticated rejoinder.

Another requirement for writing dialogue appropriate to character is to give the various people of your play speeches that establish them as unique individuals. If the lines you write do not reflect the differences that separate people, your dialogue is defective. There are a number of ways in which unique characters may be revealed through dialogue. One is the *content* of the line. It reveals the drives and values that dominate the character.

If you look back to Chapter 12, you will see how the dialogue Reginald Rose gave to the characters in his TV play *Twelve Angry Men* made them distinct and different persons.

A second factor distinguishing people is *word choice*. Words reflect a character's educational and cultural background and provide clues to personality. A shallow person may be revealed through the constant use of meaningless clichés and empty repet-

itive phrases, a thoughtful one by precise and eloquent use of language.

Differences in *sentence structure* help further to distinguish people. Mistakes in grammar and short staccato sentences, often left incomplete, tell the audience that a character lacks culture and poise. Longer, more rounded sentences suggest an educated person who retains control of a situation.

Closely allied to structure is the overall *rhythm* of the speeches. Rhythm is a product of the choice of words and the structure of the sentences. Excellent examples of the way rhythm can reveal character can be found in Tennessee Williams' *A Streetcar Named Desire*. Blanche, the impractical visionary trembling on the verge of a mental breakdown, who tries not to think about the harsh realities confronting her, speaks with a rhythm that has the flowing cadences of poetry. Her brutish, primitive brother-in-law Stanley, in contrast, uses language that is abrupt and staccato in its underlying pattern.

In writing dialogue, however, it is not enough simply to distinguish characters from one another. A given character reacts in different ways to the various developments of the play. Dialogue is deficient if it does not convey these different emotional states to the audience. The dramatist must try to earn the accolade a reviewer gave to John P. Marquand: "His characters not only always speak as if they were themselves and nobody else, but as if they were themselves at a particular time and place and will never be quite the same again."[4]

In some ways the playwright faces a much sterner challenge in writing dialogue than a short-story writer or novelist does. The fiction writer can say, "He won her with charming words." Dramatists have no such easy escape. They must contrive those charming words.

Purposeful and Economical Dialogue

As we have noted, much of the conversation of everyday life rambles without direction, accomplishing no other purpose than that of filling an empty space with sound. Dramatists may include some small talk of this nature to promote the illusion of normal speech, but most of the dialogue they write should be big talk, the talk that deals with matters vital to the story. Most dialogue should be purposefully designed to reveal character, advance the story, or illuminate the theme. If it does none of these things and cannot be justified as small-talk dressing which provides an echo of reality, then it should be resolutely eliminated.

Another important attribute of dialogue is economy. Drama does not reflect life in its entirety, but distills its essence. The dramatist must condense conflicts to their essentials, sometimes capturing the illusion of years, without belaboring the audience with all the verbiage. Compression, concentration, and selection are vital necessities. Morton Wishengrad, writer of many scripts for the distinguished radio series *Eternal Light*, emphasized this need when he said, "Good dialogue should sound like a pair of boxers trading blows, short, swift, muscular, monosyllabic."[5]

Natural and Unobtrusive Exposition
Since a dramatist can present directly only part of the crisis that is the play's main concern, a major problem is to give the audience the rest of the information it needs to understand the story. Dialogue is the main tool for providing this exposition, although narration, titles, movement, and business may also be used.

The Need for Exposition   Introducing needed information into dialogue naturally and unobtrusively is a difficult task, yet the dramatist should be glad that expository devices are available. Through their use primary attention can be concentrated on the high points of a crisis, thus making the play as a whole more vivid and compelling. Moreover, by encompassing a larger segment of human experience than that actually presented in the play, exposition helps to give the dramatized events greater significance and breadth.

Exposition plays a particularly vital role in the opening scenes. These are some of the questions that need answering: Who are the characters? What kind of people are they? What is the place, the time, and the period? What in the past and the present is causing this crisis? All background information is not necessarily revealed at the beginning, of course. Exposition must be provided at regular intervals.

In plays of an earlier era, audiences sometimes were informed about the situation by a character who addressed the audience directly or delivered a soliloquy, as Richard does at the opening of Shakespeare's *Richard III*. Narration is used today on occasion to accomplish this function. Expository scenes at the beginning of plays were common in the past. There was no drama or conflict in these scenes; they were all explanation. Presenting exposition in this way is not artful; an obvious recital of facts is a clumsy way to begin a play. The skilled writer will weave essential facts into dramatic scenes in such a way that the listener absorbs them without realizing it. A second reason for avoiding expository scenes is that they are a poor means of seizing attention. Clash, not facts, arouses interest.

Rules for Exposition   Implanting exposition in dialogue so that it reaches the audience naturally and unobtrusively requires adherence to certain rules.

1. *Motivate the presentation of facts.* One of the commonest techniques for bringing out essential information is to create a character who draws out the facts the audience needs to know. This person must be one whom the audience can accept as a normal participant in the action, of course. Information can also be communicated by having characters give messages to servants, make telephone calls, send telegrams, or dictate letters.

Sometimes writers subject audiences to unnecessary exposition when a character tells a second character about events known to the audience but unknown to the second character. Though some repetition of this type may be unavoidable if the second character must be shown receiving the information to advance the action of the play, the writer should try to keep the repetition to the smallest amount possible.

A problem of the opposite kind occurs when a character describes events for another character who the audience realizes already knows about them. Such an exchange may be necessary, however, if the audience is to be provided essential facts. The writer must try to devise a situation that will make the exchange seem natural and reasonable. An example is a scene in which a person seeks solace or advice from another regarding a problem with which both are familiar. Emotional motivation for exposition is the best motivation there is, which leads directly to a second rule.

2. *Color the presentation of information with emotion.* One of the difficulties with exposition is that it frequently interrupts the dramatic action; the perfect solution is to make the presentation of necessary facts part of the mounting drama. In William Archer's phrase, information should be "wrung out, in the stress of the action."[6]

3. *Make the audience want the information.* The best way to motivate exposition in this way is to bring out an unusual or intriguing fact about a character or situation. Viewers with their curiosity aroused will then eagerly listen to the explanation that follows without being aware that expo-

sition is taking place. By making an audience want knowledge, a dramatist infuses the facts with added interest and significance and gives the process of exposition an excitement of its own.

Special Dialogue Problems

Thus far we have been considering the problems of creating effective dialogue that arise in the writing of almost all dramatic scripts. There are some other problems, however, that may or may not develop, depending on the nature of the play.

Gaining Authentic Flavor When characters represent specific occupations, come from a certain well-defined region, or live in a time different from the present, their speech must reflect these conditions. For example, it is not enough that physicians speak like the usual well-educated person— at least not while they are discussing a case with other physicians—and even in talking with patients, physicians are likely to use their own characteristic terms. In their language the average man's stiff neck becomes a myositis or torticollis, indigestion becomes gastritis, and nearsightedness becomes myopia. Terms like these should be inserted into the dialogue of physicians to give their speech an authentic ring. It is not necessary for the audience to know the meaning of all the words so long as the basic meaning of the sentence is clear.

How are you to know the special terms you should use? The best solution is to depend on your own personal experience. You cannot have personal contact with everything, however, even in the contemporary world, and when you write a play set in another century, obviously you must learn what terms to use through something other than direct personal experience.

There is a synthetic method for gaining authenticity that can be an acceptable substitute for actual experience. First of all, make up as large a list as you can of the special terms identified with the particular occupation, region, or time you have in mind. The best way to create this list is to get in touch with the type of people you are writing about. If personal contacts are impossible, the next best source of terms is reading. As far as plays of another period are concerned, reading must be your principal means of discovering the language that will infuse your script with the atmosphere of the past. The best sources are works written during the period, with contemporary books about the period a good secondary source. Robert Sherwood, in preparing to write *Abe Lincoln in Illinois*, studied English grammars of the 19th century and read such works as *Huckleberry Finn* and *Pickwick Papers* in search of expressions that would give a period flavor to his dialogue. If you are writing about the Elizabethan age, examine the plays of Shakespeare, Christopher Marlowe, and John Webster as well as other literature of the period. Maxwell Anderson's modern plays *Mary of Scotland* and *Elizabeth and Essex* can also serve as guides to diction and usage. Terms and expressions you will find in these sources include: *Take heed, fain, by the Queen's grace, mayhap, good my lord, good morrow, set against, I commend me, beyond all measure, I grant you, in good conscience, divers, lest, unseemly, nay, knave, avail, stand forth, constrain,* and *ere.*

With a list of appropriate terms, you are now ready to write your dialogue. By scattering expressions distinctive of a particular occupation, region, or period through your lines, you can create the language of a real-life Texan, the words of an authentic truck driver, or the rich verbiage of a genuine Elizabethan. If you can, have someone who knows the subject through personal experience check your dialogue, with special attention to usage. If you carelessly permit a Southerner to address one person as "y'all," a representative of that region will quickly correct your error.

Writing Dialect The main problem in writing dialect is similar to the one we have just considered—namely, that of finding the terms and style that will give the desired authentic flavor to a character's speeches. The needed information can be acquired in the ways we have just mentioned. Having gained a knowledge of a dialect, the writer must then decide how to indicate it in the script. A problem is that some sounds occurring in other languages cannot be symbolized by an English letter. Usually you must depend on the actor knowing how the words should be pronounced. You can provide some guidance in the way you spell the words. It is also important to reflect the basic cadence of the dialect and capture its characteristic sentence structure. The Irish, for example, tend to reverse the usual sequence of subject and predicate and then add a further inimitable touch by beginning the sentence with "it." An Irishman might say, for instance: "It's a bit of a cold I have." An actor can scarcely avoid putting an Irish flavor into that line, no matter how he pronounces the words.[7]

Writing Dialogue for Highly Emotional Scenes A problem for writers is that when people become highly emotional they often say very little and when they do, their language may not be appropriate for television. Sometimes facial expressions or bodily movements can take the place of words. When words are required the writer may find expressions that aren't profane but seem to be. Norman Corwin's radio script "Old Salt" achieved the illusion perfectly. Such phrases as "Ye scurvy dog," "Curses throttle ye," "Ye pusillanimous pantaloon," "Ye besotted gobthrasher," and "Ye lickerous, gluttonous weed-smeller" have the irresistible impact of profanity without actually being profane.

You have to be sensitive, however, to the impressions such substitutes can make. Expressions like "gleeps" or "holy barracuda" may be satisfactory for a spoof like *Batman* but in serious drama would evoke only laughter. When you write for the movies, where there are no longer any language taboos, you can use whatever words you think reflect the emotion.

Writing Tag Lines   Most of you are familiar with the expression "curtain line" as it is used in the theater to denote the line, delivered just before the fall of the curtain, that sums up, succinctly and with special impact, the meaning of what has been happening. This type of line, which occurs at the ends of acts and scenes, usually is referred to as a *tag line*. Composing effective tag lines is of the utmost importance, yet it is difficult to lay down specific rules for doing so. Tag lines should pack a special punch by summing up the point of the scene with precision and pungency and arousing suspense and expectation.

Describing the Expression of Lines
Beginning writers, convinced that their lines must be read in one certain way to gain the optimum effect, frequently fall into the habit of indicating the precise manner for speaking each line. Thus we see each sentence preceded by an adverb: *flatly, sadly, angrily*, and so on. Such description is necessary only when the content of the line does not indicate how it should be read. If the lines are well written, this need should rarely exist. A justifiable use is the description used to qualify the reading of an ironic line, which carries a meaning completely opposite to the usual meaning of the words. For example:

JANE
Did you have a good time at the party?
ANN
(IRONICALLY) Great! Simply great!

With this description, the actress knows that she must convey to the audience that the time she had at the party was exactly the opposite of great.

There are other situations in which instructions to the actor can help refine the meaning intended by the writer. But writers who find themselves qualifying every line should begin to wonder whether it is not the dialogue itself that needs some attention. A constant obbligato of *coldly, sadly,* and *warmly* may be an open advertisement of dialogue deficiencies.

NARRATION

Narration was an important element in much radio drama, but with the coming of the television form its use receded sharply and it is employed infrequently in movies. In the visual forms it is not necessary to describe what is happening for viewers who can see the action. Still, narration does have occasional uses, even in television and films, and in this section we review the contributions it can make, the types of narration, and some rules for using it.

The Functions of Narration

The main advantage of narration is that it conveys information to an audience more economically than dialogue. By employing it for exposition, the writer can use dialogue mainly to dramatize the high points of the play.

Providing Exposition   Narration can accomplish exposition in two main ways. First of all, it can *look backward* to give the information about the past essential to understanding the present. Second, narration can *carry a story forward* with great speed and efficiency.

Achieving Reinforcement   Occasionally, narration may describe what is taking place even though viewers can see what is happening. Providing information or interpretation through narration may add reinforcement that enhances the impact of a scene.

Presenting Comment   Narration can be a vehicle for presenting the writer's comment on the action directly to the audience, a privilege that is denied if the story is told exclusively in dialogue. These observations may help to enrich the meaning of a drama, but they need to be kept under restraint, for gratuitous and unnecessary comment may dull rather than sharpen the impact. Generally speaking, drama should be permitted to speak for itself.

Gaining a Filtering Effect   The usual objective of a dramatist is to extract from a situation the greatest emotional effect possible, and the best guarantee of maximum emotional intensity is dramatic treatment. Some events, however, may be so harrowing that complete dramatization makes them unbearable. In such cases, narration, by subduing vividness and realism and by interposing an intermediary between the audience and the experience, helps to tone it down and filter its effect.

Types of Narration

Because narration may be spoken in the first, second, or third person, it may be categorized in terms of the "person" in which it is presented.

The Person of Narration   The traditional type of narration is that in which a narrator, not involved in the action, tells what is happening to other people. Of the types of narration, this third-person approach is the most straightforward, the simplest, and the least "arty." Its main disadvantage is that the narrator, by getting between the audience and the action, may

weaken the dramatic impact of the story and damage its emotional intensity. A voice from outside the story has intervened; the illusion is broken; the action is suspended and emotional intensity is inevitably lessened.

There is one kind of third-person narration that does not reach the audience by voice at all, but provides information about time intervals and settings by means of title cards. A card printed "Six Months Later" or "Moscow—1917" preceding a scene can convey information efficiently that would be awkward to insert into the scene itself.

Another form of narration, which was very popular in radio and has had some use in television, is that delivered in the first person by an individual who is involved in the action. Its main advantage in radio was that it could present information to the audience without awkwardly interrupting a dialogue scene or suspending the dramatic quality of the script. The narrator remains in character, enduring the crises and emotions that are the focus of the action. Thus, dramatic continuity is sustained. No outsider has come between the audience and the emotion. At times this type of narration achieves a stream-of-consciousness effect in which the speakers reveal their innermost thoughts and feelings.

A third type of narrative presentation approaches viewers in the second person, addressing them as "you" and inviting them to visualize themselves as taking part in the action. Second-person narration was a feature of some radio dramatic series, but it has been rarely used in television. It has the disadvantage of sounding somewhat forced and artificial, lacking the naturalness of the storytelling approach inherent in the third person or of the personal testament communicated in the first person. The second person does, however, invest a program with the quality of immediacy since it makes the use of the present tense in narration easy, and it also encourages a sense of audience participation in the events.

Narrator Off and On Camera When narration is presented on television, it is usually by a narrator who does not appear on camera, at least while narrating. The narration is heard as an accompaniment to a scene or sequence of events. This technique is known as "voice-over" or VO narration.

Voice-over narration is also used in connection with the use of a production technique known as the *subjective camera*. This is an approach that, in effect, places the character inside the camera. The audience sees only what the character sees. The dialogue of the character in the camera is voiced over the scene just as the narration is.

The subjective camera does have some disadvantages. It tends to attract attention to itself as a gimmick and unless used carefully may confuse an audience. The events must also be told entirely in terms of what a single character sees and does, a requirement that places severe restrictions on the range of the story.

A rarely used narrative technique places the narrator on camera and in the scene. At intervals during the story he or she turns directly to the audience to comment on what is happening. At these points the camera may move in to exclude the rest of the scene, or a blackout effect may be used to isolate the person doing the narrating. The film *Shirley Valentine* exemplifies this technique. Much of Shirley's personality is revealed in her comments addressed to a wall, a rock, or the audience itself.

Some Rules for Writing Narration

When a script suddenly bursts into narration at a late stage in the action after having been confined up to that point entirely to dialogue, we can assume that the author has written the story into a corner and is using narration as an escape hatch. When this happens, even the most naïve listener becomes aware of a structural malfunction.

Narration should not be used haphazardly simply because the writer finds it difficult to get certain essential information to the audience in a dramatic scene. *Make the narration an integral part of the script design.*

The choice of viewpoint has an obvious bearing on the narrative technique used by the dramatist. The omniscient viewpoint usually requires a third-person narrator; character viewpoints are almost always told in the first person. The writer must be aware of the relationship between the viewpoint needed to tell the story and the narrative method being planned. *Choose the narrative approach in terms of the viewpoint.*

Narration should retain the flavor of the spoken word, although sometimes it can be written in a more elevated style than is usually appropriate for dialogue, particularly when the narration is being delivered in the third person by a noncharacter voice. It must never become pretentious or cumbersome, however. And even though it may be language that has dignity, even nobility, it must always flow from the lips with naturalness and ease. *Give narration the quality of the spoken word.*

Narration by a character in the story is an extension of the dialogue of that character. It is obvious, then, that all of the rules that apply to writing the dialogue lines apply equally to writing the narration. Narration in all instances should preserve the dramatic tone of a play and enhance its overall effect. *Write narration that fits both mood and character.*

After finishing a script, you may wonder whether you have succeeded in making your theme clear to your audience. With a narrator available, you may be tempted to use narration to explain to the audience what your story is all about. It is wiser to let the story as a whole make the point, not the narration. This does not mean that a philosophical comment by the narrator at the end of the story is always out of place. But *do not use narration for an obvious pointing of the moral.* The 1979 Francis Ford Coppola/John Milius film *Apocalypse Now* was guilty of this last fault in the eyes of some critics. One of them, Frank Rich (then with *Time*), said "The voice-over commentary becomes a makeshift panacea for the film's many other defects: it hastily clarifies plot points and states themes that Coppola has uncharacteristically failed to develop through action, dialogue, and pictures."[8]

SCRIPT FORMATS

No one format for television and radio programs has been adopted throughout the industry, but there is agreement on the basic pattern that should be followed in putting a script on paper. Within this general pattern the various broadcasting organizations and film producers develop their individual styles. When you know the general principles, you can adapt easily to the special requirements of the organization for which you work.

Formats for TV and Filmed Drama

The formats used in typing dramatic scripts for film and television tend to be somewhat more standardized than those used for nondramatic programs such as news, game shows, and music. Writers of filmed dramas shown in theaters or on television use the same basic format. It differs in some respects from the format used for dramas produced on videotape.

Filmed Drama   The excerpts from a *MacGyver* episode and from the TV drama *Sarah, Plain and Tall* that appear earlier in this chapter, and the two excerpts from a *Law and Order* episode that appear in Chapter 11 and Chapter 12, illustrate the formats used for filmed productions. Because they are shooting scripts, however, they contain

more information than you need to include in the scripts you submit to a producer. The shots are numbered, for example. Some people in the field argue that it is not necessary for the screenwriter to carry out this function. Shots can be numbered by technical experts as the script is being prepared for production. Moreover, you do not usually need to describe how cameras are to pick up the action. Decisions about the nature of shots should be left to the director in almost all instances. Only when the kind of shot used is crucial to bringing out some particular facet of your story should you make any reference to it. In most cases you can suggest appropriate shot selection simply by being specific in your description of the action. If you say, for example, that someone is seen in the distance, the director will know that a long shot is called for. A profusion of technical terms in a script is usually a sure sign that an amateur has been at work.

What you should concentrate on in writing your script is to tell your story as clearly and as interestingly as possible. In typing your basic story, there are certain rules to be observed, however. You can get a good idea of what those rules are by thinking about the information directors must have to film scripts. The items they need to know for each scene are the following:

1. The place and setting for the action, whether it takes place in an interior (INT.) or exterior location (EXT.) and whether the time is DAY or NIGHT.
2. The people in the scene (usually indicated by character designations), their dialogue, and any pertinent description of the way the lines should be read or the appearance of the characters.
3. A description of significant properties.
4. A description of significant movement or action.
5. An indication of the way the scene ends—CUT, DISSOLVE, FADE.

A scene, we remind you, is a unit in the script in which the action takes place in one setting without a break in time. A change in either of these elements requires a new scene. In most instances it is not necessary to indicate how transitions to new scenes will be made.

In typing your script observe the following rules:

1. Begin your script with a FADE IN typed at the left.
2. Type all scene listings and descriptions, any camera directions you may wish to include, and other information and directions across the page from margin to margin.
3. Type dialogue in a column about 3 inches wide running down the center of the page. Type the character's name centered above the dialogue lines, and any suggestions about line reading in parentheses below the lines and slightly to the left of the character designation.
4. Use single spacing in all dialogue, directions, and descriptions.
5. Double space between characters' speeches; between a speech and any description other than one indicating line interpretation; between scenes; and between scene transition indications (e.g., CUT) and the two scenes they affect.
6. Type the following in capital letters: Exterior and interior locations, descriptions of the setting, day or night indications, any camera shots or directions, transition methods, names of characters when indicated above the dialogue and any reference to characters in descriptive paragraphs the *first time* they are mentioned, and sound effects. Everything else should be typed in regular upper- and lower-case letters.

As mentioned earlier, filmed scripts for television are divided into acts; their number depends on the length of the show. Theater films are not usually divided into acts. In addition to the script itself, writers prepare title pages and lists of characters and sets. Scripts for hour-long TV dramas run from 50 to 70 pages, scripts for theater films about 120 pages.

An excerpt from an episode in the *Lou Grant* series illustrates one format a writer could use in typing a script for submission to a producer.

Lou Grant: "Cop"
Act One

FADE IN:
EXT. SILVERLAKE STREET—NIGHT

This neighborhood of small California houses sleeps soundly. Lights out in most houses. No cars moving down the quiet street

FEATURING ONE HOUSE

where, if someone were standing, say, on the sidewalk near the pathway to the front door, he could hear, muffled, the SOUNDS of struggle within. But no one is there to hear.

INT. HOUSE—NIGHT

The CRASH of a lamp being knocked over. Darkened forms grapple in the shadows. A wordless, adrenalin pumping, life-death struggle—desperate, very serious, very real. And because two strong people are locked in combat—vicious. More furniture is wrecked.

EXT. STREET—NIGHT

Hume's car drives up and stops in front of Lou Grant's house (for this is Lou's street in Silverlake). Lou gets out on the passenger side.

LOU

Thanks for the lift, Charlie.

HUME

You're not sore?

LOU

No, no, but the next time the Librarians Association
needs a guest speaker in a hurry, I'm busy, okay?

HUME

(smiling)

It wasn't that bad.

LOU

No, not *that* bad.
Come in for a drink and I'll tell you
this great joke I heard about the Dewey decimal system.

As Hume gets out of the car to join Lou, both men react as a motorcycle kicks into a roar in the driveway across the street, peels out, zooms past them and away down the street. The motorcycle comes closest to Lou who only gets a glimpse of the rider in the dark.
As they look around, Lou points across the street.

Filmed scripts are rehearsed and filmed shot by shot although not necessarily in the sequence that the shots appear in the script. Shots in a particular setting, for example, are usually filmed in succession even though they do not appear together in the finished production. They are then placed in the proper sequence by the editor.

Taped Television Drama The scripts for television shows produced on tape use a format somewhat different from that used for film scripts. The excerpt from the situation-comedy series *Dear John* that appears in Chapter 17 illustrates the format.

You will note that the tape format is different in several ways from the film formats. One difference is that directions for stage business are typed in capital letters. A second difference is that characters' speeches are double spaced; thus the script runs longer than a comparable film script. A half-hour script, for example, runs about forty pages. A third difference is that both dialogue and directions are typed to take up about two-thirds of the page. This leaves space for the director to indicate camera shots. Writers of taped scripts are also responsible for preparing title pages, and lists of characters and sets.

An excerpt from the daytime serial *Another World* illustrates the format used in typing scripts for taped production.

Another World
Act Two

(IRIS' SUITE, A LITTLE LATER. IRIS, NOW DRESSED, IS
SEATED AT HER DESK, WRITING THANK YOU NOTES. SHE
FINISHES ONE PAGE, PICKS UP ANOTHER AND STARES OFF)

                    IRIS
        (VO) I wish I'd known what a clever
      young man Philip is. Perhaps he's too clever.
        Why did I ever put that agreement in writing?

SOUND: DOORCHIMES RING
(IRIS LOOKS TOWARD THE DOOR, AS VIVIEN ENTERS FROM
WITHIN)

                    VIVIEN
(MOVING TOWARD DOOR)
                I'll get it!
(VIVIEN OPENS THE DOOR TO MAC AND JANICE
        Oh, hello, Mr. Cory, Mrs. Cory.

                    MAC
            Hello, Vivien.

                    VIVIEN
        It's so nice to see you.

                    MAC
        Thank you. Tracy tells me you all
      had a wonderful Christmas together.

                    VIVIEN
    Yes, sir, we sure did. How was your holiday?

                    MAC
    Very pleasant, thank you. Is Iris home?

                    VIVIEN
        Yes, sir. Come on in.
(VIVIEN TURNS)
            Mrs. Bancroft?

                    IRIS
(RISES)

Yes, Vivie, I'm right here.
(SHE MOVES TO GREET MAC AND JANICE)
What a nice surprise, Daddy.
(SHE KISSES HIM)

MAC
I hope we're not disturbing you.

IRIS
Heavens, no, I was just writing some thank-you notes.
(VIVIEN TAKES THEIR COATS)

JANICE
Welcome back, Iris.

IRIS
Thank you Janice. Don't you look pretty?

Daytime serials are usually shot in studios without an audience. Individual episodes are rehearsed and taped in a single day. Half-hour situation comedies are often taped before audiences in a session that lasts about two hours. The taping follows about five days of rehearsal. Writers divide the action into six or seven scenes, which they then separate into two acts. The scenes are taped individually in one long take by a number of cameras operating simultaneously. The order of taping is the same as that occurring in the script. The breaks between scenes are used to make whatever set and costume changes are necessary.

In examining the scripts in this book you may see terms that have not been explained. The meanings of the most common terms used in writing dramatic scripts are defined in a glossary at the end of this book. The Writers Guild has prepared a pamphlet that provides helpful information about film and tape script formats, which also includes examples. You can get information about obtaining it by writing either to Writers Guild of America, East, 555 West 57 Street, New York, NY 10019 or Writers Guild of America, West, 8955 Beverly Boulevard, Los Angeles, CA 90048.

Format for Radio Drama

We have said little about radio drama in this book because very few radio dramas are now being produced. However, the writing of radio scripts can provide students with valuable experience. Radio scripts can be produced quickly and economically, providing that production facilities are available. Thus beginning writers can find out what their work sounds like in actual production.

The objective in typing a radio script is to make instantly clear the nature of all the elements and their relationships. Radio dramas receive relatively short periods of rehearsal and there is no time for the director, cast, and crew to puzzle out weird or original hieroglyphics. There should be a clear differentiation between the material in the script that is to be spoken into the microphone and that which is not. This can be accomplished in a number of ways:

1. Type all material to be spoken in regular upper- and lowercase letters in the usual way. Type all material that is not spoken in capital letters; this includes character names, directions for reading lines, other descriptive material, music, and sound effects.

2. Put parentheses around any element inserted into a line that is not part of the line itself; this includes directions for reading the line and music and sound effects notations.
3. Indent music and sound effects descriptions beyond the point where the dialogue or narration begins.

It is essential that radio scripts be double spaced, for nothing invites an actor's misreading so much as the closely bunched letters on a single-spaced page. To facilitate the process of rehearsal, you might also use some system of numbering lines or cues so that a director can quickly indicate a spot in a script that needs attention.

The following scene from a radio adaptation of Shakespeare's *Macbeth* illustrates the format for a radio script, showing how character names, dialogue, directions to actors, sound effects, and music notations appear in the script.

MACBETH: His horrible shadow mocks me. I will tomorrow to the weird sisters. More shall they speak, for now I am bent to know by the worst means the worst.

MUSIC: TRANSITION

SOUND: WEIRD SOUND . . . CAULDRON BUBBLES . . . THUNDER . . . WIND

WITCHES: Round about the cauldron go; In the poisoned entrails throw . . .

1ST WITCH: Eye of newt . . .

2ND WITCH: And toe of frog . . .

3RD WITCH: Wool of bat . . .

1ST WITCH: And tongue of dog.

WITCHES: Double, double, toil and trouble; Fire burn and cauldron bubble.

MACBETH: (COMING ON) How now, you secret, black, and midnight hags? What is't you do?

WITCHES: A deed without a name.

MACBETH: I conjure you, by that which you profess, howe'er you come to know it answer me. Though you untie the winds, and let them fight against the churches; though the yesty waves confound and swallow navigation up even till destruction sicken—answer me what I ask you.

1ST WITCH: Speak.

2ND WITCH: Demand.

3RD WITCH: We'll answer.

MACBETH: What need I fear?

1ST WITCH: Macbeth, beware MacDuff . . . Beware the Thane of Fife. Enough! Enough!

MACBETH: For thy good caution thanks. But one word more.

2ND WITCH: Be bloody, bold, and resolute . . . Laugh to scorn the power of man. For none of woman born shall harm Macbeth.

MACBETH: Then live, MacDuff, what need I fear of thee?

3RD WITCH: Be lion-mettled, proud, and take no care who chafes, who frets, or where conspirers are. Macbeth shall never vanquished be, until Great Birnam Wood to high Dunsinane Hill shall come against him.

MACBETH: That will never be. Who can impress the forest, bid the tree unfix his earth-bound root? Macbeth shall live.

WITCHES: Double, double, toil and trouble;
Fire burn and cauldron bubble.

SOUND: WITCHES EFFECTS VANISH . . . HORSE APPROACHES . . . STOPS . . . FOOT-

STEPS APPROACH

MACBETH: Where are they? Gone? Ho! Who is this?

MESSENGER: (COMING ON) My Lord, Macbeth.

MACBETH: What is it?

MESSENGER: I bring you word. MacDuff is fled to England.

MACBETH: Time, thou anticipa'st my dread exploits. MacDuff is gone then. The

castle of MacDuff I will surprise, give to the edge o' the sword his wife,

his babes, and all unfortunate souls that trace him in his line. No boast-

ing like a fool. This deed I'll do before this purpose cool.

MUSIC: CURTAIN

QUESTIONS AND PROJECTS

1. Observe and analyze a number of TV plays with special attention to the following factors:
   (a) the techniques employed to gain attention
   (b) the minor and major suspense questions
   (c) the devices used to develop expectancy
2. In watching TV plays, movies, and stage productions, be alert to note excellent uses of the techniques of implication. Describe these uses to your class.
3. Observe TV plays or films with particular attention to their plausibility. Are there any instances in which your credulity is strained? Are there examples of faulty or excellent preparation?
4. Analyze the visualization employed in a TV play, citing the information communicated by the visualization and the specific means used to convey it.
5. Hide a microphone in a social situation and evaluate the conversation you record for its qualities as dramatic dialogue.
6. The English playwright Harold Pinter is noted for writing dialogue that reflects the pointlessness, repetitions, irrelevancies, and hiatuses of ordinary conversation. Study the dialogue in one of his plays (*The Birthday Party, The Caretaker,* for example) to determine whether, even though simulating conversation, it still possesses the direction and purpose of dramatic dialogue.
7. Evaluate the dialogue given to two diametrically different characters in a play in terms of content, word choice, structure, and rhythm.

8. Cite how specific information is made clear to the audience in a number of plays and rate this exposition for its naturalness and unobtrusiveness.

9. Make a list of the terms you would insert into the dialogue of each of the following characters to provide an aura of authenticity: (a) a physician, (b) an astronaut, (c) a baseball player.

10. Watch a number of TV plays and note the lines that end acts or scenes. Evaluate these tag lines for their effectiveness.

11. Check the narrative techniques used in a number of plays. Decide whether this narration was used as a crutch or as an integral and purposeful element in the script design.

NOTES

1. Quoted in Syd Field, *Selling a Screenplay* (New York: Delacorte Press, 1989), p. 61.

2. Eric Barnouw, *Handbook of Radio Writing* (Boston: D.C. Heath, 1939), p. 14.

3. Syd Field, *Screenplay: The Foundations of Screenwriting* (New York: Dell Publishing Co., 1982).

4. Goronwy Rees, Review of "Women and Thomas Harrow," *The Listener*, Vol. 61 (January 22, 1959), p. 180.

5. Morton Wishengrad, *The Eternal Light* (New York: Crown Publishers, 1947), p. xxvii.

6. William Archer, *Play-Making* (Boston: Small, Maynard and Co., 1912), p. 119.

7. Helpful information on dialect construction can be found in two books co-authored by Lewis Herman and Marguerite Shalett Herman: *Foreign Dialects: A Manual for Actors, Directors, and Writers* (New York: Theatre Arts Books, 1943) and *American Dialects: A Manual for Actors, Directors, and Writers* (New York: Theatre Arts Books, 1947).

8. Frank Rich, "The Making of a Quagmire," *Time*, Vol. 113 (August 27, 1979), p. 57.

The techniques for writing drama considered thus far are those employed by writers who are entirely free to create characters and plots of their own. Such complete freedom is rare these days, however, especially in television. The series they write for may demand a certain type of content or feature leading characters created by someone else. Even the basic plot developments may be dictated by a program formula. The writer's freedom may also be limited by the way in which the story appears; techniques for writing serials differ somewhat from those used in writing dramas that are completed in one program period.

Movie scripts are often created by a number of people who may not even consult with one another while the writing is going on. It is said that the writers who received an Academy Award for the script of the movie *Coming Home* met for the first time when they came to the stage the night of the ceremony to receive their Oscars. One writer may outline the story, a second may do the screen treatment, and other writers may revise the script or contribute special material.

In this chapter we review the ways in which dramatic programs are arranged for presentation on television and consider some major types of drama classified according to content. The emphasis is on the unique demands these various forms and content make on the writer.

PROGRAM ARRANGEMENTS

The program series that presents separate and distinct dramas each week is known as

CHAPTER
15

TYPES OF DRAMA

There are three kinds of audiences: thinkers who demand characterization; women who demand passion; and the mob who demand action.
VICTOR HUGO
(1802–1885)

an *anthology*. The titles of such series are broad enough to encompass material differing widely in content and style. *The American Playhouse* series, broadcast by public television stations, is an example. The pure anthology places no restriction on the writer except one of creating a drama that will fit into the allotted time period.

Often, however, producers introduce a common element into the programs that helps to identify them. This element may be the appearance of the same host, like Alistair Cooke on *Masterpiece Theatre*, the same actor portraying different roles each week, or concentration on a similar type of content.

A *series* drama is one that features the same leading characters in separate and complete stories every week. Each program deals with the same type of content. Among the characters that various series have focused on are lawyers, doctors, nurses, comedy writers, detectives, westerners, and mothers and fathers.

The creative challenge of the series writer is easier in some ways than that of the anthology writer, and in other ways it is more difficult. It is easier in that the leading characters have already been created; the general content is decided; there may be a plotting formula to follow. It is more difficult in that the series writer must respond to the particular demands that give the series its identity and individuality.

The *serial* is another common form of TV drama. It continues a story without ever bringing it to an end; there are distinct episodes in the everlasting saga, but one episode does not conclude until the next is well under way. Most serials are broadcast during the day to an audience made up largely of women. There are some nighttime examples of this type, however, among them the programs *Dallas* and *Knots Landing*. The movie serial was once a common element in Saturday afternoon film programs designed mainly for children, but the rise of television took away its audience. The special problems of writing the serial will be considered later in this chapter.

A fourth type of television drama is the *mini-series*. It tells a story in episodes broadcast several nights in a row, or at the same time and day once a week through several weeks. The subject matter, more often than not, is a novel or a book dealing with history or biography. The presentation of Alex Haley's *Roots* as a mini-series of seven episodes broadcast nightly for a week drew the largest TV audience ever assembled to that time.

Other notable mini-series were Herman Wouk's adaptations of his novels. *The Winds of War* and *War and Remembrance*, and the adaptation of Larry McMurtry's novel *Lonesome Dove*.

ADAPTATIONS

Many of the scripts written for TV, radio, or the movies are based on material first created in another form—novels, short stories, biographies, histories, or stage plays. We now discuss the special problems that confront writers when they are preparing scripts founded on other works.

A Definition of Terms

A number of different terms are used to denote scripts having their origin in whole or in part in material written by others. The choice of term depends on the strictness with which the writer of the broadcast version adheres to the original work. The greatest degree of faithfulness to the original author's work is implied in the term *adaptation*. Perhaps the best way to describe the obligation of adapters is to say they should try to write their scripts just as the original writers would have written them had they been working in the new medium. That obligation is similar to the translator's, who must convey the ideas and feelings expressed in one language with as little change as possible. Some changes are necessary, however, to accommodate the material to the demands of the new medium. Adapters, then, have two main responsibilities: They must retain as far as possible the impact and qualities of the original, and at the same time they must make the changes called for by the demands of the new medium. They must, in other words, be as faithful to the original as the new medium permits them to be. As George Wells, writer of more than 400 adaptations, put it:

If the original is by James Hilton, the adapter must strive to write in the style of Mr. Hilton. If it is a work by Conrad, he may have to dress in sea boots and oilskins. His quill must laugh with Mark Twain and chuckle with Sir James Barrie; it must be dipped in bitterness for Eugene O'Neill and in sentiment for Dickens.[1]

In some instances writers do not attempt to write scripts that are completely faithful to the original works, but make changes dictated by their own ideas and invention. Such scripts should not be called adaptations. The term to be used depends on the degree to which the new version has departed from the old. A script deriving a major share of its inspiration from the original work is usually described as being *based* on that work. The expression *freely adapted* is also used in the same way. When the original material merely provides a springboard for the dramatist's imagination, the term *suggested by* provides the most appropriate description.

The rest of this section deals with the principles and techniques that apply in preparing adaptations. The writing of the freer versions involves the use of methods employed in creating original plays, which were described in previous chapters.

Changes Made by Adapters

Even though your aim in writing an adaptation is to deliver the work to the audience with the impact inherent in the original, you will discover that you spend most of your time making changes in it. It is true that portions of the original can sometimes be carried over intact—a narrative section or a portion of dialogue, for example—but in most cases you will have to shorten it, lengthen it, translate it from one form into another, or alter it in some other way.

Shortening the Material Of all the changes adapters must make, the most common one is to compress the material they find in the original work. A characteristic of dramatization is that it takes more time to depict a given incident than any other literary form—occasionally as much time as that same incident takes in real life. This means that a drama cannot cover nearly so much material as a short story of the same length. In a single paragraph, the story writer may cover centuries of time, refer to events calling for a multitude of sets, or describe scenes involving thousands of characters. When Pat Conroy, for example, took up the task of adapting his novel *The Prince of Tides* into a screenplay, he had to condense a 567-page book that was dense with plot and featured many secondary characters into a film with a reasonable running time.

Eliminating Scenes Removing an entire scene from a story is one obvious way of shortening it. This technique is used in preparing a feature film for TV projection when the film runs longer than the time period allotted to the program. In the same

way, a writer doing an adaptation looks for scenes that can be removed from the original work without materially damaging the story. Generally, however, adapting must extend beyond this mere cutting of scenes into a process that involves revision of the entire work.

Eliminating Part of the Plot A full-length play or novel that develops one or more subplots in addition to developing the main plot of the story often can be shortened by eliminating the subplots. Ibsen's play *A Doll's House* deals primarily with the relationship between Nora and her husband Torvald, but it also includes a subplot involving Dr. Rank. This subplot adds much to the overall effect of this play, but it can be removed without seriously affecting the telling of the main story. It usually is better to eliminate a subplot than to try to squeeze both it and the main plot into a relatively brief period. In removing a subplot, you must be careful that you perform a clean operation. To avoid confusing the audience, you must avoid any references to incidents that took place as part of the material you have omitted.

Eliminating or Fusing Characters When subplots are cut, characters are often cut also. In the suggested adaptation of *A Doll's House*, the character of Dr. Rank does not even appear. Even when plot material is not actually eliminated, it is often possible to cut characters or to make one character do the work of two or three. This fusing of characters works particularly well in translating Shakespearean plays into broadcast versions, since several minor Shakespearean characters often perform essentially the same function.

In adapting a book of a panoramic nature, such as a *David Copperfield*, you may be reduced to covering just one incident or a series of incidents that illuminate one of the themes in the book. One adaptation of the Dickens work, for example, concentrated only on the love life of David Copperfield. From all of the myriad incidents in the book *Pinocchio*, a 15-minute radio adaptation treated only those that bore on the little puppet's experiences in learning to tell the truth.

Condensing Scenes   In many instances, the substance of a scene may be needed to maintain story coherence, but all the details in the original work need not be included. A great deal of compression can be accomplished by pruning action and exposition not essential to the story. In making decisions about what to keep and what to discard, there are two considerations to be kept in mind: First, what will the audience expect to hear; what characters and scenes in the original work are the most popular? Second, what parts of the material being adapted are most suitable for translation into a dramatic medium?

Translating the Material   The conversion of material written in one literary form into a form suitable for a broadcast or film presentation is known as translation. Most adaptations require this type of change at one point or other.

Translation into Dialogue   Writers who adapt stories or books into dramatic form find that often they must turn material appearing in the original work as narration or description into dialogue. Washington Irving's "The Legend of Sleepy Hollow," for example, contains not one single dialogue exchange, and in the whole story there are only two spoken lines, both uttered by people who are alone at the time. Turning this work into a drama requires virtually complete translation of the material into dialogue. In writing this dialogue, the writer faces the challenge of presenting essential information without making the lines sound heavy with exposition. Dialogue in adaptations must sound as lifelike and natural as it does in any dramatic form.

Translation into Narration   When three-act plays are being adapted into a shorter television form, the opposite technique may be used, namely, the translation of certain points revealed in dialogue into narration. The scenes thus treated, of course, should not portray the key events of the story. The emotional impact of important scenes needs to be preserved intact by presenting them in their original dramatic form.

Translation into Sound Effects and Music   Sound effects and music have their principal use in radio adaptations, but they also have a place in television. The major function of music is to emphasize effects that are accomplished primarily through other means, for rarely does music communicate meaning directly.

Translation into Sets, Costumes, Business, and Action   One of the advantages of television is that visual means sometimes can be used to depict in an instant what a writer of fiction may have taken pages and pages to convey. In most cases the need for converting a storyteller's description into visual elements is completely evident, but because the visual can communicate meaning so clearly and so economically, the adapter also should be alert to employ visual devices where their use may not be so obviously indicated.

Lengthening the Material   Adapters rarely have to lengthen the material they are treating, though there are instances when some expansion may be necessary. This is particularly true when the subject of the adaptation is a Bible story. Many are so pithily told that only their bare outlines exist in the original version. Often adapters must invent surrounding incidents, and even characters, in order to give the story enough body for dramatic presentation.

Adapters may have to add new scenes for other reasons. Sometimes they must introduce information not appearing in the original version. Poe's story "The Cask of Amontillado" portrays an act of revenge without explaining what motivated it. Most dramatizers of this story feel it necessary to fill in this detail. Cutting material from a script may demand the creation of a new scene to serve as a bridge between the two sections of the story.

One thing you should avoid is adding material or making arbitrary changes simply because you believe they will improve the story. One student doing an adaptation of Guy de Maupassant's classic story "The Necklace" decided that the writer had slighted the events that took place after the supposed diamond necklace had been lost. He therefore invented a conflict between the man and wife precipitated by their misfortune. The resulting script bore little relationship to the original, and de Maupassant's ironic twist at the end, the whole point of the story, was de-emphasized to the verge of extinction.

Making Other Modifications   There are a number of changes adapters must make simply because the public is more permissive with what can be said or done in some media than it is with others. Differences in the essential nature and special requirements of the various media also dictate certain changes.

The Taboos of Broadcasting   A good example of the different standards of permissiveness under which the media operate can be found in the use of what is generally considered profane or indecent language. The public is willing to tolerate language in stage plays, movies, and fiction that it will not accept in television. Changes in the language of works adapted to television sometimes must be made to conform to the prevailing taboos.

There is also a greater public concern about the effect of violence in television than there is about the effect of violence in other media. This concern reaches its peak when the audience includes children. For this reason the violence occurring in the material being adapted often must be toned down. A TV adaptation of "Hansel and Gretel" provides an example. As told by the Brothers Grimm, the original story ended when the witch was pushed into the oven by her intended victim Hansel. The adapter, Yasha Frank, felt that permitting her to remain in the oven and be cooked into extinction conjured up a picture too horrible for young children to endure. He, therefore, showed the witch peeking out of the oven unharmed, and even suggested that her searing experience might reform rather than destroy her. The adapter also made another change in the original story prompted by his concern for its effect on children. In the Grimm Brothers' story it was the cruel stepmother who lured Hansel and Gretel into the forest in the hope that they would perish. Feeling that he should not thus vilify stepmothers, the adapter made the witch and her assistants the ones who did the luring.

A film adaptation of a Bible story that violated the taboos felt by many people was Martin Scorsese's *The Last Temptation of Christ*. In the eyes of some religious groups he made Christ too worldly, particularly in portraying his sexual feelings, and they demanded that the film be boycotted.

Another fact to keep in mind in deciding whether to translate certain material into dramatic form is that action often becomes more vivid in drama than when told in story form. One of literature's most spine-chilling experiences is provided by Lord Dunsany's "Two Bottles of Relish," a story that tells how a murderer disposed of his victim's body by cannibalism. You might look this story up and decide whether it is suitable for translation into dramatic form. Alfred Hitchcock, who made a specialty of horror in the movies and television programs he directed, recognized that some stories suitable for printing in a book are too shocking or grotesque for presentation on television.[2] Were Hitchcock working today, however, he might have made a different decision, for times seem to have changed.

The Need for Getting Attention Immediately The necessity for catching audience attention may demand certain rearrangements of the material to be adapted. If the original writer has begun the story slowly, the adapter may have to move an exciting scene forward in the action and then introduce the necessary exposition after audience interest has been awakened.

The Need for Language That Speaks Well Even where dialogue exists in the original work, some modifications may be required before it is suitable for dramatic presentation. What may read well on the printed page often sounds cumbersome when it is put into the mouths of actors. Consider this passage from Poe's story "Morella," which appears here just as Poe wrote it, except that character designations have been added.

MORELLA: I am dying, yet shall I live.
HUSBAND: Morella!
MORELLA: I repeat that I am dying, but within me is a pledge of that affection—ah, how little!—which thou didst feel for me, Morella. And when my spirit departs shall the child live—thy child and mine, Morella's. But thy days shall be days of sorrow—that sorrow which is the most lasting of impressions, as the cypress is the most enduring of trees.
HUSBAND:
Morella! Morella! How knowest this?

Poe was assuredly a literary genius possessed of piercing insight into the macabre and perverse. Yet unless you wish to attempt to capture completely the archaic style of his writing, it is obvious that you need to modernize the language.

Sometimes you need not rewrite dialogue, but you may have to distribute it in a different way. Writers of books and short stories often give their characters long, uninterrupted speeches. If you are to achieve naturalness and a real-life quality, you must break these speeches up to secure more frequent interchange among the characters. You also may have to modernize the descriptive sections of stories, particularly those written in another period, before you give them to a radio or TV narrator.

Deciding whether to modify existing dialogue or narrative passages is one of the most difficult decisions confronting an adapter. Some of the material in Poe's stories, for example, needs to be rewritten, and some does not. Much of the dialogue in "The Cask of Amontillado" is marked by a crispness and direction that makes it ideal just as it is for inclusion in a television or radio version. And it would be difficult for an adapter to compose better narration than that already existing in "The Tell-Tale Heart."

Radio's Lack of the Visual Writers of radio adaptations frequently encounter unusual problems because they must make action clear to an audience that can see nothing. They are most likely to overlook this responsibility when adapting stage, movie, or television plays. Remembering that in these media some dialogue is clear only because the audience can see what is happening, the adapter must put into the dialogue of the radio adaptation the facts the listener needs to understand the scene. The problem is to provide this information without being obvious about it. Radio dialogue must give eyes to the listener, but it must do so unobtrusively.

Steps in Adaptation

When you set out to adapt some other person's work into a television, radio, or film script, you will be wise to follow a well-organized procedure instead of attacking the problem on a hit-or-miss basis. Only in that way can you be assured of a satisfactory result.

Choosing Material for Adaptation

You make your first critical decision when you decide on the material you plan to adapt. You should realize that some stories can be told satisfactorily only in the medium of their original creation. "The Pit and the Pendulum" of Edgar Allan Poe is an example of such a work. Most of this story deals with the thoughts and experiences of one man alone in a dungeon as he endures tortures of mind and body directed at him by hidden persecutors. The hero is never named and the nature of his offense, which led to his condemnation by the Inquisition, is not revealed. At the end of the story General LaSalle dashes to the rescue with not even a hint earlier that he might be on his way.

People reading the story often are not aware of these problems. By keeping our attention focused on the reeking pit, on the razor-sharp pendulum, and on the red-hot walls moving in to destroy their victim, Poe achieved a unity of impression that makes nothing else seem to matter. The dramatic form, perhaps unfortunately, does not provide an opportunity for concentration of this intensity. Audiences expect leading characters to be named; when a man is condemned they want to know what he has done; and drama usually requires relationships between people during some part of the story.

Hollywood provides another example of this problem. It was decided to adapt Tom Wolfe's novel *Bonfire of the Vanities* into a movie despite the opinion of some that it could not be successfully translated into film.

The doubters turned out to be prophetic. The movie, though it featured some of the most popular actors of the day (Bruce Willis, Melanie Griffith, and Tom Hanks), was one of the costliest failures in Hollywood history.

As a beginner you would do well to turn to less challenging material. It is better to learn the craft of adaptation with works that are easily translatable into a dramatic medium. Only when you have mastered the basic techniques of the craft should you attack problems that have thus far defeated even the most inventive minds.

Securing the Rights

After choosing the subject matter for adaptation, you must consider next the question of who owns the rights. You may use freely only material that is no longer under copyright. You must secure permission to adapt any material protected by copyright, and you must reach an agreement with the holder of the rights regarding the conditions under which the use is to take place. If you fail to get permission to adapt material owned by someone else, you may get some writing experience from your effort, but you are likely to end up with nothing else except a lawsuit. We describe the provisions of the current copyright law in Chapter 19.

Studying the Material

If you are to deliver to a broadcast or movie audience the sense and feeling of another person's creation, it is obvious that you must become as familiar with it as if you had created it yourself. You must understand every character in the story; you must know what their values are; you must recognize the motivations driving them; you must have a thorough understanding of the plot structure and the relationship between the main and subplots; you must have a clear conception of the story's theme, for it will be your responsibility to project that theme in your adaption.

Planning and Writing the Adaptation
The next step is to decide what material in the original can be included in your adaptation. Wise selection is the principal key to the adapter's success. You must then determine what changes are needed to convert this material into a version that can be broadcast or filmed and prepare to create whatever new sequences may be required to bridge the gaps your changes have left. When these decisions have been made, they should be incorporated into a plan that can guide the writing of the script. This plan can be similar in design to the one used in writing any dramatic script.

Evaluating the Result When you have written your first draft, you must evaluate it carefully to determine whether you have been faithful to the first author's intent. Even when you have adhered as strictly as you can to the original material, you may feel that you have failed to capture the full impact generated by the original material, or you will sense that there is a somewhat different quality to this effect when the story is presented in the new medium. If you have used all of your craftsmanship to prepare a faithful adaptation, you should accept this deterioration philosophically. It is sometimes an inevitable product of the process of adaptation itself. In some instances, you cannot make the changes that an adaptation requires without doing some damage to the story. A half-hour adaptation obviously cannot communicate the depth of experience inherent in a three-act play. And it may be, as has been noted, that the original story and medium are so inextricably linked that to separate one from the other inevitably filters the effect.

There are occasions, however, when just the opposite of this result takes place. It turns out that the new medium transmits the story more effectively than the original medium did. Thus, without intending to, you produce a greater work of art than the original writer produced.

ACTION AND CRIME DRAMA

One of the most popular kinds of drama in both television and the movies is the type that focuses primarily on physical action. Though its popularity has gone up and down through the years as public tastes have changed, action dramas in some form have always been available to those who want them. They can be classed into a number of categories, which, though different in important respects, also share certain characteristics which confront writers with common problems.

Westerns

Developed by the motion picture industry on a foundation laid down by the dime novels and the Wild West shows of the late 19th century, the western flourished in both the early days of the movies and television. There was a period in the 1950s, in fact, when as many as 11 westerns were scheduled on television during prime time. In the years that followed, their number gradually dwindled until virtually none were being produced for either television or the movies. In the late 1980s there was a revival of sorts with the appearance of such new western series as *Guns of Paradise* and *The Young Riders*.

The classic western is an idealized drama whose story bears little relation to life as it really existed in the old West. Exemplified by the title character in the movie *Shane*, its hero is a transcendent figure who, representing the forces of good, rides into town to meet and vanquish the forces of evil before disappearing into the mists on the trail, to be seen no more. The motives of the villain, whose machinations make his exploits necessary, are often as cloudy as those of the hero, but one thing is clear; he is all bad and the hero is all good. Other stock characters of the classic western are the derelict professional—the lawyer, doctor, or minister—who betrays the creed of his profession except perhaps for one glorious, soul-restoring moment; the effete Easterner who, disdaining the use of violence, is often humiliated or killed; the anemic good woman who is generally the schoolmarm; and the bad woman who works in the saloon. The climactic moment of the western is the final confrontation between the hero and the villain, which often takes place on a street deserted by the rest of the townspeople, who cower in fear behind doors and windows. The classic western *High Noon* is an example, and so is the more recent *Silverado* of Lawrence Kasdan.

This stock pattern was modified to some extent with the development of the so-called "adult" western, a type best exemplified by *Gunsmoke*, which began on radio and ran on television for more than two decades. It revealed a West somewhat closer to what it really was, where virtue did not always triumph and the problems were not solved by the simple application of heroic violence. Characterization is more important in this form; the figures in the drama often take time to consider and discuss the situation; the hero is sometimes torn by doubt and indecision, he experiences fear, and he is not always victorious.

Police Dramas

Stories based on police investigations featuring chases and shootouts are standard fare in television and the movies. The violence they involve has disturbed some people; they persist, however, because the stark conflict between crime and the law that is central to their plots attracts many viewers.

Settings and characters have many variations. *Hill Street Blues* and the *Dirty Harry* movie series focused on a big-city police force, *In the Heat of the Night* on police work in a small Southern town. At times the spotlight was on motorcycle cops, women police officers, and special investigative squads. In some instances the leading character was a private investigator, as in *Magnum P.I.*, but the story remained one of confrontation between good and evil. Some police stories mix humor and drama, as the film *Beverly Hills Cop* did.

Other Adventure Dramas

Many other adventure dramas featuring neither cowboys nor police officers share with westerns and police dramas an emphasis on physical action. The heroes of spy dramas, for example, like those of the western, are masters of violence, and the villains who oppose them are as sinister and as faceless as any unshaven bushwhacker who waylays the hero in a western draw. Many other dramas set in diverse times and places fall into the action category.

Writing Action Dramas

Most action dramas involve a struggle to attain a goal. Their characters noticeably lack the reflection and deliberation characteristic of those in decision-centered dramas. Pursuit is a central element in many action dramas and the narrative line is brisk and simple. The key to the writer's success is the ability to devise exciting action and to maintain nerve-wracking suspense. The highest points are reached when the hero, apparently caught without a chance of escape, manages to evade the trap through the exercise of great ingenuity or strength. A distinguishing feature of the *MacGyver* series was that the hero usually succeeded in extricating himself from what appeared to be hopeless dilemmas through his mastery of mechanical devices. With the emphasis on action, the delineation of character takes second place. Usually, the writer plots the adventures first and then creates the characters needed to carry out the plot. If any of the characters has distinctiveness and individuality, it is the hero or heroine, the person whose strength, courage, ingenuity, or intuition overcomes the difficulties or solves the problem. Yet even this characterization is often a narrow one, being presented only in those elements that are specifically connected with the plot elements of the story.

The Drama of Detection

A special type of crime story is one in which the audience's interest is focused on the process through which a brilliant detective solves a perplexing crime with a series of breathtaking deductions. Edgar Allan Poe originated the type and the tradition has been carried on by many writers, among them A. Conan Doyle, whose creation, Sherlock Holmes, has become synonymous with "The Great Detective" throughout the world. Immensely popular in books and short-story form, the classic detective story has appeared less often in dramatic form. One reason is that drama demands emotional values and a story that turns on the solving of an ingenious puzzle is largely an intellectual exercise. There have been some notable successes, however, among them *Perry Mason*, which had a nine-year network run, and the *Columbo* series, which has been broadcast at intervals for many years. In *Murder, She Wrote* the *de facto* detective is a woman who writes mystery novels. In a number of series lawyers carried out the detective function, among them *Perry Mason, Matlock,* and the district attorney in *Jake and the Fatman.* The PBS *Mystery* series has broadcast dramatizations of Doyle's Sherlock Holmes stories and stories focusing on the deductive feats of Hercule Poirot and Jane Marple, characters created by Agatha Christie. All of these detectives and many others have appeared in feature movies. Stories about the Scotland Yard detective Adam Dalgliesh, a creation of contemporary writer P. D. James, have also been featured on the *Mystery* series.

Writing the Detective Drama

Crime stories in which the emphasis is on the steps leading to the solution of a crime are usually plotted backwards. You must begin by figuring out the circumstances of the crime. This involves deciding who is to be killed, who is to do the killing, how the murder is to be committed, and the place it occurs. Of particular importance at this time is devising a distinctive idea or gimmick which will give the story some degree of individuality. This special idea may be an unusual method of committing the crime, an original way of concealing the body, a unique method of escape by the culprit, a point of law turned either to the detective's or to the criminal's advantage, a surprising motive, or an unusual or particularly ingenious method of solving the crime.

Your next task is to develop the process through which detection takes place. The elements in this process are: (1) to confront the detective with the crime; (2) to produce the information needed to solve it; (3) to arrive at a solution; and (4) to provide whatever final explanation may be necessary.

One of the strongest traditions of the detective story is to surprise the audience in some way at the end of the story. Usually this is achieved through the revelation of a person no one suspected as the perpetrator of the crime. In some stories the audience knows who the criminal is, as was the case in the *Columbo* series, and the surprise arises from the detective's revelation of the clues that pointed to the culprit. Ingenious use of the technique of gradual revelation is the principal means of achieving surprise in telling a detective story. The best detective stories are those in which this final revelation causes all the other facts to fall into place, thus making the solution completely understandable without further explanation.

One problem a writer faces is to play fair with the audience by revealing the clues the detective finds without at the same time killing surprise by telegraphing the solution to the crime. There are a number of ways of including clues without indicating their significance:

1. Divide the clue from its application to the story by a period of time, thus disguising the connection between the two.
2. Include an important clue among a number of other casual incidents which belong in the story but have no particular relevance to the solution of the crime.
3. Deflect the audience's attention from a clue by following its presentation immediately with exciting action.
4. Present an item of information that actually has no relevance at the point it is introduced but becomes meaningful only when the detective connects it to the crime.

Characterization in the detective story is less important than the development of a plot that will puzzle and intrigue viewers. Still, the great writers of these stories have often created detectives whose unique habits and personality quirks have made them memorable characters. Among them are the eccentric Sherlock Holmes and Hercule Poirot, the vain Belgian who emphasized the use of "the little gray cells." Developing a full characterization of the guilty person is also important, for it helps viewers to understand the pattern of traits and values that played a part in motivating the crime.

THE FANTASY

The fantasy is a drama of events that, measured by natural law and available knowledge, could not actually take place. Other dramas, in contrast, portray events that could occur even though they have not. A drama is not a fantasy simply because it exists in the imagination of the writer, for all drama is to some degree imaginative, nor is it drama that is merely highly improbable. A drama is a fantasy only if it portrays events or phenomena that could not possibly have happened. It is on this basis that any drama taking place at some future time is usually considered a fantasy.

Types of Fantasies

The largest class of fantasies includes those stories that involve some application of sheer magic. Their diversity is great, presenting characters ranging from the frightening monster created by *Frankenstein* to the entrancing love story of *Beauty and the Beast*, and involving moods varying from the chilling horror of *Dracula* to the inimitable drolleries of *Alice's Adventures in Wonderland*.

Stories of the supernatural include that large group of legends usually known as ghost stories and tales involving a phenomenon like telepathy, which extends psychological power beyond the limits usually recognized by scientists.

The writers of many fantasies have imagined the world as it might exist in some future period, as the makers of the *Star Wars* movies and the *Star Trek* television programs and movies did. A principal element in these productions was the speculation that other beings inhabit the worlds out in space. Some works of this nature were produced not merely to entertain readers but also to establish philosophical points about modern life and culture. The conjecture that periods of time do not occur consecutively but exist concurrently is the foundation for stories in which an individual travels from one level of time to another. This was the fantastic premise underlying the *Back to the Future* films and the television series *Quantum Leap*. Another popular type of fantasy is one that projects future developments that could arise from natural laws already established. Sometimes actual scientific discoveries have been foreshadowed by stories of this type. The nuclear submarine of our day was described in many of its details by Jules Verne in his fantasy *Twenty Thousand Leagues Under the Sea*, written in the 19th century. The Disney company adapted it into a memorable movie.

Some stories rest on the borderline between fantasy and other types of drama. A good example is Henry James' *The Turn of the Screw* (dramatized for the stage and movies as *The Innocents*). From one point of view this story may be accepted as a powerful tale of ghosts and therefore a fantasy; from another the events may be explained as delusions affecting its chief characters, an interpretation that makes this story not a fantasy at all but a tragic story of disordered minds.

A story revolving around an event that seems to be clearly fantastic in nature, but which turns out in the end to have a rational explanation is also a borderline fantasy. A story portraying ghosts who turn out to be illusions contrived by natural means is an example. Another example was a drama presented on *The Twilight Zone*. It told of space explorers, shot from the earth in a rocket vehicle, who landed on a planet they could not identify. Most of the program portrayed their exploration of the strange land into which they had been catapulted. In the end it was revealed that their space vehicle had actually returned to Earth. The weird landscape in which they had landed was that of the Nevada desert.

Writing the Fantasy

A number of general approaches may be used in plotting the fantasy; it may be goal centered or decision centered, or it may be the type of plot designed to reveal the explanation of some mysterious event or strange phenomenon. Since the quality that distinguishes the fantasy from other types of stories is the existence of an assumption that defies accepted natural law or existing conditions, it follows that the unique problems inherent in plotting the fantasy are connected with the manipulation of this fantastic premise. The writer should have a clear idea of its nature, and it should play an important part in the development of the story.

One might think that because fantasies are based on an event or premise that defies natural law, the writer doesn't have to worry about maintaining believability. Actually it is just as important to make fantastic stories plausible as it is with any other type of dramatic writing. What happens is that the writer and the audience strike a bargain; for the purposes of the drama the viewers agree to accept the fantastic premise, but in all other respects they demand that the depiction of events and characters be convincing and believable. This applies to the fantastic premise itself. The writer must stay within the limits it imposes.

Realizing the full potential inherent in the fantastic premise is the greatest challenge facing the writer of fantasies. The idea that a certain individual had the power to destroy his enemies merely by shouting, "Drop dead!" at them was the starting point for one fantasy. This idea alone was not enough for a completely developed drama, however. Fortunately, the writer was equal to the task of inventing the twist he needed to bring his story to a satisfactory conclusion. As the play ended, the character visited a canyon in the far West, and in exultation at his ascendency over mankind he screamed to the heavens, "Drop dead! Drop dead!" Unfortunately for him, the words were reflected from the canyon walls and their author was killed by the malign power of this own echo.

A device for developing plotting ideas, which is especially well suited to creating fantasies, is to ask the question, "What if?" In the case of the fantasy, of course, the "What if?" is directly related to a fantastic premise. "What if?" questions that could lead to fantasies are the following: What if the world's population continues increasing at the present rate? What if scientists actually conquer aging? What if we succeed in contriving machines to do all of our work? What if a person goes back in time and meets his own parents as teenagers. It was this idea that gave *Back to the Future* its special impact.

DOCUDRAMA

A prominent element in broadcasting and movie schedules is a type of drama that either dramatizes factual material or presents a story inspired by actual events and the lives of real people, but which also includes events and characters invented by the writer. The term docudrama, which refers in an overall way to dramatic material having a factual basis, is used to identify both these types. Docudrama differs from the documentary, which we discussed in an earlier chapter, in that in the docudrama, actors portray the contemporary people or historical personages involved in the events, whereas in the documentary the people themselves appear and the events are real, not dramatized. The documentary, moreover, usually explores a current problem, whereas docudramas may merely tell the story of a life or an event. A script that focuses on dramatizing the life of a real person is biographical in nature; one centering on past events is historical. Since both con-

front writers with similar types of problems, we shall consider them together.

Biographical and Historical Drama

The writing of drama telling about an actual person or reflecting events that really took place requires some special talents. To the inventiveness needed by all writers must be added the skill to find information, the discernment to select the significant and dramatic facts from the material available, and the power to translate them into strong, arresting drama. To begin with there are often serious obstacles to discovering the necessary facts. Sometimes the historical record is a sparse one; we know for sure only a few isolated facts about the life of William Shakespeare, for instance. Speculation and inference must fill in the rest of his story. Even when a great deal is known about a person, there may be gaps in the record which keep us from knowing why or how a subject acted in a particular situation. A second obstacle to discovering the truth is the existence of conflicting information. A third obstacle for writers who must turn out scripts in short order is lack of time. They cannot spend five years researching and writing, as Catherine Drinker Bowen did in composing her biography of John Adams.

Obstacles there may be, but it is clear that people aspiring to write what is true must carry out a diligent and organized program of research. They must assemble as much information as they can in the time they have, more than they can possibly, use, for only then do they have the opportunity to select the material that will give the maximum point and purpose to the script. They must have the imagination and energy to follow leads. They must keep a special lookout for material that is particularly appropriate for presentation in the dramatic form. This becomes largely a task of finding those revealing details that will convert figures of the past into living, breathing human beings. The makers of the docudrama *Separate But Equal*, whose plot we analyzed in Chapter 11, succeeded brilliantly in accomplishing this objective.

Writing Biographical and Historical Drama

In addition to presenting facts about a person or event, the writer of biographical or historical drama must create a play that has the elements necessary for all successful drama—the capacity to catch and sustain attention, vivid characters, a well-constructed plot, and the power to arouse emotions.

Reflecting the Truth   Having discovered the truth about a person or event, the next task is to reflect that truth in a script. Writers must do this even though they cannot escape inventing some of the material. Dialogue is a good example. There is usually no way of knowing precisely what historical characters actually said during a given episode, but if dramatists are not granted the privilege of devising words to clothe a situation, there can be no drama. They must rely on invention also when there are gaps in the information needed to complete the dramatization. Always, of course, this invention should be consistent with what is known. The dialogue they devise should communicate the import of the situation as it actually took place and should be in keeping with the style and character of the people speaking.

It may be tempting sometimes to improve the story with invented incidents or character anecdotes. You should never introduce anything that warps the truth or make changes that distort the historical records. It is also a mistake to begin research with a firm theory about what the truth is, for you may find yourself overemphasizing the facts that support your theory and discounting those that conflict with it. This is the error many felt Oliver Stone made in constructing the script for his film *JFK*. Though critics applauded his technical virtuosity in directing and editing the picture, many criticized him for making it appear that his speculation regarding the assassination of John Kennedy was actually fact. This feeling was summed up in a comment made by Ronald Steel in *The New Republic*. "Because of the director's ability to cut, splice, fuse, restage, and invent, it is virtually impossible for a viewer of this film to tell if he is seeing a real or a phony event."[3]

Distortion in a docudrama can also result when biographers attempt to shield from public view significant information about a contemporary subject because it is shocking or unpleasant. Equally undesirable is the use of unsubstantiated rumors that may be lurid or sensational to pump up interest. When writers indulge in either practice, they are on the road to creating fiction.

Selecting Material   The next task is to select the facts to be presented in the play. Selection is essential, for even the longest dramatization is not long enough to include everything about a subject. If writers could present everything about a subject, they still should not do so, for selection and emphasis are part of their function as artists. Their obligation is to select the material which, after imaginative arrangement, will provide the work with unity and meaning and invest it with dramatic power.

Plotting   The procedures that have been described for plotting all dramas can be applied to biographical and historical dramas. Many of them can be made to turn on the struggle for a goal or the making of decisions. In some cases neither of these approaches works and a unique plotting formula must be discovered that will fit the material. This is particularly true of the historical drama in which the event rather than the person dominates.

Maintaining Interest One problem in dealing with a well-known person or event is that the audience already knows how the story came out. Developing suspense under such circumstances is virtually impossible, but there are other techniques for arousing and maintaining the interest of the audience. One of these techniques is to take full advantage of the fact that you are dealing in truth. George Roy Hill and John Whedon, the writers of the television version of *A Night to Remember*, the book about the sinking of the *Titanic,* used this device. In the opening moments of this script a narrator speaks to the audience as follows: "What you will see actually took place. It is as accurate as man can reconstruct that night. This is not fiction. It is fact."

Another way of stimulating interest is to develop expectancy through the use of the technique of foreshadowing. The audience may know most of what happened, but its interest in seeing it happen can be sharpened through this means. The technique of gradual revelation, used in combination with foreshadowing, can reinforce the effect. In an early part of the TV version of *A Night to Remember*, the audience is told that the *Titanic* has lifeboats for only a fraction of its passengers and crew. Later this information is made more specific: There is room in the lifeboats for only one-third of the ship's complement. The existence of icebergs in the path of the *Titanic* is referred to in the first minutes of the drama. The crew and passengers ignore the warnings, but the viewers do not. They know what happened later and they shiver with expectancy. The process that led to the sinking of the *Titanic* is handled with consummate skill, again through the use of

gradual revelation. Not until late in the script, for example, does the designer of the ship admit that the gash in the side is so long that the ship must inevitably sink. Up to this point even sophisticated viewers could, in their imagination, entertain some hope. The skill of the writers has provided them with the feeling of living through those moments on the *Titanic* as they might have been experienced by someone who was actually on board.

Characterization If a biographical drama fails to bring its chief character vividly to life, it fails almost completely. The task for writers is primarily one of character revelation. The character exists. Their task is to discover the character and then transmit this vision to an audience.

Characterization for the writers of historical drama is not quite so crucial, for the emphasis is likely to be on the events rather than on the people. Providing these events with an adequate exposition actually may take most of the time they have at their disposal. If they can, however, they should try to present historical figures who are more than mere stereotypes. Vivid characters revealed in depth can invest the cold facts of history with warmth and humanity.

Factual Drama with Fictional Elements

In addition to dramas dealing with real people and actual happenings, docudramas also include the type that, while remaining true to the overall record, also includes invented characters and events. The TV mini-series *Holocaust*, which dramatized the experience of Jews during the Nazi period, is a good example of the type. It contrasted the experience of a Jewish family as it endured the horrors of the concentration camps with that of a German citizen, who, under the influence of Nazi doctrine, was gradually transformed from a decent human being into a sadistic S.S. officer. The main characters were not historical personages; their kind did exist in Nazi Germany, however, and the events they experienced reflected those that actually took place during the Nazi period. Some historical personages were characters in the story, among them Heinrich Himmler, the head of the secret police.

The distinction between the docudrama that includes fictional elements and biographical and historical drama is a significant one for writers. It is obvious that there is much greater room for invention in writing a script in which some events and characters are invented than there is in writing a script that must remain completely faithful to the lives of people who really lived and to the events they experienced. In other ways, however, writers face similar challenges in writing the two types. Writers of any scripts with a factual basis cannot escape the task of research if they are to reflect truthfully the period in which their stories are set, whether it is a contemporary or historical one. Their characters, moreover, must be people whose values and traits are comparable to those possessed by historical people of the period. The essential task of all writers of docudrama, as David Wolper, a leading producer of the type expressed it, is to interpret reality in a creative way.

THE DAYTIME SERIAL

One of the most enduring forms of broadcast drama is the daytime serial, often called soap opera because so many of its sponsors are soap makers. Established on radio in the early 1930s, it soon became the most important element in morning and afternoon programming. Television eventually drove the radio serial from the air, as it did almost all radio drama, but by the time the last of them disappeared in the early 1960s, the TV

version was occupying as important a place in daytime schedules as had its radio counterpart. At first the episodes were 15 minutes long, just as radio serial episodes had been, but they gradually expanded until most now run for 60 minutes.

Of all of the dramatic forms, soap operas have been subjected to the most withering attack. In many instances they have even been ridiculed by those involved in producing them. Max Wylie, an author of books on broadcast-writing who at one time wrote radio serials, once turned on the hand that fed him by deriding them as a "gloomy, watery, wailing, histrionic procession of Virtue, Irresolution, and Just-Plain-Bilge."[4] A few critics have seen some merit in them, however. The distinguished media critic Gilbert Seldes described serials as radio's single notable contribution to the art of fiction,[5] and another prominent critic, Marya Mannes, in an otherwise scathing article, remarked on the ingenuity of the plotting and the fine ear for natural dialogue displayed by their writers.[6]

Whatever their merits or demerits may be, they attract millions of listeners. Former Supreme Court Justice Thurgood Marshall was said to be a regular listener to *Days of Our Lives*, and other reputed soap opera fans have included novelists Dan Wakefield and P. G. Wodehouse, artist Andy Warhol, singer Sammy Davis, Jr., and former Texas governor John Connally. Many college students are also counted among their devoted listeners.

The criticism leveled against daytime serials is not irrelevant to those who write them, but it is not the function of this book to determine their status as an art form or to discuss their social implications. Our concern is with the peculiar characteristics of soap operas and the special techniques employed in writing them. The prototype for today's serial is the model developed in radio. In some respects, however, the TV form has established conventions quite different from its radio predecessor. We now examine the TV daytime serial with particular attention to the characteristics that distinguish it from other types of drama.

The Viewing Situation

One circumstance requiring special consideration by writers is the fact that no one can view every episode of a serial. It must be written so that the members of the audience can follow the story despite the gaps in their viewing. In addition to missing an episode here and there, regular viewers may also miss a substantial number of episodes consecutively because of vacations. They expect to pick up the story on their return without undue loss of orientation. Even the viewing of a given episode, taking place as it does during the working day, is likely to be interrupted by household emergencies. Writers must also remember that domestic chores may keep people from watching the screen constantly; they must try to make it possible for the audience to keep track of what is happening through sound and dialogue alone.

The Serial Idea   The first response to the peculiarities of the viewing situation can be said to be the serial idea itself—the telling of a story that, in defiance of the Aristotelian dictum, has no beginning, no middle, and no end, but goes on and on forever. This characteristic is particularly effective in luring back to the program listeners who may have been absent for a considerable period of time, for they will quickly recognize the characters and their same old problems, even though the specific complications may have changed. It is this change in the nature of the complications that provides whatever independent stories there are in the structure of the serial. A dilemma of some type provides the core around which each sequence is unified; the overall story maintains its never-ending character, however, because one problem is never completely resolved until another descends.

Constant Tension   With previous listeners pulled back to the program by the nature of the serial form itself, the task of the writer is to generate an immediate renewal of interest. This need leads to another characteristic quality of the daytime serial—the maintenance of tension at a constant fever pitch. There must be "perpetual emotion," as someone has said. Conventional dramas have their flow and ebb; excitement rises to the climax but is dispersed with a resolution which permits the audience to relax. The writer of the serial cannot afford any lulls in the action. A listener who tuned in to find the heroine free from jeopardy and at peace might find no reason to continue listening. Broadcasters have discovered that domestic happiness is fatal to the daytime serial. Writers must never be deflected from their primary task of creating anxiety and suffering.

The continuous emphasis on misfortune in the soap serial means that the kind of life it portrays—although ostensibly that of normal, everyday people—is characterized by wide variations from the norm. The stories are replete with intrigue, vicious gossip, marital infidelity, crime, financial chicanery, and catastrophic diseases. Amnesia, temporary blindness, strange attacks of paralysis, and tropical fevers abound. Almost no one ever gets the common cold or comes down with something as mundane as the "flu." Another rare experience endured by few people in real life is to be accused of and stand trial for murder. Such an event is commonplace in the lives of soap-opera characters. When the story moves from the home out into the community, it is usually into a hospital or courtroom.

One marked trend in daytime serials is that the conduct of the characters has become much more uninhibited than it once was. In the days of radio the heroines were scarcely permitted to think about men in sexual terms before marriage, much less engage in illicit relations. Now bedroom scenes involving unmarried couples have become commonplace on the regular networks. Some cable networks are producing serials that go still further in breaching the barriers against the use of sensational material and unconventional characters.

The Repetitiousness of Serials The lack of continuous listening forces on writers the necessity of repeating elements of the story over and over again so that a viewer who has missed an episode or two may be immediately informed of the current situation. One device is to repeat a given revelation in a number of different scenes, a technique that not only helps to orient the occasional viewer but also wrings the last ounce of dramatic effect from each disclosure. This repetition, although it is necessary, does give the serial what is perhaps its most distinctive characteristic—an incredible slowness of movement. It is the dragging tempo of life itself rather than the foreshortened pace of drama. As Gilbert Seldes said, the serial is "the only dramatic art form in which nothing ever happens between the acts."[7] Soap operas are filled with scenes that seem to change the situation without actually moving it ahead.

Another device for orienting intermittent listeners is the expository scene, which is more frequent in the soap opera than in any other type of drama. This is particularly true of the TV serial, which has dispensed with the announcer of radio, who used to sum up the current situation before each day's episode began. The information a listener needs must now be inserted in the dialogue of the opening scenes. Thus, in serials there is a constant discussion of the situation, a continual retracing of the past.

The Characters of Serials

The creation of characters who almost become real people for their audiences is important in all dramatic writing but it is particularly crucial for the soap opera. William Bell, who was at one time the principal writer for *Days of Our Lives* and originated and guided the writing of *The Young and the Restless* thinks that effective characterization is the key to a soap opera's success. It is the characters who reach and touch people's lives and sometimes bring them to tears. For some they actually cross the boundary from fiction into reality. The solitude in which the reception of most daytime serials takes place is one factor contributing to this effect. The characters become company for those who are alone, being accepted almost as neighbors who come to visit for a while. Thus, many habitual viewers talk about the people of the soap serials as if they really existed. When they get married or have babies, some viewers for whom the distinction between dramatic creations and real-life characters has become blurred, flood the networks with gifts and letters of congratulation. Even radio serials in which characters become known only through their voices, evoked this kind of response.

Plotting the Serial

There are a number of steps in the plotting of a daytime serial. Writers must first plan the overall sweep of events making up the story. They must then design the sequences, extending over a number of weeks, that center on particular dilemmas. Finally, they must devise and write each day's episode. The writing of soap operas is a collaborative project. In many instances a senior writer maps out plotting lines for as much as a year ahead and records them in what is sometimes called a "Bible." With this "Bible" as their guide, other writers then work out the individual episodes and write the scripts.

Designing Sequences Most radio serials revolved around one leading character, whose current predicament provided the focus for a given plotting sequence. The line memorization and extensive rehearsal required in television make it impossible to center the serial on a focal character who appears every day. The single-character soap-opera titles of radio—such as *Ma Perkins*—have, therefore, given way to the umbrellalike appellations of television—*Another World, Days of Our Lives, As the World Turns*—which permit the treatment of any type of subject matter the writer chooses to treat and the inclusion of an unlimited number of principal characters. With the multiplication of characters has come a multiplication of entanglements: Characters have their own particular problems and at the same time they become involved in the problems of others.

A summary of some of the character relationships and plot elements of the serial *Days of Our Lives* provides a good example of the complex relationships and story material common to TV soap operas. The members of two families dominate the series. One is headed by the venerable Dr. Tom Horton, former head of Hope Memorial Hospital. His wife Alice serves as a volunteer in the hospital and operates a restaurant whose profits are dedicated to supporting a theater enterprise. Plotting threads involve their children, their children's children, and even the children of those children. The other unit is the Brady family. The senior members operate a fish market and their two sons and two daughters play key roles in the serial. The stories of the two families intertwine. One of the Brady sons, Bo, was married at one time to a great-granddaughter of the Hortons, for example. A myriad of other characters

impinge on the lives and fortunes of the members of these two families as they move in and out of the stories. One of the most prominent was the charismatic yet evil Victor Keriakis, who exerts a malign influence on both families.

The complex relations that characterize soap operas are exemplified in the marriages of Dr. Horton's daughter Addie and her daughter Julie, which took place in the early years of the series. Addie, after a marriage that produced Julie, married a man named Doug Williams. After Addie's death, Julie then married her stepfather. Another entanglement involved two of Dr. Horton's sons, Mickey and Bill. Mickey, once married to Laura, presumably fathered her son Mike. After Mickey and Laura's divorce, it turned out that the actual father of the boy was Mickey's brother Bill, who then married Laura.

These complications by no means cover the complete web of relationships existing among the numerous characters in *Days of Our Lives*. It would take many pages to describe all of them in their entirety. They constitute a maze in which one life is intersected by another to produce complications which are, in turn, affected by other people who produce even further complications. The writers carry several different stories along at the same time; while one entanglement is being resolved, another entanglement is coming into being. The existence of a number of stories that are developing simultaneously provides a natural means of maintaining suspense. Just as the tension in one of the stories rises to a boiling point, the writer can leave it and take up the story of another group of characters, while the audience continues to worry about the problems of the first group.

Sometimes writers must invent developments that are not directly inspired by the necessity of telling a good story. The resurrection of a character named Marlene after her presumed death and the appearance of a second character named Roman Brady in *Days of Our Lives* are good examples. The writers created these complications because the actors portraying the parts, who had left the cast some years ago to pursue other opportunities, signaled their interest in returning. Because they had been among the serial's most popular performers, the producer instructed the writers to invent developments that would make their return feasible.

Other extraneous factors also affect the writing of serials. As already noted, the appearances of leading characters are limited to avoid demanding too much burdensome line memorization and rehearsal. The reverse of this problem may also be a factor. Contracts with actors sometimes specify that they be assigned a certain amount of work. The writers must design plots that will permit the producer to meet this guarantee.

Planning the Episodes Having designed the basic stories, the final task of the writer is to parcel them out, first, in the weekly portion of five episodes, then in the daily episodes, and lastly in the four- or five-minute portions that come between the commercials. Each of these sequences must end on a point of strain so that the interest of the viewer will be carried through the interruption. The greatest suspense must be generated on Friday to sustain interest through the weekend. This means that as the serial proceeds through the week, there is high tension on Monday which gradually lets down through Wednesday, a day often devoted to bringing the audience up to date on developments, followed by another buildup to a high point on Friday. Within this pattern, tension is brought up at the end of each episode and again at the end of each scene, but the peaks are lower, of course, than those developed at the end of the week. To develop these peaks the writer must become an expert in the construction of tag lines—those lines that, in a statement or a question, crystallize viewers' interest and suspense and intensify their desire to see the next development.

PRIME-TIME SERIALS

The prime-time serial was not unknown to radio—*One Man's Family*, for example, was broadcast in the evening for many years—but the form reached its full flowering in the TV era when *Dallas* began its long run in 1978. For five years it ranked either first or second in audience ratings. Its success in attracting audiences motivated others to produce serials for nighttime audiences, among them *Dynasty, Knot's Landing,* and *Falconcrest*. When *Dallas* and *Dynasty* completed their runs in the early 1990s, the form went into at least a temporary decline, but it is likely that serials like these will continue to be produced.

The evening serial shares a number of characteristics with the daytime counterpart. The principal one, of course, is the serial technique itself. An essential element in its use is the cliff-hanger technique that leaves audiences waiting breathlessly for the next episode. As we noted in an earlier chapter, *Dallas* even used this technique to carry audience interest through the summer hiatus by leaving hanging the question of "Who shot J. R.?" The program that answered the question in the fall drew one of the largest audiences in American TV history. This success prompted other series producers to devise season-ending cliff-hangers.

The dramatic material with which daytime and evening serials deal is similar. The characters in *Dallas,* for example, were preoccupied with money, power, sex, and family. As the serial went on, brother double-crossed brother, quirky sexual relationships developed, new family members fought for acceptance, unexpected relatives suddenly showed up, and business rivals conspired against each other.

In some ways the two forms differ, however. Evening soap operas repeat or refer to previous incidents less often than the daytime variety because they can count on more constant viewing. And because only one production a week is required rather than five, the leading characters can appear in every episode. For example, Larry Hagman, who played J. R., the corrupt and immoral schemer of the *Dallas* series, appeared in virtually every episode.

QUESTIONS AND PROJECTS

1. In your opinion, which is the more difficult writing challenge: to adapt a difficult story for radio or television presentation, or to create an original script?
2. Compare the movie adaptations of *Presumed Innocent* and *Patriot Games* with the novels by Scott Turow and Tom Clancy to determine what changes were made by the adapters.
3. Write a half-hour radio or TV version of Shakespeare's *Macbeth* that tells the basic story clearly without the use of a narrator.
4. Study Conrad Aiken's story of childhood insanity, "Silent Snow, Secret Snow." Decide whether this story could be successfully converted into a radio or television drama and, if so, explain how you would adapt it.
5. Analyze a detective drama or story to determine what clues were made available to the audience and how the solution was gradually revealed through the story's course.
6. Create the foundation for a fantasy by developing a fantastic premise through asking the question: What if?

7. In your opinion, how far may the dramatist writing historical or biographical plays go in inventing material to fill out the dramatic situation?
8. Develop a biographical or historical theme you would like to establish and plan a script that will communicate it to an audience.
9. Watch a daytime serial for a week at the beginning of the term and define the dilemmas of the characters. Return to the serial at the end of the term and define the plot movement that has taken place.
10. Watch a few episodes of a daytime serial and a prime-time serial. Analyze the similarities and differences in the techniques and approaches they use.

NOTES

1. George Wells, "Radio's Strangest Bird," in *Off Mike*, edited by Jerome Lawrence (New York: Duell, Sloan and Pearce, 1944), p. 89.
2. Alfred Hitchcock, *12 Stories They Wouldn't Let Me Do on TV* (New York: Dell Publishing Co., 1957).
3. Ronald Steel, "Mr. Smith Goes to the Twilight Zone," *The New Republic*, February 3, 1992, p. 30.
4. Max Wylie, *Radio and Television Writing* (New York: Holt, Rinehart and Winston, 1950), p. 289.
5. Gilbert Seldes, *The Great Audience* (New York: Viking Press, 1951), p. 115.
6. Marya Mannes, "Massive Detergence," *The Reporter*, July 6, 1961, p. 41.
7. Gilbert Seldes, *The Great Audience*, p. 115.

PART

IV

Writing Comedy

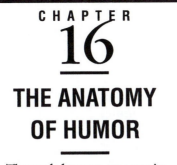

Through humor, we see in what seems rational, the irrational; in what seems important, the unimportant.

CHARLES CHAPLIN (1889–1977)

Programs in which comedy is a major ingredient have been important in broadcasting since the early 1930s. For many years in succession during the period of radio's dominance, 10 of the first 15 programs in audience popularity were comedy programs. Comedy continues to hold its place in the television era as one of the most important elements in the broadcasting bill of fare.

In the opening months of the 1991–1992 television season, some 35 shows in which comedy was a major ingredient appeared on the prime-time schedules of the regular networks. During this same period the popularity of stand-up comedy on the late-night schedules of the regular networks and on cable networks seemed to be growing. In the movie industry comedy has played an equally important role. From the beginning, actors who appeared in comedy films were among the industry's best-known stars and the prominence of such performers has continued to the present day.

Turning out scripts for stand-up comedians, situations comedies, and film comedies can provide rich rewards for those who can respond to the special demands such writing imposes. Laying down principles for achieving success as a comedy writer, however, involves unusual difficulties.

Laughter, to begin with, is an intensely personal experience. What is funny to one person may not be funny to another person at all. As Jean Kerr, a playwright and humorist, put it, "In many ways what makes you laugh is as private as what makes you cry."

E. B. White put his finger on a second problem when he said, "Humor can be dissected as a frog can, but the thing dies in the process and the innards are discouraging to any but the pure scientific mind." Explaining the point in a joke does kill the fun, and yet we cannot understand its mechanism unless we take it apart to see how it works. The analyses that follow may spoil a number of jokes for you even though they have made millions laugh, and it could even dampen the fun in future jokes.

A third problem is that many jokes are funny in the context in which they are heard, but when they are repeated outside of that situation, they lose their mirth-provoking power. You undoubtedly have had the chastening experience of describing to your friends what seemed to be a hilarious incident at the time it happened only to have them greet your story with nothing more than frowns or puzzled looks. A comedy program develops its own atmosphere of fun in which even a poor joke may seem funnier than it really is.

Finally, we should recognize that analyzing humor, although it is an intriguing exercise in itself, may contribute little to an individual's ability to write comedy programs. The possession of natural talent is more important to the person who turns out comedy scripts than it is to the writer of any other kind of material. To make an audience laugh, your view of events and people must be eccentric. What others see as round you must see as a little out of round. The monloguist Steven Wright, who makes frequent appearances on television, is a good example. In one routine he told an audience that it wasn't heights that frightened him, but widths; in another he wondered what life would be like for birds if feathers tickled them.

One trait that characterizes many comedians is that they can't seem to help being funny. When we asked Phyllis Diller for permission to use a line from one of her comedy routines, she wrote an amusing letter which included a funny story explaining how that particular line had come into existence. To our request to Henry Morgan for United States and world rights for the use of some of his material, the comedian replied, "You may also use it on the nearby planets."

Woody Allen is another person to whom laugh lines come naturally. Even in the fifth grade he wrote themes so droll that his teacher pointed him out to other teachers. Allen says that funny responses occur to him as an instinctive reaction to a situation.

Still, with all the comedy lines that must be created every week to satisfy the appetite of television and the movies, writers cannot simply sit back and wait for funny lines to come to them. Understanding what makes people laugh may help you get the process of writing started. Such knowledge, moreover, though it cannot give you a comic sense, may help you to sharpen its edge and realize its full potential.

THE ROOTS OF LAUGHTER

A number of people have tried to devise a theory that would explain the motivation for all laughter. The theories differ to some extent, but each one identifies elements found in situations that makes people laugh. It seems reasonable to assume that comedy writers who insert these elements into their scripts will succeed in producing laughter, provided the presentation is effective and the atmosphere is congenial to humor. Let us review these elements and illustrate them by references to jokes and comedy situations.

Triumph

An element that can be discerned in many comedy situations is a condition of triumph; we laugh to express the feeling of superiority or elation accompanying it. The particular kind of triumph we experience may be one of several varieties.

Triumph in a Fight   The most primitive type of laughter is that which issues from the throats of people who have been victorious in a fight. Besides expressing their feeling of joy, it helps them dissipate the energy and strain they have mobilized in preparation for the battle. The losers in the struggle accomplish the demobilization of resources in just the opposite way; they weep. Albert Rapp, in his book *The Origins of Wit and Humor*, expressed the belief that all laughter can be traced back to this primitive roar of triumph. He described laughter as an essentially hostile reaction which is born out of hatred and aggressiveness. If there were no hostility in people, he argued, there would be no laughter and no need for it.

Vicarious Triumph   Few people actually engage in personal combat these days, but there is still a great deal of laughter motivated by feelings of triumph because we participate vicariously in the success of the victor. Those who see the struggle directly identify themselves with one of the participants, usually the winner, and they laugh in unison with that person. It is not even necessary to see the actual conflict, for evidence of a struggle substitutes for the scene as a whole and triggers a laugh reaction. That is why the possessor of a black eye, the obvious loser in a struggle, is almost universally greeted with giggles. Other manifestations of defeat call for the same reaction. We titter when someone trips and stumbles because these actions recall the moment in a fight when the defeated one is beaten to the ground. If the person who stumbles is stuffy or dignified, we laugh even harder, for the sharp contrast between dignity and discomfiture enlarges our feeling of superiority.

Generally, of course, we laugh only at the minor mishaps of others but greet those afflicted by major misfortunes with sympathy and help. Thus we laugh at a man when he falls down, but we stop laughing if he fails to get up. It seems clear, however, that this sympathetic reaction is a thin veneer on a more primitive response. Young children often laugh uproariously at other people's misfortunes, and their idea of a joke is to inflict pain or embarrassment on some other person. The sight of a disabled or misshapen person may send them into gales of merriment because they have not yet learned that such an outburst is improper. Reactions of this type are not limited to children, however. In some cultures, witnesses to floggings and even to executions have been seen convulsed with laughter. The literature of our own western civilization contains many examples of laughter provoked by the damaged, the battered, the deformed, and the crippled. Laughter at physical misfortune, as an expression of vicarious triumph, appears to be elemental in people.

Triumph Through Words A struggle does not necessarily involve physical combat but may be fought with words alone, particularly in a civilized situation. A clever person with a rapier thrust of wit may achieve a triumph as complete as that of the caveman who batters his adversary to the ground with a club. Once, for example, an old lady was greeted by an insolent young man as follows:

"Good morning, Mother of Asses."

"Good morning, my son," she replied. We can imagine that she went down the road shaking with laughter at her triumph in this duel of wits.

Often a feeling of triumph can be achieved without winning a duel of wits but simply by making fun of someone or something. It follows that much humor is based entirely on derision. In fact, it is estimated that 70 percent of all humor is of this type. Critics of plays, television programs, and movies often make insulting remarks about the productions they review. A drama critic named Percy Hammond once made this comment in his review of a stage musical: "So far I have knocked everything except the chorus girls' knees and nature anticipated me there." That is pure, undiluted ridicule. Moreover, it is savage. During an appearance on the *Today* show, the movie critic Gene Shalit criticized the acting in a film he was reviewing by saying: "After the screen tests were given, they must have given the parts to the losers."

The important place of derision in comedy can be observed in the routines of many of the comedians who present monologues. Phyllis Diller's comment that her husband Fang "lost so much blood after cutting himself shaving that his eyes cleared up" is an example of sheer venom. In a retort attributed to Groucho Marx, "I never forget a face, but I'll make an exception in your case," the attempt to belittle is obvious. The comedian Don Rickles even makes fun of his audiences during his nightclub appearances.

Politicians are a frequent target of derisive humor. During his first months in office, Vice-President Dan Quayle must surely have gritted his teeth every time such comedians as Jay Leno or David Letterman went on the air, for their monologues were peppered with barbs directed at him. This onslaught was stimulated by some statements Quayle made that didn't quite make sense. During one television interview he said, for example, "I stand by all the misstatements I've made." The monologuists weren't content with merely reporting Quayle's actual stumbles, however. They embellished reality with quotations they made up and then attributed to him. In one instance, one of them said that Quayle had expressed satisfaction about studying Latin in high school because he was taking a trip to Latin America and would be able to speak to the people in their native language.

Among the professions, lawyers are the most common butts of offensive humor. One story making the rounds is that lawyers are now replacing white rats as the subjects of laboratory experiments for three reasons: There are more lawyers than white rats, you sometimes develop affection for a white rat, and there are still some things white rats won't do. Even places are made the subject of ridicule. In one of his monologues Jay Leno said that a group in Washington, D.C., had given up trying to set up a Christmas crèche. They had searched the city diligently, but had been unable to find either three wise men or a virgin.

Triumph of Getting the Point   A kind of triumph implicit in much comedy that is quite different from what has been discussed thus far is the feeling of superiority experienced when one sees the point of a story. This type off triumph alone seems to be an important factor in causing a laugh response to many jokes. It is one of the reasons we laugh at puns—if we do. Richard Sheridan, when asked to explain the difference between a man and woman, replied, "Madame, I cannot conceive." The feat of discerning Sheridan's double meaning gives us a feeling of satisfaction and we laugh.

The importance of letting listeners get the point on their own is illustrated by what happens when we explain a story to people who have failed to get the joke. Having been denied the feeling of triumph that comes from seeing the point themselves, listeners almost never laugh. This fact has two lessons for comedy writers. First, they must make adroit use of the technique of implica-

tion. Skillful comedy writers provide clues to ideas, but they do not directly express the ideas themselves. Audience members then put the clues together to arrive at the ideas on their own. One idea that writers for Jack Benny, an early radio and television comedian, wanted to establish was that he was incredibly stingy. In one instance they did this by showing that his home was equipped with a pay telephone to which he directed his guests when they wanted to make a call. In the situation comedy *Golden Girls,* one character trait of Rose, the character played by Betty White, was her naïveté about sexual matters. This fact was not explained directly, but was communicated by showing Rose responding innocently to double entendres and suggestive situations. The second rule for writers is that they must avoid following their punch lines with an explanation, trusting their listeners to get the point on their own.

Triumph Over Restraint   The gratification we experience when we conquer a repression is still another form of triumph that causes laughter. That is why employees at a company picnic laugh so uproariously when someone, under the special rules that come into being for such an occasion, makes fun of the boss. For the same reason, college students howl with glee at even the feeblest joke on their professor. And Protestants listen to jokes about their ministers and Catholics to jokes about their priests with particular relish. Another way of breaking restraints is to use four-letter words in comedy routines. Sometimes the word itself can cause audiences to laugh even when no joke is involved. This comedy technique cannot yet be used on regular television stations and networks, of course, but it is often employed in night clubs and on cable networks. A similar effect was attained when the situation comedy *All in the Family* broke a long-standing taboo by permitting its leading character, Archie Bunker, to use racial epithets.

The greatest triumph over repression comes when a joke contains a sexual implication, for such a reference breaks through the most rigid taboos that society can muster. For this reason, humor with sexual overtones is likely to elicit the loudest outburst of all. In fact, sexual references alone, unsupported by any other humorous element, often seem sufficient in themselves to make many people laugh. The type of triumph involved in breaking this taboo can also reinforce the effect of jokes that are funny for other reasons. Richard Sheridan's pun about the difference between men and women gains impact because it nudges into the area of the forbidden.

Surprise

A second element found in many laugh-provoking situations is surprise. Switching suddenly from one train of thought to another causes surprise and therefore provokes laughter. The changes producing this effect are of various types.

Changes in Context The novelist Arthur Koestler (*Darkness at Noon*) once said that we laugh because an event we had previously believed to belong in one context is suddenly seen to belong in another. A good example of this effect lies in the reply the actor John Barrymore made when he was asked whether Hamlet was really in love with Ophelia. "Only in the Chicago Company," Barrymore replied. Another example of this technique occurred in a *Golden Girls* episode. When a knock was heard, Blanche asked Rose to see who it was. As Rose was peering through the peephole, Dorothy asked her who was at the door. "I am," Rose replied brightly. The same kind of switch is evident in the story about the high-school girl who was filling out a college application form. In the blank in which she was supposed to list her high-school graduation date, she wrote "Bill Arnold." The former coach of the Denver Broncos, John Ralston, switched contexts when he said that he had resigned because of illness and fatigue. The fans, he explained, were sick and tired of him.

Puns Changes in context often occur because many of the words we use have more than one meaning. Using the same word to communicate two different meanings is called a pun. The following joke illustrates the technique. "Two old maids went for a tramp in the woods. The tramp got away." Sometimes puns occur accidentally when a word one person interprets figuratively is given a literal meaning by another. Told that "schools and parents ought to get closer together," a father replied, "I certainly agree because then I wouldn't have so far to walk to PTA meetings."

Puns are used more to call forth laughter than any other comedy technique. The programs of one of the early radio comedians, Ed Wynn, were composed almost entirely of a series of puns. Many writers have been habitual punsters. Shakespeare's plays are filled with puns. Even when Mercutio, a character in *Romeo and Juliet*, was stabbed, Shakespeare could not resist having him describe the effect of his wound with a pun: "Ask for me tomorrow and you shall find me a grave man."

Puns are not universally admired. They have been called the lowest form of humor. Their defenders have pointed out that this does not mean that they are beneath contempt but rather that they are the foundation on which a great deal of humor is built. Yet the questions persist: Are puns worthy of the perpetrator? Are puns really funny? Do they deserve to be greeted with laughs or with groans?

The answer seems to be that some puns are funny and some are not. The funny ones are those that help communicate a richness of meaning and effect. The unfunny ones are those that involve only a play on words but nothing much more than that. The jokes, "One Turk meeting another one said, 'I don't remember your name, but your fez is familiar,'" or the definition of a music lover as a stereotype are thin and unsatisfying. They deserve to be greeted with groans, rather than laughter.

Another characteristic of the funny pun is that it has the quality of spontaneity. It seems to spring naturally from the situation. The labored, artificial pun produced by dint of great effort and careful prearrangement is usually not very funny. "A radio announcer has small hands because he needs wee paws for station identification" is an example of a forced pun. Jean Kerr put what she says is the only pun she ever contrived in this category. It involved a remark made to a monsignor who had been waiting for many years to become a bishop, "Long time, no See."

Changes in Direction Performers and writers often make us laugh by seeming to take us down one road and then suddenly switching to another road altogether. Drama critic George Jean Nathan used this technique in one of his reviews. "This is a play for the ages—the ages from five to ten." Goodman Ace, a radio and television writer and performer, at one time wrote a weekly column for *Saturday Review*. In one of them he said that when he saw in the *Reader's Digest* that cigarettes were bad for one's health, he decided to give up reading the *Reader's Digest*.

Children often make us laugh by taking us in unexpected directions. An example was the little girl whose aunt told her that an angel had brought her baby brother. When the aunt asked whether she'd like to see the new baby, the girl replied, "First of all, I'd like to see the angel."

Changes in Meaning. Sometimes a comedian can achieve a surprise that causes laughter by leading listeners to expect a meaning and then leaving them with no meaning at all. This happens when a statement that seemed logical at first suddenly collapses into nonsense. The comment by the Canadian humorist Stephen Leacock, "The legendary Bulbecks were a fabulous race, half man, half horse, half bird," makes us laugh because it suddenly derails our rational train of thought. The horse in Groucho Marx's statement, "I'd horsewhip you if I had a horse," seems to have a certain logical significance until we recognize that it is a complete irrelevancy. The famous baseball player Yogi Berra gained his greatest fame as a fount of statements that seem meaningful on the surface but which further contemplation reveals as sheer absurdities. He is supposed to have said, for instance, "Nobody goes to that restaurant anymore. It's too crowded."

The so-called "Irish bull" is another example of humor arising from ideas whose logical inconsistencies and contradictory statements leave the listener with no meaning at all. The following "bulls" illustrate the mirth-provoking potentialities of a single idea straining to go in opposite directions at the same time. An Irish parishioner chided one of his fellows for not attending services with these words: "If you'd been in church this morning and saw how few were there, you would have been ashamed to have been absent." A distracted father on a trip with his child said to his whining offspring; "The next time I take you anywhere I'll leave you home." Then there are the words of the Irish architect: "Where will you find any modern building that has lasted as long as the old ones?"

Incongruity

A third major ingredient in many laugh-provoking situations is an incongruity. We tend to laugh at the approximation of two elements that do not naturally belong together. Another way of stating this point is to say that we laugh at the incompatible, the absurd, the outlandish, and the grotesque. Even a mere contrast may make us laugh. The fact that Stan Laurel was thin and Oliver Hardy was fat enhanced the humor of their comedies.

Incongruity and Surprise   It might be argued that incongruity should not be thought of as a separate factor in the stimulation of laughter but merely as one of the techniques that creates surprise. It is true that putting incongruous elements together is often unexpected and thus causes an audience to laugh. This was true of one of the most famous cartoons ever printed in *The New Yorker*. It showed a mother trying to persuade her child to eat his food. "It's broccoli, dear," she said. "I say it's spinach," replied the youngster, "and I say to hell with it!"[1] The adult-sounding response of the child unquestionably surprises us. Its incongruity compounds our amusement. An episode of *The Cosby Show* provides a further example of this technique. It featured the character played by Cosby, Dr. Huxtable, in a serious conversation with his very young granddaughter Olivia. To a question put to her by her grandfather, the tiny girl responded solemnly, "May I be frank?" The audience in the studio exploded in laughter.

There are jokes, however, in which the incongruity, not the surprise it may produce, appears to be the essential element. This was true of an exchange in a Ring Lardner story in which a little boy asked his father: "'Are you lost, Daddy?' 'Shut up,' he explained." It is the incongruity of the "explained" that makes us laugh. The child characters in Charles Schulz's comic strip *Peanuts* regularly use a complex language style and express ideas whose sophistica-

tion and maturity are quite out of keeping with their age. Readers are no longer surprised by this peculiarity. Its incongruity still makes them laugh, however. Sheer incongruity seemed to be at the root of a scene in an episode of *The Bob Newhart Show*. It showed a clown dressed in his full regalia being counseled by psychologist Robert Hartley (Bob Newhart). What troubled the clown was that people kept laughing at him.

Mistakes and Incongruity   Mistakes in language often create incongruities that make us laugh. A good example is the so-called spoonerism, named after a certain Reverend Spooner, who was often guilty of interchanging the syllables of words. At the end of a wedding service, he is reputed to have said, "It is kisstomary to cuss the bride." The Reverend Spooner was not the only victim of this type of error. Mel Allen, introducing a show sponsored by a tobacco company, said blithely, "It's smipe poking time, gentlemen," and Ben Grauer closed a program with the statement, "We are deepful grately for your being here." Some comedians consistently employ gross mispronunciation as a comedy technique. The most celebrated practitioner of this technique, of course, was Richard Sheridan, who in *The Rivals* created Mrs. Malaprop, a character whose very name has come to symbolize the humorous misuse of words.

Incongruity Through Exaggeration   A common technique for introducing incongruity into a situation is to exaggerate it. This is supposed to be a peculiarly American form of humor, but its use is not limited to this country. When the English writer Noel Coward sent a picture of the Venus de Milo to one of his friends and said, "This is what will happen to you if you don't stop biting your nails," he was employing this technique.

Johnny Carson often made use of exaggeration to generate laughter during his monologue on *The Tonight Show*. He might say, for example, "While I was in Europe, I stayed at the biggest hotel I've ever seen." "How big was it?" an audience member was certain to scream. "Well, it was so big that when I called room service I had to use long distance." Or Carson might comment that he had a very fat friend. "How fat is he?" someone would shout. "Well, he's so fat that he had to let out the shower curtain," Carson would respond. The pianist and raconteur Victor Borge used visual exaggeration in one of his comedy presentations now preserved on videotape. During one episode the soprano he was accompanying suddenly hit a note so high and piercing that the startled Borge fell off the piano bench. He scrambled to his feet, opened the cover of the bench and took out a seat belt.

Many people who recall the Jack Benny program remember the vault in which he kept his money. It was a masterpiece of exaggeration. Located deep beneath his home, it was approached through a long tunnel, barricaded at regular intervals with heavy metal doors, and reinforced with chains. The sound of these doors being opened one by one as Jack Benny approached his vault is one of the memorable recollections of radio. But the stroke of genius in this routine was the creation of the guard Ed, who spent his life in the abyss below, guarding Benny's money. If the audience had not laughed before, it could always be depended on to explode when lonely Ed asked plaintively, "How are things on the outside?"

Exaggeration carried to its furthest extreme becomes sheer absurdity, which also has marked power to make people laugh. Stephen Leacock's famous line that the young man "flung himself upon his horse and rode madly off in all directions" illustrates the laugh-provoking capacity of utter nonsense. The delightful inconsistency of Samuel Goldwyn in discussing the naming of a motion-picture character brings a smile to our lips. "Let's not call the hero Joe," said Sam. "Every Tom, Dick, and Harry is called Joe."

The television comedian Sid Caesar often extended a simple act into an outlandish exaggeration. As a doctor he did not merely tap the patient's chest, but his shoulder, his arm, his hand, and even the floor. Then he ended up by saying, "Your trouble is termites."

Incongruity Through Understatement

A direct opposite of the technique of exaggeration is the introduction of incongruity by understating a situation or underreacting to it. This technique is supposed to be English in its origin, and it is true that some English writers, particularly P. G. Wodehouse, were unusually skilled in employing it, but Americans have also used understatement with telling effect. When Mark Twain said, "The reports of my death are grossly exaggerated," he was employing understatement.

The technique of underreacting to a situation is akin in its effect to that of understatement. The comedians of the silent film era were notable for their use of it. One of Buster Keaton's characteristic techniques was to keep a stony, fixed expression on his face no matter what indignities or perils were being visited upon him. Another favorite comedy device of the movies was to stand unresisting while someone committed mayhem upon one's person.

One of the early Woody Allen movies, *Take the Money and Run*, provides a good example of the technique of underreaction. The inept character played by Allen decides to rob a bank. The note he shoves through the window says that he has a gun, but instead of responding to the threat he poses, the teller follows her normal procedure by saying that she will have to get the manager's okay before she can release any funds. The manager continues the pattern of underreaction to the menace of the situation by pointing out that Allen has misspelled some of the words in his holdup note. Allen is attempting to defend his literacy when the police arrive.

Combining the Techniques

We have pointed out that in most laugh-provoking situations we can find an element of triumph, surprise, or incongruity. It is also clear that in many of them we can find more than one of these elements. As we have seen, the introduction of an incongruity often creates surprise. It may also add other elements. A small-town newspaper once carried the following news item: "A traveler would have missed the noon train yesterday, had he not stepped on a peach pit at the head of the depot stairs." Understatement is the primary reason for the humor of this statement but it also contains other laugh-producing factors—the use of implication which permits readers the triumph of fashioning the image of what happened in their own minds and the vision of a person falling ignominiously down a flight of steps, suggesting triumph in a fight.

The multiplication of the comedy elements in a situation often enhances its power to produce mirth. A line from a script by Fred Allen, one of the pioneer radio comedians, illustrates this fact. In one program Allen commented, "Next Sunday the Reverend Dr. Jones will preach on 'Skiing on the Sabbath' or 'Are Our Young Women Backsliding on Their Week-ends?'" This line, first of all, arouses a ludicrous picture in the listener's mind. Some degree of surprise also develops as the listener perceives that the last line has a double meaning. In addition, there are two elements of triumph: one is the satisfaction that arises from divining the play on words involved in the two puns, and the second is

victory over repression inherent in the implied reference to a portion of the human anatomy whose mention in the period the Fred Allen program was being broadcast was usually taboo.

VARIETIES OF HUMOR

The term *humor* is often used as an overall term that covers all of the material that makes us laugh. Humor, however, can be divided into several categories, one of which is also called humor, particularly when it is compared with wit. One characteristic of wit is abruptness. The payoff comes quickly and the material exists mainly for that final funny line, which is often the only part of the routine that provokes laughter. Humor, in contrast, is longer and develops in a more leisurely manner. Laughter bubbles along the way, rising gradually in intensity until the final laugh explodes. Peggy Noonan, a speech writer for Presidents Ronald Reagan and George Bush, has said, "Wit penetrates; humor envelops."

Another characteristic of wit is that it is often derisive. Prime examples of wit, in the eyes of many, are those occasions when one person cuts down another in a dazzling exhibition of word play. Humor, on the other hand, is usually gentler, more human, and more understanding. Besides making us laugh, it often provides meaningful insights into the nature of human experience. Humor may thus be considered deeper and more lasting in its effect than wit. The line, "It should be the function of medicine to make us die young as late as possible" in addition to making us smile, also may cause us to think. So, too, may the title a speaker gave to his lecture, "Is there intelligent life on Earth?" We move from wit to humor when comedy goes beyond the creation of mere gags to establish characters and ideas of enduring significance.

Again, the film work of Woody Allen illustrates this progression. *Take the Money and Run* strung together a series of gags which were funny in themselves, but which provoked little appreciation or understanding of people and events. The main character's inept attempts at crime produced many laughs, but he remained a caricature who lacked real-life dimension and depth. Allen's later movies, such as *Annie Hall* and *Manhattan,* though still providing laughs, also presented a number of inimitable and complex characters and portrayed in moving detail the relationships among them.

Dorothy Parker, the short-story writer and essayist, made a further distinction between wit and the wisecrack. She said, "Wit has truth in it; wisecracking is simply calisthenics with words." Other categories of humor are parody, satire, and burlesque. Parody is an imitation of a serious work for humorous effect. Satire exposes or ridicules human folly. Jay Leno and Mark Russell are among the preeminent contemporary satirists. Their targets are often the foibles and misadventures of political figures. A burlesque is a presentation that mocks or ridicules a person or event. It is usually broader in its approach than satire. Many of the sketches produced on *Saturday Night Live* are of the burlesque variety.

QUESTIONS AND PROJECTS

1. Analyze the jokes in a stand-up comedy routine for the elements of triumph, surprise and incongruity.
2. Carry out this same procedure in analyzing a situation comedy.
3. Watch some current situation comedies to determine whether they depend primarily on gags or situations to create laughs.
4. Who among the current stand-up comedians do you think are the funniest, and why?
5. A secretary to a psychiatrist once told her boss that someone who claimed to be invisible was waiting to see him. "Tell him I can't see him," the psychiatrist said. Do you think this joke is funny? If so, can you discern the elements that made you laugh?
6. Watch an episode of *Saturday Night Live* and decide whether the various episodes can be categorized as parody, burlesque, or satire.

NOTES

1. Caption for a Carl Rose drawing, Copyright © 1928, 1956, *The New Yorker.*

Creating comedy material is one of the most demanding tasks writers can face, particularly when it must be produced on a regular schedule. Generations of comedy writers have testified to the anguish this effort entails. When they reach an impasse, they cannot turn to a magic formula whose use guarantees the creation of material certain to make audiences laugh. Nothing can take the place of an instinctive feel for what is funny. Knowing standard approaches to creating comedy, however, can help writers make the most of the talent they possess. They should also recognize that different types of comedy confront them with different types of challenges. Finally, a group of criteria for evaluating their work can help them sharpen its effectiveness.

CHAPTER
17

CREATING COMEDY MATERIAL

Television is a medium of entertainment which permits millions of people to listen to the same joke at the same time and yet remain lonesome.
T. S. Eliot (1888–1965)

TYPES OF COMEDY

Humorous ideas can be communicated both by what people do and what they say. In the silent-film era, comedians had to rely almost entirely on physical action to make audiences laugh, though some jokes were conveyed by means of subtitles. Charlie Chaplin, the premier comedian of the period, was funny because of what he *did.* The development of sound for motion pictures opened the door to speech, of course. In his movies Bob Hope produced much of his comedy through what he *said,* though he also used some physical action. Most comedy uses a mix of these two elements.

In the television field, the major comedy forms are situation comedy, sketches, and stand-up routines. Those who write situation comedies must not only be masters of the art of writing jokes, but they must also be able to create characters and a plot, build suspense, enlist audience sympathy for the characters, make those characters believable within the confines of the comedy idea, construct a story that immediately engages the attention of viewers, carry them forward on a rising plane of interest to a climax, and provide a sound and satisfying resolution.

Writers of this form use two main comedy techniques to generate laughs—the gag or wisecrack and the development of funny situations. Most situation comedies use both, but some emphasize one technique more than the other. There were few gags on *The Cosby Show,* for example. The humor arose mainly from the mirth-provoking interactions of the various members of the Huxtable family. Each episode of *Golden Girls,* in contrast, is replete with gags. In one of them, Blanche said disparagingly to Rose, "Your hair looks as if it has been colorized by Ted Turner." *Cheers* uses both gags and funny situations. The entry of Norm, the rotund occupant of the corner bar stool, is often marked by a gag. In one instance he was asked as he came in, "What are you up to, Norm?" His answer, "My ideal weight if I were eleven feet tall."

A characteristic of the gag is that it is funny even when it is taken out of context. This is not true of lines that depend on the development of situations for their humor. They are often very funny but the humor can be appreciated only if the situation is known. Consider these two lines which were delivered near the conclusion of an episode of *Maude.* A man said to a woman, "Glad to have known you." The woman replied, "It was my pleasure." The studio audience exploded in laughter. The situation that produced this reaction began with the fact that the woman, played by Rue McClanahan, did not know that her husband had an identical twin brother. When he showed up while her husband was away, she took him for her husband and went to bed with him. Thus the lines that concluded their encounter vibrated with funny double meanings.

Another type of comedy script depends on a series of sketches to create laughs. Usually there is no overall idea that unites them; emphasizing gags, each sketch features characters and situations completely separate from the others. They are usually more exaggerated than those found in the weekly situation comedies and often approach the grotesque, as in the *Saturday Night Live* series. Sometimes programs of this nature include music and dance as well as comedy sketches, in which case they are known as variety programs.

Sketch comedy is not nearly so prominent as it once was. Besides being used on *Saturday Night Live,* it survives on occasional Bob Hope specials. Carol Burnett, whose sketch program was a popular TV attraction of the 1970s, tried the form again in 1991 but the series was canceled after four weeks.

The practitioners of stand-up comedy differ widely in their approaches. Some try to maintain continuity in their presentations by building one idea on another. Those who talk about family life or relate personal experiences often tell complete stories. Others dart from one comic idea to another without trying to establish any connection between them. The monologues of Steven Wright and Jay Leno exemplify this approach. Stand-up comedians also differ widely in the material they use. The idiosyncrasies of spouses figure prominently in the monologues of Phyllis Diller and Alan King.

The humor of Leno and Mark Russell finds its inspiration in news events, particularly those involving political figures. This type of humor is called topical.

THE WRITING ROUTINE

The way in which comedy material is produced differs to some extent depending on the nature of the comedy itself. Those who produce monologues for stand-up comedians face challenges somewhat different from those confronting the creators of situation comedy, for example. The basic objective for all, however, is the same—making people laugh.

Team Writing

One condition that distinguishes the writing of comedy from the writing of many other types of scripts is that in most instances the material is created by teams rather than by a single person. When Jack Benny first went on the air he had only one writer. He soon expanded the number to four. Bob Hope regularly employed seven writers to prepare material not only for his television programs but also for his appearances before servicemen, at dinners, and at benefits. Fifteen writers contributed material to his film *The Princess and the Pirate.* The credits for situation comedies almost always list more than one writer. The reason for the team approach seems to be that creating material that will make people laugh is difficult for a person sitting alone at a typewriter. The presence of other minds is required to create an atmosphere congenial to the invention of jokes, and a writer needs to bounce comedy ideas at other people to test their effectiveness. Their reactions, in turn, trigger new comedy inventions, and thus a script is slowly built, one joke inspiring another. Teams may work together from the beginning, or each member may work independently on a specific part of the script. Usually they put it all together in a final meeting.

Writing Gags or Jokes

Making Connections   The first responsibility of gag writers is to incorporate in their material one or more of the elements of humor discussed in the previous chapter. The second is to lead audiences into making a connection between what the comedian or performer says and an item of information known by the audience. This connection is what is known as the *point* of the joke. Grasping it gives the listeners satisfaction and is a primary reason for their laughter. If comedians telegraph this point or explain it, audiences are not likely to laugh. Listeners must be permitted to arrive at the point themselves from clues the comedian provides.

A joke told by Leno during one of his monologues illustrates the process. It was based on two events that had recently been in the news. The first was that President George Bush had sufficiently recovered from a slight heart disorder to resume his normal exercise program. The second was that Bush's then chief of staff, John Sununu, had improperly used a government limousine to travel to New York to see his dentist. Leno's comment was, "President Bush went jogging today. He had to. John Sununu was using the car." The audience laughed because it made the connection between this comment and the two news events we have described.

Often jokes connect, not with news events, but with items of general information. In one of his monologues Johnny Carson told about a clown who was trying to escape from prison. The trouble was that when the spotlight hit him, he tried to sweep it up. And when he finally did reach the getaway car, 26 clowns were already in

it. To get the point to these jokes, the audience must connect them with two of the routines clowns use in their circus performances. A commonly known geographical fact provides the point for a Woody Allen joke: "My girl friend was a streetwalker in Venice, but she drowned."

The Importance of Audience Knowledge

If audiences don't know the facts on which the joke is based, they obviously won't laugh. A person unaware that Venice is a canal city would only be puzzled by Allen's remark. In one of his books, Peter DeVries comments: "Love is an art. I thought you might notice my craft ebbing." Most people are not likely to laugh on hearing this joke, although its self-deprecatory tone may cause them to smile. The few who know that a German neurologist named Richard von Krafft-Ebing wrote a notable book about sex can be counted on to laugh uproariously, however. They make a connection that escapes most people and satisfaction at their own erudition enhances their reaction.

In the movie *The In-Laws,* Peter Falk played a character who, as a CIA agent, was given to concocting outlandish schemes. In one scene a mention of the Bay of Pigs operation brought from Falk the proud comment, "That was my idea." The young people in the audience with no memory of this event didn't laugh. The older people, remembering what a catastrophe the 1961 Bay of Pigs operation was, guffawed. Johnny Carson, in a monologue, said that when Abraham Lincoln rose to give his speech at Gettysburg he originated the phrase now heard at Academy Award presentations, "May I have the envelope, please." A stony silence greeted this joke. The audience wasn't familiar with the historical fable that Lincoln wrote his speech on the back of an envelope while he was traveling by train to Gettysburg. Carson tried to rescue the situation by reminding his listeners of this fact, but it was too late. The audience members didn't laugh because they had failed to make the connection on their own.

Double-barreled Jokes Most monologuists feel that they have reached the pinnacle of success when they manage to squeeze more than one laugh out of the same comic idea. The following joke illustrates the technique:

Margaret Thatcher told George Bush that before appointing people to her cabinet, she gave them a little intelligence test. She asked John Major, for example, to answer the riddle: "He's not my brother, but he is my father's son. Who is he?" "He's me," Major answered and was promptly appointed to the Thatcher cabinet.

George Bush decided to give Dan Quayle the same test. Quayle responded nervously, "Let me get back to you," and then called Henry Kissinger. "He's me," Kissinger said when he heard the riddle. "It's Henry Kissinger," Quayle told George Bush. "No, no, you stupid ninny," Bush replied. "It's John Major."

The Quayle reference to Henry Kissinger will get the first laugh. An even bigger one is likely to follow when Bush corrects him.

Switching Jokes The demand for comedy material is so prodigious that writers must develop special techniques for creating it. Each monologue presented by Jay Leno, for example, requires the writing of from 15 to 20 new jokes. Often writers build resources by establishing a file of jokes. Milton Berle claims to have collected more than six million of them. Usually these jokes are not recycled in their original forms, since they would be recognized by many people as old jokes. To disguise them a process called "switching" is used. This means appropriating the basic point of the joke but casting it in another context. Consider this joke for example.

A woman told her friend that her husband was suffering from the delusion that he was a chicken. "Why don't you take him to a psychiatrist and have him cured?" the friend asked. "I'd like to," the woman replied, "but then what would we do for eggs?"

This basic joke has been used many times with many variations.

Many switches have been worked on the joke that is often looked on as the prototype of all jokes: "Who was that lady I saw you with last night? That was no lady, that was my wife." There is the musician's version: "Was that an oboe I saw you playing last night? That was no oboe, that was my fife"; the kitchen version: "Was that a ladle I saw you using last night? That was no ladle, that was my knife"; the magician's version: "Who was that lady I saw you saw last night? That was no lady, that was my half-sister." And then there is this shortened version: "Who was that lady I saw you outwit last night?"

At times, it is the form rather than the substance of a joke that is recycled. The previously noted comment of former football coach John Ralston, "I retired because of illness and fatigue; the fans were sick and tired of me," has its counterpart in Milton Berle's gag: "The company accountant is shy and retiring. He's shy a quarter of a million dollars. That's why he's retiring." Sometimes comic ideas are switched by reversing them. In the early silent film *Sherlock, Jr.,* Buster Keaton became part of the movie he was projecting. Woody Allen reversed this idea in *The Purple Rose of Cairo* when Tom, the character played by Jeff Daniels, walked out of the screen and into the theater.

Comedy Topics

Writers often use the same topics over and over again. Their nature changes with the years. At one time references to Brooklyn in

New York, to Hamtramck in Detroit, and to Pismo Beach in California could draw laughs. So could jokes about mothers-in-law, old maids, and women's hats. These topics are now outdated but jokes about marriage and particularly about the peccadilloes of husbands and wives still persist. References to spinach used to produce laughs. Because of George Bush's expressed distaste for it, broccoli has now replaced spinach as a comedy topic.

Repeating Jokes

Sometimes writers desperate for comedy material simply use jokes over again without bothering to switch them or present them from a new angle. It is a common practice for film comedians to use routines that work successfully in more than one film. In one of his monologues, Henny Youngman said that a girl had kept him awake one night knocking on his door. Finally he had to get up and let her out. This joke has also been used by the writers of situation comedies.

Writing Situation Comedies

Conceiving the Series Idea The first requirement for writing a successful situation comedy is to develop a basic frame or premise around which all of the episodes in the series can turn. It obviously must be one that has a significant laugh-producing potential. One of the situation comedies now viewed as a classic of the form is *The Dick Van Dyke Show.* Its creator, Carl Reiner, achieved a master stroke when he made three of its characters writers for a TV comedy show. This provided an automatic springboard for putting gags into the script. Many situation comedies are based on the activities and relationships in different types of families, among them: *The Cosby Show, Roseanne, Married with Children,* and *The Simpsons.* Another situation-comedy classic,

All in the Family, created a fruitful source of comedy by putting blue-collar, right-wing Archie Bunker in juxtaposition with his ultra-liberal son-in-law. *Empty Nest* found its fun in the difficulties that develop when older children remain at home. *Full House* chronicled the attempts of three unattached males to cope with a houseful of little girls. A similar idea underlay the film *Three Men and a Baby* and its sequel *Three Men and a Little Lady.*

In some situation comedies the unifying element is a place. This was true of *The Mary Tyler Moore Show,* in which most of the action occurred in a TV newsroom, and of *Cheers,* whose locale was a Boston bar. A unique entry in the field was *Seinfeld,* which combined situation comedy with humorous monologues. The title character used the experiences portrayed in the dramatic portions of the program as a foundation for the jokes presented in his stand-up routines.

Sometimes an unexpected development takes a series in a direction different from the one originally envisioned. *Family Matters* began as a program that focused on a Chicago cop and his family. Then a character who was scheduled at first for just one appearance began to take over. He was Steve Urkel, the nerdish character played by Jaleel White. The producers soon recognized his comedy potential and brought him back again and again. With each appearance his role increased until his antics became the show's centerpiece.

Conceiving the Episode Idea Once the overall frame for a series has been defined, writers must come up with a premise for each of its episodes. If this core idea has enough laugh-producing possibilities, the writing of the show itself may be a relatively easy task. One idea that has inspired episodes in a number of situation comedies is the inadequacy with which some husbands respond when their pregnant wives go into labor. This idea was at the center of two of the most memorable episodes from the *I Love Lucy* and *Dick Van Dyke* series. Another *Dick Van Dyke Show* that almost wrote itself was one in which an artist painted the face of Dick's wife onto the body of a nude woman and then displayed the picture in the city's art museum. Dick's desperate efforts to keep his friends from seeing the painting provided the fun.

A show some have characterized as the most hilarious ever written was presented as an episode in the *Mary Tyler Moore* series. Its success arose directly from the brilliance of its concept. The somewhat macabre story began with the fact that a rogue elephant had killed the station's clown Chuckles while he was walking in a parade dressed as a peanut. To Mary's horror, the newsroom staff began making jokes about the tragedy, even to saying that it was a good thing no one else in the parade was dressed as a peanut because "you can't stop with just one."

Mary denounced them for their unfeeling reaction to their colleague's sad end. During the funeral, however, when the minister began describing how Chuckles had died it was Mary who could not control her laughter while her newsroom companions maintained a respectful silence.

It is not enough, of course, merely to invent a premise for a show. A script must still be written that will take full advantage of its laugh-producing potential. The episodes in the situation comedy *Dear John,* which began its fourth year on network television in 1991 as an NBC offering, usually revolved around the title character's misadventures with women. In one of them John Lacey, the English teacher played by Judd Hirsch, went out on a blind date, ending the encounter with what he thought was a one-night stand in his apartment. To his dismay, he soon discovered that the woman had in fact fallen for him, and, believing that her feelings were reciprocated, had moved into his apartment. She even went so far as to invite her mother for a visit and called in a repairman to fix the TV set. Most of the script dealt with John's effort to get rid of her. This idea might have been enough to sustain the story. The writers took it one step further, however. As the closing scene of the script reveals, they produced even more merriment by suddenly reversing the situation.

Dear John: "John's Blind Date"
ACT TWO, SCENE J

FADE IN:

INT. JOHN'S HALLWAY/LIVING ROOM—THAT NIGHT
(John, Louise, Kate)

(THE ELEVATOR DOORS OPEN AND JOHN, LOUISE AND KATE STEP OUT. THEY CROSS TO JOHN'S DOOR.)

> JOHN
> I really appreciate you guys helping me out like this.

> LOUISE
> Think nothing of it.

                           KATE
           Now just let us in and wait out here, while
           we talk to her.
(JOHN PUTS HIS KEY IN THE DOOR.)

                          LOUISE
           I hope she's decent.

                           JOHN
           If she was decent, she would've left last
           week.

(JOHN OPENS THE DOOR. KATE AND LOUISE ENTER AND CLOSE THE DOOR BEHIND THEM.
AFTER A BEAT, HE TRIES TO LISTEN AT THE DOOR. AFTER ANOTHER BEAT, THE DOOR
OPENS AND KATE POKES HER HEAD OUT.)

                           KATE
              John.

(JOHN FOLLOWS KATE INTO THE APARTMENT. LOUISE ENTERS FROM THE KITCHEN.)

                          LOUISE
           I'm afraid she's not here, John.

                           JOHN
           That's impossible. Suzanne?

(HE CROSSES INTO BEDROOM. KATE CROSSES TO TV AND PICKS UP A FOLDED PIECE OF
STATIONERY. A BEAT AND HE RE-ENTERS.)

                           JOHN
           Her clothes are gone.

                           KATE
           Oh, John . . .

(SHE BECKONS HIM OVER.)

                           JOHN
           What? . . .

                           KATE
(READING NOTE)
              "Dear John . . . "

(JOHN REACTS AS WE HEAR THE FIRST TWO WORDS OF THE "DEAR JOHN" THEME SONG.)

SFX: "DEAR JOHN" THEME SONG

> JOHN
> No, no! Stop it! Not another Dear John let-
> ter. Not again. I don't wanna hear this.

> KATE
> "I never wanted to hurt you. But when I
> first set eyes on . . ."

(KATE TRIES TO SMOTHER HER LAUGHTER.)

> LOUISE
> Kate, really. This is not funny.

(LOUISE GRABS THE NOTE. AFTER A BEAT, SHE TRIES TO SMOTHER HER LAUGHTER.)

> LOUISE (CONT'D)
> She left you for the TV repairman.

(THEY BOTH LAUGH.)

> JOHN
> Oh, terrific. You think this is funny?!

> KATE
> But there's good news. He's not charging
> you for the repairs.

(THEY ARE NOW IN HYSTERICS.)

> JOHN
> Thanks for your support.

> KATE
> John, you wanted her out and she's out.

> JOHN
> But not like this. She dumped me. Isn't
> there any justice? It was my turn to dump.

> LOUISE
> Oh, John. She probably didn't know.

> JOHN
> It's not fair. How could she walk away

from me like this? I told that woman I
loved her!

                KATE
    I knew it, I knew it, I knew it.

(THE TWO WOMEN HIGH-FIVE IN FRONT OF JOHN. HE REACTS, SHEEPISHLY, AS WE:)

FADE OUT

END OF SHOW

Revising the Script   Scripts for situation comedies go through a number of drafts before production begins. Poor jokes are eliminated or improved, new jokes are added, and the whole show is sharpened or polished. Sometimes new writers are brought in to "punch up" the material, as the saying goes. This process of revision goes on even during the rehearsal period. Writers often stay up through the night reworking material that the actual reading of lines has shown to be deficient. The scripts for *The Cosby Show* regularly underwent changes that affected 50 to 60 percent of the content after rehearsal began. In fact, some of the lines spoken by Bill Cosby did not reach their final form until he said them during the taping.

Writing Sketches

Much of what we have said about the writing of situation comedy can also be applied to the writing of sketches. The key step is the selection of the premise. If it is one that can produce funny developments, the writers are well on the road to success. Even the best of writers, however, are not likely to squeeze humor out of a premise that lacks comedy potential.

One series that still features comedy sketches is *Saturday Night Live.* In one program an impersonation of President George Bush talking about the 1991 recession turned into a single-person sketch. The premise was that to encourage the retail buying he believed would cure the nation's economic ills, the president became a pitchman for a variety of products—a Salad Shooter, a beaded car seat cushion, even a six-pack of beer. Another sketch in the same program was a take-off on support groups which bring people together to talk about such serious personal problems as a painful divorce or the loss of loved ones. The problem for those in the SNL sketch, however, was that they were all suffering from bad haircuts. The incongruity implicit in these two premises—a president pitching products on television and a support group treating a trifling matter with deadly seriousness—provided the script writers with ample opportunities to generate laughs.

EVALUATING COMEDY MATERIAL

The forms of comedy are so diverse and the art of humor so complex that distinguishing the qualities characteristic of effective comedy writing is a difficult task. Still, there are some questions that writers can ask about the first draft of a script that can help to measure its comic potentialities and provide ideas for improving them.

Basic Elements

Does the comedy material manifest one or more of the elements that constitute the roots of all laughter? A sketch that fails to reflect some element of triumph, incongruity, or surprise is not likely to amuse. If it reflects all three of them, it is almost certain to be funny. Sometimes writers create material that masquerades as humor but which falls flat because it contains none of these elements or contains an element that is too feeble in its effect. Merely using a word in two different ways, for example, does not necessarily create a joke, as the following sequence indicates.

HE: I really like roast beef and potatoes best.
SHE: Why don't you try something different occasionally—broiled quail, for instance.
HE: I quail at the thought.

Switching the meaning of the word "quail" in this exchange incorporates very little surprise and suggests no incongruity or triumph. It is not a joke. We may smile but only because the speaker has shown a little ingenuity and not because he has appealed to our comic sense. On the other hand, consider this example.

SHE: Do you like bathing beauties?
HE: I don't know. I never bathed any.

This is a joke because the switch in the meaning of the word involves a major element of surprise.

The surprise, moreover, is accompanied by the suggestion of an idea that is usually suppressed, thus adding an element of triumph.

Arrangement

Is the material arranged in a way that will secure the maximum possible effect? A joke is a delicate entity which a clumsy arrangement can easily damage. One thing that broadcast writers must be particularly careful about is to put the point of the story at the very end of the last line of the exchange, or part of the story may be covered by laughter

that is triggered too soon. This point can be illustrated by rewriting an episode from a Jack Benny program which took place while Jack and Mary Livingstone were sitting beside a swimming pool. As originally written the radio program dialogue went like this:

JACK: It's a little embarrassing to say the least, but your bathing suit is a bit snug and skimpy.
MARY: If you don't like it, go in and take it off.

Consider what would happen if Mary's line had been written as follows:

MARY: Go in and take it off if you don't like it.

This version might still get a laugh but it would likely be a bit muffled and indecisive. The point has come too soon to permit a clean reaction.

Giving the point away before the audience has had a chance to build up any expectation is another type of error. There is a story about a man who went to see a doctor because he was tired and run down.

DOCTOR: There's really nothing the matter with you. All you need is a little relaxation. Why don't you take the night off and go see Jay Leno?
MAN: But I AM Jay Leno.

Consider what would happen if you told the audience before this dialogue exchange that the man who came into the doctor's office was Jay Leno. All other elements would remain the same, but you would ruin the joke by depriving the audience of the opportunity to be surprised.

Economy

Have you presented the material with the maximum economy? Unnecessary words can clutter a story so much that its effect will be seriously damaged. When George Burns told this story—"Two friends of mine have had eight sets of twins. They make book-ends for a living. It's affected their whole lives"—the audience members began laughing in the middle of the last sentence. They didn't need it to see the point. This doesn't mean that you cannot condense too much. Some stories gain much of their effect from the repetition of certain key phrases or ideas. To eliminate this repetition might blunt most of the joke's point.

Naturalness

Do your jokes spring from the situation as if there were an inevitability about them, as if they were happening in spite of themselves, so to speak? Nothing is more inimical to the production of laughter than a labored, contrived effect. As we have noted before, one reason we often groan at puns rather than laugh at them is their air of ponderous contrivance. Yet a writer cannot gain the qualities of effortlessness and spontaneity in comedy writing without much hard work. That is the paradox. Intense labor is needed to arrive at an unlabored effect.

Clarity

Is your material completely clear? In no other form of writing is complete understanding by the audience so essential to arriving at the ultimate effect. There will be no laughter at all if people do not understand. As we pointed out earlier in this chapter, one requirement is that the audience know the item of information with which the joke connects. Another is that the joke be clear in its spoken form. Most people need to see the following joke in print to get its point. "You can tell that overweight is hereditary. It shows up in your jeans."

Suddenness

Can your audience see what you mean instantly? Suddenness is an essential attribute of comic writing. If an audience must ponder before seeing the point, the laugh is lost. The triple pun in the story about the Texas boys who called their ranch Focus because it's where the sons raise meat (sun's rays meet) is probably too complex to generate immediate laughter. This is also true of the joke about the mother who belonged to an organization called DAM, Mothers Against Dyslexia. The audience must know to begin with that dyslexics frequently reverse the order of words. Then they must connect this knowledge with the reversal in the joke. Ogden Nash's dazzling play on words in the following lines may be almost too clever for audiences to appreciate soon enough to laugh:

> I am a conscientious man, when I throw rocks at sea birds I leave no tern unstoned,
> I am a meticulous man, and when I portray baboons I leave no stern untoned![1]

Appropriateness

Is your comedy writing appropriate to the situation? This question has a number of possible applications. If you are writing for a specific comedian, you must write material that fits his or her style. The gags of a Bob Hope, for example, all seem to have been invented by the same mind, so consistent in style are they, and yet through the years many different writers have produced them. If the comedy vehicle is drama, the humor must be appropriate to the characters and the situation. It is true that we allow comedy writers a little more leeway in this regard than we do the writer of serious drama, but complete irrelevancy is undesirable, and the best jokes are those inspired by the character or situation. The medium of transmittal or the locale in which humor is produced are also factors that affect its appropriateness. Audiences in comedy clubs tolerate material far rawer in its content than audiences of network television are willing to accept, for example. Comedy that goes too far for the situation in which it occurs may shock rather than amuse. With the boundaries of what can and cannot be said constantly changing in a society undergoing a revolution in mores, writers must have an extraordinary sensitivity to what falls within the bounds of good taste and acceptability and what exceeds it.

QUESTIONS AND PROJECTS

1. Listen to a stand-up comedian and identify the items of information that connect with the material being presented.
2. View a number of situation comedies and state the premise for each show in one sentence. Decide whether these premises were fruitful sources of comedy values.
3. Write the funniest gag line you can think of for each of the following straight lines: (a) My brother is so lazy that . . . ; (b) My uncle is so rich that . . . ; (c) My aunt is such a hypochondriac that. . . .
4. Write three switches on each of the following jokes:
   (a) One man told another that he played chess with his dog every night. "You mean to say your dog plays chess," said the first man, "Why that's wonderful." "What's so wonderful?" replied the first man, "I beat him regularly two out of three."
   (b) A dying woman called her husband to the bedside and said, "Dave, I know you don't like my sister Ellen but I hope you'll invite her to ride with you to the funeral." The husband, much moved, replied, "I'll do it for you, Dorothy, but it'll spoil my day."
5. Write a three-minute monologue for a stand-up comedian.

NOTES

1. From the poem, "Everybody's Mind to Me a Kingdom Is or A Great Big Wonderful World Its," from *The Private Dining Room* (1953). Reprinted by permission of Little, Brown and Company and Curtis Brown, Ltd., New York.

PART

V
———

Writing for
Children

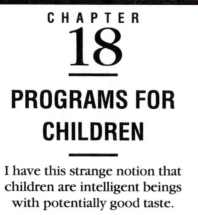

CHAPTER
18

PROGRAMS FOR CHILDREN

I have this strange notion that children are intelligent beings with potentially good taste.

ROBERT KEESHAN
(CAPTAIN KANGAROO)

Young boys and girls are among the most avid consumers of television programs. While a wide range of social factors influences the amount of time individual children spend before their television sets, researchers agree that by the time children enter kindergarten they have become purposeful viewers, committing approximately three hours a day to favorite shows. Pre-adolescents grow increasingly dependent on television for entertainment and surrogate companionship. By the time children graduate from high school, they have spent more time watching television than in any other single activity except sleeping.

The effect of spending so much time watching television and the influence programs may have on children is a subject of public concern. Television has been attacked on a number of counts, among them that it is a passive experience which lures children from more fruitful activities; that it warps values by presenting a distorted picture of people and events; and that it causes emotional damage which may even lead to juvenile delinquency. Television is criticized also because its tremendous potentialities are dedicated primarily to attaining commercial purposes, instead of being used to enlarge the child's vision of the world. The authors share the opinion that those who write programs for children bear a particular responsibility toward this most impressionable of audiences. It is our hope they will respond to the wisdom of one of the foremost scholars on the effects of televised violence, Professor George Gerbner, long-time dean of the Annenberg School of Communications at the University of Pennsylvania. Gerbner says: "Whoever tells the stories controls the culture. And television tells most of the stories to most of the people most of the time."

Much of the agitation, it is true, is aroused not by programs written especially for children but by adult-oriented programs that children view. This only deepens the responsibility of those who direct the programs they write specifically to audiences of young people. They need not accept all of the objections to current programming as valid, but they must at least be alert to the practices that some people have found questionable. They also need some understanding of childhood itself and a knowledge of the program content and writing techniques best adapted to meeting the child's unique needs.

This discussion focuses on television because it has replaced both theatrical movies and radio as the medium for presenting material specifically designed for young children. Among moviemakers, the Walt Disney organization regularly produces films adapted to the needs and interests of preteen youngsters. Most of these movies are also shown eventually on the Disney television channel. The Children's Television Workshop and Nickelodeon are among the most famous and prolific suppliers of children's quality television programs. Radio, once a patron of children's dramatic imaginings, no longer figures as a program supplier for young audiences. What has become a growing commercial market, however, is the recording of stories on audiotape, as well as videotape.

THE NATURE OF CHILDHOOD

In answering the question "What is a child?" it is certainly too naïve to say that a child is simply a little adult. On the other hand, many of the attributes that characterize adult life exist in embryo in the child.

Limited Experience

Some of the differences between adults and children are obvious to everyone. A young child clearly lacks the large reservoir of experience that is characteristic of an adult. One consequence of direct concern to the writer is the limited vocabulary of children. Another is that they cannot discern relationships which may be perfectly clear to an older person. They tend to see items in an experience as separate and unconnected and they may have special problems in understanding time sequences. They are primarily aware of the present and their own existence in it, and it is difficult for them to conceive of a world of which they were not a part. The concept of future time is even more difficult for them to comprehend. Their lack of sophistication also causes them to assign roles to people as they are familiar with them in real life, and violations of these concepts may create confusion. Stories that portray children carrying out heroic actions may perplex them, for they see children as relatively powerless persons who are dependent on others for their well-being.

Seeing Life in Simple Terms

A second major difference between adults and children is that children see the world in essentially simple terms instead of in the complex terms of adults. Children do not comprehend the shades and nuances of character that are actually true to life; rather, they see people in absolute colors as being good or bad and they understand only the most obvious of motives. They also tend to see events literally, often through a filter of feelings induced by a range of experiences, among them: inclusion, exclusion, dependency, independence, kindness, cruelty, protection and abandonment.

Another quality in children is their attachment to nature. Environmentalists at heart, they personify living things, especially trees and animals. The prolific Dr. Seuss brought to this reality a formula for success. Shel Silverstein's *The Giving Tree* likewise has stood the test of a time. The story begins with an apple tree and a little boy loving one another. The tree's love remains constant, while the boy becomes fickle and demanding with the passage of years, taking everything and returning nothing other than the trust that the tree will provide for all his needs. While adults may find opportunities to point out to their offspring the boy's selfishness and the tree's failure to discipline him, children will delight in the security of the tree's constant, caring presence in the boy's life.

Writing for children differs most significantly from writing for adults in that programs targeting adults draw basically on the same vocabulary and reservoir of understandings common to grown-ups, whether they are 25 or 80 years of age. If writing for children embraces ages two to 15, then that task addresses the most diverse staircase in human development. Wonder and curiosity increase, as does the need to test limits of expression and behavior. Vocabularies expand, attention spans increase, and interests change. As they progress through childhood they will find themselves moving away from *Sesame Street* and *Mister Rogers' Neighborhood* which invite them to participate in learning activities. As they advance through elementary and junior high school, they will be drawn to *The Wonder Years* and *DeGrassi High,* which allow viewers to observe how their peers handle relationships and solve related problems.

Accepting Fantasy on Its Own Terms

Very young children do not realize that happenings in a fantasy are only make believe; they accept them as true. Millions of children for a period in their lives actually believe in that most fantastic of creatures, Santa Claus. A child seeing a man shot in a movie may believe that a man really had to be shot to make the scene. Some children even think the characters in a television program are little people who live and sleep in the set behind the screen.

Young children have no problem in equalizing different forms of life: human, animal, inanimate and supernatural. Dorothy and her dog Toto, when uprooted by a cyclone from their home in Kansas, accept the companionship of a brainless scarecrow, a heartless tin man, and a cowardly lion. Together they travel the yellow brick road in search of *The Wizard of Oz.* Dorothy is able to eliminate her greatest adversary, the wicked witch, by dousing her with a pail of water. This "solution" raises the question about violence in fantasy. Does Dorothy's action make her a killer? In *Hansel and Gretel* children are inclined to cheer when the vicious witch dies howling in the oven. Is this acceptable? Should children be brought into the world of *Cinderella,* whose misery stems from every child's worst nightmare, the death of her mother? Should they be allowed to ponder the wicked stepmother left in control by an absentee father, or the heartless stepsisters who treat her cruelly? And is it wise to make Cinderella dependent on a rich young prince for her release from misery?

Are these concerns of any importance to those who care about children? Despite these and other considerations, the dominant wisdom recognizes that, in the minds of most children, the complexities perceived by adults are reduced to a simple struggle between good and evil. In all the fairy tales cited here, in the end, evil is punished and good rewarded.

Psychoanalyst Bruno Bettelheim, who worked extensively with children, attributed the extraordinary popularity of Cinderella, one of the world's most cherished fairy tales, to its connection to "the inner experiences of the young child in the throes of sibling rivalry, when he feels hopelessly outclassed by his brothers and sisters." Patricia O'Toole, in a an article published in a special edition of *Newsweek* honoring the 20th anniversary of Disney World, states: "Children share Cinderella's yearning to have their inner goodness discovered by those with the power to make them happy."[1] Her other observations include the recognition that children in fairy tales, physically unable to overcome most of the giants who threaten or abuse them, win the unequal battles by using their intelligence. She notes further that, from a child's perspective, "every adult is a giant, a creature of prodigious strength and boundless authority," issuing orders, setting limits, force feeding, assigning punishments, and transporting them to places they don't wish to go.

Repetitions

A third major difference between adults and children is that children enjoy repetitions of the same experience much more than adults do. Most children delight in hearing the same story read over and over again in exactly the same way and complain bitterly if the reader varies the presentation in the slightest degree. Children watch, as if-fascinated, a television cartoon they have already seen many times before. They give close attention to a routine that opens every sequence of a favorite program and listen to each repetition of its theme song as though it were a new experience. Mister Rogers, for example, opens every one of the programs in the *Mister Rogers' Neighborhood* series by coming through the front door, changing his suit-coat for a sweater and his shoes for sneakers, all the while singing his "Won't You Be My Neighbor?" song. The constant repetition of this folksy approach makes children feel comfortable and secure. The *Mickey Mouse* theme, repeated at great length at the end of each program, may have driven some parents close to madness, but their children seemed to enjoy every syllable of it.

Differences in Children

Thus far we have been thinking of children as if they were all cast from the same mold. Actually, the differences between boys and girls of one age and those of another, and the differences even among children of the same age group, may be as profound as the differences that distinguish adults from children. Writers must take these differences into account. It is impossible, of course, to adapt to all of the individuals who may be in their audience, but they should have a good idea of the general age level toward which they are aiming. They do not have to worry about whether their listeners are boys or girls, for their interests and needs before adolescence are virtually identical.

There is, however, one difference which may possibly reflect sexist attitudes learned by children. Young boys, studies report, are unwilling to accept young girls in lead roles. The 1991 fall season had none. Stations were not willing to risk low ratings, and writers were not expected to apply their creativity to advancing sexual equality. What is lacking is not the possibility of success in challenging sexual stereotypes, but the supply of courage to enter the competitive arena.

Peggy Charren, founder of Action for Children's Television (ACT), disagrees with the report. The problem, she suggests, is not the miscasting of heroic figures, but the dearth of really good stories. The appeal of the most attractive programs, in her judgment, does not lie in whether boys or girls portray the stronger roles. It comes from the way in which the authors present the children. To do justice to them and achieve excellence in storytelling, authors themselves need to perceive children for what they are. They are not miniature adults, not boys and girls who can't handle ideas, but important people whose worth must be respected and who deserve to be taken seriously. She advises against envisioning young audiences as separate entities, grouped as minorities, one sex or the other, or members of an ethnic class.

Authors in the print medium have succeeded in presenting attractive heroines. Bob Munsch and Michael Martchenko collaborated on *The Paper Bag Princess,* the former providing the story and the latter the art. (Martchenko admits, however, to engaging the cooperation of his five-year-old daughter Holly as "consultant on dragons.")

Elizabeth, the beautiful, elegantly dressed heroine, was cheerfully anticipating her forthcoming marriage to Prince Ronald when a dragon destroyed her castle, breathed destructive fire on all her clothes and kidnapped the prince.

Elizabeth does not waste any time swooning; instead, she decides to pursue the dragon and rescue her prince. Her wardrobe in ashes, she slips into a brown paper bag and, covered with soot, follows the dragon's fiery trail. He responds to her persistent knocking by assuring her that he finds princesses especially delicious. Instead of fleeing, Elizabeth shouts a challenge: "Is it true that you are the smartest and fiercest dragon in the whole world?"

Trapped in his own macho image, the dragon responds to her invitations by showing off his strength. When he is exhausted from his efforts, Elizabeth steps over him, enters the dragon's cave and discovers her imprisoned Prince Ronald.

The pretty prince ignores her courage and genius and, concentrating on her disheveled appearance, chides her, "Elizabeth, you are a mess. You smell like ashes, your hair is all tangled, and you are wearing

a dirty old paper bag. Come back when you are dressed like a real princess."

Elizabeth, who was fearless in the face of a fiery giant, expresses an observation of her own: "Ronald, your clothes are really pretty and your hair is very neat. You look like a real prince, but you are a bum."

The happy ending is that they didn't get married after all.

When an animation company purchased *The Paper Bag Princess* for adaptation as a half-hour cartoon, they intended to change the ending. Elizabeth, in dumping Prince Ronald, was to begin her search for a substitute prince. Munsch persuaded the animators not to alter the ending because, to do so, would be to rob this spunky heroine of her independence.

Action-
Liz delivers 1st "UGH" O.S. then steps in with 2nd

Dialogue-
"UGH UGH"

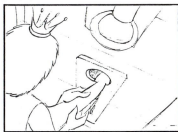

Action-
Liz unlocks door
Click

Dialogue-

Action-
Liz reaches up for knocker
TRK in.

Dialogue-
"Will someone get me out of here!?"

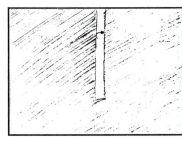

Action-
Liz pulls on door. It starts to move at tail.

Dialogue-
". . . and I mean *now*!"

Action-
Start all black
Door opens
Creak

Dialogue-
"Ronald?"

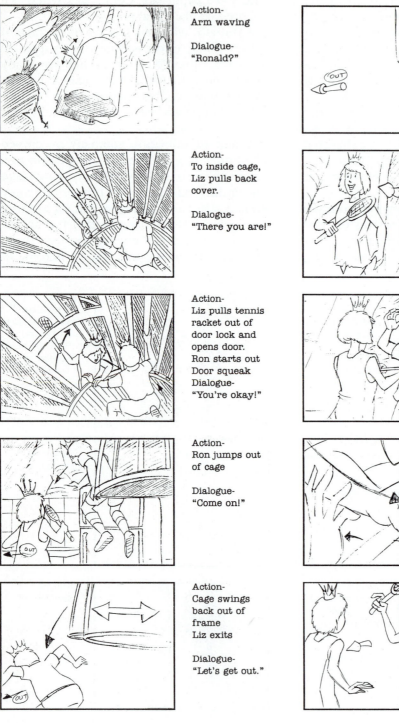

Action-
Arm waving

Dialogue-
"Ronald?"

Action-
To inside cage,
Liz pulls back
cover.

Dialogue-
"There you are!"

Action-
Liz pulls tennis
racket out of
door lock and
opens door.
Ron starts out
Door squeak
Dialogue-
"You're okay!"

Action-
Ron jumps out
of cage

Dialogue-
"Come on!"

Action-
Cage swings
back out of
frame
Liz exits

Dialogue-
"Let's get out."

Action-
Cage swings
back in.
Ron exits.

Dialogue-
". . . of here!"

Action-
Elizabeth and
Ronald walk out
of cave.

Action-
Liz turns to pre-
sent Ronald with
his racket.

Dialogue:
"Thank--"

Action-
As Ronald
snatches racket

Dialogue-
"--you."

Action-
Liz steps back

Dialogue-
"Elizabeth, why
are you dressed
like that?"

Action-
Liz looks hurt

Dialogue-
"Your hair is all
dirty . . ."

Action-
. . . then leans
forward

Dialogue:
"Well, Ronald
. . ."

Action-
Elizabeth wig-
gles her toes

Dialogue-
". . . you don't
have any shoes
on . . ."

Dialogue-
". . . Your hair
is all nice. . ."

Action-
Dragon's tail
slowly exits

Dialogue-
"You're wearing
an ugly
paperbag, and
you smell like a
dragon's ear!"

Action-
Pulls at his shirt

Dialogue-
"Your clothes
are all pretty
. . . but . . ."

Action-
Ronald gestures
with his hand to
leave

Dialogue-
"Come back and
rescue me when
your dressed
like a *real*
princess."

Dialogue-
"*You* are a
bum!"

Action-
Stunned, Liz
blinks twice
quickly . . .

Action-
Liz prods Ron

Dialogue-
". . . and I will
not marry. . ."

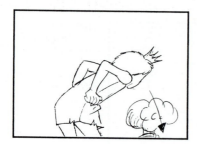

Action-
Ron falls down
O.S.
Thump

Dialogue-
". . . a bum!"

Action-
Dragon lifts his
head, surprised.

Dialogue-
"The dragon
looked at Eliza-
beth . . ."

221.

RONALD (OS)
(desperately)
Will somebody help me get out of here? And I mean now!

ANGLE DOWN tunnel towards door as it CREAKS open. Elizabeth is silhouetted in doorway.

FADE TO BLACK.

ELIZABETH (O.S.)
Ronald?

INT. DRAGON'S KITCHEN. DAY.
Ronald's POV as the cloth is lifted from the cage revealing Elizabeth.

226.

ELIZABETH
(delighted)
Ronald!

FULL SHOT of Elizabeth yanking the tennis racquet from the lock. Ronald sits with his arms crossed, looking disgusted.

226.

ELIZABETH
(delighted)
There you are.

He starts to crawl out.

ELIZABETH (CONT'D)
You're okay.

Elizabeth grabs him by the hand and zips o.s.

227.

ELIZABETH (CONT'D)
Come on, let's get out of here.

Ronald rubberbands o.s. after her.

45   EXT. DRAGON'S CAVE ENTRANCE—DAY

FULL SHOT as Elizabeth emerges from the cave, still carrying the tennis racquet. She turns
to watch an irritated Ronald emerge. He snatches his racquet from her hand.

> RONALD
> (snapping)
> Thank you.

Ronald leans into her, eyeing her.

> RONALD
> (admonishing)
> Elizabeth, why are you dressed like that?

ANGLE BEHIND Ronald, as he points from the top of his head to her feet with his tennis racquet. Elizabeth looks down.

> RONALD (CONT'D)
> . . . Your hair is all dirty, you don't have any shoes on . . .

FULL SHOT as he throws his hands up. Elizabeth is shocked.

> RONALD (CONT'D)
> . . . you're wearing an ugly paper bag and you smell like a dragon's ear.

ON Ronald, fans himself with his tennis racquet. The Dragon in b.g. opens one eye and looks
at him.

> RONALD (CONT'D)
> Come back and rescue me when you're dressed like a real princess.

PAN OVER to Elizabeth still taken aback. She blinks.

231.   ELIZABETH (CONT'D)
> Well, Ronald! (beat)
> (peeved, her hands on her hips)
> Your hair is all nice, your clothes are all pretty. You look like a nice guy, but . . .

FULL SHOT of Elizabeth and Ronald as she stiffens, clenches her fists and leans into him.

> ELIZABETH (CONT'D)
> (shouting)
> You are a *bum*! And I will not marry a bum!

Early Childhood   One generalization which seems obvious is that the younger children are, the more limited is their fund of experience, but this is not the only variable. Another factor distinguishing children of different ages is the relationship of the child to the world outside. Children of preschool age see themselves as the focus of the universe and in a completely self-centered way relate what is happening entirely to their own needs and concerns. One of the main ways in which they discover themselves is through their responses to others, and of these responses the most common is imitation. The writer can never afford to disregard the imitativeness of childhood.

Writers also need to realize children are going through a process of finding themselves in the world at large. They often feel insecure and wonder how other people are accepting them. They frequently experience doubts about their own worth. The program *Mister Rogers' Neighborhood* makes a special point of providing children with self-assurance by emphasizing each person's unique individuality. At the end of many programs, Mister Rogers tells his young viewers, "You are special. There's only one person in this whole world just like you."

Writers of children's programs, paid for in the way most television is—by the insertion of commercials at intervals throughout the program—need to recognize that most young children lack the sophistication to distinguish commercials from program content. If the commercials follow the program segments without a perceptible break, child viewers are likely to think that the advertising message is coming to them from a program personality. In the opinion of some critics, they are, therefore, more likely to be influenced by the appeal than they would be by what they recognize as a commercial.

Another characteristic of young children is that they remain interested in one subject for only a brief period. Most programs for

children adapt to this short attention span by scheduling many different segments in a single program and using a variety of techniques to produce them. *Sesame Street,* a program aimed at preschool children, includes as many as 50 different segments in its one-hour running time and uses, among its techniques, live action, puppets, animation, stop-action photography, music, and sound effects. *Captain Kangaroo* employed the same approach. Rarely did a unit on this program last longer than five minutes, and the program switched constantly back and forth among live action cartoons, puppets, and films. A rundown of a broadcast would list not only these various program elements but also the breaks for commercials.

The programs discussed thus far are those primarily aimed at children who have not yet started regular school, although the appeal of both *The Giving Tree* and *The Paper Bag Princess* defy age limitations. As children mature, their interest in themselves is gradually supplemented by an interest in the world outside. An important step in this process occurs when children first go to school and people outside their immediate family begin to assume an important role in their lives. They feel a strong need to associate with people of their own age and become interested in sports, both as participants and as observers. The world around them begins to attract their attention, a matter of critical significance to the writer, for at this stage the child develops intense curiosity about what things are, how they work, and where they come from.

Later Childhood   The interest of older children continues to range out from their immediate environment, both in time and space, and they become curious about events in the past and even about worlds that may exist among the stars. Stories of foreign lands and facts about them attract children of this age, and they also become interested in the lives of great men and women. Nine-year-old children distinguish clearly between the real and the fantastic, and although they still may indulge in make-believe thinking, they know they are only pretending.

As children enter adolescence, they discover the world of popular music as heard on radio, CDs, and tapes. For many, headphones become a substitute for the pacifier. The writer of children's scripts, however, need not be concerned about this age, as audience surveys show that adolescents are not interested in programs written specifically for them, but instead view almost exclusively programs designed for general audiences and adults. The exception is MTV.

Originally intended for the 12- to 25-year-old market, music videos increasingly attract younger children. Many contain material more explicit and irreverent than anything imagined in the 1960s and 1970s, or available now on commercial television channels during prime-time programming hours. The best evidence of the impact of MTV on young people is their perplexity that their guardians and teachers are disturbed by the violence, bigotry, and sexual behavior on such videos. These themes, formerly regarded as shameful by ordinary people, fail to offend MTV's target audience.

Adult Values in the Child

It is important for the writers of children's scripts to appreciate the differences that distinguish their audience from the one of adults, but it is just as important to recognize their great similarities. Children and adults turn to a television program for much the same reason—to escape the humdrum routine of their everyday existence. They want to be taken into a world outside the one that immediately surrounds them, to feel the excitement of rousing adventure, to savor the stimulation of new knowledge, to experience the emotional arousal that effective drama can accomplish. The vicarious enjoyment in the forbidden which helps to explain the great popularity of crime drama among adults is also a factor in children's listening. One of the appeals of clown programs for young children is that clowns can do things the child is not permitted to do. They can mumble and stumble, drop things, and make a mess of themselves and their surroundings.

Delight in comedy is another common characteristic of both children and adults. Most people, whatever their age, like to laugh and have fun. One of the attractions of the programs produced by the Children's Television Workshop, *Sesame Street* and *The Electric Company,* is the fun they provide their listeners. Both programs have serious educational objectives; the lessons, however, are lightened with comedy so that children laugh even as they learn. A sketch from one of *The Electric Company* programs, which aim to teach reading skills and language usage to children from seven to 10, illustrates how humor can cap a serious lesson. The following episode occurred as one of a number of sequences designed to teach the meaning and use of the word *or.*

The Electric Company

VIDEO	*AUDIO*
A MAN IS SITTING AT A TABLE IN A RESTAURANT QUIETLY EATING HIS DINNER.	

THE DOOR OPENS AND A ROBBER
WEARING A MASK COMES IN.
HE POINTS HIS GUN AT THE DINER.
LETTERS ABOVE CHARACTERS

| | ROBBER |
| | Your money or your life. |

YOUR MONEY *OR*
YOUR LIFE

| | DINER |
| | Your money or your life? |

AS BEFORE
YOUR MONEY *OR*
YOUR LIFE

| | ROBBER |
| | That's right. Your money or your life. |

AS BEFORE
YOUR MONEY *OR*
YOUR LIFE

| | DINER |
| | All right. I'll take your money. |

ROBBER REACHES INTO HIS POCKET
AND HANDS THE DINER HIS WALLET.
DINER GETS UP AND LEAVES.
ROBBER STANDS IN CONFUSION,
THEN RUEFULLY REMOVES HIS MASK
FROM HIS FACE AS HE SAYS

| | ROBBER |
| | This didn't work out the way I intended it to. |

Among the elements that attracted audiences to *Captain Kangaroo* for more than a quarter of a century were the lighthearted humor and spirit of fun that imbued each broadcast. The following segment from one of the programs in this series illustrates how comedy helps to make the program enjoyable to young children.

Captain Kangaroo
"To Grandmother's House"
Script by Harry Crossfield
(c) 1978 by Robert Keeshan Associates
By Permission of Robert Keeshan Associates

A FOREST SETTING: A CLEARING WITH TREES AND A COUPLE OF TREE STUMPS. LUMPY AND GUS ENTER. LUMPY AS FRIAR TUCK AND GUS AS LITTLE JOHN.

GUS:
I'm tired, Friar Tuck. I have to rest.

LUMPY:
I wonder where we are?

GUS:

I would say off hand, that we are lost in the forest.

THEY SIT ON THE TREE STUMPS.

LUMPY:

I think you're right, Little John. What are we going to do? We're supposed to drop in on Robin Hood's grandmother.

GUS:

How are we going to drop in if we can't find her house? Maybe we should call her.

LUMPY: (CALLING)

Oh Grandmother! Grandmother!

OFF CAMERA BOB MAKES A TARZAN YELL. GUS AND LUMPY REACT.

GUS:

That's grandmother?

BOB SWINGS THROUGH FRAME ON A VINE. (IN ROBIN HOOD COSTUME WITH HAT WITH FEATHER)

LUMPY:

That doesn't look like grandmother to me. It's Robin Hood.

BOB SWINGS THROUGH AGAIN, MAKES A TARZAN YELL AND OUT OF FRAME. <u>SE:</u> CRASH. GUS AND LUMPY GO OVER AND HELP BOB UP.

LUMPY:

Robin, what are you doing?

BOB:

Just trying to get into the swing of things.

GUS:

Are you all right?

BOB:

Aside from a little bent feather, I'm perfect. Have you dropped in on my grandmother?

LUMPY:

We can't find your grandmother's house.

BOB:

Oh, Friar John and Little Tuck, what would you do without me?

GUS.

Robin, that's Friar Tuck and Little John.

SE: TELEPHONE RING
What's that?

BOB:

Oh excuse me, it's the phone.

BOB GOES OVER TO A WALL PHONE ON A TREE AND PICKS UP RECEIVER.

BOB:

Hello. Sherwood Forest, Robin Hood speaking. I'm sorry you have the wrong forest.

BOB HANGS UP PHONE.

LUMPY:

Who was that?

BOB:

Bambi calling his mother. Well OK, let's get started. Follow me.

An activity satisfying to both adults and children is actual participation in a program: The adult who shouts out the answer to quiz questions before the guests on the program do is enjoying an experience similar to that of the preschool child who claps and sings along with the television cast. Knowing how much children like to anticipate answers with their own responses, the producers of programs such as *Sesame Street* sometimes delay giving an answer until their young viewers have had a chance to shout it out first.

THE CONTENT OF CHILDREN'S PROGRAMS

A helpful guide for the person who aspires to write for children is to note what broadcasters have done for children in the past and what they are doing today. It should be recognized, however, that such an examination cannot provide final answers to all the questions. Some programs represent clear adaptations to the special needs and characteristics of children, but the suitability of other practices is hotly debated. One problem is that concern for the child runs head on into commercial considerations; unfortunately, some programs considered most undesirable for children are also the most likely to attract them.

ACT and numerous parents' groups have vigorously protested programs designed as a marketing showcase for products, such as the G.I. Joe series. A second, related problem is that many thoughtful adults object to the brutal, negative values projected by that and similar bellicose programs.

Basic Subject Matter

The Television Information Office at one time surveyed the television stations of the nation to discover what programs they produced for at-home viewing by children between the ages of four and 12. The results of this survey, published in the book *For the Young Viewer,* provide a good index to the range of subjects covered by various children's programs.

Exploration   Many TV programs appeal directly to the urge of children to explore—to find out about themselves, their neighborhood, and the world. Two generations of children who grew up in *Mister Rogers' Neighborhood* enjoyed being guided into other neighborhoods and into the Neighborhood of Make Believe. The success of that program lies in some measure in the balance between the faraway and the familiar.

The range of programs in the category of discovery and exploration is wide. Travel to other lands and visits to such places in the community as zoos, museums, hospitals, public buildings, state fairs, and factories may be featured, but exploration is not limited merely to places. Programs explore the past to make children acquainted with historical personages and events; they introduce them to the discoveries of science; they take them into the world of the theater; they tell them about sports; some simply help them to examine ideas and traditions. Program hosts or guides include real people, puppets and muppets, animated cartoons, and characters conceived by computer graphics.

Orientation   Having found out about the world through exploration, children now need help in making their adjustment to it. A number of programs aim to orient children by teaching them what they can expect from the world and what is expected from them in return. Many such programs therefore deal with manners, morals, and health practices.

One of the chief aims of *Mister Rogers' Neighborhood* is to help young children cope with everyday feelings such as sadness

when friends leave, fear of the doctor, jealousy provoked by the arrival of a new baby, or the anger that comes from being frustrated. Fred Rogers sees programs treating subjects of this nature as an ally for parents and teachers.

At the heart of many of the above-mentioned concerns is the technique of conflict resolution, surely an important consideration for people of all ages. Fred Rogers brought this topic to its ultimate concern when during a week of his *Mister Rogers' Neighborhood* programs which premiered in 1983 and is repeated each year, he devoted five programs to peace making. One specifically fostered the avoidance of war between the people of the Neighborhood of Make Believe and the inhabitants of Southwood. A synopsis of one of the program follows:

Mister Rogers, following the usual opening song, greeting, and ritual, empties a box of building blocks onto a table and out of them constructs a bridge.

He next takes his TV neighbors to a factory where marbles are made, from ground glass to packaged product.

Then in the Neighborhood of Make Believe, he presents a story about suspicion, spies, and peace soldiers. According to the story line, King Friday jumps to the conclusion that Southwood was making bombs, so he decides that his Neighborhood should make bombs, too. Because Lady Aberlin and Lady Elaine Fairchilde don't think that's a good idea, he dispatches them, along with Bob Dog, as a delegation to Southwood to find out what Southwood is making out of numerous parts it has been buying from Cornflake S. Pecially's factory. He dubs them his "soldiers of peace."

What they discover is friendly people, much like themselves, who welcome them and display the bridge they are making out of the parts.

While the peace soldiers are enjoying their visit at Southwood, the King worries that they are away too long. He decides to send troops to rescue them, only to be informed that the Neighborhood of Make Believe has no soldiers, only generals. At that moment the trio returns with an enthusiastic report about their newly discovered good neighbors.

In response, King Friday says, "I am shocked, sadly bewildered am I."

"Why?" they ask.

"Because I should have done what you peace soldiers did before I ever trained the generals or built the bombs. I don't know how I could have been so thoughtless."

So ends the threat of war. The King admits that his ancestors will be so proud that they avoided a war because it's better that way.

Then, with strains of "The Star Spangled Banner" in the background, they say, "Good news. No bombs bursting anywhere, Trolley. Rejoice."

Mister Rogers returns with his closing song and a few final thoughts:

"I was just thinking that even games like marbles and block building need rules. If a person threw a marble or a block at another person, that could really hurt. So one rule is no throwing things at other people to hurt them. Rules are very, very important. Not just for games but for all things, even big things, like countries. Countries have to have rules to protect people too. And some day you'll be helping to make the rules for your country. I trust you'll make the best kind you know how."

Doing The purpose of some programs is to stimulate children to engage in worthwhile activity. In a sense such programs reverse the direction of exploratory programs; instead of taking the child outside the home to visit other places and peoples, they bring talented people into the home to lead the child into rewarding activities. Children may be taught to improve skills they have already developed, such as maintaining proper posture, or spelling, or they may be introduced to new skills such as painting, folk dancing, making puppets, training pets, or carving soap.

Storytelling A large number of children's programs, perhaps the largest number of all, are designed to tell a story. These programs may range from those employing very simple formats to those engaging in a complete dramatic presentation.

Multipurpose A number of programs are not limited to one type of content but fuse several elements into a program that seeks a variety of goals. This is particularly true of the longer programs. Because the attention span of children is very short, as we have noted, their interest might drift away if one segment is continued for too long a time. Therefore a typical program of this type might present a short film about another land (exploration); have a brief discussion on a topic such as "How do you act if you don't get the Christmas gifts you expected?" (orientation); teach the proper way to swing a baseball bat (doing); and close with a cartoon story (storytelling). The *Captain Kangaroo* program was of this type. One problem in such programs is maintaining unity. A colorful personality like Captain Kangaroo helps to establish some connection between the segments when there is no overall theme to provide linkage.

The Problem of Violence

One of the perennial controversies in television revolves around the question whether the violence so common in programs is harmful to children. Modern social critics periodically rethink the depiction of violence even, as indicated earlier, in classic tales, such as *Cinderella* and *The Wizard of*

Oz. The writer of plays for children cannot escape this problem merely by excluding violence from the work, for to do so would eliminate an element intrinsic to the dramatic form. The question is, how much violence is permissible and what kind? The findings of some research studies provide little help because they often conflict. Based on experiments they conducted, some researchers have concluded that viewing aggression incites violent behavior in children, either by inviting direct imitation or by planting ideas that lead eventually to violence. Other scholars, equally reputable, as a result of their research reached a directly contrary conclusion—that viewing violence is actually beneficial to children because it helps to defuse their potentially violent behavior. Thus, they argue, violence has a cathartic effect.

In the light of these conflicting results, the best guidance for writers appears to lie in the findings of two extended studies, one directed by Wilbur Schramm in the United States and the other by Hilde Himmelweit in Great Britain. Though conducted independently, the two studies reached remarkably similar conclusions. Among the findings, which provide a reasonable and workable guide for writers, were the following:

1. Stylized or ritual violence, such as that occurring in cartoons or western dramas, usually does not frighten children. Shooting seems not to be disturbing except to very young children because the bullet cannot be seen, but the use of knives can be frightening because children can see the weapon and its effect and they may vicariously feel the wound.
2. Violence that takes place in an unfamiliar setting is less likely to be frightening than violence that can be imagined as happening in the child's own home or street. The sight of a dark room or a stormy night or a glimpse of a face peer-

ing in at a window may terrify children because it brings back the fears they feel in their own dark bedrooms.
3. The magnitude of a disaster is less important to children than the prospect of hurt to someone with whom they identify or feel attachment. The threat of injury or death to children or to a beloved animal such as *Lassie* is particularly agitating.
4. Characters with clearly defined traits are less likely to arouse fears than those who seem to be ambivalent in their motives and actions. Children feel more secure when they can immediately tell the "good guys" from the "bad guys." Characters who seem to have both good and bad qualities may confuse children even if they do not disturb them.
5. A program in a series that follows a rigidly established pattern is less likely to be frightening than an individual show even though the series drama may contain a great deal of violence. Because the child is familiar with the conventions of the series, he or she has the security of knowing the pattern of events and can have confidence in the final supremacy of the hero figure.
6. The knowledge that events are make believe rather than real reduces fear. As has been mentioned, this distinction is more difficult to maintain with younger than it is with older children; the age of a child is therefore an important factor. A small boy listening to a radio adaptation of Oscar Wilde's "The Selfish Giant" burst into tears when the giant finally died because he was too young to discount what he heard and reacted to it as if it were real. The tendency of young children to become totally absorbed by what they see and hear means that they should not be exposed to situations that are highly emotional or violent or in which tension is prolonged for too long

a time. Heavy music, dead silence, ticking clocks, or sudden noises may make a scene intolerable to children. Graphic portrayals of torture are likely to be especially disturbing. Shrieks of agony or other evidences of pain should be avoided.

Later studies, including one which in 1982 updated the Surgeon General's report of a decade earlier, offered compelling evidence of a causal connection between viewing and committing violence. The numbers involved in imitation were relatively small; however, more disturbing was the finding that regular viewing of televised violence contributes to a desensitization which numbs viewers to the real sufferings and needs of others.

In the mid-1980s, the American Psychiatric Association, which represents 60,000 psychologists, took a stand against televised violence. Members testified before Congress that 25 years of research had demonstrated the negative effects of video violence on human behavior. In 1985 the APA passed a resolution encouraging parents to monitor and control their children's television viewing; it requested industry representatives to adopt a responsible attitude in reducing direct imitative violence and in providing better programming for children, and it urged industry, government and private foundations to support research aimed at reducing the effects of high levels of televised violence on children.[2]

It sometimes happens that writers may be assigned the task of adapting material that is usually thought of as being for children even though it contains violent scenes and characters. The classic children's story "Rumpelstiltskin" as told by the Brothers Grimm features one of the most unsavory characters in literature: a king who threatens to kill a young girl unless she can produce gold and who decides to marry her only when she has satisfied his avariciousness. Other tales, among them some included in the *Arabian Nights,* are even more bloodthirsty. It is well to remember that many of these stories were not written originally for children at all but for adults. Turning them into TV offerings suitable for children, particularly when we remember that dramatic treatment intensifies the effect of violence, often requires some modification of the original character and plots.

Other Undesirable Content

Violence in children's shows has been the most common target of criticism, but it is not the only one. In an unusual exercise in self-examination, the National Broadcasting Company at one time organized a Children's Program Review Committee and then published its criticism even though many of the complaints applied to shows then being carried by NBC. On the basis of the committee's report, NBC established the following standards:

1. Do not portray as acceptable action that would be forbidden at home and which might have a bad effect on the relationship between children and parents.
2. Avoid bad grammar and poor pronunciation except when they are given a clear character identification.
3. Eliminate overdone and destructive slapstick and such crudities as calling on performers to play the trombone with a mouth filled with watermelon.
4. Refrain from an overemphasis on money and exorbitant rewards for successes that are simply the result of chance.
5. Be careful that the information included on programs is accurate and expressed in terms the child can understand. Misguided enlightenment can be worse than none at all.

Writers should avoid another type of content also, not because it is harmful to children but because it does not interest them. That subject is romance. Children realize that men and women fall in love and get married, but the subtler meanings of the emotion are beyond their understanding and interest. Anyone who has heard a group of children at a Saturday movie matinee groan when a love scene starts will appreciate the soundness of this suggestion.

Including Positive Values

Most people considering children's programs think about what to avoid, but it is just as important to consider what to include. The old National Association of Broadcasters (NAB) *TV Code* suggested that "programs should contribute to the sound, balanced development of children to help them achieve a sense of the world at large and informed adjustments to their society." It added that programs should stress "positive sets of values which will allow the child to become a responsible adult, capable of coping with the challenges of maturity." It also argued that the TV industry should take into account the fact that "children may constitute a substantial segment of the audience watching programs designed primarily for adults."

The NBC committee report, referred to earlier, in addition to listing undesirable content, also criticized the lack of balance in children's programs and suggested more of the following: how-to-do-it shows, field trips to interesting, instructive places, music, greater contact with people and customs of other countries, hobby material, simple storytelling, child-animal series, and adventure stories other than westerns.

One of the best descriptions of positive values in children's programs was prepared by Dr. Fred Rainsberry while he was supervisor of School Broadcasts and Youth Programming for the Canadian Broadcasting Corporation (CBC). The main points of that policy statement were as follows:

1. Because children's programs play a part in determining the artistic taste and social attitude of adults of the future they should: (a) communicate traditional and essential values, (b) include vital material that will add to the child's stature as an experiencing person, (c) help the child to develop a sense of social responsibility.
2. Programs should take advantage of the child's urge to imitate, the type of imitation that will have a significant creative and developmental effect.
3. Programs should preserve the creative and spontaneous urge to self-expression, an urge that can be ruined by dull and tasteless programming.
4. Programs must be based on an understanding of current trends in culture.

At one time the CBC produced its own version of the American puppet show *Howdy Doody*. The way in which the program differed from its American counterpart illustrated some of the CBC's policies with respect to children's programs. In comparison to the American, the Canadian *Howdy Doody* was slower-paced and less noisy; it substituted nature films for segments of old movies; it made the lead a disciplined person rather than a blatant exhibitionist; it included more music; it eliminated tension; it substituted whimsy for frenzy.

There is still disagreement among the producers of children's programs about what might be called the proper noise level. *Bozo the Clown* is a program produced independently by various local stations which, in effect, rent the idea of the program from a national syndication company. The creators of this concept apparently believe that noise and exaggerated activity attract children, for Bozo is a loud, aggressive exhibitionist. The producers of *Mister Rogers' Neighborhood,* on the other hand, believe in a low-key approach to young children. Mister Rogers is always soft-spoken and genuine when he talks to his audience. The *Captain Kangaroo* program adopted the same understated approach. Though others on the program sometimes became noisy and excited, Captain Kangaroo was consistently calm and measured no matter what was happening.

One word of warning is necessary with respect to the execution of high-minded principles such as those of the CBC. In endeavoring to include concrete values in their scripts, writers may fall into the distressing error of moralizing. This is no more palatable to children than it is to adults. As we have noted before, a child tunes in a television set to seek entertainment, relaxation, excitement, and release from humdrum living. Moral and educational values must be achieved incidentally to the major goal of entertaining the child.

Akin to the mistake of moralizing is that most pernicious of faults—writing down to children. Patronizing a child is the worst mistake a writer can make. Obviously you have to write in terms of the child's understanding, but you should nevertheless communicate your own sense of enjoyment in the subject. Children quickly detect a supercilious attitude, and they deeply resent it.

Reflecting "Progressive" Attitudes

As writers of children's programs moved into the 1990s, some seemed to be responding to criticism of male dominance and the emphasis on violence in problem solving. Steven Spielberg, who gave children of all ages the endearing extraterrestrial, *E. T.,* also produced *Tiny Toon Adventures.* This par-ody of the often violent cartoon series *Bugs Bunny and Friends* employs child instead of animal cartoon characters. Although some violence is present in *Tiny Toons,* most episodes have the cast tackling problems together, instead of resorting to aggressive action. Warner Brothers' *Bugs Bunny* frequently mentions family members but often they are male. The occasional female may be introduced as another character's mother, whose role is minor. Sometimes Bugs appears dressed as a female ("in drag," some observe) to deceive his enemies. Quite often he ends by embracing them. One of Bugs' counterparts in *Tiny Toons,* by contrast, is a female who possesses a wit and cunning similar to that of Bugs.

In the action-adventure cartoon, *He-Man and the Masters of the Universe,* She-Ra is a princess with magical capabilities. It is she who gave He-Man the forces that empower him.

Writers have also begun to enter the child's most terrifying field of fears by dealing with the subject of death. Television, like the audiences it targets, rarely addresses this topic with ease, perhaps because, for many, it is fraught with mystery and pain, and it evokes a sense of helplessness.

Television doesn't deny death. By the time children living in the United States have reached the age of 14, they will have witnessed the televised killings of approximately 13,000 human beings. Only a small percentage of these deaths is followed by survivors mourning the loss of loved ones, attending funerals, or engaging in other rituals so important to the survivors' healing process. Death ends on a note of inevitability or deserved punishment.

The death of a pet can be as traumatic for a young child (and sometimes an adult) as the death of a relative. An episode of *The Cosby Show* brought the Huxtable family to a bathroom funeral for "Mr. Fish." Although it may have seemed hilarious to the audience, that sequence provided rare insights into the pain that accompanies the death of another, the appropriateness of grieving, and the need for people who love one another to stand together at a time of loss.

Another fish became famous in death in *Mister Rogers' Neighborhood.* Mister Rogers, in discussing the death of his fish on the public television children's show, allowed children to see his sadness as he said, "It's okay to be sad when someone you love dies."

The producers of *Sesame Street* confronted the issue of the death of a beloved person when Will Lee died of a heart attack. The character he portrayed, Mr. Hooper, the friendly neighborhood grocer, would certainly be missed by the children for whom he had become real. Having dismissed the consideration that they simply write him out of the series, they produced an episode that would explain his death. In a sensitively executed scenario, Big Bird learns that "when people die, they don't come back."

Some years later *The Muppets* suffered a similar tragedy and learned a painful lesson when their beloved creator Jim Henson died after a brief illness. He had given voice and life to the endearing Kermit the Frog. As in the case of *Sesame Street* viewers, the Muppets also shared a sorrow as they were given some understanding of the meaning of death and the value of life.

Some programs engaging child actors in series designed for general audiences inherently teach acceptance of people whose lives or cultures may be different from the experience of many of their viewers. Corky, a young man with Down syndrome (in real life as well as on television), each week shows what a mildly retarded person can accomplish, given the support of a loving family. As a key character in *Life Goes On,* Corky demonstrates that goodness, generosity, and responsibility are not synonymous with superior intelligence alone.

Brooklyn Bridge, a situation-comedy series, presents children from different backgrounds (Jewish and Catholic) struggling to be friends despite the fears and prejudices of their parents and grandparents. Humor is one of the defenses against bigotry in this program.

Life Goes On and *Brooklyn Bridge* communicate pro-social values, less by preaching than by example.

The themes of loneliness and alienation suffered by adults are often endured by children as well. Two storybook classics, *The Secret Garden* by Frances Hodgson Burnett and *The Velveteen Rabbit* by Margery Williams, are among the many wonderfully successful adaptations that have brought television audiences stories long cherished by readers. An excellent rendition of *The Velveteen Rabbit* features the voice of actress Meryl Streep over the original illustrations in the book. Pianist George Winston provides musical accompaniment. The story of the lonely little boy whose best friend is a stuffed toy bunny, remains an intergenerational favorite. Child and toy share sickness, endure separation and estrangement, and in the end each experiences a different rite of passage.

SPECIFIC WRITING TECHNIQUES

Writing a script for children does not require radical new approaches or techniques that differ basically from those already covered in previous chapters. If you are writing a drama mainly designed to entertain children, you would use the techniques described in the chapters on dramatic writing. If you are writing a program aimed at achieving some educational value, you would review the techniques covered in the chapter on educational programs. They apply as much to children's scripts as they do to programs meant for general audiences. This does not mean that you need make no changes at all. The responsibility of the broadcaster for contributing to their proper growth and development does call, however, for some adaptations in the usual techniques.

The Structure of the Program

Many children's programs, particularly those aimed at the youngest age group, are built around the telling of a story. In television a number of visual techniques can be used to illustrate the story: the narrator drawing pictures while talking; still pictures; animation; puppets; and actors appearing in silhouette or in dramatic scenes. Some successful programs like *The Muppets* and *Sesame Street* combine puppets and people, including popular entertainment figures. Then, blending fantasy and reality, writers devise situations in which puppets and guests interact in believable relationships. A radio or audio narration may feature only a storyteller, or it may add such devices as music at transition points; sound effects; actors to read voices; a proxy listener to ask questions of the narrator; and dramatic scenes. Many stories for children are completely dramatized, of course. Other programs of a nonfiction type employ a wide variety of visual and sound effects to achieve their purposes.

One factor of great importance in planning a program's structure is the amount of money available to pay for production. Few groups have the resources possessed by the Children's Television Workshop when it began producing *Sesame Street*. Before the first program went on the air, it had received $8 million in grants to support the first year's activity. With this money it could match in polish and production effectiveness the commercials which helped to provide a model for the techniques it employed in teaching letter and number concepts to young children. Most educational groups cannot afford the animation, professional assistance, and special effects that characterize *Sesame Street*. Ingenious people, however, have created program ideas of great appeal to children. Furthermore they have demonstrated that these concepts can be produced by groups with limited resources.

A good example of such a program is *The Friendly Giant*. It was created by Bob Homme for station WHA-TV in Madison, Wisconsin, and later was produced by the Canadian Broadcasting Corporation with the originator of the program continuing to play the title character and write the scripts. The set is made up of tiny farm buildings and houses and miniature furniture and animals. Standing in this set, Homme appears to be a giant of tremendous proportions. He is a friendly giant, however, who carries on interesting, enlightening, and amusing conversations with animal puppets about a great variety of topics, among them word usage, distant lands, government, and values in living. The giant often shows pictures to illustrate the topic of the conversations. The production does not involve complicated techniques, yet it is highly effective.

In developing a series for children, there are a number of points to keep in mind. Maintain a simple and coherent program structure which follows a consistent pattern from week to week so that children know what to expect. The scripts written for *Mister Rogers' Neighborhood* illustrate the application of this principle. After showing an interesting real object and discussing the day's subject for a while, Mister Rogers gives several perspectives of it through a film demonstration, an interview with a guest, or a visit to a neighbor. He might talk about making bread, for example, and then take his young viewers to a bakery to see bread mixed and baked. The middle segment is the Neighborhood of Make Believe, an imaginary place clearly distinguished with the words "Let's pretend" and with a transitional device such as a miniature trolley. In the make-believe portion the puppets and people reflect more about the subject of the program. The program always returns to the real world of Mister Rogers' living room where he interprets the theme further and sings his goodbye song. This pattern is followed with little variation from program to program.

If the program is dramatic, keep the story line as direct as possible by developing a few scenes completely rather than by writing a staccato succession of short scenes. Start the main story promptly and provide enough action and excitement to hold attention, for suspense and urgency are as important as they are in adult drama.

Present as few major characters as possible to avoid complicating the child's problem of keeping track of people. Introduce them early and keep them consistent. You should be careful in naming your characters. One common mistake is choosing a bizarre name such as Nicodemus Nimbletoes, which carries little meaning to a child. A funny character name can be an asset to a program but only if it is funny to the child.

Since the attention span of children is shorter than that of adults, you should vary the content and pace as much as possible and avoid encompassing too much information in one broadcast. Generally, you should keep in mind the youngest children toward whom you are aiming your program and try to make it meaningful and interesting to them. This does not mean that children will not enjoy programs meant for another group; it has been discovered that some children, particularly the brighter ones, like the challenge of viewing programs meant for older children.

Relating to the Child's Experience

The child's limited fund of experience and lack of sophistication require a number of adaptations. It is obvious that the language used in a children's program should be simpler and more direct than that used for adults. One important requirement is a careful attention to vocabulary. This does not mean that you should use only words the child already knows, for to do so would nullify the contribution that broadcasts can make to the growth of a child's vocabulary, but you should introduce new words so that their meaning becomes clear from the context. For young children, nouns, verbs, and pronouns are the most important parts of sentences, and adverbs and adjectives should be used sparingly. Keep grammatical structure simple, particularly for the very young child. Avoid dialects if possible, for they are not easily understood.

Children's craving to find out about the world around them provides you with an automatic hold on their attention, but you can lose it quickly if you present new material in such a way that bewilderment rather than enlightenment results. Introduce fresh ideas by connecting them with something the child already knows. A sketch from *Sesame Street* illustrates how a new concept, the letter *J,* was described by comparing it with something most children are familiar with—the shape of a fishhook.

SESAME STREET
THE LETTER J

VIDEO	AUDIO
PICTURE OF TWO SMALL BOYS SITTING AND TALKING	FIRST BOY What's happening, man? SECOND BOY I don't know.

	FIRST BOY
LETTER J APPEARS	What's that?
FROM TOP OF SCREEN	SECOND BOY
	I don't know
	FIRST BOY
	It looks like a fishhook.
	MAN (VOICE-OVER)
J ENLARGES AND BOYS	It's not a fishhook!
HUDDLE TOGETHER	It's a J.
	BOYS (TOGETHER)
	Yeah!
J MOVES TO LEFT	MUSIC UP—VOICE-OVER
LITTLE MAN WALKS	Once upon a time a guy named Joe
OVER TO J AND LIES IN	Noticed a June bug on his toe
HOOK—SEES BUG ON	Put it in a jar and started to go
TOE	
GETS OFF J, PUTS BUG	
IN JAR	
JUDGE ENTERS FROM	But here comes the judge and said, "No, no, no."
RIGHT	
JOE JUMPS	But Joe said, "Why?" and started to jump
JOE DANCES ON TREE	And danced a jig on an old tree stump
STUMP	
JOE JOGS TO LEFT OF	And jogged along to the city dump
SCREEN	
JOE PUTS BUG IN TIRE	Where he jammed the June bug in a tire pump
PUMP	
JUDGE APPEARS AND	And the judge caught up and started to wail.
HITS JOE ON HEAD	Said to Joe, "Justice will prevail."
WITH GAVEL	
JOE IN COURTROOM	And the Jury met and set the bail
JOE BEHIND BARS.	And Joe got an hour in the city jail.
	FIRST BOY
	So that's the letter J.
CUT BACK TO TWO	
BOYS SITTING THEN	
LIE DOWN LOOKING	
UP AT J	
	SECOND BOY
	It still looks like a fishhook.
	FIRST BOY
	You know what else we learned?
	SECOND BOY
BOYS SIT UP	Yeah. Don't jive a judge by jamming a June bug.
WORDS STARTING	
WITH J APPEAR AS	
THEY ARE SPOKEN	

When you present problems in a program, they should be ones that can be related to the real or easily imagined experiences of children. A program on bereavement, for example, should begin by referring to the grief that comes from the loss of a pet, which most children either undergo or can understand, rather than to the grief aroused by the loss of family members, which many people experience only after becoming adults.

Because children have difficulty with the concept of time, you must be especially careful when time concepts are involved. Programs should proceed chronologically if possible, for children expect a story to move forward. If it moves backward, they are likely to be confused, which means that the flashback technique should be used sparingly if at all. For the same reason avoid extreme shifts in time and space and be sure that transitions are simple and clear.

QUESTIONS AND PROJECTS

1. Consider how the interests and capabilities of children in the four-to-eight age group differ from those in the nine-to-12 age group. Then suggest two subjects or stories particularly adapted to the needs of each group.

2. What is your personal response to the often-heard criticism that television purveys too much violence, especially for children?

3. Watch a TV program designed for children with special attention to vocabulary. Decide whether the language is simple enough for children to follow the program yet sufficiently challenging to expand their vocabulary.

4. The familiar stories "Bluebeard" and "The Emperor's New Clothes" present difficulties of different types for the writer who proposes to adapt them into dramas for children. Read these stories, decide what the problems are, and indicate how you would deal with them in adaptations.

5. Suggest subjects for children's programs in each of the following content categories: exploration, orientation, doing, storytelling, and multipurpose.

NOTES

1. Patricia O'Toole, "Ever-Ever Land," *Newsweek*, Fall/Winter 1991, pp. 38–40.
2. Robert Liebert and Joyce Sprafkin, *The Early Window: Effects of Television on Children and Youth*, 3rd ed. (Washington, D.C.: Pergamon Press, 1988).

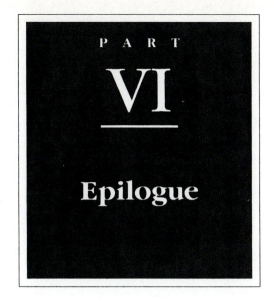

PART

VI

Epilogue

If you have now reached a stage where, as historian Walter Prescott Webb said, you believe that you have something to say, that it is worth saying, and that you can say it better than anyone else, you may qualify as a script writer. You cannot realize that aspiration to the fullest, however, unless you find someone to employ you. You may well find that meeting this challenge is even more difficult than the task of writing itself. Even if you do find employment, you will discover that your creative talent cannot be exercised without restraint. State and federal laws, the conventions of society, and the nature of the industries for which you work all restrict what you can put into your script.

CHAPTER 19

CAREER OPPORTUNITIES AND RESTRICTIONS

Talent goes into the first draft and the art into the drafts that follow.

JOHN LE CARRÉ

THE EMPLOYMENT OF WRITERS

The employment situations for writers differ widely. There are variations in the status they hold in the organization for which they work and the pay they receive. Another matter of great concern is the protection of writers' interests in the material they have created.

Classes of Employment

Writers who are permanently attached to the staff of a broadcasting organization and are paid on a regular weekly or monthly basis instead of being paid per script are known as *staff writers*. They are the ones who turn out most of the newscasts, commercials, and gen-eral continuities broadcast by networks and stations. At the other end of the spectrum are *freelance writers,* who have no connection with a broadcasting organization and no assurance that a script on which they may have spent many hours of work will find a market. They are paid only if the script they submit to a station, network, production organization, or advertising agency is accepted. Freelance writers often work at other occupations because the sale of scripts is too irregular to earn them a living; for some of them writing is merely a hobby.

An excellent, though limited, opportunity for freelance writers exists in the area of episodic television. People designing new or continuing series assemble an ad hoc staff of writers for a season, roughly 40 weeks of work, usually beginning in May or June. They assemble producers, story editors, and script consultants to write for particular episodes.

Ideally, the first batch of scripts will be ready by August, anticipating broadcasts beginning in late September. Every few months the staff will break for a brief vacation, allowing the executive producer to evaluate the team. Each hiatus results in the retention or dismissal of staff members based upon their ability to work effectively and collaboratively.

The disadvantage of so fluid a situation is obvious; however, people who spend a few years with a hit show will very likely discover doors opening to them over the next years. Story editors often move up to become producers, and networks will welcome their pitches for new series.

Writers who secure a contract to do a particular piece of writing are known as *commissioned writers*. Like freelance writers, they are paid by the script but, like staff writers, they are assured that once designated to do a particular piece of writing, they will be paid for their work even if it is never broadcast. Most writers of this type receive their commissions on the basis of story ideas or treatments submitted to a script editor. Occasionally a freelance writer may submit a script for use in a regular series, but the rate of acceptance is very low. Commissioned writers, like freelance writers, may create scripts as a side line.

The Pay of Writers

A topic of absorbing interest to young writers is the amount of money that can be earned in broadcasting, and yet it is one of the most difficult subjects on which to make generalizations. Of the three classes of writers just discussed, staff writers are likely to receive the least amount of money per page but they have the advantage of being on a regular salary. The size of this salary is related to the size of the market area in which they work. News or continuity writers in a small community earn much less than those working for a station in a large city. Staff writers for networks and national advertising and production agencies usually earn the highest incomes. The annual earnings of a skilled advertising copywriter who works for a national agency may even approach the six-figure mark. Commissioned writers, by virtue of the reputation that caused them to be commissioned, are likely to receive the most money per page of script. Freelance writers will not receive as much money per page as the commissioned writer, but they may receive more than staff writers. In total income from writing, however, they may fall below the staff writer because they sell only an occasional script.

The Writers Guild of America, which represents radio, TV, and film writers, has established minimum fees which vary with the length and nature of the script. Established writers are paid more than the minimum. The income from a given script, moreover, may not be restricted to that received for a single broadcast. If the program is repeated, the writer receives residual payment according to terms established by the Writers Guild. A further source of income may be the adaptation of an original script into a movie or stage version. Success in writing may also be a stepping stone toward other positions in the media which pay even better than writing. Norman Lear, who began as a writer, increased his income substantially when he became the producer of *All in the Family*. Those who have been successful in writing for one medium frequently move on to lucrative careers writing for another.

Protecting the Writer's Interest

Writers have sometimes been exploited by unscrupulous producers, the violations ranging from the outright theft of ideas or scripts, to inadequate compensation for scripts, or no payment at all for reusing them. The Writers Guild of America was organized to establish a set of rules for protecting writers' interests, and it now has contracts with the major radio and television networks, film companies, and production agencies. Membership in the Guild is open only to those who have established their professional credentials by selling scripts. They pay an initiation fee and dues based on the income they earn from writing. Besides carrying on activities that benefit its members, the Guild also provides some services for writers who are not yet eligible to join.

The contracts the Guild negotiates with the industry vary according to the nature of the writing and the relationship the writer has with the employer. The contract for staff news writers, for example, is different from that negotiated for writers who write plays on a commissioned basis. The various documents are too lengthy to cover in detail, but a review of some of the points they deal with indicates the kind of conditions with which writers and the Writers Guild are concerned.

In addition to negotiating the minimum fees paid for scripts for both original and subsequent presentations, which we have already mentioned, the Guild deals with other important matters. It prohibits employers from inviting writers to submit scripts on speculation, a system under which the writer is paid only if the script turns out to be satisfactory in the employer's eyes. A commissioned script for live or taped production must be used within a specified time after its delivery or the writer is free to sell it elsewhere, even though the producer who commissioned it has already paid for it. Guild contracts also contain references to the nature of the writer's credits, the requirements for rewriting the original submission, the payment of traveling expenses, the writer's privilege of attending rehearsals, the conditions affecting collaboration, and the rights of the producer and the writer in the sale of the script for subsidiary uses.

One thing that worries writers a great deal is the possibility that their scripts or ideas will be stolen. A major form of protection is the Copyright Act, which is designed to maintain property rights for a specified period of time for material people create. In 1978 a revision of the copyright law went into effect that established the period of copyright protection as the life of the material's creator plus 50 years. Sometimes writers do not bother to copyright their scripts, relying instead on other measures to protect their work. We describe these methods shortly. If you do decide to copyright your script, you should put a copyright notice on it as soon as you exhibit, display, or sell it. This notice should include three elements: (1) the copyright symbol "©" or the word "copyright," or the abbreviation "copr."; (2) the year of its first publication; (3) your name as the copyright owner. On publication, you should also register your work with the Copyright Office by sending it two copies of the work and paying the required fee. The address is: Register of Copyrights, Library of Congress, Washington, D.C. 20559.

You can copyright only complete scripts. Even titles cannot be copyrighted, although in some circumstances the courts have ruled that people have property rights in certain titles. Ideas for scripts and treatments cannot be protected by copyright, however. In an effort to protect both ideas and complete scripts, the Writers Guild maintains a Registration Service. Members and nonmembers who have developed ideas or written scripts for radio and television programs and for films may, for a fee, file descriptions or scripts with the Registration Service, where they are kept in files available to no one except their creators. The address is: Writers Guild Registration Office, 8955 Beverly Boulevard, Los Angeles, California 90048.

This service does not provide absolute protection but it helps to answer two questions frequently at issue when plagiarism or theft is being alleged: When did the idea or script come into existence, and who had access to it? Another technique used by some writers is to mail a copy of the script to themselves by registered mail and keep the package unopened unless the question of the time of authorship arises.

While the date on the postmarked envelope is essential for those who use the registered mail technique, the date on a script can be lethal to its author. Two potential problems merit consideration: First, an old date suggests rejection by others to whom the script may have been submitted; second, anyone intent upon stealing your ideas may simply backdate their own rendition of your script. The latter, according to a past vice president of the Writers Guild, rarely happens.

GETTING STARTED AS A WRITER

If the first question of an aspiring writer is: "How much do writers get paid for scripts?" the second is: "How do I get started as a writer?" Both questions are equally difficult to answer. There is, in fact, no well-defined route to a career as a writer in broadcasting.

David Black, a writer and producer of the *Law and Order* series, says, "The best way to break in is to be a friend of the producer." Friendship, he explains, is just the beginning. When he's developing a series, he looks first to his own circle of friends, especially journalists and novelists. He explains: "You need stories."

In a sense, the individual who seeks a position as a staff writer has the easiest task. As in the news field, potential staff writers apply to the head of the script department or to a director of the specific programs for which they wish to write. Usually they must call or write for an appointment, send or bring a résumé of their experience, samples of their work, and be prepared to audition. This audition generally involves a five-minute, on-the-spot writing of a given type of material—news, dialogue, commercial, and so on.

The route to employment for the freelance or commissioned writer is not as well defined as it is for staff writers. A beginner might think that the best way to bring a script to the attention of producers is to send it to them by mail. The catch to this approach is that producers generally refuse to open envelopes containing scripts from unknown writers. They fear that even if they find the script completely unacceptable and return it, they will be sued later for filching the idea and using it in a script prepared by another writer. It is true that ideas and even scripts actually have been appropriated by producers in the past, and on occasion the courts have awarded the injured writer substantial damages. It is equally true, however, that two people may think of similar ideas at the same time, and the appearance of two scripts with the same basic premise does not necessarily indicate that one writer has stolen an idea from the other. Establishing the ownership and originality of ideas is one of the most difficult of legal problems, and most producers try to avoid becoming caught in courtroom tangles by simply refusing to look at scripts submitted by strangers.

Though selling a script by mailing it to a producer is almost impossible, an occasional sale is made in this way. If you do take this route, you must obtain a release form and submit it with your script. Release forms differ from place to place but their objective is the same—namely, to protect the producer from being sued. In the release form you affirm that the script is an original work, that the company to which you send it is not responsible for plagiarism or damage suits, and that it has no obligation to you. You may also be asked to recognize the fact that others may have developed scripts along the same general lines as yours. Be sure to include a stamped, self-addressed envelope or your script will not be returned. As a safety measure, keep a copy of the script in your files.

With securing direct access to producers through the mail a virtual impossibility, the beginning writer must use the services of an intermediary to have a script considered. These intermediaries, or literary agents as they are called, are known to producers, and their participation in the process provides some assurance that producers will not be confronted by vexatious lawsuits. The agent's willingness to submit a script also indicates that it is of professional quality and has some relationship to the producer's need for material, though it may not finally be accepted, of course. For the services they provide, agents usually receive 10 percent of the fee the writer is paid for the script.

Unfortunately, beginning writers may find it almost as difficult to find an agent willing to submit their scripts as it is to reach the producer directly. Agents are interested only in representing writers whose scripts they can sell, for that is the way they profit from their efforts. For that reason, they usually accept as clients only those writers who have already had scripts accepted for production. Lawrence Kasdan, whose talent became obvious when he wrote and directed such films as *Body Heat, The Big Chill, Silverado,* and *Grand Canyon,* spent five years working in an advertising agency before he could find an agent willing to represent him. Beginners must persist until they can find agents who are willing to look at the work of newcomers to the field in the hope that they will discover new talent. When you submit your work to agents, be sure to include stamped, self-addressed envelopes.

The Writers Guild lists agents it approves in a publication that is available for a small fee. The Guild publishes at the beginning of each TV season a list of the shows to be produced. Those series that seek scripts from outside the production staff are specially identified and the nature of the series is described. With this as a guide, writers may prepare scripts and then seek agents to submit them. Both this list and the agent's lists are available from: Writers Guild of America West, 8955 Beverly Boulevard, Los Angeles, California 90048.

One of the best ways for new writers to gain access to a producer is to find some kind of work in a production organization. First scripts are often brought to a producer's desk by the clerk in the mailroom, by the extra who is appearing in the productions, or by the stenographer who types someone else's scripts. Occasionally, contact can be made through an intermediary who works in the organization; cousins, uncles, and brothers have paved the way to production for relatives outside the organization.

In addition to making contact with script editors and producers easier, employment in a production organization is important to writers for two other reasons. First of all, it gives them the opportunity to gain general knowledge of broadcasting and to learn specifically about the particular needs and demands of the company they work for. Second, if the script is accepted, they will be available, as writers are often expected to be, to participate in the rewriting process that goes on during rehearsals.

Once writers have established themselves and can gain direct access to the production staff, their problems measurably diminish. Beginners may spend many hours writing a script that is rejected, not because it lacks professional quality, but because it does not fit the concept of the show. Those on the inside can often test their ideas in a personal conference with producers or story editors. If the idea is unsuitable, the writer can find that out before wasting time turning out a complete script. If it is suitable, a commitment is often made calling for a treatment, a first draft, and a final draft, each of which can be accepted or rejected by the producer, and each of which, under Writers Guild regulations, is paid for. Once writers have become firmly established, they often present their ideas orally to producers. This process is called *pitching.* They usually only have a few minutes to make their presentations, which means that they must describe their ideas as succinctly as possible. Those that can be expressed in just a few words are called *high-concept* ideas. Ideas for scripts are also presented in written form. A *synopsis* sums up the basic idea and describes the characters and plot in just a page or two. Longer descriptions that may run for six or more pages are called *treatments* or *scenarios.*

Beginners are likely to think only of markets in the United States, but Americans often write for radio, TV, and film producers outside this country. Writers seeking to market their work should not overlook the opportunities that may exist in other parts of the English-speaking world. Canadian and British production organizations frequently purchase the work of writers who live in the United States.

Beginners, contemplating the barriers producers and agents erect to protect themselves from amateurs, may feel they have little chance of breaking into the field. This feeling is not entirely unreasonable; breaking in is very difficult. It may be of some comfort to realize, however, that some half a hundred beginners do get a script accepted for the first time every year. If this did not happen, the entertainment industry would soon run out of writing talent. It may be helpful to realize also that if you have the talent to write material that will attract and entertain audiences, producers are as anxious to discover you as you are to be discovered. Note the importance of talent, however. No person who turns out amateurish, unpolished scripts will ever become a successful writer. Persistence is also necessary. Writers confident of their talent must keep trying to surmount the barriers designed to discourage the untalented.

Oliver Stone, writer and director of such films as *Platoon* and an Academy Award-winning screenwriter, during one period in his career wrote 11 scripts, none of which he succeeded in selling. It took him 10 years to find a producer for the script of *Platoon,* which eventually won the Academy Award as the best picture of 1986.

THE NATURE OF THE INDUSTRIES

Writers, no matter what their medium, must respond to requirements that may, in fact, prevent them from realizing their full creative potential. The major influence as far as commercial broadcasting is concerned is that most of the scripts a writer turns out have only a secondary role: They exist merely for the purpose of attracting an audience so that the program can accomplish its primary goal of selling goods. A network program that fails to attract about a third of the people who are watching television is almost certain to be dropped. The audience requirements for local shows and specialized programs may be somewhat less demanding, but few can ignore the verdict of the audience rating, which finally determines whether most programs will live or die.

The movie industry operates on a basis that is somewhat different from that of the broadcasting industry in that films exist for themselves rather than merely being lures to attract audiences for commercials. (The practice of showing commercials as part of movie bills, though spreading, is not yet widespread enough to be a significant factor in the situation.) Films still must attract audiences, however, if their makers are to survive. Because it is difficult to determine why a given movie succeeds or fails, occasional failures may be forgiven, but writers in the long run must be able to create scripts that a significant number of people are willing to pay to see performed. This commercial emphasis, though unlike the one in broadcasting, is an all-important factor. In one instance writers are subject to the tyranny of the audience rating; in the other they are subject to the tyranny of the box office.

RESTRICTIONS ON WRITERS

Writers in all media operate under certain restrictions that limit their freedom to write as they might otherwise choose. Radio and television, which are primarily controlled by the Communications Act of 1934 and its amendments, are bound by the severest restrictions, films by the loosest. The limitations on cable TV fall somewhere in between. One reason for the greater restrictions on radio and television is that broadcasters use frequencies generally considered to be public property. The Communications Act requires that the programs they transmit serve the *public interest, convenience,* and *necessity.* A second reason is that most radio and television programs come into the home, often entering uninvited on the heels of other programs. Families frequently watch them together. A third reasons is that the audience is very diverse, containing people of widely different ages, classes, occupations, and races. These facts dictate restraint in the kind of material presented.

You might wonder why cable programs, which are also watched by families and diverse groups of people, don't operate under the same restrictions. The main reason is that the facilities used to transmit programs are privately owned rather than being in the public domain, as radio and television frequencies are. Cable operators are therefore not subject to the public-interest requirement that restrains broadcasters.

Offensive Language and Situations

During the past 25 years there has been a revolution in the nature of the language and subject matter people are willing to accept in various types of media presentations. It is difficult to believe now that the expression "holy cow" was once cut from a radio script because it was too daring and the words "Out, damned spot" were removed from the broadcast version of Shakespeare's *Macbeth.*

Though words considered to be offensive are used much more freely in broadcasts than they once were, not all the restrictions have disappeared. A provision in the U.S. Criminal Code prohibits the transmission of obscene, indecent, or profane language by means of radio communications (which also includes television broadcasting). It is difficult, however, to determine just what these words or their synonyms mean. Courts, including the U.S. Supreme Court, grapple regularly with the problem of defining them. No clear-cut definition has yet emerged. Supreme Court Justice Potter Stewart said, for example, that although he could not define pornography, he knew it when he saw it. Federal Communications Commissioner Robert E. Lee remarked somewhat plaintively, "Least of all do I have a clear understanding of what constitutes obscenity in broadcasting."

The situation, to say the least, is fluid. As the 1980s came to a close the FCC seemed to be taking a stricter stance when it fined a number of stations for broadcasting obscene and indecent programs. On the other hand, the use of graphic sexual terms in the transmission of both the confirmation hearing of Supreme Court Justice Clarence Thomas, which involved claims of sexual harassment by Anita Hill, and the trial of William Kennedy Smith for rape seemed to open the door to greater use of these terms in regular broadcasts.

At one time broadcasters could look for some guidance to their own organization, the National Association of Broadcasters (NAB), which regularly published codes of good practice. In a move surprising to many people, the Justice Department ruled that these codes violated the antitrust laws, and in 1982 they were dropped. Even when they existed, stations and networks were ultimately responsible for deciding what constituted appropriate situations and language. In carrying out this prickly chore, they must always be sensitive to the constant shifts in public attitudes.

The situation as far as films are concerned is quite different. There are now no restrictions on the language that can be used and almost none on the actions that can be performed. This marks a significant change from what used to be the case. In the 1930s the Motion Picture Association of America (MPAA) adopted a highly restrictive code that severely limited the freedom of writers and producers. Even married people could not be shown in bed together and writers had to make clear that those who committed crimes were punished for their transgressions. When some producers began defying this code, the MPAA finally abandoned it and set up a rating system in its place. The Association's Code and Rating Administration reviews each new film and gives it a rating indicating the type of audience for which it is appropriate. A rating of G means that the film is suitable for all audiences. Pictures rated PG are open to all who want to buy tickets, but the rating warns parents that the inclusion of certain language and behavior suggests that parents should use discretion in permitting young people to see the picture. An R rating bars admittance to children younger than 17 unless they are accompanied by an adult. When this restriction began to cut down the size of audiences, the MPAA introduced the PG-13 rating, which indicated that the subject matter was inappropriate for children younger than 13. The newest rating, NC-17, prohibits children younger than 17 from seeing the movie under any circumstances. It replaced the X rating, which had been taken over by the makers of

pornographic films to designate films that were sexually explicit throughout. Although ratings change in definition and influence, what remains constant is a concern for the effect of programs and movies upon young and vulnerable viewers, those members of society most entitled to protection by responsible adults.

The fact that moviemakers and television broadcasters operate under different standards sometimes creates problems when movies are presented on television. Broadcasters often have to edit out offensive language and situations. Sometimes scenes in movies are shot in two versions—one for theaters and one for television. This technique is called *covering*.

Just as the restraints governing language and action have loosened in recent years, so have the restraints on what can be advertised. Commercials for products that deal with the most intimate parts and functions of the human body can be heard or seen at all hours of the day and night. All restrictions have not vanished, however. There is an agreement among broadcasters not to present commercials for hard liquor, although advertising for wine and beer is permitted. There is also an odd restraint on what can be done in a beer commercial—the performers are almost never shown actually drinking it. Congress has intervened to prevent the advertising on radio and television of another widely used product, the cigarette, because of the Surgeon General's verdict that cigarette smoking is injurious to health. Later Congress instituted a similar ban against the advertising of smokeless tobacco. The AIDS epidemic has diminished the taboo against the advertising of condoms.

Offending Audience Members

Another challenge facing writers is to avoid offending various groups in the audience. In considering this problem we usually think first about minority groups. A decision that writers sometimes must make at the very beginning is to decide what to call them.

Naming Races   In the past 100 years there have been several changes in the terms used to designate the race that most publications now refer to as *black* or *African-American*. Terms that many now frown upon still linger, however, in the names of such august organizations as the National Association for the Advancement of Colored People (NAACP) and the United Negro College Fund. In 1931, the *New York Times* began capitalizing *Negro* (the Spanish and Portuguese word for black), and most dictionaries shortly followed this example. In line with this precedent, some publications now capitalize *Black* when it refers to race. To be consistent, it would seem that publications capitalizing *Black* should also capitalize *White* when referring to race.

The most recent entry in this area is the term *African-American*. Those who advocate its use argue that it is preferable to other labels because it denotes a particular historical and cultural background. Recent studies indicate, however, that members of this racial group are divided in their preferences. The practices of publishers and broadcasters also differ. Some have adopted the *African-American* term, some use *black* (or *Black*), and some use both.

The problem of choosing terms for other races or minority groups is not as difficult as the one we have just discussed. *Hispanic* is now the label chosen by many in designating those who speak Spanish or Portuguese, although *Chicano* and *Latino* also have their adherents. The term *Indian,* while still highly popular, has given some ground to *Native American* as the fashionable term for referring to America's original inhabitants, and *Oriental* has been displaced in most instances by *Asian-American.*

Avoiding Stereotypes   The practice of ascribing the same characteristics, values, and positions in society to all members of a certain race, nationality, or group is called stereotyping. As we pointed out in Chapter 12, it should be avoided because it perpetuates false ideas about people and denies what every human should enjoy, the right to be considered a unique individual with characteristics that make each person different from anyone else.

In the past few years awareness of the damaging effect of stereotypes increased sharply. Because stereotypes first take shape in scripts, writers more than most must realize their use often involves slurs against ethnic and racial groups which denigrate their standing in society. Eliminating stereotypes, however, is not easy; it is a task calling for constant vigilance.

Writing About People with Disabilities
When you write about people with disabilities, you must be particularly sensitive about the words you use. As with the naming of races, one problem is to decide what to call them. Some refer to them as "physically, mentally or emotionally challenged people," for example. The main thing to remember is that people in this group want to be remembered for their accomplishments, personalities, and character, not for their disabilities or the symbols of their handicaps. Brother Nick Curry, S.J., founder of the National Theater for the Handicapped, an acting school and talent pool for physically challenged individuals, objects, for instance, to camera shots taken through the spokes of a wheelchair. This approach shifts the attention of the audience from the competence of the actor to what may be an unrelated physical condition. Disabilities should not even be mentioned unless they are crucial to a story. Guidelines for writing about people with disabilities can be obtained from the following: Media Project,

Research and Training Center on Independent Living, BCR/3111 Haworth, University of Kansas, Lawrence, Kansas 66045 (*Phone:* 913-842-7694).

These guidelines recommend that certain words are preferable to others. Saying that a person is "confined to a wheelchair" is unacceptable. It is better to say "uses a wheelchair." The guidelines further recommend against describing the disabled as either "pathetic" or "overachievers." The objective should always be to establish them as complex personalities who give as well as receive.

Avoiding Sexism

Much of what we have said about the kind of writing that might offend the diverse groups in our society also applies to the treatment of women. They have suffered as much from stereotyping as anyone. The commercial that points the finger at women as the family members solely responsible for carrying out onerous household chores is an example. So are TV series that consistently place women in subservient roles and assign all positions of authority to men. The rise of the feminist movement has thrown the spotlight on such practices, and they are now much less common than they once were.

Sometimes, however, sexism goes in the other direction. Writing in the *New York Times,* Bernard Goldberg pointed out that the TV program *Roseanne* consistently portrayed the father as a clumsy dolt. He also cited a commercial showing a husband and wife playing tennis: *He* plays so awkwardly that the ball keeps hitting him in the head; *her* game, in contrast, is crisp and controlled, presumably because she eats the right kind of cereal. Goldberg argued that even though such instances of sexism do not provoke the barrage of complaints incited by material offensive to women, they nevertheless deserve examination.[1]

Selecting Pronouns   Although it is surely true that many words can get us into trouble, leading anywhere from personal misunderstandings to full-scale wars, it is probable that the most troublesome villains, as far as sexism is concerned, are pronouns. The main problem is that English does not have a neutral personal pronoun in the singular that can be used to designate either a man or a woman. The battle of the pronouns may even reach to the heavens when descriptions of God are involved. Some people may protest when sermons use a masculine pronoun in referring to God, even though most theologies state that God is neither male nor female, but spirit. Scripture abounds in gender-related images, spun and translated through generations of writers. Jesus taught his followers to pray to "Our Father," but he sometimes also used feminine images of God's care for creation— for example, a mother hen longing to gather her chicks under her wings.

There are also difficulties with more earthbound references. It was once the practice of writers to refer to activities involving both men and women with a masculine pronoun. Twenty-five years ago we might have written, "The audience for this textbook is not restricted to aspiring script writers, for who does not want to improve his writing skills?" The *his* implies to some that only men want to become better writers, which is obviously untrue. Moreover, it is seen as discriminatory because it places men in the dominant role.

What is the way out of this difficulty? The substitution of the feminine counterpart of *his* suggests a reverse sexism. To alternate between *his* and *her* is not only inconsistent; it is blatantly foolish. *Her/his* or *his/her* gets tedious, and constructions like s/he smack of contrivance. *Itself* is patently unacceptable because it neuters both sexes, hardly a desirable outcome. "For who does not want to improve *their* writing skills" is grammatically incorrect. A singular antecedent requires a singular pronoun. It is possible, of course, to cast the verb in the passive voice, "For who does not wish to be improved as a writer?" This avoids the problem but weakens the expression. Passive voice, successfully employed in print, makes speech sound stilted and therefore should be used sparingly, because speech is what broadcasting is about. Fortunately, the plural personal pronouns are neutral. The solution to the problem in most instances is simply to turn singular subjects into plurals. The use of the plural neutral pronoun thus becomes grammatically correct. This revision of our sample sentence, while lumbering a bit, represents a compromise between what might be considered the ideal and the expedient: "The audience for this textbook is not restricted to aspiring scriptwriters, for what students do not want to improve their writing skills?"

Sometimes this solution cannot be used because the situation has an essentially singular context. The discussion of a parent's relationship with a child is an example. In such instances, the only recourse is to employ the somewhat clumsy "he or she" or "she or he" usages. Another approach is to repeat the subject of the sentence instead of using a pronoun.

Other Language Considerations
Choosing the right pronoun is important but writers also need to be alert to other language practices that can give their work a sexist tone. One is the habit of employing a special term to identify gender when the activities of women are being discussed. Sexist terms that have been or should be abandoned include *authoress, aviatrix, stewardess, male nurse,* and *woman doctor.* The *New York Times Stylebook* recommends: "In referring to women, avoid words or phrases that seem to imply that *The Times* views men as the norm and women the exception, or descriptions that would be irrelevant if the subject were male."

The *Associated Press Stylebook* directs its writers to afford women the same treatment they would men in all areas of coverage, adding: "Physical descriptions, sexist references, demeaning stereotypes, and condescending phrases should not be used." Advising that copy should not assume maleness when both sexes are involved, they urge their writers to use alternate terms. *Newsmen* is easily replaced by *reporters* for example. The AP cautions against expressions of surprise that an attractive woman can be professionally accomplished. Neither should copy "gratuitously mention family relationships when there is no relevance to the subject." It suggests using the same standards for men and women in deciding whether to include references to personal appearances or professional and marital status.

Controversial Issues

Because a program exists primarily to sell goods, its capacity to enrich the hearts and minds of its viewers tends to be a secondary consideration. If a TV play incorporates an honest statement about life that in the advertiser's view may inhibit the sale of products, the honest statement usually must be sacrificed. The result is that plays dealing with controversial public issues are likely to be banned or modified because of their potential to offend certain members of an audience or to arouse the sensitivity of the advertiser. The programs underwritten by corporations for use by public broadcasting stations have been largely those that ignore the contemporary issues of the day. These corporations instead support programs that deal with historical and literary subjects which are likely to offend no one. The commercial networks have had the same difficulty in attracting advertisers for their documentaries. Advertisers worry that the hostility aroused in some viewers by documentary treatment of certain issues may be transferred to their products.

Problems of this type also afflict programs of entertainment. When *thirtysomething* presented an episode involving a homosexual relationship, a number of advertisers canceled their commercials. The same thing happened to an episode of *China Beach* in which one of the leading characters had an abortion. When the time came to rerun these episodes, the ABC network decided not to schedule them a second time. It is obvious that writers invite rejection when they deal with subjects about which people are passionately divided.

The Violence Issue

One of the perennial issues in American broadcasting is the amount of violence shown on television and in films. There is naturally much public anxiety about the effect it may have on viewers, particularly children. This concern is regularly fanned by such researchers as George Gerbner, who for many years counted the number of violent acts occurring on various television shows and indicated whether the amount of violence was going up or down. Other researchers turn out studies suggesting that violence may provoke certain types of undesirable action in those who view it. Though studies thus far have failed to prove that violence has a precise effect that can be identified and predicted, there is no doubt that many people feel that watching it is harmful. Some groups like the PTA, the American Medical Association, and ACT (Action for Children's Television) agitate constantly against violence in television. It is estimated that by age 18 the average American has seen 200,000 violent acts on television, 40,000 of them murders. The movies, which often depict violence with an explicit realism far exceeding that shown on television, add many more violent acts to the total. The amount of violence in movies and on TV is increasing. The movie *Die Hard* turned 18 fictional human beings into corpses; its sequel *Die Hard 2* increased this number to 264. Accompanying this trend is a sharply increasing amount of violence in society as a whole. Although researchers have not been able to establish a direct connection between the two, it is difficult to believe there is none. A Gallup poll conducted in March 1991 showed that 68 percent of those questioned believe violence in the movies influences some of those who see it to commit violent acts.[2]

This issue is of great concern to writers, especially dramatists, because drama by its very nature involves violence. That statement may be shocking to those who share the public dismay at the amount of violence in TV and films, but it is true, nevertheless. The essence of drama is conflict and conflict breeds violence. To write effective drama, you must engulf people in difficulties, you must arouse their passions, you must incite them to conflict. If you do these things, you will provoke violence. If you fail to do them, you will have no drama.

Another factor in the situation is that although violence in television and film is routinely condemned, it appears to fascinate millions of people. The film *The Silence of the Lambs* is a case in point. Adapted from the Thomas Harris novel of the same name, it featured two repulsive murderers, one who skinned his victims and another who ate them. Some considered the material so revolting that it could not be filmed, yet when it was brought to the screen with unrelenting and chilling faithfulness to the original, it became one of the big hits of 1991 and subsequently swept the major Academy Awards.

There is no easy answer to the problem of dealing with the violence issue, particularly when the medium is television. Simply insisting that violence is inherent in drama does not solve the problem. As is the case with other taboos, the writer must walk the narrow line between doing what is acceptable and what will be condemned. It is obvious that gratuitous violence should be avoided, although drawing the line between violence that is necessary to the story and that which is indiscriminately piled on often requires a fine exercise of discrimination. The presentation of sheer brutality, however, is not only unacceptable, but it may also blunt the attainment of the dramatist's goal by blurring the issues with excess.

Violence is often most effective in achieving a dramatic purpose when it is imagined rather than seen. What the writer concentrates on is the effect of the violence, not the violence itself. This was the approach followed by the Greeks in presenting their dramas. Violent acts generally took place off stage; it was considered improper to expose them to the viewers' eyes. From this practice comes the word *obscene,* which condemns the revelation of an act or word that should take place only away from the scene.

Violence, moreover, need not necessarily be physical. Words that slash and tear are violent; a man walking tensely out of a house leaving his weeping wife behind him is indulging in a violent act. Sometimes the conflict may not provoke an actual outburst, but boiling beneath the surface and threatening to explode, it pervades the drama with a potential violence that creates tension and excitement. To abstain from the use of violence entirely is not a solution to the problem, for as we explained earlier, drama needs some violence to be effective. Writers cannot be successful if they restrict themselves to writing what one sponsor is supposed to have requested, "happy plays about happy people with happy problems."

Copyright

Previously in this chapter we cited the Copyright Law as a statute that protects the right of writers and other creators to profit from their creative effort. The Copyright Law also constitutes a severe restriction on writers in that it severely limits their right to incorporate material under copyright in their own work. The only condition under which writers may use another's copyrighted work or substantial portions of it, is to receive permission from the copyright holder. In many instances this permission is granted only after the payment of a fee.

There is one circumstance in which writers may use a small portion of another's work without receiving permission. This use is allowed under a provision in the Copyright Law known as the "fair use" principle. Under this provision, writers engaged in such activities as scholarly research, teaching, news reporting, and criticism may use short excerpts from copyrighted material without authorization. In interpreting this provision, the point to remember is that any unauthorized use of a work that jeopardizes the right of creators to profit from their effort is prohibited. Those who are thinking about using copyrighted material obviously should know the precise nature of the restraints. If you are in doubt, you should seek expert advice.

Laws Prohibiting Defamation

Other laws that substantially restrict the freedom of writers are state statutes prohibiting defamation. This offense occurs when some person or group makes false statements that tend to damage the reputation of other individuals or groups by holding them up to hatred or contempt or impugns their competency in a trade or calling. Spoken defamation is known as slander, written as libel. The written form usually involves higher penalties than the spoken because its relative permanence and wider circulation inflicts greater damage. The wide dissemination of derogatory statements made possible by radio and television has caused many authorities to consider them libelous in their impact and therefore subject to the higher penalties.

Defamation is a civil rather than a criminal offense, and those damaged must therefore seek recompense by bringing civil suits against people who have injured them. The truth of a statement is generally considered to be an absolute defense against a charge of defamation. In some states an exception to this rule is made when damaging but true stories are circulated for the purely malicious purpose of destroying a person's reputation. Decisions of the Supreme Court have modified the application of state laws prohibiting defamation in a number of instances. Under what came to be known as the "Sullivan rule," public officials cannot recover damages for a defamatory falsehood unless it is made with "actual malice." Later decisions applied this rule to celebrities. Another decision relieved writers of responsibility for defamation even when a statement is false if the intent of the material is purely satirical.

The Right of Privacy

Some states have laws designed to protect the privacy of their citizens. They resemble defamation statutes but are somewhat vaguer in definition. Programs that invade people's solitude, use their pictures without their consent, delve into their pasts, intrude into their homes, picture them in a false light, or reveal private information about them may invite the application of these laws. Proof that the facts are true is not necessarily a defense against a charge that the right of privacy has been violated. Producers of programs depicting true events have paid damages in the past because they ignored this right. Most news organizations protect the privacy of those who claim to be rape victims by refusing to divulge their names, for example.

Writers must always be alert to avoid damaging people's reputations with statements that are false or that improperly invade their privacy. News writers must be especially careful in the words they use to report alleged crimes. If they become careless, they may find themselves subjected to major damage suits.

LIVING WITH RESTRICTIONS

Though writers may chafe at any restraints on their activities, few would seek the elimination of all restrictions. It is generally recognized that copyright laws advance the interests of all writers. Laws that protect people from falsehoods damaging to their reputations and ward off invasions of their privacy work for everybody's good. The same can be said of the restrictions designed to suppress racism and sexism. It is equally clear that stereotyping should be discouraged because it unfairly represents the place and contributions of certain individuals and groups. Most also agree that there is some justification in placing limits on violence and the nature of the language, situations, and subjects suitable for broadcasting.

What does irritate some writers, especially those who create dramas and documentaries, is what some think of as an unreasonable concern about offending anyone in the audience. As we pointed out earlier, this causes documentary producers to shy away at times from treating subjects thought to be too controversial and may prevent dramatists from pursuing themes they want to explore or developing the characters and plots they believe best suit their artistic purposes. One thing to remember is that these restrictions are not absolute. ABC, for example, presented a documentary in 1990 that dealt with one of the most controversial issues it would be possible to choose—gun control. We analyzed this documentary in Chapter 4. It should be remembered also that opinions about what is appropriate in broadcast drama are also constantly changing. What may have been unacceptable yesterday may be acceptable today.

One development that has reduced restraints on writers is that advertisers no longer have the absolute control over programs that they once exercised. They can still refuse to sponsor programs of which they disapprove, of course, but they no longer edit scripts. In the past advertisers sometimes resorted to extreme measures to keep from reminding audiences of a competitor's name. To cite an example, at one time the meat-packing company, Armour, would not allow the word *swift* to be used in any of the programs it sponsored. The Swift company promptly retaliated by putting a similar ban on the word *armor*. Current writers can also be glad that equally bizarre restrictions established by the formulators of TV and movie codes have disappeared.

It may well be that writers tend to exaggerate the effect of restrictions on the quality of their work. Reginald Rose and Rod Serling, two pioneer television dramatists, complained constantly about what they described as ridiculous restrictions. Yet though they worked under restraints much more severe than those existing now, many of the scripts they turned out are regarded as classics. One thing writers who think they have a good idea should do is to avoid censoring themselves. Oscar Katz, a programming executive for CBS in the 1960s, recounts an incident that illustrates the

point. One of the writers for a series he was producing, *The Defenders,* suggested a story idea dealing with abortion. The writer was defensive, believing that the network would never permit production of the story. Katz advised him not to censor himself but to draw up a treatment and submit it to the Standard and Practices Division, a polite title for the network censor. Much to the writer's surprise, the subject was approved and *The Defenders* became one of the first series to deal with a topic formerly prohibited.

QUESTIONS AND PROJECTS

1. Conduct research to discover the steps taken by contemporary TV and film writers to reach their present positions. Obtain information about their educational backgrounds, methods of gaining entry into the field, and their present status as writers.
2. Should the system used to rate movies also be applied to television programs?
3. Do you believe that the standards of acceptability now applied to programs broadcast by TV stations and networks should also apply to programs transmitted by cable networks?
4. Do you think there is too much violence in television programs and movies, and, if so, what would you do to rectify the situation?

NOTES

1. Bernard R. Goldberg, "TV Insults Men, Too," *New York Times,* National Edition, March 14, 1989, p. 19.
2. Peter Plagens, "Violence in Our Culture," *Newsweek,* April 1991, p. 48.

GLOSSARY OF TERMS

The following are terms every television and screen writer should know. Those explained within the text have not been repeated here.

angle   Camera on person, place or thing—the subject of the shot. Angles may be high, wide, low, and so forth.

another angle   A variation of the previous shot, also called *new angle*.

antagonist   The person, force, or element obstructing a character's attainment of a goal.

audio   Speech, sound, music elements.

breakdown   A step-by-step delineation of the elements—action, dialogue, setting—in the scenes making up a script.

close shot   Provides a feeling of nearness to the subject.

crane shot   A moving shot from a camera fixed to a mobile arm.

CU   Close up. Provides a somewhat tighter view than does the close shot.

cut   Instantaneous transition from one shot to the next.

dissolve   The gradual replacement of one shot with another.

dolly shot   The camera moves as it picks up the scene, usually in or out.

edit   To select takes from those made during the taping or filming and arrange them into a completed production.

establishing shot   Provides a general view of the elements in a scene.

EXT.   An exterior location.

fade   A change from black to the picture (FADE IN) or from the picture to black (FADE OUT).

favoring   A shot that emphasizes a particular person, thing, or scene element.

follow shot   The camera moves to keep the emphasis on a particular element.

FX   Special effects.

insert   A shot put into a tape or film to show a scene element in close up.

INT.   An interior location.

intercut   Quick back-and-forth transitions between two or more shots.

LS   Long shot.

master scene   A shot showing the major elements in a scene.

MS   Medium shot.

moving shot   Focuses on a moving element in a scene.

one, two, three shot   Signifies the number of people in a shot.

OS   Over the shoulder. A shot taken from behind one character into the face of another.

pan   Movement of the camera on its pedestal from side to side.

parallel action   Quick switches back and forth between action occurring in two different settings simultaneously.

POV   Point of view. A shot taken from the perspective of a particular character in a scene.

premise   The basic idea that provides the springboard for a film, series, or series episode.

process shot   Action filmed against the tape or film of an appropriate background.

protagonist   A leading character who attracts the greatest audience sympathy or interest; the focal character.

rear projection   The projection from behind onto a translucent screen of a scene to provide the background for a process shot.

reverse angle   A transition from one perspective in a scene to its direct opposite.

scenario   A now-outdated term for the narrative exposition of a story or its breakdown of scenes. See *treatment*.

segue   A transition from one element to another. Usually refers to sound or music.

sequence   A succession of related shots or scenes.

sequence or step outline   A breakdown of the scenes or shots making up a script.

shooting script   A script in which the director has indicated the kind of shots to be used. The blueprint for the production.

SOF   Sound on film.

SOT   Sound on tape.

scene   A sequence of action occurring in one place without a break in time. May include several different shots.

set ups   A series of shots that provide variations of the master scene.

stock shot   A sequence taken from a library of films or tapes. Also called *file footage*.

shot   The picture taken during a single run of the camera.

storyboard   A succession of drawings showing the shots to be used in a commercial; drawings showing the shots to be used in filming or taping a story.

super   Superimposure. Inserting one image over another.

take   Same as *shot*.

tilt   The movement up and down of a camera on its pedestal.

treatment   A narrative, in the present tense, of a film or television story.

trucking shot   The camera moves laterally as it picks up a scene.

video   Refers to the visual elements in a script.

VO   Voice over.

zoom   The movement into or away from the scene. May be done electronically or by moving the camera.

BIBLIOGRAPHY

GENERAL WORKS

Barnouw, Eric, *Handbook of Radio Writing* (Boston, D.C. Heath and Co., 1948).

Barzun, Jacques, *Simple and Direct* (New York: Harper and Row, 1975).

Block, Mervin, *Writing Broadcast News: Shorter, Sharper, Stronger* (Chicago: Bonus Books, 1987).

Fox, Walter, *Writing the News* (New York: Hastings House, 1978).

Freeman, Morton, *A Treasury for Word Lovers* (Philadelphia: ISI Press, 1983).

French, Christopher, W., Eileen Alt Powell, and Howard Angione, eds., *The Associated Press Stylebook and Libel Manual* (New York: The Associated Press, 1985).

Garvey, Daniel E., and William L. Rivers, *Broadcast Writing* (New York: Longman, 1982).

_____, *Broadcast Writing Workbook* (New York: Longman, 1982).

_____, *Newswriting for the Electronic Media* (Belmont, Calif.: Wadsworth, 1982).

Hall, Mark W., *Broadcast Journalism: An Introduction to News Writing,* 3d Ed. (New York: Hastings House, 1978).

Hilliard, Robert, *Writing for Television and Radio,* 5th Ed. (Belmont, Calif.: Wadsworth, 1991).

Hood, James R., and Brad Kalbfeld, eds., *The AP Broadcast News Handbook* (New York: The Associated Press, 1982).

Kilpatrick, James J., *The Writer's Art* (Kansas City: Andrews, McMeel and Parker, 1984).

MacDonald, R. H., *A Broadcast News Manual of Style* (White Plains, N.Y.: Longman, Inc., 1987).

Maloney, Martin, and Paul Max Rubenstein, *Writing for the Media* (Englewood Cliffs, N.J.: Prentice-Hall, 1980).

Mayeux, Peter E., *Writing for the Broadcast Media* (Boston: Allyn and Bacon, 1985).

Mencher, Melvin, *Basic News Writing,* 3d Ed. (Dubuque, Iowa: Wm. C. Brown, 1989).

Miller, Casey, and Kate Swift, *The Handbook of Nonsexist Writing,* 2d Ed. (New York: Harper & Row, 1988).

Morris, William, and Mary Morris, *Harper Dictionary of Contemporary Usage* (New York: Harper & Row, 1975).

Newsom, Doug, and James A. Wollert, *Media Writing: Preparing Information for the Mass Media,* 2d Ed. (Belmont, Calif.: Wadsworth, 1988).

Orlik, Peter B., *Broadcast Copywriting,* 4th Ed. (Boston: Holbrook Press, 1990).

Rawson, Hugh, *A Dictionary of Euphemisms and Other Doubletalk* (New York: Crown, 1981).

Roberts, William H., *The Writer's Companion* (Boston: Little, Brown, 1985).

Semmelmeyer, Madeline, and Donald Bolander, *Instant English Handbook* (New York: Dell, 1990).

Smeyak, G. Paul, *Broadcast News Writing,* 2d Ed. (New York: Macmillan, 1983).

Strunk, William, and E. B. White, *The Elements of Style,* 3d Ed. (New York: Macmillan Co., 1979).

Walters, Roger L., *Broadcast Writing: Principles and Practices* (New York: Random House, 1988).

Webb, Robert A., ed., *The Washington Post Deskbook on Style* (New York: McGraw-Hill Book Co., 1978).

Wylie, Max, *Radio Writing* (New York: Farrar and Rinehart, 1939).

_____, *Writing for Television* (New York: Cowles Book Co., 1970).

NON-DRAMATIC WRITING

Advertising Age scripts. The Collector's Bookstore, 1708 N. Vine, Hollywood, Calif. 90029.

Baker, Stephen, *The Advertiser's Manual* (New York: John Wiley & Sons, 1988).

Baldwin, Huntley, *How to Create Effective TV Commercials,* 2d Ed. (Lincolnwood, Ill.: NTC Business Books, 1989).

Barnouw, Eric, *Documentary: A History of the Non-Fiction Film* (New York: Oxford University Press, 1974).

_____, *The Sponsor: Notes on a Modern Potentate* (New York: Oxford University Press, 1978).

Barsom, Richard M., *Nonfiction Film* (New York: E. P. Dutton, 1973).

Biagi, Shirley, *Interviews That Work,* 2d Ed. (Belmont, Calif.: Wadsworth, 1991).

Bittner, John R., and Denise Bittner, *Radio Journalism* (Englewood Cliffs, N.J.: Prentice-Hall, 1977).

Bland, Michael, *The Executive's Guide to TV and Radio Appearances* (White Plains, N.Y.: Knowledge Industry Publications, 1980).

Bluem, A. William, *Documentary in American Television: Form, Function, Method* (New York: Hastings House, 1964).

Book, Albert C., Norman D. Cary, and Stanley I. Tannenbaum, *The Radio and Television Commercial* (Chicago: NTC Business Books, 1989).

Brady, John, *The Craft of Interviewing* (Cincinnati: Writer's Digest, 1976).

Butler, Matilda, and William Paisley, *Women and the Mass Media* (New York: Human Sciences Press, 1980).

Cavett, Dick, and Christopher Porterfield, *Cavett* (New York: Harcourt Brace Jovanovich, 1974).

"Code of Ethics," *This is Your Radio-Television News Directors Association.* (Washington, D.C.: Radio-Television News Directors Association, 1966).

Cohen, Akiba A., *The Television News Interview* (Newbury Park, Calif.: Sage Publications, 1987).

Coleman, Ken, *So You Want to be a Sportscaster?* (New York: Hawthorne Books, 1973).

Costello, G. F., and G. N. Gordon, *Teach with Television: A Guide to Instructional TV* (New York: Hastings House, 1965).

Diament, Lincoln, *The Anatomy of a Television Commercial* (New York: Hastings House, 1971).

———, *Television's Classic Commercials: The Golden Years* (New York: Hastings House, 1971).

Elliot, Deni, *Responsible Journalism* (Newbury Park, Calif.: Sage Publications, 1986).

Epstein, Laurily Keir, *Women and the News* (New York: Hastings House, 1978).

Fabe, Maxene, *TV Game Shows* (Garden City, N.Y.: Doubleday and Co., 1980).

Fang, Irving E., *Television News, Radio News,* 4th Ed. Rev. (St. Paul: Rada Press, 1985).

Fates, Gil, *What's My Line: The Inside Story of TV's Most Famous Panel Show* (Englewood Cliffs, N.J.: Prentice-Hall, 1978).

Frank, Milo O., *How to Get Your Point Across in 30 Seconds* (New York: Simon and Schuster, 1986).

Frank, Reuven, *Out of Thin Air: The Invention and History of Network News* (New York: Simon and Schuster, 1991).

Friendly, Fred W., *Due to Circumstances Beyond Our Control* (New York: Random House, 1967).

Gans, Herbert J., *Deciding What's News* (New York: Pantheon Books, 1979).

Garrett, Annette, *Interviewing: Its Principles and Methods* (New York: Family Association of America, 1982).

Gayeski, Diane, *Corporate and Instructional Video* (Englewood Cliffs, N.J.: Prentice-Hall, 1983).

Gordon, George N., *Classroom Television: New Frontiers in ITV* (New York: Hastings House, 1970).

Gronbeck, Bruce C., et al., *Principles and Types of Speech,* 11th Ed. (Glenview, Ill.: Scott, Foresman, 1990).

Grove, George, *Dictionary of Music and Musicians,* Eric Blom, ed. (New York: St. Martin's Press, 1955).

Hagerman, William, *Broadcast Advertising Copywriting* (Boston: Focal Press, 1989).

Hall, Jim, *Mighty Minutes: An Illustrated History of Television's Best Commercials* (New York: Harmony Books, 1984).

Hammond, Charles M., *The Image Decade: Television Documentary, 1965–1975* (New York: Hastings House, 1981).

Hausman, Carl, *Institutional Video* (Belmont, Calif.: Wadsworth, 1991).

Hecht, Ben, and Charles MacArthur, *The Front Page* (New York: Samuel French, 1955).

Heighton, Elizabeth J., and Don R. Cunningham, *Advertising in the Broadcast Media,* 2d Ed. (Belmont, Calif.: Wadsworth Press, 1984).

Hewitt, John, *Our Words: Writing for Broadcast News* (Mountain View, Calif.: Mayfield Publishing Co., 1988).

Higgins, Denis, *The Art of Writing Advertising* (Lincolnwood, Ill.: NTC Business Books, 1990).

Iuppa, Nicholas V., and Karl Anderson, *Advanced Interactive Video Design* (Stoneham, Mass.: Focal Press, 1988).

Jacobs, Lewis, ed., *The Documentary Tradition* (New York: W. W. Norton and Co., 1979).

Jeweler, A. Jerome, *Creative Strategy in Advertising* (Belmont, Calif.: Wadsworth, 1989).

Johnston, Carla, *Election Coverage: Blueprint for Broadcasters* (Boston: Focal Press, 1991).

Johnston, Donald F., *Copyright Handbook,* 2d Ed. (New York: Bowker, 1982).

Jung, Carl G., *Man and His Symbols* (New York: Doubleday, 1969).

Kendrick, Alexander, *Prime Time* (Boston: Little, Brown and Co., 1969).

Klages, Karl W., *Sportscasting* (Logan, Utah: Sports-casters, 1963).

Klatell, David A., and Norman Marcus, *Sports for Sale* (New York: Oxford University Press, 1988).

Kleppner, Otto, *Advertising Procedures,* 7th Ed. (Englewood Cliffs, N.J.: Prentice-Hall, 1980).

Klevers, Anita, *Women in Television* (Philadelphia: Westminster Press, 1975).

Marshall, Wes, E. B. Eiselein, John Thomas Duncan, and Raul Gamez Bogarin, *Fiesta: Minority Television Programming* (Tucson: University of Arizona Press, 1974).

Martin, David N., *Romancing the Brand: The Power of Advertising and How to Use It* (New York: American Management Association, 1989).

Marzolf, Marion, *Up from the Footnote: A History of Women Journalists* (New York: Hastings House, 1977).

Maslow, Abraham H., *The Farthest Reaches of Human Nature* (Magnolia, Mass.: Peter Smith, 1983).

Mathias, Harry, and Richard Patterson, *Electronic Cinematography* (Belmont, Calif.: Wadsworth, 1985).

McCavitt, William, *Television Production Handbook* (Overland Park, Kans.: Intertec Publishing, 1983).

Meeske, Milan D., and R. C. Norris, *Copywriting for the Electronic Media* (Belmont, Calif.: Wadsworth, 1987).

Meppen, Adrian, Ted White, and Steve Young, *Broadcast News Writing* (New York: Macmillan, 1984).

Naisbitt, John, and Patricia Audurdene, *Megatrends Two Thousand* (New York: Morrow, 1990).

Nelson, Harold, and Dwight Jeeter, *Law of Mass Communications* (Mineola, N.Y.: Foundation Press, 1989).

North, Donald, *Designing the Effective Message* (Dubuque, Iowa: Kendall/Hunt, 1989).

Ogilvy, David, *Confessions of an Advertising Man* (New York: Atheneum Publishers, 1963).

_____, *Ogilvy on Advertising* (New York: Random House, 1985).

Overbeck, Wayne, and Rick D. Pullen, *Major Principles of Media Law* (Fort Worth: Harcourt Brace Jovanovich College Publishers, 1993).

Parsloe, Eric, *Interactive Video* (Cheshire, U.K.: Epic Industrial Communications, 1983).

Passman, Arnold, *The Deejays* (New York: Macmillan Co., 1971).

Pember, Don R., *Mass Media Law* (Dubuque, Iowa: Wm. C. Brown, 1989).

Percival, Fred, and Henry Ellington, *A Handbook of Educational Technology* (New York: Kogan Page, Nichols, 1988).

Powers, Ron, *The Newscasters* (New York: St. Martin's Press, 1977).

Price, Jonathan, *The Best Thing on TV: Commercials* (New York: Viking Press, 1978).

Reeves, Rosser, *Reality in Advertising* (New York: Knopf, 1985).

Rivers, William L., *Finding Facts: Interviewing, Observing, Using Reference Sources* (Englewood Cliffs, N.J.: Prentice-Hall, 1975).

Routt, Edd, *Dimensions of Broadcast Editorializing* (Blue Ridge Summit, Pa.: TAB Books, 1974).

_____, James B. McGrath, and Frederick A. Weiss, *The Radio Format Conundrum* (New York: Hastings House, 1978).

Sack, Robert D., *Libel, Slander and Related Problems* (New York: Practicing Law Institute, 1980).

Schulberg, Bob, *Radio Advertising: The Authoritative Handbook* (Lincolnwood, Ill.: NTC Business Books, 1989).

Small, William, *To Kill a Messenger: Television News and the Real World* (New York: Hastings House, 1970).

Smith, David L., *Video Communication* (Belmont, Calif.: Wadsworth, 1991).

Stasheff, Edward, Rudy Bretz, John Gartley, and Lynn Gartley, *The Television Program,* 5th Ed. (New York: Hill and Wang, 1976).

Steenland, Sally, "Those Daytime Talk Shows," *Television Quarterly,* Vol. xxiv, No. iv, 1990.

Stephens, Mitchell, *Broadcast News: Radio Journalism and an Introduction to Television* (New York: Holt, Rinehart and Winston, 1980).

Stewart, Charles J., and William B. Cash, Jr., *Interviewing: Principles and Practices,* 4th Ed. (Dubuque, Iowa: Wm. C. Brown, 1985).

Stokes, Judith Terenco, *The Business of Nonbroadcast Television* (White Plains, N.Y.: Knowledge Industry Publications, 1988).

Stone, Vernon, and Bruce Hinson, *Television Newsfilm Techniques* (New York: Hastings House, 1974).

Stonecipher, Harry W., *Editorial and Persuasive Writing* (New York: Hastings House, 1976).

Strong, William S., *The Copyright Book: A Practical Guide* (Cambridge, Mass.: MIT Press, 1984).

Sugar, Bert Randolph, *The Thrill of Victory: The Inside Story of ABC Sports* (New York: Hawthorne Books, 1978).

Swallow, Norman, *Factual Television* (New York: Hastings House, 1966).

Turnbull, Robert B., *Radio and Television Sound Effects* (New York: Rinehart and Co., 1951).

Tyrell, R. W., *The Work of the Television Journalist* (New York: Hastings House, 1972).

Wainwright, Charles Anthony, *Television Commercials* (New York: Hastings House, 1970).

Walters, Barbara, *How to Talk with Practically Anybody about Practically Anything* (Garden City, N.Y.: Doubleday and Co., 1970).

Williamson,, Daniel R., *Newsgathering* (New York: Hastings House, 1979).

Willis, Edgar E., *A Radio Director's Manual* (Ann Arbor: Campus Publishers, 1961).

Wurtzel, Alan, *Television Production* (New York: McGraw-Hill Book Co., 1979).

Yellin, David G., *Special: Fred Freed and the Television Documentary* (New York: Macmillan Co., 1973).

Yoakum, Richard, and Charles F. Cremer, *ENG: TV News and the New Technology* (New York: Random House, 1985).

Zettl, Herbert, *Television Production Handbook,* 3d Ed. (Belmont, Calif.: Wadsworth Press, 1976).

Ziegler, Sharilyn K., and Herbert H. Howard, *Broadcast Advertising,* 2d Ed. (Columbus, Ohio: Grid, 1984).

Films/Videocassettes

ABC Notebook: Making the News, 24 minutes (Coronet/MTI Film and Video). This film on the criteria used for selecting the news contains actual news footage and a panel discussion with high school students led by Roone Arledge and Peter Jennings.

Basic Television Terms: A Video Dictionary, 17 minutes (Pyramid, 1977).

Basic Film Terms: A Visual Dictionary, 15 minutes (Pyramid, 1970).

Big Bucks: A Look at Television Commercials, 30 minutes (Great Plains ITV Library, University of Nebraska, 1979). A behind-the-scenes look at the making of a nationally aired soft drink commercial, from planning through filming to broadcast and audience testing.

Bottle Babies, 26 minutes, Peter Krieg (Teldok Films; Tricontinental, 1975). A documentary on the effects of marketing western-style baby formulas in Africa.

The Camera, 22 minutes, Saul J. Turell and Jeff Lieberman (Janus Films; Perspective Films, 1975).

The Car of Your Dreams, 18 minutes (Pyramid Film and Video). A guide through 36 years of television automobile advertising from 1948 to 1984.

The Celia Nachatovitz Diamant Memorial Library of Classic Television Commercials (Chair, Dept. of Television and Radio, Brooklyn College of the City University of New York).

Child Abuse: Cradle of Violence, 20 minutes, J. Gary Mitchell (Motorola, 1976).

Clio Award-Winning TV Commercials, 50–60 minutes (Clio Enterprises).

A Day Without Sunshine, 60 minutes, Robert Thurber (Florida, Public Broadcasting; National Council of Churches, 1976). An update of Edward R. Murrow's *Harvest of Shame.*

A Dose of Reality, 16 minutes, Suzanne St. Pierre (CBS News: Carousel, 1977). Interview from *60 Minutes.* A nurse discusses the dying person's needs.

The Edited Image, 22 minutes, Saul J. Turell and Jeff Lieberman (Janus Films; Perspective Films, 1975).

Film: The Art of the Impossible, 25 minutes (Learning Corporation of America, 1972).

The Fire Next Door, 52 minutes (CBS News: Carousel Films, 1977).

Harvest of Shame, 54 minutes (CBS News: McGraw-Hill, 1960). The famous Edward R. Murrow–Fred Friendly documentary on the plight of migrant farm workers.

Hospice, 38 minutes (Behr Cinematography; St. Christopher's, 1976).

Inside Advertising, 17 minutes (Film Communicators, 1983). Documents the production of a TV commercial from planning to finished spot.

Interviews and Interviewers, 57 minutes, Pacifica Foundation Tape Library). Studs Terkel and Elsa Knight Thompson discuss techniques of the trade.

Joseph Campbell and the Power of Myth with Bill Moyers. A production of Public Affairs Television, Inc., and Alvin H. Perlmutter, Inc. Six-part series. Information: Mystic Fire Video, P.O. Box 30869, Dept. TR, New York, N.Y. 10011.

Lorraine Hansberry: The Black Experience in the Creation of Drama, 35 minutes (Films for the Humanities, 1975).

Making the News Fit, 28 minutes (Cinema Guild). This film examines how journalists covered the war in El Salvador, and the relationship between press coverage and foreign policy.

Media Probes: Political Spots, 30 minutes (Time-Life Video, 1981).

Media Probes: TV News, 30 minutes (Time-Life Video, 1981). The drive for ratings, ratings challenges, a discussion with a news consultant, and the use of a jet helicopter are covered in this film.

News (Indiana University AudioVisual Center, 1977). A series of six titles which tells the story of people who gather and report the news, including Jack Anderson, Bill Bradlee, Walter Cronkite, Bill Moyers, George Will, and others.

News, Features and Sports: It's In the Writing, 20 minutes (Kent Johnson Productions). Instructional videotape that explores the development of three stories through the writing and rewrite process.

1984 Presidential Campaign TV Political Commercials, 45 minutes (L. Patrick Devlin, Dept. of Speech Communication, University of Rhode Island).

The Public Mind with Bill Moyers: The Truth About Lies, 1989. A production of Public Affairs Television, Inc., and Alvin H. Perlmutter, Inc.

Secrets of Effective Radio Advertising (Tony Schwartz, BBC).

Shaping News for the Consumer, 17 minutes (Phoenix/BFA Films and Video, 1975). Discusses the advantages and disadvantages of various news sources.

Sixty Second Spot, 25 minutes, Harvey and Dotty Mandlin (Pyramid, 1973).

Structure of the News Film Story, 20 minutes, John Schultz (CMC, 1973). Morton Dean illustrates the building of a news film story.

The Television Newsman, 28 minutes, Charles Braverman (Pyramid Films, 1975).

Telling the Story: The National Public Radio Guide to Radio Journalism (National Media Programs). A package of six audio cassette programs and a textbook which covers the art and craft, theory and practice, ethics and pragmatics, legal underpinnings, and marketing of news and information radio.

TV: The Anonymous Teacher, 15 minutes (United Methodist Communications: Media Action Research Center; Episcopal Church; Mass Media Films, 1976).

TV Ads: Our Mini Myths, 16 minutes (Clio Enterprises; Pyramid, 1977).

TV News: Behind the Scenes, 27 minutes (EBEC, 1973).

TV News: Measure of the Medium, 16 minutes (Shana Corp., BFA, 1971).

Trip to Nowhere, 52 minutes (NBC; NBCEE, 1970). A documentary on drug use among high school students.

Who Are the DeBolts and Where Did They Get 19 Kids?, 72 minutes (Korty Films and Charles Schultz Creative Associations: Pyramid, 1977).

DRAMATIC WRITING

Allen, Robert C., Speaking of Soap Operas (Chapel Hill, N.C.: North Carolina Press, 1985).

Armer, Alan A., Writing the Screenplay (Belmont, Calif.: Wadsworth, 1988).

Bluestone, George, Novels into Film (New York: Simon and Schuster, 1966).

Blum, Richard, Television Writing from Concept to Contract (New York: Hastings House, 1980).

Burr, Kenneth, and Joseph Gillis, The Screenwriter's Guide: The Handbook for Film and Television Sales (New York: Zoetrope, 1982).

Chayefsky, Paddy, Television Plays (New York: Simon and Schuster, 1955).

Cousin, Michelle, Writing a Television Play (Boston: The Writer, 1975).

Egri, Lajos, The Art of Dramatic Writing, Rev. Ed. (New York: Simon and Schuster/Touchstone, 1980).

Field, Syd, Screenplay: The Foundations of Screenwriting (New York: Dell Publishing Co., 1979).

_____, The Screenwriter's Workbook (New York: Dell Publishing Co., 1984).

_____, Selling a Screenplay (New York: Delacorte Press, 1989).

Foote, Horton, Harrison, Texas (New York: Harcourt, Brace & World, 1956).

Goldman, William, Adventures in the Screen Trade (New York: Warner, 1983).

Hailey, Arthur, Close-up on Writing for Television (Garden City, N.Y.: Doubleday and Co., 1960).

Herman, Lewis, and Marguerite Shalett Herman, American Dialects: A Manual for Actors, Directors, and Writers (New York: Theatre Arts Books, 1947).

_____, Foreign Dialects: A Manual for Actors, Directors, and Writers (New York: Theatre Arts Books, 1943).

Hill, George Roy, and John Whedon, "A Night to Remember," in The Prize Plays of Television and Radio 1956 (New York: Random House, 1957).

Kaminsky, Stuart M., with Mark Waller, Writing for Television (New York: Dell Publishing Co., 1981).

Kerr, Walter, How Not to Write a Play (New York: Simon and Schuster, 1956).

_____, Tragedy and Comedy (New York: Simon and Schuster, 1967).

Kittredge, William, and Steven M. Krause, eds., Stories into Film (New York: Harper and Row, 1979).

LaGuardia, Robert, The Wonderful World of TV Soap Operas (New York: Ballantine Books, 1974).

Matrazzo, Donna, The Corporate Scriptwriting Book, Rev. Ed. (Portland, Oreg.: Communicon, 1985).

Maugham, W. Somerset, "The Vagrant Mood," in The Decline and Fall of the Detective Story (New York: Doubleday and Co., 1953).

McMurtry, Larry, Film Flam (New York: Simon and Schuster, 1987).

Miller, William, Screenwriting for Narrative Film and Television (Boston: Hastings House, 1980).

Nash, Constance, and Virginia Oakey, The Screenwriter's Handbook (New York: Barnes and Noble, 1978).

Packard, William, *The Art of Screenwriting* (New York: Paragon House Publishers, 1987).

Poteet, G. Howard, *Published Radio, Television, and Film Scripts: A Bibliography* (Troy, N.Y.: Whiston Publishing Co., 1975).

Rilla, Wolf, *The Writer and the Screen* (New York: William Morrow and Co., 1974).

Rodger, Ian, *Radio Drama* (London: Macmillan, 1983).

Root, Wells, *Writing the Script* (New York: Holt, Rinehart and Winston, 1979).

Rose, Reginald, *Six Television Plays* (New York: Simon and Schuster, 1956).

Rouveral, Jean, *Writing for the Soaps* (Cincinnati, Ohio: Writer's Digest Books, 1984).

Samples, Gordon, *The Drama Scholars Index to Plays and Filmscripts,* Volume 1 (Metuchen, N.J.: Scarecrow Press, 1974).

_____, *The Drama Scholars Index to Plays and Filmscripts,* Volume 2 (Metuchen, N.J.: Scarecrow Press, 1979).

Stedman, Raymond William, *The Serials: Suspense and Drama by Installment* (Norman: University of Oklahoma Press, 1971).

Swain, Dwight V., with Joye R. Swain, *Film Scriptwriting,* 2d Ed. (Boston: Focal Press, 1988).

Trapnell, Coles, *Teleplay: An Introduction to Television Writing* (San Francisco: Chandler Publishing Co., 1966).

Vale, Eugene, *The Technique of Screenplay Writing* (New York: Grosset and Dunlap, 1972).

Van Druten, John, *Playwright at Work* (New York: Harper and Row, 1953).

Wishengrad, Morton, *The Eternal Light* (New York: Crown Publishers, 1947).

Films/Videocassettes

Guilty by Suspicion, 1991.

Sarah, Plain and Tall (Hallmark Hall of Fame).

Story of a Writer, 25 minutes (Wolper; Sterling, 1963). Ray Bradbury discusses his writing.

Thelma and Louise, 1991.

COMEDY WRITING

Allen, Steve, *The Funny Men* (New York: Simon and Schuster, 1956).

Eastman, Max, *The Enjoyment of Laughter* (New York: Simon and Schuster, 1957).

Gruner, Charles R., *Understanding Laughter: The Workings of Wit and Humor* (Chicago: Nelson-Hall, 1978).

Harmon, Jim, *The Great Radio Comedians* (Garden City, N.Y.: Doubleday and Co., 1970).

Josepberg, Milt, *Comedy Writing for Television and Hollywood* (New York: HarperCollins, 1987).

Lax, Eric, *On Being Funny: Woody Allen and Comedy* (New York: Manor Books, 1977).

Leacock, Stephen, *Humor* (New York: Dodd, Mead and Co., 1935).

Maltin, Leonard, *The Great Movie Comedians* (New York: Crown Publishers, 1978).

Rapp, Albert, *The Origins of Wit and Humor* (New York: E. P. Dutton and Co., 1951).

Rosenblatt, Roger, "What Brand of Laughter Do You Use?" *The New York Times,* Section 2, Nov. 17, 1991, H5.

"Take my Wife. Please. Thank you. How Nice." *The New York Times,* Living Arts Pages, Jan. 2, 1991, C1.

Wertheim, Alfred, *Radio Comedy* (Oxford University Press, 1979).

Wilde, Larry, *How the Great Comedy Writers Create Laughter* (Chicago: Nelson-Hall, 1976).

Films/Videocassettes

Closed Mondays, 8 minutes, Will Venton, Bob Gardiner (Pyramid Films, 1974). Animated comedy-parable.

Great Radio Comedians, I, 35 minutes; *Great Radio Comedians, III,* 27 minutes (WNET/13: Contemporary/McGraw-Hill, 1972).

Woody Allen: An American Comedy, 30 minutes (Harold Mantell: Films for the Humanities, 1977).

WRITING FOR CHILDREN

Cater, Douglas, and Stephen Strickland, *TV Violence and the Child* (New York: Russell Sage Foundation, 1975).

"Children and Television: Growing Up in a Media World," *Media and Values* (Center for Media and Values, Los Angeles), No. 52–53, Fall 1990/Winter 1991.

Garry, Ralph, F. B. Rainsberry, and Charles Winick, eds., *For the Young Viewer* (New York: McGraw-Hill Book Co., 1962).

Harmony, Maureen, ed., *ACT's Guide to TV Programming for Children* (Cambridge, Mass.: Ballinger Publishing Co., 1977).

Himmelweit, Hilde, T. Oppenheim, and Pamela Vince, *Television and the Child* (London: Oxford University Press, 1958).

Howe, Michael J. A., *Television and Children* (Hamden, Conn.: Linnet Books, 1977).

Lesser, Gerald, *Children and Television: Lessons from Sesame Street* (New York: Random House, 1974).

Lesser, Harvey, *Television and the Preschool Child: A Psychological Theory of Instruction and Curriculum Development* (New York: Academic Press, 1977).

Liebert, Robert M., John M. Neale, and Emily S. Davidson, *The Early Window: Effects of Television on Children and Youth* (Elmsford, N.Y.: Pergamon Press, 1973).

Melody, William, *Children's Television: The Economics of Exploitation* (New Haven: Yale University Press, 1973).

O'Toole, Patricia, "Ever-Ever Land," *Newsweek* special issue (New York: Fall/Winter 1991).

Palmer, Edward L., *Television and American Children* (New York: Oxford University Press, 1988).

Schramm, Wilbur, *Television in the Lives of our Children* (Stanford: Stanford University Press, 1961).

Films/Videocassettes

Stories!, 14 minutes (Churchill, 1977). Children use their imaginations to make up a collaborative story.

Big Henry and the Polka Dot Kid, 33 minutes (LCA, 1976). A story for children.

CAREERS IN BROADCASTING AND FILM

Alves, Jeff, *How to Break into the Film Business: Production Assistant Handbook* (Sherman Oaks, Calif.: Alves Co., 1990).

Blanksteen, Jane, and Avi Odeni, *TV: Careers Behind the Screen* (New York: John Wiley and Sons, Inc., 1987).

Callow, Ridgeway, et al., *You Can Make It: An Insider's Guide to a Hollywood Career* (Grass Valley, Calif.: Tetragram, 1991).

Head, Sydney, *Broadcasting in America,* 3d Ed. (Boston: Houghton Mifflin Co., 1976).

Hines, William E., *Job Descriptions: Responsibilities and Duties for the Film & Video Craft Categories & Classifications,* Rev. Ed. (Los Angeles: Ed-Venture, 1984).

Jackson, Gregory, *Getting into Broadcast Journalism: A Guide to Careers in Radio and TV* (New York: Hawthorne Books, 1975).

Jurek, Ken, *Careers in Video: Getting Ahead in Professional Television* (White Plains, N.Y.: Knowledge Industries Publications, Inc., 1989).

Katahn, T. L., *Reading for a Living: How to Be a Professional Story Analyst for Film & Television* (Pacific Palisades, Calif.: Blue Arrow Books, 1990).

Keller, Barbara B., *Film, Tape & TV: Where Do I Fit In?* (Great Neck, N.Y.: Keller International Publishers, 1985).

Reed, Maxine K., and Robert Reed, *Career Opportunities in Television, Cable & Video,* 3d Ed. (New York: Facts on File, 1990).

Shaw, William H., *Presenting Entertainment Arts: Stage, Film, Television* (Dubuque, Iowa: Kendall-Hunt Publishing Co., 1983).

Timmons, W. Milton, *Orientation to Cinema—The Complete Guide to Career Planning, Vol. I. A Survey of the Industry for Beginning TV & Film Students,* Rev. Ed. (Van Nuys, Calif.: Academic Associates, 1988).

_____, *Orientation to Cinema—The Complete Guide to Career Planning, Vol. II. A Survey of the Industry for Beginning TV & Film Students* (Van Nuys, Calif.: Academic Associates, 1988).

INDEX

PERMISSIONS AND ACKNOWLEDGMENTS

CHAPTER 2

TV Commercial Pictureboard for Bell South, "Churchill." *Copyright, 1991. Reprinted with permission of Bell South Corporation.*

Radio Commercial for the Wellness Plan, "Newton." *Courtesy of the Wellness Plan* and *Stone, August, Baker Communications Company Advertising Agency.*

Radio Commercial for *Time*, "College Daze." *Courtesy of Time Magazine.*

TV Commercial Storyboard for Energizer Batteries, "Pink Rabbit." *Courtesy of Eveready Battery Company, Inc.*

TV Commercial Pictureboard for Hallmark Cards, "Mrs. Lagow's Gift." *Courtesy of Hallmark Cards, Inc.*

TV Commercial Pictureboards for Kellogg's Crispix, "Science Experiments A & B." *Courtesy of Kellogg Company.*

TV Commercial Pictureboard for Kellogg's Frosted Flakes, "Shadows/Congressman." *Courtesy of Eveready Battery Company, Inc.*

TV Commercial Script for Energizer Batteries, "Pink Rabbit." *Courtesy of Energizer Battery Company, Inc.*

TV Commercial Script for Nike Shoes, "Jordan/Finals A.C." *Courtesy of Nike, Inc. and Wieden and Kennedy Advertising Agency.*

TV Promotion Script for Channel 7. *Courtesy of WXYZ-TV/Channel 7/Detroit.*

TV Promotion Script for Channel 2. *Courtesy of Carla Gaines, Assistant News Director, WJBK-TV 2.*

TV Public Service Announcement for Juvenile Diabetes Foundation, "Mother and Child." *Courtesy of Young and Rubicam, Inc; Copy—Mike Robertson; Art Direction—Ray Groff.*

TV Promotional Announcement for WQED, Public Television Station. *Courtesy of WQED, Pittsburgh.*

Radio Public Service Announcement, "Anti-Smoking —Koch." *Courtesy of Tony Schwartz, Media Creator and Consultant.*

Radio Public Service Announcement, "Anti-Smoking —Reynolds." *Courtesy of Tony Schwartz, Media Creator and Consultant.*

CHAPTER 3

Introductions for Radio Interview Program "Focus," WJR. *Courtesy of W. Hal Youngblood, Executive Producer, WJR Detroit.*

Introductions to Programs One and Five of "*Joseph Campbell and the Power of Myth with Bill Moyers:* 'The Hero's Adventure' and 'Love and the Goddess.'" *Courtesy* Joseph Campbell and the Power of Myth with Bill Moyers. *Alvin H. Perlmutter, Inc. and Public Affairs Television.*

Introduction to "Day at Night." James Day's Conversation with Anne Sexton. *Courtesy of James Day, Publivision, Inc.*

Excerpt from "Jane Pauley's Real Life Interview with Oprah Winfrey." *Transcript Courtesy of National Broadcasting Company, Inc. and "Real Life with Jane Pauley."* © 1991 National Broadcasting Co. All Rights Reserved.

Segments from "The Mike Cuthbert Radio Call-In Show." *Courtesy of WAMU-FM Public Radio, The American University.*

CHAPTER 4

Excerpt from TV Feature "Good Friends," on *CBS Sunday Morning. Copyrighted CBS, Inc. Reprinted by Permission. All Rights Reserved.*

TV Feature, "Consumer Report." *Courtesy of Asa Aarons/WDIV-TV Detroit.*

Excerpt from *60 Minutes* segment "That's the Law." *Courtesy of 60 Minutes.*

Excerpt from ABC Documentary "Peter Jennings Reporting: Guns." *Courtesy of ABC News.*

Excerpt from Documentary "Who Are the DeBolts and Where Did They Get Nineteen Kids?" *Courtesy of Dorothy DeBolt and John Korty.*

Excerpt from Documentary "Reading, Writing and Reefer." *Courtesy of Robert Rogers, NBC News.*

CHAPTER 5

Format for Semi-Scripted Show. *Courtesy of Edward Stasheff.*

Excerpt from TV Educational Program "The Next Few Steps: Preparing for Total Hip Replacement." *Courtesy of Joyce B. Williams, R.N., M.A., Writer/Producer. Copyright, 1989. Catherine McAuley Health System, Ann Arbor, Michigan.*

CHAPTER 6

TV Editorial "Productivity and the Sanitation Workers," WPIX-TV. *Courtesy of Richard N. Hughes,*

Editorialist for WPIX-TV, 11 WPIX Plaza, New York, NY 10017.

Radio Editorial "The Ravages of Rape-I," KGO Radio. *Courtesy of Michael Luckoff, General Manager, KGO Radio, San Francisco.*

TV Feature "Advertising," presented on *60 Minutes* by Andy Rooney. *Courtesy of Andrew A. Rooney, CBS News.*

Radio Commentary "The Osgood File: Avoiding the S's," presented by Charles Osgood on CBS. *Copyrighted CBS, Inc. Reprinted by Permission. All Rights Reserved.*

Radio Commentary "The Osgood File: HIV Nightmare." *Copyrighted CBS, Inc. Reprinted by Permission. All Rights Reserved.*

Radio Commentary "The Osgood File: The Fur War." *Copyrighted CBS, Inc. Reprinted by Permission. All Rights Reserved.*

Radio Commentary by Mort Crim on *One Moment Please.* "Open Letter to Michael Landon." *Courtesy of Mort Crim, Senior Editor.*

Radio Commentary "The Death of Three Astronauts," presented on CBS News by Eric Sevareid. *Copyrighted by CBS, Inc. Reprinted by Permission. All Rights Reserved.*

TV Commentary "Censorship in the Persian Gulf War," presented by John Chancellor on PBS during The Columbia Journalism Awards. *Courtesy of John Chancellor, Senior Commentator, NBC News.*

TV Commentary "Milepost." Charles Kuralt on *CBS Sunday Morning. Copyrighted by CBS, Inc. Reprinted by Permission. All Rights Reserved.*

TV Film Review "Silence of the Lambs," presented by Joel Siegel on *Good Morning, America.* Courtesy of *Good Morning America, ABC-TV.*

TV Media Review "PBS P.O.V." presented by John Leonard on *CBS Sunday Morning. Copyrighted by CBS, Inc. All Rights Reserved. Reprinted by Permission.*

Radio Commentary "Winning Isn't Everything," presented by Sister Camille D'Arienzo on WINS. *Courtesy of All News 1010 WINS Radio, New York City.*

Radio Commentary "The Poor and the Panhandlers," presented by Rabbi Marc Tanenbaum on WINS. *Courtesy of All News 1010 WINS Radio, New York City.*

CHAPTER 7

Radio News Slug Examples, written by Mike Lopiparo. *Courtesy of All News 1010 WINS Radio, New York City.*

TV News Stories "Cameras in the Courtroom" and "A Special Wish," presented by Ellen Fleysher on WNBC-TV. *Scripts Courtesy of WNBC-TV, National Broadcasting Company, Inc. © 1991. All Rights Reserved.*

TV News Story "Viet Vets," presented by Mary Murphy on WCBS-TV. *Courtesy of WCBS-TV, Columbia Broadcasting System. All Rights Reserved.*

TV News Story "Sharp Shooting," presented by Lis Daily on WISH-TV. *Courtesy of Lis Daily, WISH-TV Reporter.*

TV Newscast, News Center 4. *Courtesy of WNBC-TV, New York.*

CHAPTER 8

Radio Sports Feature from *Bob Costas with the Inside Sports Magazine,* "Rick Monday Stops Flag Burners." *Courtesy of "Inside Sports Magazine," Olympia Radio Network, Bob Costas—Host; Dave Cohen—Producer/Writer.*

Excerpt from Radio Sports Report *courtesy of Paul Greenberg, Sportscaster, 1010 WINS Radio, New York City.*

TV Sports Feature by Jack Whitaker, ABC-TV, "Kentucky Derby 1991." *Courtesy of Jack Whitaker, ABC Sports.*

Excerpt from TV Sports Feature on *CBS Sunday Morning,* "Bill Geist Report: Shuffleboard." *Copyrighted CBS, Inc. Reprinted by Permission. All Rights Reserved.*

TV Sports Feature by Andrea Joyce "Jimmy Connors." *Courtesy of Andrea Joyce, 1991 U.S. Open/CBS Sports.*

CHAPTER 9

Pop Music Radio Continuity by Meridith Gottlieb. *Courtesy of Meridith Gottlieb, Writer.*

Excerpt from Radio Music Continuity for *Music of the Masters. Courtesy of WUOM, Ann Arbor, Michigan.*

Excerpt from Radio Music Continuity for "A Case of Unmistaken Identity," presented by Karl Haas. *Courtesy of Karl Haas, WJR, Detroit.*

Rundown for Radio Music Continuity "A Jazz Sampler for 1941," presented by Hazen Schumacher. *Courtesy of Hazen Schumacher.*

Radio Music Continuity for *Money, Machines, and Music! Courtesy of WUOM, Ann Arbor, Michigan.*

Excerpt from Variety Show "The Song and Dance Man," presented on the *Bell Telephone Hour. Courtesy of Henry Jaffe Enterprises.*

CHAPTERS 11 AND 12

Excerpts from "Life Choice," an Episode in the *Law and Order* series. *Courtesy of Universal Television. Teleplay by David Black and Robert Stuart Nathan. Story by Dick Wolf. The permission to reprint the excerpt in this text from the teleplay "Life Choice" does not extend the permission to any user of this text to copy said excerpt in whole or in part, or to perform said excerpt in whole or in part. All rights in said excerpt except the non-exclusive North American and world reprint rights in the English language are specifically reserved by the copyright owner of said teleplay. Copyright 1990.*

CHAPTER 12

Dialogue Excerpts from the TV Play "Twelve Angry Men" by Reginald Rose. *Reprinted by Permission of International Creative Management. Copyright 1956 by Reginald Rose.*

CHAPTER 13

Excerpt from the TV Adaptation of Walter Lord's Book *A Night to Remember* by George Roy Hill and John Whedon. *Courtesy of George Roy Hill.*

CHAPTER 14

Excerpt from "Coma," an Episode in the *MacGyver* series. *Courtesy of Henry Winkler/John Rich Productions in association with Paramount Pictures Corporation. Story by Anthony Rich, Teleplay by John Sheppard. Copyright, 1990.*

Excerpt from "Sarah, Plain and Tall," a Presentation in the *Hallmark Hall of Fame* series. *Courtesy of Hallmark Cards, Inc. Copyright Self Productions Inc. and Trillium Productions, Inc.*

Excerpt from "Cop," an Episode in the *Lou Grant* series. *Courtesy of MTM Enterprises.*

Excerpt from *Another World. Courtesy of Procter and Gamble Productions, Inc.*

Excerpt from a Radio Adaptation of Shakespeare's *Macbeth. Adaptation by Edgar E. Willis—as broadcast on WUOM, Ann Arbor, Michigan.*

CHAPTER 17

Excerpt from a Situation Comedy Episode, "John's Blind Date," in the series *Dear John. Courtesy of Hal Cooper. Written by Mike Milligan and Jay Moriarty; Directed by Hal Cooper.*

CHAPTER 18

Excerpt and Partial Storyboard from *The Paper Bag Princess,* Filmed Adaptation from Robert Munsch's Book. *Courtesy of Cinar. A Cinar Production in association with Crayon Animation, Montreal, Canada.*

Segment from *The Electric Company. Courtesy of Children's Television Workshop.*

Excerpt from "To Grandmother's House," a Program in the *Captain Kangaroo* series. *By Permission of Robert Keeshan Associates.*

Segment from Episode 1524 of *Mister Rogers' Neighborhood.* © 1983 Family Communications, Inc.